How Can It Be
GLUTEN FREE
Cookbook Collection

Also by America's Test Kitchen

The Complete Plant-Based Cookbook
Meat Illustrated
The Complete One Pot
Cooking for One
Bowls
The Complete Summer Cookbook
Vegetables Illustrated
The Side Dish Bible
Foolproof Fish
100 Techniques
Easy Everyday Keto
Everything Chocolate
The Perfect Pie
How to Cocktail
Spiced
The Ultimate Burger
The New Essentials Cookbook
Dinner Illustrated
America's Test Kitchen Menu Cookbook
Cook's Illustrated Revolutionary Recipes
Tasting Italy: A Culinary Journey
Cooking at Home with Bridget and Julia
The Complete Mediterranean Cookbook
The Complete Vegetarian Cookbook
The Complete Cooking for Two Cookbook
The Complete Diabetes Cookbook
The Complete Slow Cooker
The Complete Make-Ahead Cookbook
Just Add Sauce
How to Braise Everything
How to Roast Everything
Nutritious Delicious
What Good Cooks Know
Cook's Science
The Science of Good Cooking
The Perfect Cake
The Perfect Cookie
Bread Illustrated
Master of the Grill
Kitchen Smarts
Kitchen Hacks
100 Recipes: The Absolute Best Ways to Make the True Essentials
The New Family Cookbook
The America's Test Kitchen Cooking School Cookbook

The Cook's Illustrated Baking Book
The Cook's Illustrated Cookbook
The America's Test Kitchen Family Baking Book
America's Test Kitchen Twentieth Anniversary TV Show Cookbook
The Best of America's Test Kitchen (2007–2021 Editions)
The Complete America's Test Kitchen TV Show Cookbook 2001–2021

Toaster Oven Perfection
Mediterranean Instant Pot
Cook It in Your Dutch Oven
Vegan for Everybody
Sous Vide for Everybody
Air Fryer Perfection
Multicooker Perfection
Food Processor Perfection
Pressure Cooker Perfection
Instant Pot Ace Blender Cookbook
Naturally Sweet
Foolproof Preserving
Paleo Perfected
The Best Mexican Recipes
Slow Cooker Revolution Volume 2: The Easy-Prep Edition
Slow Cooker Revolution
The America's Test Kitchen D.I.Y. Cookbook

THE COOK'S ILLUSTRATED ALL-TIME BEST SERIES
All-Time Best Brunch
All-Time Best Dinners for Two
All-Time Best Sunday Suppers
All-Time Best Holiday Entertaining
All-Time Best Appetizers
All-Time Best Soups

COOK'S COUNTRY TITLES
Big Flavors from Italian America
One-Pan Wonders
Cook It in Cast Iron
Cook's Country Eats Local
The Complete Cook's Country TV Show Cookbook

FOR A FULL LISTING OF ALL OUR BOOKS
CooksIllustrated.com
AmericasTestKitchen.com

Praise for America's Test Kitchen Titles

"The sum total of exhaustive experimentation . . . anyone interested in gluten-free cookery simply shouldn't be without it."
NIGELLA LAWSON ON *THE HOW CAN IT BE GLUTEN-FREE COOKBOOK*

Selected as the Cookbook Award Winner of 2019 in the Health and Special Diet Category
INTERNATIONAL ASSOCIATION OF CULINARY PROFESSIONALS (IACP) ON *THE COMPLETE DIABETES COOKBOOK*

"Diabetics and all health-conscious home cooks will find great information on almost every page."
BOOKLIST (STARRED REVIEW) ON *THE COMPLETE DIABETES COOKBOOK*

"This is a wonderful, useful guide to healthy eating."
PUBLISHERS WEEKLY ON *NUTRITIOUS DELICIOUS*

"True to its name, this smart and endlessly enlightening cookbook is about as definitive as it's possible to get in the modern vegetarian realm."
MEN'S JOURNAL ON *THE COMPLETE VEGETARIAN COOKBOOK*

"The book offers an impressive education for curious cake makers, new and experienced alike. A summation of 25 years of cake making at ATK, there are cakes for every taste."
THE WALL STREET JOURNAL ON *THE PERFECT CAKE*

"The editors at America's Test Kitchen pack decades of baking experience into this impressive volume of 250 recipes. . . . You'll find a wealth of keeper recipes within these pages."
LIBRARY JOURNAL (STARRED REVIEW) ON *THE PERFECT COOKIE*

"Cooks with a powerful sweet tooth should scoop up this well-researched recipe book for healthier takes on classic sweet treats."
BOOKLIST ON *NATURALLY SWEET*

"Here are the words just about any vegan would be happy to read: 'Why This Recipe Works.' Fans of America's Test Kitchen are used to seeing the phrase, and now it applies to the growing collection of plant-based creations."
THE WASHINGTON POST ON *VEGAN FOR EVERYBODY*

"As with previous titles from America's Test Kitchen, this keto-focused volume is a solid collection of rigorously tested recipes. . . . The dishes are easy to source and prepare, and nutritional information is included for each recipe, as are menu plans for those new to the program. This information-packed volume rises above the rest of the keto cookbooks."
PUBLISHERS WEEKLY ON *EASY EVERYDAY KETO*

"Some books impress by the sheer audacity of their ambition. Backed up by the magazine's famed mission to test every recipe relentlessly until it is the best it can be, this nearly 900-page volume lands with an authoritative wallop."
CHICAGO TRIBUNE ON *THE COOK'S ILLUSTRATED COOKBOOK*

"The 21st-century *Fannie Farmer Cookbook* or *The Joy of Cooking*. If you had to have one cookbook and that's all you could have, this one would do it."
CBS SAN FRANCISCO ON *THE NEW FAMILY COOKBOOK*

"The go-to gift book for newlyweds, small families, or empty nesters."
ORLANDO SENTINEL ON *THE COMPLETE COOKING FOR TWO COOKBOOK*

"This book upgrades slow cooking for discriminating, 21st-century palates—that is indeed revolutionary."
THE DALLAS MORNING NEWS ON *SLOW COOKER REVOLUTION*

"Some 2,500 photos walk readers through 600 painstakingly tested recipes, leaving little room for error."
ASSOCIATED PRESS ON *THE AMERICA'S TEST KITCHEN COOKING SCHOOL COOKBOOK*

"If you're a home cook who loves long introductions that tell you why a dish works followed by lots of step-by-step hand holding, then you'll love *Vegetables Illustrated*."
THE WALL STREET JOURNAL ON *VEGETABLES ILLUSTRATED*

"A one-volume kitchen seminar, addressing in one smart chapter after another the sometimes surprising whys behind a cook's best practices. . . . You get the myth, the theory, the science, and the proof, all rigorously integrated as only America's Test Kitchen can do."
NPR ON *THE SCIENCE OF GOOD COOKING*

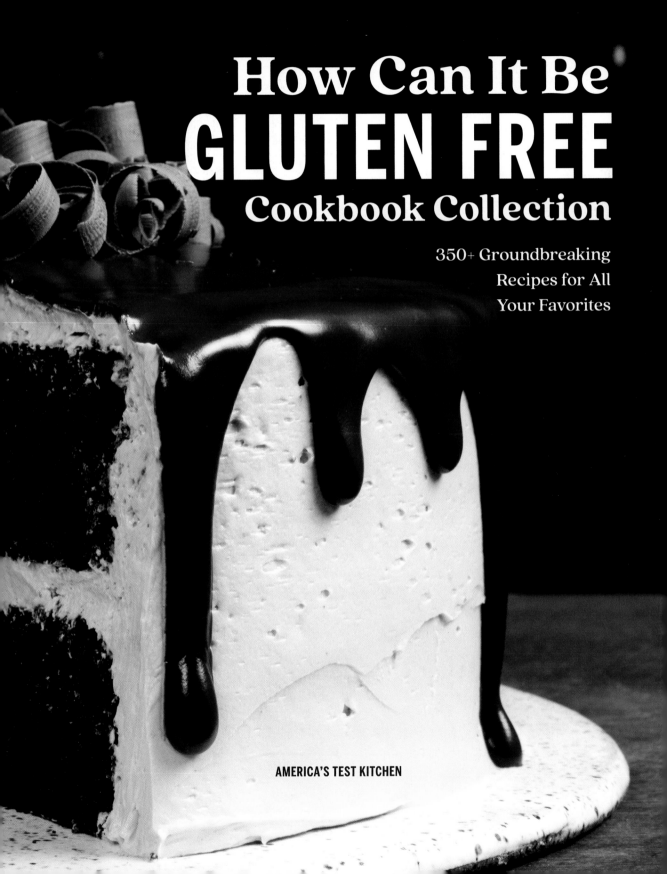

How Can It Be
GLUTEN FREE
Cookbook Collection

350+ Groundbreaking Recipes for All Your Favorites

AMERICA'S TEST KITCHEN

How Can It Be Gluten Free Cookbook Collection
combines recipes previously published in
The How Can It Be Gluten Free Cookbook,
Volumes 1 and 2.

Library of Congress Cataloging-in-Publication
Data has been applied for.

ISBN 978-1-948703-50-5

AMERICA'S TEST KITCHEN

21 Drydock Avenue, Boston, MA 02210

Manufactured in the United States of America

10 9 8 7 6 5 4 3 2 1

Distributed by Penguin Random House
Publisher Services

Tel: 800.733.3000

PICTURED ON FRONT COVER: Almond Granola
with Dried Fruit (page 104), Bagels (page 314),
Whole-Grain Blueberry Muffins (page 62),
Currant Scones (page 72), and Coffee Cake
(page 84)

EDITORIAL DIRECTOR, BOOKS: Adam Kowit

EXECUTIVE FOOD EDITOR: Dan Zuccarello

DEPUTY FOOD EDITOR: Stephanie Pixley

EXECUTIVE MANAGING EDITOR: Debra Hudak

SENIOR EDITORS: Louise Emerick, Andrew Janjigian,
Suzannah McFerran, Sara Mayer

ASSOCIATE EDITORS: Sebastian Nava, Anne Wolf

TEST COOKS: Danielle DeSiato-Hallman, Meaghen Walsh

ASSISTANT TEST COOK: Amanda Rumore

CONTRIBUTING EDITORS: Elizabeth Carduff, Cheryl Redmond

ASSISTANT EDITOR: Brenna Donovan

EDITORIAL ASSISTANT: Emily Rahravan

DESIGN DIRECTOR: Lindsey Timko Chandler

DEPUTY ART DIRECTOR: Allison Boales

PHOTOGRAPHY DIRECTOR: Julie Bozzo Cote

PHOTOGRAPHY PRODUCER: Meredith Mulcahy

SENIOR STAFF PHOTOGRAPHERS: Steve Klise, Daniel J. van Ackere

STAFF PHOTOGRAPHER: Kevin White

ADDITIONAL PHOTOGRAPHY: Carl Tremblay

FOOD STYLING: Daniel Cellucci, Catrine Kelty, Marie Piraino,
Sally Staub

PHOTOSHOOT KITCHEN TEAM

    PHOTO TEAM MANAGER: Alli Berkey

    LEAD TEST COOK: Eric Haessler

    ASSISTANT TEST COOKS: Matthew Fairman, Hannah Fenton,
Jacqueline Gochenouer, Cecelia Jenkins

ILLUSTRATIONS: Jay Layman

SENIOR MANAGER, PUBLISHING OPERATIONS: Taylor Argenzio

IMAGING MANAGER: Lauren Robbins

PRODUCTION AND IMAGING SPECIALISTS: Tricia Neumyer,
Dennis Noble, Amanda Yong

COPY EDITORS: Cheryl Redmond and Jeff Schier

PROOFREADER: Vicki Rowland

INDEXER: Elizabeth Parson

CHIEF CREATIVE OFFICER: Jack Bishop

EXECUTIVE EDITORIAL DIRECTORS: Julia Collin Davison and
Bridget Lancaster

CONTENTS

Welcome to America's Test Kitchen

This book has been tested, written, and edited by the folks at America's Test Kitchen, where curious cooks become confident cooks. Located in Boston's Seaport District in the historic Innovation and Design Building, it features 15,000 square feet of kitchen space, including multiple photography and video studios. It is the home of *Cook's Illustrated* magazine and *Cook's Country* magazine and is the workday destination for more than 60 test cooks, editors, and cookware specialists. Our mission is to empower and inspire confidence, community, and creativity in the kitchen.

We start the process of testing a recipe with a complete lack of preconceptions, which means that we accept no claim, no technique, and no recipe at face value. We simply assemble as many variations as possible, test a half-dozen of the most promising, and taste the results blind. We then construct our own recipe and continue to test it, varying ingredients, techniques, and cooking times until we reach a consensus. As we like to say in the test kitchen, "We make the mistakes so you don't have to." The result, we hope, is the best version of a particular recipe, but we realize that only you can be the final judge of our success (or failure). We use the same rigorous approach when we test equipment and taste ingredients.

All of this would not be possible without a belief that good cooking, much like good music, is based on a foundation of objective technique. Some people like spicy foods and others don't, but there is a right way to sauté, there is a best way to cook a pot roast, and there are measurable scientific principles involved in producing perfectly beaten, stable egg whites. Our ultimate goal is to investigate the fundamental principles of cooking to give you the techniques, tools, and ingredients you need to become a better cook. It is as simple as that.

To see what goes on behind the scenes at America's Test Kitchen, check out our social media channels for kitchen snapshots, exclusive content, video tips, and much more. You can watch us work (in our actual test kitchen) by tuning in to *America's Test Kitchen* or *Cook's Country* on public television or on our websites. Download our award-winning podcast *Proof*, which goes beyond recipes to solve food mysteries (AmericasTestKitchen.com/proof), or listen in to test kitchen experts on public radio (SplendidTable.org) to hear insights that illuminate the truth about real home cooking. Want to hone your cooking skills or finally learn how to bake—with an America's Test Kitchen test cook? Enroll in one of our online cooking classes. And you can engage the next generation of home cooks with kid-tested recipes from America's Test Kitchen Kids.

Our community of home recipe testers provides valuable feedback on recipes under development by ensuring that they are foolproof. You can help us investigate the how and why behind successful recipes from your home kitchen. (Sign up at AmericasTestKitchen.com/recipe_testing.)

However you choose to visit us, we welcome you into our kitchen, where you can stand by our side as we test our way to the best recipes in America.

- FACEBOOK.COM/AMERICASTESTKITCHEN
- TWITTER.COM/TESTKITCHEN
- YOUTUBE.COM/AMERICASTESTKITCHEN
- INSTAGRAM.COM/TESTKITCHEN
- PINTEREST.COM/TESTKITCHEN

AMERICASTESTKITCHEN.COM

COOKSILLUSTRATED.COM

COOKSCOUNTRY.COM

ONLINECOOKINGSCHOOL.COM

AMERICASTESTKITCHEN.COM/KIDS

GLUTEN-FREE BASICS

Introduction

Our first gluten-free cookbook was published to a groundswell of support from our fans and supporters around the country, as well as from many people who had never bought a book developed by our test kitchen but who were desperate for gluten-free recipes that were reliable and tasted great. Although we're not in the business of prescribing diets or offering up medical advice, engineering foolproof recipes for great food is what we do best, and we delivered recipes—everything from pancakes to pizza—that tasted as good as their wheat counterparts.

We asked for and got lots of feedback on our first book, from ideas for recipes (bagels were often mentioned) to pleas for whole-grain recipes and dairy-free recipes to nutritional information for every recipe. Our second gluten-free book addressed all of these wishes, including a versatile and healthful whole-grain gluten-free flour blend.

With the publication of this new, combined volume, you now have our entire gluten-free collection—the result of many years of research and recipe tests—at your fingertips. Throughout our recipe development process, we were guided by a set of clear goals.

DEVELOP gluten-free recipes for favorite foods that typically rely on wheat in some form. In addition to the obvious cakes, cookies, breads, and pizzas, we wanted to tackle recipes like fried chicken (usually made with a flour coating), eggplant Parmesan (with a bread-crumb coating), and meatloaf (which often includes bread for moisture).

CREATE a versatile alternative to all-purpose flour that could be used not only in the recipes in this book, but as a starting point for reworking readers' favorite recipes. Our ATK All-Purpose Gluten-Free Flour Blend uses easy-to-find ingredients and produces baked goods that taste as good as their wheat-based counterparts.

CREATE a whole-grain gluten-free flour blend that would allow us to create hearty baked goods that rival those made with traditional whole-wheat flour, including recipes for pancakes and waffles, a rustic boule, pecan bars, and free-form tart dough. Our ATK Whole-Grain Gluten-Free Flour Blend features teff flour, which adds both a nutritional boost and a robust flavor to baked goods.

TEACH readers about the wide range of gluten-free grains (everything from amaranth to millet) now sold in supermarkets. Many cooks are unfamiliar with these grains, and our test kitchen explains how to buy, store, and cook them, offering up approachable, appealing recipes for the most versatile grains.

RATE key gluten-free supermarket ingredients that make cooking—and eating—easier, including the wide variety of gluten-free pastas and sandwich breads now on the market. We also explored substitutions for pantry staples, such as soy sauce, that are typically made with wheat.

DEVELOP dairy-free variations for dozens of our recipes and summarize our findings so readers can tailor their own recipes to be dairy-free.

As the test kitchen was working on this book, we sent the most important (and most difficult) recipes out to volunteer recipe testers—home cooks like you. In all, we received more than 2,500 written reports from this army of gluten-free testers. Thank you. Your feedback helped identify techniques that needed to be described in more detail as well as recipes that needed to be reworked.

If you have comments or questions about this book, we'd love to hear from you. Visit howcanitbeglutenfree.com where we have posted answers to the most frequently asked questions. If your questions aren't answered there, you can email us at glutenfree@americastestkitchen.com.

The Science of Gluten

Before you attempt to cook without gluten, it's helpful to understand what gluten does in various recipes. Let's start with the most common source of gluten—wheat flour—which is the main ingredient in everything from pasta and pizza to cakes and cookies.

WHEAT FLOUR 101

Flour is milled from wheat berries, which contain starches, proteins, and fats. There are two main proteins in wheat flour—glutenin and gliadin. Glutenin is a very large, loosely coiled protein, while gliadin is a much smaller and tightly coiled sphere. Glutenin provides most of the strength and elasticity in dough, allowing it to bounce back after it has been stretched. Gliadin, on the other hand, provides the stretch.

DEFINING GLUTEN

In dry flour, these proteins are basically lifeless strands wrapped around granules of starch. But they begin to change shape when they come in contact with water, a process called hydration. Once moistened, the individual protein molecules (the glutenin and gliadin) begin to link up with one another to form long, elastic chains called gluten. These strands of gluten combine to form a membrane-like network. The network engulfs swollen starch granules and gas bubbles (created by yeast, chemical leaveners like baking powder, or foams like whipped egg whites), stretching as the batter or dough rises and then bakes, giving the finished cake or loaf its structure and chew.

GLUTEN DEVELOPMENT

There are several factors that can affect gluten development. The first is the flour itself. Bread flour is milled from high-protein wheat, which means it's capable of developing more gluten, or structure, which is perfect for chewy artisan loaves. In contrast, cake flour is made from soft wheat with a low protein content. As a result, cake flour produces less gluten, making it perfect for tender cakes. All-purpose flour has a relatively high protein content of 10 to 12 percent, depending on the brand. Bread flours have even more protein, generally 12 to 14 percent. Cake flour has just 6 to 8 percent protein. Second, the amount of water can affect gluten development. Basically, the more water in a dough or batter, the stronger and more elastic the gluten strands. Why does this matter? If the gluten strands are strong and elastic, they can support the starch granules and air bubbles that hydrate and swell as the dough rises and bakes, producing an airier bread with good chew.

The third variable is the mixing time. A muffin batter that is gently stirred will develop less gluten than a bread dough beaten in a stand mixer for 10 minutes. More stirring equals more gluten, which equals more structure and chew.

What Is Gluten?

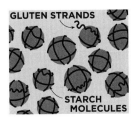

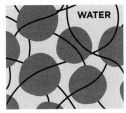

Wheat flour contains two types of protein strands, glutenin and gliadin, wrapped around starch granules.

When flour is combined with water, the protein strands unwind and link together to form a membrane-like network, which is called gluten.

Strategies for Replacing Wheat Flour

Before you remove the flour from your favorite recipes, you need to consider the role the flour is playing in those recipes in order to devise a successful substitute. Remember that flour contains both protein and starch, and the kind of substitute you will need when trying to convert a recipe to be gluten-free will vary because some recipes rely on one but not the other element. Let's look at the three most common roles played by wheat flour.

FLOUR THICKENS

In sauces, gravies, soups, and stews, wheat flour plays the role of thickener. Flour is 75 percent starch; when its starch granules are heated in these dishes, they absorb water, swell, and eventually burst, releasing a starch molecule called amylose that diffuses throughout the solution, trapping additional water and forming a gelatinous network. This is how a few tablespoons of flour turn chicken stock into gravy.

Some thickeners, like cornstarch, are pure starches and contain more amylose than flour. Purity affects not only thickening power but performance. Cornstarch is more fickle than flour; for instance, overwhisking pastry cream made with cornstarch can break the bonds of the starch gel and thin out the custard. In contrast, the proteins and lipids in flour dilute its capacity to form starch gels, so that more flour is needed for thickening. But these non-starch compounds also act as binders, ensuring that the liquid not only thickens but also stays thick.

For these reasons, simply replacing flour with a pure starch doesn't always work. Large quantities of pure starch can impart a gritty texture to dishes. We had this problem when developing our recipe for pot pie—the amount of cornstarch needed to thicken the filling to the proper consistency gave the sauce a gritty mouthfeel. Luckily, there are other gluten-free starches besides cornstarch, including arrowroot (derived from a tropical tuber of the same name), potato starch, and tapioca starch (derived from cassava, another tropical tuber). In the end, we didn't find a single replacement for flour as a thickener but, given all the options, we had no trouble finding an excellent work-around.

FLOUR COATS

In addition to its use as a thickener, flour can also be used as a coating in dishes like fried chicken or pan-fried pork chops. The starches in the flour are responsible for most of the browning and crisping, while the proteins in the flour help the coating cling to the surface of the food. The proteins also create chew, or texture, in the fried or baked coating.

Cornstarch is traditionally used as a coating in many recipes, from tempura to onion rings, so replacing the wheat flour in our recipes with cornstarch was a start. However, since cornstarch contains almost no protein, we had to rely on other ingredients to help the coating adhere and/or give it a chewy texture.

In our pan-fried pork chop recipe, we used the sticky proteins in the meat itself to help bind the coating to the chops. Simply cutting a very shallow crosshatch pattern into the meat released these sticky proteins and ensured that the crisp cornstarch and cornflake crust stayed put. In our fried chicken recipe, we added cornmeal (a good source of protein) as well as an egg to the coating. Some baking powder and baking soda also helped the coating to puff in the hot oil and create a crisp crust with the requisite chew.

Finally, in recipes like eggplant Parmesan and chicken fingers that rely on a bread-crumb coating, we were able to use gluten-free sandwich bread (dried in the oven first to make the crumbs less sticky) in combination with cornstarch (which improved overall coverage and increased browning and crispness). As with thickeners, we didn't find one direct substitute for flour as a coating ingredient but here, too, we had no trouble finding solutions that worked.

FLOUR BUILDS STRUCTURE

The main use for flour in the home kitchen is as a structural agent in baked goods. It's here that the gluten performs an essential function, as the ability of the proteins in wheat flour to expand and trap gas bubbles is key in many baked goods. Finding a replacement to replicate these structural functions using gluten-free ingredients was especially challenging because most options contain less protein.

In a baked good such as a muffin, the starch granules in wheat flour absorb moisture and swell as the batter is being prepared. The strands of gluten bond together and surround the starch granules. Gluten is particularly elastic and strong, especially when heated. This highly organized and strong network of gluten gives the muffin its structure and shape. Compared with wheat flour, gluten-free flours generally contain less protein and their protein is less elastic, so they don't do as good a job of organizing and holding the swollen starch granules. Most gluten-free flours also contain an even higher starch content, which means they can impart a gritty texture to baked goods. In effect, there's too much starch and not enough protein.

These differences mean that no single gluten-free flour behaves like wheat flour. To achieve the same (or at least similar) results, it's necessary to use a combination of gluten-free flours and starches to take advantage of their different properties. In addition, it's helpful to incorporate other ingredients that boost the effectiveness of their protein. Xanthan gum, for instance, acts like glue, helping cement the protein network in gluten-free flour. Emulsifiers such as nonfat milk powder can help the flour to hydrate more readily, which promotes the swelling of the starch granules and the bonding of the protein strands. Emulsifiers can also make gluten-free flour more compatible with fat—something that wheat flour does better than other flours. Why is this important? Many baked goods (think cookies, cakes, even muffins) contain a lot of fat for flavor and moistness. If the flour doesn't absorb fat well, the baked good can be both greasy (from the unabsorbed fat) and dry (because the starches are not properly coated with fat).

TIPS FOR SUCCESSFULLY MAINTAINING A GLUTEN-FREE DIET

If you're new to a gluten-free diet, you will want to pick up some good resources to help teach you how to read a product label and find hidden sources of gluten. Here are the key challenges, in brief.

Check Ingredients: Many foods are made with an ingredient that contains gluten. This list includes the obvious (traditional sandwich bread and Italian pasta) and the less obvious (such as soy sauce—which is typically made with soybeans and wheat—and some brands of baking powder). You will need to learn which ingredients are typically made with wheat-based ingredients, and then to read labels carefully.

Review Processing: Other foods can be processed in facilities that also handle wheat and as a result may contain trace amounts of gluten—even though the food contains no wheat. This can be an issue with foods like cornmeal or oats. If you have celiac disease or another reason to avoid foods with even trace amounts of gluten, you need to read labels carefully to make sure naturally gluten-free foods, like oats, have not been processed in the same machines used to grind wheat.

Separate and Safe: Likewise, as a cook, you need to think about cross-contamination if you're trying to eliminate all gluten, even trace amounts, from your diet. If you're preparing dishes with wheat as well as gluten-free recipes in the same kitchen, you need to be vigilant about washing measuring tools, bowls, cutting boards, and your hands.

As we developed gluten-free baked goods, much of our testing was aimed at solving both grittiness and weak structure. And because most home cooks don't want to stock a dozen flours and starches and use a customized blend for each recipe, we decided to develop as many recipes as possible using one all-purpose or whole-grain gluten-free flour blend.

The ATK All-Purpose Gluten-Free Flour Blend

G-F TESTING LAB

RICE FLOURS	We had the best results using Bob's Red Mill white rice flour and brown rice flour. See page 23 for more information.
POTATO STARCH	Be sure to use potato starch, not potato flour. Alternatively, 7 ounces (1¼ cups plus 2 tablespoons) sweet white rice flour, or 7 ounces (1¾ cups) arrowroot starch/flour/powder can be substituted for the potato starch. We had better results using sweet rice flour in quick breads, cakes, and cookies, and using arrowroot starch in yeast breads.
TAPIOCA STARCH	Tapioca starch is also sold as tapioca flour; they are interchangeable.
MILK POWDER	You can omit the milk powder, but baked goods won't brown as well and they will taste less rich. Alternatively, you can substitute soy milk powder.

✓ WHY THIS RECIPE WORKS

The decision to develop our own all-purpose blend came about after we tested a variety of other published recipes and store-bought blends, none of which worked universally well in all types of baked goods. Our ideal blend would have a rich, round flavor with enough protein to provide baked goods with a good chew and decent browning, and we wanted the ingredients to be easy to find. We also decided to leave out any binders, such as xanthan or guar gum, so that we could add them as needed to individual recipes. Most blends are based on one of three ingredients: rice flour, sorghum flour, or bean flour. We didn't like the bean- or sorghum-based flour blends; they worked well structurally but had off-flavors. Rice flour was clearly the best choice for building our own versatile flour blend, and white rice flour was ideal because of its neutral flavor and smooth texture. We knew that the blend would need a few other ingredients in addition to white rice flour. Individual gluten-free flours and starches absorb water, swell, and gel at different temperatures and to different degrees, creating more or less structure, more or less readily. Combining white rice flour with other types of starch essentially combined the properties of each to make the blend work better in a wide array of recipes. We added brown rice flour because it has an earthy flavor and gave the baked goods some welcome heft. Cornstarch didn't work well because it made the baked goods taste very starchy. Instead we liked tapioca starch, because it provided chew and elasticity, as well as potato starch, which helped with tenderness and binding. To find the ideal ratio of white rice flour, brown rice flour, tapioca starch, and potato starch, we baked many batches of muffins and cookies (upward of a thousand) with slightly altered flour and starch proportions. In the end, we found that too much brown rice flour made baked goods gritty, too much tapioca starch made them dense, and too much potato starch gave them crumbly textures. We liked a basic formula of 4 parts white rice flour, 1 part brown rice flour, 1 part potato starch, and ½ part tapioca. Tinkering with these amounts a bit further helped us land closer to the final proportions, but we were still having some structural problems. Suspecting that our flour blend needed a protein boost, we considered adding one of the following three ingredients: calcium carbonate, powdered egg whites, or nonfat milk powder. Calcium carbonate (the active ingredient in Tums) is added to many gluten-free breads, so we tried crushing and adding some tablets, but ultimately the hassle factor outweighed the slight tenderness it added. Powdered egg whites added a big boost in terms of structure but imparted an unpleasant, meringue-like flavor. The nonfat milk powder, however, helped with structure, tenderness, and browning and added rich and caramel-like flavor; it also helped temper the starchiness. Now we had a balanced and versatile blend that would perform well in many different types of recipes.

ATK All-Purpose Gluten-Free Flour Blend

MAKES 42 OUNCES (ABOUT 9⅓ CUPS)

If you don't bring the flour to room temperature before using, the recipe may not work as expected.

- 24 ounces (4½ cups plus ⅓ cup) white rice flour
- 7½ ounces (1⅔ cups) brown rice flour
- 7 ounces (1⅓ cups) potato starch
- 3 ounces (¾ cup) tapioca starch
- ¾ ounce (3 tablespoons) nonfat milk powder

Whisk all ingredients together in large bowl until well combined. Transfer to airtight container and refrigerate for up to 3 months or freeze for up to 6 months. Bring to room temperature before using.

The ATK Whole-Grain Gluten-Free Flour Blend

G-F TESTING LAB

TEFF FLOUR	We used teff flour made by Bob's Red Mill during our testing. We also tested several other brands of teff flour and found that they all worked equally well.
RICE FLOURS	We had the best results using Bob's Red Mill brown rice flour and sweet white rice flour. See page 23 for more information.
GROUND GOLDEN FLAXSEEDS	We had good results with Bob's Red Mill ground golden flaxseeds. Do not substitute ground brown flaxseeds because its flavor will be too strong. Do not attempt to grind flaxseeds yourself because you will not be able to grind them fine enough.

✓ WHY THIS RECIPE WORKS

In addition to our ATK All-Purpose Gluten-Free Flour Blend, we wanted a whole-grain flour blend that loosely mimicked the flavor, color, and texture of whole-wheat flour. We started by testing a variety of store-bought blends and published blend recipes to get the lay of the land. Surprisingly, most whole-grain blends we tested produced decent baked goods, but none of them had a deep, hearty, "wheaty" flavor. In fact, when we set up a blind taste test and pitted baked goods made with these whole-grain blends against our own all-purpose blend, most tasters could not tell the difference. We knew we could do better. As with our all-purpose blend, we wanted the whole-grain blend to use five ingredients or less, and we didn't want to include any binders such as xanthan or guar gum. Also, we wanted to keep this blend as allergy-friendly as possible and avoid milk powder, oat flour, and potato starch. Finally, we wanted whole-grain flours to make up more than 50 percent of our blend. The world of gluten-free whole-grain flours is fairly large, but we quickly narrowed it down to just eight options—amaranth, brown rice, buckwheat, coconut, millet, quinoa, sorghum, and teff. We ran these flours through a series of tests to help identify their flavors and textures and confidently eliminated buckwheat, quinoa, and coconut flours from the race because they all tasted too distinctive for a blend. Moving forward with teff, brown rice, sorghum, millet, and amaranth, we began a series of tests that paired them together in various configurations, round-robin style, to see what worked best. We also added some tapioca starch to the mix, knowing that we'd finesse the type and amount of starch later. As we moved through this intense round of testing (during which time we produced over 600 muffins), teff flour consistently came out on top for its hearty chew, darker color, and wheat-like flavor. Brown rice flour also ranked well because its mild flavor and texture smoothed out the rough edges of the teff. Sorghum, millet, and amaranth all fell out of the testing along the way—the sorghum consistently made muffins dry and tough, while the millet and amaranth added an unwelcome aftertaste and a grainy texture. Working with a ratio of 3 parts teff flour to 1 part brown rice flour, we put the tapioca under the spotlight and tested it against a few other starches including arrowroot, sweet white rice flour, and cornstarch. Tasters unanimously preferred the clean flavor and smooth, nongritty texture of sweet white rice flour over the others, and we settled on 3 parts teff flour and 1 part brown rice flour to ⅔ part sweet white rice flour. Finally, we turned our attention to a somewhat random group of secret ingredients that are sometimes added to blends in small amounts to add flavor, help with browning, or boost the protein content to make the blend stronger. Our secret list included ground flax, chia, and hemp seeds and pea powder isolate. We loved ground golden flaxseeds because they added a well-rounded, wheaty flavor and richness to both muffins and cookies. After 126 tests and more cookies and muffins than any one person could consume in a year, we nailed down the ingredients in our whole-grain blend: 3 parts teff flour, 1 part brown rice flour, 1 part ground golden flaxseeds, and ⅔ part sweet white rice flour.

ATK Whole-Grain Gluten-Free Flour Blend

MAKES 45 OUNCES (ABOUT 10 CUPS)

If you don't bring the flour to room temperature before using, the recipe may not work as expected.

- **24 ounces (5¼ cups) teff flour**
- **8 ounces (1¾ cups) brown rice flour**
- **8 ounces (2⅓ cups) ground golden flaxseeds**
- **5 ounces (1 cup) sweet white rice flour**

Whisk all ingredients together in large bowl until well combined. Transfer to airtight container and refrigerate for up to 3 months or freeze for up to 6 months. Bring to room temperature before using.

What About Store-Bought Flour Blends?

In traditional baking recipes, the brand of flour isn't terribly important. That's because all brands of all-purpose flour (as well as bread flour) contain the same single ingredient—wheat flour. Yes, protein levels in the wheat will vary among different brands, but this has minimal impact on the finished product.

In gluten-free baking recipes that call for a gluten-free flour blend, the brand of flour will have significant impact on the final baked good. That's because each brand of flour blend, whether all-purpose or whole-grain, relies on a mix of different ingredients, yielding cookies, cakes, breads, and muffins with varying textures, colors, and flavors.

TESTING ALL-PURPOSE FLOUR BLENDS

To get a sense of the range of possible outcomes, we tested 10 store-bought all-purpose gluten-free flour blends in three of our well-vetted recipes—chocolate chip cookies, blueberry muffins, and sandwich bread. Twenty tasters from our test kitchen participated in these blind taste tests, which also included samples of each recipe made with the ATK flour blend (the control). Tasters were asked to rate how close each sample came to the control.

THE RESULTS

For the most part, all of the blends worked in these recipes—that is, they made cookies, muffins, and loaves of bread that at least looked the part. However, there were significant textural and flavor differences (see the charts on pages 11 and 12). Our two favorite brands are made with neutral-tasting rice flour. Brands that ended up at the bottom of the rankings tend to include ingredients with more personality, such as sorghum or bean flours, which were detectable in the baked goods. Based on these tastings, we divided these 10 flour blends into two groups: recommended replacements for the ATK flour blend and those recommended with reservations.

RECOMMENDED ALL-PURPOSE FLOUR BLENDS

For the best results with recipes in this book, we recommend that you use the ATK flour blend. It was designed especially for these recipes. It's also cheaper than store-bought blends and more convenient, since you can make it in bulk rather than buying little boxes.

If shopping for five ingredients and spending less than 5 minutes to combine them is too much bother, we recommend that you use King Arthur Gluten-Free All-Purpose Flour in recipes that call for an all-purpose flour blend. Our second choice is Betty Crocker All-Purpose Gluten Free Rice Flour Blend. (This product wasn't available when we developed recipes for our first book but based on our experience testing the Betty Crocker blend in all the recipes in our second book, we can say with confidence that it will also work in the recipes from our first book.)

All of our recipes have also been tested with Bob's Red Mill GF All-Purpose Baking Flour, the most widely available brand in the United States. While we don't love its beany, earthy notes, it can be the only choice in many markets, and therefore we deemed it important to understand how this flour blend worked in our recipes. It's an acceptable choice in nearly all of our recipes, with the exception of Yeasted Doughnuts (page 92), Popovers (page 96), Baguettes (page 294), Bagels (page 314), and Rugelach (page 398).

REMEMBER TO WEIGH

If you decide to use a store-bought all-purpose flour blend, we strongly recommend that you weigh it. Because each blend is made with different ingredients, it packs into dry cup measures differently. A scale ensures that you have the right amount of flour—no matter the brand.

A WORD ON WHOLE-GRAIN FLOUR BLENDS

We could not find a store-bought whole-grain flour blend that delivered the same earthy, "wheaty" flavor as our blend. We don't recommend using any store-bought blends in recipes that call for our whole-grain blend.

Rating All-Purpose Flour Blends

We tested these 10 store-bought blends in three of our own gluten-free recipes—blueberry muffins, chocolate chip cookies, and sandwich bread—and compared them to baked goods made using the ATK All-Purpose Gluten-Free Flour Blend. Here are the results:

RECOMMENDED

These two blends performed very similarly to the ATK All-Purpose Gluten-Free Flour Blend in most of the recipes throughout this book. Look for more details in the G-F Testing Lab notes that accompany each recipe.

BRAND		INGREDIENTS	TASTERS' COMMENTS
	KING ARTHUR Gluten-Free All-Purpose Flour PRICE: $7.95 for 1.5-lb box ($5.30/lb)	White Rice Flour, Tapioca Flour, Potato Starch, Brown Rice Flour, Calcium Carbonate, Niacinamide (a B vitamin), Reduced Iron Thiamin Hydrochloride (vitamin B¹), Riboflavin (vitamin B²)	Across the board, this blend performed well in terms of both delivering good structure and having a neutral, not-too-starchy flavor. It finished in the top three for all tests. A few tasters found it too sweet in cookies and muffins, but overall it won out for its superior flavor. Many noted a grainy, gritty texture, but not enough to push it to the bottom of any tastings.
	BETTY CROCKER All-Purpose Gluten Free Rice Flour Blend PRICE: $3.75 for 1-lb box	Rice Flour, Potato Starch, Tapioca Starch, Guar Gum, Salt	In all three of our tests, this blend was ranked highly, particularly in the chocolate chip cookies. Overall, the blend won out for having a flavor very similar to our homemade blend. In terms of texture, a handful of tasters noted a "bouncy" texture in muffins and a "gummy" crumb in breads. However, the overall versatility of the blend kept it near the top in all of our tastings.

RECOMMENDED WITH RESERVATIONS

These eight blends (listed alphabetically and not in order of performance) all produced edible baked goods in the tasting; however, some worked better than others. We cannot guarantee that these blends will work as a replacement for the ATK All-Purpose Gluten-Free Flour Blend with the exception of Bob's Red Mill, which we tested in the recipes in this book and found to be an acceptable substitute with a few exceptions (see below). It will add a noticeable bean flavor in most instances.

BRAND		INGREDIENTS	TASTERS' COMMENTS
	AUTHENTIC FOODS GF Classical Blend PRICE: $15.79 for 3-lb bag ($5.26/lb)	Brown Rice Flour, Potato Starch, Tapioca Flour	This blend fared well in producing muffins, but failed to satisfy tasters when baked into cookies and bread. Due to the relatively high proportion of potato starch in the mix, tasters found the bread and cookies to be "doughy" and "pasty." The blend also changed the way the baked goods performed in the oven, producing "squat" muffins and cookies that "didn't spread."
	BOB'S RED MILL GF All-Purpose Baking Flour PRICE: $4.29 for 1.5-lb bag ($2.86/lb)	Garbanzo Bean Flour, Potato Starch, Tapioca Flour, Sorghum Flour, Fava Bean Flour	Our tasters did not like the distinctive taste of bean flour in their baked goods. There were complaints that items tasted "stale," and most panelists picked up strong "earthy" notes. Structurally speaking, muffins were "dense" and "crumbly," cookies spread into very thin crisps, and while bread had a "good structure," many noted that it was "dry."

RECOMMENDED WITH RESERVATIONS (continued)

BRAND	INGREDIENTS	TASTERS' COMMENTS
 **CUP4CUP Multipurpose Flour** PRICE: $19.95 for 3-lb bag ($6.65/lb)	Cornstarch, White Rice Flour, Brown Rice Flour, Nonfat Milk Powder, Tapioca Flour, Potato Starch, Xanthan Gum	Made up primarily of cornstarch, this blend left a starchy coating on the tongue and produced a "tight" texture in baked goods. Many tasters complained about the samples being "gummy." The cookies fared better than the muffins, in part because the sugar seemed to mask the presence of the cornstarch.
GLUTINO Gluten Free Pantry All Purpose Flour PRICE: $4.55 for 1-lb box	White Rice Flour, Potato Starch, Tapioca Starch, Pea Hull Fiber, Acacia Gum, Rice Protein	Since this blend includes some of the most unusual ingredients we've seen in any blend (pea hull fiber, acacia gum, and rice protein), we were interested to see how it would perform in our recipes. Unfortunately, the added ingredients came along with flavors that weren't appreciated by tasters. Muffins had a "bitter vegetal" note, cookies had a distinct "bean" flavor, and the bread tasted "sour."
 **LIVING NOW Gluten-Free All-Purpose Flour** PRICE: $4.49 for 1-lb box	White Rice Flour, Brown Rice Flour, Tapioca Flour, Potato Starch, Potato Flour, Cellulose	Producing muffins that were "heavy" and "dusty," cookies that tasters called "gritty" and "biscuit-y," and bread with an "odd flavor" and "lemon-like aftertaste," this blend fell short in flavor and texture. The blend produced "almond-y" and "nutty" tastes in the finished products that many found to be welcome in muffins and cookies, but out of place in bread.
PAMELA'S All-Purpose Flour Artisan Blend PRICE: $7.98 for 1.5-lb bag ($5.31/lb)	Brown Rice Flour, Tapioca Flour, White Rice Flour, Potato Starch, Sorghum Flour, Arrowroot Flour, Sweet Rice Flour, Xanthan Gum	Although tasters were partial to the muffins made with this blend, chocolate chip cookies and sandwich bread fared poorly in our testing. Many noted the samples had a "grainy" quality and the bread had an "off vegetal flavor."
PILLSBURY Best Multi-Purpose Gluten Free Flour Blend PRICE: $9.42 for 2-lb bag ($4.71/lb)	Rice Flour, Potato Starch, Pea Fiber, Tapioca Starch, Xanthan Gum	While tasters were partial to the "sweet buttery flavor" of baked goods made with this flour blend, the "gritty" texture of the flour distracted from the taste. Cookies were "crunchy," while muffins had a "strange coarseness," and loaves of bread were "tough and chewy." All of the samples failed to rise as much as the control, resulting in squat breads and muffins.
TRADER JOE'S Baker Josef's Gluten Free All Purpose Flour PRICE: $3.99 for 1-lb bag	Brown Rice Flour, Potato Starch, Rice Flour, Tapioca Flour	Bread made with the Trader Joe's blend was one of the favorites of the tasting panel; the chocolate chip cookies and blueberry muffins, however, didn't stand up against the rest. Our bread loaves had a "good structure," "tall rise," and a "tender" crumb. Cookies and muffins "lacked structure," "spread" during baking, and had an "off aftertaste" that bothered tasters.

Gluten-Free Cooking: Test Kitchen Discoveries

During the years we spent in the kitchen testing gluten-free recipes, we learned that cooking without wheat really is different. In many cases, we had to reinvent recipes and employ new techniques. Here are some of our key discoveries, which may be helpful if you are trying to adapt recipes already in your repertoire to work without wheat flour.

Thickening stays the same: In recipes where a tablespoon or two of flour is used as a thickener, you can generally use a gluten-free flour blend in a one-to-one replacement. This includes most stews and pan sauces. As with wheat flour, let the gluten-free flour cook for a minute before whisking in the liquid. This will cook out some of the raw, starchy flavor in the flour.

If you use cornstarch: You can also thicken liquids with cornstarch rather than flour. However, you must first turn cornstarch into a slurry by mixing it with cold water, and then use this slurry at the end of the cooking process. In general, you will need less cornstarch than flour.

For dusting proteins: Many breaded foods (everything from fried chicken and pork chops to eggplant Parmesan) are made with a bound breading—that is, they are dusted with flour, dipped in eggs or dairy, and then coated with crumbs. For the "dusting" part of the equation, cornstarch is a good replacement for the flour.

Make your own breading: We weren't terribly impressed with the brands of gluten-free bread crumbs that we tested. We had better luck taking our top-rated gluten-free sandwich bread and then grinding it into crumbs. Note that fresh bread crumbs should be dried in the oven before being used as a coating (see page 209 for more information).

Consider cornflakes: Cornflakes (as long as they are produced in a gluten-free facility) are another option that can be used in place of bread crumbs to top casseroles and such, though they are a bit sweeter than bread crumbs.

Replace soy sauce with tamari: Any recipe made with soy sauce (which generally contains wheat) can be made with tamari sauce (which generally does not contain wheat). A one-to-one replacement will work in most recipes.

Gluten-Free Baking: Keys to Success

Traditional baking is an exact science with time-honored techniques. When it comes to gluten-free baking, however, many new factors come into play and often key tenets of standard baking no longer apply. From measuring flour and proofing bread to determining leaveners, baking times and temperatures, and more, we had to break from tradition to develop great-tasting and foolproof gluten-free recipes. Here is a summary of what we learned.

1 THE BLEND YOU CHOOSE MAKES A HUGE DIFFERENCE

You can't plug just any gluten-free flour blend into the recipes in this book and expect them to work. (Similarly, you can't plug one of our blends into another recipe and expect it to work there either.) No two gluten-free blends are the same; they can contain wildly different ingredients—from rice and bean flours to seeds and gums—and in varying amounts. This means that the blend and the recipe need to be matched up; if they're not compatible, you'll just be wasting your time. For those of you who just can't resist the convenience of a premade blend, we offer store-bought alternatives to our all-purpose blend; you'll find recipe-specific information in the G-F Testing Lab attached to each recipe. We were unable, however, to find an acceptable store-bought substitute for our whole-grain gluten-free flour blend.

CUPCAKES
In simple yellow cupcakes, some gluten-free blends work better than others, but none tasted as good as the version made with the ATK blend.

ATK ALL-PURPOSE BLEND
Cupcake rises extremely well, with slight doming. Crumb is fine and very tender.

KING ARTHUR
Cupcake is denser and doesn't rise as well. Tastes slightly starchy

BETTY CROCKER
Cupcake rises well but crumb is dry and crumbly. Tastes slightly pasty.

BOB'S RED MILL
Cupcake rises well but crumb is coarser and more crumbly. Distinct bean flavor.

SANDWICH BREAD
In our Whole-Grain Sandwich Bread (page 272), no whole-grain gluten-free blend came close to the flavor and texture of bread made with the ATK blend.

ATK WHOLE-GRAIN BLEND
Bread rises tall, with just the right open texture.

CUP4CUP WHOLESOME FLOUR BLEND
Bread is more squat and dense.

2 FINELY GROUND RICE FLOURS YIELD BETTER RESULTS

Throughout all of our testing, we found that different brands of white and brown rice flours (the former is in our all-purpose blend, and the latter is used in both of our flour blends) have slightly different grinds that affect how well our recipes work and taste. Note that because our all-purpose flour blend has three times more white rice flour than brown rice flour, the brand you choose (and its grind) can have a big impact on the success of your baked goods. Depending on the brand, the grind can range from very fine to a tad gritty. In the end, we found that finely ground flours work best in both our all-purpose gluten-free flour blend (page 7) and our whole-grain gluten-free flour blend (page 9). By comparison, the rice flours with coarser grinds (such as Arrowhead Mills and Hodgson Mills brown rice flour) will have trouble absorbing the liquid and fat and will retain their gritty texture. We found Bob's Red Mill rice flours (the most widely available brand of white and brown rice flour) to have the finest grind, although several other flours were acceptable, including EnerG (white and brown), Living Now (white), and King Arthur (brown). (Note that Goya brand rice flours are not gluten-free.) If you use another brand of rice flour, the texture should be close to that of cornstarch, with no more than a hint of grit. In the photos below, you can see the difference that finely and coarsely ground flours make in a simple chocolate chip cookie recipe.

COOKIES MADE WITH ARROWHEAD MILLS RICE FLOURS
Cookies spread too much and seemed to fry in unabsorbed fat, resulting in a candy-like texture.

COOKIES MADE WITH BOB'S RED MILL RICE FLOURS
Cookies spread nicely and had just the right balance of crisp edges and chewy centers.

3 GLUTEN-FREE FLOURS REQUIRE SPECIAL MEASURING TECHNIQUES

Most home bakers use the dip-and-sweep method when measuring flour, but this doesn't work well with gluten-free flours and starches. One reason is that these flours and starches are finer than wheat flours, making them hard to pack evenly and consistently into a measuring cup. Also, they are often sold in small bags or boxes, so it is hard to maneuver a measuring cup inside the package without creating a mess or unevenly packing the cup. The simple solution is to just use a scale and weigh the flours instead of relying on wavering volume measurements. **We strongly recommend that you use a scale when baking from this book.** If you insist on using measuring cups, we found the following method delivers the most uniform results.

1. Place sheet of paper towel on counter and set measuring cup in center.

2. Spoon flour into cup, occasionally shaking cup to settle flour, until flour is mounded over rim. Do not tap cup or pack flour.

3. Using flat edge (like back of butter knife), scrape away excess flour to level.

4. Use paper towel to help funnel excess flour back into bag/container.

4 **USING LESS BUTTER AND OIL MINIMIZES GREASINESS AND IMPROVES STRUCTURE**
Gluten-free flours don't absorb fat as readily as wheat flour does. In high-fat recipes, such as cookies, cakes, and pie dough, simply replacing the wheat flour with an equal amount of gluten-free flour doesn't work. The baked goods are often much too greasy, which not only makes them unappetizing but can affect how cookies spread in the oven or determine whether pie dough holds its shape when baked. When reworking conventional recipes with gluten-free flour, we often trimmed a few tablespoons of butter or oil. You can easily see the difference in these two double-crust pies: One has been made with a traditional amount of fat, and the other has been made with a reduced amount of fat.

PIE DOUGH
MADE WITH
20 TABLESPOONS
BUTTER

PIE DOUGH
MADE WITH
16 TABLESPOONS
BUTTER

5 **OTHER INGREDIENTS CAN SUPPLY RICHNESS**
While using less butter or oil solved the greasiness problem in many recipes, this also made them less rich. In some cases, we compensated by adding another rich ingredient, such as cream cheese, sour cream, white chocolate, or even almond flour.

6 **BINDERS ADD STRUCTURE**
Binders (such as egg, xanthan gum, and ground psyllium husk) are crucial in gluten-free baking because the flours and starches are not able to form the strong, elastic bonds necessary for structure and height. Almost every baking recipe in the book includes an extra egg for this reason, and we even include them in recipes that don't traditionally call for eggs, such as Baguettes (page 294). Xanthan gum is also added to most of our baking recipes for extra structure and strength. The xanthan is more important in some recipes than in others; you can omit it if making muffins but not if making cookies, as you can see in the photos of White Chocolate–Macadamia Nut Cookies (page 361) below. We've noted the binder's level of importance in the G-F Testing Lab that accompanies each recipe. For more information on how to substitute different binders, see The Use of Binders on page 31.

COOKIES MADE
WITHOUT
XANTHAN GUM

COOKIES MADE
WITH XANTHAN GUM

7 EXTRA LEAVENERS HELP DOUGHS RISE PROPERLY

Gluten-free batters and doughs have a weaker protein structure than those made with wheat flour. This means that they have a harder time holding on to air bubbles from yeast and baking powder, and so they often bake up heavy and dense. Adding a little extra leavener, such as baking powder or baking soda, can help prevent this. Also, we've found that yeast bread often benefits from the addition of baking powder or baking soda to give the loaves a small height boost, as you can see in the sandwich bread below.

SANDWICH BREAD MADE WITH YEAST ALONE

SANDWICH BREAD MADE WITH YEAST AND BAKING POWDER

8 GLUTEN-FREE FLOUR DOESN'T BROWN AS WELL AS WHEAT FLOUR

To improve browning as well as add richness, we included milk powder in our all-purpose blend. A few recipes, such as sandwich bread, benefited from the addition of even a bit more milk powder. We sometimes added baking soda to help with browning, and often we sprinkled sugar on top of things (such as muffins) to encourage browning.

9 MIXING BATTERS LONGER PROVIDES STRUCTURE

While traditional recipes often warn against overmixing to avoid building up excess structure in delicate batters (such as muffins and cakes) so that they don't turn rubbery, we found the opposite to be true of gluten-free batters. In fact, we often found ourselves trying to get the batters to have more structure so that they would have a better rise and a nicer chew, and could support stir-ins, such as blueberries. The gluten-free blueberry muffins below show the difference between an undermixed batter and a well-mixed batter in terms of both overall height and the ability to support berries evenly throughout the muffin.

MUFFIN MADE USING TRADITIONAL MIXING METHOD

MUFFIN MADE USING LONGER MIXING METHOD

10 **RESTING BATTERS AND DOUGHS HAS MULTIPLE BENEFITS**
Early on in our testing, we were commonly plagued by a sandy texture in our quick-cooking baked goods. (It was not noticeable in our baked goods with long baking times.) We tested lots of theories on how to get rid of this grit (grinding the flours further in a food processor, soaking them in water, heating them up before making the batter), but nothing worked well. Then, almost by accident, we found that letting the batters sit for 30 minutes before baking made all the difference. It simply gave the flours and starches time to absorb the liquid and soften before baking. It also helped batters become thicker and doughs to firm up so that they were less sticky. You can see the dramatic difference this made in the Whole-Grain Pancakes (page 42) below. Be sure to cover the bowl of batter tightly with plastic wrap so that it doesn't dry out as it rests.

**PANCAKES MADE
WITHOUT RESTED
BATTER**

**PANCAKES MADE
WITH RESTED BATTER**

11 **THE FASTER THE RISE, THE BETTER**
When working with gluten-free yeast breads, you want them to rise as quickly as possible before the starches begin to set and the dough becomes stiff. As the dough stiffens, which happens as soon as the abundant starches in gluten-free flours absorb liquid, it becomes more difficult for the air bubbles produced by the yeast to move evenly throughout the dough. As a result, breads can be dense with a gummy layer along the bottom of the loaf. We use a superfast rising technique that blooms instant yeast in warm, sweetened water before adding it to the dough, and then starts the one and only rise in a warm (but turned-off) oven; see page 274 for more information. This technique results in a taller loaf with an open, even texture versus bread made traditionally with a longer, two-stage rising technique, which results in a denser, more squat loaf with a gummy bottom.

**BREAD USING
TRADITIONAL
LONG RISE**

**BREAD USING
SUPERFAST RISING
TECHNIQUE**

12 **CUSTOMIZED PANS ENSURE THE BEST SHAPE AND COLOR**
With many gluten-free baked goods, we needed some creative solutions to get rolls to hold their shape and breads to rise tall, and to keep cookies from burning. For our Hamburger Rolls (page 303), we made our own aluminum foil collars, much like professional ring molds, to help the rolls stay round; for Honey-Millet Sandwich Bread (page 275), we used a slightly smaller loaf pan (8½ by 4½ inches) but then wrapped a foil collar around the top of the pan in order to get a nice tall loaf. And for some baked goods, we found that we needed to use two baking sheets (one nestled inside another) to prevent burning. Don't ignore these instructions, or you'll likely be very unhappy with the results.

**HAMBURGER ROLL
MADE WITHOUT
FOIL COLLAR**

**HAMBURGER ROLL
MADE WITH FOIL
COLLAR**

13 **VISUAL CUES ALONE ARE NOT RELIABLE**
Knowing when a cake or bread is perfectly done and ready to come out of the oven can be tricky. This is especially true with gluten-free baking because traditional techniques (like a clean toothpick or pressing on the top of a cake) aren't always accurate indicators. Even when fully cooked, gluten-free baked goods often look underdone, are slightly wet inside, and feel soft to the touch. Only when they cool do the starches set and firm up. We always list visual cues to help identify when something is fully baked, but we often find that timing is a more reliable way to determine doneness, so if you don't have one, invest in a kitchen timer. Obviously, if your oven runs hot or cold, these times will not be accurate, so be sure to use a good oven thermometer.

1. A timer is often the best way to tell when your gluten-free baked goods are done because visual cues can be misleading.

2. A well-calibrated oven is crucial for gluten-free baking. Use a good oven thermometer and place it as close to the center of the oven as possible.

14 **EXTRA LIQUID IMPROVES TEXTURE**
The high starch content of gluten-free flour can impart a gritty texture to baked goods. We found that many gluten-free batters and doughs need more liquid to hydrate the flour blend properly, eliminate grittiness, and achieve a less dense or dry texture.

15 **PATIENCE PAYS OFF**
For recipes with an increased liquid content, it is very important to drive off this extra moisture during baking or you'll wind up with a gummy texture. This is why many of our recipes have long baking times. Some of our recipes even instruct you to bake beyond the time that a toothpick inserted into the baked good comes out clean. Whole-Grain Gingerbread Coffee Cake (page 88) is such a recipe; if you pull this cake out of the oven too soon, it will have a very mushy texture.

COFFEE CAKE BAKED UNTIL TOOTHPICK COMES OUT CLEAN

COFFEE CAKE BAKED 20 MINUTES PAST POINT THAT TOOTHPICK COMES OUT CLEAN

16 **SMALL BATCHES ARE BEST**
Gluten-free baked goods don't last as long as regular baked goods, so don't make big batches of cookies or muffins and expect them to stay fresh for days. We provide storage guidelines for various types of baked goods throughout the book.

Troubleshooting Gluten-Free Recipes

After thousands of kitchen tests, we have a sense of what problems are likely to occur when you attempt to make a conventional baked good gluten-free. The tips on this page offer advice for common problems we encountered during our recipe development. Note that every baking recipe is a unique formula, so these solutions won't work in all cases. Think of this information as a starting point when problem-solving in your kitchen.

TYPE OF RECIPE	COMMON PROBLEM	POSSIBLE SOLUTION
Pancakes	Dense, gummy texture	Lower burner or griddle temperature and extend cooking time to help pancakes cook through without getting too brown
Muffins/Quick Breads	Crumbly texture	Add extra egg and use binder, like xanthan gum
	Dense texture	Use more leavener
	Gritty texture	Let batter rest for 30 minutes before baking
	Dry texture	Add additional liquid or sour cream
	Mushy center	Lower oven temperature and extend baking time
Drop Cookies	Excessive spread	Add binder and let dough rest
	Gritty texture	Let dough rest for 30 minutes before baking
	Greasy	Use less butter and swap in a portion of almond flour
	Overly crisp texture	Use more brown sugar, less white sugar
	Overly soft texture	Use superfine sugar and leave cookies in turned-off oven after baking for several minutes to dry out
	Airy, hollow texture	Use melted butter instead of creaming it
	Burnt bottoms	Before baking, place baking sheet of cookies inside second sheet for extra insulation on bottom
Cakes	Greasy mouthfeel	Swap in sour cream, chocolate, or cream cheese for some of fat
	Dense crumb	Reduce amount of fat, use additional liquid, use additional baking powder, use additional egg
	Gummy center	Lower oven temperature and extend baking time; swap out some of liquid for sour cream
	Edges of cake are tough	Line sides and bottom of cake pan with parchment paper
	Cake doesn't release	When parchment is not an option, make paste of butter and flour blend and brush into pan
Pie/Tart Dough	Crumbly texture	Add binder, such as xanthan gum
	Not flaky	Add small amount of rice vinegar
	Dry, difficult dough	Process butter more thoroughly during mixing
Yeast Breads	Dough doesn't rise	Add extra liquid; use instant yeast and bloom yeast in warm, sweetened water; make proofing box (see page 273)
	Dense crumb	Add ground psyllium husk
	Gummy, wet crumb	Lower oven temperature and extend baking time
	Squat loaves	Use smaller loaf pan and add foil collar
	Bread sinks after baking	Leave bread in turned-off oven after baking to dry out

The Use of Binders

Because there is less protein in gluten-free flours than in wheat flours, gluten-free flours are not capable of forming the strong network required to stretch and surround starch granules. In our testing, we found that gluten-free flours required some help from a binder, generally in the form of xanthan gum, guar gum, or powdered psyllium husk. (See pages 24–25 for detailed descriptions of each.) These ingredients strengthen protein networks in baked goods and make them more elastic. In effect, they act as the glue that gives gluten-free baked goods the proper shape.

XANTHAN GUM AND GUAR GUM

We tested both xanthan gum and guar gum in muffins, cakes, cookies, brownies, and fresh pasta as well as in pie dough and tart dough, and we preferred xanthan gum in every application. In many cases the differences were slight, but the guar gum produced baked goods that were a bit more pasty and/or starchy. Also, baked goods made with xanthan had a longer shelf life than those made with guar. That said, guar gum produced good results in almost every case other than tart dough and fresh pasta.

CHIA SEEDS

We tested adding ground chia seeds to muffins, cookies, and pie crust in lieu of xanthan gum. They were moderately successful in the muffins but added a mushy texture and unwelcome flavor. In the cookies and pie crust, they didn't add enough structure to the dough; the cookies melted completely into greasy puddles, and the pie crust was very cracked and crumbly. We don't recommend them as a binder.

PSYLLIUM HUSK IN YEASTED RECIPES

Powdered psyllium husk is especially effective at creating a more open and airy crumb. In extensive kitchen tests, we found it was the only choice in yeast breads and pizza. It produced breads with a bit of chew and a better rise. And its earthy flavor (which might seem out of place in a sugar cookie) worked beautifully in bread recipes. So why does psyllium work better than either gum in yeast breads? It binds more effectively with water, and there's a lot of water in bread dough. As a result, psyllium does a better job of strengthening the protein network so it is capable of holding in lots of gas and steam during baking.

PSYLLIUM HUSK IN NONYEASTED RECIPES

We tried psyllium husk in nearly a dozen other recipes. In most cases it worked fine but not quite as well as xanthan gum, in part because so much more of it is required. In recipes with less moisture than bread dough (such as muffins, cookies, fresh pasta, pie dough, or tart dough), the psyllium produced a drier texture and a coarser crumb, and its hearty flavor seemed a little out of place in some cases (especially popovers and shortbread). That said, it was a good substitute for xanthan if you want a more "natural" option.

OUR APPROACH

Other than our yeast breads, which rely on psyllium husk, the majority of the baked goods in this book call for a small amount of xanthan gum. We know that some people have a hard time digesting xanthan, so here are some guidelines for those who want to swap it with something else. You can replace xanthan with an equal amount of guar or twice as much psyllium in most recipes in this book. The one exception is drop cookies, where xanthan does a better job of controlling spread. In our cookie recipes, we suggest replacing xanthan with three times as much guar or five times as much psyllium.

Substitution Formulas

	SUBSTITUTIONS
Baked Goods (except Drop Cookies)	1 teaspoon xanthan gum =
	1 teaspoon guar gum =
	2 teaspoons psyllium powder
Drop Cookies	1 teaspoon xanthan gum =
	3 teaspoons guar gum =
	5 teaspoons psyllium powder

The Gluten-Free Pantry

If you are serious about gluten-free baking, you'll want to stock your pantry with the flours and starches that make up our versatile flour blends as well as those that are used in many of our recipes. Below you will find a list of these flours and starches as well as other helpful ingredients—such as leaveners and binders, grains and seeds, and rice and gluten-free pasta—that are essential when preparing gluten-free baked goods and savory foods.

Many of the ingredients listed in this section are sold in all supermarkets. Other items (like rice flour and teff flour) are sold in natural foods stores and well-stocked supermarkets, or you can buy them online directly from manufacturers. Bob's Red Mill makes many of the flours and starches listed below and is the brand we stock in the test kitchen. Amazon also sells most of the products listed below.

FLOURS AND STARCHES

Because protein is an important component in any flour, we have included this information below. (The percentage will vary according to how the flour is processed.) Wheat flour has 6 to 13 percent protein. Like the flours, each starch behaves differently—they are not interchangeable. Most of these starches already will be familiar to you, and you'll find that you use them in a variety of roles for both cooking and baking applications.

Almond Flour: Almond flour has a mild flavor that is subtly sweet and nutty. It is high in protein and has a coarse texture. Almond flour is usually made with blanched almonds, while almond meal can be made with blanched almonds or almonds with their skins on. That said, some manufacturers, including Bob's Red Mill, use both terms on their packaging, so read labels carefully. We prefer flour (or meal) made from blanched almonds since the lighter color tends to be more versatile. Almond flour is a good choice for rustic cakes, and we have found that it is particularly helpful in cookie recipes, like our Linzer Cookies (page 381), where a small amount contributes richness, heft, and fat without adding a noticeable flavor. You can make your own almond flour by grinding blanched almonds in a food processor.
Protein: 21%
Where to Store It: Refrigerator or freezer

Buckwheat Flour: Buckwheat, despite its name, is not related to wheat but is in fact an herb. Made by grinding the plant's triangular seeds, buckwheat flour (and all buckwheat products) has a noticeably earthy flavor and dark color. Its most familiar uses are in the traditional Russian yeast-raised pancakes known as blini and as the base of soba noodles. It is also a good option for making crepes. Because of its strong flavor, it is best used in combination with another flour. (See also Buckwheat Groats and Kasha on page 26.)
Protein: 13%
Where to Store It: Refrigerator or freezer

Chickpea (Garbanzo Bean) Flour: Made by grinding whole dried chickpeas, this flour has a distinct bean flavor and darker color and is more often seen in dishes outside the United States, particularly in the Middle East, France, and Italy.
Protein: 20%
Where to Store It: Refrigerator or freezer

Cornstarch: This refined product, made from the starchy endosperm of corn, has a neutral flavor and has long been used as a thickener for sauces and gravies. Some gluten-free recipes use it in large quantities in baked goods, but we found that this approach can impart a starchy texture. In addition, cornstarch is low in nutrients, so using it by the cupful isn't terribly appealing.
Where to Store It: Pantry

Masa Harina: This fine, mild-flavored flour is made from dried masa, the corn-flour dough used throughout Latin America. Masa is made from hominy (dried corn kernels) that are cooked in water with slaked lime until tender. The hominy is then ground to a flour and mixed with more water and fat (usually lard or shortening) to form a dough. Since fresh masa has a short life, many cooks make masa by adding water to masa harina. Maseca (the name translates as "dried masa") is sold in most supermarkets.
Protein: 11%
Where to Store It: Pantry or freezer

Millet Flour: This light, powdery, pale yellow flour is ground from a seed that is believed to be the first domesticated cereal grain. Millet has a sweet, corn-like flavor and is suitable in both savory and sweet applications. Millet flour has more protein than rice flour, so we often use it to help build structure in doughs; too much, however, can leave a starchy taste, so we add it in small quantities. You can grind your own millet flour from the seeds using a spice grinder; just be sure to rinse and dry the seeds before grinding, and grind in batches until it reaches a fine, powdery consistency.
Protein: 10%
Where to Store It: Refrigerator or freezer

Oat Flour: Made by grinding oats to a powder, this flour has a subtle, slightly sweet whole-grain flavor. It adds a welcome wheatiness to sandwich bread, and because it is high in protein it helps build structure in breads. You can grind old-fashioned rolled oats in a food processor or spice grinder for about 1 minute to make your own oat flour. We also tested a number of widely available brands of oat flour and found they all performed equally well in our breads, with the exception of "toasted" oat flour. We do not recommend using toasted oat flour in our recipes; the dough will be stickier and more difficult to work with, and breads will be darker in color and denser in texture. Oats are a gluten-free grain, but they're often processed in facilities that also process wheat, which creates cross-contamination issues. When buying oat flour, make sure to check the label. Alternatively, you can substitute sorghum flour for oat flour in our bread recipes. We developed our recipes using Bob's Red Mill Gluten-Free Whole-Grain Oat Flour.
Protein: 17.5%
Where to Store It: Refrigerator or freezer

Potato Starch: Made by dehydrating a slurry of water and peeled potatoes, potato starch provides structure, along with tenderness and binding power. However, it requires a higher baking temperature (and thus more time and moisture) than tapioca starch (see page 00) to reach its maximum viscosity. This makes it most useful in longer-cooking baked goods that have more moisture, like muffins or quick breads (tapioca starch is more effective in cookies). Do not confuse it with potato flour, which is made

from cooked unpeeled potatoes and has a definite potato flavor. If you have a nightshade allergy and cannot use potato starch, we found that sweet white rice flour or arrowroot starch is the best substitute for potato starch in our ATK All-Purpose Gluten-Free Flour Blend.

Where to Store It: Pantry

Rice Flour, Brown: Since it still contains the bran, brown rice flour has more fiber, fat, and protein than white rice flour. It has a sandy texture like white rice flour, but a nuttier, earthier flavor (just like brown rice in comparison with white rice). Because of its fat content, brown rice flour has a short shelf life and should not be stored in the pantry. Look for brown rice flour that is as finely ground as possible. For best results when making recipes in this book, we recommend using Bob's Red Mill Brown Rice Flour.

Protein: 7.5%
Where to Store It: Refrigerator or freezer

Rice Flour, White: Made from rice after the bran and germ have been removed, white rice flour has a neutral flavor, light color, and somewhat sandy texture. It is affordable and fairly easy to find, and it has a long shelf life. Look for white rice flour that is as finely ground as possible, with little or no grit. For best results when making recipes in this book, we recommend using Bob's Red Mill White Rice Flour.
Protein: 5%
Where to Store It: Pantry

Rice Flour, Sweet White: Despite its name, sweet white rice flour isn't actually sweet, but it is much starchier than white rice flour. It is ground from a variety of white rice, called glutinous rice (no, it doesn't contain gluten), that contains a higher percentage of starch than white rice flour does. Because of its starchiness, this flour acts as an effective binder, so much so that we included a small amount of sweet rice flour in our whole-grain gluten-free flour blend. Look for sweet white rice flour that is as finely ground as possible, with little or no grit. For best results when making recipes in this book, we recommend using Bob's Red Mill Sweet White Rice Flour.

Protein: 6%
Where to Store It: Pantry

Sorghum Flour: Largely unknown in the United States, sorghum flour is a commonly used ingredient around the rest of the world, and for good reason. It is high in protein, fiber, and iron and has a mild flavor, making it a great addition to both savory and sweet applications; it is also used to make gluten-free beer. We've found that it is a good substitute for oat flour in our recipes, not only because of its mild flavor profile, but also because of the comparable protein boost it lends baked goods. There is sorghum flour and "sweet" white sorghum flour. We tested a wide variety of available brands in our recipes for Maple-Sorghum Skillet Bread (page 324) and Popovers (page 96) and found that while we noticed slight variations in grind, color, and flavor across brands, they all performed acceptably in both recipes. For best results when making recipes in this book, we recommend using Bob's Red Mill "Sweet" White Sorghum Flour.
Protein: 12%
Where to Store It: Refrigerator or freezer

Tapioca Starch: Made from the starchy tuberous root of the cassava plant, this white powder provides chew, elasticity, and structure to baked goods. Tapioca starch is sometimes labeled tapioca flour even though it contains no protein and is a pure starch. Products with either label can be used in our recipes.
Where to Store It: Pantry

Teff Flour: Teff flour, which anchors our whole-grain flour blend, is high in protein and therefore helps provide structure in baked goods. It is made from the tiny grains of an ancient cereal grass primarily grown in Ethiopia and Eritrea. Teff flour has a deep brown color and a mild, earthy, wheaty flavor with hints of molasses. We tested a number of brands, which performed equally well in our whole-grain gluten-free flour blend. We developed our recipes using Bob's Red Mill Teff Flour.
Protein: 12.5%
Where to Store It: Refrigerator or freezer

BINDERS AND LEAVENERS

In the absence of gluten's structural power, leaveners become absolutely critical in creating the necessary amount of lift and browning in baked goods. Many of the recipes in this book rely on multiple leaveners and, in some cases, comparatively large quantities of them. Binders such as xanthan gum, guar gum, and psyllium husk are essential for replacing structure typically provided by gluten. See page 21 for more information on our testing of these binders.

Baking Soda: Containing just bicarbonate of soda, baking soda provides lift to cakes, muffins, and other baked goods, both traditional and gluten-free. When baking soda, which is alkaline, encounters an acidic ingredient (such as sour cream, buttermilk, or brown sugar), carbon and oxygen combine to form carbon dioxide. The tiny bubbles of carbon dioxide then lift up the dough. In addition to lift, baking soda helps cookies spread and improves browning in everything from cornbread to fried chicken. For information on how baking soda helps promote tender gluten-free yeast breads, see page 308.
Where to Store It: Pantry

Baking Powder: Baking powder creates carbon dioxide to provide lift to baked goods. Cooks use baking powder rather than baking soda when there is no natural acidity in the batter. The active ingredients in baking powder are baking soda and an acidic element, such as cream of tartar. It also contains cornstarch to absorb moisture and keep the powder dry. These three ingredients are naturally gluten-free; however, wheat starch is sometimes used in place of the cornstarch, so make sure to check the ingredient list on the nutritional label. Also note that some brands may be produced in a facility that also processes wheat; this information will also be noted on the label. We've had good luck using Rumford and Clabber Girl brands, both of which are gluten-free. As with baking soda, baking powder is sometimes added to savory breaded or fried coatings for improved texture and chew.
Where to Store It: Pantry

Cream of Tartar: This fine white powder is sold in small bottles in the spice aisle, but it's not actually a spice. Cream of tartar is a by-product of the wine-making process. It is used to help stabilize egg whites when they are whipped. This is especially important in gluten-free recipes, which often depend on whipped egg whites for structure and height. How does cream of tartar work? As an acid, it lowers the pH of the egg whites. This slows down the process by which the proteins link up and form a foam. The longer it takes for the proteins to link up, the stronger the foam will be—and a stable foam is key to tall cakes and sturdy meringues.
Where to Store It: Pantry

Guar Gum: A powder derived from the ground endosperm of guar seeds, guar gum is high in fiber so it is often sold as a laxative. It works like xanthan gum in adding structure and thickening, although it does impart a slightly starchy texture to baked goods. We prefer to use xanthan gum rather than guar gum, but the two are interchangeable in most recipes. See page 21 for information on using guar gum in place of xanthan gum.
Where to Store It: Pantry

Nonfat Milk Powder: This shelf-stable dehydrated dairy product is in our all-purpose flour blend. It is helpful in gluten-free baking because it acts as an emulsifier, which contributes to structure by helping proteins and starches hydrate more readily so that they can then swell and form networks more effectively. It helps gluten-free flours become more compatible with fat. It also adds dairy flavor, and the lactose and milk proteins help with browning.
Where to Store It: Pantry

Powdered Psyllium Husk: Psyllium seed husk powder is one of the major components of Metamucil and Colon Cleanse. Its chemical composition is similar to that of xanthan gum, but it has a higher viscosity, so it is able to bind water even more effectively. We have found that psyllium interacts strongly with the proteins in gluten-free flours, creating a sturdy network capable of holding in lots of gas and steam during baking, and it provides a strong enough structure to support highly leavened bread once the bread cools. It adds wheat flavor that works well in breads where "whole-wheat" flavor is appropriate. We tested a number of widely available brands of powdered psyllium husk in our sandwich breads and found that their performance varied. Some breads did not rise as well and therefore were denser, while others were a bit more wet and gummy. Two brands, Yerba Prima and The Vitamin Shoppe, turned the breads a purplish gray; however, this did not affect the flavor of the breads. We had the best luck using Now Foods Psyllium Husk Powder.
Where to Store It: Pantry

Xanthan Gum: Made by using the microorganism *Xanthomonas campestris* to ferment simple sugars, xanthan gum is used widely as a thickener and stabilizer in commercial products like prepared salad dressings and toothpaste. It serves many roles in gluten-free baking. Because gluten-free flours have less protein than wheat flours and are not capable of forming the same network required to stretch and surround starch granules, they need reinforcement. Xanthan gum strengthens these networks and also makes them more elastic. Essentially, adding xanthan gum is like adding glue to the proteins in gluten-free flour. It also increases the shelf life of baked goods. Yes, xanthan gum is expensive, but you only need a little bit. See page 21 for more information about substitutions for xanthan gum.
Where to Store It: Refrigerator or freezer

Yeast: Throughout this book we call for instant or rapid-rise yeast, which, unlike active dry yeast, does not require proofing. However, we found that when we proofed it, the yeast got to work even faster, which was key when getting many of our gluten-free breads to rise faster and taller. To substitute active dry yeast for instant yeast, use 25 percent more active dry yeast and follow the proofing instructions in the recipe. For example, if the recipe calls for 1 teaspoon of instant yeast, use 1¼ teaspoons of active dry.
Where to Store It: Refrigerator (and pay attention to the expiration date)

GRAINS AND SEEDS

The world of grains is a big one—which is a great thing for those who can't eat gluten. The list below offers a wide range of options for making interesting side dishes, main dishes, and more. In chapter 2 you will find recipes using many of these gluten-free grains. In addition to grains, this list includes the seeds that can be ground into flour or used whole in baked goods and other recipes.

Amaranth: Amaranth, a staple of the Incas and Aztecs, is second only to quinoa for protein content among grains and seeds. Amaranth has a complex flavor that's very nutty and earthy. It is often dry-toasted before being cooked and can be prepared like porridge or rice. The whole seeds can also be popped like popcorn.

Buckwheat Groats and Kasha: Buckwheat, despite its name, is not related to wheat but is in fact an herb that is related to sorrel and rhubarb.

Buckwheat has an assertive flavor and can be found in several forms. Hulled, crushed buckwheat seeds are known as buckwheat groats, and because of their high carbohydrate content they are generally treated like a grain. Grayish green in color, groats have a mild, earthy flavor. They are often eaten as a staple like rice and are baked into puddings and porridges. Buckwheat's triangular seeds can also be ground to make flour.

Kasha is buckwheat groats that have been roasted. This process gives kasha a darker color and a noticeably earthier and roasty flavor that some people love, and others don't. Kasha is often served pilaf-style and as a hot cereal and is traditionally used in blintzes, combined with pasta to make a traditional Eastern European Jewish dish called kasha varnishkas, and included as part of a filling for pastries known as knishes.

Cornmeal and Polenta: For many consumers, buying cornmeal used to mean picking up a container of Quaker, or perhaps (especially if you lived in the South) a stone-ground local variety. But at most supermarkets today, you've got a lot more options to sort through: fine-, medium-, and coarse-ground; instant and quick-cooking; whole-grain, stone-ground, and regular. Whether you are making cornbread, pancakes, polenta, or a rustic Italian-style cake, different recipes require different grinds and types of cornmeal. What you use can make a big difference. Make sure to read—and buy—carefully.

Flaxseeds: Flaxseeds are similar in size to sesame seeds and have a sweet, wheaty flavor. They are naturally gluten-free and are sold in most supermarkets both whole and ground. Flaxseeds are one of the highest sources known for the omega-3 fatty acid called alpha-linolenic acid (ALA), which is found only in certain plant foods and oils and must be supplied in our diet for good health. There are two types of flaxseeds: brown and golden. We chose to use golden flaxseeds in our whole-grain flour blend, as their milder, nutty flavor complemented the teff flour. Whole seeds have a longer shelf life, but we preferred ground flaxseeds in our whole-grain gluten-free flour blend and breads because we use them as a flour rather than as a stir-in. As an added bonus, grinding flaxseeds improves the release of nutrients.

Millet: Believed to be the first domesticated cereal grain, this tiny cereal grass seed has a long history and is still a staple in a large part of the world, particularly in Asia and Africa. The seeds can be ground into flour or used whole. Millet has a mellow corn flavor that works well in both savory and sweet applications, including breads and pan-fried cakes. It can be cooked pilaf-style, pasta-style for a grain salad, or turned into a creamy breakfast porridge. To add texture to baked goods, try incorporating a small amount of millet into the batter (see Honey-Millet Sandwich Bread on page 275).

Oats: From breakfast table to cookie jar, this nutritious cereal grass is a versatile part of the gluten-free diet. But be careful when buying oats; they're often processed in facilities that also process wheat, which creates cross-contamination issues. It's therefore critical to make sure you are buying oats that are processed in a gluten-free facility. Oats come in several forms: groats (see below), old-fashioned rolled oats, steel cut, and instant.

Oat Berries (Oat Groats): Labeled either oat berries or oat groats, this gluten-free whole grain is simply whole oats that have been hulled and cleaned. They are the least processed oat product (other forms are processed further, such as being rolled flat, cut, or ground). Because they haven't been processed, they retain a high nutritional value. They have an appealing chewy texture and a mildly nutty flavor. Oats are usually thought of as a breakfast cereal, but oat berries make a great savory side dish cooked pilaf-style and can be cooked like risotto for a rich, satisfying main dish.

Quinoa: Quinoa originated in the Andes Mountains of South America, and while it is generally treated as a grain, it is actually the seed of the goosefoot plant. Sometimes referred to as a "supergrain," quinoa is high in protein, and its protein is complete, which means it possesses all of the amino acids in the balanced amounts that our bodies require. Beyond its nutritional prowess, we love quinoa for its irresistible crunchy texture, nutty taste, and ease of preparation.

White quinoa is the most commonly found variety of these tiny seeds, but red and black varieties are increasingly available. White quinoa, the largest seed of the three, has a slightly nutty, vegetal flavor with a hint of bitterness; it also has the softest texture of the three quinoas. The medium-size red seeds offer a heartier crunch, thanks to their additional seed coat, and a predominant nuttiness. Black quinoa seeds, the smallest of the three, have the thickest seed coat. They are notably crunchy and retain their shape the most during cooking. These seeds have the mildest flavor, with a hint of molasses-like sweetness. You can use white and red quinoa interchangeably in our quinoa pilaf recipes and other side dishes or salads. However, white quinoa is best for dishes like cakes and patties because it is starchier and will hold together better. Black quinoa is better off in recipes specifically tailored to its distinctive texture and flavor. Unless labeled "prewashed," quinoa should always be rinsed before cooking to remove its protective layer (called saponin), which is unpleasantly bitter.

Quinoa Flakes: Quinoa flakes are simply quinoa seeds that have been rolled flat into thin flakes. They are growing in popularity as an alternative to instant oatmeal for a nutritious hot breakfast cereal. They can also be used in baked goods and granola. Quinoa flakes can be found in the cereal aisle of your grocery store, near the instant oatmeal.

STORING GRAINS

To prevent open boxes and bags of grains from spoiling in the pantry, store them in airtight containers and, if you have space, in the freezer. This is especially important for whole grains, which turn rancid with oxidation.

RICE

In the gluten-free kitchen, rice is a lifesaver. There are many varieties on the market and many ways to prepare rice: as a simple side dish, an appealing salad, or a hearty main course when paired with multiple vegetables, or even as hearty rice cakes, as with our Miso Brown Rice Cakes (page 124).

Arborio Rice: Arborio, the variety of medium-grain rice that we use in the test kitchen to make risotto, was once grown exclusively in Italy. Now widely available, these stubby, milky grains have a high starch content, which is what enables them to make such creamy risotto.

Basmati Rice: Prized for its nutty flavor and sweet aroma, basmati rice is eaten in pilafs and biryanis and with curries. Indian basmati is aged for a minimum of a year, though often much longer, before being packaged. Aging dehydrates the rice, which translates into grains that, once cooked, expand greatly. We don't recommend American-grown basmati.

Black Rice: Like brown rice, black rice is sold unhulled. But only black rice contains anthocyanins, the same antioxidant compounds found in blueberries and blackberries. These compounds are what turn the rice a deep purple as it cooks. Note that black rice is especially easy to overcook. To keep it from turning mushy, we have found that boiling it in an abundance of water (similar to cooking pasta) is the best approach.

Brown Rice: All rice (except wild rice) starts out as brown rice. Each grain of rice is made up of an endosperm, germ, bran, and a protective outer hull or husk. Brown rice is simply rice that has been husked and cleaned. Considered a whole grain, brown rice has more fiber and vitamins than white rice, along with a firmer texture and a nuttier, earthier flavor. Keep in mind that the bran and germ contain oils that shorten the rice's shelf life. Brown rice takes longer to cook than white rice because it requires more time to allow water to penetrate the bran.

Brown rice comes in three grain sizes: short, medium, and long. Long-grain brown rice, the best choice for pilafs, cooks up fluffy with separate grains. Medium-grain brown rice is a bit more sticky, perfect for risotto, paella, and similar dishes. Short-grain brown rice is the most sticky, ideal for sushi and other Asian dishes where getting the grains to clump together is desired.

Jasmine Rice: Native to Thailand and a staple in Southeast Asian cuisine, jasmine rice has an aroma similar to basmati rice, but the texture is stickier and moister and the grain size is much smaller. Compared with other varieties of long-grain rice, jasmine rice tends to cook up relatively soft and sticky, though it maintains a slightly firm chew. Because it clumps together when cooked, jasmine rice works well in stir-fries. It's also nice in soups.

White Rice: White rice is husked and cleaned like brown rice, but then the germ and bran are removed. This makes the rice cook up faster and softer, and it's more shelf-stable, but the process also removes much of the fiber, protein, and other nutrients, as well as flavor.

Like brown rice, white rice can be long-, medium-, or short-grained. The category of long-grain white rice includes aromatic varieties such as basmati and jasmine as well as generic long-grain rice. The grains are slender and measure four to five times longer than they are wide. Long-grain white rice cooks up light and fluffy, with firm, distinct grains, making it good for pilafs and salads.

Medium-grain white rice includes a wide variety of specialty rices, including many Japanese and Chinese brands, used to make risotto and paella. The grains are fat and measure two to three times longer than they are wide. Medium-grain white rice cooks up a bit sticky, and when simmered the grains clump together, making this rice a common choice in Chinese restaurants. With the exception of sushi, we don't eat much short-grain white rice in this country. The grains are almost round, and the texture is quite sticky and soft when cooked.

Avoid converted rice, which is parboiled during processing. This tan-colored rice cooks up too separate in our opinion, and the flavor seems a bit off.

Wild Rice: North America's only native grain, this aquatic grass grows naturally in lakes and is cultivated in paddies in Minnesota, California, and Canada. Its smooth grains have a remarkably nutty, savory depth and a distinct chew that make this rice an ideal choice for a hearty side dish or addition to soup. Cook wild rice at a bare simmer and check it often: It can go from chewy and underdone to mushy and "blown out" in a matter of minutes.

GLUTEN-FREE PASTA

Just because you're no longer eating wheat doesn't mean that pasta is off the menu. There are two routes you can take: Asian noodles that traditionally don't contain wheat and gluten-free approximations of classic Italian pasta.

Dried Italian-Style Pasta: We ran extensive taste tests of gluten-free spaghetti and rotini (see page 34). In subsequent work in the test kitchen, we had excellent results with other shapes manufactured by Jovial, the winner of our spaghetti tasting. As with wheat pasta, we found that cooking times listed on packages of gluten-free pasta are often inaccurate. You must taste pasta often as it cooks. Also note that gluten-free pasta goes from al dente to mush even faster than wheat-based pasta, so err on the side of undercooking the noodles. We often call for reserving some of the starchy cooking water to help loosen sauces. Place a measuring cup in the colander so you remember not to pour all the cooking water down the drain.

Lasagna Noodles: Gluten-free lasagna noodles are available in both no-boil and boil-before-use forms. We found that no-boil gluten-free noodles varied considerably; some brands were thick and cooked up gummy, while others were thin and fragile. We had better luck using noodles that we boiled. There are just a few brands on the market. We had the most success with Tinkyada; they were tender once cooked and held up well, while other brands were incredibly fragile. Boil them for a bit less time than the package instructions indicate so they don't fall apart. After boiling and draining the noodles, toss them with a teaspoon of olive oil and spread them out in a single layer on a baking sheet to prevent sticking.

Rice Noodles: Pasta made from rice flour and water is used in a variety of dishes in Southeast Asia and southern China. Flat rice noodles come in two widths: a medium-width (¼-inch-wide) noodle and a larger (⅜-inch-wide) noodle. Round rice noodles also come in more than one size, but we prefer the thinner rice vermicelli. Don't follow the package directions, which often call for boiling. Such treatment will turn these delicate noodles into a gummy, mushy, unappealing mess. You'll get the most reliable results by steeping these noodles in hot water. Place the noodles in a very large bowl, cover them with very hot tap water, and stir to separate the individual strands. Let the noodles soak until they are softened, pliable, and limp but not fully tender, 20 minutes for vermicelli or narrow flat noodles, or 35 to 40 minutes for wide flat noodles. Drain the noodles and use as directed.

Soba Noodles: Soba noodles possess a rich, nutty flavor and a delicate texture. They get their flavor from buckwheat flour. Be aware that many brands also contain wheat, which not only keeps the price down but gives the noodles more structure. Make sure to read the label and look for those that contain buckwheat flour only. Soba noodles should be cooked like Italian-style pasta. Since they are often used in Asian-inspired recipes that include salty ingredients like tamari, there is often no need to salt the water.

Cooking Grains

Creating variety in your diet with gluten-free grains doesn't need to be an issue; however, properly cooking those grains could be if you simply follow the package instructions. We've spent plenty of time in the test kitchen working with these grains and fine-tuning our techniques to ensure you get the best results every time.

There are two basic ways to cook grains: either with a measured amount of water or in abundant water. The latter method (called the pasta method) is best for larger grains that take a long time to cook: Simply boil them in a big pot of salted water and drain when tender. With so much water in the pot, there's no risk of the pot running dry. And all that water ensures even, thorough cooking. For smaller grains, like rice and millet, we cook them with a measured amount of water in a covered pot over low heat, using either the absorption or the pilaf method (however, we have a unique oven method for cooking brown rice; see our recipe on page 115). Once all the water has been absorbed, the grains are done. In general, we prefer the pilaf method because it adds a nutty, toasted flavor. However, the absorption method can work well in dishes where the grains will be seasoned aggressively once they are cooked.

Most grains should be rinsed before cooking to remove surface starch, detritus, or bitter coatings. (We prefer to buy quinoa labeled "prewashed," but if you're unsure, rinse it anyway to be sure to remove its saponin coating.) In some cases, we go on to dry the grains after rinsing since soggy grains can throw off the water-to-grain ratio. Also, soggy grains are hard to toast, which we do when cooking grains pilaf-style to deepen their flavor.

For the absorption or pilaf method, make sure to use a sturdy, heavy-bottomed saucepan with a tight-fitting lid. Following are the general directions; refer to the chart on the opposite page for specific water amounts.

PASTA METHOD

This method is well suited to larger grains (like oat berries) because it guarantees even cooking. In some cases, toasting the grains before adding the water lends a flavor boost. Grains cooked this way are ready to use in salads and soups. To quickly cool boiled grains for a salad, rinse them with cold running water.

Bring 2 quarts water to boil in Dutch oven. Stir in 1 cup rinsed grains and 1 teaspoon salt. Return to boil, reduce heat to low, and simmer until grains are tender. Drain in strainer in sink. Let sit in strainer for 5 minutes before using (or pat dry with paper towels) to remove excess moisture.

ABSORPTION METHOD

This is the simplest way to prepare small grains like millet and quinoa. It's ideal when using these grains in salads. If you want fluffy rather than sticky grains, place a clean, folded dish towel between the pot and lid during the resting step to absorb excess moisture.

Combine 1 cup rinsed and dried grains, water, and ½ teaspoon salt in medium saucepan. Bring mixture to simmer, then reduce heat to low, cover, and simmer until grains are tender and liquid is absorbed. Off heat, let sit, covered, for 10 minutes. Fluff with fork and serve.

PILAF METHOD

Toasting the grains in fat develops nutty flavor (however, we toast quinoa in a dry pan since toasting in fat makes it taste slightly bitter). You can also sauté spices and aromatics before adding grains; swap in chicken broth for some of the water; and/or stir in fresh herbs before serving. If you want fluffy rather than sticky grains, place a clean, folded dish towel between the pot and lid during the resting step to absorb excess moisture.

Heat 1 tablespoon unsalted butter or oil in medium saucepan over medium-high heat until melted or shimmering, according to recipe. Add 1 cup rinsed and dried grains and toast until lightly golden and fragrant, about 3 minutes. Add ½ teaspoon salt and water. Bring mixture to simmer, then reduce heat to low, cover, and simmer until grains are tender and liquid is absorbed. Off heat, let sit, covered, for 10 minutes. Fluff with fork and serve.

Formulas for Cooking Grains

Use this chart to determine the amount of water and the cooking time needed to prepare 1 cup of grains. If you're using the absorption or pilaf methods, the grains should first be rinsed and dried well; if you're using the pasta method, simply rinse the grains. You can cook 2 or 3 cups of raw grains using the pasta method by increasing the water to 4 quarts; the cooking time will be the same. You can cook 2 cups of grains using the absorption or pilaf method by doubling the amount of water and salt; the cooking time might require a few extra minutes.

GRAIN	METHOD(S)	WATER	SALT	TIME	YIELD
Buckwheat Groats	Pasta	2 quarts	1 teaspoon	10–12 minutes	2¾ cups
Kasha (Roasted Buckwheat Groats)	Absorption or Pilaf	2 cups	½ teaspoon	10–15 minutes	3 cups
Millet	Absorption or Pilaf	2 cups	½ teaspoon	15–20 minutes	2¼ cups
Oat Berries (Oat Groats)	Absorption or Pilaf	1⅓ cups	¼ teaspoon	30–40 minutes	2¾ cups
	Pasta	2 quarts	½ teaspoon	45–50 minutes	2¾ cups
Quinoa (any color)	Absorption or Pilaf	1 cup plus 3 tablespoons	½ teaspoon	18–20 minutes	2¾ cups
Long-Grain White Rice, Jasmine, Basmati	Absorption or Pilaf	1½ cups	½ teaspoon	16–18 minutes	3 cups
	Pasta	2 quarts	1 teaspoon	12–17 minutes	3 cups
Long-Grain Brown Rice	Pasta	2 quarts	1 teaspoon	25–30 minutes	2½ cups
Wild Rice	Pasta	2 quarts	1 teaspoon	35–45 minutes	2½ cups

RINSING AND DRYING GRAINS

1. Rinse grains in fine-mesh strainer under cool water until water runs clear, occasionally stirring grains around lightly with your hand. Set strainer over bowl to drain until needed.

2. If drying grains, line rimmed baking sheet with clean dish towel and spread rinsed grains over towel. Let grains dry for 15 minutes.

3. To easily and neatly remove grains from towel, pick up towel by corners and gently shake grains into bowl.

Gluten-Free Sandwich Bread

When you're avoiding gluten, it's tough to give up toast and sandwiches—and if a recipe calls for bread slices or crumbs, you're really out of luck. That's where gluten-free supermarket bread can step in. While fresh loaves are scarce, the freezer section of most supermarkets is usually packed with many gluten-free options for both white and multigrain or whole-grain breads. When we first evaluated white sandwich bread several years ago, we tasted eight products and found only one to recommend. We later revisited the world of white sandwich breads with a taste test of five products and also tried multigrain/whole-grain options to see if they would fare any better.

GOOD NEWS/BAD NEWS

Among brands of white sandwich bread, two were subpar in every application. Even toasting and buttering them could not make these samples palatable. The other three breads were acceptable, though tasters still had quibbles with texture or flavor. On the multigrain front, we were pleasantly surprised by the positive response from tasters; two brands received high praise and were deemed "actually really good!" while three more fell into our Recommended with Reservations category. (Since our second taste test, one brand, Udi's, has reformulated its products; because of this, we have omitted their white and whole-grain breads from our results.)

TAKING A CLOSER LOOK

At first glance you might assume the multigrain breads fared so much better because they had an abundance of hearty grains and fiber. But in most instances, these breads looked like their gluten-free white bread counterparts (with the exception of those with a smattering of seeds or grains that were visible in the crust or floating within the mostly white interiors). To be labeled "multigrain," breads only have to contain more than one type of grain—and that can be in the form of refined flours, which lack the fibrous bran and nutrient-rich germ. In fact, our favorite "multigrain" gluten-free bread, Glutino Gluten Free Multigrain Bread, contains no fiber or protein at all, a sign that it contains no whole grains. By contrast, the second-place bread, Three Bakers 7 Ancient Grains Whole Grain Bread, Gluten-Free contains 4 grams of protein and 10 grams of fiber in a 100-gram serving (equivalent to about three slices). These two breads are our favorites from both tastings; despite their multigrain and whole-grain labels, in our opinion these breads are so much like white bread that they are interchangeable whether you are simply making a sandwich or using them as part of a recipe such as when making bread crumbs or a breakfast casserole.

BROWN RICE IS NICE

What was clear across both tastings was that brown rice flour, with its flavorful germ and fibrous bran, made better breads. Among the white sandwich breads, our top three breads all used brown rice flour, while the bottom-ranking breads used white rice flour, which has no fiber to help create structure, and far less flavor. All the multigrain breads we tested used brown rice flour.

WORTH ITS SALT AND FAT

Another common theme was that salt goes a long way toward enhancing flavor. Our top-ranked white sandwich bread had the second-highest level of salt; our winning multigrain bread also had plenty of salt, while the lowest-ranked breads had the least sodium. The amount of fat in these breads also mattered: more fat means more flavor (and with these gluten-free breads, it helped create an interior crumb that was fluffy and moist). Glutino Gluten Free Multigrain Bread, the winner, has 12 grams of fat per 100-gram serving, or 3.5 grams per slice.

THE BOTTOM LINE

Gluten-free breads labeled multigrain or whole-grain are a better bet than white breads. For gluten-free bread with the best flavor and texture, we recommend you reach for the breads ranked the highest in our multigrain sandwich bread tasting.

Rating Gluten-Free Sandwich Breads

Our tasting panel tasted each sample of white bread three times: plain, then toasted with butter, and finally baked with eggs in our recipe for strata. The scores from the tastings were averaged to determine overall rankings. Multigrain breads were tasted twice: plain and then toasted with butter. The scores from both tastings were averaged to determine overall rankings.

WHITE BREADS
RECOMMENDED WITH RESERVATIONS

CANYON BAKEHOUSE Mountain White Gluten Free Bread
PRICE: $5.00 for 18-ounce loaf
PROTEIN (100 G SERVING): 3 g   CARBOHYDRATES: 44 g
FAT: 4 g   SODIUM: 412 mg
DIETARY FIBER: 6 g   SUGARS: 9 g
TASTERS' COMMENTS: "I like this most of all," one taster wrote. "Amazingly close to regular bread!" agreed another. "Slightly sweet" and "nutty," it had a texture that was "softer," "the best chew of the bunch," albeit "a hint mushy," or "gummy/slimy," even when it was toasted. Baked in strata, it "holds its shape well," though some found it "spongy."

THREE BAKERS Whole Grain White Bread, Gluten Free
PRICE: $6.79 for 17-ounce loaf
PROTEIN (100 G SERVING): 3 g   CARBOHYDRATES: 44 g
FAT: 4 g   SODIUM: 338 mg
DIETARY FIBER: 7 g   SUGARS: 4 g
TASTERS' COMMENTS: "This doesn't have much flavor," one taster wrote, which was the consensus of our panel. As for texture, it was "sandy," "crumbly," and "very chewy, not in a good way, almost marshmallow-y" when served plain; "very disappointing." Baked in strata, its flavor was "neutral, mildly sweet," but "the bread dissolved too much" and became "pasty."

MULTIGRAIN BREADS
RECOMMENDED

THREE BAKERS 7 Ancient Grains Whole Grain Bread, Gluten-Free
PRICE: $5.99 for 17-oz loaf
PROTEIN (100 G SERVING): 4g Carbohydrates: 63 g
FAT: 4 g Sodium: 412 mg
DIETARY FIBER: 10 g   SUGARS: 6 g
TASTERS' COMMENTS: With "a yeasty, rich flavor," "crust that is very chewy," and "seeds and grains that add interest," this bread was appealing to tasters. Toasted, this loaf had "nice crunch" but became "gummy in the middle."

MULTIGRAIN BREADS
RECOMMENDED WITH RESERVATIONS

CANYON BAKEHOUSE 7-Grain Bread, Gluten-Free
PRICE: $5.49 for 18-oz loaf
PROTEIN (100 G SERVING): 6 g Carbohydrates: 41 g
FAT: 4 g Sodium: 309 mg
DIETARY FIBER: 6 g   SUGARS: 6 g
TASTERS' COMMENTS: "Nutty" and "slightly sweet," this loaf had "normal bread flavor." Toasted, it was much less successful: "a little off—sort of sweet and turns mushy quickly in my mouth."

KINNIKINNICK MULTIGRAIN BREAD, GLUTEN-FREE
PRICE: $4.99 for 16-oz loaf
PROTEIN (100 G SERVING): 5 g Carbohydrates: 35 g
FAT: 11 g Sodium: 316 mg
DIETARY FIBER: 9 g   SUGARS: 2 g
TASTERS' COMMENTS:
This bread was deemed "very light" with "no chew" to the interior but a "substantial" crust.

Italian-Style Dried Gluten-Free Pasta

When we first evaluated gluten-free spaghetti several years ago, the vast majority of products were based on rice—either alone or in combination with corn or quinoa. Unfortunately, most of those pastas were gritty and grainy or dissolved into a mushy, gummy mess. We found only one product with a flavor and texture we could unreservedly recommend. When we revisited these products for our second gluten-free book, we hoped that, given the number of new companies jumping on the gluten-free bandwagon, we might have better luck. To find out, we pitted our top two scorers against six new products. More recently, we explored a new category of gluten-free pasta: legume-based pasta.

NEW BRANDS, SAME PROBLEMS

Our original rice-based favorite, Jovial Organic Brown Rice Spaghetti, remained impressive at our second tasting, with its pleasantly neutral, chewy yet tender noodles. But to our dismay, the majority of the rice-based brands again failed to meet our expectations. As before, many products were unpleasantly "pasty" and "gummy" with "zero chew" and some of them practically disintegrated. Our old runner-up fell into the other end of the texture spectrum, cooking up unacceptably "rubbery" and "chewy." A newcomer, made with a combination of corn and rice flours, joined our brown rice favorite at the top. Although corn starch tends to leak out of pasta as it cooks, causing soggy, sticky noodles, this pasta, from Barilla, remained "intact" and had an "al dente" texture thanks to mono- and diglycerides. These stabilizers help hold the starches together and keep the pasta tender.

PROTEIN AND FIBER

For all types of pasta, protein is the most important factor in determining texture, but fiber also plays a role. All of our spaghetti contained adequate protein: between 4 and 6 grams per serving. However, gluten-free pastas don't behave in exactly the same ways as pastas made with white or whole-wheat flour. Although particles of fiber can interfere with the protein bonds in wheat pasta and cause it to weaken during cooking, rice fiber plays a helpful role in gluten-free pasta—to a point. The ideal combination turns out to be a relatively high amount of protein (at least 4 grams) and a fiber content that's less than half that amount. Our two favorite rice-based brands have roughly the ideal protein to fiber ratio; both remained intact but tender after cooking. The rest

of the samples, all of which had been soft and mushy or gritty and grainy, had a near-equal ratio of protein to fiber.

WHAT ABOUT LEGUMES?

Chickpeas, lentils, and dried beans have been popping up in all kinds of products, including pasta. To find out if legume pasta was worth the hype, we tasted eight nationally available products: two chickpea pastas, four lentil pastas, one mung bean pasta, and one pasta made with chickpeas and lentils. We settled on easily available rotini or spiral shapes and tasted them plain, with tomato sauce, and with pesto. In the plain tasting, the pasta made from mung beans was deemed "bitter" and "grassy." The more subtle lentil and chickpea pastas scored higher, with tasters describing them as "earthy," "nutty," and "slightly sweet." In addition to lentil flour, our winner contains rice flour, which gives it a notably neutral flavor. Some tasters compared it to wheat pasta.

TEXTURE IS KEY

Flours made from legumes contain no gluten and less starch than wheat flour, so some manufacturers add ingredients such as tapioca, xanthan gum, pea protein, rice flour, or quinoa flour in an attempt to mimic the texture of wheat pasta. These additives all improve the moisture-retaining qualities of the pasta, keeping the noodles hydrated and chewy. Some, such as pea protein and xanthan gum, also improve cohesiveness. Tasters commented that our two higher-rated products, which included one or more of these additives, were "tender," "chewy," and "smooth." Lower-rated pastas, which were panned as "gummy," "dry," and "crumbly," didn't contain any additives.

Rating Italian-Style Dried Gluten-Free Pastas

Our panel tasted each sample twice—cooked in salted water and tossed with canola oil, then again served with our favorite tomato sauce. The scores from the two tastings were averaged to determine overall rankings. Our panel tasted the legume pastas plain, with Quick Tomato Sauce, and in our recipe for Pasta with Pesto, Potatoes, and Green Beans.

The following products were not recommended in our original tasting and have not been reformulated: Bionaturae Organic Gluten Free Spaghetti; Ancient Harvest, Gluten Free, Spaghetti Style; Tinkyada Pasta Joy Ready Brown Rice Pasta, Spaghetti Style; Rustichella d'Abruzzo Organic Corn Spaghetti; DeLallo Gluten Free Corn & Rice Spaghetti; DeBoles Gluten Free Rice Spaghetti Style Pasta.

RICE-BASED PASTAS
RECOMMENDED

JOVIAL Organic Gluten Free Brown Rice Spaghetti
PRICE: $3.49 for 12-oz box ($0.29 per oz)
INGREDIENTS: Organic Brown Rice Flour, Water
TASTERS' COMMENTS: Our original favorite again emerged at the top of our rankings, thanks to a high ratio of protein to fiber. These delicate and thin strands had a "neutral, pleasant" flavor and "al dente texture" that combined for gluten-free spaghetti that was deemed "just like regular pasta."

BARILLA Gluten Free Spaghetti
PRICE: $2.69 for 12-oz box ($0.22 per oz)
INGREDIENTS: Corn Flour, Rice Flour, Mono- and Diglycerides
TASTERS' COMMENTS: With four times more protein than fiber and helpful emulsifiers, this spaghetti boasted a cohesive and "springy" texture much like traditional pasta. Some astute tasters identified a cornlike sweetness, but since the corn flour is combined with rice flour, its flavor was deemed pleasantly "neutral."

RICE-BASED PASTAS
RECOMMENDED WITH RESERVATIONS

DELALLO Gluten Free Whole Grain Rice Spaghetti
PRICE: $5.19 for 12-oz bag ($0.43 per oz)
INGREDIENTS: 100% Brown Rice Flour
TASTERS' COMMENTS: The texture of these small, skinny noodles was pleasant enough, but our panel was ambivalent about the flavor. While some described it as having an "earthy" or "whole wheat flavor," many tasters thought this spaghetti tasted "stale" or even "cardboard-y."

LEGUME-BASED PASTAS
RECOMMENDED

MODERN TABLE Rotini
PRICE: $3.67 for 8-oz box ($0.46 per oz)
INGREDIENTS: Red lentil flour, white rice, pea protein
TASTERS' COMMENTS: Our top-rated legume pasta won tasters over with its "smooth" texture. "It still held its shape but had some chew," said one taster. This pasta is the only one in our lineup that contained rice flour, which gave it a neutral flavor and texture that most closely resembled traditional pasta. Overall tasters said this product "tastes surprisingly like regular pasta!"

BANZA Chickpea Rotini
PRICE: $2.86 for 8-oz box ($0.36 per oz)
INGREDIENTS: Chickpeas, tapioca, pea protein, xanthan gum
TASTERS' COMMENTS: The flavor of this pasta was "neutral" and "slightly buttery." Our tasters liked it better when served with pesto than when served with tomato sauce. As one taster put it, the pesto "is a great match that brings out the best in the noodles." The addition of tapioca, pea protein, and xanthan gum helped improve the pasta's structure by providing moisture, structure, and cohesion.

CHICKAPEA Spirals
PRICE: $3.88 for 8-oz box ($0.48 per oz)
INGREDIENTS: Organic Chickpea Flour, Organic Lentil Flour
TASTERS' COMMENTS: Tasters enjoyed this pasta both served with tomato sauce and served with pesto. One noted that its "flavor was good and not too strong, which helped the pesto shine." However, given their lack of additives, these spirals had a few textural issues. As one taster wrote, "It remains mostly firm but becomes a bit mushy and separated/grainy when chewed."

Making Recipes Dairy-Free

Many people on a gluten-free diet also have other food allergy issues, including the inability to digest dairy. In fact, one of the comments we heard most from gluten-free home cooks is that they'd like to know more about how to make recipes that are both gluten-free and dairy-free. So, in response, we came up with dairy-free variations for many of the recipes in this book. There were only two types of recipes that occasionally stumped us: those that used three or more types of dairy, and those that depended heavily on dairy for flavor and texture, such as cheesecake or pie dough. We used only the ATK gluten-free flour blends in our dairy-free testing; we don't recommend using a store-bought flour blend when making recipes dairy-free. You can omit the milk powder from our all-purpose blend, but for better results substitute soy milk powder. Remember that substitutions affect not just flavor but also texture. While you might think that canola oil spread tastes fine on toast, it will behave quite differently than butter in a cookie recipe, affecting how the cookies spread and brown.

BUTTER

The texture and flavor of butter play a big role in many baked goods. To figure out how to replace it, we tested a number of dairy-free butter options in a handful of gluten-free recipes. We tried vegetable oil and coconut oil along with several Earth Balance products including Vegan Buttery Sticks, Vegan Shortening Sticks, and Coconut Spread. The vegetable oil and Earth Balance Vegan Buttery Sticks both worked quite well. The coconut oil also worked well but had a distinctive flavor that we knew would work only in coconut-flavored baked goods, such as Coconut-Cashew Muffins (page 66). Earth Balance Shortening Sticks and Coconut Spread fell short on flavor or tasted plasticky.

Vegetable oil is our preferred substitution for melted butter and browned butter in most recipes. It works particularly well when the recipe has another strong flavor.

Earth Balance Vegan Buttery Sticks are a good substitution for solid or softened butter. It also works well when a "buttery" flavor is important to the recipe; however, this product tastes fairly salty (so reduce or eliminate salt called for in the recipe).

Coconut oil is a good replacement for solid, softened, or melted butter in recipes, although it has a distinctive coconut flavor.

MILK

Dairy-free milks on the market today include those made from soy, rice, hemp, oats, quinoa, almonds, hazelnuts, cashews, and coconut. Right off the bat, we took hemp, oat, quinoa, and cashew milk off our list because at the time they were just too difficult to find. We tested the remaining milks in gluten-free muffins and cookies, and found that soy milk and almond milk worked best. Soy milk is leaner than almond milk, which makes it an ideal replacement for low-fat milk. Rice milk is more watery and gave the baked goods an overly starchy and gummy texture. The flavor of coconut milk is too specific to make it a basic milk substitute.

BUTTERMILK

We found it easy to make a buttermilk substitution by combining soy or almond milk with a dash of distilled white vinegar or lemon juice. This works best when the buttermilk is not the main flavor but rather just a background note, as in Date-Nut Bread (page 78).

TO MAKE 1 CUP OF DAIRY-FREE BUTTERMILK: Mix 1 cup of unsweetened soy or almond milk with 1 tablespoon of distilled white vinegar or fresh lemon juice.

HEAVY CREAM

There are dozens of dairy-free cream options, including coffee creamers made of hydrogenated oil as well as more natural creamers made of soy, almonds, cashews, or coconut. We tested these more natural creamers and preferred the mild flavor of plain soy creamer. None of them can be whipped.

WHIPPED CREAM

Since none of the heavy cream replacements we tried can be whipped, we tested several store-bought whipped products, including Soyatoo! Soy Whip and Soyatoo! Rice Whip, and homemade coconut whipped cream made using coconut fat from a can of coconut milk. Tasters didn't like Soyatoo!'s Rice Whip but found their Soy Whip to be a decent substitute for whipped cream. The homemade coconut whipped cream was also a decent substitute, although it uses a partial can of coconut milk and has a notice-able coconut flavor. Note that while soy whip is naturally gluten-free, the Soyatoo! brand is not labeled gluten-free.

COCONUT WHIPPED CREAM

Refrigerate a 10-ounce can of regular (not low-fat) coconut milk for a few hours, and chill a mixing bowl and beaters in the freezer for at least 20 minutes. Using a spoon, skim only the top layer of cream from the coconut milk (about ¾ cup) and combine with 1½ teaspoons sugar, ½ teaspoon vanilla, and a pinch of salt in the chilled bowl. Beat the mixture on low speed until small bubbles form, about 30 seconds, then increase the speed to high and beat until the mix-ture thickens and forms light peaks, about 2 minutes.

YOGURT

We tested coconut milk yogurt, soy milk yogurt, and Greek-style almond milk yogurt in several of our gluten-free recipes. The almond milk yogurt was the least successful, producing biscuits with a strong, funky flavor and a gummy texture, and muffins that were mushy. Soy milk yogurt worked fine in the muf-fins, but the biscuits turned out drier and crumbly. In general, however, we found soy milk yogurt to be a decent substitution for plain whole-milk yogurt even though it produced slightly dry baked goods. We prefer coconut milk yogurt, which performed well in both recipes; surprisingly, we could not taste the coconut flavor.

SOUR CREAM

A number of our recipes rely on sour cream to add richness and moisture. We found a variety of dairy-free brands on the market, including Tofutti Better Than Sour Cream, Weyfair, Vegan Gourmet, and Green Valley, and put them all to the test using some of our own gluten-free recipes. Although these products are thicker than regular sour cream, they all worked well. For this book, we used Tofutti Better Than Sour Cream for all of our testing.

CREAM CHEESE

We used cream cheese in some gluten-free cake and cookie recipes to help add structure, richness, and chew. We tested two brands of dairy-free cream cheese in our recipes: Tofutti Better Than Cream Cheese and Vegan Gourmet Cream Cheese. Both seemed more rubbery than regular cream cheese, but they worked equally well as dairy-free substitutes. In our Cream Cheese Frosting (page 499), they both produced a frosting with a slightly thinner, silkier texture. We used Tofutti Better Than Cream Cheese for all of our testing.

CHOCOLATE

Finding dairy-free chocolate is not easy if you want to make sure that it was produced in a gluten-free facility. We found a few brands online (including Scharffen Berger and Milkless) and tested them in several of our chocolate chip cookie and chocolate cake recipes. In the end, we found that all of the dairy-free bar chocolates worked well in our cake recipes. We also found that the bars could be chopped and used in place of chips in cookies. Dairy-free chips worked well as stir-ins for the cook-ies but didn't work as a swap for the bar chocolate in any of the cakes. Look for dairy-free chocolate products online.

A GOOD START

Buttermilk Pancakes

FLOUR SUBSTITUTION	King Arthur Gluten-Free Multi-Purpose Flour 10½ ounces = **1⅔ cups plus ¼ cup**	Bob's Red Mill GF All-Purpose Baking Flour 10½ ounces = **2 cups plus 2 tablespoons**

Note that pancakes made with Bob's Red Mill will be flatter and will have a distinct bean flavor.

WHY THIS RECIPE WORKS

Just because you need to avoid gluten doesn't mean you can't enjoy a leisurely Saturday morning pancake breakfast. But you can't just take a basic traditional recipe and plug in gluten-free flour—the results will be dense and gummy. We found that using both baking powder and baking soda, something we do with traditional pancake recipes as well, was key to keeping our gluten-free pancakes light and tender and ensuring they rose properly. But that wasn't quite enough. Instead of adding whole eggs to the batter, we separated the eggs, whipped the whites to stiff peaks, and gently folded them in. Yes, this step takes a few extra minutes, but it delivers gluten-free pancakes that are light, fluffy, and tender. Buttermilk gives these pancakes a nice tang and helps ensure a light, fluffy texture; see page 43 for buttermilk substitutes. To make blueberry pancakes, sprinkle 1 tablespoon berries over surface of each pancake immediately after adding the batter to the skillet, and cook as directed. You can add raspberries or blackberries the same way, as long as you chop any large berries.

Buttermilk Pancakes

MAKES SIXTEEN 3-INCH PANCAKES; SERVES 6

10½	ounces (2⅓ cups) ATK All-Purpose Gluten-Free Flour Blend (page 7)
1	teaspoon salt
1	teaspoon baking powder (see page 24)
½	teaspoon baking soda
1¾	cups buttermilk
2	large eggs, separated
4	tablespoons unsalted butter, melted and cooled
2	tablespoons sugar
1-2	teaspoons vegetable oil

1. Adjust oven rack to middle position and heat oven to 200 degrees. Spray wire rack set inside rimmed baking sheet with vegetable oil spray; place in oven. Whisk flour blend, salt, baking powder, and baking soda together in large bowl. In separate bowl, whisk buttermilk, egg yolks, and melted butter until combined.

2. Using stand mixer fitted with whisk, whip egg whites on medium-low speed until foamy, about 1 minute. Increase speed to medium-high and whip whites to soft, billowy mounds, about 1 minute. Gradually add sugar and whip until glossy, stiff peaks form, 2 to 3 minutes.

3. Whisk buttermilk mixture into flour mixture until batter has thickened and no lumps remain, about 1 minute. Gently fold in whipped egg whites until just combined and few streaks remain.

4. Heat 1 teaspoon oil in 12-inch nonstick skillet over medium heat until shimmering, 3 to 5 minutes. Using paper towels, carefully wipe out oil, leaving thin film of oil on bottom and sides of pan. Using ¼ cup batter per pancake, portion batter into skillet and cook until bottoms of pancakes are brown and top surfaces start to bubble, 2 to 3 minutes. Flip pancakes and cook until second side has browned, 1 to 2 minutes longer. Serve immediately or transfer pancakes to wire rack in preheated oven (don't overlap). Repeat with remaining batter, using remaining oil as needed.

TEST KITCHEN TIP

Why Preheating the Skillet Matters

Did you fully preheat your skillet? We call for preheating it (with a teaspoon of oil) for a full 3 to 5 minutes; this step isn't one you can shortcut. A cooking surface that hasn't been allowed to heat up properly will produce pale, dense pancakes. If you aren't sure how hot the cooking surface is, cook a test pancake to get the lay of the land. After a few minutes in the pan, large bubbles should appear in the batter, indicating the pancake is ready to be flipped over. If the pancake isn't browned when flipped, your cooking surface needs to be hotter. Alternatively, if the pancakes are overly browned, you need to turn down the heat. Adjust the heat accordingly, give it a few minutes to preheat properly, and try again. If you own an electric griddle, set it to 325 degrees and lightly grease the cooking surface once it is fully preheated.

Whole-Grain Pancakes

G-F TESTING LAB

FLOUR SUBSTITUTION	Do not substitute other whole-grain blends for the ATK Whole-Grain Gluten-Free Flour Blend; they will not work in this recipe.
BAKING POWDER	Not all brands of baking powder are gluten-free; see page 24 for more information.
RESTING TIME	Do not shortchange the batter's 30-minute rest; if you do, the pancakes will be dense.

✓ WHY THIS RECIPE WORKS

Whole-grain pancakes are often overly virtuous and not well balanced in terms of richness and whole-grain flavor. We set out to make a pancake that was earthy-tasting but that also had a rich, buttery flavor. Our whole-grain flour blend has a lot of teff flour, which adds a robust flavor much like traditional whole-wheat flour. But in a simple pancake the flavor was a little too robust, so to balance it we tested a variety of sweeteners including honey, brown sugar, and granulated sugar. The honey and brown sugar added too much moisture and resulted in gummy pancakes, but granulated sugar provided the best balance of sweetness while also helping with the structure, making airier pancakes. As for the dairy, we are fans of buttermilk in pancakes for its characteristic tang but in combination with our whole-grain blend it made pancakes that were a bit sour. We tried using whole milk but it made our pancakes too dense. Low-fat milk, however, hydrated the starches in the blend perfectly and lightened up the pancakes. Typically, pancake recipes include just one egg, but an additional egg helped with structure and richness here. Processing the eggs along with the other liquid ingredients helped us get additional lift from the eggs. We found that a combination of butter and oil worked best in these pancakes; butter alone, while adding flavor, made the pancakes gummy because it also includes water. Swapping out some of the butter for vegetable oil, which is a pure fat, gave us the best of both worlds: buttery flavor and a crisp exterior and moist interior. Finally, letting the batter rest for 30 minutes ensured that the starch granules in the flour softened uniformly, eliminating grittiness and also allowing the flours to become fully hydrated for pancakes that were not dense or gummy. Do not substitute skim or whole milk in this recipe.

Whole-Grain Pancakes

MAKES EIGHTEEN 3-INCH PANCAKES; SERVES 4 TO 6

12 ounces (2⅔ cups) ATK Whole-Grain Gluten-Free Flour Blend (page 9)

1¾ ounces (¼ cup) sugar

2¼ teaspoons baking powder

¾ teaspoon salt

2½ cups 1 or 2 percent low-fat milk, plus extra as needed

2 large eggs

2 tablespoons unsalted butter, melted and cooled

¼ cup vegetable oil

1 teaspoon vanilla extract

1. Set wire rack in rimmed baking sheet. Adjust oven rack to middle position, place prepared sheet on rack, and heat oven to 200 degrees.

2. Whisk flour blend, sugar, baking powder, and salt together in large bowl. Process milk, eggs, melted butter, 2 tablespoons oil, and vanilla in blender until frothy, about 1 minute. Whisk milk mixture into flour mixture until well incorporated and no lumps remain, about 1 minute. Cover bowl with plastic wrap and let batter rest at room temperature for 30 minutes.

3. Heat 1 teaspoon oil in 12-inch nonstick skillet over medium-low heat until shimmering, 3 to 5 minutes. Using paper towels, wipe out oil, leaving thin film in pan. Using ¼-cup measure, portion pancakes into pan, spreading each immediately into 3-inch round using back of spoon; you will fit about 3 pancakes in pan. Cook until first side is golden and bubbles on surface begin to break, 2 to 3 minutes.

4. Flip pancakes and cook until second side is golden, 1 to 2 minutes. Serve or transfer to wire rack in oven. Repeat with remaining oil and batter, whisking extra milk into batter as needed to loosen.

VARIATION
Dairy-Free Whole-Grain Pancakes

We prefer the flavor and texture of these pancakes made with soy milk but almond milk will also work; do not use rice milk.

Substitute unsweetened soy milk for milk, and vegetable oil for melted butter.

Buckwheat Blueberry Pancakes

G-F TESTING LAB

FLOUR SUBSTITUTION	King Arthur Gluten-Free Multi-Purpose Flour 7 ounces = **1¼ cups**	Bob's Red Mill GF All-Purpose Baking Flour 7 ounces = **1¼ cups plus 2 tablespoons**
	Note that pancakes made with Bob's Red Mill will be flatter and will have a distinct bean flavor.	

✓ WHY THIS RECIPE WORKS

Naturally gluten-free buckwheat flour is the main ingredient in Russian blini and can be used to make hearty, slightly savory American-style pancakes. Buckwheat has an assertive flavor, so we knew that substituting just a few ounces for some of the gluten-free flour blend in our Buttermilk Pancakes (page 41) would provide the nutty, slightly earthy flavor we were after without going overboard. Because buckwheat flour is slightly heavier than our gluten-free flour blend (think wheat flour compared to all-purpose), it was no surprise that our first batch of pancakes cooked up flat and gummy. Adding an extra whipped egg white to the batter gave our pancakes the proper rise. The tang of the buttermilk in our original pancake recipe competed with the flavor of the buckwheat, so we swapped it out for whole milk (and dropped the baking soda because it worked in tandem with the buttermilk). Sweeter, more complexly flavored honey in lieu of granulated sugar, plus a pinch of cinnamon, helped to balance and round out the flavors.

Buckwheat Blueberry Pancakes

MAKES SIXTEEN 3-INCH PANCAKES; SERVES 6

7	ounces (1⅓ cups plus ¼ cup) ATK All-Purpose Gluten-Free Flour Blend (page 7)
3½	ounces (¾ cup) buckwheat flour
2	teaspoons baking powder (see page 24)
1	teaspoon salt
½	teaspoon ground cinnamon
1¾	cups whole milk
3	large eggs, separated
4	tablespoons unsalted butter, melted and cooled
2	tablespoons honey
1–2	teaspoons vegetable oil
5	ounces (1 cup) blueberries

1. Adjust oven rack to middle position and heat oven to 200 degrees. Spray wire rack set inside rimmed baking sheet with vegetable oil spray; place in oven. Whisk flour blend, buckwheat flour, baking powder, salt, and cinnamon together in large bowl. In separate bowl, whisk milk, egg yolks, melted butter, and honey until combined.

2. Using stand mixer fitted with whisk, whip egg whites on medium-low speed until foamy, about 1 minute. Increase speed to medium-high and whip until stiff peaks form, 3 to 4 minutes.

3. Whisk milk mixture into flour mixture until batter has thickened and no lumps remain, about 1 minute. Gently fold in whipped egg whites until just combined and few streaks remain.

4. Heat 1 teaspoon oil in 12-inch nonstick skillet over medium heat until shimmering, 3 to 5 minutes. Using paper towels, carefully wipe out oil, leaving thin film of oil on bottom and sides of pan. Using ¼ cup batter per pancake, portion batter into skillet and sprinkle 1 tablespoon blueberries over each pancake. Cook until bottoms of pancakes are brown and top surfaces start to bubble, 2 to 3 minutes. Flip pancakes and cook until second side has browned, 1 to 2 minutes longer. Serve immediately or transfer pancakes to wire rack in preheated oven (don't overlap). Repeat with remaining batter, using remaining oil as necessary.

SMART SHOPPING **Buckwheat Flour**

Buckwheat, despite its name, is not related to wheat. It is actually an herb, and its seeds are ground to make flour (the kernels can also be hulled and crushed to make groats; kasha is simply toasted buckwheat groats). Buckwheat is native to Russia, where it is used to make that country's traditional small yeast-raised pancakes known as blini. Buckwheat has a strong, earthy flavor, so here we use buckwheat flour in combination with our gluten-free flour blend. Buckwheat products can be found in natural food stores and well-stocked supermarkets. For information on buckwheat groats and kasha, see page 26.

Fluffy Oat Pancakes

OAT FLOUR   Oats are a gluten-free grain, but they're often processed in facilities that also process wheat, which creates cross-contamination issues. When buying oats or oat flour, make sure to check the label. We use Bob's Red Mill Gluten-Free Whole-Grain Oat Flour. For more information on oat flour, see page 23.

BAKING POWDER   Not all brands of baking powder are gluten-free; see page 24 for more information.

✓ WHY THIS RECIPE WORKS

The beauty of these hearty oat pancakes is that they don't require a gluten-free flour blend; plus, they are supereasy to make—all you need is store-bought oat flour, a blender, and a few pantry ingredients. We first tried grinding our own gluten-free oats but found that we just couldn't get the grind fine enough—our pancakes were turning out rather heavy and dense. We switched to store-bought oat flour (which is ground very fine), and the texture improved dramatically. For lift, we needed 2½ teaspoons of baking powder because of the high protein content and heaviness of the oat flour; for flavor we added cinnamon and nutmeg, which paired nicely with the hearty oat flavor. We started out using whole milk, but it had too much fat and weighed down our pancakes; switching to low-fat milk kept them light and airy. We knew we wanted eggs and a little butter for richness. Just one egg did not create enough structure to provide lift for our pancakes, so we added an extra yolk, which also gave them more flavor. To get lift from the eggs, we whipped them until frothy in a blender along with the other liquid ingredients. We tried brown sugar, maple syrup, and honey as alternative sweeteners, but they all made the texture too dense. Plain old granulated sugar gave us the best combination of sweetness and structure. Do not substitute skim or whole milk in this recipe.

Fluffy Oat Pancakes

MAKES SIXTEEN 3-INCH PANCAKES; SERVES 4

- 9 ounces (3 cups) oat flour
- 2½ teaspoons baking powder
- 2¼ teaspoons ground cinnamon
- ¾ teaspoon salt
- ¼ teaspoon ground nutmeg
- 1½ cups 1 or 2 percent low-fat milk, plus extra as needed
- ¼ cup (1¾ ounces) sugar
- 3 tablespoons unsalted butter, melted and cooled
- 1 large egg plus 1 large yolk
- 2¼ teaspoons vanilla extract
- 5 teaspoons vegetable oil

1. Set wire rack in rimmed baking sheet. Adjust oven rack to middle position, place prepared sheet on rack, and heat oven to 200 degrees.

2. Whisk oat flour, baking powder, cinnamon, salt, and nutmeg together in large bowl. Process milk, sugar, melted butter, egg and yolk, and vanilla in blender until frothy, about 1 minute. Whisk milk mixture into flour mixture until well incorporated and no lumps remain, about 1 minute.

3. Heat 1 teaspoon oil in 12-inch nonstick skillet over medium-low heat until shimmering, 3 to 5 minutes. Using paper towels, wipe out oil, leaving thin film in pan. Using ¼-cup measure, portion pancakes into pan, spreading each immediately into 3-inch round using back of spoon; you will fit about 3 pancakes in pan. Cook until first side is golden and bubbles on surface begin to break, about 3 minutes.

4. Flip pancakes and cook until second side is golden, about 3 minutes. Serve or transfer to wire rack in oven. Repeat with remaining oil and batter, whisking extra milk into batter as needed to loosen.

VARIATION

Dairy-Free Fluffy Oat Pancakes

We prefer the flavor and texture of these pancakes made with soy milk but almond milk will also work; do not use rice milk.

Substitute unsweetened soy milk for milk, and vegetable oil for melted butter.

Johnnycakes

G-F TESTING LAB

CORNMEAL	The test kitchen's favorite cornmeal for most applications, including this recipe, is finely ground Whole-Grain Arrowhead Mills Cornmeal. This brand has been processed in a gluten-free facility, but not all brands are. Make sure to read the label. See page 26 for more information.
RESTING TIME	Do not shortchange the batter's 15-minute rest; if you do, the pancakes will be gritty.

✔ WHY THIS RECIPE WORKS

Johnnycakes, a Rhode Island specialty, are rich, crisp corn cakes that are a naturally gluten-free alternative to pancakes. Made from little more than cornmeal and water, they should be crisp on the outside and creamy in the middle. To avoid a gritty or sandy texture, we found that, after we combined the dry ingredients and then whisked them into boiling water and stirred in some butter, we needed to let the batter sit for 15 minutes to soften the grains for a consistently smooth interior. To ensure that they didn't fall apart when flipped in the pan, we let the johnnycakes set completely on the first side before gently turning and flattening them so they would be evenly cooked throughout. Johnnycakes are best served warm with maple butter (or maple syrup) for breakfast, or as a side dish for soups and stews. Do not try to turn the johnnycakes too soon or they will fall apart. If you prefer crispier johnnycakes, press them thinner in step 5.

Johnnycakes

MAKES TWELVE 3-INCH JOHNNYCAKES; SERVES 3 TO 4

- 1 **cup (5 ounces) stone-ground cornmeal**
- 2 **teaspoons sugar**
- ¾ **teaspoon salt**
- 2¾ **cups water, plus extra as needed**
- 2 **tablespoons unsalted butter**
- 2 **tablespoons vegetable oil**

1. Set wire rack in rimmed baking sheet. Adjust oven rack to middle position, place prepared sheet on oven rack, and heat oven to 200 degrees.

2. Whisk cornmeal, sugar, and salt together in bowl. Bring water to boil in large saucepan. Slowly whisk in cornmeal mixture until no lumps remain, and cook until thickened, about 30 seconds. Off heat, whisk in butter. Pour batter into bowl, cover with plastic wrap, and let batter rest at room temperature until slightly firm, about 15 minutes.

3. Rewhisk batter until smooth. Batter should be consistency of mashed potatoes; if not, whisk in 1 to 2 tablespoons extra hot water as needed.

4. Heat 1 tablespoon oil in 12-inch nonstick skillet over medium heat until shimmering. Using greased ¼-cup measure, portion 6 cakes into pan. Cook until edges are crisp and golden brown, 6 to 8 minutes.

5. Carefully flip cakes and press with spatula to flatten into 2½- to 3-inch rounds. Cook until well browned on second side, 5 to 7 minutes. Serve or transfer to wire rack in oven. Repeat with remaining oil and batter, whisking extra hot water into batter as needed to loosen.

VARIATION

Dairy-Free Johnnycakes

Substitute 1 tablespoon Earth Balance Vegan Buttery Sticks for both tablespoons of butter.

Maple Butter

MAKES ¼ CUP

If using salted butter, omit the salt.

- 4 **tablespoons unsalted butter, softened**
- 1 **tablespoon maple syrup**
- ¼ **teaspoon salt**

Whisk all ingredients together in bowl. (Butter can be refrigerated for up to 1 week.)

TEST KITCHEN TIP **Shaping Johnnycakes**

1. Use greased ¼-cup dry measuring cup to carefully portion 6 mounds of batter into hot pan.

2. When edges are crisp and brown, carefully flip cakes and gently flatten with spatula.

Lemon Ricotta Pancakes

G-F TESTING LAB

FLOUR SUBSTITUTION	King Arthur Gluten-Free Multi-Purpose Flour 3½ ounces = ½ **cup plus 2 tablespoons**	Bob's Red Mill GF All-Purpose Baking Flour 3½ ounces = ⅔ **cup**

Note that pancakes made with Bob's Red Mill will be heavier and not as delicate as they should be, and they will have a distinct bean flavor.

WHY THIS RECIPE WORKS

Lemon ricotta pancakes stand apart from the classic versions with their light and creamy interior that is almost soufflé-like, and a subtle milky flavor. While ricotta adds creamy flavor and texture to these pancakes, it also adds weight. To keep the pancakes light, we folded four whipped egg whites into the batter. We also used a combination of baking soda and lemon juice for an extra boost not only to ensure the right ethereal rise, but also to provide a clean, bright flavor that balanced the milky richness of the ricotta. Still, these pancakes seemed a little heavier than we wanted, so we minimized the amount of flour blend, getting it down to just 3½ ounces. We like these pancakes plain or with a drizzle of honey, but we also threw together a quick fruit topping.

Lemon Ricotta Pancakes

MAKES TWELVE 4-INCH PANCAKES; SERVES 4

3½	ounces (¾ cup) ATK All-Purpose Gluten-Free Flour Blend (page 7)
½	teaspoon baking soda
½	teaspoon salt
9	ounces (1 cup) whole-milk ricotta cheese
2	large eggs, separated, plus 2 large egg whites
⅓	cup milk
1	teaspoon grated lemon zest plus 4 teaspoons juice
½	teaspoon vanilla extract
2	tablespoons unsalted butter, melted and cooled
	Pinch cream of tartar
1¾	ounces (¼ cup) sugar
1-2	teaspoons vegetable oil

1. Adjust oven rack to middle position and heat oven to 200 degrees. Spray wire rack set in rimmed baking sheet with vegetable oil spray; place in oven. Whisk flour blend, baking soda, and salt together in medium bowl, and make well in center. Add ricotta, egg yolks, milk, lemon zest and juice, and vanilla and whisk until combined. Stir in melted butter.

2. Using stand mixer fitted with whisk, whip egg whites and cream of tartar on medium-low speed until foamy, about 1 minute. Increase speed to medium-high and whip whites to soft, billowy mounds, about 1 minute. Gradually add sugar and whip until glossy, soft peaks form, 1 to 2 minutes. Transfer ⅓ of whipped egg whites to batter and whisk gently until mixture is lightened. Using silicone spatula, gently fold remaining egg whites into batter.

3. Heat 1 teaspoon oil in 12-inch nonstick skillet over medium heat until shimmering, 3 to 5 minutes. Using paper towels, carefully wipe out oil, leaving thin film of oil on bottom and sides of pan. Using ladle or ¼ cup measure, portion batter, leaving 2 inches between each portion. Using back of ladle (or spoon, if using measuring cup), gently spread each portion into 4-inch round. Cook until edges are set and first side is deep golden brown, about 2½ minutes. Flip pancakes and continue to cook until second side is golden brown, about 2½ minutes longer. Serve immediately or transfer to wire rack in preheated oven (don't overlap). Repeat with remaining batter, using remaining oil as necessary.

Pear-Blackberry Pancake Topping

MAKES 3 CUPS

3	ripe pears, peeled, cored, halved, and cut into ¼-inch pieces
1	tablespoon sugar
1	teaspoon cornstarch
	Pinch salt
	Pinch ground cardamom
5	ounces (1 cup) blackberries, berries halved crosswise if large

Combine pears, sugar, cornstarch, salt, and cardamom in bowl and microwave until pears are softened but not mushy and juices are slightly thickened, 4 to 6 minutes, stirring once halfway through microwaving. Stir in blackberries.

Sweet Crepes

G-F TESTING LAB

FLOUR SUBSTITUTION	King Arthur Gluten-Free Multi-Purpose Flour 5½ ounces = **1 cup**	Bob's Red Mill GF All-Purpose Baking Flour 5½ ounces = **1 cup plus 2 tablespoons**
	Note that crêpes made with Bob's Red Mill will be slightly gummier and will have a distinct bean flavor.	

✓ WHY THIS RECIPE WORKS

A traditional crêpe batter relies on 1 cup of flour, 1½ cups of milk, three eggs, and 2 tablespoons of butter (plus salt and sugar), so we swapped in our gluten-free flour blend and cooked up a batch. The results were close, but a bit rubbery. Reducing the number of eggs to two made the crêpes more tender and delicate. As with traditional crêpes, it was crucial to heat the pan properly—if it was too hot, the batter set up before it evenly coated the surface, yielding a crêpe marred by thick, spongy patches and holes; if too cool, the crêpe was pale (read: bland) and too flimsy to flip without tearing. To ensure steady, even cooking, we slowly heated the oiled skillet over low heat for at least 10 minutes. (Crêpes give off steam as they cook, but if at any point the skillet begins to smoke, remove it from the heat immediately and turn down the heat.) Adding just enough batter to coat the pan's bottom, and using the tilt-and-shake method to distribute the batter, ensured browned, flavorful crêpes that were perfectly thin and easy to flip without tearing. To allow for practice, the recipe yields 10 crêpes; only eight are needed for the filling.

Crepes with Lemon and Sugar

SERVES 4

- ½ teaspoon vegetable oil
- 5½ ounces (1¼ cups) ATK All-Purpose Gluten-Free Flour Blend (page 7)
- 3 tablespoons plus ½ teaspoon sugar
- ¼ teaspoon salt
- 1½ cups whole milk
- 2 large eggs
- 2 tablespoons unsalted butter, melted and cooled
- Lemon wedges

1. Place oil in 10-inch nonstick skillet and heat over low heat for at least 10 minutes. While skillet is heating, whisk flour blend, 1½ teaspoons sugar, and salt together in medium bowl. In separate bowl, whisk together milk and eggs. Add half of milk mixture to dry ingredients and whisk until smooth. Add melted butter and whisk until incorporated. Whisk in remaining milk mixture until smooth.

2. Using paper towel, wipe out skillet, leaving thin film of oil on bottom and sides of pan. Increase heat to medium and let skillet heat for 1 minute. After 1 minute, test heat of skillet by placing 1 teaspoon batter in center and cook for 20 seconds. If mini test crêpe is golden brown on bottom, skillet is properly heated; if too light or too dark, adjust heat accordingly and retest.

3. Whisk batter to recombine and pour scant ¼ cup batter into far side of pan and tilt and shake gently until batter evenly covers bottom of pan. Cook crêpe without moving it until top surface is dry and crêpe starts to brown at edges, loosening crêpe from side of pan with silicone spatula, about 25 seconds. Gently slide spatula underneath edge of crêpe, grasp edge with fingertips, and flip crêpe. Cook until second side is lightly spotted, about 20 seconds. Transfer cooked crêpe to wire rack, inverting so spotted side is facing up. Return pan to heat and heat for 10 seconds before repeating with remaining batter, whisking batter often to recombine. As crêpes are done, stack on wire rack.

4. Sprinkle upper half of 1 crêpe with 1 teaspoon sugar. Fold unsugared bottom half over sugared half, then fold into quarters. Transfer sugared crêpe to serving plate. Continue with remaining crêpes and sugar. Serve immediately, passing lemon wedges separately.

VARIATIONS

Crepes with Bananas and Nutella

Omit sugar and lemon wedge in step 4. Spread 1 teaspoon Nutella over half of each crêpe, then distribute three to four ¼-inch-thick banana slices atop the Nutella. Fold crêpes into quarters.

Crepes with Honey and Toasted Almonds

Omit sugar and lemon wedge in step 4. Drizzle 1 teaspoon honey over half of each crêpe and sprinkle with 2 teaspoons finely chopped toasted sliced almonds and pinch salt. Fold crêpes into quarters.

Buttermilk Waffles

G-F TESTING LAB

FLOUR SUBSTITUTION	King Arthur Gluten-Free Multi-Purpose Flour 12 ounces = **1⅔ cups plus ½ cup**	Bob's Red Mill GF All-Purpose Baking Flour 12 ounces = **2¼ cups plus 2 tablespoons**
	Note that waffles made with Bob's Red Mill will be somewhat darker and will have a slight bean flavor.	

People often think waffle and pancake batters are interchangeable, and while we don't agree with that in the test kitchen, we thought our gluten-free pancake batter (page 40) would at least serve as a good jumping-off point for a waffle recipe. Waffles made with this batter—which includes two whipped egg whites and multiple leaveners—came off of the waffle iron with a crisp shell and a hollow interior. Clearly we had too much lift, so we eliminated the baking powder and stopped separating the eggs and whipping the whites. For more structure, we increased the amount of flour. While these waffles were better, they were a little on the heavy side. Increasing the number of eggs from two to three fixed the problem, giving the batter the heft, volume, and richness it needed without making the waffles leaden. This batter baked up into waffles with a crisp exterior and a substantial interior that was moist, with just the right amount of chew. Buttermilk gives these waffles a nice tang and helps ensure a light texture. We prefer the crisper texture of these waffles when made in a Belgian waffle iron, but a classic iron will also work, though it will make more waffles.

Buttermilk Waffles

MAKES FIVE 7-INCH BELGIAN WAFFLES

- 12 ounces (2⅔ cups) ATK All-Purpose Gluten-Free Flour Blend (page 7)
- 2 tablespoons sugar
- ½ teaspoon salt
- ½ teaspoon baking soda
- 1¾ cups buttermilk
- 3 large eggs
- 4 tablespoons unsalted butter, melted and cooled

1. Heat waffle iron according to manufacturer's instructions.

2. Whisk flour blend, sugar, salt, and baking soda together in medium bowl. In separate bowl, whisk buttermilk, eggs, and melted butter until combined. Whisk buttermilk mixture into flour mixture thoroughly until batter has thickened and no lumps remain, about 1 minute (batter will be thick).

3. Bake waffles according to manufacturer's instructions (use about ⅓ cup batter for 7-inch round iron and generous ¾ cup for Belgian waffle iron). Repeat with remaining batter. Serve immediately.

TEST KITCHEN TIP **Buttermilk Substitutes**

If you do not have buttermilk on hand, that's not a problem. There are a couple of options for making buttermilk substitutions. For our waffles and Buttermilk Pancakes (page 40), both of which call for 1¾ cups buttermilk, mix ½ cup milk with 1¼ cups yogurt and substitute this mixture for the 1¾ cups buttermilk in the recipe. Both whole-milk and low-fat yogurt will work.

While too thin to use in our waffle and pancake batters, a mixture of lemon juice and milk is often used as a buttermilk substitute in other recipes. For 1 cup buttermilk, mix 1 cup whole milk with 1 tablespoon white vinegar or lemon juice.

Whole-Grain Waffles

G-F TESTING LAB

FLOUR SUBSTITUTION	Do not substitute other whole-grain blends for the ATK Whole-Grain Gluten-Free Flour Blend; they will not work in this recipe.
BAKING POWDER	Not all brands of baking powder are gluten-free; see page 24 for more information.
RESTING TIME	Do not shortchange the batter's 30-minute rest or the waffles will be dense.
COOKING TIME	These waffles may require a longer cooking time than usual.
ADDING FRUIT	For berry waffles, sprinkle 1 tablespoon berries (chopped if large) over surface of each waffle immediately after adding batter to waffle iron, and cook as directed.

WHY THIS RECIPE WORKS

We wanted a gluten-free whole-grain waffle recipe that produced crisp-on-the-outside, moist-on-the-inside waffles. We liked the idea of a classic buttermilk waffle, but unfortunately buttermilk tasted harsh in combination with our hearty whole-grain blend. We swapped out the buttermilk for low-fat milk, preferring the leaner, thinner batter along with the milder flavor. However, removing the buttermilk, the acidic component of this recipe, altered the effectiveness of the baking soda, which is acid-activated. This led to doughy, dense waffles. After numerous tests of combinations of baking powder and baking soda, we found that we liked baking powder alone the best. It gave the waffles a lighter structure and a fluffy rise. But we still noticed a slightly gritty texture. Letting the batter sit at room temperature for 30 minutes allowed the starch granules to hydrate and soften before hitting the waffle iron. Although this step made for a less gritty waffle, the starches absorbed much of the moisture, so we increased the amount of milk to allow the starches to fully hydrate without turning our batter to cement. Our last challenge was to create a crisp exterior. Even straight out of the waffle iron, our waffles were soft. It turns out the interior moisture was making its way to the surface, causing our waffles to feel doughy from edge to edge. Since butter contains some water, and since fat repels moisture, we traded the butter for pure fat in the form of vegetable oil. Waffles made with oil were significantly crispier than those made with butter, but we missed the rich, buttery flavor that complemented the whole-grain blend so well. So instead we swapped in vegetable oil for only half of the butter, and this resulted in waffles that had a crisp exterior encasing a light interior, plus rich flavor. We prefer the crisper texture provided by a Belgian waffle iron, but a classic waffle iron will also work, though it will make more waffles. Do not substitute skim or whole milk in this recipe.

Whole-Grain Waffles

MAKES FOUR 7-INCH BELGIAN WAFFLES; SERVES 4

- 12   ounces (2⅔ cups) ATK Whole-Grain Gluten-Free Flour Blend (page 9)
- 1¾ ounces (¼ cup) sugar
- 1   teaspoon baking powder
- ½   teaspoon salt
- 2   cups 1 or 2 percent low-fat milk, plus extra as needed
- 3   large eggs
- 2   tablespoons unsalted butter, melted and cooled
- 2   tablespoons vegetable oil
- 1   teaspoon vanilla extract

1. Set wire rack in rimmed baking sheet. Adjust oven rack to middle position, place prepared sheet on oven rack, and heat oven to 200 degrees.

2. Whisk flour blend, sugar, baking powder, and salt together in large bowl. In separate bowl, whisk milk, eggs, melted butter, oil, and vanilla together until combined. Whisk milk mixture into flour mixture until well incorporated, batter has thickened, and no lumps remain, about 1 minute. Cover bowl with plastic wrap and let batter rest at room temperature for 30 minutes.

3. Heat waffle iron and cook waffles according to manufacturer's instructions, until each waffle is deep golden brown and has crisp, firm exterior (use about 1 cup batter for Belgian waffle iron and scant ¾ cup for 7-inch round iron). Serve or transfer to wire rack in oven. Repeat with remaining batter, whisking extra milk into batter as needed to loosen.

VARIATION
Dairy-Free Whole-Grain Waffles

We prefer the flavor and texture of these waffles made with almond milk but soy milk will also work; do not use rice milk.

Substitute unsweetened almond milk for milk, and vegetable oil for melted butter.

Blueberry Muffins

G-F TESTING LAB

FLOUR SUBSTITUTION	King Arthur Gluten-Free Multi-Purpose Flour 11 ounces = **2 cups**	Bob's Red Mill GF All-Purpose Baking Flour 11 ounces = **1⅔ cups plus ½ cup**
	Note that muffins made with King Arthur will have a slightly starchy aftertaste and gritty texture; muffins made with Bob's Red Mill will be somewhat darker and will have a distinct bean flavor.	
XANTHAN GUM	The xanthan gum can be omitted, but the muffins will be more crumbly, with slightly less structure, and they will be a little more difficult to get out of the pan.	
RESTING TIME	Do not shortchange the 30-minute rest for the batter; if you do, the muffins will be gritty.	

Even the best traditional bakeshops often come up short when they attempt to make gluten-free muffins—the results are usually gritty, crumbly, and pale. We set out to make a golden-domed gluten-free muffin that also had a tender, delicate interior. To fix the grittiness, we found that resting the batter before baking hydrated the flour and softened its texture—but we had to be careful because the longer we let the batter sit, the more dense the muffins were and the less they rose. While we typically use two eggs in a muffin recipe, this thick batter needed three eggs to achieve the proper richness and structure. For the liquid component, we were after something that would help create a moist crumb and also lend some flavor. A few tests with various dairy options proved that plain whole-milk yogurt was the answer (you can use low-fat yogurt, but the muffins will be a little drier). Finally, sprinkling the muffins with turbinado sugar before they went into the oven helped create the browned tops we were after. You can substitute an equal amount of fresh raspberries or chopped strawberries for the blueberries. Frozen berries, rinsed well and blotted dry with paper towels, will also work; however, the berries will bleed slightly into the batter. See page 60 for tips on portioning the muffin batter into the prepared tin.

Blueberry Muffins
MAKES 12 MUFFINS

11	ounces (1¾ cups plus ⅔ cup) ATK All-Purpose Gluten-Free Flour Blend (page 7)
1	tablespoon baking powder (see page 24)
½	teaspoon salt
¼	teaspoon ground cinnamon
¼	teaspoon xanthan gum
5¼	ounces (¾ cup) granulated sugar
8	tablespoons unsalted butter, melted and cooled
½	cup plain whole-milk yogurt
3	large eggs
1	teaspoon vanilla extract
7½	ounces (1½ cups) blueberries
2	tablespoons turbinado sugar

1. Whisk flour blend, baking powder, salt, cinnamon, and xanthan gum together in large bowl. In separate bowl, whisk granulated sugar, melted butter, yogurt, eggs, and vanilla together until well combined. Using silicone spatula, stir egg mixture into flour mixture until thoroughly combined and no lumps remain, about 1 minute. Gently fold in blueberries until evenly distributed (batter will be thick and stiff). Cover bowl with plastic wrap and let batter rest at room temperature for 30 minutes.

2. Adjust oven rack to middle position and heat oven to 375 degrees. Spray 12-cup muffin tin with vegetable oil spray. Using ice cream scoop or large spoon, portion batter evenly into prepared muffin tin. Sprinkle turbinado sugar over top. Bake until muffins are golden and toothpick inserted in center comes out clean, 16 to 20 minutes, rotating pan halfway through baking.

3. Let muffins cool in muffin tin on wire rack for 10 minutes. Remove muffins from tin and let cool for 10 minutes before serving. (Muffins are best eaten warm on day they are made, but they can be cooled, then immediately transferred to zipper-lock bag and stored at room temperature for up to 1 day. To serve, warm in 300-degree oven for 10 minutes. Muffins can also be wrapped individually in plastic wrap, transferred to zipper-lock bag, and frozen for up to 3 weeks. To serve, remove plastic and microwave muffin for 20 to 30 seconds, then warm in 350-degree oven for 10 minutes.)

TEST KITCHEN TIP **Cooling and Storing Gluten-Free Quick Breads**

Like their traditional counterparts, our gluten-free muffins, quick breads, and coffee cake should be cooled in the tin or pan for a short stint once they come out of the oven. This gives them time to set up, reducing the chance they'll break when you remove them. Then let them cool further, as directed in the recipe, before serving.

However, don't let them sit out for an extended time—our gluten-free muffins, quick breads, and coffee cake may taste as good as versions made with all-purpose flour, but their shelf life is shorter. The high starch content in gluten-free flour absorbs moisture much more quickly than traditional all-purpose flour does, making these baked goods dry and crumbly fairly quickly. Consequently, we highly recommend eating them as soon as they are cooled. Letting them sit out even a couple of hours beyond our recommended times makes a big difference in quality.

If you want to store leftovers, we found that they will all keep acceptably well for a day or two at room temperature (don't refrigerate them, as this only makes them drier). Quick breads and coffee cake don't freeze well, but muffins freeze quite nicely (and you can conveniently thaw them individually as needed). To avoid a starchy aftertaste, we also learned that reheating leftover muffins and quick breads is a must.

1. Once baked, cool in tin/pan on wire rack for time noted in recipe, then remove and let cool as directed. Serve or store immediately.

2. To store muffins for up to 1 day, immediately transfer cooled muffins to zipper-lock bag and store at room temperature. To store quick breads for up to 2 days, immediately wrap in plastic wrap and store at room temperature. To serve, warm in 300-degree oven for 10 to 15 minutes.

3. To store muffins for up to 3 weeks, wrap each muffin individually in plastic wrap, transfer to zipper-lock bag, and freeze. To serve, remove plastic and microwave muffin for 20 to 30 seconds, then warm in 350-degree oven for 10 minutes.

TEST KITCHEN TIP **Pay Attention to Portioning**

Not only does portioning the muffin batter haphazardly result in muffins that are of various sizes—some may overflow the cups while others look awkwardly small—but it also means the muffins may cook unevenly. We like to use a ⅓-cup dry measuring cup, large spoon, or spring-loaded #16 ice cream scoop. Whichever tool you use to portion the batter, spray it with vegetable oil spray so that the batter slides off easily.

For neat, evenly sized muffins, portion ⅓ cup batter into each cup using measuring cup or ice cream scoop, then circle back and evenly distribute remaining batter with spoon.

Muffins

Muffins are one of the first things many people learn to bake because they're quick (no waiting for yeast to do its job), the ingredients are usually straightforward, and you don't need any special equipment. But as simple as they seem, bad muffins, and bad muffin recipes, abound. Try to make them gluten-free and you've got a host of new problems on your hands. Here's how we made gluten-free muffins that can hold their own against the best of the traditional versions.

1. ADD AN EXTRA EGG AND YOGURT: We typically use two eggs in a traditional muffin recipe, but for various reasons this gluten-free batter needed three. First, the extra egg boosted the flavor and richness, which was a must because the starch granules in gluten-free flour absorb a lot of flavor. Second, the egg provided more moisture and structure, which our thick batter required for the proper rise and a moist, tender crumb. When it came to the liquid component, whole-milk yogurt, like the egg, provided a flavor boost and helped add moisture.

2. ADD XANTHAN GUM: Xanthan gum acts as a binding agent, providing the structure and stability that traditional baked goods usually get from the gluten protein (see page 21 for more about xanthan gum). While our muffins will work without it, they will be a little more crumbly and harder to get out of the pan. We think adding just ¼ teaspoon delivers a superior muffin.

3. STIR, STIR, STIR: The most common pitfall in traditional muffin making is overmixing, because it works the gluten in the flour, and this leads to a tough, tunneled interior rather than a uniform, fluffy texture. Overworking the gluten was obviously not a concern with our gluten-free muffins. In fact, we discovered we needed to be more worried about undermixing. All that starch in the gluten-free flour blend made the muffin batter dense and thick. We had to stir the mixture for a full minute to ensure the leaveners and xanthan gum were evenly distributed.

4. LET THE BATTER SIT: Our early versions had a gritty texture—the result of gluten-free flour's higher starch content. Starch is very slow to absorb water, so if the batter goes straight into the oven right after it's mixed, the starch granules clump together and absorb water only on their surface. The result is a muffin with a noticeably gritty texture. Letting the batter sit at room temperature allowed those granules to hydrate and soften uniformly before baking. But you can overhydrate the starches, making the muffins denser and squat. Don't let the batter rest for more than 30 minutes.

Whole-Grain Blueberry Muffins

G-F TESTING LAB

FLOUR SUBSTITUTION	Do not substitute other whole-grain blends for the ATK Whole-Grain Gluten-Free Flour Blend; they will not work in this recipe.
BAKING POWDER	Not all brands of baking powder are gluten-free; see page 24 for more information.
XANTHAN GUM	The xanthan can be omitted, but the muffins will be crumbly and more difficult to get out of the pan.
RESTING TIME	Do not shortchange the batter's 30-minute rest; if you do, the muffins will be gritty.

WHY THIS RECIPE WORKS

We set out to create a tender blueberry muffin using our whole-grain gluten-free flour blend to deliver earthy, nutty flavor. Our starting point was testing types and amounts of liquid, as we knew this would significantly affect the texture of the muffins. We settled on yogurt, which added moisture without making the batter too loose. We needed a full cup, but it added a sour flavor. Instead we swapped in a little heavy cream for some of the yogurt, which nicely hydrated the flours and made the texture more substantial. However, the muffins were still a bit gritty and dense. To fix this, we needed to make the batter more loose, because the flours in the whole-grain blend absorbed more liquid as the batter sat. As with our regular gluten-free blueberry muffin batter, this thick batter needed three eggs to achieve the proper richness and structure. To get an open crumb we quickly learned that we needed both baking powder and baking soda; muffins made with both leaveners were lighter in texture, and they had a domed top and were more golden brown than muffins made with just baking powder. This was because the baking soda helped neutralize the acid in the yogurt, which in turn allowed the baking powder to function more effectively. You can substitute frozen berries, rinsed well and blotted dry with paper towels; however, they will bleed slightly into the batter. See page 60 for tips on how to portion the muffin batter into the prepared tin and how to store the muffins after baking to preserve freshness.

Whole-Grain Blueberry Muffins
MAKES 12 MUFFINS

- 12 ounces (2⅔ cups) ATK Whole-Grain Gluten-Free Flour Blend (page 9)
- 4 teaspoons baking powder
- ¾ teaspoon baking soda
- ¾ teaspoon salt
- ¾ teaspoon ground cinnamon
- ¼ teaspoon xanthan gum
- 7 ounces (1 cup) granulated sugar
- 10 tablespoons unsalted butter, melted and cooled
- ½ cup plain whole-milk yogurt
- ⅓ cup heavy cream
- 3 large eggs
- 1½ teaspoons vanilla extract
- 7½ ounces (1½ cups) blueberries
- 2 tablespoons turbinado sugar

1. Whisk flour blend, baking powder, baking soda, salt, cinnamon, and xanthan gum together in large bowl. In separate bowl, whisk granulated sugar, melted butter, yogurt, cream, eggs, and vanilla together until well combined. Using silicone spatula, stir butter mixture into flour mixture until thoroughly combined and no lumps remain, about 1 minute (batter will be thick). Gently fold in blueberries. Cover bowl with plastic wrap and let batter rest at room temperature for 30 minutes.

2. Adjust oven rack to middle position and heat oven to 375 degrees. Spray 12-cup muffin tin with vegetable oil spray. Portion batter evenly into prepared muffin tin. Sprinkle turbinado sugar over top. Bake until muffins are golden and toothpick inserted in center comes out clean, 20 to 22 minutes, rotating pan halfway through baking.

3. Let muffins cool in pan for 10 minutes, then remove from pan and let cool on wire rack for 10 minutes longer. Serve.

VARIATION
Dairy-Free Whole-Grain Blueberry Muffins
We prefer the flavor and texture of these muffins made with coconut milk yogurt but soy milk yogurt will also work. We had good luck using Silk Soy Creamer.

Increase baking powder to 5 teaspoons. Substitute ½ cup vegetable oil for melted butter, plain coconut milk yogurt for whole-milk yogurt, and plain soy creamer for heavy cream.

Cranberry-Orange Pecan Muffins

FLOUR SUBSTITUTION	King Arthur Gluten-Free Multi-Purpose Flour 11 ounces = **2 cups**	Bob's Red Mill GF All-Purpose Baking Flour 11 ounces = **1⅔ cups plus ½ cup**
	Note that muffins made with King Arthur will have a slightly starchy aftertaste and gritty texture; muffins made with Bob's Red Mill will be somewhat darker and will have a distinct bean flavor.	
XANTHAN GUM	The xanthan gum can be omitted, but the muffins will be more crumbly, with slightly less structure, and they will be a little more difficult to get out of the pan.	
RESTING TIME	Do not shortchange the 30-minute rest for the batter; if you do, the muffins will be gritty.	

WHY THIS RECIPE WORKS

With a successful gluten-free Blueberry Muffin recipe (page 59) under our belts, we decided to try a different take using a similar base. We swapped whole cranberries in for the blueberries, and added pecans for nutty flavor and texture. The tartness of whole cranberries overwhelmed some bites (and was absent in others), so we pulsed the cranberries in the food processor to temper their punch and ensure they were more evenly distributed. We started testing with 1 cup of pecans, but this amount made our muffins too dense and heavy. But cutting back to ½ cup wasn't enough. We didn't want to sacrifice any more pecan flavor, so we ground the pecans in the food processor. This gave us a nut flour that we could add to the flour blend. And since we already had the food processor out, we decided to see if we could streamline things and prepare the batter in it rather than combining ingredients by hand in mixing bowls. The results were great: The muffins were perfectly tender and light and had a nutty flavor throughout. Because the nuts made our batter a bit denser and added fat, we needed to increase the oven temperature from 375 to 400 degrees to ensure the rise and nicely domed tops. Finally, a touch of orange zest added sweetness and brightness that complemented the cranberries. If fresh cranberries aren't available, substitute frozen: Microwave them in a bowl until they're partially but not fully thawed, 30 to 45 seconds. Plain low-fat yogurt will work just fine in this recipe, although the muffins will be a bit drier.

Cranberry-Orange Pecan Muffins
MAKES 12 MUFFINS

- 8 **ounces (2 cups) cranberries**
- 5¼ **ounces (¾ cup) granulated sugar**
- ½ **cup pecans, toasted**
- 2 **teaspoons grated orange zest**
- 11 **ounces (1¾ cups plus ⅔ cup) ATK All-Purpose Gluten-Free Flour Blend (page 7)**
- 1 **tablespoon baking powder (see page 24)**
- ½ **teaspoon salt**
- ¼ **teaspoon xanthan gum**
- 8 **tablespoons unsalted butter, melted and cooled**
- ½ **cup plain whole-milk yogurt**
- 3 **large eggs**
- 2 **tablespoons turbinado sugar**

1. Pulse cranberries in food processor until very coarsely chopped, 4 to 5 pulses. Transfer to bowl and set aside. Process granulated sugar, pecans, and orange zest in now-empty food processor to coarse sand, 10 to 15 seconds. Add flour blend, baking powder, salt, and xanthan gum and pulse until well combined, 5 to 10 pulses.

2. Whisk melted butter, yogurt, and eggs together in large bowl until well combined. Add to food processor and process until thoroughly combined and no lumps remain, about 30 seconds. Transfer to now-empty bowl and fold in chopped cranberries (batter will be thick and stiff). Cover bowl with plastic wrap and let batter rest at room temperature for 30 minutes.

3. Adjust oven rack to middle position and heat oven to 400 degrees. Spray 12-cup muffin tin with vegetable oil spray. Using ice cream scoop or large spoon, portion batter evenly into prepared muffin tin. Sprinkle turbinado sugar over top. Bake until muffins are golden and toothpick inserted in center comes out clean, 16 to 20 minutes, rotating pan halfway through baking.

4. Let muffins cool in muffin tin on wire rack for 10 minutes. Remove muffins from tin and let cool for 10 minutes before serving. (Muffins are best eaten warm on day they are made, but they can be cooled, then immediately transferred to zipper-lock bag and stored at room temperature for up to 1 day. To serve, warm in 300-degree oven for 10 minutes. Muffins can also be wrapped individually in plastic wrap, transferred to zipper-lock bag, and frozen for up to 3 weeks. To serve, remove plastic and microwave muffin for 20 to 30 seconds, then warm in 350-degree oven for 10 minutes.)

Coconut-Cashew Muffins

G-F TESTING LAB

FLOUR SUBSTITUTION	King Arthur Gluten-Free Multi-Purpose Flour 9 ounces = **1½ cups plus 2 tablespoons**	Betty Crocker All-Purpose Gluten Free Rice Blend 9 ounces = **1½ cups plus ⅓ cup**
	Muffins made with King Arthur will have a tighter crumb and not rise as well; muffins made with Betty Crocker will have a slightly pasty texture.	
BAKING POWDER	Not all brands of baking powder are gluten-free; see page 24 for more information.	
XANTHAN GUM	The xanthan can be omitted, but the muffins will be crumbly and more difficult to get out of the pan.	
RESTING TIME	Do not shortchange the batter's 30-minute rest; if you do, the muffins will be gritty.	

✔ WHY THIS RECIPE WORKS

We set out to create a golden-domed coconut-cashew muffin with a moist, tender interior and rich, nutty flavor. For our basic muffin base, we found that, as with many of our other gluten-free muffins, it benefited from the additional structure, moisture, and richness gained by using three eggs instead of two; the extra egg boosted the flavor (the starch granules in gluten-free flour absorb so much flavor) and provided moisture, which this thick batter needed for a proper rise. To infuse our muffins with coconut flavor we started by mixing sweetened flaked coconut into the batter, but we didn't like the texture their long strands created. Pulsing the coconut in a food processor created smaller bits that distributed evenly throughout the batter. As for the cashews, tossing chopped cashews into the batter weighed it down, and the nut flavor was lackluster. Since we already had the food processor out, we tried processing the cashews into a nut flour that we could add to the flour blend. We liked the soft, light texture this gave us, but the muffins had an underwhelming cashew flavor. Increasing the amount of cashews from ½ cup to 1¼ cups provided the ideal balance of toasted coconut flavor and rich nuttiness. Finally, sprinkling the muffins with untoasted coconut and chopped cashews before baking gave them an appealingly crunchy top. Be sure to grease the muffin tin thoroughly, as these muffins tend to stick. See page 60 for tips on how to portion the muffin batter into the prepared tin and how to store the muffins after baking to preserve freshness.

Coconut-Cashew Muffins
MAKES 12 MUFFINS

- 1⅔ cups sweetened flaked coconut
- 8 tablespoons unsalted butter, melted and cooled
- 3 large eggs
- ½ cup plain whole-milk yogurt
- 2 tablespoons water
- ½ teaspoon vanilla extract
- 5¼ ounces (¾ cup) sugar
- 1¼ cups roasted cashews, chopped
- 9 ounces (2 cups) ATK All-Purpose Gluten-Free Flour Blend (page 7)
- 1 tablespoon baking powder
- ½ teaspoon salt
- ¼ teaspoon xanthan gum

1. Adjust oven rack to middle position and heat oven to 375 degrees. Spread 1⅓ cups coconut over rimmed baking sheet and bake, stirring frequently, until lightly golden, 7 to 10 minutes. Let coconut cool for 15 minutes, then pulse in food processor until finely chopped, about 10 pulses; transfer to bowl. In separate bowl, whisk melted butter, eggs, yogurt, water, and vanilla together.

2. Process sugar and 1 cup cashews in now-empty food processor to coarse sand, 10 to 15 seconds. Add flour blend, baking powder, salt, and xanthan gum and pulse until well combined, 5 to 10 pulses. Add butter mixture and process until thoroughly combined and no lumps remain, about 30 seconds. Transfer mixture to large bowl and fold in toasted, chopped coconut (batter will be thick and stiff). Cover bowl with plastic wrap and let batter rest at room temperature for 30 minutes.

3. Spray 12-cup muffin tin thoroughly with vegetable oil spray. Portion batter evenly into prepared muffin tin. Combine remaining ¼ cup cashews with remaining ⅓ cup untoasted coconut and sprinkle over muffins. Bake until muffins are golden and toothpick inserted in center comes out clean, 18 to 20 minutes, rotating pan halfway through baking.

4. Let muffins cool in pan for 10 minutes, then remove from pan and let cool on wire rack for 10 minutes longer. Serve.

VARIATION
Dairy-Free Coconut-Cashew Muffins
We prefer the flavor of these muffins made with coconut milk yogurt but soy milk yogurt will also work.

Substitute vegetable oil for butter, and ⅔ cup plain coconut milk yogurt for whole-milk yogurt.

Corn Muffins

FLOUR SUBSTITUTION	King Arthur Gluten-Free Multi-Purpose Flour 7½ ounces = **1¼ cups plus 2 tablespoons**	Betty Crocker All-Purpose Gluten Free Rice Blend 7½ ounces = **1½ cups**
	Muffins made with King Arthur will have a tighter crumb; muffins made with Betty Crocker will have a tighter crumb and the edges will be less crisp.	
CORNMEAL	Not all brands of cornmeal are gluten-free; see page 26 for more information.	
BAKING POWDER	Not all brands of baking powder are gluten-free; see page 24 for more information.	
XANTHAN GUM	The xanthan can be omitted, but the muffins will be more crumbly.	
RESTING TIME	Do not shortchange the batter's 30-minute rest; if you do, the muffins will be gritty.	

WHY THIS RECIPE WORKS

For gluten-free corn muffins with a tender crumb, we started with the classic corn muffin ratio of two parts flour to one part cornmeal using our all-purpose gluten-free flour blend, but we found ourselves with crumbly, starchy, and bland muffins. By tipping the scale to use almost equal parts cornmeal and flour blend, we were able to create a moister crumb with a more powerful corn flavor. Unfortunately, we still had a slightly dry and lean muffin on our hands. We tried adding an extra egg, but that resulted in an overwhelming eggy flavor that overpowered the sweet corn-flavored base. Instead, we increased the milk and sour cream amounts to provide the necessary moisture and emulsified fats. In order to get an appealingly crisp edge, we brushed the tops of the muffin batter with melted butter and started baking them at 500 degrees. Halfway through baking, we reduced the oven temperature to 400 degrees, which allowed the interiors time to fully cook while the tops finished crisping up. Now we had rustic-looking gluten-free corn muffins with crisp, buttery edges, a soft but firm interior crumb, and a bold, sweet corn flavor. See page 60 for tips on how to portion the muffin batter into the prepared tin and how to store the muffins after baking to preserve freshness.

Corn Muffins
MAKES 12 MUFFINS

7½	ounces (1⅔ cups) ATK All-Purpose Gluten-Free Flour Blend (page 7)
6⅔	ounces (1⅓ cups) stone-ground cornmeal
1½	teaspoons baking powder
1	teaspoon baking soda
½	teaspoon salt
¼	teaspoon xanthan gum
1⅓	cups sour cream
5¼	ounces (¾ cup) sugar
⅔	cup whole milk
2	large eggs
10	tablespoons unsalted butter, melted and cooled

1. Whisk flour blend, cornmeal, baking powder, baking soda, salt, and xanthan gum together in medium bowl. In separate bowl, whisk sour cream, sugar, milk, eggs, and 8 tablespoons melted butter together until well combined. Using silicone spatula, stir sour cream mixture into flour mixture until thoroughly combined and no lumps remain, about 1 minute. Cover bowl with plastic wrap and let batter rest at room temperature for 30 minutes.

2. Adjust oven rack to middle position and heat oven to 500 degrees. Spray 12-cup muffin tin with vegetable oil spray. Portion batter evenly into prepared muffin tin. Brush remaining 2 tablespoons melted butter over top. Bake muffins for 7 minutes.

3. Reduce oven temperature to 400 degrees, rotate muffin tin, and continue to bake muffins until golden brown and toothpick inserted in center comes out clean, about 7 minutes.

4. Let muffins cool in pan for 10 minutes, then remove from pan and let cool on wire rack for 10 minutes longer. Serve.

VARIATION
Dairy-Free Corn Muffins

We prefer the flavor and texture of these muffins made with soy milk but almond milk will also work; do not use rice milk.

Use dairy-free sour cream. Substitute unsweetened soy milk for milk, and vegetable oil for melted butter. Add 2 additional tablespoons sugar to sour cream mixture in step 1.

Millet–Cherry Almond Muffins

G-F TESTING LAB

FLOUR SUBSTITUTION	King Arthur Gluten-Free Multi-Purpose Flour 11 ounces = **2 cups**	Bob's Red Mill GF All-Purpose Baking Flour 11 ounces = **1⅔ cups plus ½ cup**
	Note that muffins made with King Arthur will have a slightly starchy aftertaste and gritty texture; muffins made with Bob's Red Mill will be somewhat darker and will have a distinct bean flavor.	
XANTHAN GUM	The xanthan gum can be omitted, but the muffins will be more crumbly and will have slightly less structure, and they will be a little more difficult to get out of the pan.	
RESTING TIME	Do not shortchange the 30-minute rest for the batter; if you do, the muffins will be gritty.	

WHY THIS RECIPE WORKS

After developing a couple of muffin recipes with a classic profile—blueberry and cranberry-nut (see pages 58 and 64)—we set out to make one with a more rustic profile. Incorporating a gluten-free grain plus some dried fruit into our batter seemed like a good route to take. We started with our blueberry muffin batter, then stirred in millet seeds and dried cherries. We quickly discovered that a little millet went a long way—too much created a crunchy, distracting texture. Just ¼ cup of millet lent the right nutty flavor and crunch. When it came to the fruit, the muffins clearly needed the plump, juicy bursts of fresh or frozen fruit because the dried cherries turned out hard and chewy. Six ounces of frozen cherries gave the muffins the right sweet-tart punch. Almond extract was just the right finishing flavor touch that complemented the cherries and the millet. Do not thaw the cherries or your batter will turn purple. When fresh cherries are in season, you can substitute 6 ounces fresh sweet cherries, pitted and chopped coarse, for the frozen cherries. Plain low-fat yogurt will work just fine in this recipe, although the muffins will be a bit drier.

Millet–Cherry Almond Muffins

MAKES 12 MUFFINS

- 11 ounces (1¾ cups plus ⅔ cup) ATK All-Purpose Gluten-Free Flour Blend (page 7)
- 1 tablespoon baking powder (see page 24)
- ½ teaspoon salt
- ¼ teaspoon xanthan gum
- 5¼ ounces (¾ cup) granulated sugar
- 8 tablespoons unsalted butter, melted and cooled
- ½ cup plain whole-milk yogurt
- 3 large eggs
- ½ teaspoon almond extract
- 6 ounces frozen sweet cherries, chopped coarse
- ¼ cup millet, rinsed
- 2 tablespoons turbinado sugar

1. Whisk flour blend, baking powder, salt, and xanthan gum together in large bowl. In separate bowl, whisk granulated sugar, melted butter, yogurt, eggs, and almond extract together until well combined. Using silicone spatula, stir egg mixture into flour mixture until thoroughly combined and no lumps remain, about 1 minute. Gently fold in cherries and millet until evenly distributed (batter will be thick and stiff). Cover bowl with plastic wrap and let batter rest at room temperature for 30 minutes.

2. Adjust oven rack to middle position and heat oven to 375 degrees. Spray 12-cup muffin tin with vegetable oil spray. Using ice cream scoop or large spoon, portion batter evenly into prepared muffin tin. Sprinkle turbinado sugar over top. Bake until muffins are golden and toothpick inserted in center comes out clean, 16 to 20 minutes, rotating pan halfway through baking.

3. Let muffins cool in muffin tin on wire rack for 10 minutes. Remove muffins from tin and let cool for 10 minutes before serving. (Muffins are best eaten warm on day they are made, but they can be cooled, then immediately transferred to zipper-lock bag and stored at room temperature for up to 1 day. To serve, warm in 300-degree oven for 10 minutes. Muffins can also be wrapped individually in plastic wrap, transferred to zipper-lock bag, and frozen for up to 3 weeks. To serve, remove plastic and microwave muffin for 20 to 30 seconds, then warm in 350-degree oven for 10 minutes.)

Currant Scones

G-F TESTING LAB

FLOUR SUBSTITUTION	King Arthur Gluten-Free Multi-Purpose Flour 7½ ounces = **1¼ cups plus 2 tablespoons**	Betty Crocker All-Purpose Gluten Free Rice Blend 7½ ounces = **1½ cups**
	Scones made with King Arthur will have a stickier dough and taste slightly chewy; scones made with Betty Crocker will be starchy and taste slightly rubbery.	
BAKING POWDER	Not all brands of baking powder are gluten-free; see page 24 for more information.	
XANTHAN GUM	Xanthan is crucial to the structure of the scones; see page 21 for more information.	
RESTING TIME	Do not shortchange the dough's 30-minute rest; if you do, the scones will be harder to shape, they will spread, and they will taste gritty.	

WHY THIS RECIPE WORKS

Even the best traditional bakeshops often come up short when they attempt to make gluten-free scones—the results are usually gritty, crumbly, and pale. We set out to make a light and tender scone with a buttery flavor and gentle sweetness. To fix the crumbly texture we found that a two-part solution worked best. A small amount of xanthan gum acted as a binding agent and provided the structure and stability we were missing, while an egg added additional structure along with moisture and elasticity. For scones with a light, not dense, texture, we added a full tablespoon of baking powder, and to eliminate grittiness we found that resting the dough for 30 minutes before shaping the scones hydrated the flour and softened its texture. The resting step also helped thicken the wet dough a bit and made it easier to shape. For our dairy component, we noticed that scones made with milk or cream spread way too much, and the dough was difficult to work with. Switching to thicker sour cream solved those problems. To achieve a golden crust and a nice rise, scones are typically baked at a high temperature, but we struggled to get a nice color on the tops of the scones without burning the bottoms. Lowering the oven temperature seemed like a natural solution, but we needed to bake them so long that they dried out. We had better luck preheating the oven at a high temperature and dropping it down slightly when putting the scones in the oven. We also found that using a second baking sheet as insulation kept the bottoms from burning. Make sure to preheat your oven before you make the dough. Other types of dried fruit, such as cranberries, apricots, or raisins, can be chopped fine and substituted for the currants if desired.

Currant Scones

MAKES 6 SCONES

7½	ounces (1⅔ cups) ATK All-Purpose Gluten-Free Flour Blend (page 7)
3	tablespoons plus 1½ teaspoons sugar
1	tablespoon baking powder
¼	teaspoon salt
¼	teaspoon xanthan gum
6	tablespoons unsalted butter, cut into ½-inch pieces and chilled
⅓	cup dried currants
⅔	cup sour cream
1	large egg

1. Adjust oven rack to upper-middle position and heat oven to 500 degrees. Line rimmed baking sheet with parchment paper and place in second baking sheet. Lay large sheet of parchment paper flat on counter and spray with vegetable oil spray.

2. Pulse flour blend, 3 tablespoons sugar, baking powder, salt, and xanthan gum in food processor until combined, about 5 pulses. Add butter and pulse until fully incorporated and mixture resembles very fine crumbs with no butter pieces visible, about 10 pulses. Transfer mixture to large bowl and stir in currants.

3. In separate bowl, whisk together sour cream and egg until combined. Using silicone spatula, stir sour cream mixture into flour mixture until no dry bits of flour remain. Cover bowl with plastic wrap and let dough rest at room temperature for 30 minutes. (Do not let dough rest for longer than 30 minutes.)

4. Using wet hands, transfer dough to prepared parchment on counter. Clean and wet hands again. Pat dough into 6-inch round about 1 inch thick. Spray knife with vegetable oil spray and cut dough into 6 equal wedges. Arrange scones on prepared baking sheet and sprinkle remaining 1½ teaspoons sugar over top.

5. Reduce oven temperature to 425 degrees and bake scones until golden brown, 12 to 14 minutes, rotating sheet halfway through baking. Transfer scones to wire rack and let cool for 20 minutes before serving. (Scones can be wrapped individually in plastic wrap and frozen for up to 1 month; unwrap and thaw in microwave for 20 to 30 seconds, then refresh in 350-degree oven for 10 to 15 minutes.)

VARIATION

Dairy-Free Currant Scones

We had good luck using Tofutti Better Than Sour Cream.

Omit salt and use dairy-free sour cream. Substitute Earth Balance Vegan Buttery Sticks for butter. Increase sugar to ¼ cup in step 2.

TEST KITCHEN TIP **Making Scones**

The dough for the scones is fairly sticky, so using wet hands, greased parchment, and a greased knife makes shaping the dough easier.

1. Pulse dry ingredients in food processor until combined. Add butter and pulse until fully incorporated and mixture looks like very fine crumbs with no visible butter.

2. In separate bowl, whisk together sour cream and egg until combined. Using silicone spatula, stir sour cream mixture into flour and currant mixture until no dry bits of flour remain.

3. Cover bowl with plastic wrap and let dough rest at room temperature for 30 minutes.

4. With wet hands, transfer dough to large sheet of parchment paper greased with vegetable oil spray. Clean and wet hands again, then pat dough into 6-inch round about 1 inch thick.

5. Spray knife with vegetable oil spray and cut dough into 6 wedges.

6. Arrange scones on prepared baking sheet and sprinkle remaining 1½ teaspoons sugar over top.

Currant Scones

We wanted a recipe for gluten-free scones that were sweet, but not overly so, with a fluffy and delicate interior crumb. To achieve the same high rise and delicate crumb as traditional scones, we had to rework the recipe slightly.

1. REIN IN THE SUGAR AND FAT: To keep the sweetness level in check and make the scones less chewy, we reduced the amount of sugar to just a few tablespoons. And since the starches in the gluten-free flour blend don't absorb fat as readily as traditional flour does, we swapped out the milk for sour cream. The sour cream added richness and flavor without making the scones greasy, because it contains a more emulsified fat that doesn't leach out during baking.

2. ADD XANTHAN GUM AND AN EGG FOR STRUCTURE: While traditional scones rely on gluten for structure, we had to find another source. Adding xanthan gum (as we had done in other recipes) helped reinforce the weak structure in the gluten-free flours and helped retain moisture to prevent the scones from becoming dry and crumbly. An egg provided additional structure along with moisture and elasticity.

3. DOUBLE UP ON THE SHEET PANS: Because we were placing the scones in a very hot oven, the bottoms were getting overly browned. Since we needed the hot oven for the rise, the only solution for protecting the bottom of the scones was to use a second baking sheet as insulation.

4. BAKE HIGH, THEN LOW: Hoping to get scones with good height and a tender crumb, we preheated our oven to 500 degrees to maximize "oven spring," which is the final burst of rising that happens when water vaporizes into steam and the air in the dough heats up and expands. The more oven spring, the lighter the crumb; with very little oven spring, you end up with a denser texture. After placing the scones in the oven we lowered the temperature to 425 degrees to ensure the crust would not burn before the interior cooked through.

Banana Bread

G-F TESTING LAB

FLOUR SUBSTITUTION	King Arthur Gluten-Free Multi-Purpose Flour 9½ ounces = **1¾ cups**	Bob's Red Mill GF All-Purpose Baking Flour 9½ ounces = **1¾ cups plus 2 tablespoons**
	Note that bread made with King Arthur will be slightly denser; bread made with Bob's Red Mill will be denser and darker, and will have a distinct bean flavor.	
XANTHAN GUM	The xanthan gum can be omitted, but the banana bread will be more crumbly and have less structure.	

✓ WHY THIS RECIPE WORKS

For the ultimate banana bread, we wanted to pack in as much banana flavor as possible without turning out a mushy loaf. We found we could smash five bananas into a single loaf. The key was eliminating some of their moisture. We microwaved the bananas until they started to break down, then moved them to a fine-mesh strainer to drain. Reducing the released liquid gave us an intense syrup that we could mix into the batter without adding excess water. To ensure the dense batter rose properly, we found we had to add a full tablespoon of baking powder plus baking soda. Xanthan gum ensured that our loaf had enough structure and stability. Stirring the batter for 1 minute before transferring it to the loaf pan ensured that all the ingredients were thoroughly incorporated and that the thick batter was properly aerated. Unlike our muffin recipes, this wetter batter did not need to be rested to hydrate the flour; the extra moisture plus the longer baking time prevented any grittiness. The test kitchen's preferred loaf pan measures 8½ by 4½ inches; if you use a 9 by 5-inch loaf pan, start checking for doneness 5 minutes early.

Banana Bread

MAKES 1 LOAF

9½	ounces (2 cups plus 2 tablespoons) ATK All-Purpose Gluten-Free Flour Blend (page 7)
1	tablespoon baking powder (see page 24)
1	teaspoon baking soda
½	teaspoon salt
¼	teaspoon xanthan gum
5	large very ripe bananas (about 1¾ pounds), peeled
8	tablespoons unsalted butter, melted and cooled
2	large eggs
5¼	ounces (¾ cup packed) light brown sugar
1	teaspoon vanilla extract
½	cup walnuts, toasted and chopped (optional)
2	teaspoons granulated sugar

1. Adjust oven rack to middle position and heat oven to 350 degrees. Grease 8½ by 4½-inch loaf pan. Whisk flour blend, baking powder, baking soda, salt, and xanthan gum together in large bowl.

2. Microwave bananas in separate bowl, covered, until they have softened and released liquid, about 5 minutes. Transfer bananas to fine-mesh strainer placed over medium bowl and let drain, stirring occasionally, about 15 minutes (you should have ½ to ¾ cup liquid).

3. Transfer banana juice to medium saucepan and cook over medium-high heat until reduced to ¼ cup, about 5 minutes. Return reduced juice to bowl, add bananas, and mash with potato masher until mostly smooth. Whisk in melted butter, eggs, brown sugar, and vanilla.

4. Using silicone spatula, stir banana mixture into flour mixture until thoroughly combined and no lumps remain, about 1 minute. Gently fold in walnuts, if using. Scrape batter into prepared pan and sprinkle granulated sugar evenly over loaf.

5. Bake until toothpick inserted in center comes out clean, 55 minutes to 1¼ hours. Let bread cool in pan on wire rack for 15 minutes. Remove bread from pan and let cool for at least 1 hour before serving. (Banana bread is best eaten on day it is baked, but bread can be cooled, immediately wrapped in plastic wrap, and stored at room temperature for up to 2 days. To serve, warm in 300-degree oven for 10 to 15 minutes.)

TEST KITCHEN TIP

Top Bananas Are Black Bananas

For maximum flavor, be sure to use very ripe, heavily speckled (or even black) bananas. If you like, you can freeze overly ripe bananas, one at a time, and save them expressly for use in this recipe. Thawed frozen bananas will release their liquid without the need for microwaving, so you can skip that step and put them directly into the fine-mesh strainer, then continue as directed.

Date-Nut Bread

G-F TESTING LAB

FLOUR SUBSTITUTION	King Arthur Gluten-Free Multi-Purpose Flour 10 ounces = **1½ cups plus ⅓ cup**	Betty Crocker All-Purpose Gluten Free Rice Blend 10 ounces = **2 cups**
	Bread made with King Arthur will be quite delicate and crumbly; bread made with Betty Crocker will be slightly wet and pasty.	
BAKING POWDER	Not all brands of baking powder are gluten-free; see page 24 for more information.	
XANTHAN GUM	The xanthan can be omitted, but the bread will be more crumbly and have less structure.	

✅ WHY THIS RECIPE WORKS

The dense texture and unmitigated sweetness of most date breads, whether gluten-free or not, can ruin an otherwise delicious breakfast treat. We wanted a lightly sweet bread, studded equally with dates and nuts, that was also moist and tender. To start, we simply swapped in our all-purpose gluten-free flour blend for regular all-purpose flour in one of our favorite recipes from our archives. Unsurprisingly, the loaf we sliced into a few hours later was dense and pasty, and it crumbled apart during slicing. The recipe we started from used buttermilk, but not enough, yet going up on buttermilk helped only to a point: As we increased the overall amount of buttermilk, the loaf became more moist, but it also became correspondingly wet and dense. We found 1 cup provided the best balance, though we were still plagued by a slightly dry, overly tender loaf. Adding an extra egg helped to add moisture and richness without weighing down the rise, and it also contributed binding power so we could easily cut clean slices from the loaf. To create a more open, tender crumb we took a closer look at the combination of baking powder and baking soda in our bread. Baking soda reacts with acidic ingredients, like buttermilk, to produce carbon dioxide, which creates rise in baked goods. Increasing the overall amount of baking soda from 1 to 1½ teaspoons created an even, open crumb, and, as added insurance against a heavy bread, we decreased the overall amount of dates from 10 ounces to just 6 ounces, resulting in a light, just slightly sweet, and tender date bread. The test kitchen's preferred loaf pan measures 8½ by 4½ inches; if you use a 9 by 5-inch loaf pan, start checking for doneness 10 minutes early.

Date-Nut Bread
MAKES 1 LOAF

- 10 ounces (2¼ cups) ATK All-Purpose Gluten-Free Flour Blend (page 7)
- 1½ teaspoons baking soda
- 1 teaspoon baking powder
- ½ teaspoon salt
- ¼ teaspoon xanthan gum
- 1 cup buttermilk
- 5¼ ounces (¾ cup packed) dark brown sugar
- 6 tablespoons unsalted butter, melted and cooled
- 2 large eggs
- 1 cup pitted dates, chopped
- 1 cup walnuts, toasted and chopped

1. Adjust oven rack to middle position and heat oven to 350 degrees. Grease 8½ by 4½-inch loaf pan.

2. Whisk flour blend, baking soda, baking powder, salt, and xanthan gum together in large bowl. In separate bowl, whisk buttermilk, sugar, melted butter, and eggs together until well combined. Using silicone spatula, stir buttermilk mixture into flour mixture until thoroughly combined and no lumps remain, about 1 minute. Fold in dates and walnuts.

3. Scrape batter into prepared pan and smooth top. Bake until deep golden brown and toothpick inserted in center comes out clean, about 1 hour, rotating pan halfway through baking.

4. Let bread cool in pan for 20 minutes, then remove from pan and let cool on wire rack for 1 hour before serving. (Cooled bread can be wrapped in plastic wrap and stored at room temperature for up to 2 days; refresh in 300-degree oven for 10 to 15 minutes.)

VARIATION
Dairy-Free Date-Nut Bread

We prefer the flavor and texture of this bread made with soy milk but almond milk will also work; do not use rice milk.

Substitute 1 cup unsweetened soy milk mixed with 1 tablespoon distilled white vinegar (or lemon juice) for buttermilk. Substitute vegetable oil for melted butter.

Pumpkin Bread

G-F TESTING LAB

FLOUR SUBSTITUTION	King Arthur Gluten-Free Multi-Purpose Flour 5½ ounces = **1 cup**	Bob's Red Mill GF All-Purpose Baking Flour 5½ ounces = **1 cup plus 2 tablespoons**

Note that bread made with King Arthur will be slightly denser; bread made with Bob's Red Mill will be denser and darker, and will have a slight bean flavor.

WHY THIS RECIPE WORKS

Pumpkin bread is usually boring. No loaf is remarkably bad, but none is remarkably good. We wanted a pumpkin bread that not only was gluten-free but also had just the right texture—neither too dense nor too cakey—and that had a rich pumpkin flavor tempered by sweetness and enhanced (not obscured) by spices. Our first task was to improve the raw metallic flavor of canned pumpkin puree. Cooking it (along with the spices) on the stovetop gave it a richer, fuller flavor. The only problem was that this process also drove off some of the moisture and increased its sweetness—the flavors were out of balance. Adding buttermilk solved the dryness problem, and incorporating cream cheese into the mix regained some of the tanginess that the sweetness was overpowering. Since we had to melt the cream cheese, we just added it to the pan of hot puree, achieving the dual goals of melting it and cooling the puree. Once the puree was cool, we were able to use the pot as the mixing bowl. After adding the flour blend and leaveners to our puree mixture, we continued stirring for a full minute to ensure they were thoroughly incorporated into the thick pumpkin puree mixture. Stirring for this amount of time also guaranteed the batter was properly aerated, giving our bread a good rise. Unlike our muffin recipes, this wetter batter did not need to be rested to hydrate the flour; the extra moisture plus the longer baking time prevented any grittiness. A handful of toasted and chopped walnuts gave the loaf some textural contrast and nice flavor. The test kitchen's preferred loaf pan measures 8½ by 4½ inches; if you use a 9 by 5-inch loaf pan, start checking for doneness 5 minutes earlier than advised in the recipe. You can substitute milk for the buttermilk if you don't have buttermilk.

Pumpkin Bread
MAKES 1 LOAF

- 5½ ounces (1¼ cups) ATK All-Purpose Gluten-Free Flour Blend (page 7)
- ¾ teaspoon baking powder (see page 24)
- ¼ teaspoon baking soda
- 7½ ounces canned pumpkin puree (¾ cup)
- ¾ teaspoon ground cinnamon
- ½ teaspoon salt
- ⅛ teaspoon ground nutmeg
   Pinch ground cloves
- 3½ ounces (½ cup) granulated sugar
- 3½ ounces (½ cup packed) light brown sugar
- ¼ cup vegetable oil
- 2 ounces cream cheese
- 2 large eggs
- 2 tablespoons buttermilk
- ½ cup walnuts, toasted and chopped fine

1. Adjust oven rack to middle position and heat oven to 350 degrees. Grease 8½ by 4½-inch loaf pan. Whisk flour blend, baking powder, and baking soda together in bowl.

2. Combine pumpkin puree, cinnamon, salt, nutmeg, and cloves in medium saucepan over medium heat. Cook, stirring constantly, until mixture is reduced to ¾ cup, 2 to 4 minutes.

3. Off heat, stir in granulated sugar, brown sugar, oil, and cream cheese until combined. Let mixture stand for 5 minutes. Whisk until no visible pieces of cream cheese remain and mixture is homogeneous.

4. Whisk together eggs and buttermilk in separate bowl. Add egg mixture to pumpkin mixture and whisk to combine. Stir flour mixture into pumpkin mixture until thoroughly combined and no lumps remain, about 1 minute. Fold walnuts into batter.

5. Scrape batter into prepared pan. Bake until toothpick inserted in center comes out clean, 45 to 50 minutes. Let bread cool in pan on wire rack for 20 minutes. Remove bread from pan and let cool for at least 1½ hours before serving. (Pumpkin bread is best eaten on day it is baked, but bread can be cooled, immediately wrapped in plastic wrap, and stored at room temperature for up to 2 days. To serve, warm in 300-degree oven for 10 to 15 minutes.)

Whole-Grain Chai Spice Bread

G-F TESTING LAB

FLOUR SUBSTITUTION	Do not substitute other whole-grain blends for the ATK Whole-Grain Gluten-Free Flour Blend; they will not work in this recipe.
BAKING POWDER	Not all brands of baking powder are gluten-free; see page 24 for more information.
XANTHAN GUM	The xanthan can be omitted, but the bread will be more crumbly and slightly denser.

✓ WHY THIS RECIPE WORKS

For a quick-bread recipe using our whole-grain flour blend, we looked to the modern flavor of chai spice to match our flour's earthy profile. It can be difficult to create harmony among the spices found in chai (cinnamon, cardamom, ginger, clove, and sometimes even black pepper), so instead we steeped chai-flavored tea bags in warm milk and then incorporated the spiced milk into the batter for well-rounded flavor. In our initial testing we used brown sugar as our sweetener but found that the rich, molasses-like flavor muddled the chai spices. Switching to granulated sugar gave our bread a cleaner flavor. To give this dense, hearty bread some lift, we ramped up the baking powder to a whopping 4 teaspoons. We also found it necessary to add extra liquid in order to hydrate and soften the whole-grain flours. Unfortunately, all this additional liquid left the bread with a wet, spongy texture. To dry it out, we continued to bake the bread 10 minutes beyond the point at which a toothpick inserted in the center came out clean. The downside of the increased baking time, however, was crumbly bread that didn't slice cleanly. Luckily, adding a smidgen of xanthan gum fixed this. The test kitchen's preferred loaf pan measures 8½ by 4½ inches; if you use a 9 by 5-inch loaf pan, start checking for doneness 10 minutes early.

Whole-Grain Chai Spice Bread

MAKES 1 LOAF

- 1¼ cups whole milk
- 3 chai-flavored tea bags
- 12 ounces (2⅔ cups) ATK Whole-Grain Gluten-Free Flour Blend (page 9)
- 4 teaspoons baking powder
- 1½ teaspoons salt
- ¼ teaspoon xanthan gum
- 7 ounces (1 cup) plus 1 tablespoon sugar
- 8 tablespoons unsalted butter, melted and cooled
- 2 large eggs
- 1 teaspoon vanilla extract
- ½ cup walnuts, toasted and chopped (optional)

1. Adjust oven rack to middle position and heat oven to 325 degrees. Grease 8½ by 4½-inch loaf pan. Bring milk to simmer in saucepan over medium-high heat. Remove pot from heat, add tea bags, and steep until fragrant, 4 to 6 minutes. Discard tea bags.

2. Whisk flour blend, baking powder, salt, and xanthan gum together in large bowl. In separate bowl, whisk spiced milk, 1 cup sugar, melted butter, eggs, and vanilla together until well combined. Using silicone spatula, stir milk mixture into flour mixture until thoroughly combined and no lumps remain, about 1 minute. Fold in walnuts, if using.

3. Scrape batter into prepared pan, smooth top, and sprinkle with remaining 1 tablespoon sugar. Bake until toothpick inserted in center comes out clean, 60 minutes to 1 hour 10 minutes, rotating pan halfway through baking, then continue to bake for 10 minutes longer.

4. Let bread cool in pan for 20 minutes, then remove from pan and let cool on wire rack for 1 hour before serving. (Cooled bread can be wrapped in plastic wrap and stored at room temperature for up to 2 days.)

VARIATION

Dairy-Free Whole-Grain Chai Spice Bread
We prefer the flavor and texture of this bread made with soy milk but almond milk will also work; do not use rice milk.

Substitute unsweetened soy milk for milk, and vegetable oil for melted butter.

SMART SHOPPING **Chai Tea**

Chai is a fragrant Indian black-tea blend that often includes cardamom, cinnamon, clove, ginger, and black pepper, though the exact formulation can vary from brand to brand; you can find it in any supermarket. We tested this recipe with several brands of caffeinated and decaffeinated chai, and they all worked equally well.

Coffee Cake

G-F TESTING LAB

FLOUR SUBSTITUTION	King Arthur Gluten-Free Multi-Purpose Flour 12 ounces = **1⅔ cups plus ½ cup**	Bob's Red Mill GF All-Purpose Baking Flour 12 ounces = **2¼ cups plus 2 tablespoons**
	Note that cake made with Bob's Red Mill will be slightly denser and darker, and will have a slight bean flavor.	
XANTHAN GUM	The xanthan gum can be omitted, but the coffee cake will be more crumbly and slightly more dense and it will not rise as well.	

WHY THIS RECIPE WORKS

A coffee cake that feeds a crowd is perfect for Sunday brunches or holiday breakfasts. Most cake recipes cream butter and sugar, beat in eggs, and then alternate additions of dry ingredients and wet. While that method is great for producing a fluffy yellow cake, we wanted a coffee cake with a dense, rich crumb. Adding the butter with a portion of the sour cream to the dry ingredients, mixing for a few minutes, then adding the rest of the liquid was key: It ensured the fat was evenly distributed (the flour clumped when we added butter and all the liquid at once), and because this approach reduced the mixing time—which meant less air was beaten into the batter—it delivered exactly the crumb we wanted. To avoid a greasy cake we found it essential to use less butter than you'd find in a traditional coffee cake; unlike the proteins in all-purpose flour, the starches in our gluten-free flour blend can't absorb as much fat. For the baking pan, we liked the simplicity of a round cake pan (rather than a tube or Bundt pan), but our cake sank in the middle and didn't cook through. A tube pan was essential, as the center tube, which conducts heat, ensured an even rise and a cake that cooked through evenly. The biggest hurdle was figuring out the streusel filling and topping. A classic streusel was too heavy for our cake—the high-starch gluten-free flour blend didn't offer the same structure or stability of all-purpose flour—and it sank as it baked. Instead, we took a portion of the batter, added cinnamon and nutmeg, then swirled this spiced batter into the plain batter in the pan. For a topping, a simple glaze plus candied nuts added texture and visual appeal the cake needed.

Coffee Cake

SERVES 12 TO 16

CAKE

- **4   large eggs**
- **1½ cups sour cream**
- **3½ teaspoons vanilla extract**
- **12   ounces (2⅔ cups) ATK All-Purpose Gluten-Free Flour Blend (page 7)**
- **8¾ ounces (1¼ cups) granulated sugar**
- **1   tablespoon baking powder (see page 24)**
- **1   teaspoon salt**
- **¾ teaspoon baking soda**
- **¼ teaspoon xanthan gum**
- **8   tablespoons unsalted butter, cut into ½-inch pieces and softened**
- **1   tablespoon ground cinnamon**
- **¼ teaspoon ground nutmeg**

TOPPING AND GLAZE

- **½ cup pecans, chopped fine**
- **2   tablespoons granulated sugar**
- **½ teaspoon ground cinnamon**
-     **Pinch salt**
- **2   tablespoons unsalted butter, melted and cooled**
- **4   ounces (1 cup) confectioners' sugar**
- **5   teaspoons milk**
- **1   teaspoon vanilla extract**

1. FOR THE CAKE: Adjust oven rack to lowest position and heat oven to 350 degrees. Grease 16-cup tube pan. Whisk eggs, 1 cup sour cream, and 1 tablespoon vanilla together in bowl.

2. Using stand mixer fitted with paddle, mix flour blend, granulated sugar, baking powder, salt, baking soda, and xanthan gum on low speed until combined. Add remaining ½ cup sour cream and butter and mix until dry ingredients are moistened and few large butter pieces remain, about 1½ minutes. Gradually add egg mixture in 3 additions, beating for 20 seconds after each addition, scraping down bowl as needed. Increase speed to medium-high and beat until batter is light and fluffy, about 1 minute. Give batter final stir by hand (batter will be thick).

3. Measure 1 cup batter into bowl and whisk in remaining ½ teaspoon vanilla, cinnamon, and nutmeg. Pour remaining batter into prepared pan. Drop spoonfuls of spiced batter over top. Using butter knife, and working once around pan, gently fold batters together to make large swirls of spice inside cake; do not overmix.

4. Bake until cake feels firm to touch and skewer inserted in center comes out clean, 45 to 55 minutes. Let cake cool in pan on wire rack for 30 minutes. Run thin knife around edge of cake to loosen. Remove cake from pan and let cool on rack, about 1 hour. (Do not turn off oven.)

5. FOR THE TOPPING AND GLAZE: Meanwhile, line rimmed baking sheet with parchment paper. Combine pecans, granulated sugar, cinnamon, and salt in small bowl. Stir in melted butter until well combined. Transfer pecan mixture to prepared sheet and bake until golden, about 15 minutes. Let pecan mixture cool, then break into small pieces. In separate bowl, whisk confectioners' sugar, milk, and vanilla together until smooth. Pour glaze evenly over top of cooled cake, then sprinkle with pecan topping. Let glaze set for 20 minutes before serving. (Coffee cake is best eaten on day it is baked, but cake can be cooled, immediately wrapped in plastic wrap, and stored at room temperature for up to 2 days.)

TEST KITCHEN TIP **Making Coffee Cake**

Our recipe rethinks the usual streusel filling and topping. Here are the key steps.

1. Transfer 1 cup batter to separate bowl and whisk in vanilla, cinnamon, and nutmeg.

2. Pour remaining batter evenly into greased 16-cup tube pan. Using 2 spoons, drop spoonfuls of spiced batter on top.

3. Using butter knife and working around pan only once, gently fold batters together to make large swirls of spice inside cake; do not overmix.

4. After baking cake and letting it cool for 30 minutes in pan on wire rack, run paring knife around edge of cake to loosen, then flip out onto wire rack.

5. After preparing nut mixture, spread mixture over parchment-lined rimmed baking sheet and bake until golden. Let cool, then break into small pieces.

6. Whisk together glaze, then drizzle over cooled cake and sprinkle with topping. Let glaze set 20 minutes before serving.

Putting the Streusel in Coffee Cake

THE PROBLEM The test kitchen's traditional sour cream coffee cake starts with a rich, ultra-moist cake as its base. A streusel made with flour, brown and granulated sugars, cold butter, cinnamon, and chopped pecans gets swirled into this rich batter, and more gets sprinkled over the top. The result is a decadent, pleasantly rich and dense cake with crisp, crunchy, melt-in-your-mouth streusel inside and on top. At the outset, we thought the biggest challenge to making a gluten-free coffee cake would be the cake itself. We quickly discovered that the cake was the easy part. Incorporating the warm spices, sugar, and nuts—as a streusel or otherwise—turned out to be the main hurdle.

A SINKING FEELING We started with the same streusel ingredients as our traditional recipe and simply swapped in our gluten-free flour blend for all-purpose flour. Once baked, this cake had a layer of streusel that had sunk to the bottom of the pan, and the topping portion had caved into the middle. Clearly our gluten-free cake batter didn't have the same stability as our traditional version. We learned that this is because of the abundance of starch and limited amount of protein in the blend. In a cake made with all-purpose flour, the gluten begins to form a strong structure as it heats in the oven and at a certain temperature the structure becomes rigid, even when hot. But for starch to form a rigid structure, the granules have to absorb water and swell when heated, then cool to form a fairly strong gel—while hot, the starch gel is not strong enough to hold much weight. We wondered, How much weight could our gluten-free version take? Testing a slew of options was the only way to find out.

LIGHTENING UP To retain all the flavor and texture but lessen the weight, we omitted the flour (about 4 ounces) from the streusel for our next test. This helped, but the mixture still sank. Next we tried cutting back on the butter. Our traditional streusel calls for 2 tablespoons; it's not much, but we wondered if it was making our mixture too wet, thus causing it to sink into the cake and take the spices, sugar, and nuts with it. But the mixture sank again, both in the middle of the cake and on top. As a final resort, suspecting the nuts were too heavy, we decided to try swapping them out for oats, an ingredient often used in gluten-free streusels. We hoped that they would add nuttiness and texture but not much weight. But they likewise sank—and also were unappealingly chewy—so they didn't make the cut.

SPICE SWIRL It was time to come at the problem from a new angle. We abandoned the streusel entirely and instead took a cue from marble-style cakes. We prepared the coffee cake batter as usual, then took a portion of it and stirred in plenty of cinnamon, as well as nutmeg and vanilla. We spooned the spiced batter over the plain and ran a knife through it in a zigzag motion around the pan. But this led to overmixing—we ended up with a nearly homogeneous cake that lacked the visual appeal a swirl of spice would provide, and the spice flavor was faintly distributed throughout instead of being a swirl with a potent punch. Next we tried a circular folding motion to gently swirl the spiced batter into the plain batter. Success—this technique left a thin but distinct trail that was visually appealing and packed plenty of flavor.

TACKLING THE TOPPING Our spiced batter swirl delivered a cake with the right warm-spice flavor and some great visual appeal, but we still needed a solution for the topping. We wondered if we could make a sugar-centric topping that could lock a handful of nuts in place in the heat of the oven. A mixture of butter, granulated sugar, cinnamon, and nuts was a failure—a dusty, dry mix that didn't adhere to the baked cake at all. We then switched to turbinado sugar instead of the granulated because it melts more readily and contains a small amount of moisture not present in granulated sugar, but one test proved this alternative to be equally unsuccessful.

THE SOLUTION THAT STUCK After a lot of flops, we landed on a two-part approach that applied the topping after baking, when the cake would have enough structure not to collapse. While the cake cooled, we made a candied nut topping by baking a mix of pecans, sugar, cinnamon, salt, and melted butter. Then we drizzled the baked, cooled cake with a simple confectioners' sugar–based glaze and sprinkled our candied spiced pecans over the top. Once the glaze set, it locked the nuts in place. Together with our swirl of spiced cake, we had a coffee cake with the visual appeal, texture, and flavor—inside and out—that we were after.

Whole-Grain Gingerbread Coffee Cake

G-F TESTING LAB

FLOUR SUBSTITUTION	Do not substitute other whole-grain blends for the ATK Whole-Grain Gluten-Free Flour Blend; they will not work in this recipe.
BAKING POWDER	Not all brands of baking powder are gluten-free; see page 24 for more information.
XANTHAN GUM	The xanthan can be omitted, but the cake will be crumbly and more difficult to get out of the pan.

✔ WHY THIS RECIPE WORKS

For a wholesome version of a brunch favorite, we set our sights on developing a rich gluten-free gingerbread-flavored coffee cake using our whole-grain flour blend. The traditional creaming method yielded a gritty, gummy brick of a cake. We tried whipping the batter longer, which aerated it more, yet the cake was still dense because the sour cream we used to moisten the cake created a very thick, dense batter. Switching to a combination of ½ cup sour cream and 1½ cups milk got us closer, but our cake still wasn't rising enough—and it was also now very wet. A hefty amount of baking powder plus the addition of baking soda helped, but the extra liquid we added to hydrate the flours and loosen the batter meant that the cake would need an extended baking time. We baked it until a skewer came out clean, and then continued to bake it for an additional 20 minutes for a cake that was still moist, with a tender crumb. Topped with a coffee-flavored glaze, this cake makes a satisfying morning treat. Do not substitute low-fat or nonfat milk in this recipe.

Whole-Grain Gingerbread Coffee Cake
SERVES 12 TO 16

CAKE

- 1½ cups whole milk, room temperature
- ½ cup sour cream, room temperature
- 3 large eggs, room temperature
- 12 ounces (2⅔ cups) ATK Whole-Grain Gluten-Free Flour Blend (page 9)
- 5 teaspoons baking powder
- 2 teaspoons ground ginger
- 1½ teaspoons salt
- 1½ teaspoons baking soda
- 1 teaspoon ground cinnamon
- ½ teaspoon ground allspice
- ½ teaspoon ground cloves
- ½ teaspoon ground nutmeg
- ¼ teaspoon xanthan gum
- 8¾ ounces (1¼ cups) granulated sugar
- 10 tablespoons unsalted butter, softened

GLAZE

- 3 tablespoons whole milk
- 1 tablespoon instant espresso or instant coffee
- 7 ounces (1¾ cups) confectioners' sugar

1. FOR THE CAKE: Adjust oven rack to middle position and heat oven to 350 degrees. Grease 12-cup nonstick Bundt pan. Whisk milk, sour cream, and eggs together in bowl. In separate bowl, whisk flour blend, baking powder, ginger, salt, baking soda, cinnamon, allspice, cloves, nutmeg, and xanthan gum together.

2. Using stand mixer fitted with paddle, beat sugar and butter on medium-high speed until light and fluffy, about 3 minutes. Reduce mixer speed to low and gradually add egg mixture, about 1 minute, scraping down bowl as needed (batter may look curdled). Gradually add flour mixture and mix until incorporated. Scrape down bowl, increase speed to medium-high, and beat until batter is light and fluffy, about 6 minutes.

3. Give batter final stir by hand. Transfer batter to prepared pan. Bake cake until skewer inserted in center comes out clean, 45 to 50 minutes, then continue to bake for 20 minutes longer.

4. Let cake cool in pan for 30 minutes, then remove from pan and let cool on wire rack for 1 hour.

5. FOR THE GLAZE: Whisk 2 tablespoons milk and espresso together until dissolved. Whisk in sugar until smooth. Gradually add remaining 1 tablespoon milk as needed until glaze is thick but pourable. Pour glaze over cooled cake, letting it drip down sides, and let set for 10 minutes. Serve. (Cake can be stored in airtight container for up to 2 days.)

VARIATION

Dairy-Free Whole-Grain Gingerbread Coffee Cake

Almond milk can be substituted for the soy milk; do not use rice milk.

Substitute unsweetened soy milk for milk and Earth Balance Vegan Buttery Sticks for butter. Use dairy-free sour cream. Reduce salt to 1 teaspoon.

New York–Style Crumb Cake

FLOUR SUBSTITUTION	King Arthur Gluten-Free Multi-Purpose Flour 6 ounces = ¾ **cup plus ⅓ cup**	Betty Crocker All-Purpose Gluten Free Rice Blend 6 ounces = ⅔ **cup plus ½ cup**
	Cake made with King Arthur will be slightly greasy and won't rise as well, and the crumbs on top will melt together; cake made with Betty Crocker will be springy and slightly dense.	
XANTHAN GUM	The xanthan can be omitted, but the cake will be slightly drier and more crumbly, and it won't store as well.	

WHY THIS RECIPE WORKS

This buttery cake is a balance between the tender cake and the thick layer of spiced crumb topping. To develop a gluten-free version, we knew we'd need to first focus on the cake and find a way to add structure, since gluten-free flours are lower in protein. We were after a cake with a dense, rich, and buttery crumb that could support a substantial topping. To make a sturdier cake, we subbed in our gluten-free flour blend and added an extra egg and yolk to the test kitchen's original recipe. For buttery flavor, we stuck with 6 tablespoons of butter. To solve the wetness issue, we swapped out the buttermilk for sour cream, which added richness without making our batter overly wet. The topping proved to be more of a hurdle than we expected. With gluten-free flour it became too sandy and was not cohesive. We tried a few options to fix this, and surprisingly an egg yolk was the winner. It kept our topping moist yet still distinct and crumbly.

New York–Style Crumb Cake
SERVES 8

TOPPING

- 8 tablespoons unsalted butter, melted and still warm
- 2⅓ ounces (⅓ cup) granulated sugar
- 2⅓ ounces (⅓ cup packed) dark brown sugar
- 1 large egg yolk
- ¾ teaspoon ground cinnamon
- ⅛ teaspoon salt
- 6 ounces (1⅓ cups) ATK All-Purpose Gluten-Free Flour Blend (page 7)

CAKE

- 6 ounces (1⅓ cups) ATK All-Purpose Gluten-Free Flour Blend (page 7)
- 3½ ounces (½ cup) granulated sugar
- ½ teaspoon baking soda
- ¼ teaspoon salt
- ¼ teaspoon xanthan gum
- 6 tablespoons unsalted butter, cut into 6 pieces and softened
- ½ cup sour cream
- 2 large eggs plus 1 large yolk
- 1 teaspoon vanilla extract
  Confectioners' sugar, for serving

1. FOR THE TOPPING: Whisk melted butter, granulated sugar, brown sugar, egg yolk, cinnamon, and salt in bowl to combine. Stir in flour blend with silicone spatula until mixture resembles thick, cohesive dough; set aside.

2. FOR THE CAKE: Adjust oven rack to upper-middle position and heat oven to 325 degrees. Cut 16-inch length of parchment paper (or aluminum foil) and fold lengthwise to 7-inch width. Spray 8-inch square baking pan with vegetable oil spray and fit parchment into pan, pushing it up sides; allow excess to overhang edges of pan.

3. Using stand mixer fitted with paddle, mix flour blend, granulated sugar, baking soda, salt, and xanthan gum on low speed to combine. Add butter, 1 piece at a time, and continue to mix until mixture resembles moist crumbs with no visible butter chunks remaining, 1 to 2 minutes. Add sour cream, eggs and yolk, and vanilla; increase mixer speed to medium-high and beat until batter is light and fluffy, about 1 minute, scraping down bowl as needed.

4. Scrape batter into prepared pan and smooth top. Break topping into large pea-size pieces and sprinkle evenly over batter. Bake until crumbs are golden and wooden skewer inserted in center of cake comes out clean, 35 to 40 minutes, rotating pan halfway through baking.

5. Let cake cool in pan for 30 minutes. Remove cake from pan using parchment sling and transfer to platter. Dust with confectioners' sugar before serving. (Cake can be stored in airtight container at room temperature for up to 3 days.)

VARIATION

Dairy-Free New York–Style Crumb Cake
In topping, substitute Earth Balance Vegan Buttery Sticks for butter and omit salt. In cake, omit salt, substitute Earth Balance Vegan Buttery Sticks for butter, and use dairy-free sour cream.

Yeasted Doughnuts

G-F TESTING LAB

FLOUR SUBSTITUTION	Do not substitute other all-purpose blends for the ATK All-Purpose Gluten-Free Flour Blend; they will not work in this recipe.
PSYLLIUM HUSK	Psyllium is crucial to the structure of the doughnuts; see page 21 for more information.
BAKING POWDER	Not all brands of baking powder are gluten-free; see page 24 for more information.
XANTHAN GUM	Xanthan is crucial to the structure of the doughnuts; see page 21 for more information.

WHY THIS RECIPE WORKS

If there is one thing many people crave when they need to eat gluten-free, it's a great yeasted doughnut, one with a slightly crisp exterior and a tender interior. Using our gluten-free flour blend as the base proved to be the perfect start, as the potato starch in the blend created a tender crumb and the tapioca starch added elasticity. After our first test, we went down on fat by decreasing the amount of butter by 2 tablespoons and using low-fat milk instead of whole, which gave us a rich dairy flavor without weighing down the dough. To keep the doughnuts together, we first tried adding just xanthan gum, but we needed too much and the doughnuts became tough. A combination of xanthan gum and powdered psyllium husk gave us a nice chew. For a rich yeasty flavor we used a full tablespoon of yeast but added baking powder and baking soda to help the doughnuts rise and maintain their shape during proofing and frying. To get the quickest possible rise before the gluten-free flours absorbed all of the liquid, we jump-started the yeast in warmed milk and let the doughnuts rise in a warmed oven for the first 10 minutes. After just 30 minutes of rising (10 minutes in the oven and 20 on the counter), the doughnuts were ready to fry. We dropped them into 350-degree oil (which is a standard frying temperature), but in just 30 seconds the doughnuts' exteriors began to burn. We tried frying them for less time, but the interiors remained raw. Lowering the frying temperature to 325 degrees allowed us to fry the doughnuts longer, which ensured that the interiors and exteriors were done at the same time. Although a lower frying temperature would traditionally cause doughnuts to absorb more oil and become greasy, gluten-free flours do not absorb fat as readily as wheat flour does, so this was not a problem. If you don't have a doughnut cutter, you can improvise with two biscuit cutters: Use a standard cutter (about 2½ inches) for cutting out the doughnuts, and a smaller one (about 1¼ inches) for cutting out the holes. Do not substitute nonfat or whole milk in this recipe.

Yeasted Doughnuts

MAKES ABOUT 10 DOUGHNUTS AND 10 HOLES

- ¾ cup 1 or 2 percent low-fat milk, warmed to 110 degrees
- 1 tablespoon instant or rapid-rise yeast
- 2⅓ ounces (⅓ cup) plus 1 teaspoon granulated sugar
- 4 tablespoons unsalted butter, melted and cooled
- 2 large eggs
- 12½ ounces (2¾ cups) ATK All-Purpose Gluten-Free Flour Blend (page 7)
- 2 teaspoons powdered psyllium husk
- 1½ teaspoons baking powder
- ½ teaspoon xanthan gum
- ¼ teaspoon baking soda
- ¼ teaspoon salt
- ¼ teaspoon ground nutmeg
- 3–4 quarts peanut or vegetable oil
- 1½ cups confectioners' sugar, for coating

1. Adjust oven rack to middle position and heat oven to 200 degrees. As soon as oven reaches 200 degrees, turn it off. (This will be warm proofing box for dough. Do not mix dough until oven has been turned off.) Lay large sheet parchment paper flat on counter and grease with vegetable oil spray. Line baking sheet with parchment paper and dust with flour blend.

2. Combine milk, yeast, and 1 teaspoon granulated sugar in bowl and let sit until bubbly, about 5 minutes. Whisk in melted butter and eggs. In stand mixer fitted with paddle, mix flour blend, psyllium husk, baking powder, xanthan gum, baking soda, salt, nutmeg, and remaining ⅓ cup granulated sugar on low speed until combined. Slowly add yeast mixture and let dough come together, about 1 minute, scraping down bowl as needed. Increase speed to medium and beat until sticky and uniform, about 6 minutes.

3. Using wet hands, transfer dough to greased parchment. Clean and wet hands again, then pat dough to ½-inch thickness. Using 2½- or 3-inch floured doughnut cutter, cut out doughnuts; twist cutter to help release dough and reflour cutter as needed. Transfer doughnuts and holes to prepared baking sheet; gather and repeat dough scraps as needed.

4. Cover doughnuts loosely with plastic wrap, place on middle rack in warmed oven, and let rise for 10 minutes; do not let plastic touch oven rack. Remove doughnuts from oven and continue to let rise on counter for 20 more minutes.

5. Add oil to large Dutch oven until it measures 2 inches deep and heat over medium-high heat to 325 degrees. Line wire rack with paper towels. Working with half of doughnuts at a time, fry until golden brown, about 30 seconds per side for holes and 45 to 60 seconds per side for doughnuts.

6. Transfer fried doughnuts to prepared wire rack and let cool for at least 10 minutes. Place confectioners' sugar in bowl. Dip both sides of each doughnut in sugar, then gently shake off excess. Serve.

VARIATIONS
Dairy-Free Yeasted Doughnuts
Do not substitute almond or rice milk for the soy milk.

Substitute ½ cup unsweetened soy milk mixed with ¼ cup water for milk, and Earth Balance Vegan Buttery Sticks for butter. Reduce salt to ⅛ teaspoon.

Cinnamon Sugar–Glazed Doughnuts
Substitute granulated sugar for confectioners' sugar and mix with 1 tablespoon ground cinnamon.

Vanilla-Glazed Doughnuts
Increase confectioners' sugar to 3 cups and combine with ½ cup buttermilk (or 5 tablespoons water for dairy-free) and ¼ teaspoon vanilla extract in bowl to make smooth glaze. Dip both sides of each doughnut in glaze to coat, letting excess drip back into bowl; return doughnuts to rack and let glaze set for 15 minutes before serving.

Chocolate-Glazed Doughnuts
Increase confectioners' sugar to 2 cups and combine with 4 ounces melted semisweet or bittersweet chocolate and ½ cup half-and-half to make smooth glaze. Dip both sides of each doughnut in glaze to coat, letting excess drip back into bowl; return doughnuts to rack and let glaze set for 15 minutes before serving.

TEST KITCHEN TIP **Cutting Doughnuts**

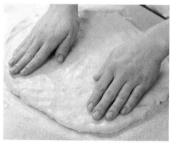

1. Using wet hands, transfer dough to greased parchment. Clean and wet hands again, then pat dough until ½ inch thick.

2. Using 2½- or 3-inch floured doughnut cutter, cut out doughnuts; twist cutter to help release dough. Reflour cutter as needed.

3. Transfer doughnuts and holes to baking sheet lined with floured parchment.

Yeasted Doughnuts

We wanted a great doughnut that was crunchy on the outside, tender yet sturdy on the inside, laced delicately with nutmeg, and lightly sweetened. To achieve the tender, light chew we were looking for we had to rely on a number of tricks. Here is what we learned.

1. USE THREE LEAVENERS: Since gluten-free flours are lower in protein, doughs can't hold on to air bubbles as well, so to achieve a nice rise for our doughnuts we needed a combination of leaveners: baking powder, baking soda, and yeast. And we needed a short proofing time because otherwise the flour blend absorbed the available liquid, creating a tough doughnut. To speed along the activity of the yeast, we dissolved it in warmed milk with a little sugar. The quick 30-minute proofing time is then helped along by the baking powder and baking soda.

2. GO LOW-FAT FOR A HIGHER RISE: Although traditionally we'd use whole milk to add richness to doughnuts, its fat weighed down our gluten-free doughnuts, preventing them from rising because the starches in gluten-free flours don't absorb fat as well as wheat flour does. Using low-fat milk easily solved this problem and gave us the higher-rising and moist doughnuts we were after.

3. PROOF IN THE OVEN: A drafty or cold room can extend rising times, and since our gluten-free blend does not provide the luxury of a long proofing time (the flour absorbs more liquid as it sits, making the dough thick and heavy), we created a more reliable environment by heating the oven to 200 degrees and then turning it off while we prepared the dough. At this point the oven was the perfect temperature for proofing the dough without killing the yeast.

4. FRY AT A LOWER TEMPERATURE: When we deep-fry food, the oil is generally held between 350 and 375 degrees. When using our gluten-free flour blend, we have to overhydrate the dough to accommodate the high amount of starches in the blend, and this means the doughnuts need to fry longer. We found that frying the doughnuts at the lower temperature of 325 degrees allowed the outside to crisp at the same rate that the inside cooked and dried out. If the oil crept above 350 degrees, the outside cooked way too quickly, leaving us with a raw interior.

Popovers

FLOUR SUBSTITUTION	King Arthur Gluten-Free Multi-Purpose Flour 4½ ounces = **½ cup plus ⅓ cup**	Betty Crocker All-Purpose Gluten Free Rice Blend 4½ ounces = **1 cup**
	Popovers made with Betty Crocker will be shorter, rubbery, and lack air pockets.	
XANTHAN GUM	Xanthan is crucial to the structure of the popovers; see page 21 for more information.	
SORGHUM FLOUR	Sorghum flour and sweet white sorghum flour will both work in these popovers. The grind, color, and flavor of the sorghum flour will vary slightly from brand to brand; however, all five of the brands we tried produced decent popovers. We had good luck using Bob's Red Mill "Sweet" White Sorghum Flour.	

WHY THIS RECIPE WORKS

The perfect popover soars to towering heights, but only if you get the baking method and ingredients just right. We wanted a popover that not only was gluten-free, but also had a nice rise and a custardy interior. Classic recipes contain as few as four ingredients: flour, milk, eggs, and butter, but the structure of the popover is mostly created by a higher-protein flour (like bread flour). Protein content is especially important when making popovers to ensure their trademark high rise and crisp crust. We knew our gluten-free flour blend would need help because the starches in our blend melt during baking. After making batches of popovers by adding a variety of high-protein flours to our blend, such as oat, millet, and amaranth, we found that adding a small amount of sorghum flour provided enough protein to give us a nice rise without imparting a distinct flavor. The rise was then reinforced by the batter's high liquid content (from the eggs, milk, and butter), which created a lot of steam in the oven, but we wanted our popovers to rise even higher. Reducing the amount of milk made them dry; switching to low-fat milk made for a higher-rising and moist popover. We also decreased the amount of butter from 4 to 2 tablespoons, which was enough to give them rich, buttery flavor without weighing down the dough. Now for our mixing method. We preferred mixing the batter in a blender for its ease and convenience, as we had a very loose dough (more like a pancake batter). We had one last problem to tackle to ensure our popovers were reaching their full potential: the oven temperature. Popovers baked at a high oven temperature became too crusty on the outside before the inside had a chance to set. We had the best results baking the popovers for 35 minutes at 400 degrees to initiate the rise, then turning the oven down to 350 degrees so the interior would be done at the same time as the crust. We then poked a hole in the top of the popovers when they were done cooking to allow the steam to escape, and this kept the crisp structure intact. Do not substitute skim or whole milk in this recipe.

Popovers
MAKES 6 POPOVERS

- 1¼ cups 1 or 2 percent low-fat milk
- 4 large eggs
- 2 tablespoons unsalted butter, melted and cooled
- 4½ ounces (1 cup) ATK All-Purpose Gluten-Free Flour Blend (page 7)
- 1 ounce (¼ cup) sorghum flour
- ½ teaspoon salt
- ¼ teaspoon xanthan gum

1. Adjust oven rack to middle position and heat oven to 400 degrees. Spray 6-cup popover pan with vegetable oil spray. Process milk, eggs, and melted butter in blender until completely incorporated, about 30 seconds.

2. Whisk flour blend, sorghum flour, salt, and xanthan gum together in bowl. Add flour mixture to egg mixture in blender and process until smooth, about 1 minute. Portion batter evenly into prepared popover pan (batter will not quite reach top of cups). Bake until popovers are golden brown, about 35 minutes.

3. Without opening oven door, reduce oven temperature to 350 degrees and continue to bake until popovers are deep golden brown, about 20 minutes longer.

4. Transfer pan to wire rack, poke each popover with skewer, and let cool for 2 minutes. Remove popovers from pan and serve warm.

10-Minute Steel-Cut Oatmeal

✓ WHY THIS RECIPE WORKS

Oats are a great gluten-free option, and most oatmeal fans agree that the steel-cut style offers the best flavor and texture. However, many balk at the 40-minute cooking time, especially when all you want is a quick breakfast. We decreased the morning-of cooking time to only 10 minutes by stirring our steel-cut oats into boiling water the night before. This allowed the grains to hydrate and soften overnight. In the morning, all we had to do was add more water (fruit juice or milk also worked) and simmer the mixture for about 5 minutes. A brief rest off the heat ensured it had the perfect consistency. Whether eaten plain or with a handful of our favorite toppings, this recipe finally made great oatmeal a weekday option. The oatmeal will continue to thicken as it cools; if you prefer a looser consistency, thin the oatmeal with boiling water. Customize your oatmeal with toppings such as brown sugar, toasted nuts, maple syrup, or dried fruit.

10-Minute Steel-Cut Oatmeal
SERVES 4

    4 cups water
    1 cup gluten-free steel-cut oats
    ¼ teaspoon salt

1. Bring 3 cups water to boil in large saucepan over high heat. Remove pan from heat; stir in oats and salt. Cover pan and let stand overnight.

2. Stir remaining 1 cup water into oats and bring to boil over medium-high heat. Reduce heat to medium and cook, stirring occasionally, until oats are softened but still retain some chew and mixture thickens and resembles warm pudding, 4 to 6 minutes. Remove pan from heat and let stand for 5 minutes. Stir and serve, passing desired toppings separately.

VARIATIONS
Apple-Cinnamon 10-Minute Steel-Cut Oatmeal
Increase salt to ½ teaspoon. Substitute ½ cup apple cider and ½ cup whole milk for water in step 2. Stir ½ cup peeled, grated sweet apple, 2 tablespoons packed dark brown sugar, and ½ teaspoon ground cinnamon into oatmeal with cider and milk. Sprinkle each serving with 2 tablespoons coarsely chopped toasted walnuts.

Cranberry-Orange 10-Minute Steel-Cut Oatmeal
Increase salt to ½ teaspoon. Substitute ½ cup orange juice and ½ cup whole milk for water in step 2. Stir ½ cup dried cranberries, 3 tablespoons packed dark brown sugar, and ⅛ teaspoon ground cardamom into oatmeal with orange juice and milk. Sprinkle each serving with 2 tablespoons toasted sliced almonds.

Carrot Spice 10-Minute Steel-Cut Oatmeal
Increase salt to ¾ teaspoon. Substitute ½ cup carrot juice and ½ cup whole milk for water in step 2. Stir ½ cup finely grated carrot, ¼ cup packed dark brown sugar, ⅓ cup dried currants, and ½ teaspoon ground cinnamon into oatmeal with carrot juice and milk. Sprinkle each serving with 2 tablespoons coarsely chopped toasted pecans.

SMART SHOPPING **Know Your Oats**

Yes, oats are a gluten-free grain, but they're often processed in facilities that also process wheat, which creates cross-contamination issues. It's critical to make sure you are buying oats that are processed in a gluten-free facility; check the label when shopping. Once you've narrowed the oats field to gluten-free, you'll find there are a variety of options—but not all of them make for a good bowl of oatmeal. Groats are whole oats that have been hulled and cleaned. They are the least processed oat product, but we find them too coarse for oatmeal. Steel-cut oats are groats that have been cut crosswise into coarse bits. They're our preference for making oatmeal; they cook up creamy yet chewy, with a rich, nutty flavor. Rolled oats (often labeled "old-fashioned") are groats steamed and pressed into flat flakes. Rolled oats cook faster than steel-cut but make for a gummy, lackluster bowl of oatmeal; they are best saved for granola and baking.

Millet Porridge with Maple Syrup

✔ WHY THIS RECIPE WORKS

The mellow corn flavor and fine texture of tiny millet seeds make them extremely versatile in both savory and sweet applications. We'd already discovered a small amount could add appealing texture to baked goods (see Millet–Cherry Almond Muffins on page 70), but a little research revealed it could be used in myriad other types of dishes. Going through its long history (as far back as the Stone Age!), we made a short list of the breakfast options and settled on developing a sweet millet porridge, a traditional staple for Germans and Russians. We started by cooking the seeds in plenty of liquid until they turned tender, then added more liquid (in the form of milk) and continued to cook the millet, uncovered, to encourage the swollen seeds to burst and release their starch. This delivered a porridge with just the right creamy consistency. We settled on cooking the millet in 3 cups of water until it was almost tender, then added milk to the pot to finish cooking it through and add richness. Simple flavorings of maple syrup and cinnamon, plus a little salt, were all our porridge needed to turn it into an appealing morning meal. We prefer this porridge made with whole milk, but low-fat or skim milk can be substituted. For more information on millet, see page 26.

Millet Porridge with Maple Syrup
SERVES 4

- 3   cups water
- 1   cup millet, rinsed (see page 26)
- ⅛   teaspoon ground cinnamon
- ⅛   teaspoon salt
- 1   cup whole milk
- 3   tablespoons maple syrup

1. Bring water, millet, cinnamon, and salt to boil in medium saucepan over high heat. Reduce heat to low, cover, and cook until millet has absorbed all water and is almost tender, about 20 minutes.

2. Uncover and increase heat to medium, add milk, and simmer, stirring frequently, until millet is fully tender and mixture is thickened, about 10 minutes. Stir in maple syrup and serve.

VARIATIONS

Millet Porridge with Dried Cherries and Pecans
Substitute 2 tablespoons packed brown sugar for maple syrup. Stir in ½ cup dried cherries and ½ cup chopped, toasted pecans along with brown sugar in step 2.

Millet Porridge with Coconut and Bananas
Omit cinnamon and maple syrup. Substitute coconut milk for whole milk. Stir in 2 sliced bananas, ½ cup shredded, toasted coconut, and ½ teaspoon vanilla just before serving.

Hot Quinoa Breakfast Cereal

G-F TESTING LAB

QUINOA

We like the convenience of prewashed quinoa. If you buy unwashed quinoa (or if you are unsure if it's washed), quinoa should be rinsed before cooking to remove its bitter protective coating (called saponin); see page 27. We developed this recipe using white quinoa; we don't recommend using red or black quinoa here.

WHY THIS RECIPE WORKS

Given quinoa's availability, great nutritional profile, appealing nutty flavor, and quick cooking time, it seemed like a shoo-in for a great breakfast. We skipped toasting the quinoa to keep the flavor profile on the neutral side so that it could work with a variety of stir-ins, and also because we wanted to keep this morning recipe simple. To deliver the consistency we were after, we used a 2:1 ratio of liquid to quinoa and then cooked the quinoa until it partially broke down. We started by cooking it with 1 cup of water until it was almost done, then we added a cup of almond milk (for a little richness and flavor boost) and continued to cook until the milk was mostly absorbed and the quinoa had the consistency of porridge. With the technique down, we looked at flavorings. Honey, almonds, and blueberries were a good trio, and we used almond milk to reinforce the nut flavor. Sweet-tart raspberries paired well with mildly nutty sunflower seeds and maple syrup, while golden raisins, brown sugar, pistachios, and cardamom gave us an appealing version with a slightly Indian profile. If you prefer, replace almond milk with an equal amount of whole milk.

Hot Quinoa Breakfast Cereal with Blueberries and Almonds

SERVES 6

1	cup prewashed white quinoa
1	cup water
⅛	teaspoon salt
1	cup almond milk, plus extra for serving
5	ounces (1 cup) fresh blueberries
½	cup whole almonds, toasted and chopped
1	tablespoon honey

1. Bring quinoa, water, and salt to simmer in medium saucepan. Reduce heat to low, cover, and continue to simmer until quinoa is just tender, 15 to 17 minutes.

2. Uncover, stir in milk, and cook, stirring often, until milk is mostly absorbed and quinoa has consistency of porridge, about 10 minutes. Stir in blueberries, almonds, and honey. Serve, adding additional milk as needed to adjust consistency.

VARIATIONS

Hot Quinoa Breakfast Cereal with Raspberries and Sunflower Seeds

Substitute whole milk for almond milk. Substitute raspberries for blueberries, toasted sunflower seeds for almonds, and maple syrup for honey.

Hot Quinoa Breakfast Cereal with Golden Raisins and Pistachios

Substitute whole milk for almond milk. Substitute ½ cup golden raisins for blueberries, shelled pistachios for almonds, and 2 tablespoons packed brown sugar for honey. Add pinch ground cardamom along with raisins in step 2.

TEST KITCHEN TIP Toasting Nuts and Seeds

Toasting nuts and seeds maximizes their flavor and takes only a few minutes. To toast a small amount (1 cup or less) of nuts or seeds, put them in a dry skillet over medium heat. Shake the skillet occasionally to prevent scorching and toast until they are lightly browned and fragrant, 3 to 8 minutes. Watch the nuts closely because they can go from golden to burnt very quickly. To toast a large quantity of nuts, spread the nuts in a single layer on a rimmed baking sheet and toast in a 350-degree oven. To promote even toasting, shake the baking sheet every few minutes, and toast until the nuts are lightly browned and fragrant, 5 to 10 minutes.

Three-Grain Breakfast Porridge

G-F TESTING LAB

QUINOA
We like the convenience of prewashed quinoa. If you buy unwashed quinoa (or if you are unsure if it's washed), give it a rinse before cooking to remove its bitter protective coating (called saponin). We developed this recipe using white quinoa; we do not recommend using red, rainbow, or black quinoa here. For more information on quinoa, see page 27.

✓ WHY THIS RECIPE WORKS

For this hearty three-grain porridge, we chose a blend of quinoa, millet, and amaranth. Finding a harmonious balance among these three grains posed a bit of a challenge. Equal amounts of each resulted in porridge that was completely overwhelmed by the amaranth's licorice flavor. A mix of mostly quinoa, slightly less millet, and a tiny amount of amaranth put us on the right track, but our porridge was now bitter from all of the quinoa. Equal parts quinoa and millet (½ cup), along with a ¼ cup of amaranth, gave us a harmonious balance of textures and flavors. Millet, with its mellow corn flavor and fine, starchy texture was balanced by the nutty, earthy flavors of quinoa, while the amaranth added bold anise flavor and an intriguing caviar-like texture. Since each of these grains absorbs liquid differently, our next challenge was to figure out how to cook them together perfectly. After testing numerous ratios of liquid to grains and various simmering times, we pinpointed the perfect compromise of 30 minutes of cooking and five cups liquid to 1¼ cups grains. The high amount of liquid encouraged the grains to swell and some to burst and release their starches. This delivered a porridge with a creamy texture. However, the lengthy 30-minute simmering time was off-putting for what was meant to be a quick breakfast. The solution was stirring the grains into boiling water the night before. This allowed the grains to hydrate and soften overnight. As a bonus, we found that the assertive licorice flavor of the amaranth mellowed over the course of the night and the grains released starches to create an appealing consistency. In the morning, all we had to do was add milk and simmer the mixture for about 10 minutes. Stirring in golden raisins and warm spices, and finishing with a bit of honey, accentuated the millet's sweetness, balanced the often-bitter quinoa, and tamed the somewhat assertive flavor of the amaranth.

Three-Grain Breakfast Porridge

SERVES 4

- 4 cups water
- ½ cup millet, rinsed
- ½ cup prewashed white quinoa
- ¼ cup amaranth, rinsed
- ½ teaspoon salt
- 1 cup whole milk, plus extra as needed
- ¾ cup golden raisins
- ½ teaspoon ground cinnamon
- ⅛ teaspoon ground nutmeg
- 2 tablespoons honey

1. Bring water to boil in large saucepan over high heat. Remove pan from heat and stir in millet, quinoa, amaranth, and salt. Cover pan and let sit at room temperature overnight.

2. Stir in milk, raisins, cinnamon, and nutmeg and bring to simmer over medium-high heat. Reduce heat to medium-low and simmer uncovered, stirring occasionally, until grains are fully tender and mixture is thickened, 8 to 10 minutes.

3. Stir in honey and adjust consistency with hot milk as needed; porridge will thicken as it sits. Serve.

VARIATIONS

Dairy-Free Three-Grain Breakfast Porridge
Substitute unsweetened soy milk, almond milk, or rice milk for milk.

Three-Grain Breakfast Porridge with Blueberries and Maple
Omit raisins. Substitute 3 tablespoons maple syrup for honey. Stir in 1½ cups fresh blueberries with maple syrup.

Three-Grain Breakfast Porridge with Tahini and Apricots
Substitute ½ cup finely chopped dried apricots for raisins and ground cardamom for nutmeg. Increase honey to 3 tablespoons. Stir in ¼ cup tahini with milk. Sprinkle each serving with 2 tablespoons chopped toasted pistachios.

Almond Granola with Dried Fruit

G-F TESTING LAB

OATS   Do not use quick oats; they have a dusty texture that doesn't work in this recipe. Make sure to buy old-fashioned rolled oats (see page 27 for more information) that have been processed in a gluten-free facility.

✔️ WHY THIS RECIPE WORKS

Granola is a great staple in the gluten-free pantry, ideal not just as an energy-packed breakfast cereal, but also for topping yogurt or serving as a satisfying afternoon snack. Store-bought granola is often loose and gravelly, and/or infuriatingly expensive. We wanted to make our own granola at home, with big, satisfying clusters and a crisp texture. The secret was to pack the granola mixture firmly into a rimmed baking sheet before baking. Once it was baked, we had a granola "bark" that we could break into crunchy clumps of any size. Chopping the almonds by hand is the first choice for superior texture and crunch. If you prefer not to hand-chop, substitute an equal quantity of slivered or sliced almonds. (A food processor does a lousy job of chopping whole nuts evenly.) Use either a single type of your favorite dried fruit or a combination.

Almond Granola with Dried Fruit
MAKES ABOUT 9 CUPS

⅓ cup maple syrup
2⅓ ounces (⅓ cup packed) light brown sugar
4 teaspoons vanilla extract
½ teaspoon salt
½ cup vegetable oil
5 cups gluten-free old-fashioned rolled oats
2 cups whole almonds, chopped coarse
2 cups raisins or other dried fruit, chopped

1. Adjust oven rack to upper-middle position and heat oven to 325 degrees. Line rimmed baking sheet with parchment paper.

2. Whisk maple syrup, sugar, vanilla, and salt together in large bowl. Whisk in oil. Fold in oats and almonds until thoroughly coated.

3. Transfer oat mixture to prepared sheet and spread across sheet into thin, even layer (about ⅜ inch thick). Using stiff metal spatula, compress oat mixture until very compact. Bake until lightly browned, 40 to 45 minutes, rotating pan halfway through baking.

4. Remove granola from oven and cool on wire rack to room temperature, about 1 hour. Break cooled granola into pieces of desired size. Stir in raisins. (Granola can be stored in airtight container for up to 2 weeks.)

TEST KITCHEN TIP **Making Chunky Granola**

For granola with nice substantial chunks, we found it was key to pack it into the baking sheet and to avoid stirring.

1. Spread oat mixture onto parchment-lined baking sheet, then press down firmly with spatula to create compact layer.

2. Bake granola at 325 degrees for 40 to 45 minutes, rotating pan halfway through baking; do not stir.

3. Let granola cool, then break into pieces.

Quinoa Granola

G-F TESTING LAB

QUINOA FLAKES	Quinoa flakes can be found in the cereal aisle of your grocery store, near the instant oatmeal.
QUINOA	We like the convenience of prewashed quinoa. If you buy unwashed quinoa (or if you are unsure if it's washed), give it a rinse before cooking to remove its bitter protective coating (called saponin). You can use either white, red, rainbow, or black quinoa here. For more information on quinoa, see page 27.

Oat-free granola is the allergen-friendly answer to traditional oat granola. Most of the recipes we found were packed with supergrains and seeds like chia, flaxseed, and quinoa, and while we loved the crunch the quinoa added, we found that chia had an off-putting flavor and the slippery flaxseeds were overpowering. Quinoa flakes cut the tough texture of raw quinoa and added a more delicate crunch without tempering the earthy flavor, which we found appealing. Almonds and sunflower seeds were mild enough to pair well with quinoa, while unsweetened flaked coconut lent enough flavor without making our granola too sweet. To enhance the coconut flavor, we turned to coconut oil instead of vegetable oil, and this added nutty flavor without being cloying. Maple syrup and a hefty amount of vanilla rounded out the warm, rich flavor of our granola. We loved our new granola so much we decided to create a couple of variations. Pecans and chocolate paired well with the earthy flavor of the quinoa, while pepitas, golden raisins, and a dash of cayenne gave our granola a little spice without being overpowering. We prefer to chop the almonds by hand for large, evenly chopped pieces. You can substitute vegetable oil for the coconut oil if desired.

Quinoa Granola with Sunflower Seeds and Almonds

MAKES ABOUT 9 CUPS

- ⅔ **cup maple syrup**
- 4 **teaspoons vanilla extract**
- ½ **teaspoon salt**
- ¼ **cup coconut oil, melted**
- 2 **cups whole almonds, chopped coarse**
- 2 **cups unsweetened flaked coconut**
- 1 **cup quinoa flakes**
- 1 **cup quinoa, rinsed**
- 1 **cup raw sunflower seeds**
- 2 **cups dried cherries or other dried fruit, chopped**

1. Adjust oven rack to upper-middle position and heat oven to 325 degrees. Line rimmed baking sheet with parchment paper.

2. Whisk maple syrup, vanilla, and salt together in large bowl. Whisk in oil. Fold in almonds, coconut, quinoa flakes, quinoa, and sunflower seeds until thoroughly coated.

3. Transfer mixture to prepared baking sheet and spread into thin, even layer. Using stiff metal spatula, press on quinoa mixture until very compact. Bake until deep golden brown, 50 to 60 minutes, rotating pan halfway through baking.

4. Remove granola from oven and let cool on wire rack for about 1 hour. Break cooled granola into pieces of desired size. Stir in dried fruit and serve. (Granola can be stored in airtight container at room temperature for up to 2 weeks.)

VARIATIONS

Quinoa Granola with Pecans, Espresso, and Chocolate

To make dairy-free, use dairy-free chocolate chips.

Add 1 teaspoon instant espresso powder to maple syrup mixture in step 2. Substitute pecans for almonds, and mini chocolate chips for dried cherries.

Quinoa Granola with Pepitas, Cayenne, and Golden Raisins

Add ¼ teaspoon cayenne pepper to maple syrup mixture in step 2. Substitute raw pepitas for sunflower seeds, and golden raisins for dried cherries.

SMART SHOPPING **Coconut Oil**

Coconut oil is made by extracting oil from the meat of fresh coconut. It is a semisolid fat, which means that it remains solid at room temperature; we don't recommend keeping it in the fridge, since it gets very hard. This oil has a mild, nutty flavor that adds richness to many sorts of dishes, from vegetables to baked goods. It is touted as a healthy fat because it is made up primarily of heart-healthy saturated fats. In terms of flavor, unrefined coconut oil has a stronger coconut flavor than refined coconut oil.

GRAINS

Coconut Rice with Bok Choy and Lime

G-F TESTING LAB

RICE   We prefer the nutty flavor and fluffy texture of basmati rice in this recipe; however, long-grain white, jasmine, or Texmati rice can be substituted with good results. For more information on basmati rice, see page 28.

✓ WHY THIS RECIPE WORKS

Rich, creamy coconut rice is served around the globe as a cooling accompaniment to spicy curries, stir-fries, and more. This dressed-up version features baby bok choy along with aromatic lemongrass, lime, and cilantro. Following the traditional method, we cooked basmati rice in coconut milk along with lemongrass, which steeped in the liquid and lent its flavor as the rice simmered. We found that cooking our rice in straight coconut milk didn't provide enough moisture and resulted in crunchy, uncooked grains. Folding in coconut milk after cooking our rice left us with overly sticky clumps of rice that offered very little coconut flavor. By thinning our coconut milk with water we had perfectly cooked rice, with individual grains and fragrant coconut flavor. To ensure the hearty bok choy stalks turned tender by the time the rice was fully cooked, we sautéed them in the pan along with some minced shallot before adding the rice, water, coconut milk, and lemongrass. When the rice was mostly done, we stirred in bright lime zest and juice and fresh cilantro along with the delicate bok choy greens. The last 3 minutes of cooking on the stovetop gently wilted the greens and infused the rice with lime and cilantro flavors.

Coconut Rice with Bok Choy and Lime

SERVES 4 TO 6

- 2 teaspoons vegetable oil
- 2 heads baby bok choy (4 ounces each), stalks sliced ½ inch thick and greens chopped
- 1 shallot, minced
- 1½ cups basmati rice, rinsed
- 1½ cups water
- ¾ cup canned coconut milk
- 1 lemongrass stalk, trimmed to bottom 6 inches and bruised with back of knife
  Salt and pepper
- 2 tablespoons minced fresh cilantro
- 1 teaspoon grated lime zest plus 2 teaspoons juice

1. Heat oil in large saucepan over medium-high heat until shimmering. Add bok choy stalks and shallot and cook, stirring occasionally, until softened, about 2 minutes.

2. Stir in rice, water, coconut milk, lemongrass, and 2 teaspoons salt and bring to boil. Reduce heat to low, cover, and simmer gently until liquid is absorbed, 18 to 20 minutes.

3. Fold in cilantro, lime zest and juice, and bok choy greens, cover, and cook until rice is tender, about 3 minutes. Discard lemongrass. Season with salt and pepper to taste, and serve.

TEST KITCHEN TIP **Preparing Lemongrass**

1. After trimming top and bottom of each stalk, peel and discard dry outer layer until moist, tender inner stalk is exposed.

2. Smash peeled stalk with back of chef's knife or meat pounder to release maximum flavor.

TEST KITCHEN TIP **Rinsing Rice and Grains**

Rinse rice or grains in fine-mesh strainer under cool water until water runs clear, occasionally stirring rice or grains around lightly with your hand. Let drain in strainer until needed.

Basmati Rice Pilaf

G-F TESTING LAB

RICE   Because of its nutty flavor and fluffy texture, basmati rice is our first choice for pilaf. That said, long-grain white, jasmine, or Texmati rice can be substituted with good results. For more details about basmati rice, see page 24.

Rice is a staple in any gluten-free pantry, but no one wants plain rice or, worse, rice that's improperly cooked, night after night. Though simple, rice pilaf—fragrant and fluffy, perfectly steamed and tender—takes plain rice to the next level. Recipes for pilaf abound, but none seem to agree on the best method for guaranteeing these results; many espouse rinsing the rice and soaking it overnight to maximize grain elongation and prevent the grains from breaking, but we wondered if this extra work was really necessary for a simple rice dish. Rinsing the rice removed excess starch, ensuring separate rather than clumpy grains, but soaking was a failure—it actually resulted in mushy rice and unevenly sized and broken grains. Sautéed onion, cooked in the pot before adding the rice, lent sweetness. We then added the rice, sautéed it for a few minutes to give it a toasted, extra-nutty flavor; this step also helped to produce more discrete grains. And when it came to the liquid, instead of following the traditional 1:2 ratio of rice to water, we found that using a little less water delivered better results.

Basmati Rice Pilaf

SERVES 4 TO 6

1	tablespoon extra-virgin olive oil
1	small onion, chopped fine
	Salt and pepper
1½	cups basmati rice, rinsed (see page 31)
2¼	cups water

1. Heat oil in large saucepan over medium heat until shimmering. Add onion and ¼ teaspoon salt and cook, stirring occasionally, until onion is softened, about 5 minutes.

2. Stir in rice and cook, stirring often, until grain edges begin to turn translucent, about 3 minutes. Stir in water and bring to simmer. Reduce heat to low, cover, and continue to simmer until rice is tender and water is absorbed, 16 to 18 minutes.

3. Remove pot from heat and lay clean folded dish towel underneath lid. Let sit for 10 minutes. Fluff rice with fork, season with salt and pepper to taste, and serve.

VARIATIONS
Herbed Basmati Rice Pilaf
Add 2 minced garlic cloves and 1 teaspoon minced fresh thyme to pot with rice. Before covering rice with dish towel in step 3, sprinkle ¼ cup minced fresh parsley and 2 tablespoons minced fresh chives over top.

Basmati Rice Pilaf with Peas, Scallions, and Lemon
Add 2 minced garlic cloves, 1 teaspoon grated lemon zest, and ⅛ teaspoon red pepper flakes to pot with rice. Before covering rice with dish towel in step 3, sprinkle ½ cup thawed frozen peas over top. When fluffing rice, stir in 2 thinly sliced scallions and 1 tablespoon lemon juice.

Basmati Rice Pilaf with Currants and Toasted Almonds
Add 2 minced garlic cloves, ½ teaspoon turmeric, and ¼ teaspoon ground cinnamon to pot with rice. Before covering rice with dish towel in step 3, sprinkle ¼ cup currants over top. When fluffing rice, stir in ¼ cup toasted sliced almonds.

TEST KITCHEN TIP
Ensuring Fluffy Rice Pilaf

The first key steps to getting fluffy rice pilaf are selecting basmati rice, which cooks up particularly fluffy, and then rinsing the rice to remove excess starch. We also place a towel under the pan lid while the rice rests to absorb excess moisture.

Remove pot from heat and lay clean, folded dish towel under lid. Let rice sit for 10 minutes, then fluff with fork.

Hearty Baked Brown Rice

G-F TESTING LAB

RICE   You can substitute short- or medium-grain brown rice for the long-grain if desired, but the results will be a little more sticky. For more details about brown rice, see page 28.

✅ WHY THIS RECIPE WORKS

All too often brown rice cooks unevenly, with the grains on the bottom of the pot (near the burner) scorching while the grains at the top of the pot are underdone. We found that moving from the stovetop to the oven, an environment that mimics the even heat of the rice cooker, delivered perfectly cooked grains. For our foolproof approach, we brought the liquid (a combination of broth and water) to a boil on the stovetop, stirred in our rice, then transferred the pot to the oven. To add heartiness, we turned to several flavorful combinations of add-ins: red peppers and onions, black beans and cilantro, peas and feta. But after adding these ingredients to the pot with our rice, we found that we needed to tinker with the liquid-to-rice ratio a bit more. Increasing the amount of liquid ensured that the rice cooked through perfectly every time. Fresh herbs, added just before serving, brightened the dish and balanced the earthiness of the rice. To make this vegetarian, substitute vegetable broth for chicken broth.

Hearty Baked Brown Rice with Onions and Roasted Red Peppers
SERVES 4 TO 6

4	teaspoons extra-virgin olive oil
2	onions, chopped fine
2¼	cups water
1	cup chicken broth
1½	cups long-grain brown rice
	Salt and pepper
¾	cup chopped jarred roasted red peppers
½	cup minced fresh parsley
1	ounce Parmesan cheese, grated (½ cup)
	Lemon wedges

1. Adjust oven rack to middle position and heat oven to 375 degrees. Heat oil in Dutch oven over medium heat until shimmering. Add onions and cook, stirring occasionally, until well browned, 12 to 14 minutes.

2. Add water and broth, cover, and bring to boil. Off heat, stir in rice and 1 teaspoon salt. Cover, transfer pot to oven, and bake rice until tender, 65 to 70 minutes.

3. Remove pot from oven and uncover. Fluff rice with fork, stir in roasted red peppers, and replace lid; let sit for 5 minutes. Stir in parsley and ¼ teaspoon pepper. Serve, passing Parmesan and lemon wedges separately.

VARIATIONS

Hearty Baked Brown Rice with Black Beans and Cilantro
Substitute 1 finely chopped green bell pepper for 1 onion. Once vegetables are well browned in step 1, stir in 3 minced garlic cloves and cook until fragrant, about 30 seconds. Substitute 1 (15-ounce) can black beans for roasted red peppers and ¼ cup minced fresh cilantro for parsley. Omit Parmesan and substitute lime wedges for lemon wedges.

Hearty Baked Brown Rice with Peas, Feta, and Mint
Reduce amount of olive oil to 1 tablespoon and omit 1 onion. Substitute 1 cup thawed frozen peas for roasted red peppers, ¼ cup minced fresh mint for parsley, and ½ teaspoon grated lemon zest for pepper. Omit Parmesan and sprinkle with ½ cup crumbled feta before serving.

SMART SHOPPING **Long-Grain Brown Rice**

Brown rice is essentially a less-processed version of white rice. For a product with so little processing, we wondered if the brand of brown rice really mattered. We tasted five brands of long-grain brown rice prepared two ways: steamed in a rice cooker and baked in the oven. While most were fairly neutral in flavor, one brand boasted distinct nutty and toasty flavors. In both taste tests, Goya Brown Rice Natural Long Grain Rice came out on top—though by a slim margin. What separated it from the rest of the group was a bolder, more distinct flavor.

Wild Rice Pilaf

G-F TESTING LAB

RICE   See page 31 for information on rinsing the wild rice and white rice.

WHY THIS RECIPE WORKS

Properly cooked wild rice is chewy yet tender, and pleasingly rustic—not crunchy or gluey, like the wild rice so many recipes produce. We wanted to figure out how to turn out properly cooked wild rice with fluffy pilaf-style results every time. In the end, we found that simmering the wild rice in plenty of liquid and then draining off any excess was the most reliable method. Cooking times from batch to batch were variable, so we started checking for doneness after 35 minutes. For the liquid, using water alone resulted in a muddy flavor. A combination of water and chicken broth performed much better. Mild yet rich, the broth tempered the rice's muddiness and brought out its earthy, nutty flavors. We also added some white rice to balance the wild rice's strong flavor profile.

Wild Rice Pilaf with Pecans and Cranberries
SERVES 6 TO 8

1¾	cups chicken broth
2½	cups water
2	bay leaves
8	sprigs fresh thyme, divided into 2 bundles, each tied together with kitchen twine
1	cup wild rice, picked over and rinsed
3	tablespoons unsalted butter
1	onion, chopped fine
1	large carrot, peeled and chopped fine
	Salt and pepper
1½	cups long-grain white rice, rinsed
¾	cup dried cranberries
¾	cup pecans, toasted and chopped coarse
4½	teaspoons minced fresh parsley

1. Bring broth, ¼ cup water, bay leaves, and 1 bundle thyme to boil in medium saucepan over medium-high heat. Add wild rice, cover, and reduce heat to low; simmer until rice is plump and tender and has absorbed most of liquid, 35 to 45 minutes. Drain rice in fine-mesh strainer to remove excess liquid. Remove bay leaves and thyme. Return rice to now-empty saucepan, cover, and set aside.

2. Meanwhile, melt butter in medium saucepan over medium-high heat. Add onion, carrot, and 1 teaspoon salt and cook, stirring frequently, until vegetables are softened but not browned, about 4 minutes. Add white rice and stir to coat grains with butter; cook, stirring frequently, until grains begin to turn translucent, about 3 minutes. Meanwhile, bring remaining 2¼ cups water to boil in small saucepan or in microwave. Add boiling water and second thyme bundle to rice and return to boil. Reduce heat to low, sprinkle cranberries evenly over rice, and cover. Simmer until all liquid is absorbed, 16 to 18 minutes. Off heat, remove thyme and fluff rice with fork.

3. Combine wild rice, white rice mixture, pecans, and parsley in large bowl and toss with silicone spatula. Season with salt and pepper to taste; serve immediately.

VARIATION
Wild Rice Pilaf with Scallions, Cilantro, and Almonds
Omit dried cranberries. Substitute ¾ cup toasted sliced almonds for pecans and 2 tablespoons minced fresh cilantro for parsley. Add 2 thinly sliced scallions and 1 teaspoon lime juice with almonds.

SMART SHOPPING **Wild Rice**

When we tasted five brands, textural differences stood out the most. Some cooked up springy and firm, while others blew out. The differences come from the way the rice is processed. To create a shelf-stable product, manufacturers heat the grains by either parching or parboiling, which gelatinizes their starches and drives out moisture. To parch, manufacturers load the rice into cylinders that spin over a fire, but this is an inexact process that produces "crumbly" results. Parboiling, however, steams the grains for more uniform gelatinization, which translates into rice that cooks more evenly. The top three brands, including our winner, Goose Valley Wild Rice, were all parboiled.

Black Rice Salad

G-F TESTING LAB

BLACK RICE	Do not substitute other types of rice for the black rice in this recipe. For more information on black rice, see page 28.

✐ WHY THIS RECIPE WORKS

Black rice, also known as purple rice or forbidden rice, is an ancient grain that was once reserved for the emperors of China. It has a delicious roasted, nutty taste and is used in anything from salads to dessert puddings. We decided to use it in a simple salad, and to stick with its decidedly Asian roots we paired it with crunchy snap peas, peppery radishes, cilantro, and a ginger-sesame vinaigrette. Our major obstacle was finding the right method for cooking the rice, as it is easy to overcook. We discovered that the best way to keep it evenly cooked was to cook it like pasta, in lots of boiling water, giving it space to move around. Once it was cooked and drained, we drizzled it with a little vinegar for a boost of flavor and let it cool completely on a rimmed baking sheet. This ensured perfectly cooked grains that had the expected chew of black rice, and without any mushiness. Once the rice had cooled, we tossed it with our vinaigrette, peas, radishes, and peppers. A bit of minced cilantro brought a fresh vibrancy to the finished salad.

Black Rice Salad with Snap Peas and Ginger-Sesame Vinaigrette

SERVES 4 TO 6

- 1½ cups black rice
  Salt and pepper
- 3 tablespoons plus 1 teaspoon rice vinegar
- 2 teaspoons minced shallot
- 2 teaspoons honey
- 2 teaspoons Asian chili-garlic sauce
- 1 teaspoon grated fresh ginger
- ¼ cup extra-virgin olive oil
- 1 tablespoon toasted sesame oil
- 6 ounces sugar snap peas, strings removed and halved
- 5 radishes, trimmed, halved, and sliced thin
- 1 red bell pepper, stemmed, seeded, and chopped fine
- ¼ cup minced fresh cilantro

1. Bring 4 quarts water to boil in large pot over medium-high heat. Add rice and 1 teaspoon salt and cook until rice is tender, 20 to 25 minutes. Drain rice, spread onto rimmed baking sheet, drizzle with 1 teaspoon vinegar, and let cool for 15 minutes.

2. Whisk remaining 3 tablespoons vinegar, shallot, honey, chili-garlic sauce, ginger, ¼ teaspoon salt, and ⅛ teaspoon pepper together in large bowl. Whisking slowly, drizzle in olive oil and sesame oil until combined. Add cooled rice, snap peas, radishes, bell pepper, and cilantro and toss to combine. Season with salt and pepper to taste, and serve.

TEST KITCHEN TIP

Trimming Snow and Snap Peas

Using paring knife and thumb, snip off stem end of pea, then pull stem end along flat side of pod to remove string.

SMART SHOPPING **Black Rice**

Also sold under the name purple rice, black rice is sold unhulled and has a high fiber content similar to that of brown rice. But only black rice contains anthocyanins, the same antioxidant compounds in blueberries and blackberries. These compounds turn the rice a deep purple as it cooks.

Brown Rice Bowls

G-F TESTING LAB

RICE
We prefer the fluffy texture of long-grain brown rice in this recipe; however, short- or medium-grain brown rice can be substituted with good results. For more information on brown rice, see page 28.

✓ WHY THIS RECIPE WORKS

We were after a version of the now-popular rice bowls that pairs nutty brown rice with roasted vegetables. To start, we tossed sweet carrots with za'atar and roasted them, first covered and then uncovered, until they were tender and spotty brown. When we uncovered the carrots, we also spread sliced kale over the top of them. Briefly roasting the kale gave it great flavor and an appealingly crisp texture. While the vegetables were roasting, we baked the rice alongside them in the oven, a hands-off method that delivered distinct grains of rice. After portioning the rice and vegetables into bowls, we drizzled everything with a shallot vinaigrette and topped each bowl with a fried egg. For an accurate measurement of boiling water, bring a full kettle of water to a boil and then measure out the desired amount.

Brown Rice Bowls with Roasted Carrots, Kale, and Fried Eggs

SERVES 4

- 2 cups boiling water
- 1 cup long-grain brown rice, rinsed
  Salt and pepper
- 5 carrots, peeled, halved crosswise, then halved or quartered lengthwise to create uniformly sized pieces
- ⅓ cup extra-virgin olive oil
- 2 teaspoons za'atar
- 8 ounces kale, stemmed and sliced into 1-inch-wide strips
- 2 tablespoons red wine vinegar
- 1 small shallot, minced
- 4 large eggs

1. Adjust oven racks to upper-middle and lower-middle positions and heat oven to 375 degrees. Combine boiling water, rice, and ¾ teaspoon salt in 8-inch square baking dish and cover tightly with aluminum foil. Bake rice on lower rack until tender, 45 to 50 minutes. Remove rice from oven, uncover, and fluff with fork. Cover with dish towel and let sit for 5 minutes.

2. Meanwhile, toss carrots, 1 tablespoon oil, za'atar, ¼ teaspoon salt, and ⅛ teaspoon pepper together in bowl. Spread carrots onto parchment paper–lined baking sheet, cover with foil, and roast on upper rack for 20 minutes.

3. Toss kale, 1 tablespoon oil, ¼ teaspoon salt, and ⅛ teaspoon pepper together in bowl. Remove foil from carrots and spread kale over top. Continue to roast vegetables, uncovered, until carrots are spotty brown and tender and edges of kale are lightly browned, about 15 minutes.

4. Portion brown rice into individual bowls and top with roasted vegetables. Whisk vinegar, shallot, and 3 tablespoons oil together in bowl and season with salt and pepper to taste. Drizzle vinaigrette over rice and vegetables; cover and set aside.

5. Heat remaining 1 teaspoon oil in 12-inch non-stick skillet over low heat for 5 minutes. Crack eggs into 2 small bowls (2 eggs per bowl) and season with salt and pepper. Increase heat to medium-high and heat until oil is shimmering. Working quickly, pour eggs into skillet, cover, and cook for 1 minute. Remove skillet from burner and let sit, covered, 15 to 45 seconds for runny yolks, 45 to 60 seconds for soft but set yolks, and about 2 minutes for medium-set yolks. Top each bowl with fried egg and serve immediately.

TEST KITCHEN TIP **Frying Eggs**

While skillet heats, crack eggs into 2 small bowls (2 eggs per bowl) and season with salt and pepper. Working quickly, position bowls on either side of skillet and add eggs simultaneously.

SMART SHOPPING **Za'atar**

This spice mixture is used frequently in the Middle East and the Mediterranean region to season meats and vegetables. It traditionally includes ground dried herbs such as thyme and oregano, spices such as cumin, and sumac, salt, and toasted sesame seeds.

Indonesian-Style Fried Rice

RICE   We prefer the delicate, perfumed flavor of jasmine rice in this recipe; however, long-grain white, basmati, or Texmati rice can be substituted with good results. For more information on jasmine rice, see page 28.

✓ WHY THIS RECIPE WORKS

Nasi Goreng is an Indonesian version of fried rice seasoned with chile paste and sweet soy sauce, and garnished with fried shallots, egg, and vegetables. Since sweet soy sauce is made using wheat, we needed a substitute. Simply switching out the soy sauce for gluten-free tamari left much to be desired in terms of flavor. But a mixture of molasses, dark brown sugar, tamari, and fish sauce was the perfect alternative. To get distinct grains of rice, this dish is traditionally made with day-old rice, but we were able to mimic this effect by rinsing the rice thoroughly, sautéing it with oil before cooking, and chilling the cooked rice in the fridge before finishing the dish. For the vegetables, we liked broccoli florets, steamed in the skillet until crisp-tender. Finally, we created a few garnishes by making a simple omelet and frying thinly sliced shallots until golden. If Thai chiles are unavailable, substitute two serranos or two medium jalapeños. To make this dish less spicy, use fewer chiles. Serve with wedges of cucumber, tomato, and lime.

Indonesian-Style Fried Rice

SERVES 6

RICE

2	tablespoons vegetable oil
2	cups jasmine rice, rinsed
2⅔	cups water

STIR-FRY

7	large shallots, peeled
5	green or red Thai chiles, stemmed
4	garlic cloves, peeled
3	tablespoons packed dark brown sugar
3	tablespoons molasses
3	tablespoons gluten-free tamari
3	tablespoons fish sauce
	Salt
4	large eggs
½	cup vegetable oil
1	pound broccoli florets, cut into 1-inch pieces
¼	cup water
4	scallions, sliced thin

1. FOR THE RICE: Cook oil and rice in large saucepan over medium heat until hot, 1 to 2 minutes. Stir in water and bring to boil. Reduce heat to low, cover, and simmer gently until rice is tender and water is absorbed, 16 to 18 minutes. Remove pot from heat, lay clean folded dish towel underneath lid, and let sit for 10 minutes. Spread cooked rice onto rimmed baking sheet and let cool for 10 minutes, then chill in refrigerator for 20 minutes.

2. FOR THE STIR-FRY: Chop 4 shallots coarse and add to food processor with chiles and garlic. Pulse mixture into coarse paste, about 15 pulses; transfer to bowl. In separate bowl, combine sugar, molasses, tamari, fish sauce, and 1¼ teaspoons salt. In third bowl, whisk eggs and ¼ teaspoon salt together.

3. Slice remaining 3 shallots thin and combine with oil in 12-inch nonstick skillet. Cook shallots over medium heat, stirring constantly, until golden and crisp, 6 to 10 minutes. Using slotted spoon, transfer shallots to paper towel–lined plate and season with salt. Pour off oil and reserve.

4. Wipe out now-empty skillet with paper towels, add 1 teaspoon reserved oil, and heat over medium heat until shimmering. Add half of eggs and tilt pan to coat bottom. Cover and cook until top is just set, about 1½ minutes. Slide omelet onto cutting board, roll up into tight log, and cut crosswise into 1-inch-wide segments; leave segments rolled. Repeat with 1 teaspoon reserved oil and remaining eggs.

5. Combine broccoli and water in now-empty skillet, cover, and cook over medium-high heat until broccoli is crisp-tender and water is absorbed, 4 to 6 minutes; transfer to small bowl. Remove rice from refrigerator and break up any large clumps.

6. Heat 3 tablespoons reserved oil in now-empty skillet over medium heat until just shimmering. Add chile mixture and cook until golden, 3 to 5 minutes. Stir in molasses mixture and bring to simmer. Fold in rice and broccoli and cook, stirring constantly, until heated through and evenly coated, about 3 minutes. Stir in scallions. Transfer to platter and garnish with omelet rolls and fried shallots. Serve.

Miso Brown Rice Cakes

G-F TESTING LAB

RICE	We prefer the fluffy texture of long-grain brown rice in this recipe; however, short- or medium-grain brown rice can be substituted with good results. For more information on brown rice, see page 28.
MISO	We prefer the rich, hearty flavor of red miso here; however, white miso can be substituted with good results. Do not substitute "light" miso. Also, note that not all types of miso are gluten-free; read the label.

✓ WHY THIS RECIPE WORKS

For these hearty rice cakes we paired long-grain brown rice with red miso and shiitake mushrooms for depth of flavor and meatiness. Although we usually cook brown rice in the oven to ensure fluffy grains, we wanted stickier rice for making the cakes. So we turned to the stovetop method, which ensured the rice released starches that helped bind the patties. Once the rice was cool, we pulsed it in a food processor to help break down the starches for even better binding. Then we mixed the rice with egg, toasted sesame oil, and the miso, plus scallions for some freshness, before forming the mixture into patties and chilling them briefly until firm. Just a few minutes in a hot skillet gave us crisp, browned rice patties. We like to serve these cakes with spicy Sriracha Mayonnaise.

Miso Brown Rice Cakes

SERVES 4

- 3 tablespoons vegetable oil
- 8 ounces shiitake mushrooms, stemmed and chopped
- 2 teaspoons grated fresh ginger
- 2 garlic cloves, minced
- 1½ cups long-grain brown rice
- 3¾ cups water
-     Salt and pepper
- 4 scallions, chopped fine
- 1 large egg plus 1 large yolk, lightly beaten
- 3 tablespoons gluten-free red miso
- 1½ teaspoons toasted sesame oil

1. Heat 1 tablespoon vegetable oil in large saucepan over medium heat until shimmering. Add mushrooms and cook until lightly browned, about 5 minutes. Stir in ginger and garlic and cook until fragrant, about 30 seconds. Add rice, water, and ½ teaspoon salt and bring to simmer. Reduce heat to low, cover, and cook, stirring occasionally, until rice is tender and liquid is absorbed, about 50 minutes. Spread rice mixture onto rimmed baking sheet and let cool for 15 minutes.

2. Pulse cooled rice mixture in food processor until coarsely ground, about 10 pulses; transfer to large bowl. Stir in scallions, egg and yolk, miso, sesame oil, ½ teaspoon salt, and ¼ teaspoon pepper until combined.

3. Line rimmed baking sheet with parchment paper and spray with vegetable oil spray. Using wet hands, divide rice mixture into 8 equal portions and pack firmly into 3½-inch-wide patties; lay on prepared sheet. Refrigerate patties, uncovered, until chilled and firm, about 30 minutes.

4. Adjust oven rack to middle position and heat oven to 200 degrees. Set wire rack in rimmed baking sheet. Heat 1 tablespoon vegetable oil in 12-inch nonstick skillet over medium-high heat until shimmering. Lay 4 rice cakes in skillet and cook until crisp and browned on both sides, about 4 minutes per side. Transfer cakes to prepared rack and keep warm in oven. Repeat with remaining 1 tablespoon vegetable oil and remaining cakes.

Sriracha Mayonnaise

MAKES ABOUT ¾ CUP

The mayonnaise can be refrigerated for up to 5 days.

- ½ cup mayonnaise
- 1 scallion, chopped fine
- 2 tablespoons Sriracha sauce
- 1 tablespoon lime juice

Combine all ingredients in bowl and serve.

SMART SHOPPING **Miso**

An essential ingredient in the Japanese kitchen, miso paste is made by fermenting soybeans and sometimes grains (such as rice, barley, or rye) with a mold called koji. Packed with savory flavor, miso is used to season everything from soups and braises to dressings and sauces. Although countless variations of the salty, deep-flavored ingredient are available, three common types are white shiro (despite its name, this miso is light golden in color), red aka, and brownish-black hatcho. Since not all types of miso are gluten-free, you must read the labels carefully.

Almost Hands-Free Risotto

G-F TESTING LAB

ARBORIO   Carnaroli rice can be substituted for the Arborio; the risotto will be softer and creamier. For more details on Arborio rice, see page 28.

Classic risotto can demand half an hour of stovetop tedium for the best creamy results. Our goal was 5 minutes of stirring, tops. First, we swapped out the saucepan for a Dutch oven, which has a thick, heavy bottom, deep sides, and a tight-fitting lid—perfect for trapping and distributing heat as evenly as possible. Typical recipes dictate adding the broth in small increments (and stirring constantly after each addition), but we added most of the broth at once and covered the pot, allowing the rice to simmer until almost all the broth had been absorbed (stirring just twice). Cooking the rice in a large amount of liquid actually agitated the grains, much like stirring. After adding the second and final addition of broth, we stirred the pot to ensure the bottom didn't cook more quickly than the top and then turned off the heat and let the rice finish cooking by residual heat. To finish, we simply stirred in butter, herbs, and a squeeze of lemon juice to brighten the flavors. This more hands-off method requires precise timing, so we strongly recommend using a timer.

Almost Hands-Free Risotto with Parmesan and Herbs
SERVES 6

   5 **cups chicken broth**
1½ **cups water**
   4 **tablespoons unsalted butter**
   1 **large onion, chopped fine**
      Salt and pepper
   1 **garlic clove, minced**
   2 **cups Arborio rice**
   1 **cup dry white wine**
   2 **ounces Parmesan cheese, grated (1 cup)**
   2 **tablespoons minced fresh parsley**
   2 **tablespoons minced fresh chives**
   1 **teaspoon lemon juice**

1. Bring broth and water to boil in large saucepan over high heat. Reduce heat to medium-low to maintain gentle simmer.

2. Melt 2 tablespoons butter in Dutch oven over medium heat. Add onion and ¾ teaspoon salt and cook, stirring frequently, until onion is softened, 4 to 5 minutes. Add garlic and cook until fragrant, about 30 seconds. Add rice and cook, stirring frequently, until grains are translucent around edges, about 3 minutes.

3. Add wine and cook, stirring constantly, until fully absorbed, 2 to 3 minutes. Stir 5 cups hot broth mixture into rice; reduce heat to medium-low, cover, and simmer until almost all liquid has been absorbed and rice is just al dente, 16 to 18 minutes, stirring twice during cooking.

4. Add ¾ cup hot broth mixture and stir constantly until risotto becomes creamy, about 3 minutes. Stir in Parmesan. Remove pot from heat, cover, and let stand for 5 minutes. Stir in remaining 2 tablespoons butter, herbs, and lemon juice. To loosen risotto, add up to ½ cup remaining broth mixture. Season with salt and pepper to taste and serve immediately.

Almost Hands-Free Risotto with Chicken and Herbs
SERVES 6

The thinner ends of the chicken breasts may be fully cooked by the time the broth is added to the rice, with the thicker ends finishing about 5 minutes later.

   5 **cups chicken broth**
   2 **cups water**
   1 **tablespoon extra-virgin olive oil**
   2 **(12-ounce) bone-in split chicken breasts, trimmed and cut in half crosswise**
   4 **tablespoons unsalted butter**
   1 **large onion, chopped fine**
      Salt and pepper
   1 **garlic clove, minced**
   2 **cups Arborio rice**
   1 **cup dry white wine**
   2 **ounces Parmesan cheese, grated (1 cup)**
   2 **tablespoons minced fresh parsley**
   2 **tablespoons minced fresh chives**
   1 **teaspoon lemon juice**

1. Bring broth and water to boil in large saucepan over high heat. Reduce heat to medium-low to maintain gentle simmer.

2. Heat oil in Dutch oven over medium heat until just starting to smoke. Add chicken, skin side down, and cook without moving until golden brown, 4 to 6 minutes. Flip chicken and cook second side until lightly browned, about 2 minutes. Transfer chicken to saucepan of simmering broth and cook until chicken registers 165 degrees, 10 to 15 minutes. Transfer to large plate.

3. Melt 2 tablespoons butter in now-empty Dutch oven over medium heat. Add onion and ¾ teaspoon salt and cook, stirring frequently, until onion is softened, 4 to 5 minutes. Add garlic and cook until fragrant, about 30 seconds. Add rice and cook, stirring frequently, until grains are translucent around edges, about 3 minutes.

4. Add wine and cook, stirring constantly, until fully absorbed, 2 to 3 minutes. Stir 5 cups hot broth mixture into rice; reduce heat to medium-low, cover, and simmer until almost all liquid has been absorbed and rice is just al dente, 16 to 18 minutes, stirring twice during cooking.

5. Add ¾ cup hot broth mixture to risotto and stir constantly until risotto becomes creamy, about 3 minutes. Stir in Parmesan. Remove pot from heat, cover, and let stand for 5 minutes.

6. Meanwhile, remove and discard skin and bones from chicken and shred meat into bite-size pieces. Gently stir shredded chicken, remaining 2 tablespoons butter, herbs, and lemon juice into risotto. To loosen risotto, add up to ½ cup remaining broth mixture. Season with salt and pepper to taste, and serve immediately.

SMART SHOPPING **Arborio Rice**

The stubby, milky grains of Arborio rice, once grown exclusively in Italy, are valued for their high starch content and the creaminess they bring to risotto. But does the best Arborio have to come from Italy? To find out, we cooked up batches of Parmesan risotto with two domestically grown brands of Arborio rice and four Italian imports. To our surprise, the winning rice, RiceSelect Arborio Rice, hails from Texas. Tasters were won over by its "creamy, smooth" grains with their "good bite."

TEST KITCHEN TIP **Easier Risotto**

We achieve the same creamy, evenly cooked risotto as that produced in traditional recipes—but with far less stirring—by adding more liquid at the outset and cooking the grains in a covered Dutch oven. A brief stir followed by a 5-minute rest provides additional insurance that the rice will be perfectly al dente.

1. After rice has absorbed wine, add portion of hot broth mixture.

2. Reduce heat to medium-low, cover pot with lid, and simmer until almost all liquid has been absorbed, stirring twice.

3. After adding more broth and stirring for 3 minutes, stir in Parmesan and let pot sit, off heat and covered, for 5 minutes.

Creamy Parmesan Polenta

✔ WHY THIS RECIPE WORKS

Polenta is a great option for a wintry, satisfying side that's also gluten-free; however, if you don't stir polenta almost constantly to ensure even cooking, it forms intractable lumps, and it can take up to an hour to cook. We wanted to get creamy, smooth polenta with rich corn flavor—but without the fussy process. From the outset, we knew that the right type of cornmeal was essential. Coarse-ground degerminated cornmeal gave us the soft but hearty texture and nutty flavor we were looking for. Taking a cue from dried bean recipes, which use baking soda to help break down the tough bean skins and accelerate cooking, we added a pinch of baking soda to our polenta. As we had hoped, the baking soda helped to soften the cornmeal's endosperm, which cut the cooking time. Baking soda also helped the granules break down and release their starch in a uniform way, so we could virtually eliminate the stirring time if we covered the pot and kept the heat on low. If the polenta bubbles or sputters even slightly after the first 10 minutes, the heat is too high and you may need a flame tamer (see page 131). Parmesan cheese and butter, stirred in at the last minute, ensured a satisfying, rich side dish. Instead of serving our polenta with a meaty ragu or grilled sausages (as is the custom in Italy), we opted to create a few hearty vegetable-based main course toppings, which can be prepared while the polenta cooks.

Creamy Parmesan Polenta

SERVES 4

7½ cups water
   Salt and pepper
   Pinch baking soda
1½ cups coarse-ground cornmeal (see page 26)
4 ounces Parmesan cheese, grated (2 cups), plus extra for serving
2 tablespoons unsalted butter

1. Bring water to boil in large saucepan over medium-high heat. Stir in 1½ teaspoons salt and baking soda. Slowly pour cornmeal into water in steady stream while stirring back and forth with wooden spoon or silicone spatula. Bring mixture to boil, stirring constantly, about 1 minute. Reduce heat to lowest possible setting and cover.

2. After 5 minutes, whisk polenta to smooth out any lumps that may have formed, about 15 seconds. (Make sure to scrape down sides and bottom of pan.) Cover and continue to cook, without stirring, until polenta grains are tender but slightly al dente, about 25 minutes longer. (Polenta should be loose and barely hold its shape; it will continue to thicken as it cools.)

3. Remove from heat, stir in Parmesan and butter, and season with pepper to taste. Let stand, covered, for 5 minutes. Serve, passing extra Parmesan separately.

Sautéed Cherry Tomato and Fresh Mozzarella Topping
MAKES ENOUGH FOR 4 SERVINGS

Don't stir the cheese into the sautéed tomatoes or it will melt prematurely and turn rubbery.

3 tablespoons extra-virgin olive oil
2 garlic cloves, peeled and sliced thin
   Pinch red pepper flakes
   Pinch sugar
1½ pounds cherry tomatoes, halved
   Salt and pepper
6 ounces fresh mozzarella cheese, cut into ½-inch cubes (1 cup)
2 tablespoons shredded fresh basil

Heat oil, garlic, pepper flakes, and sugar in 12-inch nonstick skillet over medium-high heat until fragrant and sizzling, about 1 minute. Stir in tomatoes and cook until just beginning to soften, about 1 minute. Season with salt and pepper to taste and remove from heat. Spoon tomato mixture over individual portions of polenta, top with mozzarella, sprinkle with basil, and serve.

G-F TESTING LAB

CORNMEAL   Coarse-ground degerminated cornmeal such as yellow grits (with grains the size of couscous) works best in this recipe. Avoid instant and quick-cooking products, as well as whole grain, stone-ground, and regular cornmeal. Not all brands of cornmeal are processed in a gluten-free facility; make sure to read the label. For more details on cornmeal, see page 26.

Broccoli Rabe, Sun-Dried Tomato, and Pine Nut Topping

MAKES ENOUGH FOR 4 SERVINGS

- ½ **cup oil-packed sun-dried tomatoes, chopped coarse**
- 3 **tablespoons extra-virgin olive oil**
- 6 **garlic cloves, minced**
- ½ **teaspoon red pepper flakes**
  Salt
- 1 **pound broccoli rabe, trimmed and cut into 1½-inch pieces**
- ¼ **cup chicken broth**
- 3 **tablespoons pine nuts, toasted**

Heat sun-dried tomatoes, oil, garlic, pepper flakes, and ½ teaspoon salt in 12-inch nonstick skillet over medium-high heat, stirring frequently, until garlic is fragrant and slightly toasted, about 1½ minutes. Add broccoli rabe and broth, cover, and cook until rabe turns bright green, about 2 minutes. Uncover and cook, stirring frequently, until most of broth has evaporated and rabe is just tender, 2 to 3 minutes. Season with salt to taste. Spoon broccoli rabe mixture over individual portions of polenta, sprinkle with pine nuts, and serve.

Wild Mushroom and Rosemary Topping

MAKES ENOUGH FOR 4 SERVINGS

If you use shiitake mushrooms, they should be stemmed. To make this topping vegetarian, replace the chicken broth with an equal amount of vegetable broth.

- 2 **tablespoons unsalted butter**
- 2 **tablespoons extra-virgin olive oil**
- 1 **small onion, chopped fine**
- 2 **garlic cloves, minced**
- 2 **teaspoons minced fresh rosemary**
- 1 **pound wild mushrooms (such as cremini, shiitake, or oyster), trimmed and sliced thin**
- ⅓ **cup chicken broth**
  Salt and pepper

1. Heat butter and oil in 12-inch nonstick skillet over medium-high heat until shimmering. Add onion and cook, stirring frequently, until onion softens and begins to brown, 5 to 7 minutes. Stir in garlic and rosemary and cook until fragrant, about 30 seconds.

2. Add mushrooms and cook, stirring occasionally, until juices release, about 6 minutes. Add broth and salt and pepper to taste; simmer briskly until sauce thickens, about 8 minutes. Spoon mushroom mixture over individual portions of polenta and serve.

TEST KITCHEN TIP **Making a Flame Tamer**

To ensure even cooking, it's important to cook polenta over very gentle heat. If your stove runs hot, use a flame tamer (a metal disk that fits on top of the burner and helps regulate heat output) to keep the polenta from simmering too briskly. If you don't have a flame tamer, you can easily make one.

Take long sheet of heavy-duty aluminum foil and shape it into 1-inch-thick ring that will fit on your burner. The ring should be of even thickness so that pot will rest flat on it.

TEST KITCHEN TIP **Making Polenta**

Slowly pour cornmeal into water in steady stream while stirring back and forth with wooden spoon or silicone spatula to prevent cornmeal from clumping.

Quinoa Pilaf

G-F TESTING LAB

QUINOA   We like the convenience of prewashed quinoa. If you buy unwashed quinoa (or if
you are unsure if it's washed), quinoa should be rinsed before cooking to remove
its bitter protective coating (called saponin) and dried on a towel; see page 31. We
developed this recipe using white quinoa. Red quinoa will work, but because its seed
coat is thicker, the grains have a crunchier texture. Black quinoa's seed coat is even
thicker than that of red quinoa; we don't recommend it for this recipe.

✓ WHY THIS RECIPE WORKS

Quinoa, often called a "supergrain" because of its great nutritional profile, has an appealingly firm bite and a nutty flavor, and it is easy to prepare, generally requiring 15 to 20 minutes of hands-off cooking. For a pilaf-style side dish, we toasted the quinoa prior to adding liquid; this ensured plump individual grains and also brought out its nutty flavor. Next, we considered the cooking liquid. Water was passable, but chicken broth better complemented the quinoa's flavor. After the quinoa had simmered, we pulled the pan off the heat and let it sit, covered, to allow the grains to steam. The result was evenly cooked, fluffy quinoa with just the right bite. We particularly like a combination of thyme and parsley in this recipe, but mint, tarragon, chives, or cilantro are also good choices.

Quinoa Pilaf with Herbs and Lemon
SERVES 4 TO 6

- 1½ cups prewashed quinoa
- 2 tablespoons unsalted butter, cut into 2 pieces
- 1 small onion, minced
- ¾ teaspoon salt
- 1¾ cups water
- 3 tablespoons chopped fresh herbs
- 1 tablespoon lemon juice

1. Toast quinoa in medium saucepan over medium-high heat, stirring frequently, until quinoa is very fragrant and makes continuous popping sound, 5 to 7 minutes. Transfer quinoa to bowl and set aside.

2. Return now-empty saucepan to medium-low heat and melt butter. Add onion and salt; cook, stirring frequently, until onion is softened and light golden, 5 to 7 minutes.

3. Increase heat to medium-high, stir in water and quinoa, and bring to simmer. Cover, reduce heat to low, and simmer until grains are just tender and liquid is absorbed, 18 to 20 minutes, stirring once halfway through cooking. Remove pot from heat and let sit, covered, for 10 minutes. Fluff quinoa with fork, stir in herbs and lemon juice, and serve.

VARIATIONS

Quinoa Pilaf with Chile, Queso Fresco, and Peanuts

Add 1 teaspoon chipotle powder and ¼ teaspoon ground cumin with onion. Substitute ½ cup crumbled queso fresco, 2 scallions, sliced thin, and ½ cup roasted unsalted peanuts, chopped coarse, for herbs. Substitute 4 teaspoons lime juice for lemon juice.

Quinoa Pilaf with Apricots, Pistachios, and Aged Gouda

Add ½ teaspoon ground coriander, ½ teaspoon grated lemon zest, ¼ teaspoon ground cumin, and ⅛ teaspoon black pepper with onion. Stir in ½ cup dried apricots, chopped coarse, before letting quinoa sit for 10 minutes in step 3. Substitute ½ cup shelled pistachios, chopped coarse, 2 ounces aged Gouda, shredded, and 2 tablespoons chopped fresh mint for herbs.

Quinoa Pilaf with Olives, Raisins, and Cilantro

Add ¼ teaspoon ground cumin, ¼ teaspoon dried oregano, and ⅛ teaspoon ground cinnamon with onion. Add ¼ cup golden raisins when stirring halfway through cooking in step 3. Substitute ⅓ cup pimento-stuffed green olives, chopped coarse, and 3 tablespoons minced fresh cilantro for herbs. Substitute 4 teaspoons red wine vinegar for lemon juice.

Quinoa Pilaf with Shiitakes, Edamame, and Ginger

Substitute 2 tablespoons vegetable oil for butter. Substitute whites of 4 scallions, minced, 4 ounces shiitake mushrooms, stemmed and sliced thin, and 2 teaspoons grated fresh ginger for onion. Stir in ½ cup cooked shelled edamame before letting quinoa sit for 10 minutes in step 3. Substitute 4 scallion greens, sliced thin, for herbs. Substitute 4 teaspoons rice vinegar and 1 tablespoon mirin for lemon juice.

Rainbow Quinoa Pilaf

QUINOA   We like the convenience of prewashed quinoa. If you buy unwashed quinoa (or if you are unsure whether it's washed), give it a rinse under cold water to remove its bitter protective coating (called saponin) and spread the seeds out over a dish towel to dry before cooking. We developed this recipe using rainbow quinoa, which is also sometimes labeled tricolor quinoa. You can substitute white or red quinoa for the tricolor quinoa without changing the cooking time; do not substitute black quinoa. For more information on quinoa, see page 27.

✓ WHY THIS RECIPE WORKS

Quinoa, with its great nutritional profile, appealing texture and flavor, and ease of preparation, makes a hearty pilaf-style dish that lends itself to countless variations. We wanted to create a substantial side-dish pilaf based on tricolor, or rainbow, quinoa. Brightly colored carrots and rainbow chard echoed the vibrant colors found in the quinoa and stood up to its bold flavor. After toasting the quinoa, we simmered it with the carrots and chard stems and then pulled the pan off the heat and let it sit. This resting time gave us the opportunity to gently cook our chard leaves by spreading them out over the quinoa before covering the pan and allowing the grains' heat to soften the leaves. While the chard leaves wilted, the quinoa became perfectly fluffy. We then stirred in fresh citrus juice for a bright punch of acidity.

Rainbow Quinoa Pilaf with Swiss Chard and Carrots

SERVES 4 TO 6

1½	cups prewashed rainbow quinoa
10	ounces rainbow Swiss chard, stems sliced thin, leaves cut into 1-inch pieces
2	carrots, peeled and cut into ¼-inch pieces
1	shallot, minced
2	tablespoons vegetable oil
	Salt and pepper
1	garlic clove, minced
1	teaspoon minced fresh thyme or ¼ teaspoon dried
1¾	cups water
4	teaspoons lemon juice

1. Toast quinoa in large saucepan over medium-high heat, stirring often, until fragrant and makes continuous popping sounds, 5 to 7 minutes; transfer to bowl.

2. Add chard stems, carrots, shallot, oil, and ¾ teaspoon salt to now-empty pot and cook over medium-low heat until vegetables are softened, 5 to 7 minutes. Stir in garlic and thyme and cook until fragrant, about 30 seconds.

3. Stir in water and toasted quinoa, increase heat to medium-high, and bring to simmer. Reduce heat to low, cover, and simmer gently until grains are just tender and liquid is absorbed, 18 to 20 minutes, stirring once halfway through cooking.

4. Off heat, place chard leaves over top, cover, and let sit until chard is wilted, about 10 minutes. Add lemon juice, season with salt and pepper to taste, and fluff gently with fork to combine. Serve.

VARIATION

Rainbow Quinoa Pilaf with Red Bell Pepper, Lime, and Cilantro

Omit chard. Substitute 1 red bell pepper, cut into ½-inch pieces, for carrots; add to pot with shallot and cook until softened, 3 to 5 minutes. Let pilaf rest off heat as directed in step 4. Substitute 1 tablespoon lime juice for lemon juice. Stir in 3 tablespoons chopped fresh cilantro before serving.

TEST KITCHEN TIP **Preparing Swiss Chard**

1. Cut away leafy portion from stem using chef's knife, and slice stems thin.

2. Stack several leaves, slice crosswise, then cut into 1-inch pieces.

Quinoa Salad with Bell Pepper and Cilantro

G-F TESTING LAB

QUINOA   We like the convenience of prewashed quinoa. If you buy unwashed quinoa (or if you are unsure if it's washed), quinoa should be rinsed before cooking to remove its bitter protective coating (called saponin) and dried on a towel; see page 31. We used white quinoa to develop this recipe. Red quinoa will work, but because its seed coat is thicker, the grains have a crunchier texture. Black quinoa's seed coat is even thicker than that of red quinoa; we don't recommend it for this recipe.

WHY THIS RECIPE WORKS

Easy to prepare in advance and quick to assemble, quinoa salad makes a great fresh-tasting weekday lunch or picnic food. But too often the grains are either overcooked or unevenly cooked, and the resulting salad is clumpy or gritty. Toasting the quinoa in a dry pot helped to deepen its flavor. The liquid then went into the pot and the quinoa was covered and simmered gently until it was nearly tender, then spread over a rimmed baking sheet to cool. This ensured the grains (quinoa is actually a seed, but it is treated as a grain) didn't overcook and stayed fluffy and separate. Inspired by quinoa's Peruvian roots, we decided to give our salad a Latin flavor profile. Red bell pepper, jalapeño, and cilantro provided fresh flavors as well as color, sweetness, and some heat, and adding lime juice and cumin to the dressing brought it all together. After the 12-minute simmer in step 1, there will still be a little bit of water in the pan; it will be absorbed as the quinoa cools. To make this dish spicier, add the chile seeds.

Quinoa Salad with Red Bell Pepper and Cilantro

SERVES 4

- 1 cup prewashed quinoa
- 1½ cups water
  Salt and pepper
- ½ red bell pepper, stemmed, seeded, and chopped fine
- ½ jalapeño chile, stemmed, seeded, and minced
- 2 tablespoons finely chopped red onion
- 1 tablespoon minced fresh cilantro
- 2 tablespoons lime juice
- 1 tablespoon extra-virgin olive oil
- 2 teaspoons Dijon mustard
- 1 garlic clove, minced
- ½ teaspoon ground cumin

1. Toast quinoa in medium saucepan over medium-high heat, stirring frequently, until quinoa is lightly toasted and aromatic, about 5 minutes. Stir in water and ¼ teaspoon salt and bring to simmer. Reduce heat to low, cover, and continue to simmer until quinoa has absorbed most of water and is nearly tender, about 12 minutes. Spread quinoa out over rimmed baking sheet and set aside until tender and cool, about 20 minutes.

2. When quinoa is cool, transfer to large bowl. Stir in bell pepper, jalapeño, onion, and cilantro. In separate bowl, whisk lime juice, oil, mustard, garlic, and cumin together, then pour over quinoa mixture and toss to coat. Season with salt and pepper to taste, and serve. (Quinoa salad can be refrigerated for up 1 day.)

SMART SHOPPING
The Many Colors of Quinoa

In just the past few years, quinoa has moved beyond the shelves of natural food stores and can be found at most supermarkets. And while at one time you typically saw only white (or golden) quinoa, you'll notice that red and black (or a mixture of the three) are also increasingly available. White quinoa has the largest seeds of the three varieties. It has a nutty, vegetal flavor with a hint of bitternesss; white quinoa is also the softest of the three types. Medium-size red quinoa offers a heartier crunch and more prominent nuttiness. (Some of our tasters called it the "brown rice" of the quinoa world.) Black quinoa is the smallest of the three and has the thickest seed coat. As a result, black quinoa retains its shape during cooking and is very crunchy. Our tasters found the texture a bit sandy, although they liked the mild flavor that has hints of molasses. Red and white quinoa can be used interchangeably in pilaf and salad recipes. However, for our quinoa patties (see page 141), use white quinoa since only the softer white grains hold together enough to make a cohesive patty. We think black quinoa is best used in recipes tailored for its distinctive texture and flavor.

Quinoa, Black Bean, and Mango Salad

QUINOA   We like the convenience of prewashed quinoa. If you buy unwashed quinoa (or if you are unsure whether it's washed), give it a rinse under cold water to remove its bitter protective coating (called saponin) and spread the grain out over a dish towel to dry before cooking. You can substitute red quinoa for the white quinoa without changing the cooking time; do not use black quinoa. For more information on quinoa, see page 27.

✅ WHY THIS RECIPE WORKS

We wanted to feature the delicate texture and nutty flavor of quinoa in a fresh-tasting salad hearty enough for a main course. We started by toasting the quinoa to bring out its flavor before adding liquid to the pan and simmering the seeds until nearly tender. We then spread the quinoa over a rimmed baking sheet so that the residual heat would finish cooking it gently as it cooled, giving us perfectly cooked, fluffy grains. Black beans, mango, and bell pepper lent the salad heartiness, bright flavor, and color. A simple but intense dressing with lime juice, jalapeño, cumin, and cilantro gave this dish the acidity needed to keep its flavors fresh. We also added scallions and avocado for bite and creaminess.

Quinoa, Black Bean, and Mango Salad with Lime Dressing

SERVES 4 TO 6

- 1½ cups prewashed white quinoa
- 2¼ cups water
- Salt and pepper
- 5 tablespoons lime juice (3 limes)
- ½ jalapeño chile, stemmed, seeded, and chopped
- ¾ teaspoon ground cumin
- ½ cup extra-virgin olive oil
- ⅓ cup fresh cilantro leaves
- 1 red bell pepper, stemmed, seeded, and chopped
- 1 mango, peeled, pitted, and cut into ¼-inch pieces
- 1 (15-ounce) can black beans, rinsed
- 2 scallions, sliced thin
- 1 avocado, halved, pitted, and sliced thin

1. Toast quinoa in large saucepan over medium-high heat, stirring often, until fragrant and makes continuous popping sounds, 5 to 7 minutes. Stir in water and ½ teaspoon salt and bring to simmer. Reduce heat to low, cover, and simmer gently until most of water has been absorbed and quinoa is nearly tender, about 15 minutes. Spread quinoa onto rimmed baking sheet, let cool for 20 minutes, then transfer to large bowl.

2. Process lime juice, jalapeño, cumin, and 1 teaspoon salt in blender until jalapeño is finely chopped, about 15 seconds. With blender running, add oil and cilantro and process until smooth and emulsified, about 20 seconds.

3. Add lime-jalapeño dressing, bell pepper, mango, beans, and scallions to cooled quinoa and toss to combine. Season with salt and pepper to taste. Serve, topping individual portions with avocado.

TEST KITCHEN TIP **Cutting Up a Mango**

1. After trimming both ends of mango, stand mango on end and cut off remaining skin in thin strips from top to bottom.

2. Cut down along each side of flat pit to remove flesh.

3. Trim any remaining flesh off sides of pit. Once removed from pit, flesh can be cut into pieces as desired.

Quinoa Patties

G-F TESTING LAB

QUINOA   We like the convenience of prewashed quinoa. If you buy unwashed quinoa (or if you are unsure if it's washed), quinoa should be rinsed before cooking to remove its bitter protective coating (called saponin) and dried on a towel; see page 31. White quinoa was used to develop this recipe. Do not substitute red or black quinoa; the patties will not hold together.

We set out to develop a recipe for quinoa patties with bright, fresh flavors and enough add-ins to make them hearty and satisfying. While we liked the earthy flavor of red quinoa, no matter how long we cooked it, it simply didn't soften enough to form cohesive patties. Classic white (or golden) quinoa performed much better, and upping the amount of cooking liquid delivered even more cohesive patties since the quinoa cooked up extra moist. We skipped the usual toasting step, which encourages the individual grains to separate rather than stick together. As for the binders, we tried mashed beans and potatoes, a variety of cheeses, bread, and processing some of the quinoa itself—but only the duo of a whole egg plus one yolk and cheese were successful. Chilling the formed patties for 30 minutes further ensured that they stayed together. Baking was an appealing hands-off cooking method, but the heat of the oven dried them out. It was much easier on the stovetop to create a crust on the exterior while maintaining a moist interior. Because the patties needed at least 8 minutes on each side to set up and cook through, cooking them over medium heat prevented burning but still resulted in a nice crust.

Quinoa Patties with Spinach and Sun-Dried Tomatoes

SERVES 4

- ½ cup oil-packed sun-dried tomatoes, chopped coarse, plus 1 tablespoon oil
- 4 scallions, chopped fine
- 4 garlic cloves, minced
- 2 cups water
- 1 cup prewashed white quinoa
- 1 teaspoon salt
- 1 large egg plus 1 large yolk, lightly beaten
- 2 ounces baby spinach, chopped (2 cups)
- 2 ounces Monterey Jack cheese, shredded (½ cup)
- ½ teaspoon grated lemon zest plus 2 teaspoons juice
- 2 tablespoons extra-virgin olive oil

1. Line rimmed baking sheet with parchment paper. Heat tomato oil in large saucepan over medium heat until shimmering. Add scallions and cook until softened, 3 to 5 minutes. Stir in garlic and cook until fragrant, about 30 seconds. Stir in water, quinoa, and salt and bring to simmer. Reduce heat to medium-low, cover, and continue to simmer until quinoa is tender, 18 to 20 minutes. Remove pot from heat and let sit, covered, until liquid is fully absorbed, about 10 minutes. Transfer to large bowl and let cool for 15 minutes.

2. Add sun-dried tomatoes, egg, egg yolk, spinach, Monterey Jack, lemon zest, and lemon juice to cooled quinoa and mix until uniform. Divide mixture into 8 equal portions (about ½ cup each), pack firmly into ½-inch-thick patties (about 3½ inches wide), and place on prepared sheet. Refrigerate, uncovered, until patties are chilled and firm, about 30 minutes.

3. Heat 1 tablespoon olive oil in 12-inch non-stick skillet over medium heat until shimmering. Carefully lay 4 patties in skillet and cook until well browned on first side, 8 to 10 minutes. Gently flip patties and continue to cook until golden on second side, 8 to 10 minutes.

4. Transfer patties to plate and tent loosely with aluminum foil. Return now-empty skillet to medium heat and repeat with remaining 1 tablespoon olive oil and remaining 4 patties. Serve.

TEST KITCHEN TIP **Cooking Quinoa Patties**

To keep patties from falling apart, wait until they are well browned before attempting to flip them.

Carefully lay 4 chilled patties in hot skillet. Cook until set up and well browned on first side, 8 to 10 minutes. Gently flip patties. Cook until golden on second side, 8 to 10 minutes.

Kasha Pilaf with Caramelized Onions

✓ **WHY THIS RECIPE WORKS**

Kasha (buckwheat groats that have been roasted) has a deep, earthy flavor and a tender bite that make it a great fall or winter side dish for pairing with chicken or beef roasts. But we quickly learned that these kernels cook to an unappealing mush when simply simmered in liquid. Some research revealed that kasha kernels are often cooked with a beaten egg or egg white before the liquid is added to keep the kernels separate and firm. We wondered if vinegar, which we often add to the pot with dried lentils and beans to keep them from blowing out, would do the same thing (and keep things simpler). We gave it a shot; it made a big step in the right direction. But white vinegar's flavor was far too strong here. A couple tablespoons of milder, bright lemon juice worked perfectly. However, some grains were still breaking down too much, so we evaluated the cooking method next. Up to this point, we were bringing the kasha and liquid to a boil together, then reducing the heat and simmering until the kasha was cooked through—just as we do when we prepare a pilaf. In the end, waiting to add the kasha until the liquid was already at a boil solved the issue with blowouts. To balance the kasha's strong grassy flavor, we added plenty of sweet caramelized onions (which we cooked in the pan before preparing the kasha), along with garlic, parsley, and pine nuts. Use a gentle hand when stirring in the add-ins at the end, as the kasha will become pasty if mixed too vigorously.

Kasha Pilaf with Caramelized Onions

SERVES 4 TO 6

3	tablespoons extra-virgin olive oil
2	onions, chopped
	Salt and pepper
3	garlic cloves, minced
3	cups water
1½	cups kasha, rinsed (see page 26)
2	tablespoons lemon juice
¼	cup pine nuts, toasted
2	tablespoons minced fresh parsley

1. Heat 1 tablespoon oil in large saucepan over medium heat until shimmering. Add onions and ¼ teaspoon salt and cook, stirring occasionally, until browned, 10 to 15 minutes. Add garlic and cook until fragrant, about 30 seconds. Stir in ¼ cup water, scraping up any browned bits; transfer onion mixture to bowl.

2. Add remaining 2¾ cups water to now-empty pan and bring to boil. Stir in kasha, lemon juice, and 1 teaspoon salt and return to simmer. Reduce heat to low, cover, and simmer until liquid is absorbed, about 10 minutes. Remove pot from heat and lay clean folded dish towel underneath lid. Let sit for 10 minutes.

3. Fluff kasha with fork and gently stir in onion mixture, pine nuts, parsley, and remaining 2 tablespoons oil until just combined. Season with salt and pepper to taste. Serve.

SMART SHOPPING **Kasha**

Buckwheat, despite its name, is not related to wheat. It is actually an herb. In addition to being ground to make buckwheat flour, the kernels of its triangular seeds can be hulled and crushed to make groats (see pages 22 and 26 for more on flour and groats). Kasha is buckwheat groats that have been roasted to bring out their flavor and aroma. Kasha is often used in blintzes, knishes, and varnitchkes, or to make pilaf and hot cereal. Because kasha, unlike groats, has a fairly bold flavor and a distinctly earthy smell, we find that it pairs best with fall- and winter-inspired dishes like roasted meats. Buckwheat products can be found in natural food stores and well-stocked supermarkets.

Creamy Cheesy Millet

✓ WHY THIS RECIPE WORKS

After turning millet into a satisfying breakfast porridge (see our recipe on page 99), we realized it wasn't a far leap to use these tiny seeds to prepare a rustic, savory side dish similar to a creamy polenta. However, it wasn't just a matter of making some savory ingredient additions to a stripped-down version of the porridge. The porridge had a texture that was slightly set up, like oatmeal, and we wanted looser results for this dish. While we'd cooked our porridge in 3 cups of water and then simply stirred in 1 cup of milk at the end for some richness, we found the millet broke down only so much, even with additional cooking. To get looser results, we had to start the millet in 5 cups of liquid (we settled on 4 cups of water and 1 cup of milk). This made all the difference. We slightly overcooked the millet, just as we had done for our porridge, so that the seeds burst and released their starch, creating the right creamy consistency. Since millet is very mild, we stirred in a good amount of Parmesan and basil to ensure this dish had plenty of flavor.

Creamy Cheesy Millet

SERVES 4 TO 6

- 1 tablespoon extra-virgin olive oil
- 1 shallot, minced
- 2 garlic cloves, minced
- 1 cup millet, rinsed and dried on a towel (see page 31)
- 4 cups water
- 1 cup whole milk
  Salt and pepper
- 2 ounces Parmesan cheese, grated (1 cup)
- 2 tablespoons shredded fresh basil

1. Heat oil in large saucepan over medium heat until shimmering. Stir in shallot and cook until softened, about 2 minutes. Add garlic and cook until fragrant, about 30 seconds. Stir in millet and cook, stirring often, until fragrant and lightly browned, about 2 minutes.

2. Stir in water, milk, and 1 teaspoon salt and bring to boil. Reduce heat to low, cover, and simmer, stirring occasionally, until thick and porridgy, about 20 minutes. Uncover and continue to cook, stirring frequently, until millet is mostly broken down, 8 to 10 minutes.

3. Off heat, stir in Parmesan until melted. Sprinkle with basil and season with salt and pepper to taste. Serve.

SMART SHOPPING Millet

Believed to be the first domesticated cereal grain, this tiny cereal grass seed has a long history and is still a staple in a large part of the world, particularly Asia and Africa. The seeds can be ground into flour or used whole. Millet has a mellow corn flavor that makes it work well in both savory and sweet applications, including flatbreads, puddings, and pan-fried cakes. It can be cooked pilaf-style or turned into a creamy breakfast porridge or polenta-like dish (as in the recipe on this page) by slightly overcooking the seeds, which causes the seeds to burst and release starch.

Curried Millet Pilaf

G-F TESTING LAB

MILLET   See page 26 for more details on millet.

WHY THIS RECIPE WORKS

Once we had two creamier millet dishes in our arsenal (see Millet Porridge with Maple Syrup, page 99, and Creamy Cheesy Millet, page 143), we set out to feature the tiny seeds in a pilaf-style dish. Toasting the millet before simmering the seeds in water gave them some nutty depth, and after some testing, we landed on a 2:1 ratio of liquid to millet, which ensured evenly cooked, fluffy seeds. Since millet is a staple in Middle Eastern and Indian cuisines, we turned to that part of the world to inspire the flavor profile of our pilaf, adding basil, mint, raisins, almonds, and curry powder. To finish, we served it with a dollop of yogurt for richness and an appealing cooling counterpoint to the heat of the curry. We prefer whole-milk yogurt in this recipe but low-fat yogurt can be substituted if desired. We have found that millet, unlike other grains, can become gluey if allowed to steam off heat. Once all the liquid has been absorbed, use a gentle hand to stir in the basil, raisins, almonds, and scallion greens, and then immediately serve this pilaf.

Curried Millet Pilaf

SERVES 4 TO 6

1	tablespoon extra-virgin olive oil
3	scallions, white and green parts separated, sliced thin
1	teaspoon curry powder
1½	cups millet, rinsed and dried on a towel (see page 31)
3	cups water
	Salt and pepper
½	cup chopped fresh basil and/or mint
¼	cup raisins
¼	cup sliced almonds, toasted
½	cup plain yogurt

1. Heat oil in large saucepan over medium heat until shimmering. Add scallion whites and curry and cook until fragrant, about 1 minute. Stir in millet and cook, stirring often, until lightly browned, about 2 minutes.

2. Stir in water and ¾ teaspoon salt and bring to boil. Reduce heat to low, cover, and simmer until liquid is absorbed, 15 to 20 minutes.

3. Off heat, using fork, gently stir in basil, raisins, almonds, and scallion greens until just combined. Season with salt and pepper to taste. Serve, dolloping individual portions with yogurt.

SMART SHOPPING **Curry Powder**

Though blends can vary dramatically, sweet curry powder (also known as mild) combines as many as 20 different ground spices, herbs, and seeds, the staples being turmeric, coriander, cumin, black and red pepper, cinnamon, cloves, fennel seeds, cardamom, ginger, and fenugreek. Neither too sweet nor too hot, our winning blend is Penzeys Sweet Curry Powder, which sets the standard for a balanced yet complex curry powder.

Millet Salad with Corn and Queso Fresco

MILLET For more information on millet, see page 26.

The mellow corn flavor and fine texture of tiny millet seeds make them extremely versatile in savory applications. We set out to feature the small seeds in a grain-style salad that would enhance the sweet flavor of the millet. The seeds release starch as they cook, which can create large clumps. We found that using 3 quarts of boiling water to quickly cook the millet resulted in distinctive individual pieces of the cooked seeds. Spreading out the millet in a single layer on a baking sheet allowed it to cool and prevented any further clumping. With our cooking method nailed down, we set out to build the flavors of our salad. We stirred in corn to complement the millet's natural flavor and to add texture, while the addition of cherry tomatoes, queso fresco, and a minced jalapeño gave the salad a Southwestern flavor profile that paired well with the corn. We whipped up a quick vinaigrette using lime zest and juice to dress our salad and add brightness. A small amount of mayonnaise helped to emulsify the dressing and more evenly coat the millet. Chopped fresh cilantro added a bit of freshness and color in the finished salad. For more spice, reserve, mince, and add the ribs and seeds from the jalapeño.

Millet Salad with Corn and Queso Fresco

SERVES 4 TO 6

- 1 **cup millet**
  Salt and pepper
- 1 **teaspoon grated lime zest plus**
  2½ tablespoons juice (2 limes)
- 2 **teaspoons honey**
- ½ **teaspoon mayonnaise**
- 3 **tablespoons extra-virgin olive oil**
- 8 **ounces cherry tomatoes, quartered**
- ½ **cup frozen corn, thawed**
- 1½ **ounces queso fresco, crumbled (⅓ cup)**
- ¼ **cup chopped fresh cilantro**
- 1 **jalapeño chile, stemmed, seeded,**
  and minced

1. Bring 3 quarts water to boil in large pot. Add millet and 1 teaspoon salt and cook until grains are tender, about 20 minutes. Drain millet, spread onto rimmed baking sheet, drizzle with ½ tablespoon lime juice, and let cool for 15 minutes.

2. Whisk lime zest and remaining 2 tablespoons juice, honey, mayonnaise, and ¼ teaspoon salt together in large bowl. Whisking constantly, drizzle in oil. Add cooled millet and toss to combine. Fold in cherry tomatoes, corn, queso fresco, cilantro, and jalapeño. Season with salt and pepper to taste, and serve.

VARIATIONS
Millet Salad with Oranges, Olives, and Almonds

Omit tomatoes, corn, queso fresco, cilantro, and jalapeño. Substitute orange zest for lime zest, and sherry vinegar for lime juice. Fold in 2 oranges, peeled and cut into ½-inch pieces, ⅓ cup chopped pitted green olives, ⅓ cup toasted sliced almonds, and 2 tablespoons chopped fresh oregano before serving.

Millet Salad with Endive, Blueberries, and Goat Cheese

Omit tomatoes, corn, queso fresco, cilantro, and jalapeño. Omit lime zest and substitute champagne vinegar for lime juice. Fold in 2 heads thinly sliced Belgian endive, 1½ cups blueberries, ¾ cup chopped toasted pecans, and 1 cup crumbled goat cheese before serving.

Millet Cakes with Spinach and Carrots

G-F TESTING LAB

MILLET   For more information on millet, see page 26.

WHY THIS RECIPE WORKS

Millet makes a perfect base for pan-fried cakes because the seeds burst as they cook, releasing starch and becoming sticky. We liked the combination of millet and curry, and adding spinach and carrots along with shallot and garlic created a highly flavorful but nicely balanced mixture. Though millet holds together well on its own, we found that the addition of an egg and plain yogurt was helpful in keeping the cakes together during cooking. Chilling the formed cakes further ensured that they were sturdy and easy to handle. As for the cooking method, baking dried out the cakes, so we pan-fried them, which created a flavorful crust on the exterior while maintaining a moist interior. Be sure to let the uncooked cakes chill for 30 minutes or they will break apart during cooking. Serve with yogurt sauce.

Millet Cakes with Spinach and Carrots
SERVES 4

- 1 cup millet, rinsed
- 2 cups water
  Salt and pepper
- 3 tablespoons vegetable oil
- 1 shallot, minced
- 6 ounces (6 cups) baby spinach, chopped
- 2 carrots, peeled and shredded
- 2 garlic cloves, minced
- 2 teaspoons curry powder
- ¼ cup plain whole-milk yogurt
- 1 large egg, lightly beaten
- 2 tablespoons minced fresh cilantro

1. Combine millet, water, and ½ teaspoon salt in large saucepan and bring to simmer over medium heat. Reduce heat to low, cover, and simmer gently until grains are tender and liquid is absorbed, 15 to 20 minutes. Remove pot from heat and let millet sit, covered, for 10 minutes; transfer to large bowl.

2. Heat 1 tablespoon oil in 12-inch nonstick skillet over medium heat until shimmering. Add shallot and cook until softened, about 3 minutes. Stir in spinach and carrots and cook until spinach is wilted, about 2 minutes. Stir in garlic, curry powder, ½ teaspoon salt, and ¼ teaspoon pepper and cook until fragrant, about 30 seconds. Transfer to bowl with millet. Wipe out now-empty skillet with paper towels.

3. Stir yogurt, egg, and cilantro into millet mixture until well combined. Using wet hands, divide mixture into 8 equal portions, pack firmly into 3½-inch-wide patties, and place on parchment paper–lined baking sheet. Refrigerate patties, uncovered, until chilled and firm, for at least 30 minutes or up to 2 hours.

4. Adjust oven rack to middle position and heat oven to 200 degrees. Set wire rack in rimmed baking sheet. Heat 1 tablespoon oil in now-empty skillet over medium heat until shimmering. Lay 4 cakes in skillet and cook until crisp and browned on both sides, 5 to 7 minutes per side. Transfer cakes to prepared rack and keep warm in oven. Repeat with remaining 1 tablespoon oil and remaining cakes. Serve.

VARIATION

Dairy-Free Millet Cakes with Spinach and Carrots
Substitute plain soy milk yogurt or coconut milk yogurt for whole-milk yogurt.

Cucumber-Yogurt Sauce
MAKES ABOUT 2½ CUPS

Cilantro, mint, parsley, or tarragon can be substituted for the dill if desired. To make this sauce dairy-free, substitute soy milk yogurt or coconut milk yogurt.

- 1 cup plain whole-milk yogurt
- 2 tablespoons extra-virgin olive oil
- 2 tablespoons minced fresh dill
- 1 garlic clove, minced
- 1 cucumber, peeled, halved lengthwise, seeded, and shredded
  Salt and pepper

Whisk yogurt, oil, dill, and garlic together in medium bowl. Stir in cucumber and season with salt and pepper to taste. Serve. (Sauce can be refrigerated for up to 2 days.)

Buckwheat Tabbouleh

G-F TESTING LAB

BUCKWHEAT   Mild-tasting buckwheat groats work better in this recipe than kasha (roasted buckwheat groats). See page 26 for more information on kasha.

✔ WHY THIS RECIPE WORKS

Featuring parsley, bulgur (a product of the wheat berry), mint, and chopped tomatoes tossed in a bright lemon vinaigrette, classic Mediterranean tabbouleh has a refreshing flavor profile that makes it a great light side. All we had to do was find a gluten-free substitute with a clean flavor to use in lieu of the bulgur. In the end, we landed on buckwheat groats. Millet, though similar in appearance to bulgur, was too starchy and clumpy. Kasha, which is roasted buckwheat groats, added a deep earthiness that overwhelmed the delicate flavor profile of tabbouleh. The buckwheat groats (the same kernels as kasha but raw rather than roasted) lent a mild, appealing earthiness to our salad that didn't dominate. As for the cooking method, the pilaf approach seemed like the best option at first, but it produced groats that were too starchy and gummy. Boiling the kernels in plenty of water was a much better solution. Some of the starch washed away in the cooking water, giving us separate, evenly cooked kernels. For the herbs, we wanted plenty of fresh, peppery parsley; 1½ cups made just enough of a presence and balanced well with ½ cup of fresh mint. To ensure undiluted, bright flavor in the final tabbouleh, we salted the tomatoes to rid them of excess moisture before tossing them into the salad.

Buckwheat Tabbouleh
SERVES 4

- ¾ cup buckwheat groats, rinsed (see page 31)
  Salt and pepper
- 3 tomatoes, cored and cut into ½-inch pieces
- 2 tablespoons lemon juice
  Pinch cayenne pepper
- ¼ cup extra-virgin olive oil
- 1½ cups minced fresh parsley
- ½ cup minced fresh mint
- 2 scallions, sliced thin

1. Bring 2 quarts water to boil in large saucepan. Stir in buckwheat and 1 teaspoon salt. Return to boil, then reduce to simmer and cook until tender, 10 to 12 minutes. Drain buckwheat, transfer to bowl, and let cool 15 minutes.

2. Meanwhile, toss tomatoes and ¼ teaspoon salt in bowl. Transfer to fine-mesh strainer, set strainer in bowl, and let stand for 30 minutes, tossing occasionally.

3. Whisk lemon juice, cayenne, and ¼ teaspoon salt together in large bowl. Whisking constantly, drizzle in oil.

4. Add drained tomatoes, cooled buckwheat, parsley, mint, and scallions; toss gently to combine. Cover and let sit at room temperature until flavors blend, about 30 minutes or up to 2 hours. Toss to recombine and season with salt and pepper to taste. Serve.

SMART SHOPPING **Buckwheat**

Despite its name, buckwheat is not related to wheat. It is actually an herb. In addition to being ground to make buckwheat flour, the kernels of its triangular seeds can be hulled and crushed to make groats. These groats have a relatively mild, grassy flavor, making them a good side dish to a variety of entrées. Buckwheat groats cook relatively quickly, making them a good option for weeknight meals. Buckwheat products can be found in natural food stores and well-stocked supermarkets.

Buckwheat Bowls with Lemon-Yogurt Sauce

G-F TESTING LAB

BUCKWHEAT GROATS	Do not substitute kasha (roasted buckwheat groats) for the buckwheat groats in this recipe. For more information on buckwheat groats, see page 26.

✓ WHY THIS RECIPE WORKS

For a whole-grain take on rice bowls, we swapped out the rice for whole buckwheat groats and paired the grain with snow peas, ripe avocado, and toasted, spiced sunflower seeds. We first tried kasha, the roasted form of buckwheat groats, but its deep earthiness overwhelmed the delicate flavor profile of the finished dish. Turning to raw buckwheat groats lent a mild, appealing earthiness to our grain bowl that didn't dominate the other ingredients. To keep the cooking method easy, we simply boiled the buckwheat in a large pot of water until it was tender, then tossed it with a bright lemon-mint dressing. While the buckwheat cooked, we sautéed the snow peas with some coriander and toasted the sunflower seeds with lots of warm spices. Lastly, we made a quick lemony yogurt sauce to drizzle over the top.

Buckwheat Bowls with Lemon-Yogurt Sauce

SERVES 4

YOGURT SAUCE

- ½ cup plain whole-milk yogurt
- 1 tablespoon minced fresh mint
- ½ teaspoon grated lemon zest plus 1 tablespoon juice
- ¼ teaspoon salt
- ⅛ teaspoon pepper

BUCKWHEAT AND VEGETABLES

- 1½ cups buckwheat groats
  Salt and pepper
- ¼ cup extra-virgin olive oil
- ¾ teaspoon ground coriander
- 8 ounces snow peas, strings removed and halved
- ¼ cup raw sunflower seeds
- ⅛ teaspoon ground cumin
- 1 teaspoon grated lemon zest plus 2 tablespoons juice
- 1 tablespoon minced fresh mint
- ½ teaspoon Dijon mustard
- 1 avocado, halved, pitted, and cut into ½-inch pieces

1. FOR THE YOGURT SAUCE: Whisk all ingredients together in bowl, cover, and refrigerate until needed.

2. FOR THE BUCKWHEAT AND VEGETABLES: Bring 2 quarts water to boil in large pot. Add buckwheat and 1 teaspoon salt and cook until tender, 10 to 12 minutes; drain and transfer to large bowl.

3. Meanwhile, heat ½ tablespoon oil in 12-inch nonstick skillet over medium-high heat until just smoking. Stir in ½ teaspoon coriander and cook until fragrant, about 20 seconds. Add snow peas and ¼ teaspoon salt and cook until peas are spotty brown, about 3 minutes; transfer to bowl with buckwheat.

4. Add ½ tablespoon oil, sunflower seeds, cumin, remaining ¼ teaspoon coriander, and ¼ teaspoon salt and cook over medium heat until seeds are toasted, about 2 minutes; transfer to plate and let cool.

5. In separate bowl, whisk lemon zest and juice, mint, and mustard together. Whisking constantly, drizzle in remaining 3 tablespoons oil. Season with salt and pepper to taste, pour over buckwheat mixture, and toss to coat. Portion buckwheat into individual bowls, top with avocado and spiced sunflower seeds, and drizzle with yogurt sauce. Serve.

VARIATION

Dairy-Free Buckwheat Bowls with Lemon-Yogurt Sauce
In sauce, substitute plain soy milk yogurt or coconut milk yogurt for whole-milk yogurt.

Oat Berry Pilaf

G-F TESTING LAB

OAT BERRIES — Oat berries may also be labeled oat groats. Not all oat berries are processed in a gluten-free facility, so make sure to read the label.

WHY THIS RECIPE WORKS

While we think of oats mostly as part of a wholesome breakfast, oat berries—whole oats that have been hulled and cleaned but not processed—have a pleasant chew and are the perfect gluten-free replacement for farro or wheat berries. We wanted a satisfying oat berry pilaf with hearty add-ins. To cook the oat berries, we opted not to toast them since they naturally have a nutty flavor, and instead added the water and oat berries to the pan after sautéing some shallot. After testing various amounts of water and oat berries, we settled on a 4:3 ratio (2 cups water to 1½ cups oat berries). Creamy, pungent Gorgonzola seemed like it would be a nice balance to the earthy oat berries' nutty flavor, so we started there for our add-ins. First we tried stirring the Gorgonzola into the oat berries once they were cooked, but the result was a thick, gluey mixture. It was better to wait and simply sprinkle the cheese over the oat berries just before serving. The addition of tart cherries and tangy balsamic vinegar cut through the richness and strong flavors, while parsley gave our pilaf the freshness it needed.

Oat Berry Pilaf with Walnuts and Gorgonzola

SERVES 4 TO 6

- 1 tablespoon extra-virgin olive oil
- 1 shallot, minced
- 2 cups water
- 1½ cups oat berries (groats), rinsed (see page 31)
- Salt and pepper
- ¾ cup walnuts, toasted and chopped
- ½ cup dried cherries
- 2 tablespoons minced fresh parsley
- 1 tablespoon balsamic vinegar
- 2 ounces Gorgonzola cheese, crumbled (½ cup)

1. Heat oil in large saucepan over medium heat until shimmering. Add shallot and cook, stirring occasionally, until softened, about 2 minutes. Stir in water, oat berries, and ¼ teaspoon salt and bring to simmer. Reduce heat to low, cover, and continue to simmer until oat berries are tender but still slightly chewy, 30 to 40 minutes.

2. Remove pot from heat and lay clean folded dish towel underneath lid. Let sit for 10 minutes. Fluff oat berries with fork and fold in walnuts, cherries, and parsley. Drizzle with vinegar. Transfer pilaf to serving bowl. Sprinkle Gorgonzola over top and season with salt and pepper to taste. Serve.

SMART SHOPPING Oat Berries

Labeled either oat berries or oat groats, this gluten-free whole grain is simply whole oats that have been hulled and cleaned. They are the least processed oat product (other forms are processed further, such as being rolled flat, cut, or ground). Because they haven't been processed, they retain a high nutritional value. They have an appealing chewy texture and mildly nutty flavor. Oats are usually thought of as a breakfast cereal, but oat berries make a great savory side dish cooked pilaf-style.

Oat Berry Salad

G-F TESTING LAB

OAT BERRIES   Oat berries may also be labeled oat groats. Not all oat berries are processed
in a gluten-free facility, so make sure to read the label. See page 27 for more
information on oat berries.

Chewy, nutty oat berries make a great side dish (see our pilaf recipe on page 155), but we also thought these qualities were worth highlighting in a main-course salad. Cooking the oat berries in a large amount of water, pasta style, then draining and rinsing them under cold water to stop the cooking, gave us the chewy, tender berries we were after. For the leafy component of our dinner salad, peppery arugula paired well with the nutty oat berries, and we added chickpeas for a little more heft and complementary nutty flavor and creamy-firm texture. Roasted red peppers added sweetness, and creamy feta lent the right richness and salty bite. A simple lemon and cilantro vinaigrette spiked with cumin, paprika, and cayenne provided the perfect amount of spice and brightness.

Oat Berry, Chickpea, and Arugula Salad

SERVES 4 TO 6

- 2 **tablespoons lemon juice**
- 2 **tablespoons minced fresh cilantro**
- 1 **teaspoon honey**
- 1 **garlic clove, minced**
- ¼ **teaspoon ground cumin**
  Salt and pepper
- ⅛ **teaspoon paprika**
  Pinch cayenne pepper
- 3 **tablespoons extra-virgin olive oil**
- 1 **cup oat berries (groats), rinsed (see page 31)**
- 1 **(15-ounce) can chickpeas, rinsed**
- ½ **cup jarred roasted red peppers, drained, patted dry, and chopped**
- 2 **ounces feta cheese, crumbled (½ cup)**
- 6 **ounces (6 cups) baby arugula**

1. Whisk lemon juice, cilantro, honey, garlic, cumin, ¼ teaspoon salt, paprika, and cayenne together in bowl. Whisking constantly, drizzle in oil; set aside.

2. Bring 2 quarts water to boil in large saucepan. Add oat berries and ½ teaspoon salt, partially cover, and cook, stirring often, until tender but still chewy, 45 to 50 minutes. Drain oat berries and rinse under cold running water until cool. Transfer oat berries to large bowl.

3. Stir in chickpeas, roasted red peppers, and feta. Whisk vinaigrette to re-emulsify, then drizzle dressing over oat berry mixture and toss to combine. (Oat berry mixture can be refrigerated overnight; bring to room temperature before proceeding.) Add arugula and gently toss to combine. Season with salt and pepper to taste. Serve.

SMART SHOPPING **Chickpeas**

Popular particularly in Mediterranean, Middle Eastern, and Indian cuisines, canned chickpeas are a favorite among canned beans in the test kitchen because they hold up well to cooking. However, our tasters found that many brands are bland or have bitter and metallic flavors. They preferred those that were well seasoned and had a creamy yet "al dente" texture. Pastene Chickpeas came out on top.

Oat Berry and Mushroom Risotto

G-F TESTING LAB

OAT BERRIES   Oat berries may also be labeled oat groats. Not all oat berries are processed in a gluten-free facility; read the label. For more information on oat berries, see page 27.

✓ WHY THIS RECIPE WORKS

We set out to create a satisfying whole-grain version of risotto using hearty oat berries, which we thought would be a good stand-in for Arborio rice. Once cooked, the oat berries released just enough starch to lightly thicken our cooking liquid to the perfect risotto-like consistency even without the addition of butter or cheese. We wanted a satisfying risotto with hearty add-ins, and mushrooms seemed like the perfect match for our oat berries. We began by browning onions and mushrooms. Using both cremini and dried porcini mushrooms added a meaty richness to the finished risotto. Then we added oat berries, toasting them to reinforce their naturally nutty flavor. A bit of fresh thyme and garlic provided the aromatic backbone as we built the flavorful base of the dish. Chicken broth complemented the flavor of the mushrooms and seasoned the oat berries as they cooked; using all broth resulted in a salty risotto, but cutting the broth with some water was an easy fix. Once the grains were tender and the risotto thickened, we stirred in lemon juice to brighten the flavor, while parsley gave our risotto the freshness it needed. White mushrooms can be substituted for the cremini. Serve with grated Parmesan cheese.

Oat Berry and Mushroom Risotto
SERVES 4 TO 6

- 1 tablespoon extra-virgin olive oil
- 1 onion, chopped fine
- Salt and pepper
- 8 ounces cremini mushrooms, trimmed and quartered
- ½ ounce dried porcini mushrooms, rinsed and minced
- 3 garlic cloves, minced
- 1 teaspoon minced fresh thyme or ¼ teaspoon dried
- 1½ cups oat berries
- 2½ cups chicken broth
- 1½ cups water
- 2 tablespoons chopped fresh parsley
- 2 teaspoons lemon juice

1. Heat oil in large saucepan over medium heat until shimmering. Add onion and ½ teaspoon salt and cook until onion is softened, about 5 minutes. Stir in cremini and porcini mushrooms, increase heat to medium-high, and cook until cremini begin to brown, about 4 minutes. Stir in garlic and thyme and cook until fragrant, about 30 seconds.

2. Stir in oat berries and cook until lightly toasted, about 2 minutes. Stir in broth and water, scraping up any browned bits, and bring to simmer. Reduce heat to low and simmer, stirring often, until oat berries are tender and liquid is mostly evaporated and thickened, 30 to 40 minutes.

3. Off heat, stir in parsley and lemon juice. Season with salt and pepper to taste, and serve.

TEST KITCHEN TIP
Making Oat Berry Risotto

Reduce heat to low and simmer, stirring often, until oat berries are tender and liquid is mostly evaporated and thickened, 30 to 40 minutes.

Polenta Fries

G-F TESTING LAB

INSTANT POLENTA This recipe uses instant polenta, which has a much shorter cooking time than traditional polenta; do not substitute traditional polenta. Also, not all types of instant polenta are processed in a gluten-free facility; read the label. We had good luck using Pastene Instant Polenta in this recipe.

For a fresh take on how to use gluten-free polenta, we found that if we cooked polenta and then chilled it until firm, we could slice it into thin sticks that would become crisp when fried. We began our testing using instant polenta, to minimize time on the stove. Stirring oregano and lemon zest into the fully cooked polenta lent an aromatic backbone to our fries and helped to brighten the flavor. We then poured our flavored polenta into a straight-sided 13 by 9-inch baking pan to set up in the refrigerator for easy slicing. Once our fries were cut, we looked at methods for cooking them. Deep frying resulted in fries that clumped together and stuck to the bottom of the pot, but pan frying resulted in perfectly crisp fries with a tender and fluffy interior. We seasoned the fries lightly with salt as they came out of the pan. We like to serve these fries with Herb Mayonnaise, but they also taste good with marinara sauce, Sriracha Mayonnaise (page 125), or even ketchup.

Polenta Fries

SERVES 4

- 4 **cups water**
  Salt and pepper
- 1 **cup instant polenta**
- 2 **teaspoons minced fresh oregano or**
  ½ **teaspoon dried**
- 1 **teaspoon grated lemon zest**
- ½ **cup vegetable oil**

1. Line 13 by 9-inch baking pan with parchment paper and grease parchment. Bring water to boil in large covered saucepan and add 1 teaspoon salt. Slowly add polenta in steady stream while stirring constantly with wooden spoon. Reduce heat to low and cook, uncovered, stirring often, until polenta is soft and smooth, 3 to 5 minutes.

2. Off heat, stir in oregano and lemon zest and season with salt and pepper to taste. Pour polenta into prepared baking dish. Refrigerate, uncovered, until firm and sliceable, about 1 hour. (Polenta can be covered and refrigerated for up to 1 day.)

3. Gently flip chilled polenta out onto cutting board and discard parchment. Cut polenta in half lengthwise, then slice each half crosswise into sixteen ¾-inch-wide fries. (You will have 32 fries total.)

4. Adjust oven rack to middle position and heat oven to 200 degrees. Set wire rack in rimmed baking sheet. Heat oil in 12-inch nonstick skillet over medium heat until shimmering and edge of polenta sizzles when dipped in oil. Working in batches, fry half of polenta until crisp and beginning to brown, 6 to 7 minutes per side. Transfer to prepared rack, season lightly with salt, and keep warm in oven. Repeat with remaining polenta and serve warm.

Herb Mayonnaise

MAKES 1¼ CUPS
Mayonnaise can be refrigerated for up to 2 days.

- 1 **cup mayonnaise**
- 2 **tablespoons minced fresh basil**
- 1 **tablespoon minced fresh parsley**
- 1 **tablespoon lemon juice**
- 2 **teaspoons chopped fresh chives**
  Salt and pepper

Combine all ingredients in bowl, season with salt and pepper to taste, and serve.

TEST KITCHEN TIP **Making Polenta Fries**

1. Flip chilled polenta onto cutting board and discard parchment. Cut polenta in half lengthwise, then slice each half crosswise into sixteen ¾-inch-wide fries.

2. Working in batches, fry half of polenta until crisp and beginning to brown, 6 to 7 minutes per side, and transfer to wire rack set in rimmed baking sheet.

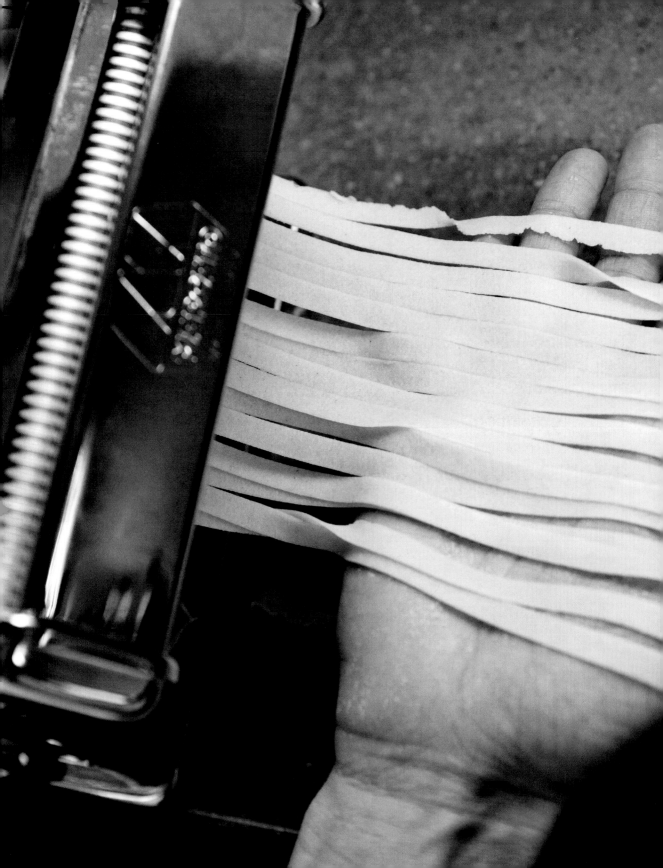

PASTA

Fresh Pasta

G-F TESTING LAB

BROWN RICE FLOUR	Not all brands of brown rice flour are milled the same way. We strongly recommend using a finely ground flour such as Bob's Red Mill. See page 23 for details on buying brown rice flour.
TAPIOCA STARCH	Tapioca starch is often labeled tapioca flour. See page 25 for more details on this ingredient.
XANTHAN GUM	Do not omit the xanthan gum; it is crucial to the structure of the pasta dough. For more information, see page 21.

WHY THIS RECIPE WORKS

Dried pasta (made with or without wheat) isn't always the best choice, especially for refined cream and butter sauces. So how do you make great fresh pasta without wheat flour—one of only two ingredients in the classic recipe (the other is eggs)? We started by testing as many different flours as possible. In the end we settled on a combination of brown rice flour for structure and tapioca starch for elasticity. Our traditional pasta recipe uses three whole eggs. However, since gluten-free pasta is more brittle, we found we needed to add a fourth egg to ensure that the noodles would set up properly once cooked. Xanthan gum was a must for structure, while a little oil made the dough easier to roll out. We developed a few sauces (see page 168) that could be put together quickly and offered good flavor but didn't outshine our fresh noodles. It takes just seconds to make pasta dough in the food processor, but you can use a stand mixer if you prefer. Combine the dry ingredients on low speed, then add the eggs and oil and mix on medium-low until the dough comes together in a rough ball, about 10 seconds. You will need a manual pasta machine to make this recipe. Do not attempt to roll this pasta with just a rolling pin; it will be too difficult to get the pasta thin enough, and the dough will be much more likely to tear. We make fettuccine here, but you can also follow the recipe through step 4 and shape the pasta sheets into farfalle or garganelli following the steps on page 169.

Fresh Pasta

MAKES ABOUT 1 POUND PASTA; SERVES 4 TO 6

- 7½ ounces (1⅔ cups) brown rice flour, plus extra for rolling
- 2½ ounces (½ cup plus 2 tablespoons) tapioca starch
- 1 tablespoon xanthan gum
- ½ teaspoon salt
- 4 large eggs
- 1 tablespoon extra-virgin olive oil

1. Pulse brown rice flour, tapioca starch, xanthan gum, and salt in food processor until combined. Add eggs and oil and process until dough forms and clears sides of bowl, about 10 seconds.

2. Transfer dough to clean counter and knead until dough comes together, about 30 seconds. (Dough should hold together but won't be smooth.) Shape dough into 6-inch-long cylinder. Cut cylinder into 6 equal pieces and cover with plastic wrap.

3. Working with 1 piece of dough at a time (keeping remaining dough covered), shape into 4-inch square using rolling pin and your hands. Using manual pasta machine, run flattened dough through widest setting twice. Fold ends of dough toward middle to re-form 4-inch square, press to seal, and feed open side of dough once more through widest setting. Repeat folding and rolling on widest setting 2 or 3 more times, until edges of dough are even.

4. Narrow setting and continue to run dough through each setting twice, until dough is translucent and thin enough that you can clearly see outline of your hand through dough. (If dough begins to stick and tear, dust sheet with brown rice flour and roll through same setting until smooth. If dough becomes too long to manage, cut in half crosswise.)

5. If not already done, cut sheet in half. Run each piece through cutter for fettuccine, lay pasta on dish towel in baking sheet, and cover with plastic wrap. Repeat steps 3 through 5 with remaining dough. (Noodles can be held for 2 hours before cooking.)

TO COOK PASTA: Bring 4 quarts water to boil in large pot. Add pasta and 1 tablespoon salt and cook, stirring often, until tender but still al dente, about 2 minutes. Reserve 1 cup cooking water. Drain pasta, return to pot, toss with sauce and reserved cooking water as needed, and serve immediately.

TO MAKE AHEAD: Spread pasta out evenly over baking sheet (avoid clumps). Transfer sheet to freezer and chill until pasta is firm, about 1 hour. Transfer pasta to zipper-lock bag and freeze for up to 2 weeks. Cook frozen pasta straight from freezer as directed.

TEST KITCHEN TIP **Making Fresh Gluten-Free Pasta**

The process for making gluten-free pasta is similar to the one used to make fresh pasta with wheat flour, but the dough is softer and tears more easily. Support the dough with one hand while feeding it through the machine. Also, don't let the dough drape over the machine because it can tear from its own weight.

1. After kneading dough briefly, shape it into 6-inch cylinder.

2. Divide into 6 equal pieces. Cover pieces of dough with plastic wrap to prevent drying.

3. Working with 1 piece at a time, shape dough into 4-inch square using rolling pin and your hands.

4. Using manual pasta machine, run flattened dough through widest setting twice.

5. Fold ends of dough toward middle to re-form 4-inch square and press to seal.

6. Feed open side of dough through widest setting. Repeat folding and rolling 2 or 3 more times until edges are even.

7. Narrow setting and run dough through machine twice. Narrow setting and repeat, continuing to roll dough through each setting twice, until dough is thin enough that you can clearly see outline of your hand through dough.

8. If dough begins to stick and tear, dust sheet with brown rice flour and roll through same setting until smooth. If dough becomes too long to manage, cut in half crosswise and work with each piece individually.

9. If not already done, cut sheet in half crosswise. Make fettuccine noodles by running each sheet of pasta through wide cutter on pasta machine (each noodle will measure ⅛ to ¼ inch across).

Fresh Pasta

Homemade pasta dough has so few ingredients that we knew coming up with a gluten-free alternative with the same delicate flavor and chew would be daunting. Getting the ingredients right as well as developing a reliable rolling method turned out to be trickier than we imagined. Here's what we learned.

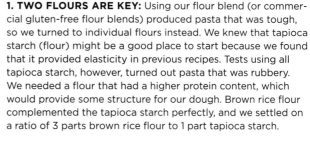

1. TWO FLOURS ARE KEY: Using our flour blend (or commercial gluten-free flour blends) produced pasta that was tough, so we turned to individual flours instead. We knew that tapioca starch (flour) might be a good place to start because we found that it provided elasticity in previous recipes. Tests using all tapioca starch, however, turned out pasta that was rubbery. We needed a flour that had a higher protein content, which would provide some structure for our dough. Brown rice flour complemented the tapioca starch perfectly, and we settled on a ratio of 3 parts brown rice flour to 1 part tapioca starch.

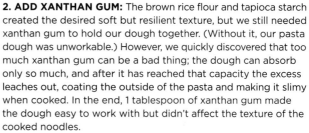

2. ADD XANTHAN GUM: The brown rice flour and tapioca starch created the desired soft but resilient texture, but we still needed xanthan gum to hold our dough together. (Without it, our pasta dough was unworkable.) However, we quickly discovered that too much xanthan gum can be a bad thing; the dough can absorb only so much, and after it has reached that capacity the excess leaches out, coating the outside of the pasta and making it slimy when cooked. In the end, 1 tablespoon of xanthan gum made the dough easy to work with but didn't affect the texture of the cooked noodles.

3. AN ADDITIONAL EGG AND OLIVE OIL: Eggs are traditional in pasta recipes (we use three in our established recipe), and we found that four were necessary for our gluten-free recipe. The eggs provided a rich flavor and texture (without which the dough didn't set up properly once cooked). In addition, the moisture they contributed to the raw dough made it easier to roll out. We noticed, however, that the cut pasta became brittle if we didn't cook it right away. A tablespoon of olive oil solved this problem and made the dough even more pliable and easier to roll out.

4. ROLL AND ROLL AGAIN: Our gluten-free pasta dough was much more likely than traditional pasta dough to tear and stick to the rollers of our manual pasta machine. Sprinkling our sheet of dough with a little brown rice flour helped, but we had real success when we rolled the sheet of dough through each setting on the pasta machine an additional time. This second pass through the machine smoothed out any imperfections and created a more cohesive sheet. We also found that holding the dough while rolling it through, and not letting it drag along the back of the pasta machine, prevented the dough from tearing.

Sauces for Fresh Pasta

Fresh Pasta al Limone

SERVES 4 TO 6

 WHY THIS RECIPE WORKS

With its clean, simple flavor profile featuring lemon and olive oil, this classic Italian sauce comes together as easily as a vinaigrette and is a great match for fresh pasta. Stirring in grated Parmesan cheese slightly thickened the sauce so that it could coat the pasta properly, while a generous amount of basil lent color and a necessary herbal balance. Finally, we found that just a bit of butter helped to round out the flavors.

⅓ cup extra-virgin olive oil
2 teaspoons grated lemon zest plus ¼ cup juice (2 lemons)
1 garlic clove, minced to paste
   Salt and pepper
2 ounces Parmesan cheese, grated (1 cup)
1 recipe Fresh Pasta (page 164)
½ cup shredded fresh basil
2 tablespoons unsalted butter, softened

1. Whisk oil, lemon zest and juice, garlic, and ½ teaspoon salt together in large bowl, then stir in Parmesan until thick and creamy; cover and set aside.

2. Meanwhile, bring 4 quarts water to boil in large pot. Add pasta and 1 tablespoon salt and cook, stirring often, until tender but still al dente, about 2 minutes. Reserve 1 cup cooking water, then drain pasta and return it to pot. Add sauce, basil, and butter and toss to combine, adding reserved cooking water as needed to adjust consistency. Season with salt and pepper to taste, and serve immediately.

Fresh Pasta with Tomato–Brown Butter Sauce

SERVES 4 TO 6

 **WHY THIS RECIPE WORKS**

While most tomato sauces start with olive oil, we put browned butter to work here for a nuttier, just-rich-enough sauce that would work well with our homemade fresh pasta. After browning the butter we added garlic for depth and then our tomatoes; processing whole canned tomatoes before incorporating them delivered a sauce with the proper consistency. Simmering the sauce for less than 10 minutes thickened it just enough; we then finished with sherry vinegar (adding it at the end preserved its bright flavor) and more butter. When browning the butter, make sure to use a skillet with a traditional (not a dark nonstick) finish. Butter can go from brown to burnt quickly, and the light finish of the pan will help you see the color change.

1 (28-ounce) can whole peeled tomatoes
4 tablespoons unsalted butter, cut into 4 pieces
2 garlic cloves, minced
½ teaspoon sugar
   Salt and pepper
2 teaspoons sherry vinegar
1 recipe Fresh Pasta (page 164)
3 tablespoons chopped fresh basil
   Grated Parmesan cheese

1. Process tomatoes and their juice in food processor until smooth, about 30 seconds. Melt 3 tablespoons butter in 12-inch skillet over medium-high heat, swirling occasionally, until butter is dark brown and releases nutty aroma, about 1½ minutes. Stir in garlic and cook for 10 seconds. Stir in processed tomatoes, sugar, and ½ teaspoon salt and simmer until sauce is slightly reduced, about 8 minutes. Off heat, whisk in remaining piece butter and vinegar. Season with salt and pepper to taste; cover to keep warm.

2. Meanwhile, bring 4 quarts water to boil in large pot. Add pasta and 1 tablespoon salt and cook, stirring often, until tender but still al dente, about 2 minutes. Reserve 1 cup cooking water, then drain pasta and return it to pot. Add sauce, ¼ cup reserved cooking water, and basil to pot with pasta; toss to combine, adding remaining cooking water as needed to adjust consistency. Season with salt and pepper to taste, and serve immediately, passing Parmesan separately.

Fresh Pasta Alfredo

SERVES 4 TO 6

✔ WHY THIS RECIPE WORKS

We wanted an Alfredo sauce that was rich and coated the noodles well, but we also wanted one that wasn't too heavy. The challenge was managing the heavy cream, which is usually reduced by half, making the sauce unpalatably thick. We got the best results by reducing only 1 cup of the cream and saving the remaining ½ cup to add at the end. We also used a lighter hand when adding the cheese and butter; just ¾ cup Parmesan and 2 tablespoons butter were sufficient. Try to find cream that has been only pasteurized, not ultrapasteurized. The latter tastes flat since it has been heated to a higher temperature during processing.

1½	**cups heavy cream**
2	**tablespoons unsalted butter**
	Salt and pepper
1	**recipe Fresh Pasta (page 164)**
1½	**ounces Parmesan cheese, grated (¾ cup)**
⅛	**teaspoon ground nutmeg**

1. Bring 1 cup cream and butter to simmer in large saucepan. Reduce heat to low and simmer gently until mixture measures ⅔ cup, 12 to 15 minutes. Off heat, stir in remaining ½ cup cream, ½ teaspoon salt, and ½ teaspoon pepper. Cover and set aside.

2. Meanwhile bring 4 quarts water to boil in large pot. Add pasta and 1 tablespoon salt and cook, stirring often, until tender but still al dente, about 2 minutes. Reserve 1 cup cooking water, then drain pasta and return it to pot.

3. Add cream mixture, Parmesan, and nutmeg to pot with pasta and cook over low heat, tossing to combine, until cheese is melted and sauce coats pasta, about 1 minute. Add reserved cooking water as needed to adjust consistency (sauce may look thin but will gradually thicken as pasta is served). Season with salt and pepper to taste, and serve immediately.

TEST KITCHEN TIP **Making Shaped Pastas**

Instead of cutting the pasta into fettuccine, you can follow the Fresh Pasta recipe through step 4 and then follow the steps below to make shapes from the rolled sheets. Before you begin, make sure to trim the ragged edges from the pasta sheets to create a straight edge. After shaping each piece of pasta, transfer it to a rimmed baking sheet lined with a clean dish towel. The shaped pasta should be cooked within 2 hours of being shaped. It can also be frozen like fettuccine (see directions on page 165).

1. FOR FARFALLE: Cut sheet of dough into 1 by 1½-inch rectangles using fluted cutter to cut short sides of rectangle.

2. Place index finger in center of rectangle. Using thumb and index finger of other hand, pinch in long sides until they reach finger in center of pasta. Remove finger and firmly pinch center together.

1. FOR GARGANELLI: Cut sheet of dough into 1½-inch squares. Lay square of pasta diagonally on counter or, to create ridges in pasta, on top of clean hair comb or wire rack.

2. Wrap corner of pasta around pencil, and with gentle pressure roll away from you until pasta is completely wrapped around pencil. Slide shaped pasta off pencil and repeat.

Penne with Spiced Butter and Cauliflower

G-F TESTING LAB

PASTA	Our favorite brand is Jovial Gluten Free Brown Rice Pasta (see pages 34–35 for complete tasting). Cooking times for gluten-free pasta vary from brand to brand. Make sure to taste the pasta often, as it can overcook quickly.

WHY THIS RECIPE WORKS

Cauliflower is an appealing complement to the nutty flavor and firm texture of gluten-free pasta, assuming you treat it right. We found it best to brown the cauliflower in a skillet to bring out its sweet notes, then add water to the pan, set the cover in place, and let the cauliflower steam until tender. We had to use olive oil to sauté the cauliflower because butter burned during this long cooking time. Building a butter sauce separately, and letting the butter brown, complemented the cauliflower with a deeper, nuttier flavor. A selection of warm spices added depth with minimal prep, and blooming the ground spices in the butter mellowed and deepened their flavors. We eventually settled on the combination of coriander, ginger, paprika, and just a hint of cinnamon. We tried to streamline this list but found each was a must to create just the right balance. To give the dish heft and also freshness, we then tested a few more vegetable additions. Asparagus seemed out of place, but baby spinach added the needed burst of color and a balancing earthiness. Pine nuts lent richness as well as texture, and sautéed shallots added another layer of sweetness. To keep our multicomponent sauce to one pan, we set the cauliflower aside after browning it, then used the same pan to toast the nuts and brown our butter. We then added the spices and gave them a minute to cook and mellow. A final squirt of lemon juice brightened the dish just enough and cut through the richness. When browning the butter, make sure to use a skillet with a traditional (not a dark nonstick) finish. Butter can go from brown to burnt quickly, and the light finish of the pan will help you see the color change.

Penne with Spiced Butter, Cauliflower, and Pine Nuts
SERVES 4

- 2 tablespoons extra-virgin olive oil
- 1 small head cauliflower (1½ pounds), cored and cut into 1-inch florets
- 4 shallots, sliced ½ inch thick
  Salt and pepper
- ¼ cup water
- ½ cup pine nuts, chopped
- 6 tablespoons unsalted butter, cut into 6 pieces
- 2 garlic cloves, minced
- ¾ teaspoon ground coriander
- ¾ teaspoon ground ginger
- ¾ teaspoon paprika
- ¼ teaspoon ground cinnamon
- 3 ounces (3 cups) baby spinach
- ¾ teaspoon lemon juice
- 12 ounces gluten-free penne

1. Heat oil in 12-inch skillet over medium-high heat until shimmering. Add cauliflower, shallots, and ¼ teaspoon salt and cook, stirring occasionally, until well browned and nearly tender, 12 to 15 minutes. Add water to skillet, cover, and continue to cook until cauliflower is tender, about 2 minutes. Transfer to bowl and set aside.

2. Wipe out now-empty skillet with paper towels. Add nuts and toast over medium heat, shaking skillet frequently, until fragrant and lightly brown, 3 to 5 minutes. Add butter, increase heat to medium-high, and cook, swirling occasionally, until butter is browned and releases nutty aroma, 1 to 2 minutes. Off heat, stir in garlic, coriander, ginger, paprika, and cinnamon, swirling pan until garlic and spices are fragrant, about 1 minute. Stir in cauliflower-shallot mixture, spinach, lemon juice, and ¼ teaspoon salt, cover, and let sit until spinach is wilted, about 2 minutes.

3. Meanwhile, bring 4 quarts water to boil in large pot. Add pasta and 1 tablespoon salt and cook, stirring often, until al dente. Reserve ½ cup cooking water, then drain pasta and return it to pot. Add sauce, toss to combine, and season with salt and pepper to taste. Before serving, add remaining cooking water as needed to adjust consistency.

Fusilli with Basil Pesto

G-F TESTING LAB

| PASTA | Our favorite brand is Jovial Gluten Free Brown Rice Pasta (see pages 34–35 for complete tasting). Cooking times for gluten-free pasta vary from brand to brand. Make sure to taste the pasta often, as it can overcook quickly. |

☑ WHY THIS RECIPE WORKS

The ultimate no-cook sauce, basil pesto is simple in that it requires only a few ingredients, but its simplicity also makes it a bit trickier to perfect. A great pesto should balance the flavors of each component: fresh basil, spicy garlic, nutty Parmesan, rich pine nuts, and fruity-peppery extra-virgin olive oil. To tame the raw garlic flavor, we toasted the cloves in a skillet, and while the skillet was out we toasted the nuts as well to deepen their flavor. Because the basil usually turns dark green in homemade pesto and gives the sauce a muddy appearance, we added some parsley to lend a bright green color boost. Processing everything together in the food processor delivered a sauce that retained some texture, and since we were cooking our pasta at the same time, we thinned the sauce with some reserved pasta cooking water so it would coat the pasta evenly. The pesto tended to clump when we tossed it with strand pasta; short shapes like fusilli made it easier to ensure even coverage. For sharper flavor, use Pecorino Romano cheese in place of the Parmesan. Toasting the pine nuts brings out their flavor, but don't walk away from the skillet, as pine nuts can burn rather quickly. An equal amount of another nut, such as walnuts or almonds, can be used if you prefer.

Fusilli with Basil Pesto
SERVES 4

3	garlic cloves, unpeeled
¼	cup pine nuts
2	cups packed fresh basil leaves
2	tablespoons fresh parsley leaves
⅓	cup extra-virgin olive oil
¼	cup grated Parmesan or Pecorino Romano cheese, plus extra for serving
	Salt and pepper
12	ounces gluten-free fusilli

1. Toast garlic in 8-inch skillet over medium heat, shaking pan occasionally, until garlic is softened and spotty brown, about 8 minutes. When cool enough to handle, remove and discard skin. While garlic cools, toast pine nuts in now-empty skillet over medium heat, stirring often, until golden and fragrant, 4 to 5 minutes.

2. Process garlic, pine nuts, basil, parsley, oil, Parmesan, and ¼ teaspoon salt in food processor until smooth, 30 to 60 seconds, scraping down bowl as needed. Transfer to medium bowl and season with salt and pepper to taste.

3. Meanwhile, bring 4 quarts water to boil in large pot. Add pasta and 1 tablespoon salt and cook, stirring often, until al dente. Reserve ¾ cup cooking water, then drain pasta and return it to pot.

4. Add sauce and ¼ cup reserved cooking water to pasta, toss to combine, and season with salt and pepper to taste. Add remaining cooking water as needed to adjust consistency. Serve, passing Parmesan separately.

VARIATIONS

Fusilli with Kale–Sunflower Seed Pesto
Reduce garlic to 1 clove and substitute ⅓ cup sunflower seeds for pine nuts. Reduce basil to ¾ cup and replace parsley with 1½ cups chopped kale leaves. Add ½ teaspoon red pepper flakes to processor in step 2, and increase Parmesan to ½ cup.

Fusilli with Roasted Red Pepper Pesto
Reduce garlic to 2 cloves. Omit pine nuts and basil. Add 1 cup patted dry jarred roasted red peppers, 2 tablespoons parsley, and 1 small chopped shallot to processor in step 2, and increase salt added to processor to ½ teaspoon.

Fusilli with Spring Vegetable Cream Sauce

PASTA   Our favorite brand is Jovial Gluten Free Brown Rice Pasta (see pages 34–35 for complete tasting). Cooking times for gluten-free pasta vary from brand to brand. Make sure to taste the pasta often, as it can overcook quickly.

WHY THIS RECIPE WORKS

For a vegetarian springtime pasta that could be whipped together on a weeknight, quick-cooking peas and asparagus were a good start. Leeks added sweetness, while fresh mint and thyme plus lemon zest and a splash of white wine added brightness. We started out by using vegetable broth as the base for our sauce, but while we liked the light profile it created, the broth added a slightly tinny flavor. Our dish also seemed unfinished. Using 1 cup of heavy cream instead as the base, plus a good dose of Parmesan, brought it all together into a cohesive whole and provided the richness and elegant finish the recipe needed.

Fusilli with Spring Vegetable Cream Sauce
SERVES 4

- 2 tablespoons extra-virgin olive oil
- 1 pound leeks, white and light green parts only, halved lengthwise, sliced thin, and washed thoroughly
- 3 garlic cloves, minced
- 1 teaspoon grated lemon zest
- 1½ teaspoons minced fresh thyme or ¾ teaspoon dried
- 1 pound asparagus, trimmed and cut on bias into 1-inch lengths
- ½ cup dry white wine
- 1 cup heavy cream
  Salt and pepper
- ¾ cup frozen peas
- 1 ounce Parmesan cheese, grated (½ cup), plus extra for serving
- 12 ounces gluten-free fusilli
- 2 tablespoons chopped fresh mint

1. Heat oil in 12-inch nonstick skillet over medium heat until shimmering. Add leeks and cook until softened, 5 to 7 minutes. Stir in garlic, lemon zest, and thyme and cook until fragrant, about 30 seconds.

2. Stir in asparagus and wine, bring to simmer, and cook until asparagus is crisp-tender, about 3 minutes. Add cream and 1 teaspoon salt and bring to simmer. Cook until sauce is slightly thickened, about 2 minutes. Off heat, stir in peas and Parmesan and let sit, covered, until peas are heated through.

3. Meanwhile, bring 4 quarts water to boil in large pot. Add pasta and 1 tablespoon salt and cook, stirring often, until al dente. Reserve ½ cup cooking water, then drain pasta and return it to pot. Add sauce, toss to combine, and season with salt and pepper to taste. Add reserved cooking water as needed to adjust consistency. Sprinkle with mint and serve, passing Parmesan separately.

TEST KITCHEN TIP **Preparing Leeks**

1. Trim and discard root and dark green leaves.

2. Cut trimmed leek in half lengthwise, then slice it crosswise as directed in recipe.

3. Rinse cut leeks thoroughly to remove all dirt and sand using either salad spinner or bowl of water.

Spaghetti with Puttanesca Sauce

G-F TESTING LAB

PASTA   Our favorite brand is Jovial Gluten Free Brown Rice Pasta (see pages 34–35 for complete tasting). Cooking times for gluten-free pasta vary from brand to brand. Make sure to taste the pasta often, as it can overcook quickly.

A spicy profile and minimal prep make this Neapolitan classic a quick pasta dinner that's beyond the everyday. And the strong flavors in this tomato sauce work well with the nutty notes in gluten-free pasta. That said, with a number of bold ingredients—garlic, anchovies, olives, and capers—the key to making a great Puttanesca is finding balance; a little too much of one ingredient will completely overpower the others. We found that blooming the garlic, anchovies, and red pepper flakes in olive oil helped to develop, mellow, and blend their flavors. To avoid burning the garlic, it was important to add it (and the other two ingredients) to the pan at the same time as the oil; the garlic burned when we heated the oil first. After adding the tomatoes (diced plus crushed delivered the right consistency), we simmered the sauce long enough to infuse it with flavor and thicken it slightly, but not too long because we wanted to preserve the tomatoes' sweetness and texture. Waiting to add the olives, capers, and parsley until the end kept them from disintegrating into the sauce and also ensured the sauce retained the right amount of piquant flavor. For a bit more richness, we drizzled olive oil over each bowl of pasta before serving. This dish is fairly spicy; to make it milder, reduce the amount of red pepper flakes.

Spaghetti with Puttanesca Sauce

SERVES 4

2	tablespoons extra-virgin olive oil, plus extra for serving
6	anchovy fillets, rinsed and minced
3	garlic cloves, minced
¼	teaspoon red pepper flakes
1	(28-ounce) can crushed tomatoes
1	(14.5-ounce) can diced tomatoes
½	cup pitted kalamata olives, chopped coarse
3	tablespoons minced fresh parsley
2	tablespoons capers, rinsed
	Salt and pepper
12	ounces gluten-free spaghetti

1. Cook oil, anchovies, garlic, and pepper flakes together in 12-inch skillet over medium heat, stirring often, until garlic turns golden but not brown, 1 to 2 minutes.

2. Stir in crushed tomatoes and diced tomatoes and their juice. Bring to simmer and cook until thickened slightly, 15 to 20 minutes. Off heat, stir in olives, parsley, and capers, and season with salt and pepper to taste.

3. Meanwhile, bring 4 quarts water to boil in large pot. Add pasta and 1 tablespoon salt and cook, stirring often, until al dente. Reserve ½ cup cooking water, then drain pasta and return it to pot. Add sauce and toss to combine. Add reserved cooking water as needed to adjust consistency. Drizzle individual portions with additional oil to taste. Serve.

SMART SHOPPING
Anchovy Fillets versus Paste

Because most recipes call for only a small amount of anchovies, we wondered whether a tube of anchovy paste might be a more convenient option. Made from pulverized anchovies, vinegar, salt, and water, anchovy paste promises all the flavor of oil-packed anchovies without the mess. When we tested the paste and jarred or canned anchovies side by side in recipes calling for an anchovy or two, we found little difference, though a few astute tasters felt that the paste had a "saltier" and "slightly more fishy" flavor. You can substitute ¼ teaspoon of the paste for each fillet. However, when a recipe calls for more than a couple of anchovies, stick with jarred or canned, as the paste's more intense flavor will be overwhelming. Our favorite brand of anchovies is Ortiz Oil-Packed Anchovies.

Spaghetti and Meatballs

G-F TESTING LAB

PASTA	Our favorite brand is Jovial Gluten Free Brown Rice Pasta (see pages 34–35 for complete tasting). Cooking times for gluten-free pasta vary from brand to brand. Make sure to taste the pasta often, as it can overcook quickly.
POTATO FLAKES	Make sure to buy potato flakes, not potato granules, which have a slightly metallic taste.

WHY THIS RECIPE WORKS

Traditional spaghetti and meatballs is off-limits to the gluten-free crowd, and not just because of the noodles. Classic meatballs rely on a panade—a paste made by mashing sandwich bread into milk—to keep the ground meat from becoming tough and dry. And while we didn't want to settle for substandard meatballs, we knew the fix wasn't as simple as swapping in a few slices of gluten-free bread. We'd recently tried to make a panade using gluten-free bread for meatloaf, but rather than breaking down into a paste, the gluten-free bread turned into spongy bits and delivered a meat mixture that was tough and chewy. However, we'd discovered that a surprising ingredient—potato flakes—could provide just the right tenderizing effect (see page 215 for more detail on our meatloaf recipe) and keep our mixture gluten-free. One test proved that along with buttermilk and an egg yolk for moisture and rich flavor, the potato flakes worked perfectly in our meatball recipe. To ensure meatballs with good flavor, we used a combination of ground pork (for a hint of sweetness) and ground beef. Since overworked ground beef makes tough meatballs, we waited to add it to the mixture until after we'd mixed the other ingredients together with the pork. Browning the meatballs added flavor and ensured they stayed together, while cooking them through in the sauce gave both the sauce and the meatballs a boost. We like the tang that buttermilk adds, but you can use regular milk; substitute ½ cup whole milk combined with 1½ teaspoons lemon juice or distilled white vinegar. See page 55 for more about buttermilk substitutes. Potato flakes are an instant mashed potato product made by cooking, processing, and dehydrating potatoes. Unlike potato flour, dehydrated potato flakes are less likely to clump when combined with liquid. Avoid potato granules, which have a slightly metallic taste. We find that 85 percent lean ground beef is the best option here. Fattier options (like 80 percent lean ground beef) can be a bit greasy. Leaner options will make fairly dry meatballs.

Spaghetti and Meatballs

SERVES 4

MEATBALLS

- ½ cup buttermilk
- 1 large egg yolk
- 4 ounces ground pork
- 1 ounce Parmesan cheese, grated (½ cup)
- ¼ cup instant potato flakes
- 3 tablespoons minced fresh parsley
- 2 garlic cloves, minced
- ½ teaspoon salt
- ¼ teaspoon pepper
- 12 ounces 85 percent lean ground beef
- 2 tablespoons extra-virgin olive oil

PASTA AND SAUCE

- 1 onion, chopped fine
- 4 garlic cloves, minced
- ⅛ teaspoon red pepper flakes
- 1 (28-ounce) can crushed tomatoes
- 1 (14.5-ounce) can diced tomatoes
  Salt and pepper
- 12 ounces gluten-free spaghetti
- 3 tablespoons chopped fresh basil
  Grated Parmesan cheese

1. FOR THE MEATBALLS: Whisk together buttermilk and egg yolk in large bowl. Add ground pork, Parmesan, potato flakes, parsley, garlic, salt, and pepper, and knead with your hands until mixture is thoroughly combined. Add beef and continue to knead until uniform. Gently form mixture into 1½-inch round meatballs (about 12 meatballs).

2. Heat oil in 12-inch nonstick skillet over medium heat until just smoking. Brown meatballs on all sides, about 10 minutes. Transfer meatballs to paper towel–lined plate. Pour off all but 1 tablespoon fat left in skillet.

3. FOR THE PASTA AND SAUCE: Add onion to fat left in skillet and cook over medium heat until softened, about 5 minutes. Stir in garlic and red pepper flakes and cook until fragrant, about 30 seconds.

Stir in crushed tomatoes and diced tomatoes and their juice. Bring to simmer and cook until sauce has thickened slightly, about 20 minutes.

4. Add meatballs to sauce and simmer, turning meatballs occasionally, until cooked through, about 10 minutes. Season sauce with salt and pepper to taste.

5. Meanwhile, bring 4 quarts water to boil in large pot. Add pasta and 1 tablespoon salt and cook, stirring often, until al dente. Reserve ½ cup cooking water, then drain pasta and return it to pot.

6. Add basil and several large spoonfuls of sauce (without meatballs) to pasta and toss to combine. Add reserved cooking water as needed to adjust consistency. Divide pasta among individual bowls and top each with tomato sauce and meatballs. Serve, passing Parmesan separately.

TEST KITCHEN TIP **Making Tender Gluten-Free Meatballs**

For traditional meatballs, we usually rely on the addition of a panade (a paste made with bread and milk). For our gluten-free version, we found that potato flakes made the best stand-in for the bread-based mixture. Overworked ground beef makes for dense, rubbery meatballs, so adding it last during the mixing step helps prevent overkneading. Browning the meatballs adds meaty depth and also helps them hold together, while simmering them in the sauce boosts the flavor of both the meatballs and the sauce.

1. Add ground pork, Parmesan, potato flakes, parsley, garlic, salt, and pepper to buttermilk and egg yolk, and mix until thoroughly combined. Then add ground beef and mix just until thoroughly combined.

2. After forming meatballs, brown on all sides, about 10 minutes, using tongs to gently turn meatballs as necessary. Transfer meatballs to paper towel–lined plate to drain briefly.

3. After sauce has cooked and thickened slightly, add meatballs and simmer, turning occasionally, until meatballs are cooked through, about 10 minutes.

Penne with Sausage and Red Pepper Ragu

✓ WHY THIS RECIPE WORKS

For a kid-friendly weeknight pasta dinner that would be equally satisfying to adults, we started by pairing rich Italian sausage with sweet red peppers. A can of crushed tomatoes worked well as the base and coated the pasta fairly well, but the sauce was a bit on the thin side and one-dimensional. Wine added depth without making it too boozy, while a few tablespoons of tomato paste helped to thicken it and also gave it a deeper tomato flavor. Incorporating garlic, oregano, and onion complemented the sausage and boosted the overall flavor of the sauce. Tossing in some parsley at the end gave it a little color and freshness. Make sure not to overcook the sausage in step 1. You want to cook it until it is just no longer pink; overbrowning the sausage will make it dry and tough. Our favorite brand is Jovial Gluten Free Brown Rice Pasta (see pages 34–35 for complete tasting). Cooking times for gluten-free pasta vary from brand to brand. Make sure to taste the pasta often, as it can overcook quickly.

Penne with Sausage and Red Pepper Ragu
SERVES 4

- 1 tablespoon extra-virgin olive oil
- 1 onion, chopped fine
- 1 red bell pepper, stemmed, seeded, and cut into ½-inch pieces
- 2 tablespoons tomato paste
- 3 garlic cloves, minced
- 2 teaspoons minced fresh oregano or 1 teaspoon dried
- 1 pound sweet or hot Italian sausage, casings removed
- ½ cup dry red wine
- 1 (28-ounce) can crushed tomatoes
- 12 ounces gluten-free penne
  Salt and pepper
- 2 tablespoons minced fresh parsley
  Grated Parmesan cheese

1. Heat oil in Dutch oven over medium heat until shimmering. Add onion and bell pepper and cook until softened, about 5 minutes. Stir in tomato paste, garlic, and oregano and cook until fragrant, about 30 seconds. Add sausage and cook, breaking up any large pieces with wooden spoon, until no longer pink, about 5 minutes. Stir in wine, scraping up any browned bits, and simmer until liquid has thickened, about 2 minutes.

2. Stir in crushed tomatoes, bring to simmer, and cook until sauce thickens slightly, about 30 minutes.

3. Meanwhile, bring 4 quarts water to boil in large pot. Add pasta and 1 tablespoon salt and cook, stirring often, until al dente. Reserve ½ cup cooking water, then drain pasta and return it to pot. Add sauce and parsley, toss to combine, and season with salt and pepper to taste. Add reserved cooking water as needed to adjust consistency. Serve, passing Parmesan separately.

TEST KITCHEN TIP
Removing Sausage from Its Casing

Italian sausage is sold in several forms, including links (which is most common), bulk-style tubes, and patties. If using links, remove the meat from the casing before cooking so that it can crumble into small, bite-size pieces.

To remove sausage from its casing, hold sausage firmly on one end, and squeeze sausage out of opposite end.

Penne with Weeknight Meat Sauce

G-F TESTING LAB

| PASTA | Our favorite brand is Jovial Gluten Free Brown Rice Pasta (see pages 34–35 for complete tasting). Cooking times for gluten-free pasta vary from brand to brand. Make sure to taste the pasta often, as it can overcook quickly. |

✓ WHY THIS RECIPE WORKS

A classic old-fashioned Italian meat sauce depends on hours of cooking to develop rich flavors. At the other end of the spectrum, the typical easy meat sauce turns out rubbery ground beef in a lackluster tomato sauce. We wanted a recipe that had deep flavor and tender meat, but it had to be doable on a weeknight. We started with ground beef because it was still the clear winner in terms of speed, but we ramped up our sauce's meaty flavor by adding umami-packed ingredients like mushrooms and tomato paste. We pulsed the mushrooms in the food processor to get the right texture (larger pieces seemed noticeably spongy), then sautéed them in the pot along with onions to develop plenty of flavorful fond. To keep the meat tender, we knew from test kitchen experience that tossing ground meat with baking soda and a little water, then letting it sit briefly, would help tenderize it. We also knew to skip the browning step since that would only dry the meat out and make it tough. Instead, we added it straight to the pot after adding the tomatoes. After a brief simmer, we had a weeknight meat sauce with deep flavor and tender beef. We use a food processor to make quick work of the mushrooms. If you don't own a food processor you can chop them by hand but make sure to chop them very fine.

Penne with Weeknight Meat Sauce

SERVES 4

- 1 pound 85 percent lean ground beef
- 2 tablespoons water
- Salt and pepper
- ½ teaspoon baking soda
- 4 ounces white mushrooms, trimmed and halved if small or quartered if large
- 1 tablespoon extra-virgin olive oil
- 1 onion, chopped fine
- 3 garlic cloves, minced
- 1 tablespoon tomato paste
- 2 teaspoons minced fresh oregano or 1 teaspoon dried
- ⅛ teaspoon red pepper flakes
- 1 (28-ounce) can tomato puree
- 1 (14.5-ounce) can diced tomatoes, drained
- ¼ cup grated Parmesan cheese, plus extra for serving
- 12 ounces gluten-free penne

1. Toss beef with water, 1 teaspoon salt, ¼ teaspoon pepper, and baking soda in bowl until thoroughly combined. Let sit for 20 minutes.

2. Meanwhile, pulse mushrooms in food processor until finely chopped, about 8 pulses, scraping down bowl as needed. Heat oil in large saucepan over medium-high heat until just smoking. Add processed mushrooms and onion and cook until vegetables are softened and well browned, 8 to 10 minutes.

3. Stir in garlic, tomato paste, oregano, and pepper flakes and cook until fragrant, about 30 seconds. Stir in tomato puree, diced tomatoes, ½ teaspoon salt, and ½ teaspoon pepper and bring to gentle simmer. Stir in meat mixture and cook, breaking meat into small pieces with wooden spoon, until cooked through and sauce has thickened, about 30 minutes. Stir in Parmesan and season with salt and pepper to taste.

4. Meanwhile, bring 4 quarts water to boil in large pot. Add pasta and 1 tablespoon salt and cook, stirring often, until al dente. Reserve ½ cup cooking water, then drain pasta and return it to pot. Add sauce to pasta and toss to combine. Add reserved cooking water as needed to adjust consistency. Serve, passing Parmesan separately.

SMART SHOPPING **Tomato Puree**

Tomato puree is cooked and strained to remove the tomato seeds, making it smoother and thicker than other canned tomato products. In the test kitchen we have found that tomato puree works well when we want a thick sauce. With its thick consistency and strong tomato flavor, Muir Glen Tomato Puree is our favorite.

Soba Noodles with Pork and Vegetables

G-F TESTING LAB

SOBA NOODLES   Many brands of soba noodles also contain wheat; make sure to read the ingredient label and buy noodles made with only buckwheat flour. See page 29 for more details. Do not substitute other types of noodles for the soba noodles. Note that because of the salty ingredients, we don't salt the cooking water for the noodles in this recipe.

Soba noodles have a strong flavor that demands an equally flavorful combination of sauce and add-ins. Baby bok choy lent appealing crunch, while meaty country-style pork ribs and earthy shiitake mushrooms gave the dish savory depth. For our sauce, we started with gluten-free tamari. Ordinarily, we would reach for oyster sauce for a hit of briny sweetness, but we discovered that oyster sauce contains gluten. After some tinkering, we found that a combination of brown sugar and fish sauce provided a similar flavor without the gluten. Sesame oil added nutty richness, chili-garlic sauce brought the right amount of heat, and sake contributed clean complexity. We prefer this dish made with sake, but an equal amount of vermouth can be substituted. One large head of bok choy (stems and leaves separated and sliced ½ inch wide) can be substituted for the baby bok choy; add the stems with the mushrooms, and the leaves with the cooked pork.

Soba Noodles with Pork, Shiitakes, and Bok Choy

SERVES 4

- ¼ cup gluten-free tamari or soy sauce (see page 187)
- 3 tablespoons packed brown sugar
- 2 tablespoons fish sauce
- 4 teaspoons sake (Japanese rice wine)
- 1 tablespoon Asian chili-garlic sauce
- 1 tablespoon toasted sesame oil
- 1 pound boneless country-style pork ribs, trimmed and sliced crosswise into ⅛-inch-thick strips
- 6 garlic cloves, minced
- 1 tablespoon grated fresh ginger
- 4 teaspoons vegetable oil
- 6 heads baby bok choy (4 ounces each), sliced crosswise ½ inch wide
- 10 ounces shiitake mushrooms, stemmed and quartered
- 8 ounces gluten-free dried soba noodles
- 2 scallions, sliced thin on bias

1. Whisk tamari, sugar, fish sauce, sake, chili-garlic sauce, and sesame oil together in medium bowl. Measure 3 tablespoons of mixture into separate bowl and stir in pork; cover and refrigerate for at least 15 minutes or up to 1 hour. In separate bowl, combine garlic, ginger, and 1 teaspoon vegetable oil.

2. Heat 1 teaspoon vegetable oil in 12-inch nonstick skillet over high heat until just smoking. Add half of pork in single layer and cook without stirring for 1 minute. Stir and continue to cook until browned, about 2 minutes; transfer to clean bowl. Repeat with 1 teaspoon vegetable oil and remaining pork; transfer to bowl.

3. Wipe now-empty skillet clean with paper towels, add remaining 1 teaspoon vegetable oil, and heat over high heat until just smoking. Add bok choy and mushrooms and cook, stirring often, until vegetables are browned, 5 to 7 minutes. Clear center of skillet, add garlic-ginger mixture, and mash into pan until fragrant, about 30 seconds; stir into vegetables. Stir in cooked pork with any accumulated juice. Stir in tamari mixture and simmer until sauce has thickened, about 1 minute. Remove from heat and cover to keep warm.

4. Meanwhile, bring 4 quarts water to boil in large pot. Add noodles and cook, stirring often, until tender. Reserve ½ cup cooking water, then drain noodles and return them to pot. Add pork mixture and toss to combine. Add reserved cooking water as needed to adjust consistency. Sprinkle individual portions with scallions and serve.

SMART SHOPPING
Boneless Country-Style Pork Ribs

These meaty boneless ribs have enough marbling to stay moist and flavorful during long simmering times, making them a good choice for braising, but they also cook relatively quickly, especially when cut into smaller pieces. Look for ribs that have striations of fat throughout the meat, and avoid those that look very lean.

Soba Noodles with Roasted Eggplant

SOBA NOODLES   Many brands of soba noodles also contain wheat; make sure to read the ingredient label and buy noodles made with only buckwheat flour. See page 29 for more details. Do not substitute other types of noodles for the soba noodles. Note that because of the salty ingredients, we don't salt the cooking water for the noodles in this recipe.

WHY THIS RECIPE WORKS

With its creamy texture and mild flavor, eggplant is a perfect foil to nutty buckwheat soba noodles. Roasting proved an easy, hands-off way to cook the eggplant, and tossing it with wheat-free tamari and vegetable oil beforehand helped to season it. For the sauce, we turned once again to tamari for savory richness. An oyster sauce substitute—a combination of fish sauce and brown sugar—that we'd just developed for another soba noodle recipe lent just the right briny sweetness. Asian chili-garlic sauce and toasted sesame oil provided a nice balance of sweet and spicy flavors, while a bit of sake contributed a clean flavor that gave the sauce complexity. Finishing with cilantro and sesame seeds kept the recipe simple while adding freshness, complementary nutty flavor, and visual appeal. We prefer this dish made with sake, but an equal amount of vermouth can be substituted.

Soba Noodles with Roasted Eggplant and Sesame

SERVES 4

- ¼ cup vegetable oil
- 2 pounds eggplant, cut into 1-inch pieces
- ¼ cup gluten-free tamari or soy sauce
- 3 tablespoons packed brown sugar
- 2 tablespoons toasted sesame oil
- 4 teaspoons sake (Japanese rice wine)
- 1 tablespoon Asian chili-garlic sauce
- 1 tablespoon fish sauce
- 8 ounces gluten-free dried soba noodles
- ¾ cup fresh cilantro leaves
- 2 teaspoons sesame seeds, toasted

1. Adjust oven rack to middle position and heat oven to 450 degrees. Line large rimmed baking sheet with aluminum foil and brush with 1 tablespoon vegetable oil. Toss eggplant with remaining 3 tablespoons vegetable oil and 1 tablespoon tamari in large bowl, then spread onto prepared baking sheet. Roast until well browned and tender, 25 to 30 minutes, stirring halfway through roasting.

2. In small saucepan, whisk remaining 3 tablespoons tamari, sugar, sesame oil, sake, chili-garlic sauce, and fish sauce together. Cook over medium heat until sugar has dissolved, about 1 minute; cover and set aside.

3. Meanwhile, bring 4 quarts water to boil in large pot. Add noodles and cook, stirring often, until tender. Reserve ½ cup cooking water, then drain noodles and return them to pot. Add sauce and roasted eggplant and toss to combine. Add reserved cooking water as needed to adjust consistency. Sprinkle individual portions with cilantro and sesame seeds and serve.

SMART SHOPPING

Gluten-Free Tamari and Soy Sauce

Tamari is sold alongside soy sauce on the supermarket shelf, but the two are not the same. While soy sauce is a blend of fermented wheat and soybeans, tamari traditionally is made from fermented soybeans and contains no wheat. However, some brands today do contain a little wheat, so it's still important to read the label. Tamari has a more pungent flavor than soy sauce, but we've found it usually works well as a soy sauce substitute. We have also noticed gluten-free soy sauce recently at the supermarket. This product is made with soybeans and rice rather than wheat and is another wheat-free option.

SMART SHOPPING **Asian Hot Chili Sauces**

Used both in cooking and as a condiment, these sauces come in a variety of styles. Sriracha contains garlic and is made from chiles that are ground into a smooth paste. Chili-garlic sauce also contains garlic and is similar to sriracha, but the chiles are coarsely ground. Sambal oelek is made purely from ground chiles. Without the addition of garlic or other spices, it provides heat but not the same complexity of flavor. Once opened, these sauces will keep for several months in the refrigerator.

Drunken Noodles with Chicken

RICE NOODLES   We prefer ⅜-inch-wide noodles here, but ¼-inch-wide rice noodles can be substituted (however, do not substitute other types of noodles for the rice noodles). Even if the package directions suggest boiling rice noodles, we strongly recommend that you soak them in hot tap water. The soaking time will be longer but there's no risk of overcooking these delicate noodles; while the noodles soak, you can prep the other ingredients. See page 29 for more details about buying and soaking rice noodles. If using ¼-inch-wide noodles, reduce the soaking time in step 1 to 20 minutes.

WHY THIS RECIPE WORKS

Called drunken noodles because it is a supposed hangover cure, this dish features wide rice noodles in a spicy, potent sauce and lots of basil. We soaked wide rice noodles in hot water until they were just pliable so that we could finish cooking them in the sauce and infuse them with flavor. Chicken and napa cabbage, which we quickly stir-fried one after the other, made it a filling entrée. We found that tossing the chicken with tamari and letting it sit before cooking boosted its flavor and helped to keep it moist. After setting the meat and vegetables aside, we added the noodles to the skillet, along with a mixture of tamari, lime juice, dark brown sugar, and chili-garlic sauce. Waiting to add the basil until the last minute ensured that its color stayed fresh.

Drunken Noodles with Chicken

SERVES 4

- **12 ounces (⅜-inch-wide) dried flat rice noodles**
- **12 ounces boneless, skinless chicken breasts, trimmed and sliced into ¼-inch-thick strips**
- **1 tablespoon plus ¼ cup gluten-free tamari or soy sauce (see page 187)**
- **¾ cup packed dark brown sugar**
- **⅓ cup lime juice (3 limes), plus lime wedges for serving**
- **¼ cup water**
- **¼ cup Asian chili-garlic sauce**
- **¼ cup vegetable oil**
- **½ head napa cabbage, cored and cut into 1-inch pieces (6 cups)**
- **1½ cups coarsely chopped fresh Thai basil, Italian (sweet) basil, or cilantro**
- **4 scallions, sliced thin on bias**

1. Cover noodles with very hot tap water in large bowl and stir to separate. Let noodles soak until softened, pliable, and limp but not fully tender, 35 to 40 minutes; drain.

2. Meanwhile, toss chicken with 1 tablespoon tamari in bowl, cover, and refrigerate for at least 10 minutes or up to 1 hour. In separate bowl, whisk together remaining ¼ cup tamari, sugar, lime juice, water, and chili-garlic sauce; set aside.

3. Heat 2 teaspoons oil in 12-inch nonstick skillet over high heat until just smoking. Add chicken in single layer and cook without stirring for 1 minute. Stir and continue to cook until nearly cooked through, about 2 minutes; transfer to clean bowl.

4. Add 1 teaspoon oil to now-empty skillet and heat over high heat until just smoking. Add cabbage and cook, stirring often, until spotty brown, 3 to 5 minutes; transfer to bowl with chicken.

5. Wipe now-empty skillet clean with paper towels, add remaining 3 tablespoons oil, and heat over medium-high heat until shimmering. Add drained rice noodles and tamari mixture and cook, tossing gently, until sauce has thickened and noodles are well coated and tender, 5 to 10 minutes. Stir in chicken-cabbage mixture and basil and cook until chicken is warmed through, about 1 minute. Sprinkle with scallions and serve with lime wedges.

TEST KITCHEN TIP
Slicing Chicken for Stir-Fries

To make it easier to cut, freeze the chicken for 15 minutes.

1. Slice breasts across grain into ¼-inch-wide strips that are 1½ to 2 inches long. Cut center in half so they are same length as end pieces.

2. Cut tenderloins on diagonal to produce pieces of meat about same size as strips of breast meat.

Singapore Noodles with Shrimp

G-F TESTING LAB

RICE NOODLES Do not substitute other types of noodles for the rice vermicelli here. Even if the package directions suggest boiling rice noodles, we strongly recommend that you soak them in hot tap water. The soaking time will be longer but there's no risk of overcooking these delicate noodles; while the noodles soak, you can prep the other ingredients. See page 29 for more details about buying and soaking rice noodles.

WHY THIS RECIPE WORKS

Also known as curry noodles, this dish is Asian comfort food at its best: a big bowl of tender rice vermicelli swathed in a fragrant, curry-laced sauce. Boiling the noodles was a nonstarter—we knew they would only turn sticky and gummy. Instead, we soaked them in hot water until just barely tender, then finished cooking them through at the end with the sauce. As for the curry powder, 1 tablespoon provided the right hit of flavor but didn't go overboard. To make the recipe substantial, we added shrimp; tossing them with a bit of the curry and some sugar ensured that they had great flavor and browned nicely. Once we had browned the shrimp, we set them aside and built our sauce, then returned the noodles and shrimp to the pot, along with a full cup of liquid (chicken broth provided the right savory balance) and finished cooking. Shallots and bell pepper added sweetness and texture. Finally, with minced cilantro for clean, citrusy notes and bean sprouts for crunch, this colorful dish proved both visually appealing and flavorful.

Singapore Noodles with Shrimp
SERVES 4

8	ounces dried rice vermicelli
1	pound extra-large shrimp (21 to 25 per pound), peeled, deveined, and tails removed
1	tablespoon curry powder
⅛	teaspoon sugar
2	tablespoons vegetable oil
6	shallots, sliced thin
2	red bell peppers, stemmed, seeded, and cut into ¼-inch-wide strips
2	garlic cloves, minced
1	cup chicken broth
⅓	cup gluten-free tamari or soy sauce (see page 187)
1	tablespoon mirin
1	teaspoon sriracha
4	ounces (2 cups) bean sprouts
½	cup minced fresh cilantro

1. Cover noodles with very hot tap water in large bowl and stir to separate. Let noodles soak until softened, pliable, and limp but not fully tender, about 20 minutes; drain.

2. Meanwhile, pat shrimp dry with paper towels and toss with ½ teaspoon curry powder and sugar in bowl. Heat 1 tablespoon oil in Dutch oven over high heat until just smoking. Add shrimp in single layer and cook, without stirring, until beginning to brown, about 1 minute. Stir shrimp and continue to cook until spotty brown and just pink around edges, about 30 seconds; transfer to clean bowl.

3. Add remaining 1 tablespoon oil to now-empty pot and heat over medium heat until shimmering. Add shallots, bell peppers, and remaining 2½ teaspoons curry powder and cook until vegetables are softened, 3 to 5 minutes. Stir in garlic and cook until fragrant, about 30 seconds.

4. Stir in drained noodles, shrimp with any accumulated juice, broth, tamari, mirin, and sriracha and cook, tossing gently, until noodles are well coated, 2 to 3 minutes. Stir in bean sprouts and cilantro. Serve.

TEST KITCHEN TIP Deveining Shrimp

1. Hold shrimp firmly in your hand, then use paring knife to cut down back side of shrimp, about ⅛- to ¼-inch deep, to expose vein.

2. Using tip of knife, gently remove vein. Wipe knife against paper towel to remove vein and discard.

Pad Thai with Shrimp

G-F TESTING LAB

RICE NOODLES Do not substitute other types of noodles for the rice noodles. Even if the package directions suggest boiling rice noodles, we strongly recommend that you soak them in hot tap water. The soaking time will be longer but there's no risk of overcooking these delicate noodles; while the noodles soak, you can prep the other ingredients. See page 29 for more details about buying and soaking rice noodles.

✓ WHY THIS RECIPE WORKS

With its sweet-and-sour, salty-spicy sauce, plump, sweet shrimp, and tender rice noodles, pad thai is Thailand's best-known noodle dish and it's naturally gluten-free. Making pad thai at home can be a chore thanks to a lengthy ingredient list with hard-to-find items. We found we could achieve just the right balance of flavors while keeping it simple by using a combination of fish sauce, lime juice, rice vinegar, and brown sugar for the sauce. With this flavorful base, we found we didn't even need to season the shrimp; we merely sautéed them in the pan until barely pink at the edges, then stirred them in later to finish cooking. To get the texture of the rice noodles just right, we first soaked them in hot water so they'd start to soften, then stir-fried them in the pan. Scrambled eggs, chopped peanuts, bean sprouts, and thinly sliced scallions completed our easy, authentic-tasting pad thai.

Pad Thai with Shrimp

SERVES 4

- 8   ounces (¼-inch-wide) dried flat rice noodles
- ⅓   cup water
- ¼   cup lime juice (2 limes)
- 3   tablespoons fish sauce
- 3   tablespoons packed brown sugar
- 1   tablespoon rice vinegar
- ¼   cup vegetable oil
- 12 ounces medium shrimp (41 to 50 per pound), peeled, deveined, and tails removed
- 3   garlic cloves, minced
- 2   large eggs, lightly beaten
- ¼   teaspoon salt
- 6   tablespoons chopped unsalted roasted peanuts
- 6   ounces (3 cups) bean sprouts
- 5   scallions, sliced thin on bias
    Lime wedges
    Fresh cilantro leaves
    Sriracha

1. Cover noodles with very hot tap water in large bowl and stir to separate. Let noodles soak until softened, pliable, and limp but not fully tender, about 20 minutes; drain. In separate bowl, whisk water, lime juice, fish sauce, sugar, rice vinegar, and 2 tablespoons oil together.

2. Pat shrimp dry with paper towels. Heat 1 tablespoon oil in 12-inch nonstick skillet over high heat until just smoking. Add shrimp in single layer and cook, without stirring, until beginning to brown, about 1 minute. Stir shrimp and continue to cook until spotty brown and just pink around edges, about 30 seconds; transfer to bowl.

3. Add remaining 1 tablespoon oil and garlic to now-empty skillet and cook over medium heat until fragrant, about 30 seconds. Stir in eggs and salt and cook, stirring vigorously, until eggs are scrambled, about 20 seconds.

4. Add drained noodles and fish sauce mixture. Increase heat to high and cook, tossing gently, until noodles are evenly coated. Add cooked shrimp, ¼ cup peanuts, bean sprouts, and three-quarters of scallions. Continue to cook, tossing constantly, until noodles are tender, about 2 minutes. (If necessary, add 2 tablespoons water to skillet and continue to cook until noodles are tender.)

5. Transfer noodles to serving platter and sprinkle with remaining peanuts and remaining scallions. Serve, passing lime wedges, cilantro, and sriracha separately.

SMART SHOPPING **Fish Sauce**

Fish sauce is a salty, amber-colored liquid made from fermented fish. Naturally gluten-free, fish sauce lends dishes a salty complexity that is impossible to replicate with other ingredients. Color correlates with flavor in fish sauce; the lighter the sauce, the lighter the flavor. Fish sauce will keep indefinitely without refrigeration.

Spicy Basil Noodles with Crispy Tofu

G-F TESTING LAB

RICE NOODLES	We prefer ⅜-inch-wide noodles here, but ¼-inch-wide rice noodles will work fine (however, do not substitute other types of noodles for the rice noodles). Even if the package directions suggest boiling rice noodles, we strongly recommend that you soak them in hot tap water. The soaking time will be longer but there's no risk of overcooking these delicate noodles; while the noodles soak, you can prep the other ingredients. See page 29 for more details about buying and soaking rice noodles. If using ¼-inch-wide noodles, reduce the soaking time in step 1 to 20 minutes.

WHY THIS RECIPE WORKS

This brightly flavored Thai dish combines rice noodles with plenty of basil and a spicy, aromatic sauce. For the right amount of subtle heat, we made a paste of chiles, garlic, and shallots in the food processor. Briefly cooking this paste deepened its flavor and mellowed the harshness of the raw aromatics. Fish sauce, brown sugar, lime juice, and chicken broth added sweet and savory notes. We found a full 2 cups of basil was required to provide the dish's trademark fresh flavor and color. Pan-fried tofu offered both creamy and crispy textures that paired well with the noodles, and giving it a properly crisped exterior required a two-step approach. First, we let the tofu drain on paper towels for 20 minutes and blotted it dry. Next, we tossed it in cornstarch, which encouraged browning and gave it the right crisp coating. Extra-firm tofu is the best choice here, but firm tofu will work. This dish is quite spicy; use the lesser amount of chiles if you want a less spicy dish. For more heat, add the chile seeds.

Spicy Basil Noodles with Crispy Tofu, Snap Peas, and Bell Pepper

SERVES 4

12	ounces (⅜-inch-wide) dried flat rice noodles
14	ounces extra-firm tofu, cut into 1-inch cubes
6–8	Thai, serrano, or jalapeño chiles, stemmed and seeded
6	garlic cloves, peeled
4	shallots, peeled
2	cups chicken broth
¼	cup fish sauce
¼	cup packed brown sugar
3	tablespoons lime juice (2 limes)
½	cup cornstarch
	Salt and pepper
7	tablespoons vegetable oil
6	ounces snap peas, strings removed
1	red bell pepper, stemmed, seeded, cut into ¼-inch-wide strips, and halved crosswise
2	cups fresh Thai basil or Italian (sweet) basil leaves

1. Cover noodles with very hot tap water in large bowl and stir to separate. Let noodles soak until softened, pliable, and limp but not fully tender, 35 to 40 minutes; drain. Spread tofu over paper towel–lined baking sheet, let drain for 20 minutes, then gently press dry with paper towels.

2. Pulse chiles, garlic, and shallots in food processor into smooth paste, about 30 pulses, scraping down bowl as needed. Whisk broth, fish sauce, sugar, and lime juice together in bowl.

3. Adjust oven rack to upper-middle position and heat oven to 200 degrees. Spread cornstarch into shallow dish or pie plate. Season tofu with salt and pepper, then dredge in cornstarch and transfer to plate. Heat 3 tablespoons oil in 12-inch nonstick skillet over medium-high heat until just smoking. Add tofu and cook, turning as needed, until all sides are crisp and browned, about 8 minutes; transfer to paper towel–lined plate and keep warm in oven.

4. Wipe now-empty skillet clean with paper towels, add 1 tablespoon oil, and heat over high heat until just smoking. Add snap peas and bell pepper and cook, stirring often, until vegetables are crisp-tender and beginning to brown, 3 to 5 minutes; transfer to bowl.

5. Add remaining 3 tablespoons oil to now-empty skillet and heat over medium-high heat until shimmering. Add processed chile mixture and cook until moisture evaporates and color deepens, 3 to 5 minutes. Add drained noodles and broth mixture and cook, tossing gently, until sauce has thickened and noodles are well coated and tender, 5 to 10 minutes.

6. Stir in cooked vegetables and basil and cook until basil wilts slightly, about 1 minute. (If necessary, add up to ¼ cup hot tap water, 1 tablespoon at a time, to adjust consistency.) Top individual portions with crispy tofu and serve.

COMFORT FOODS

Lasagna with Hearty Tomato-Meat Sauce

LASAGNA NOODLES	We had good luck using Tinkyada lasagna noodles (see page 29 for more details), which require boiling, but be careful not to overcook the noodles or they can fall apart when handled.

✔️ WHY THIS RECIPE WORKS

When it comes to making a gluten-free version of a classic meat-sauce lasagna, we quickly discovered that it's all about the noodles. As with wheat noodles, you have two options—no-boil and boil-before-use—when selecting among the various gluten-free options. No-boil noodles, a standard in the test kitchen when it comes to making traditional lasagna, failed us in the gluten-free universe. These noodles varied drastically from brand to brand. They came out unevenly cooked, gummy, starchy, or brittle, or they completely disintegrated. Old-fashioned boil-before-use noodles produced more consistent results, with tender noodles that held up in the oven. Still, our preferred noodles were more delicate than the traditional ones, so we made sure to boil them only until just tender, and we opted for a sauce with a smooth consistency to avoid chunks that might weigh down and break apart the noodles in the assembled casserole. Prepared along with a classic ricotta filling, this lasagna impressed everyone in the test kitchen. If you can't find meatloaf mix, you can substitute 8 ounces each of 85 percent lean ground beef and ground pork. You can use whole-milk or part-skim mozzarella and ricotta in this recipe.

Lasagna with Hearty Tomato-Meat Sauce
SERVES 6 TO 8

NOODLES AND SAUCE
- 12 gluten-free lasagna noodles (10 ounces)
-      Salt and pepper
- 4   teaspoons extra-virgin olive oil
- 1   (28-ounce) can diced tomatoes, drained
- 1   onion, chopped fine
- 6   garlic cloves, minced
- 1   pound meatloaf mix
- ¼   cup heavy cream
- 1   (28-ounce) can tomato puree

FILLING
- 16 ounces (2 cups) whole-milk ricotta cheese
- 2½ ounces Parmesan cheese, grated (1¼ cups)
- ½   cup chopped fresh basil
- 1   large egg, lightly beaten
- ½   teaspoon salt
- ½   teaspoon pepper
- 1   pound mozzarella cheese, shredded (4 cups)

1. FOR THE NOODLES AND SAUCE: Adjust oven rack to middle position and heat oven to 375 degrees. Bring 4 quarts water to boil in large pot. Add lasagna noodles and 1 tablespoon salt and cook, stirring frequently, until just tender. Drain noodles, return to pot, and toss with 1 teaspoon oil. Spread oiled noodles out on baking sheet; set aside.

2. Pulse diced tomatoes in food processor until almost smooth, about 5 pulses. Heat remaining 1 tablespoon oil in Dutch oven over medium heat until shimmering. Add onion and cook, stirring occasionally, until softened, about 5 minutes. Add garlic and cook until fragrant, about 30 seconds.

3. Stir in meatloaf mix, ½ teaspoon salt, and ½ teaspoon pepper, increase heat to medium-high, and cook, breaking up any large pieces with wooden spoon, until no longer pink, about 4 minutes. Add cream, bring to simmer, and cook, stirring occasionally, until liquid evaporates and only rendered fat remains, about 4 minutes. Stir in processed diced tomatoes and tomato puree, and bring to simmer. Reduce heat to low and simmer until sauce has thickened and is reduced to about 6 cups, 15 to 20 minutes. (Sauce can be cooled, covered, and refrigerated for up to 2 days; reheat before assembling lasagna.)

4. FOR THE FILLING: Meanwhile, combine ricotta, 1 cup Parmesan, basil, egg, salt, and pepper in bowl.

5. Spread ½ cup meat sauce evenly over bottom of 13 by 9-inch baking dish (avoiding larger pieces of meat). Arrange 3 noodles in single layer on top of sauce. Spread each noodle evenly with 3 tablespoons ricotta mixture and sprinkle entire layer with 1 cup mozzarella. Spoon 1½ cups meat sauce over top. Repeat layering of noodles, ricotta, mozzarella, and sauce two more times. For final layer, arrange remaining 3 noodles on top and cover completely with remaining 1 cup sauce. Sprinkle with remaining 1 cup mozzarella, then sprinkle with remaining ¼ cup Parmesan.

6. Cover dish tightly with aluminum foil sprayed with vegetable oil spray. Bake for 20 minutes. Remove foil and continue to bake until cheese is spotty brown and edges are just bubbling, 20 to 25 minutes longer. Let lasagna cool for 15 minutes before serving.

SMART SHOPPING **Diced Tomatoes**

Diced tomatoes are best for rustic tomato sauces with a chunky texture, such as our Spaghetti and Meatballs (page 178), Penne with Weeknight Meat Sauce (page 182), and Spaghetti with Puttanesca Sauce (page 176). Diced tomatoes may also be processed with their juice in a food processor and used in place of crushed tomatoes when called for in a recipe. They are available packed both in juice and in puree; we favor diced tomatoes packed in juice because they have a fresher flavor. Overall, our preferred brand is Hunt's Diced Tomatoes, which tasters liked most for its fresh flavor and good balance of sweet and tart notes.

TEST KITCHEN TIP **Assembling Lasagna**

1. Boil lasagna noodles until just tender, drain, and toss with olive oil. When cool enough to handle, lay noodles out flat on baking sheet.

2. Avoiding larger pieces of meat, spread ½ cup meat sauce evenly over bottom of 13 by 9-inch baking dish. Arrange 3 noodles in single layer on top of sauce.

3. Dollop each noodle with 3 tablespoons ricotta mixture, then spread evenly using back of spoon. Sprinkle entire layer with 1 cup mozzarella.

4. Spoon 1½ cups meat sauce over top of mozzarella layer. Repeat layering of noodles, ricotta, mozzarella, and sauce 2 more times.

5. For final layer, arrange last 3 noodles on top and cover with remaining sauce. Sprinkle with remaining mozzarella, then sprinkle with remaining Parmesan.

Spinach and Tomato Lasagna

WHY THIS RECIPE WORKS

To make the greens the star, we stirred some chopped spinach into a basic tomato sauce. Frozen spinach worked just as well as fresh and was easier since it didn't require washing. Next came the classic ricotta layer. Here was another opportunity to add spinach by adding it to the ricotta and egg mixture. We spread our spinach-packed ricotta between layers of noodles and tomato sauce and moved our casserole to the oven. Even though the spinach was already chopped, with so much of it in the lasagna, the texture was noticeably uneven. To avoid clumps of spinach, we used the food processor to chop it into small pieces. The ricotta layer also seemed a little thick and dry. Reserving some of the liquid from draining the spinach, then adding it to the ricotta mixture, boosted the spinach flavor of the whole lasagna and also helped make the ricotta mixture easier to spread. Since we had the food processor out for the spinach, we tried processing the ricotta with the eggs and spinach liquid before stirring in the spinach. This extra step was worth it; the ricotta mixture became appealingly smooth and creamy. You can thaw the spinach overnight in the refrigerator instead of microwaving it. But do warm the spinach liquid to help smooth the ricotta.

Spinach and Tomato Lasagna
SERVES 6 TO 8

20	ounces frozen chopped spinach
12	gluten-free lasagna noodles (10 ounces)
	Salt and pepper
2	tablespoons extra-virgin olive oil
1	onion, chopped fine
5	garlic cloves, minced
1/8	teaspoon red pepper flakes
2	(28-ounce) cans crushed tomatoes
6	tablespoons chopped fresh basil
16	ounces (2 cups) whole-milk ricotta cheese
3	ounces Parmesan cheese, grated (1½ cups)
2	large eggs
12	ounces mozzarella cheese, shredded (3 cups)

1. Adjust oven rack to middle position and heat oven to 375 degrees. Microwave spinach in large bowl, covered, until thawed, 10 to 15 minutes, stirring halfway through. Squeeze spinach dry, reserving ¼ cup liquid. Pulse spinach in food processor until ground, 8 to 10 pulses, scraping down bowl every few pulses. Wipe out large bowl with paper towels. Transfer spinach to now-empty bowl; set aside.

2. Bring 4 quarts water to boil in large pot. Add lasagna noodles and 1 tablespoon salt and cook, stirring frequently, until just tender. Drain noodles, return to pot, and toss with 1 teaspoon olive oil. Spread oiled noodles out on baking sheet; set aside.

3. Meanwhile, heat remaining 5 teaspoons oil in large saucepan over medium heat until shimmering. Add onion and cook until softened, about 5 minutes. Stir in garlic and pepper flakes and cook until fragrant, about 30 seconds. Add ½ cup processed spinach, tomatoes, 1 teaspoon salt, and ½ teaspoon pepper and cook until slightly thickened, about 10 minutes. Off heat, stir in 3 tablespoons basil.

4. Process reserved spinach liquid and ricotta in food processor until smooth, about 30 seconds. Add remaining 3 tablespoons basil, Parmesan, eggs, 1 teaspoon salt, and ½ teaspoon pepper and process until combined. Stir ricotta mixture into remaining spinach.

5. Spread 1¼ cups tomato sauce evenly over bottom of 13 by 9-inch baking dish. Arrange 3 noodles in single layer on top of sauce. Spread 1 cup ricotta mixture evenly over noodles and sprinkle entire layer with ⅔ cup mozzarella. Spoon 1¼ cups tomato sauce over top. Repeat layering of noodles, ricotta mixture, mozzarella, and tomato sauce two more times. For final layer, arrange remaining 3 noodles on top and cover completely with remaining tomato sauce. Sprinkle with remaining 1 cup mozzarella.

6. Cover dish tightly with aluminum foil sprayed with vegetable oil spray. Place on rimmed baking sheet, and bake until bubbling around edges, about 40 minutes. Remove foil and continue to bake until cheese is melted, about 10 minutes longer. Let lasagna cool for 15 minutes before serving.

Vegetable Lasagna

G-F TESTING LAB

LASAGNA NOODLES	We had good luck using Tinkyada lasagna noodles (see page 29 for more details), which require boiling, but be careful not to overcook these noodles or they will fall apart when handled.

✔ WHY THIS RECIPE WORKS

We wanted a gluten-free vegetable lasagna with tender, flavorful vegetables, great cheese flavor, and a light tomato sauce. To start, we zeroed in on eggplant and yellow squash. Roasting them intensified their flavor and rid them of excess moisture. We then found the biggest challenge to be the noodles. As in our other lasagna recipes, boil-before-use noodles produced more consistent results, with tender noodles that held up in the oven. Our preboiled noodles would not absorb much moisture during the baking time, so we had to keep sauciness to a minimum. A bright no-cook tomato sauce bound together the layers with no excess moisture. You can use whole-milk or part-skim mozzarella and ricotta in this recipe. Undercooking the vegetables in step 2 is crucial, as they continue to cook inside the lasagna. Leaving the skins on the eggplant and squash helps keep them intact and prevents them from turning mushy.

Vegetable Lasagna
SERVES 6 TO 8

NOODLES AND VEGETABLES
- 12 gluten-free lasagna noodles (10 ounces)
  Salt and pepper
- 4 tablespoons plus 1 teaspoon extra-virgin olive oil
- 1 pound eggplant, cut into ½-inch cubes
- 1 pound yellow squash, cut into ½-inch pieces
- 2 tablespoons minced fresh thyme or 1 teaspoon dried
- ¼ teaspoon red pepper flakes

TOMATO SAUCE AND CHEESE
- 1 (28-ounce) can crushed tomatoes
- ¾ cup chopped fresh basil
- 2 garlic cloves, minced
- 2 tablespoons extra-virgin olive oil
- ¼ teaspoon red pepper flakes
  Salt and pepper
- 1 pound (2 cups) whole-milk ricotta cheese

- 2½ ounces Parmesan cheese, grated (1¼ cups)
- 1 large egg, lightly beaten
- 8 ounces mozzarella cheese, shredded (2 cups)

1. FOR THE NOODLES AND VEGETABLES: Bring 4 quarts water to boil in large pot. Add lasagna noodles and 1 tablespoon salt and cook, stirring often, until just tender. Drain noodles, return them to pot, and toss with 1 teaspoon oil. Spread oiled noodles out over baking sheet.

2. Adjust oven rack 6 inches from broiler element and heat broiler. Line rimmed baking sheet with greased aluminum foil. Toss eggplant and squash with remaining 4 tablespoons oil, thyme, pepper flakes, and ¾ teaspoon salt and spread evenly over prepared baking sheet. Broil vegetables, stirring occasionally, until softened and beginning to brown but still slightly underdone, 15 to 20 minutes; let cool slightly.

3. FOR THE SAUCE AND CHEESE: Adjust oven rack to lower-middle position and heat oven to 375 degrees. Whisk tomatoes, ½ cup basil, garlic, oil, pepper flakes, and ½ teaspoon salt together in bowl. In separate bowl, combine ricotta, 1 cup Parmesan, egg, remaining ¼ cup basil, ½ teaspoon salt, and ½ teaspoon pepper.

4. Spread ¾ cup tomato sauce evenly over bottom of 13 by 9-inch baking dish. Lay 3 noodles in dish and spread 3 tablespoons ricotta mixture over each noodle. Top evenly with ½ cup mozzarella, followed by 2 cups roasted vegetables and ¾ cup tomato sauce. Repeat layering of noodles, ricotta mixture, mozzarella, vegetables, and sauce 2 more times. For final layer, arrange remaining 3 noodles on top and spread remaining ricotta mixture over noodles. Cover completely with remaining sauce, then sprinkle with remaining ½ cup mozzarella and remaining ¼ cup Parmesan.

5. Cover dish tightly with greased aluminum foil. Bake for 20 minutes. Remove foil and bake until cheese is spotty brown and edges are just bubbling, 20 to 25 minutes longer. Let lasagna cool for 25 to 30 minutes before serving.

Chicken Parmesan

G-F TESTING LAB

SANDWICH BREAD	Our favorite brand of gluten-free multigrain sandwich bread is Glutino Gluten Free Multigrain Bread (see page 33 for complete tasting). Slices of gluten-free bread can vary in size from brand to brand, so we recommend going by weight rather than by number of slices. Also, how quickly the bread toasts can vary dramatically from brand to brand; keep your eye on the crumbs as they toast in the oven.
PANKO	You can substitute 1 cup gluten-free panko for the sandwich bread in this recipe and skip the processing and toasting in step 1. Note that the panko will make a harder and slightly less flavorful coating. We had good luck using Ian's Gluten-Free Panko Bread Crumbs.

☑ WHY THIS RECIPE WORKS

Traditional chicken Parmesan is a minefield of potential problems—a soggy crust that doesn't stick, overcooked chicken, and a chewy blanket of mozzarella—so we knew that making this recipe gluten-free was sure to pose some challenges. Typically, pounded chicken cutlets are dipped in flour, then beaten egg, and finally bread crumbs to create an even, crisp coating. After they are pan-seared, the cutlets are then covered with tomato sauce and cheese and baked. Turning to the flour coating first, we found that simply replacing the flour with cornstarch worked well for a gluten-free version. As an added bonus, the additional starch helped the coating cling well to the chicken and also contributed to creating and retaining crispness. The biggest challenge was the bread-crumb coating itself. We tried using store-bought gluten-free bread crumbs but found them to vary widely among brands, with many tasting bland, dusty, and gritty overall. So for the sake of consistency, we settled on making our own fresh crumbs in the food processor. But unlike homemade bread crumbs made with wheat bread, those made with gluten-free bread didn't coat the chicken slices evenly. Because of gluten-free bread's high starch content and lack of structure, the bread crumbs broke down into sticky pieces that clumped together. The solution was to dry them out in the oven and add cornstarch, which helped eliminate clumping. To keep the cheese topping tender, we mixed the usual shredded mozzarella cheese with an equal amount of creamy fontina. We placed the mixture directly on the fried cutlets and briefly broiled them to form a waterproof layer between the crust and the sauce. This cheese barrier delivered a juicy cutlet that kept its crunch.

Chicken Parmesan
SERVES 4

- 4 ounces (4 slices) gluten-free multigrain sandwich bread, torn into quarters
- 1 ounce Parmesan cheese, grated (½ cup)
- ½ cup plus 1 tablespoon cornstarch
- ½ teaspoon garlic powder
- ⅛ teaspoon dried oregano
- 1 large egg
- 4 (3- to 4-ounce) chicken cutlets, ½ inch thick, trimmed
  Salt and pepper
- 6 tablespoons vegetable oil
- 2 ounces whole-milk mozzarella cheese, shredded (½ cup)
- 2 ounces fontina cheese, shredded (½ cup)
- 1 cup tomato sauce, warmed
- ¼ cup chopped fresh basil

1. Adjust 1 oven rack to lower-middle position and second rack 4 inches from broiler element. Heat oven to 425 degrees. Process bread in food processor until evenly ground, about 45 seconds. Spread crumbs in even layer on rimmed baking sheet and bake on lower rack, stirring often, until golden brown, about 5 minutes. Transfer crumbs to shallow dish and break up large clumps into fine crumbs. Stir in Parmesan, 1 tablespoon cornstarch, garlic powder, and oregano.

2. Set wire rack in each of 2 rimmed baking sheets and line one with several layers of paper towels. Beat egg in second shallow dish. Place remaining ½ cup cornstarch in large zipper-lock bag. Pat chicken dry with paper towels and season with salt and pepper. Working with 1 piece chicken at a time, add to bag of cornstarch and shake to coat. Remove chicken from cornstarch and shake off excess, then dip in egg, and finally coat with crumb mixture, pressing gently to adhere; lay coated chicken on unlined wire rack.

3. Heat broiler element. Heat ¼ cup oil in 12-inch nonstick skillet over medium-high heat until shimmering. Place 2 cutlets in skillet and cook, without moving them, until bottoms are crisp and deep golden brown, 1 to 2 minutes. Flip cutlets and cook on second side until deep golden brown, 1 to 2 minutes; transfer to paper towel–lined rack. Add remaining 2 tablespoons oil to skillet and repeat with remaining cutlets, lowering heat if necessary.

4. Remove paper towels underneath chicken. Combine mozzarella and fontina and sprinkle evenly over cutlets to cover completely. Broil on upper rack until cheese is melted and beginning to brown, about 2 minutes. Transfer chicken to serving platter and top each cutlet with 2 tablespoons sauce. Sprinkle with basil and serve with remaining sauce.

Quick Tomato Sauce

MAKES ABOUT 2 CUPS

This recipe makes enough sauce to top the cutlets as well as four servings of gluten-free pasta.

- 2 **tablespoons extra-virgin olive oil**
- 2 **garlic cloves, minced**
  Salt and pepper
- ¼ **teaspoon dried oregano**
  Pinch red pepper flakes
- 1 **(28-ounce) can crushed tomatoes**
- ¼ **teaspoon sugar**
- 2 **tablespoons chopped fresh basil**

1. Heat 1 tablespoon oil in medium saucepan over medium heat until shimmering. Stir in garlic, ¾ teaspoon salt, oregano, and pepper flakes and cook until fragrant, about 30 seconds. Stir in tomatoes and sugar, increase heat to high, and bring to simmer. Reduce heat to medium-low and simmer until thickened, about 20 minutes.

2. Off heat, stir in basil and remaining 1 tablespoon oil. Season with salt and pepper to taste; cover and set aside.

TEST KITCHEN TIP **Making Chicken Cutlets**

1. If tenderloin is attached to chicken breast, remove it. Also trim any excess fat, gristle, or pieces of bone where wing and ribs were attached.

2. Lay chicken breast flat on cutting board, smooth side facing up. Rest your hand on top of chicken and, using chef's knife, slice chicken in half horizontally.

3. Place cutlets, cut side up, between sheets of plastic wrap and pound gently to ½-inch thickness.

Eggplant Parmesan

✔ WHY THIS RECIPE WORKS

In past experience with classic recipes, dipping the eggplant slices in flour, then egg, then bread crumbs had always delivered an even, crisp coating that stayed in place. We found replacing the flour with cornstarch worked equally well for a gluten-free version. The coating clung well, and the starch also helped with crispness. The biggest challenge was the bread-crumb coating itself. After trying several options, we settled on making our own fresh crumbs in the food processor. But unlike traditional homemade bread crumbs, those made with store-bought gluten-free bread didn't coat the eggplant slices evenly. The solution involved both toasting the crumbs and adding some extra ingredients (see page 205 for more details). Traditionally, cooking the coated eggplant before assembling this casserole is key to keeping the coating crisp and in place. The same proved true with our gluten-free version. Baking the breaded slices in the oven was appealingly hands-off, but the eggplant turned out tasting stale. Pan frying won out, with eggplant surrounded by a perfectly light and crunchy golden exterior. Layered with a simple basil-tomato sauce, Parmesan, and mozzarella and baked, our eggplant remained crisp, tender, and flavorful—better results than with most traditional versions. Be sure to avoid saucing the outer edges of the eggplant slices in step 5 so that they remain crisp once baked. You can use whole-milk or part-skim mozzarella in this recipe.

Eggplant Parmesan
SERVES 6 TO 8

EGGPLANT
- 10 slices (about 10 ounces) gluten-free sandwich bread, torn into quarters
- 2 ounces Parmesan cheese, grated (1 cup)
- 1 cup cornstarch
  Salt and pepper
- 4 large eggs
- 1½ pounds eggplant, sliced into ¼-inch-thick rounds
- ½ cup vegetable oil, plus extra as needed

TOMATO SAUCE
- 3 (14.5-ounce) cans diced tomatoes
- 2 tablespoons extra-virgin olive oil
- 4 garlic cloves, minced
- ¼ teaspoon red pepper flakes
- ½ cup chopped fresh basil, plus 10 torn leaves for garnish
  Salt and pepper
- 8 ounces mozzarella, shredded (2 cups)
- 1 ounce Parmesan cheese, grated (½ cup)

1. FOR THE EGGPLANT: Adjust oven rack to lower-middle position and heat oven to 425 degrees. Process bread in food processor until evenly ground, about 30 seconds (you should have about 4 cups). Spread crumbs in even layer on rimmed baking sheet and bake, stirring occasionally, until golden brown, 7 to 10 minutes. Transfer crumbs to shallow dish, breaking up any large clumps into fine crumbs. (Do not turn off oven.) Stir in Parmesan, 1 tablespoon cornstarch, ½ teaspoon salt, and ¼ teaspoon pepper. Beat eggs in second shallow dish. Combine remaining cornstarch and ½ teaspoon pepper in large zipper-lock bag.

2. Set wire rack in rimmed baking sheet. Working with half of eggplant slices at a time, place eggplant in bag of cornstarch, seal bag, and shake bag to coat eggplant. Using tongs, remove eggplant pieces from bag, shaking off excess cornstarch, dip in eggs, then coat with bread crumbs, pressing gently to adhere. Place breaded eggplant slices on prepared wire rack.

3. Heat oil in 12-inch nonstick skillet over medium-high heat until shimmering. Cook eggplant in batches until well browned on both sides, about 4 minutes, flipping halfway through cooking; add extra oil to pan as needed. Transfer cooked eggplant to clean wire rack set in rimmed baking sheet.

4. FOR THE TOMATO SAUCE: Process 2 cans diced tomatoes and their juice in food processor until almost smooth, about 5 seconds. Heat oil, garlic, and pepper flakes in large saucepan over medium-high heat, stirring occasionally, until fragrant and garlic is light golden, about 2 minutes. Stir in processed tomatoes and remaining can of

G-F TESTING LAB

BREAD   You can use store-bought bread or our Classic Sandwich Bread (page 266) to make the bread crumbs. Our favorite store-bought brand is Canyon Bakehouse Mountain White Gluten Free Bread (see page 33 for complete tasting). Weights of gluten-free sandwich breads vary; if you use a different brand, we recommend going by weight rather than number of slices. The bread may clump together during toasting; make sure to break it apart into fine crumbs before breading.

diced tomatoes and their juice and bring to boil. Reduce heat to medium-low and simmer, stirring occasionally, until sauce has thickened and reduced to 4 cups, about 15 minutes. Stir in chopped basil and season with salt and pepper to taste.

5. Spread 1 cup tomato sauce evenly over bottom of 13 by 9-inch baking dish. Layer in half of fried eggplant slices, overlapping slices to fit. Spoon 1 cup sauce over eggplant and sprinkle with 1 cup mozzarella. Layer in remaining eggplant and spoon 1 cup sauce over eggplant, leaving majority of eggplant exposed, then sprinkle with remaining 1 cup mozzarella and Parmesan. Bake until bubbling and cheese is browned, 13 to 15 minutes. Let cool for 10 minutes, then scatter torn basil leaves over top and serve, passing remaining 1 cup tomato sauce separately.

TEST KITCHEN TIP **Achieving a Crisp Eggplant Coating**

Cornstarch works well in lieu of the all-purpose flour used in a traditional coating. Homemade bread crumbs made from store-bought or homemade gluten-free sandwich bread are the best breading, but because these crumbs are fluffy and sticky, you need to toast them before coating the eggplant. Adding Parmesan directly to the coating boosts flavor, while more cornstarch further boosts browning and crispness.

1. Process bread in food processor until evenly ground, about 30 seconds. (Crumbs will be sticky.)

2. Spread processed bread crumbs on rimmed baking sheet and bake, stirring occasionally, until crumbs are evenly golden brown.

3. Transfer crumbs to shallow dish, breaking up any large clumps into fine crumbs, then stir in Parmesan and cornstarch.

4. Place half of eggplant slices in bag of cornstarch, seal bag, and shake bag to coat eggplant evenly.

5. Using tongs, thoroughly coat eggplant with beaten eggs, allowing excess to drip off.

6. Dredge eggplant in bread crumbs, pressing gently to adhere and making sure all sides are evenly coated.

Easy Stovetop Macaroni and Cheese

G-F TESTING LAB

PASTA
Our favorite brand is Jovial Gluten Free Brown Rice Pasta (see pages 34–35 for complete tasting). This brand does not make a traditional macaroni shape, but it does offer caserecce, which is shaped like a very narrow, twisted, and rolled tube. Cooking times for gluten-free pasta vary from brand to brand. Make sure to taste the pasta often, as it can overcook quickly.

Our favorite version of mac and cheese is rich, cheesy, and indulgent—but it relies on a béchamel sauce for its base. This sauce, which calls for whisking milk into a butter-flour roux, ensures smooth, thick results in the final mac and cheese. For equally creamy results without the flour, we found that a can of evaporated milk plus a couple of eggs were the key to success. The evaporated milk added just the right richness and creaminess, while the eggs worked as the thickener. (We also tried half-and-half, but it lost out because it curdled.) We cooked the pasta, then returned it to the pot and added our eggs and evaporated milk with the cheese, plus a little dry mustard and cayenne for a flavor boost. Ready for the table in about 20 minutes, our gluten-free mac and cheese was not only super-cheesy and creamy but also fast and easy. You can substitute Monterey Jack or Colby cheese if desired, but the flavor will be less pronounced.

Easy Stovetop Macaroni and Cheese

SERVES 4

12	ounces gluten-free caserecce (see page 210) or elbow macaroni
	Salt and pepper
2	large eggs
1	(12-ounce) can evaporated milk
½	teaspoon dry mustard, dissolved in 1 teaspoon water
4	tablespoons unsalted butter
12	ounces sharp cheddar cheese, shredded (3 cups)
	Pinch cayenne pepper

1. Bring 4 quarts water to boil in large pot. Stir in pasta and 1 tablespoon salt and cook, stirring often, until pasta is al dente. Meanwhile, whisk eggs, half of evaporated milk, mustard mixture, and ¼ teaspoon salt together in bowl.

2. Drain pasta and return it to pot. Add butter and cook over low heat, stirring constantly, until melted. Stir in egg mixture, half of cheese, and cayenne. Cook, gradually stirring in remaining milk and cheese, until mixture is hot and creamy, about 5 minutes.

3. Let mixture sit off heat until sauce has thickened slightly, 2 to 5 minutes. Season with salt and pepper to taste. Serve.

SMART SHOPPING

Evaporated Milk versus Condensed Milk

Evaporated and condensed milk both begin the same way: by heating milk in a vacuum so that 60 percent or more of the water evaporates. The resulting thick liquid is then either given a high-temperature treatment to sterilize it, making evaporated milk, or sweetened to preserve it, making condensed milk. Both evaporated and condensed milk have about twice the concentration of fat and protein as regular whole milk. However, condensed milk is about 45 percent sugar and is used for baking—not for savory casseroles or macaroni and cheese—so make sure to pick up the right product when shopping.

Baked Macaroni and Cheese

G-F TESTING LAB

PASTA	Our favorite brand is Jovial Gluten Free Brown Rice Pasta (see pages 34–35 for complete tasting). This brand does not make a traditional macaroni shape, but it does offer caserecce, which is shaped like a very narrow, twisted, and rolled tube. Cooking times for gluten-free pasta vary from brand to brand.
BREAD	You can use store-bought bread or our Classic Sandwich Bread (page 266) to make the bread crumbs. Our favorite store-bought brand is Canyon Bakehouse Mountain White Gluten Free Bread (see page 33 for complete tasting). Weights of gluten-free sandwich breads vary; if you use a different brand, we recommend going by weight rather than number of slices. The bread may clump together during toasting; make sure to break it apart into fine crumbs before sprinkling over the pasta.

WHY THIS RECIPE WORKS

Baked macaroni and cheese is the king of all casseroles. At its finest, it emerges from the oven with a crisp crumb topping and creamy, cheesy pasta below. Our favorite traditional baked mac and cheese relies on béchamel sauce for its base. This sauce, which calls for whisking milk into a butter-flour roux, ensures smooth, creamy results in the final dish. For equally creamy results without the flour, we relied on cornstarch (first mixed with milk to prevent clumping), which thickened our sauce to the perfect consistency. (We kept our sauce mixture loose so that it could withstand the heat of the oven without drying out.) For the cheese, we found that a mix of Colby cheese (for meltability) and cheddar cheese (for rich flavor) delivered an appealing casserole that baked up smooth and creamy. Adding a little dry mustard and cayenne helped to boost the cheesy flavor even more. Now, all we needed was the perfect bread-crumb topping. The simple fix was pulsing gluten-free bread and melted butter in the food processor and then toasting the coated crumbs in the oven. Once baked on top of our casserole, the crumbs provided the ideal crisp counterpoint to our tender pasta and creamy cheese sauce. You can substitute Monterey Jack for the Colby cheese if desired, but the flavor will be less pronounced. Make sure to taste the pasta often, as it can overcook quickly.

Baked Macaroni and Cheese
SERVES 4

- **3 slices (about 3 ounces) gluten-free sandwich bread, torn into quarters**
- **2 tablespoons unsalted butter, melted, plus 4 tablespoons unsalted butter**
- **12 ounces gluten-free caserecce (see page 212) or elbow macaroni**
- **Salt and pepper**
- **2½ cups whole milk**
- **2 tablespoons cornstarch**
- **1 garlic clove, minced**
- **½ teaspoon dry mustard**
- **⅛ teaspoon cayenne pepper**
- **1 cup chicken broth**
- **12 ounces Colby cheese, shredded (3 cups)**
- **6 ounces extra-sharp cheddar cheese, shredded (1½ cups)**

1. Adjust oven rack to middle position and heat oven to 400 degrees. Pulse bread and melted butter in food processor until coarsely ground, about 12 pulses. Spread crumbs in even layer on rimmed baking sheet and bake, stirring occasionally, until lightly browned, 6 to 8 minutes. Let cool on wire rack. (Do not turn off oven.) Once crumbs have cooled slightly, break up any large clumps into fine crumbs.

2. Meanwhile, bring 4 quarts water to boil in large pot. Stir in pasta and 1 tablespoon salt and cook, stirring often, until pasta is al dente. Drain pasta and leave in colander.

3. Whisk ½ cup milk and cornstarch together in small bowl. Add remaining 4 tablespoons butter to now-empty pot and return to medium heat until melted. Stir in garlic, mustard, and cayenne and cook until fragrant, about 30 seconds. Whisk in remaining 2 cups milk and chicken broth and bring to simmer. Whisk in cornstarch mixture, return to simmer, and continue cooking, whisking often, until large bubbles form on surface and mixture is slightly thickened, 8 to 10 minutes. Off heat, gradually whisk in Colby and cheddar until completely melted. Season with salt and pepper to taste.

4. Stir drained pasta into cheese sauce, breaking up any clumps, until well combined. Pour pasta mixture into 8-inch square baking dish (or other 2-quart casserole dish) and sprinkle with bread crumbs. Bake until golden brown and bubbling around edges, about 15 minutes. Let cool for 10 minutes before serving.

All-American Meatloaf

WHY THIS RECIPE WORKS

For a tender, moist meatloaf, we've learned that the key is adding a panade—a paste of bread (or similar ingredient, such as crackers) and milk—to the meat mixture. We wanted to make an equally tender gluten-free version, but substituting store-bought gluten-free sandwich bread was a no-go. The bread never broke down into a proper paste, and it delivered a tough, chewy meatloaf. From there we tried more adventurous ingredients: ground oats (an addition found in many older recipes), corn tortillas, potato flakes, and gelatin. All produced a loaf that was nicely bound, but the potato flakes were the winner in the end. They had the right neutral flavor and blended seamlessly into the mixture, and their starchy makeup worked just like bread, absorbing liquid and keeping the loaf tender. A combination of beef and pork provided better flavor and texture than traditional store-bought meatloaf mix. Since ground beef will cook up tough if overworked, we mixed all the ingredients with the ground pork first, then worked in the ground beef.

All-American Meatloaf

SERVES 6

- ½ cup ketchup
- ¼ cup packed light brown sugar
- 4 teaspoons cider vinegar
- 1 tablespoon vegetable oil
- 2 onions, chopped fine
- 4 garlic cloves, minced
- 1 teaspoon minced fresh thyme or ½ teaspoon dried
- 2 large eggs
- ½ cup milk
- 2 teaspoons Dijon mustard
- 2 teaspoons Worcestershire sauce
- 1 teaspoon salt
- ½ teaspoon pepper
- ⅓ cup potato flakes
- ⅓ cup minced fresh parsley
- 1 pound ground pork
- 1 pound 85 percent lean ground beef

1. Adjust oven rack to upper-middle position and heat oven to 350 degrees. Fold heavy-duty aluminum foil to form 9 by 5-inch rectangle. Center foil on wire rack set in rimmed baking sheet. Poke holes in foil with skewer (about ½ inch apart). Spray foil with vegetable oil spray.

2. Stir ketchup, sugar, and vinegar together in bowl and set aside. Heat oil in 12-inch nonstick skillet over medium-high heat until shimmering. Add onions and cook until softened, about 5 minutes. Stir in garlic and thyme and cook until fragrant, about 30 seconds. Transfer to large bowl and let cool for 5 minutes.

3. Whisk in eggs, milk, mustard, Worcestershire, salt, and pepper. Stir in potato flakes and parsley. Add pork and knead with hands until thoroughly combined. Add beef and continue to knead until uniform.

4. Transfer meat mixture to foil rectangle and shape into 9 by 5-inch loaf. Brush half of ketchup mixture over meatloaf. Bake meatloaf for 40 minutes.

5. Brush meatloaf with remaining ketchup mixture and continue to bake until center of loaf registers 160 degrees, 30 to 35 minutes. Let meatloaf cool for 15 minutes before slicing. Serve.

TEST KITCHEN TIP
Avoiding Greasy Meatloaf

We cook our meatloaf free-form on a wire rack to let the rendered fat drip away. The foil, which should be coated with vegetable oil spray, ensures that the meatloaf doesn't stick.

Set rack inside rimmed baking sheet and top with 9 by 5-inch rectangle of aluminum foil. Using skewer, poke holes in foil about ½ inch apart to allow fat to drain away.

Cheesy Southwestern Meatloaf

G-F TESTING LAB

CORN TORTILLAS	Not all brands of corn tortillas are gluten-free (or processed in a gluten-free facility); read the label.
SALSA	The test kitchen's preferred brand of jarred salsa is Chi-Chi's Medium Thick and Chunky Salsa, which is gluten-free and is processed in a gluten-free facility.

WHY THIS RECIPE WORKS

For a fun twist on meatloaf, we created this South-western version. Gluten-free corn tortillas, ground in the food processor, replaced the usual panade (a mixture of bread and milk) used as the binder in meatloaf, and they added an intense corn flavor that perfectly complemented our south-of-the-border theme. The combination of ground beef and ground pork made for a tender texture and slightly sweet flavor, while a little sour cream, in addition to the eggs, helped keep the loaf moist. We flavored the meat with a combination of classic Southwestern spices and herbs: chili powder, cumin, and cilantro. Then, instead of the standard ketchup mixture, we covered the raw loaf with a little salsa mixed with brown sugar, which turned into a flavorful, sticky glaze as the loaf baked. Halfway through baking, we covered the top of the loaf with shredded pepper Jack cheese, which melted into a smooth layer. We simmered the rest of the salsa–brown sugar mixture to reduce it, and served it on the side as a sauce. To get the most flavor impact, use either medium or hot salsa. Ground pork adds tenderness and sweet-ness to the meatloaf, but you can use 2 pounds of ground beef if you prefer.

Cheesy Southwestern Meatloaf

SERVES 6

- 1 cup prepared tomato salsa
- 3 tablespoons packed brown sugar
- 4 (6-inch) corn tortillas, torn into small pieces
- ½ cup sour cream
- 3 large eggs
- 1 (4-ounce) can green chiles, drained and finely chopped
- ¾ cup chopped scallions
- ¼ cup minced fresh cilantro
- 1 tablespoon chili powder
- 1 teaspoon ground cumin
- 1 teaspoon salt
- ½ teaspoon pepper
- 8 ounces ground pork
- 1½ pounds 80 percent lean ground beef
- 4 ounces pepper Jack cheese, shredded (1 cup)

1. Adjust oven rack to middle position and heat oven to 350 degrees. Fold piece of heavy-duty aluminum foil into 10 by 6-inch rectangle. Place foil in center of wire rack and set in rimmed baking sheet. Grease foil, then poke holes with skewer about ½ inch apart (see page 215).

2. Combine salsa and brown sugar in small saucepan; set aside. Process corn tortillas in food processor until they resemble cornmeal; transfer to large bowl. Stir in sour cream, eggs, chiles, scallions, cilantro, chili powder, cumin, salt, and pepper. Add pork and knead with hands until thoroughly combined. Add beef and continue to knead until uniform.

3. Transfer meat mixture to foil rectangle and shape into 9 by 5-inch loaf. Brush with ¼ cup salsa mixture. Bake for 40 minutes.

4. Sprinkle pepper Jack on top of meatloaf and continue to bake until loaf registers 160 degrees, 30 to 35 minutes.

5. Remove meatloaf from oven and let cool slightly. Meanwhile, simmer remaining salsa mixture over medium-high heat until thickened, 3 to 5 minutes. Serve sauce with meatloaf.

Fried Chicken

G-F TESTING LAB

CORNMEAL   The test kitchen's favorite cornmeal for most applications, including this recipe, is finely ground Whole-Grain Arrowhead Mills Cornmeal. This brand is processed in a gluten-free facility, but not all brands are. Make sure to read the label. See page 26 for more details on buying cornmeal.

WHY THIS RECIPE WORKS

There's a lot of debate about the best way to make fried chicken, but it's pretty much a given that flour is going to be in the recipe. Typically, the chicken is dredged in flour, then a buttermilk-egg batter, then another coating of flour. The flour plays two basic roles. The starch in flour delivers a coating that will be brown and crisp, while the protein in flour allows the coating to cling to the chicken and stay in place. Could we develop a recipe that delivered moist chicken coated with a crisp, mahogany crust—without traditional flour helping us out? Once the chicken was brined (we knew from experience this would ensure juicy meat), we ran a battery of gluten-free coating tests to see if any could match all-purpose flour. We tried cornstarch, rice flour, potato flour, potato starch, cornmeal, and corn flour. Cornstarch produced the crispiest crust, and although it has less binding power than flour (because it contains a lot less protein), this coating still clung nicely to the chicken. However, the coating was thin and lacked flavor. Mixing the cornstarch with cornmeal delivered a more substantial and more flavorful crust that fried up perfectly. Following a classic three-step breading process, we gave the chicken a very light coating of cornstarch, then dipped it in a buttermilk-egg mixture, then dredged it in a final coating of seasoned cornstarch and cornmeal. We found that adding both baking soda and baking powder to the buttermilk produced just enough carbon dioxide to lighten the coating. Letting the dredged chicken sit for 30 minutes before frying evenly hydrated the coating and prevented any dry spots. This fried chicken fried up as juicy, crisp, and brown as the traditional standby. A whole 4-pound chicken, cut into 10 pieces (4 breast pieces, 2 drumsticks, 2 thighs, 2 wings), can be used instead of the chicken parts. Skinless chicken pieces are also an acceptable substitute, but the meat will come out slightly drier. If using kosher chicken, do not brine in step 1.

Fried Chicken

SERVES 4

	Salt
¼	cup sugar
3½	pounds bone-in chicken pieces (split breasts cut in half, drumsticks, and/or thighs), trimmed
1	cup cornstarch
1	large egg
1	teaspoon baking powder (see page 24)
½	teaspoon baking soda
1	cup buttermilk
1	cup cornmeal (see page 220)
1½	teaspoons garlic powder
1½	teaspoons paprika
¼	teaspoon cayenne pepper
3–4	quarts peanut or vegetable oil

1. Whisk 1 quart cold water, ¼ cup salt, and sugar together in large bowl until sugar and salt dissolve. Add chicken, cover, and refrigerate for 1 hour. Remove chicken from brine and pat dry with paper towels. Set wire rack in rimmed baking sheet and line plate with triple layer of paper towels.

2. Place ½ cup cornstarch in large zipper-lock bag. Beat egg, baking powder, and baking soda together in medium bowl; stir in buttermilk (mixture will bubble and foam). Whisk remaining ½ cup cornstarch, cornmeal, garlic powder, paprika, cayenne, and 1 teaspoon salt together in shallow dish.

3. Working with half of chicken at a time, place chicken in bag of cornstarch, seal bag, and shake bag to coat chicken. Using tongs, remove chicken pieces from bag, shaking off excess cornstarch, dip in buttermilk mixture, then coat with cornmeal mixture, pressing gently to adhere. Place dredged chicken on prepared wire rack, skin side up. Cover loosely with plastic wrap and let sit for 30 minutes.

4. Meanwhile, add oil to large Dutch oven until it measures about 2 inches deep, and heat over medium-high heat to 350 degrees. Adjust oven rack to middle position and heat oven to 200 degrees. Carefully place half of chicken in pot, skin side down, cover, and fry, stirring occasionally to prevent pieces from sticking together, until deep golden brown, 7 to 11 minutes. Adjust burner, if necessary, to maintain oil temperature between 300 and 325 degrees. (After 4 minutes, check chicken pieces for even browning and rearrange if some pieces are browning faster than others.) Turn chicken pieces over and continue to cook until breast pieces register 160 degrees and drumsticks and/or thighs register 175 degrees, 6 to 8 minutes. (Smaller pieces may cook faster than larger pieces. Remove pieces from pot as they reach correct temperature.) Drain chicken briefly on paper towel–lined plate, then transfer to clean wire rack set in rimmed baking sheet and keep warm in oven.

5. Return oil to 350 degrees and repeat with remaining chicken. Serve.

SMART SHOPPING **Cornmeal**

Different recipes require different grinds and types of cornmeal. Here's what you need to know.

GRIND SIZES: While some brands label their cornmeal as fine-, medium-, or coarse-ground, many may not. And what is one brand's fine grind is another brand's medium or even coarse. We consider grains that are about the size of couscous to be coarse-ground. "Regular" cornmeal (like Quaker or Arrowhead Mills) is finely ground.

WHOLE GRAIN VS. DEGERMINATED: Whole grain cornmeal has the hull and germ of each kernel still intact. Because of that, we have found it adds a full corn flavor to baked goods, but it will never completely break down in liquid. Degerminated corn kernels have had their hard hull and germ removed and cook more evenly in polenta.

STONE-GROUND: While companies like Quaker use smooth steel rollers to produce very fine, uniform cornmeal, stone grinding produces grains of varying sizes that create a more varied texture. Keep in mind that stone-ground cornmeal can be ground fine, medium, or coarse.

INSTANT AND QUICK-COOKING: These varieties have superfine grains that are parcooked in order to reduce the cooking time They cook up gluey and lack corn flavor, so we don't use them.

TEST KITCHEN TIP **Frying Chicken**

Frying can be intimidating, but it's really simple if you follow a few basic directions. The key to success is maintaining the proper temperature for the frying oil. If it's too hot, the exterior of the food will burn before the interior cooks through, but if it's too cool the coating will never crisp up and will instead be greasy. Make sure to use a candy or instant-read thermometer to ensure that your oil is at the right temperature.

1. Add oil to Dutch oven until it measures 2 inches deep. Heat oil over medium-high heat until it registers 350 degrees (this will take about 10 to 15 minutes).

2. Carefully place half of chicken pieces in hot oil and fry until deep golden brown and breasts register 160 degrees and drumsticks and/or thighs register 175 degrees.

3. Drain chicken briefly on paper towel–lined plate, then transfer to clean wire rack set in rimmed baking sheet and place in 200-degree oven while frying remaining chicken.

Batter-Fried Fish

✔ WHY THIS RECIPE WORKS

Creating batter-fried fish with a supercrisp yet light coating encasing tender, perfectly cooked fish is challenging at best; try to make it gluten-free and you better have a few tricks up your sleeve. For starters, we needed to find the right substitute for the cup of regular flour in the batter. We started by swapping in our all-purpose gluten-free flour blend for the flour, but the resulting coating was very heavy and dense. The high starch content of our blend was the reason; the starches melted when exposed to the hot oil and created a tough, unpleasant layer around our fish. We tried a variety of other flours and found we liked the flavor and texture of brown rice flour the best. We cut it with a little cornstarch, which gave us a smoother result. We also let the batter rest for a full 30 minutes to allow the flour to fully hydrate into a smooth, silky batter. Moving on to the liquid in our batter, we first tried gluten-free beer; most batters include either beer or seltzer, as the carbonation helps promote a lighter, lacier crust. But the gluten-free beers were adding a sweetness to the batter we didn't like. Seltzer, however, added the right texture but with a clean, neutral flavor. We also added baking powder to the batter to help lighten it up further, as well as some baking soda to help with the browning. But the batter wasn't sticking uniformly, and it was too thin. Dredging the fish in additional cornstarch helped the batter adhere more evenly, but our big breakthrough happened when we gave double frying a try, which allowed us to build layers of crisp coating. This technique gave us a sturdy, crunchy, golden crust without overcooking the delicate fish inside. A sweet and tangy tartar sauce was all we needed to round out the flavors of the dish. Use a Dutch oven that holds 6 quarts or more for this recipe.

Batter-Fried Fish

SERVES 4

FISH

- 1 cup brown rice flour
- ¾ cup cornstarch
- 1 teaspoon baking powder
- ½ teaspoon baking soda
  Salt and pepper
- 1¼ cups plain seltzer
- 1½ pounds cod, cut into 4-inch-long by 1-inch-thick fingers
- 3 quarts peanut or vegetable oil

TARTAR SAUCE

- ¾ cup mayonnaise
- 2 tablespoons capers, drained and minced
- 2 tablespoons sweet pickle relish
- 1 tablespoon minced shallot
- 1½ teaspoons distilled white vinegar
- ½ teaspoon Worcestershire sauce
- ½ teaspoon pepper

1. FOR THE FISH: Adjust oven rack to middle position and heat oven to 200 degrees. Set wire rack in each of 2 rimmed baking sheets and line 1 with several layers of paper towels. Whisk brown rice flour, ½ cup cornstarch, baking powder, baking soda, 1½ teaspoons salt, and ⅛ teaspoon pepper together in large bowl. Whisk in seltzer until no lumps remain, about 30 seconds. Cover bowl with plastic wrap and let sit at room temperature for 30 minutes.

2. FOR THE TARTAR SAUCE: Combine all ingredients in bowl, cover, and refrigerate until serving.

3. Spread remaining ¼ cup cornstarch in shallow dish. Pat fish dry with paper towels and season with salt and pepper. Dredge fish in cornstarch, shaking off excess, and place on unlined wire rack.

4. Heat oil in large Dutch oven over medium-high heat to 375 degrees. Working with half of fish, dip into batter, letting excess drip back into bowl, and add to hot oil. Fry fish for 1 minute, then return to unlined rack. Return oil to 375 degrees and repeat with remaining fish.

5. Return oil to 375 degrees. Working with half of fried fish, dip again in batter and fry second time until golden brown, about 2 minutes. Transfer to paper towel–lined wire rack and keep warm in oven. Return oil to 375 degrees and repeat with remaining fish. Serve with tartar sauce.

G-F TESTING LAB

BAKING POWDER	Not all brands of baking powder are gluten-free; see page 24 for more information.
RESTING TIME	Do not shortchange the batter's 30-minute rest; if you do, the coating will be too thin and will taste gritty.

Batter-Fried Fish

We wanted a batter that coated the fish well and that also resulted in a light, airy, and extra-crispy crust. To accomplish this without traditional flour, we needed to completely rework our standard recipe.

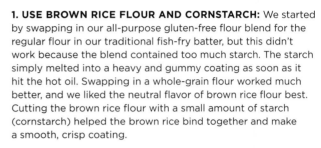

1. USE BROWN RICE FLOUR AND CORNSTARCH: We started by swapping in our all-purpose gluten-free flour blend for the regular flour in our traditional fish-fry batter, but this didn't work because the blend contained too much starch. The starch simply melted into a heavy and gummy coating as soon as it hit the hot oil. Swapping in a whole-grain flour worked much better, and we liked the neutral flavor of brown rice flour best. Cutting the brown rice flour with a small amount of starch (cornstarch) helped the brown rice bind together and make a smooth, crisp coating.

2. ADD SELTZER, NOT BEER: Many batters for fried foods contain beer because it adds a welcome wheaty flavor, and the bubbles lighten up the texture to produce a crispier crust. Unfortunately, we found that gluten-free beers (most of which are made with sorghum) don't work well as a substitute because they have a very strong, sweet flavor. Plain water also didn't work because the lack of bubbles made the batter tough and dense. So we turned to seltzer, which produced a noticeably lighter and lacier crust without adding any off-flavors.

3. LET THE BATTER REST: We figured out early on that this batter required some extra liquid for the brown rice flour to absorb, or else it had a starchy and gritty texture. The brown rice flour also needed some extra time to sit and absorb the liquid, so we added a 30-minute resting period. As the batter rested, it became thicker and clung better to the fish.

4. BATTER FISH TWICE AND FRY TWICE: Despite all our tricks, the coating on the fish was turning out a bit thin and patchy. Dredging the fish in cornstarch before dipping it in the batter helped with the patchiness, but the batter was still too thin. So we turned to a "double-fry" method whereby we battered and fried the fish twice. A first dip in the batter and a quick fry, followed by a second dip in the batter and another brief fry, made for layers of crisp coating without overcooking the fish.

New England Clam Chowder

G-F TESTING LAB

FLOUR SUBSTITUTION	King Arthur Gluten-Free Multi-Purpose Flour 2 ounces = **6 tablespoons**	Betty Crocker All-Purpose Gluten Free Rice Blend 2 ounces = **6 tablespoons**
	Chowder made with King Arthur will be a bit thicker; chowder made with Betty Crocker will be thicker and slightly starchy.	
CLAMS	We like to use cherrystone clams in this recipe; however, littlenecks or cockles will also work well. Avoid using clams larger than 4 to 5 inches in diameter, as they will be tough and will give the chowder a distinct "inky" flavor.	

WHY THIS RECIPE WORKS

There's nothing quite as comforting as a steaming bowl of creamy New England clam chowder, but it is commonly thickened with flour. Hoping for an easy fix, we simply omitted the flour, relying only on the heavy cream to give it the requisite rich body. But the chowder was just too thin and loose. In our next test, we pureed a portion of the simmered soup (before adding clams to the mix) and reduced the cream on the stovetop before stirring it in. While the soup was indeed thicker, it was lumpy and had a greasy, unsatisfying mouthfeel. We then turned to gluten-free thickeners: arrowroot, tapioca starch, cornstarch, potato starch, gelatin, and even xanthan gum. Gelatin and xanthan gum made the soup base goopy, while the individual starches produced slimy and gritty soups. Finally, we turned to our own gluten-free flour blend. We scattered 2 ounces of our blend over the vegetables we'd browned in the rendered bacon fat, and this thickened our chowder base into a velvety soup without grit or slime. Rather than deal with the pain of shucking raw clams, we simply steamed them, pulling out the meat when they just started to open to guard against overcooking. We started with bottled clam juice as our broth, then added some of the clam steaming liquid to cut the saltiness.

New England Clam Chowder

SERVES 6

- 3   cups water
- 6   pounds medium hard-shell clams, such as cherrystones, scrubbed
- 2   slices bacon, chopped fine
- 2   onions, chopped fine
- 2   celery ribs, chopped fine
- 1   teaspoon minced fresh thyme or ¼ teaspoon dried
- 2   ounces (7 tablespoons) ATK All-Purpose Gluten-Free Flour Blend (page 7)
- 3   (8-ounce) bottles clam juice
- 1½   pounds Yukon Gold potatoes, peeled and cut into ½-inch pieces
- 1   bay leaf
- 1   cup heavy cream
- 2   tablespoons minced fresh parsley
      Salt and pepper

1. Bring water to boil in Dutch oven over medium-high heat. Add clams, cover, and cook for 5 minutes. Stir clams well, cover, and continue to cook until they begin to open, 2 to 7 minutes. As clams open, transfer to large bowl; discard any that refuse to open.

2. Measure out and reserve 2 cups clam steaming liquid, avoiding any gritty sediment that has settled on bottom of pot. Remove clam meat from shells and chop coarse.

3. Clean now-empty Dutch oven, add bacon, and cook over medium heat until crispy, 5 to 7 minutes. Stir in onions and celery and cook until softened, 5 to 7 minutes. Stir in thyme and cook until fragrant, about 30 seconds. Stir in flour blend and cook for 1 minute.

4. Gradually whisk in reserved steaming liquid and bottled clam juice, scraping up any browned bits and smoothing out any lumps. Stir in potatoes and bay leaf and bring to boil. Reduce to gentle simmer and cook until potatoes are tender, 30 to 35 minutes.

5. Stir in cream and return to brief simmer. Off heat, discard bay leaf, stir in parsley, and season with salt and pepper to taste. Stir in chopped clams, cover, and let warm through, about 1 minute. Serve.

VARIATION

Quicker New England Clam Chowder
Skip steps 1 and 2. Substitute 4 (6.5-ounce) cans minced clams, drained and juice reserved, for steamed chopped clams and reserved clam steaming liquid. Add 1 teaspoon salt to pot with thyme.

Breaded Pork Cutlets

SANDWICH BREAD	Our favorite brand of gluten-free multigrain sandwich bread is Glutino Gluten Free Multigrain Bread (see page 33 for complete tasting). Slices of gluten-free bread can vary in size from brand to brand, so we recommend going by weight rather than by number of slices. Also, how quickly the bread toasts can vary dramatically from brand to brand; keep your eye on the crumbs as they toast in the oven.
PANKO	You can substitute 1 cup gluten-free panko for the sandwich bread in this recipe and skip the processing and toasting in step 1. Note that the panko will make a harder and slightly less flavorful coating. We've had good luck using Ian's Gluten-Free Panko Bread Crumbs.

✓ WHY THIS RECIPE WORKS

Since pork cutlets are so lean and mild, a flavorful coating and the right cooking method are key. To ensure the best flavor and texture, we began by making our own cutlets by cutting medallions from a pork tenderloin and then pounding them. Next, we made our own bread crumbs. We had learned previously that making bread crumbs from gluten-free bread took some work, as they break down into sticky clumps when ground; the key was to toast them in the oven to dry them out. Still, there were some clumps, creating bare spots in our breading. We solved this by adding in some cornstarch to further dry out the crumbs, which helped fill in the gaps as well as boost browning and crispness. We also mixed in some grated Parmesan cheese to add more flavor to the coating.

Breaded Pork Cutlets

SERVES 4

- 4 ounces (4 slices) gluten-free multigrain sandwich bread, torn into quarters
- 1 ounce Parmesan cheese, grated (½ cup)
- ½ cup plus 1 tablespoon cornstarch
- ½ teaspoon garlic powder
- ⅛ teaspoon dried oregano
- 2 large eggs
- 1 (1-pound) pork tenderloin, trimmed
  Salt and pepper
- 6 tablespoons vegetable oil
  Lemon wedges, for serving

1. Adjust oven rack to lower-middle position and heat oven to 425 degrees. Process bread in food processor until evenly ground, about 45 seconds. Spread crumbs in even layer on rimmed baking sheet and bake, stirring often, until golden brown, about 5 minutes. Transfer crumbs to shallow dish and break up large clumps into fine crumbs. Stir in Parmesan, 1 tablespoon cornstarch, garlic powder, and oregano. Beat eggs in second shallow dish. Place remaining ½ cup cornstarch in large zipper-lock bag.

2. Set wire rack in each of 2 rimmed baking sheets and line one with several layers of paper towels. Cut pork crosswise into 6 pieces. Place each piece, cut side up, between sheets of plastic wrap and pound gently to ⅓-inch thickness. Season pork with salt and pepper.

3. Working with 1 piece pork at a time, add to bag of cornstarch and shake to coat. Remove pork from cornstarch and shake off excess, then dip in egg, and finally coat with crumb mixture, pressing gently to adhere; lay coated pork on unlined wire rack.

4. Heat 4 tablespoons oil in 12-inch nonstick skillet over medium heat until shimmering. Place 3 cutlets in skillet and cook, without moving them, until bottoms are crisp and deep golden brown, 2 to 4 minutes. Flip cutlets and cook on second side until deep golden brown, 2 to 4 minutes; transfer to paper towel–lined rack. Add remaining 2 tablespoons oil to skillet and repeat with remaining cutlets, lowering heat if necessary. Serve with lemon wedges.

VARIATION
Lemon-Thyme Breaded Pork Cutlets

Omit oregano. Add ½ teaspoon dried thyme and 2 teaspoons grated lemon zest to bread-crumb mixture. Add 2 sprigs fresh thyme and 2 teaspoons grated lemon zest to skillet with oil and heat oil as directed; leave thyme sprigs and lemon zest in skillet when cooking pork.

TEST KITCHEN TIP **Making Pork Cutlets**

1. Cut tenderloin crosswise into 6 equal pieces, including tapered tail end (fold tip of tail underneath before pounding).

2. Place cutlets, cut side up, between sheets of plastic wrap and pound gently to ⅓-inch thickness.

Crispy Pan-Fried Pork Chops

G-F TESTING LAB

CORNFLAKES Not all brands of cornflakes are gluten-free and not all brands are processed in a gluten-free facility; make sure to read the label.

WHY THIS RECIPE WORKS

Boneless pork chops are lean and mild, a trait that often translates to bland and boring. A crunchy cornflake coating can be just the thing to give this approachable cut a boost. For a light, crisp exterior, we dipped the chops in cornstarch to absorb moisture. Buttermilk helped the cornflakes adhere, while minced garlic and mustard lent needed flavor. Two more tricks guaranteed our coating stayed in place. First, we scored the chops in a crosshatch pattern to enable the cornstarch to cling securely to the chops. And second, we let the breaded chops rest to give the cornstarch time to absorb moisture and form a thick coating that would turn crisp once cooked. We prefer natural to enhanced pork (pork that has been injected with a salt solution to increase moistness). Don't let the cooked chops drain on the paper towels for longer than 30 seconds, or the heat will steam the crust and make it soggy. Omit the sugar if using cornflakes that are already sweetened.

Crispy Pan-Fried Pork Chops
SERVES 4

- ⅓ **cup cornstarch**
- 1 **cup buttermilk**
- 1 **tablespoon Dijon mustard**
- 2 **teaspoons sugar (optional)**
- 1 **garlic clove, minced**
- 3½ **cups cornflakes**
  Salt and pepper
- 8 **(3- to 4-ounce) boneless pork chops, ½ to ¾ inch thick, trimmed**
- ⅔ **cup vegetable oil**
  Lemon wedges

1. Place cornstarch in large zipper-lock bag. In shallow dish, whisk buttermilk, mustard, sugar (if using), and garlic until combined. Process cornflakes, ¼ teaspoon salt, and ½ teaspoon pepper in food processor until cornflakes are finely ground, about 10 seconds. Transfer cornflake mixture to second shallow dish.

2. Adjust oven rack to middle position and heat oven to 200 degrees. Set wire rack in rimmed baking sheet. With sharp knife, cut 1/16-inch-deep slits on both sides of chops, spaced ½ inch apart, in crosshatch pattern. Season chops with salt and pepper.

3. Working with half of chops at a time, place chops in bag of cornstarch, seal bag, and shake bag to coat chops. Using tongs, remove chops from bag, shaking off excess cornstarch, coat in buttermilk mixture, then coat with cornflake mixture, pressing gently to adhere. Place breaded chops on prepared wire rack. Let coated chops sit for 10 minutes.

4. Heat ⅓ cup oil in 12-inch nonstick skillet over medium-high heat until shimmering. Place 4 chops in skillet and cook until golden brown and crispy, 2 to 5 minutes. Carefully flip chops and continue to cook until second side is golden brown and crispy, and center of chop registers 145 degrees, 2 to 5 minutes longer. Transfer chops to paper towel–lined plate and let drain 30 seconds on each side. Transfer to clean wire rack set in rimmed baking sheet and keep warm in oven. Discard oil in skillet and wipe clean with paper towels. Repeat process with remaining ⅓ cup oil and remaining pork chops. Serve with lemon wedges.

TEST KITCHEN TIP **Building a Sturdy Coating**

Making shallow cuts in the chops releases juices and sticky meat proteins that dampen the cornstarch and help the coating adhere.

1. With sharp knife, cut 1/16-inch-deep slits on both sides of chops, spaced ½ inch apart, in crosshatch pattern.

2. Let breaded chops sit for 10 minutes to enable cornstarch to absorb moisture and form an adhesive paste.

Crispy Chicken Fingers

G-F TESTING LAB

BREAD   You can use store-bought bread or our Classic Sandwich Bread (page 266) to make the bread crumbs. Our favorite store-bought brand is Canyon Bakehouse Mountain White Gluten Free Bread (see page 33 for complete tasting). Weights of gluten-free sandwich bread vary; if you use a different brand, we recommend going by weight rather than number of slices. The bread may clump together during toasting; make sure to break it apart into fine crumbs before breading.

✓ WHY THIS RECIPE WORKS

Fast and appealing to both kids and adults, breaded chicken fingers are a weeknight staple in many households. For a gluten-free coating that cooked up crisp, flavorful, and perfectly browned, we took a few tricks from our Eggplant Parmesan recipe (page 207). We started by processing store-bought gluten-free sandwich bread in the food processor (we knew store-bought crumbs would cook up dry and taste stale). And because these crumbs break down into fluffy, sticky clumps, we then toasted them to dry them out and give us fine, dry crumbs that coated the chicken more evenly. Still, there were some bare spots. Adding some cornstarch to the crumbs ensured an evenly browned coating. The same breading method—dipping in cornstarch, then egg, then the bread crumbs—that we'd used for our Eggplant Parmesan worked equally well here (although we skipped adding cheese to the crumbs for a simpler coating). As for the cooking method, pan-fried won out over oven-baked, delivering chicken fingers with a crisper exterior surrounding perfectly moist, flavorful chicken.

Crispy Chicken Fingers
SERVES 4

- 6 slices (about 6 ounces) gluten-free sandwich bread, torn into quarters
- ½ cup cornstarch
  Salt and pepper
- 2 large eggs
- 1½ pounds boneless, skinless chicken breasts, trimmed and cut lengthwise on slight diagonal into ¾-inch-wide strips
- ¾ cup vegetable oil

1. Adjust oven rack to lower-middle position and heat oven to 425 degrees. Process bread in food processor until evenly ground, about 30 seconds. Spread crumbs in even layer on rimmed baking sheet and bake, stirring occasionally, until golden brown, 7 to 10 minutes. Reduce oven temperature to 200 degrees.

2. Transfer crumbs to shallow dish, breaking up any large clumps into fine crumbs. Stir in 1 tablespoon cornstarch, ½ teaspoon salt, and ¼ teaspoon pepper. Beat eggs in second shallow dish. Place remaining cornstarch in large zipper-lock bag.

3. Set wire rack in rimmed baking sheet. Pat chicken dry with paper towels and season with salt and pepper. Working with half of chicken at a time, place chicken in bag of cornstarch, seal bag, and shake bag to coat chicken. Using tongs, remove chicken pieces from bag, shaking off excess cornstarch, dip in eggs, then coat with bread-crumb mixture, pressing gently to adhere. Place breaded chicken on prepared wire rack.

4. Heat oil in 12-inch nonstick skillet over medium-high heat until just smoking. Add half of chicken and cook until golden brown on all sides, 4 to 6 minutes, flipping halfway through cooking. Drain chicken briefly on paper towels, then transfer to paper towel–lined plate and keep warm in oven. Repeat with remaining breaded chicken. Serve.

TEST KITCHEN TIP **Cutting Chicken Fingers**

After trimming each chicken breast, slice it lengthwise on slight diagonal into long, ¾-inch-wide strips.

Pecan-Crusted Chicken

SANDWICH BREAD	Our favorite brand of gluten-free multigrain sandwich bread is Glutino Gluten Free Multigrain Bread (see page 33 for complete tasting). Slices of gluten-free bread can vary in size from brand to brand, so we recommend going by weight rather than by number of slices. Also, how quickly the bread toasts can vary dramatically from brand to brand; keep your eye on the crumbs as they toast in the oven. We don't recommend substituting gluten-free panko for the fresh bread crumbs in this recipe.

✓ WHY THIS RECIPE WORKS

For a twist on breaded chicken, we turned to nuts, which we thought would add a robust flavor element and appealing crunch to the breading. We started by dredging the chicken breasts in cornstarch, dipping them into an egg wash, then coating them with finely ground nuts. We then sautéed the chicken in a skillet until well browned and cooked through. Unfortunately, this didn't work. The crust tasted dense and greasy, with a gummy layer hiding underneath the breading. In addition, this heavy crust failed to stick to the chicken. To lighten up the texture of the nuts, we combined them with a handful of homemade bread crumbs. Toasting the nuts and bread crumbs together in the oven helped bring out the nut flavor and added some good crunch. We also swapped the oven for the skillet, and baked the breaded cutlets instead of sautéing them to make them less greasy. To help the breading stick better to the chicken, we employed three tricks. First, we etched a shallow crosshatch pattern into the chicken's surface which released moisture and tacky proteins from the chicken, giving the coating an exceptionally solid footing. Second, we swapped out the egg wash for buttermilk; the moisture in raw egg is bound up in its proteins, making it less available to be soaked up. Plus, we liked the subtle tang of buttermilk, along with some Dijon mustard and a little sugar, to perk up the flavor of the breading. Third, we let the breaded chicken rest, which made the coating more cohesive. Pistachios, hazelnuts, or almonds can be substituted for the pecans.

Pecan-Crusted Chicken

SERVES 4

- 1 cup pecans, chopped
- 4 ounces (4 slices) gluten-free multigrain sandwich bread, torn into quarters
- 1 tablespoon unsalted butter
- 1 shallot, minced
  Salt and pepper
- ⅓ cup cornstarch
- 1 cup buttermilk
- 1 tablespoon Dijon mustard
- 2 teaspoons sugar
- 4 (6- to 8-ounce) boneless, skinless chicken breasts, trimmed

1. Adjust oven rack to middle position and heat oven to 425 degrees. Pulse pecans and bread in food processor into coarse meal, about 30 pulses. Spread crumbs in even layer on rimmed baking sheet and bake, stirring often, until golden brown, about 5 minutes. Transfer crumbs to shallow dish and reduce oven temperature to 350 degrees.

2. Melt butter in 8-inch nonstick skillet over medium heat. Add shallot and ¼ teaspoon salt cook until softened, about 2 minutes; stir into crumbs.

3. Set wire rack in rimmed baking sheet. Place cornstarch in large zipper-lock bag. In second shallow dish, whisk buttermilk, mustard, and sugar together. With sharp knife, cut 1/16-inch-deep slits on both sides of chicken breasts, spaced ½ inch apart, in crosshatch pattern.

4. Season chicken with salt and pepper. Working with 1 piece chicken at a time, add to bag of cornstarch and shake to coat. Remove chicken from bag, shaking off excess cornstarch, then dip in buttermilk mixture, and finally coat with nut mixture, pressing gently to adhere. Lay breaded chicken on prepared wire rack and let sit for 10 minutes.

5. Bake chicken until it registers 160 degrees, 25 to 30 minutes, rotating sheet halfway through baking. Let rest 5 minutes before serving.

TEST KITCHEN TIP **Scoring Chicken Breasts**

To ensure that coating clings to chicken, use sharp knife to cut 1/16-inch-deep slits on both sides of breasts, spaced ½ inch apart, in crosshatch pattern.

Buffalo Chicken Wings

G-F TESTING LAB

BAKING POWDER   Not all brands of baking powder are gluten-free; see page 24 for more information.

WHY THIS RECIPE WORKS

We wanted to develop a recipe for roasted chicken wings that were crispy on the outside and moist and tender within, just like their fried counterpart—which usually relies on gluten. We tried rubbing the wings with baking powder and salt before they went into the oven. Baking powder acts like salt to draw out moisture from the surface of the poultry skin but also accelerates browning. More browning means crispier skin. This combination helped to draw moisture to the surface of the poultry skin. But the moisture drawn from the chicken sat as pasty beads on the skin instead of evaporating, preventing the skin from getting totally crispy. Simply blotting the wings dry with paper towels lifted away the rub, so that wouldn't work. Instead, we lowered the oven temperature to a mellow 250 degrees in order to evaporate this surface moisture without really cooking or drying out the meat. Then we cranked up the temperature and moved the wings to an upper oven rack to crisp the skin and maximize browning. The results were even better than we had hoped for: tender meat and skin that was crisp enough to pass for fried. One element remained: the sauce. Traditional Buffalo sauce is usually just Frank's RedHot Original Cayenne Pepper Sauce and butter, but we decided to add a little molasses for deeper flavor. These wings were juicy and tender, and their crispy skin held our sauce without becoming soggy. If you buy chicken wings that are already split, with the tips removed, you will need only 3½ pounds. To make this recipe dairy-free, substitute Earth Balance Vegan Buttery Sticks for the butter.

Buffalo Chicken Wings
SERVES 4 TO 6

- 4   pounds chicken wings, cut at joints, wingtips discarded
- 2   tablespoons baking powder
- ¾   teaspoon salt
- ½   cup Frank's RedHot Original Cayenne Pepper Sauce

- 4   tablespoons unsalted butter, melted
- 1   tablespoon molasses

1. Adjust oven racks to upper-middle and lower-middle positions and heat oven to 250 degrees. Set wire rack in aluminum foil–lined rimmed baking sheet. Pat wings dry with paper towels and place in large bowl. Combine baking powder and salt, sprinkle over wings, and toss to coat evenly. Arrange wings, meaty side up, in single layer on prepared wire rack.

2. Roast wings on lower rack for 30 minutes. Move wings to upper rack, increase oven temperature to 425 degrees, and roast until wings are golden brown and crispy, 40 to 50 minutes longer, rotating sheet halfway through baking.

3. Remove wings from oven and let stand for 5 minutes. Meanwhile, whisk hot sauce, melted butter, and molasses together in large bowl. Add wings to sauce, toss to coat, and serve.

VARIATION

Chicken Wings with Sweet and Spicy Thai Sauce

Substitute following sauce for hot sauce mixture in step 3: Simmer ½ cup packed brown sugar, ¼ cup lime juice (2 limes), 1 tablespoon toasted sesame oil, 1 teaspoon red pepper flakes, and 1 minced garlic clove in small saucepan over medium heat until slightly thickened, about 5 minutes. Off heat, whisk in 2 tablespoons fish sauce and transfer to large bowl.

TEST KITCHEN TIP **Prepping Chicken Wings**

1. Using chef's knife, cut through joint between drumette and wingette.

2. Cut off and discard wingtip.

Orange-Flavored Chicken

G-F TESTING LAB

SOY SAUCE   Soy sauce is traditionally a blend of fermented wheat and soybeans, but some supermarkets stock gluten-free soy sauce. Tamari is naturally gluten-free but some brands sometimes contain some wheat so it's still important to read the label. Tamari has a more pungent flavor than soy sauce, but we've found it usually works well as a substitute.

WHY THIS RECIPE WORKS

Orange-flavored chicken is a Chinese takeout classic, but most versions are more breading than chicken, and the sauce is often gloppy and lackluster. We wanted to create a gluten-free version that would be even better than the original. We started by marinating the chicken in a flavorful mixture of soy sauce, garlic, ginger, chicken broth, and fresh orange juice for bright, true orange flavor. We reserved some marinade to make our sauce, which kept our recipe streamlined. To achieve a perfect crust on our chicken—tender and yielding in places and delicately crunchy in others—we first coated the chicken pieces in egg whites and then dredged them in cornstarch. A bit of baking soda encouraged deep, flavorful browning. We prefer the flavor and texture of thigh meat for this recipe, though an equal amount of boneless, skinless chicken breasts can be used. It is easiest to grate the orange zest and remove the strips of orange zest before juicing the oranges; use a sharp vegetable peeler to remove the strips. For extra spiciness, increase the cayenne in the sauce to ½ teaspoon. The whole dried chiles are mostly for appearance, and can be omitted from the sauce with little difference in flavor. Use a Dutch oven that holds 6 quarts or more for this recipe. Sprinkle with sliced scallions and serve with white rice.

Orange-Flavored Chicken

SERVES 4

- ¾ cup chicken broth
- 1½ teaspoons grated orange zest plus 8 (2-inch) strips zest and ¾ cup juice (2 oranges)
- 6 tablespoons distilled white vinegar
- 3½ ounces (½ cup packed) dark brown sugar
- ¼ cup gluten-free soy sauce or tamari
- 3 garlic cloves, minced
- 1 tablespoon grated fresh ginger
- ½ teaspoon cayenne pepper
- 1½ pounds boneless, skinless chicken thighs, trimmed and cut into 1½-inch pieces
- 2 tablespoons water
- 5 teaspoons plus 1 cup cornstarch
- 8 small whole dried red chiles (optional)
- 3 large egg whites
- ½ teaspoon baking soda
- 3 cups peanut or vegetable oil

1. Whisk broth, grated orange zest and juice, vinegar, sugar, soy sauce, garlic, ginger, and ¼ teaspoon cayenne together in large saucepan until sugar is dissolved. Transfer ¾ cup of mixture to large zipper-lock bag, add chicken, and toss to coat; press out as much air as possible and seal bag. Refrigerate chicken for at least 30 minutes or up to 1 hour (do not marinate longer than 1 hour).

2. Meanwhile, bring remaining mixture in pot to boil over high heat. Whisk water and 5 teaspoons cornstarch together in bowl, then whisk into pot and cook until mixture is thickened, about 1 minute. Off heat, stir in orange zest strips and chiles, if using; cover and set aside.

3. Set wire rack in each of 2 rimmed baking sheets and line one with several layers of paper towels. Beat egg whites in shallow dish until frothy. Combine remaining 1 cup cornstarch, baking soda, and remaining ¼ teaspoon cayenne in large zipper-lock bag.

4. Drain chicken and pat dry thoroughly with paper towels. Working with half of chicken at a time, coat with egg whites, then transfer to bag with cornstarch and shake to coat. Shake off excess cornstarch and place on unlined wire rack.

5. Heat oil in large Dutch oven over medium-high heat until 350 degrees. Working with 1 piece of chicken at a time, add half of chicken to oil and fry until golden brown, about 5 minutes, turning chicken as needed. Transfer to paper towel–lined wire rack. Return oil to 350 degrees and repeat with remaining chicken.

6. Reheat sauce over medium heat until simmering, about 2 minutes. Add chicken and gently toss until evenly coated and heated through. Serve.

Chicken Enchiladas

G-F TESTING LAB

CORN TORTILLAS Not all brands of corn tortillas are gluten-free (or processed in a gluten-free facility); read the label.

Chicken enchiladas offer a rich and complex combination of flavors and textures, but traditional cooking methods require hours of preparation. We wanted a streamlined recipe for this popular casserole. We created a quick but flavorful red chili sauce with onions, garlic, spices, and tomato sauce. We poached the chicken directly in the sauce, which both enhanced the flavor of the sauce and ensured moist, flavorful meat for our enchilada filling. Sharp cheddar cheese complemented the rich filling nicely, while canned jalapeños and fresh cilantro rounded out the flavors and provided tang and brightness. We brushed the tortillas with oil and microwaved them to make them pliable. After experimenting with oven temperatures and times, we found that covering the assembled enchiladas and baking them at 450 degrees for 15 minutes resulted in perfectly melted cheese and kept the edges of the tortillas from drying out. Serve with sour cream, diced avocado, sliced radishes, shredded romaine lettuce, and lime wedges.

Chicken Enchiladas

SERVES 4 TO 6

- ¼ **cup vegetable oil**
- 1 **onion, chopped fine**
- 3 **tablespoons chili powder**
- 3 **garlic cloves, minced**
- 2 **teaspoons ground coriander**
- 2 **teaspoons ground cumin**
- 2 **teaspoons sugar**
- ½ **teaspoon salt**
- 1 **pound boneless, skinless chicken thighs, trimmed and cut into ¼-inch-wide strips**
- 2 **(8-ounce) cans tomato sauce**
- 1 **cup water**
- ½ **cup minced fresh cilantro**
- ¼ **cup jarred jalapeños, chopped**
- 12 **ounces sharp cheddar cheese, shredded (3 cups)**
- 12 **(6-inch) corn tortillas**

1. Heat 2 tablespoons oil in medium saucepan over medium-high heat until shimmering. Add onion and cook until softened, 5 to 7 minutes. Stir in chili powder, garlic, coriander, cumin, sugar, and salt and cook until fragrant, about 30 seconds. Stir in chicken and coat thoroughly with spices. Stir in tomato sauce and water, bring to simmer, and cook until chicken is cooked through, about 8 minutes.

2. Strain mixture through fine-mesh strainer set over bowl, pressing on chicken mixture to extract as much sauce as possible. Transfer chicken mixture to separate bowl, refrigerate for 20 minutes to chill, then stir in cilantro, jalapeños, and 2½ cups cheese.

3. Adjust oven rack to middle position and heat oven to 450 degrees. Spread ¾ cup sauce over bottom of 13 by 9-inch baking dish. Brush both sides of tortillas with remaining 2 tablespoons oil. Stack tortillas, wrap in damp dish towel, and place on plate; microwave until warm and pliable, about 1 minute.

4. Working with 1 warm tortilla at a time, spread ⅓ cup chicken filling across center of tortilla. Roll tortilla tightly around filling and place seam side down in baking dish; arrange enchiladas in 2 columns across width of dish.

5. Pour remaining sauce over top to cover completely, and sprinkle remaining ½ cup cheese down center of enchiladas. Cover dish tightly with greased aluminum foil. Bake until enchiladas are heated through and cheese is melted, 15 to 20 minutes. Serve.

Chicken and Dumplings

G-F TESTING LAB

FLOUR SUBSTITUTION	King Arthur Gluten-Free Multi-Purpose Flour 9 ounces = **1½ cups plus 2 tablespoons**	Betty Crocker All-Purpose Gluten Free Rice Blend 9 ounces = **1½ cups plus ⅓ cup**
	Dumplings made with King Arthur will be slightly gummy and dense; dumplings made with Betty Crocker will taste quite rubbery.	
XANTHAN GUM	The xanthan gum can be omitted but the dumplings will be more crumbly and will not hold together well.	
BAKING POWDER	Not all brands of baking powder are gluten-free; see page 24 for more information.	

WHY THIS RECIPE WORKS

The best chicken and dumplings boasts dumplings that are light and tender yet substantial in a brothy stew full of concentrated chicken flavor. For a gluten-free version of this comfort food classic, we started by developing a flavorful chicken and vegetable stew that was simple enough to make on a weeknight. Right off the bat we found that boneless, skinless chicken thighs were the perfect choice here because they require very little prep and are nearly impossible to overcook. After browning them, we set them aside and focused on building the stew, first sautéing chopped carrots, onions, and celery. To thicken the stew, we added 2 tablespoons of our all-purpose gluten-free flour blend and then deglazed the pan with a little sherry, which added bright flavor. After adding some chicken broth and the reserved chicken thighs, we let the stew simmer until the chicken was tender and ready to shred. Turning our attention now to the gluten-free dumplings, we first swapped in our flour blend in the usual mixture of flour, milk, melted butter, and a hefty dose of baking powder, but these dumplings simply melted into the stew. We tried adding a little xanthan gum for binding, and while these dumplings retained their shape better, they sank into the stew and had a texture that was more akin to gnocchi than to biscuits. Switching from whole milk to low-fat lightened up the batter and got us closer, but our stew still could not support the starchier dumplings. For a thicker stew, we cut back the broth to 3 cups and added more chopped carrots and celery so the dumplings could rest on a raft of chicken and vegetables while they simmered. They cooked through properly, yielding moist, tender dumplings that soaked up the sauce perfectly.

Chicken and Dumplings

SERVES 6

STEW

- **2 pounds boneless, skinless chicken thighs, trimmed**
- **Salt and pepper**
- **3 tablespoons vegetable oil**
- **4 carrots, peeled and cut into ¾-inch pieces**
- **2 celery ribs, chopped fine**
- **1 onion, chopped fine**
- **1 teaspoon minced fresh thyme**
- **2 tablespoons ATK All-Purpose Gluten-Free Flour Blend (page 7)**
- **¼ cup dry sherry**
- **3 cups chicken broth**
- **½ cup frozen peas**
- **¼ cup minced fresh parsley**

DUMPLINGS

- **9 ounces (2 cups) ATK All-Purpose Gluten-Free Flour Blend (page 7)**
- **1 tablespoon baking powder**
- **1 teaspoon salt**
- **⅛ teaspoon xanthan gum**
- **½ cup plus 1 tablespoon 1 or 2 percent low-fat milk**
- **½ cup plus 1 tablespoon water**
- **3 tablespoons unsalted butter, melted**

1. FOR THE STEW: Pat chicken dry with paper towels and season with salt and pepper. Heat 2 tablespoons oil in Dutch oven over medium-high heat until shimmering. Add chicken and brown well on both sides, 6 to 8 minutes; transfer to plate.

2. Add remaining 1 tablespoon oil, carrots, celery, onion, and thyme to fat left in pot and cook over medium heat, stirring often, until vegetables are well browned, 5 to 7 minutes. Stir in flour blend and cook for 1 minute. Stir in sherry, scraping up any browned bits. Whisk in broth, smoothing out any lumps. Stir in browned chicken and any accumulated juices, and bring to simmer. Cover, reduce heat to medium-low, and simmer until chicken registers 175 degrees, about 15 minutes.

3. Remove pot from heat. Transfer chicken to cutting board, let cool, then shred into 1-inch pieces with 2 forks. Let broth settle for 5 minutes, then skim fat from surface. Stir in shredded meat, peas, and parsley, and season with salt and pepper to taste.

4. FOR THE DUMPLINGS: Whisk flour blend, baking powder, salt, and xanthan gum together in large bowl. Microwave milk, water, and butter in separate bowl until just warm, about 1 minute. Using silicone spatula, stir warmed milk mixture into flour mixture until incorporated and no flour pockets remain; mixture will begin to bubble immediately.

5. Return stew to vigorous simmer over medium heat. Using greased tablespoon measure, spoon portions of dumpling batter evenly over top of stew; you should have about 24 dumplings. Cover, reduce heat to medium-low, and simmer vigorously until dumplings have doubled in size and toothpick inserted into center comes out clean, about 15 minutes. Serve.

VARIATION

Dairy-Free Chicken and Dumplings
In dumplings, substitute soy milk for milk and Earth Balance Vegan Buttery Sticks for butter.

TEST KITCHEN TIP **Making Chicken and Dumplings**

1. Brown chicken thighs well on both sides, 6 to 8 minutes; transfer to plate.

2. After sautéing aromatics and adding flour blend and sherry to pot, whisk in chicken broth, smoothing out any lumps. Return browned chicken to pot, cover, and simmer for about 15 minutes.

3. Transfer chicken to cutting board, let cool slightly, then shred into 1-inch pieces with 2 forks. Defat broth, then stir in shredded meat, peas, and parsley and season with salt and pepper to taste.

4. Using silicone spatula, stir warmed milk mixture into flour mixture until incorporated and no flour pockets remain; mixture will begin to bubble immediately.

5. Using greased tablespoon measure, spoon portions of dumpling batter evenly over top of vigorously simmering stew; you should have about 24 dumplings.

6. Cover, reduce heat to medium-low, and simmer vigorously until dumplings have doubled in size and toothpick inserted into center comes out clean, about 15 minutes. Serve.

Chicken Pot Pie

WHY THIS RECIPE WORKS

With its flaky pastry topping and flour-thickened gravy, chicken pot pie might be the most quintessential comfort food—so it's all the more disappointing that it's typically off-limits for anyone avoiding gluten. We knew we'd be using our own gluten-free pie dough for the topping, so we moved on to tackle finding a roux replacement that would deliver an equally velvety, rich sauce. We tested every gluten-free thickener we could think of: arrowroot, tapioca starch, potato starch, potato flour, white rice flour, gelatin, and even xanthan gum. The latter two turned the sauce gloppy and unappetizing, while most of the starches produced fillings that were slimy and oddly translucent. Finally, we turned to our own flour blend. While perhaps not as straightforward as using a single starch or flour, it amounted to minimal extra work since we needed it for the pastry topping anyway. We found that just 1½ ounces provided sufficient thickening power, and because it contains a combination of flours and starches, it didn't turn the gravy slimy, like starches alone, or gritty, like flour alone. The rest of the filling came together very easily. We followed the classic method for building the sauce, lightly browning aromatic vegetables in butter before adding tomato paste for color and flavor. We then stirred in the flour blend, making sure to cook it briefly before whisking in the chicken broth. We poached whole chicken breasts (or thighs, if you like more flavorful dark meat) in the sauce. When the chicken was cooked through, it was cooled, shredded, and stirred back into the sauce along with peas and cream. Once our classic filling was prepared, we unrolled the dough over the hot filling and popped it in the oven. But instead of baking up nice and flaky, the dough turned out gummy because of all the liquid. So instead we first parbaked the rolled-out dough until it was golden, then slid it over the filling. All the assembled pie needed was about 10 minutes in the oven to finish cooking through and unify the flaky crust and hearty, comforting filling. If you don't have a rimless baking sheet to use for baking the crust, use an inverted rimmed baking sheet.

Chicken Pot Pie

SERVES 4 TO 6

- 1 recipe Single-Crust Pie Dough (page 427)
- 4 tablespoons unsalted butter
- 1 onion, chopped fine
- 2 carrots, peeled and sliced ¼ inch thick
- 1 celery rib, sliced ¼ inch thick
  Salt and pepper
- 1 teaspoon tomato paste
- 1 teaspoon minced fresh thyme
- 1½ ounces (⅓ cup) ATK Gluten-Free Flour Blend (page 7)
- 2 cups chicken broth
- 1½ pounds boneless, skinless chicken breasts and/or thighs, trimmed
- ½ cup frozen green peas
- ¼ cup heavy cream
- 3 tablespoons minced fresh parsley
- 1 tablespoon dry sherry

1. Roll dough into 10-inch circle between 2 large sheets of parchment paper. Remove top parchment sheet. Fold in outer ½-inch rim of dough (creating 9½-inch circle). Using index finger of one hand and thumb and index finger of other hand, crimp folded edge of dough to make attractive fluted rim. Using paring knife, cut 4 oval-shaped vents, each about 2 inches long and ½ inch wide, in center of dough. Transfer dough, still on parchment, to baking sheet and chill in freezer until firm, about 15 minutes.

2. Adjust oven racks to upper-middle and lower-middle positions and heat oven to 400 degrees. Bake shaped dough on upper-middle rack until golden brown and crisp, 18 to 20 minutes. Transfer crust, still on sheet, to wire rack and let cool slightly. (Do not turn off oven.)

3. Meanwhile, melt butter in Dutch oven over medium-high heat. Add onion, carrots, celery, ¼ teaspoon salt, and ¼ teaspoon pepper and cook until tender and lightly browned, about 8 minutes. Stir in tomato paste and thyme and cook until browned, about 2 minutes. Stir in flour blend and cook until golden, about 1 minute.

G-F TESTING LAB

FLOUR SUBSTITUTION	King Arthur Gluten-Free Multi-Purpose Flour 1½ ounces = ¼ **cup**	Bob's Red Mill GF All-Purpose Baking Flour 1½ ounces = **5 tablespoons**

King Arthur makes the filling a tad starchier and Bob's Red Mill makes the filling a bit darker in color, but both options work well. King Arthur makes the crust a bit more delicate and crumbly, and it doesn't brown quite as well as our flour blend in this recipe. Bob's Red Mill makes the crust slightly drier and less tender.

4. Slowly whisk in chicken broth until no lumps remain. Add chicken, cover, and bring to simmer. Reduce heat to medium-low and continue to simmer, covered, stirring occasionally, until chicken registers 160 degrees for breasts and 175 degrees for thighs, and sauce has thickened, 15 to 18 minutes. Remove pot from heat. Transfer chicken to large bowl and let cool slightly. Using 2 forks, shred into bite-size pieces.

5. Stir peas, heavy cream, parsley, and sherry into thickened sauce, then stir in shredded chicken with any accumulated juices. Season with salt and pepper to taste. Pour mixture into 9½-inch deep-dish pie plate and place parbaked pie crust on top of filling. Bake on lower-middle rack until crust is deep golden brown and filling is bubbly, about 10 minutes. Let pot pie cool for 5 to 10 minutes before serving.

TEST KITCHEN TIP **Preparing Pot Pie Crust**

Because the pastry crust will turn gummy if baked start to finish over the hot pie filling, we roll it out to fit our pie and first parbake it alone, then slide it on top of the filling. It needs to bake only about 10 minutes longer before it's done.

1. Roll dough between 2 sheets of parchment into 10-inch circle. Remove top parchment.

2. Fold in outer ½-inch rim of dough, creating 9½-inch circle.

3. Using index finger of your hand and thumb and index finger of your other hand, crimp folded edge of dough to make fluted rim.

4. Cut 4 oval-shaped vents, each about 2 inches long and ½ inch wide, in dough. Transfer dough, still on parchment, to baking sheet and freeze until firm.

5. Bake crust, still on baking sheet, on upper-middle rack until golden brown, 18 to 20 minutes.

6. Carefully slide parbaked pie crust on top of warm filling.

Beef Pot Pie

G-F TESTING LAB

FLOUR SUBSTITUTION	King Arthur Gluten-Free Multi-Purpose Flour 1½ ounces = ¼ **cup**	Betty Crocker All-Purpose Gluten Free Rice Blend 1½ ounces = ⅓ **cup**
	Pot pie made with King Arthur will have a slightly thicker filling and a less-sturdy pie dough. Pot pie made with Betty Crocker will have a thicker, starchier filling.	
SOY SAUCE	Soy sauce is traditionally a blend of fermented wheat and soybeans, but some supermarkets stock gluten-free soy sauce. Tamari is naturally gluten-free but some brands sometimes contain some wheat so it's still important to read the label. Tamari has a more pungent flavor than soy sauce, but we've found it usually works well as a substitute.	

WHY THIS RECIPE WORKS

Beef pot pie hits all the marks as a comforting one-dish meal, with its flaky pastry topping and flour-thickened gravy—so we were determined to make version suitable for anyone avoiding gluten. As with our Chicken Pot Pie (page 243), we used our own gluten-free pie dough for the crust, and we once again found that our own all-purpose flour blend made the best roux replacement, delivering a velvety, rich sauce. Just 1½ ounces provided sufficient thickening power, and because the blend contains a combination of flours and starches, it didn't turn the gravy slimy, like starches alone, or gritty, like flour alone. The rest of the filling came together easily. When choosing a flavorful cut of meat, we found that chuck roast fit the bill without a high price tag. Browning just half of the beef before stewing imparted the rich, deep flavor of searing without overcrowding the pan and requiring the browning of two batches of beef. Sautéed mushrooms, tomato paste, beef broth, gluten-free soy sauce, and Worcestershire added even more meaty umami flavor. Instead of fully baking the pastry on the filling, we carefully shaped, chilled, and then parbaked the pastry topping until it was golden, then slid it over the filling. All the assembled pie needed was about 10 minutes in the oven to finish cooking through and unify the flaky crust and hearty, comforting filling. If you don't have a rimless baking sheet to use for baking the crust, use an inverted rimmed baking sheet.

Beef Pot Pie

SERVES 4 TO 6

1	recipe Single-Crust Pie Dough (page 427)
2¼	pounds boneless beef chuck-eye roast, trimmed and cut into ¾-inch pieces
	Salt and pepper
3	tablespoons vegetable oil
4	ounces cremini mushrooms, trimmed and quartered
2	carrots, peeled and cut into ½-inch pieces
1	onion, chopped fine
2	tablespoons tomato paste
4	garlic cloves, minced
1	teaspoon minced fresh thyme or ½ teaspoon dried
1½	ounces (⅓ cup) ATK All-Purpose Gluten-Free Flour Blend (page 7)
½	cup dry red wine
1¾	cups beef broth
1	tablespoon gluten-free soy sauce or tamari
1	tablespoon Worcestershire sauce
1	bay leaf
1	cup frozen peas

1. Roll dough into 10-inch circle between 2 large sheets of parchment paper. Remove top parchment sheet. Fold in outer ½-inch rim of dough (creating 9½-inch circle). Using index finger of one hand and thumb and index finger of other hand, crimp folded edge of dough to make attractive fluted rim. Using paring knife, cut 4 oval-shaped vents, each about 2 inches long and ½ inch wide, in center of dough. Transfer dough, still on parchment, to baking sheet and chill in freezer until firm, about 15 minutes.

2. Adjust oven racks to upper-middle and lower-middle positions and heat oven to 400 degrees. Bake shaped dough on upper-middle rack until golden brown and crisp, 18 to 20 minutes. Transfer crust, still on sheet, to wire rack and let cool slightly. Reduce oven temperature to 350 degrees.

3. FOR THE FILLING: Meanwhile, pat beef dry with paper towels and season with salt and pepper. Heat 1½ tablespoons oil in Dutch oven over medium-high heat until just smoking. Brown half of beef on all sides, 7 to 10 minutes; transfer to bowl, along with remaining unbrowned beef.

4. Add remaining 1½ tablespoons oil, mushrooms, carrots, and onion to now-empty pot and cook over medium heat until vegetables are lightly browned, about 5 minutes. Stir in tomato paste, garlic, and thyme and cook until fragrant, about 30 seconds. Stir in flour blend and cook for 1 minute. Stir in wine and cook, scraping up any browned bits, until evaporated, about 2 minutes. Slowly whisk in broth, soy sauce, and Worcestershire until no lumps remain.

5. Add beef and any accumulated juices and bay leaf to pot and bring to simmer. Cover pot, transfer to lower oven rack, and cook until beef is tender, 1¼ to 1½ hours.

6. Remove bay leaf, stir in peas, and season with salt and pepper to taste. Pour mixture into 9½-inch deep-dish pie plate and slide parbaked pie crust on top. Bake on lower rack until crust is deep golden brown and filling is bubbly, about 10 minutes. Let pot pie cool for 5 to 10 minutes before serving.

Cheese Quiche

✔ WHY THIS RECIPE WORKS

Since most quiche fillings are naturally gluten-free, the challenge of a good gluten-free quiche recipe lies squarely in the crust. We had just developed our recipe for a flaky gluten-free pie dough, so we thought baking a custardy cheese quiche filling in a parbaked crust would be a quick and easy win. To our surprise, the golden-brown parbaked crust turned unappealingly soggy after we'd filled it and returned it to the oven to cook the custard through. To preserve its light, flaky texture, we realized we needed to create a moisture barrier between the crust and the filling. Sprinkling cheese over the bottom of the crust during the last few minutes of parbaking allowed the cheese to melt into an even layer that provided the perfect defense it needed. Dry Parmesan worked best here since it didn't turn rubbery. For the filling, we opted to use cheddar since it melted seamlessly into the custard. To ensure that every bit of cheese made it into the final quiche, we added the cheddar to the pie shell before the custard since sometimes not all of the custard mixture fits into the pie shell. Even after the shell had been filled and had baked for 45 minutes, this crust was still perfectly crisp. And no one would have guessed it was gluten-free. Be sure to add the custard to the pie shell while the shell is still warm so that the quiche will bake evenly; if the crust has cooled, simply rewarm it in the oven for about 5 minutes before adding the custard. The center of the quiche will be soft and will jiggle slightly when it comes out of the oven, but the filling will continue to set (and sink somewhat) as it cools. See page 428 for details on fitting pie dough into a pie plate. This basic recipe is easy to adapt and we offer four simple variations on page 251.

Cheese Quiche
SERVES 6 TO 8

- 1   recipe Single-Crust Pie Dough (page 427)
- 1   ounce Parmesan cheese, grated (½ cup)
- 5   large eggs
- 2   cups half-and-half
- 1   tablespoon minced fresh chives
- ¼   teaspoon salt
- ¼   teaspoon pepper
- 4   ounces cheddar cheese, shredded (1 cup)

1. Roll dough into 12-inch circle between 2 large sheets of plastic wrap. Remove top plastic, gently invert dough over 9-inch pie plate, and ease dough into plate. Remove remaining plastic and trim dough ½ inch beyond lip of pie plate. Tuck overhanging dough under itself to be flush with edge of pie plate. Crimp dough evenly around edge using your fingers. Cover loosely with plastic and freeze until chilled, about 15 minutes.

2. Adjust oven rack to lower-middle position and heat oven to 375 degrees. Bake crust until light golden brown in center, about 20 minutes. Remove crust from oven, sprinkle bottom of crust evenly with Parmesan, and continue to bake until cheese has melted, about 5 minutes. Transfer pie plate to wire rack. Reduce oven temperature to 350 degrees. (Crust must still be warm when filling is added.)

3. While crust bakes, whisk eggs, half-and-half, chives, salt, and pepper together in large liquid measuring cup. Place warm pie shell on rimmed baking sheet, sprinkle cheddar into bottom of pie shell, and place in oven. Carefully pour egg mixture into shell until it reaches about ¼ inch from top edge of crust (you may have extra egg mixture).

4. Bake quiche until top is lightly browned, center is set but soft, and knife inserted about 1 inch from edge comes out clean, 35 to 45 minutes. Let quiche cool for at least 1 hour or up to 3 hours before serving.

G-F TESTING LAB

FLOUR SUBSTITUTION	King Arthur makes the crust a bit more delicate and crumbly, and it doesn't brown quite as well as our flour blend in this recipe. Bob's Red Mill makes the crust slightly drier and less tender.

VARIATIONS

Quiche Lorraine

Substitute 1 cup shredded Gruyère for cheddar. Cook 4 slices finely chopped bacon in 10-inch skillet over medium heat until crispy, about 8 minutes. Using slotted spoon, transfer bacon to paper towel–lined plate; pour off all but 2 teaspoons bacon fat left in skillet. Add 1 finely chopped small onion to skillet and cook over medium heat until lightly browned, about 5 minutes. Cool slightly, and stir into egg mixture along with bacon.

Leek and Goat Cheese Quiche

Substitute 1 cup crumbled goat cheese for cheddar. Melt 2 tablespoons unsalted butter in 10-inch skillet over medium-high heat. Add 2 finely chopped leeks, white and light green parts only, and cook until softened, about 6 minutes. Cool slightly, and stir into egg mixture.

Asparagus and Gruyère Quiche

Substitute 1 cup shredded Gruyère for cheddar and stir 1 bunch asparagus, trimmed and sliced on bias into ¼-inch-thick pieces, into egg mixture.

Spinach and Feta Quiche

Omit chives and substitute 1 cup crumbled feta for cheddar. Stir 1 (10-ounce) package frozen chopped spinach, thawed and squeezed dry, into egg mixture.

TEST KITCHEN TIP **Making Perfect Quiche**

For a crisp crust and perfectly cooked filling, we not only parbake our gluten-free crust, but also sprinkle Parmesan partway through the parbaking time to create a moisture barrier against the filling. Pouring the custard into the pie shell after it's on the oven rack is easier than trying to transfer the shell with its very liquid-y filling to the oven. Cheddar makes a good choice for the cheese in the filling because it melts well into the custard. To ensure maximum cheesy flavor, we add the cheddar before the custard because there likely wouldn't be enough room for all of it if the custard filling were poured in first. We pull the quiche from the oven before it is completely set since it will finish cooking as it cools.

1. Sprinkle Parmesan over bottom of parbaked crust and bake until just melted and set, about 5 minutes. Reduce oven temperature as directed.

2. Place warm pie shell on rimmed baking sheet, sprinkle cheddar into pie shell, and place in oven. Carefully pour egg mixture into shell until it reaches about ¼ inch from top edge of crust (you may have extra egg mixture).

3. Remove quiche from oven when top is browned and knife inserted about 1 inch from edge comes out clean. Center of quiche should jiggle slightly (it will continue to cook as it cools).

Shepherd's Pie

G-F TESTING LAB

CORNSTARCH   Cornstarch takes the place of the flour in the traditional recipe. See page 22 for details on this ingredient.

✓ WHY THIS RECIPE WORKS

We wanted a streamlined, modern take on this dish—with a flavorful gravy that coated the meat without relying on flour. Making the recipe from start to finish in a skillet kept it streamlined, and swapping in ground beef for the usual chunks of meat saved us from a lengthy braising time. To keep the meat tender, we knew from experience it would help to toss it with baking soda and water, then let it rest briefly (a trick we also used with our Penne with Weeknight Meat Sauce, page 182). In lieu of flour for thickening power, we turned to cornstarch. Combining it with a little water to make a slurry kept it from clumping and ensured that it dispersed evenly in the gravy. Don't use ground beef that's fattier than 93 percent or the dish will be greasy. You will need a 10-inch broiler-safe skillet for this recipe.

Shepherd's Pie
SERVES 4 TO 6

1½	pounds 93 percent lean ground beef
3	tablespoons water
	Salt and pepper
½	teaspoon baking soda
2½	pounds russet potatoes, peeled and cut into 1-inch chunks
4	tablespoons unsalted butter, melted
½	cup milk
1	large egg yolk
8	scallions, green parts only, sliced thin
2	teaspoons vegetable oil
1	onion, chopped
4	ounces white mushrooms, trimmed and chopped
1	tablespoon tomato paste
2	garlic cloves, minced
2	tablespoons Madeira or ruby port
1¼	cups beef broth
2	teaspoons Worcestershire sauce
2	sprigs fresh thyme
1	bay leaf
2	carrots, peeled and chopped
4	teaspoons cornstarch

1. Toss beef with 2 tablespoons water, 1 teaspoon salt, ¼ teaspoon pepper, and baking soda in bowl until thoroughly combined. Set aside for 20 minutes.

2. Meanwhile, place potatoes in medium saucepan; add water to just cover and 1 tablespoon salt. Bring to boil over high heat. Reduce heat to medium-low and simmer until potatoes are soft, 8 to 10 minutes. Drain potatoes and return to saucepan. Return saucepan to low heat and cook, shaking pot occasionally, until moisture has evaporated, about 1 minute. Remove pan from heat and mash potatoes well. Stir in melted butter. Whisk together milk and egg yolk in a small bowl, then stir into potatoes. Stir in scallions and season with salt and pepper. Cover and set aside.

3. Heat oil in broiler-safe 10-inch skillet over medium heat until shimmering. Add onion, mushrooms, ½ teaspoon salt, and ¼ teaspoon pepper and cook, stirring occasionally, until vegetables are just starting to soften, 4 to 6 minutes. Stir in tomato paste and garlic and cook until bottom of skillet is dark brown, about 2 minutes. Add Madeira and cook, scraping up any browned bits, until evaporated, about 1 minute. Add broth, Worcestershire, thyme, bay leaf, and carrots and bring to boil, scraping up any browned bits. Reduce heat to medium-low, add beef in 2-inch chunks, and bring to gentle simmer. Cover and cook until beef is cooked through, 10 to 12 minutes, breaking up meat chunks with 2 forks halfway through cooking. Stir cornstarch and remaining 1 tablespoon water together, then stir mixture into filling and continue to simmer until slightly thickened, about 1 minute. Discard thyme and bay leaf. Season with salt and pepper to taste.

4. Adjust oven rack 5 inches from broiler element and heat broiler. Place mashed potatoes in large zipper-lock bag and snip off a corner to create 1-inch opening. Pipe potatoes in even layer over filling. Smooth potatoes with back of spoon, then use tines of fork to make ridges over surface. Place skillet on rimmed baking sheet and broil until potatoes are golden brown and crusty and filling is bubbly, 10 to 15 minutes. Let cool for 10 minutes before serving.

Vegetable Pot Pie with Crumble Topping

G-F TESTING LAB

FLOUR SUBSTITUTION	King Arthur Gluten-Free Multi-Purpose Flour 5 ounces = ⅔ **cup plus ¼ cup** 3 ounces = ⅓ **cup plus ¼ cup**	Betty Crocker All-Purpose Gluten Free Rice Blend 5 ounces = **1 cup** 3 ounces = ½ **cup plus 2 tablespoons**
	Pot pie made with King Arthur will have a slightly thicker filling and a somewhat starchy-tasting crumble topping. Pot pie made with Betty Crocker will have a thicker filling and the crumble topping will be less crisp and slightly chewy.	
BAKING POWDER	Not all brands of baking powder are gluten-free; see page 24 for more information.	
RESTING TIME	Do not shortchange the topping's 30-minute rest; if you do, it will taste gritty and greasy.	

✔️ WHY THIS RECIPE WORKS

We set out to make the ultimate spring-vegetable pot pie, one that was easy and could serve a crowd. In lieu of a crust, we created a savory gluten-free crumble topping by rubbing softened butter with a mixture of our flour blend and baking powder by hand, adding Parmesan and then cream to bind it all together. For the filling, we lightly sautéed the vegetables in butter, then stirred in our flour blend for the roux, cooking it briefly before adding sherry and whisking in vegetable broth and cream. We already had prebaked the crumble to ensure that it was supercrisp before scattering it over the hot pie filling. At that point, the topped casserole needed only a mere 10 minutes to finish browning.

Vegetable Pot Pie with Crumble Topping

SERVES 6 TO 8

TOPPING

5	ounces (1 cup plus 2 tablespoons) ATK All-Purpose Gluten-Free Flour Blend (page 7)
1¼	teaspoons baking powder
¼	teaspoon salt
¼	teaspoon pepper
4	tablespoons unsalted butter, cut into ½-inch cubes and chilled
1⅓	ounces Parmesan cheese, grated (⅔ cup)
¾	cup heavy cream

FILLING

7	tablespoons unsalted butter
1½	pounds cremini mushrooms, trimmed and sliced thin
	Salt and pepper
2½	pounds leeks, white and light green parts only, halved lengthwise, sliced thin, and washed thoroughly
1¼	pounds carrots, peeled and cut into ½-inch pieces
2	pounds asparagus, trimmed and cut on bias into 1-inch lengths
4	garlic cloves, minced
3	ounces (⅔ cup) ATK All-Purpose Gluten-Free Flour Blend (page 7)
⅔	cup sherry
2½	cups vegetable broth
1	cup heavy cream
3	cups frozen peas, thawed
3	tablespoons chopped fresh tarragon
2	tablespoons grated lemon zest (2 lemons)

1. FOR THE TOPPING: Adjust oven rack to middle position and heat oven to 425 degrees. Whisk flour blend, baking powder, salt, and pepper together in large bowl. Sprinkle butter pieces over top. Using fingers, rub butter into flour mixture until it resembles coarse cornmeal. Stir in Parmesan and cream until combined. Cover bowl with plastic wrap and let rest at room temperature for 30 minutes.

2. Crumble mixture into irregularly shaped ½-inch pieces on parchment paper–lined rimmed baking sheet. Bake until starting to brown, 10 to 15 minutes, rotating sheet halfway through baking. Leave oven on.

3. FOR THE FILLING: Meanwhile, melt 4 tablespoons butter in Dutch oven over medium-high heat. Add mushrooms and ½ teaspoon salt and cook until mushrooms have released their liquid and begun to brown, 15 to 20 minutes; transfer to medium bowl.

4. Melt remaining 3 tablespoons butter in now-empty pot over medium heat. Add leeks, carrots, and 2 teaspoons salt and cook for 3 minutes. Stir in asparagus and cook until carrots and leeks are softened and asparagus is crisp-tender, 3 to 5 minutes. Stir in garlic and cook until fragrant, about 30 seconds.

5. Stir in flour blend and cook for 1 minute. Stir in sherry and cook until evaporated, about 30 seconds. Slowly whisk in broth and cream until no lumps remain. Off heat, stir in cooked mushrooms, peas, 2 tablespoons tarragon, and lemon zest. Season with salt and pepper to taste.

6. Pour filling into 13 by 9-inch baking dish and sprinkle evenly with topping. Bake until filling is bubbling and topping is well browned, about 10 minutes. Let pot pie cool for 10 minutes. Sprinkle with remaining 1 tablespoon tarragon and serve.

Strata with Spinach and Gruyère

G-F TESTING LAB

SANDWICH BREAD	Our favorite brand of gluten-free multigrain sandwich bread is Glutino Gluten Free Multigrain Bread (see page 33 for complete tasting). Slices of gluten-free bread can vary in size from brand to brand, so we recommend going by weight rather than by number of slices.
RESTING TIME	Do not shortchange the strata's 8-hour refrigerating time or else there will be pockets of raw bread in the center of the casserole.

✓ WHY THIS RECIPE WORKS

Since a classic strata breakfast casserole is all about the bread, making it gluten-free was setting the bar pretty high, especially since brands of gluten-free bread vary so widely. Also, gluten-free bread is less absorbent than regular bread, so we needed to make adjustments to the recipe because the excess liquid created a greasy, scrambled layer around the edges of the dish. We cut down overall on the amount of custard we usually use, reducing the dairy by ¼ cup and the eggs by one. We also switched from half-and-half to whole milk to combat the greasiness issue. We have used white wine previously to lighten the heaviness of dairy and decided to try that here. We cut down the amount and found that reducing it in the skillet helped to concentrate the flavor as well as keep our amount of liquid in check. We thoroughly squeezed the frozen spinach to remove excess moisture, and then sautéed it to extract even more. To determine how long our strata needed to sit before baking, we weighted it down for an hour or two but found the gluten-free bread did not absorb the custard evenly. Letting it sit overnight greatly improved its texture, and we could bake it the following morning for a perfect make-ahead breakfast.

Strata with Spinach and Gruyère

SERVES 4 TO 6

- 2 tablespoons unsalted butter
- 4 shallots, minced
  Salt and pepper
- 10 ounces frozen chopped spinach, thawed and squeezed dry
- ⅓ cup dry white wine
- 8 ounces (8 slices) gluten-free multigrain sandwich bread
- 6 ounces Gruyère cheese, shredded (1½ cups)
- 5 large eggs
- 1½ cups whole milk

1. Melt butter in 10-inch nonstick skillet over medium heat. Add shallots and pinch salt and cook until shallots are softened, about 3 minutes. Stir in spinach and cook until warmed through, about 2 minutes; transfer to plate. Add wine to now-empty skillet and simmer over medium-high heat until it has reduced by half, about 3 minutes; let cool.

2. Grease 8-inch square baking dish. Arrange half of bread in single layer in dish. Sprinkle half of spinach mixture and ½ cup Gruyère over top. Repeat with remaining bread, remaining spinach mixture, and ½ cup Gruyère to make second layer.

3. Whisk eggs, reduced wine, milk, ½ teaspoon salt, and pinch pepper together in bowl, then pour evenly over top. Cover dish tightly with plastic wrap, pressing it flush to surface. Weigh strata down and refrigerate for at least 8 hours or up to 24 hours.

4. Adjust oven rack to middle position and heat oven to 325 degrees. Meanwhile, let strata sit at room temperature for 20 minutes. Unwrap strata and sprinkle with remaining ½ cup Gruyère. Bake until edges and center are puffed and edges have pulled away slightly from sides of dish, 50 to 55 minutes. Let cool for 5 minutes before serving.

VARIATION

Strata with Sausage, Mushrooms, and Monterey Jack Cheese

Chorizo, kielbasa, or hot or sweet Italian sausage can be substituted for the breakfast sausage.

Omit spinach and substitute Monterey Jack cheese for Gruyère. Before adding shallots to skillet, add 8 ounces crumbled breakfast sausage and cook for 2 minutes, then stir in 8 ounces trimmed and sliced white mushrooms and cook until lightly browned, 5 to 10 minutes.

TEST KITCHEN TIP **Weighing Down Strata**

Cover dish tightly with plastic wrap, pressing it flush to surface. Top with second casserole dish (or trimmed piece of cardboard) and weigh it down with several heavy cans.

Tamale Pie

CORNMEAL Coarse-ground degerminated cornmeal such as yellow grits (with grains the size of couscous) works best in this recipe. Avoid instant and quick-cooking products, as well as whole-grain, stone-ground, and regular cornmeal. Not all brands of cornmeal are processed in a gluten-free facility; make sure to read the label. See page 220 for more details on buying cornmeal.

✔ WHY THIS RECIPE WORKS

With its spicy mixture of meat and vegetables—and cornbread topping that soaks up all the flavors—a good tamale pie is hard to beat. But most tamale pies rely on a cornbread layer that includes flour. We tried making a tamale pie using our own recipe for gluten-free cornbread (see page 323), spreading the batter over the prepared filling and baking the pie like a traditional recipe, but without all-purpose flour in the mix to provide structure, it disintegrated into the filling. Clearly our cornbread, while fine baked in a skillet and great served alongside a bowl of chili, didn't have the necessary structure to bake through on top of a liquid-y tamale pie filling. Looking for an alternative with a similarly rustic corn flavor, we landed on polenta. We prepared the filling in a skillet and the polenta in a separate pot and then we spread the polenta over the filling and baked it all together for about 30 minutes. For the tamale pie filling itself, we turned to a flavorful, simple combination of ground beef and black beans. A cup of Monterey Jack melted into the mixture and helped thicken it to just the right texture. Ground pork or turkey can be substituted for the beef.

Tamale Pie
SERVES 6

- 3 tablespoons vegetable oil
- 1 pound 90 percent lean ground beef
- 1 onion, chopped fine
- 1 jalapeño chile, stemmed, seeded, and minced
- Salt and pepper
- 1½ tablespoons chili powder
- 2 garlic cloves, minced
- 1½ teaspoons minced fresh oregano or ¾ teaspoon dried
- 1 (15-ounce) can black beans, rinsed
- 1 (14.5-ounce) can diced tomatoes
- 1 cup fresh or frozen corn (thawed if frozen)
- 4 ounces Monterey Jack cheese, shredded (1 cup)
- 2½ cups water
- ¾ cup coarse-ground cornmeal

1. Adjust oven rack to lower-middle position and heat oven to 375 degrees. Heat 1 tablespoon oil in 12-inch skillet over medium-high heat until just smoking. Add ground beef and cook, breaking up large clumps, until just beginning to brown, about 4 minutes.

2. Stir in onion, jalapeño, and ¼ teaspoon salt and cook until softened, about 5 minutes. Stir in chili powder, garlic, and oregano and cook until fragrant, about 30 seconds. Stir in beans, tomatoes and their juice, and corn and simmer until almost all liquid has evaporated, about 3 minutes. Off heat, stir cheese into beef mixture and season with salt and pepper to taste. Transfer mixture to 9½-inch deep-dish pie plate or 3-quart baking dish.

3. Bring water to boil in large saucepan over high heat. Add ¼ teaspoon salt, then slowly pour in cornmeal while whisking vigorously to prevent clumping. Reduce heat to medium and cook, whisking constantly, until cornmeal thickens, about 3 minutes. Stir in remaining 2 tablespoons oil.

4. Spread cornmeal mixture over top of beef mixture and seal against edge of dish. Cover with aluminum foil that has been sprayed with vegetable oil spray, and bake until crust is set and pie is heated through, about 30 minutes. Let cool for 5 to 10 minutes before serving.

Golden Cornbread and Sausage Stuffing

G-F TESTING LAB

CORNMEAL   The test kitchen's favorite cornmeal for baking is finely ground Whole-Grain
Arrowhead Mills Cornmeal. This brand has been processed in a gluten-free facility,
but not all brands are. Make sure to read the label. See page 220 for more details on
buying cornmeal.

✓ WHY THIS RECIPE WORKS

We set out to make a gluten-free cornbread stuffing that would have everyone asking for more. Using our own gluten-free cornbread recipe seemed like a reasonable starting point, but it turned to mush in a stuffing recipe. The first key was adding tapioca flour, which helps the cornbread absorb moisture without disintegrating. The second key was adding cornstarch to the broth mixture, as the cornbread soaked up the liquid like a sponge. The cornbread absorbed just enough of the cornstarch-thickened, gravylike liquid to turn into a cohesive, scoopable casserole without getting mushy. Many cornbread stuffing recipes require first baking cornbread, then drying it out so that it will hold up. To keep our recipe simple, we baked the cornbread in a thin layer in a large baking sheet, purposely overbaking it so the cornbread is dried and ready to absorb the broth.

Golden Cornbread and Sausage Stuffing

SERVES 8 TO 10

CORNBREAD

10	ounces (2 cups) cornmeal
4	ounces (1 cup) tapioca flour
1	tablespoon baking powder (see page 24)
¾	teaspoon baking soda
¼	teaspoon salt
4	large eggs
1	cup whole milk
3	tablespoons unsalted butter, melted

STUFFING

6	tablespoons unsalted butter
1	pound bulk pork sausage
2	onions, chopped fine
2	celery ribs, chopped fine
2	tablespoons minced fresh thyme
2	tablespoons minced fresh sage
2	garlic cloves, minced
3	cups chicken broth
1	cup half-and-half
1	teaspoon pepper
2	tablespoons cornstarch

1. FOR THE CORNBREAD: Adjust oven rack to middle position and heat oven to 350 degrees. Line rimmed baking sheet with parchment paper and spray with vegetable oil spray. Whisk cornmeal, tapioca flour, baking powder, baking soda, and salt together in large bowl. In separate bowl, whisk together eggs and milk, then whisk into flour mixture until combined. Stir in melted butter.

2. Spread batter evenly into prepared pan. Bake until top is deep golden brown and edges have pulled away from sides of pan, about 20 minutes, rotating sheet halfway through baking. Let cool 10 minutes, then flip out onto wire rack and let cool to room temperature. Cut cornbread into ½-inch pieces. Increase oven temperature to 400 degrees.

3. FOR THE STUFFING: Spray 13 by 9-inch baking dish with vegetable oil spray. Melt butter in large saucepan over medium-high heat. Add sausage and cook, breaking meat into small pieces, until sausage loses its raw color, about 5 minutes. Transfer sausage to very large bowl, leaving fat in pan.

4. Add onions and celery to fat in saucepan and cook over medium-high heat until softened, about 8 minutes. Stir in thyme, sage, and garlic and cook until fragrant, about 30 seconds. Whisk in 2½ cups broth, half-and-half, and pepper, and bring to simmer. Whisk together remaining ½ cup broth and cornstarch in bowl, and slowly whisk into simmering mixture. Simmer until slightly thickened, about 10 minutes.

5. Add cornbread to bowl with sausage (but don't mix it in). Pour broth mixture over cornbread and stir gently to combine, being careful not to break cornbread into smaller pieces. Cover with plastic wrap and let sit, stirring occasionally, until all liquid is absorbed, about 15 minutes. Transfer mixture to prepared baking dish. Bake until top is golden brown, about 40 minutes. Let stuffing cool for 10 minutes before serving. (Stuffing can be cooled and refrigerated for up to 1 day. Reheat, covered with foil, in 400-degree oven.)

Wild Rice Dressing

BREAD   You can use store-bought bread or our Classic Sandwich Bread (page 170) to make the bread crumbs. Our favorite store-bought brand is Udi's Gluten Free White Sandwich Bread (see page 22 for complete tasting). Weights of gluten-free sandwich bread vary from brand to brand; if you are not using Udi's, we recommend going by weight rather than number of slices. Bread may clump together during toasting; make sure to break it apart into fine crumbs.

WHY THIS RECIPE WORKS

After developing a classic Southern-style cornbread stuffing, we set out to make a wild rice stuffing that could straddle the line between rustic and elegant on the Thanksgiving table. We knew the rice would be combined with plenty of flavorful ingredients, so even though it meant a slightly diluted flavor, we settled on cooking it like pasta—in plenty of liquid—since that would guarantee even cooking and the fewest blown-out grains. A combination of chicken broth and water gave the rice the right amount of meaty flavor. To bind the grains, we wanted to use a custard for richness plus just enough gluten-free sandwich bread to hold it all together. For the custard, we tried a combination of cream and eggs, but this was too rich by itself so we added some liquid reserved from cooking the rice to lighten it up and reinforce the rice's flavor. We made gluten-free bread crumbs in the food processor from store-bought bread, then toasted the crumbs to ensure they dried out and didn't clump when we combined them with the rice. Drizzling the casserole with butter and covering it with foil before baking ensured the rice grains on top didn't dry out and infused the bread with a complementary nutty richness. Depending on the brand, wild rice absorbs varying quantities of liquid. If you have less than 1½ cups of leftover cooking liquid, make up the difference with additional chicken broth. To make this recipe vegetarian, you can substitute vegetable broth for the chicken broth.

Wild Rice Dressing

SERVES 10 TO 12

- 2   cups chicken broth
- 2   cups water
- 1   bay leaf
- 2   cups wild rice
- 10 slices (about 10 ounces) gluten-free sandwich bread, torn into pieces
- 8   tablespoons unsalted butter
- 2   onions, chopped fine
- 3   celery ribs, chopped fine
- 4   garlic cloves, minced
- 1   tablespoon minced fresh sage or 1½ teaspoons dried
- 1   tablespoon minced fresh thyme or 1½ teaspoons dried
- 1½ cups heavy cream
- 2   large eggs
- ¾   teaspoon salt
- ½   teaspoon pepper

1. Bring broth, water, and bay leaf to boil in medium saucepan over medium-high heat. Stir in rice, reduce heat to low, cover, and simmer until rice is tender, 35 to 45 minutes. Strain contents of pan through fine-mesh strainer into large liquid measuring cup. Transfer rice to bowl; discard bay leaf. Reserve 1½ cups cooking liquid.

2. Adjust oven rack to lower-middle position and heat oven to 325 degrees. Pulse 5 slices bread in food processor until only pea-size pieces remain and transfer to rimmed baking sheet. Repeat with remaining 5 slices bread and transfer to sheet. Bake bread crumbs until deep golden brown, about 15 to 17 minutes, stirring occasionally and rotating sheet halfway through baking. Let bread crumbs cool completely, about 10 minutes. (Do not turn off oven.)

3. Melt 4 tablespoons butter in 12-inch skillet over medium heat. Add onions and celery and cook until softened and golden, 8 to 10 minutes. Add garlic, sage, and thyme and cook until fragrant, about 30 seconds. Stir in reserved cooking liquid, remove from heat, and let cool for 5 minutes.

4. Whisk cream, eggs, salt, and pepper together in large bowl. Slowly whisk in onion mixture. Stir in rice and toasted bread crumbs until well combined, then transfer to 13 by 9-inch baking dish. Melt remaining 4 tablespoons butter in now-empty skillet and drizzle evenly over dressing. Cover dish with aluminum foil and bake until set, 45 to 55 minutes. Remove foil and let cool for 15 minutes. Serve. (The dressing can be cooled and refrigerated for up to 1 day. Reheat, covered with foil, in 325-degree oven.)

BREAD, PIZZA, AND CRACKERS

Classic Sandwich Bread

G-F TESTING LAB

FLOUR SUBSTITUTION	King Arthur Gluten-Free Multi-Purpose Flour 14 ounces = **2⅓ cups plus ¼ cup**	Bob's Red Mill GF All-Purpose Baking Flour 14 ounces = **2½ cups plus ⅓ cup**
	Note that bread made with King Arthur will have a slightly tighter crumb, and bread made with Bob's Red Mill will be denser and will have a distinct bean flavor.	
OAT FLOUR	If you do not have oat flour, you can process 4 ounces old-fashioned rolled oats in a food processor or spice grinder until finely ground, about 1 minute. Do not use quick oats. You can substitute sorghum or millet flour for the oat flour.	
PSYLLIUM HUSK	Do not omit the powdered psyllium husk; it is crucial to the structure of the bread. For more information, see page 21.	

WHY THIS RECIPE WORKS

Most gluten-free sandwich bread recipes turn out squat bricks with a cardboard texture. We wanted a reliable recipe that produced a light-textured sandwich loaf—something large enough to actually slice for sandwiches. We began with our classic sandwich bread mixing method in a stand mixer fitted with a dough hook but found that the bread significantly improved when we replaced the dough hook with the paddle. The starches in the gluten-free flour blend need to be hydrated, and mixing with a paddle for 6 minutes was the best way to get the job done. (At first the dough will seem very soupy, but as the starches hydrate it will become thicker and start to look like cookie dough.) To build a tall loaf with a nice crumb, we needed more protein and turned to oat flour for help. While many other recipes in this book rely on xanthan gum to provide structure, we preferred psyllium husk in this recipe (as well as in all other bread recipes) because it resulted in a more delicate crumb. Psyllium helped build a stronger protein network that trapped gas and steam—which was key to producing a tall loaf. We also liked its earthy flavor, which seemed out of place in cookies but was perfect in bread. Adding baking powder as well as the usual yeast was also key to getting a good rise. Milk is the classic choice for sandwich bread, but we achieved a better rise with water—and a lot of it. An egg and some milk powder added more protein and structure, and the milk powder was also key for flavor and browning. The high water content was essential to produce steam and enable the loaf to rise, but we found it necessary to prolong the baking time to drive off moisture once the loaf was set. (Shorter baking times yielded a gummy crumb.) To help the dough rise, we fashioned a collar out of foil and attached it to the top of the loaf pan, much as you might do when making a soufflé. Do not substitute soy milk powder for the milk powder in this recipe, as it will negatively impact the flavor and structure of the bread. Note that this recipe calls for an 8½ by 4½-inch loaf pan; if using a 9 by 5-inch loaf pan, the dough will not rise as high and the bread will not be quite as tall.

Classic Sandwich Bread
MAKES 1 LOAF

- 2 cups warm water (110 degrees)
- 2 large eggs
- 2 tablespoons unsalted butter, melted and cooled
- 14 ounces (3 cups plus 2 tablespoons) ATK All-Purpose Gluten-Free Flour Blend (page 7)
- 4 ounces (1⅓ cups) gluten-free oat flour
- 1½ ounces (½ cup) nonfat dry milk powder
- 3 tablespoons powdered psyllium husk
- 2 tablespoons sugar
- 2¼ teaspoons instant or rapid rise yeast
- 2 teaspoons baking powder (see page 24)
- 1½ teaspoons salt

1. Spray 8½ by 4½-inch loaf pan with vegetable oil spray. Whisk water, eggs, and melted butter together in bowl. Using stand mixer fitted with paddle, mix flour blend, oat flour, milk powder, psyllium, sugar, yeast, baking powder, and salt on low speed until combined. Slowly add water mixture and let dough come together, about 1 minute, scraping down bowl as needed. Increase speed to medium and beat until sticky and uniform, about 6 minutes. (Dough will resemble cookie dough.)

2. Using silicone spatula, scrape dough into prepared loaf pan and press it gently into corners with your wet hands; smooth top of dough and spray with water. Run your finger around entire edge of loaf, pressing down slightly, so that sides are about ½ inch shorter than center. Tightly wrap double layer of aluminum foil around pan so that top edge of foil rests at least 1 inch above rim of pan; secure foil collar with staples. Cover loosely with plastic wrap and let rise at room temperature until dough has risen by 50 percent (½ inch above rim of pan), about 1 hour.

3. Adjust oven rack to middle position and heat oven to 350 degrees. Remove plastic and spray loaf with water. Bake until top is golden, crust is firm, and loaf sounds hollow when tapped, about 1½ hours, rotating pan halfway through baking.

4. Transfer pan to wire rack and let bread cool for 10 minutes. Remove loaf from pan and let cool completely on rack, about 2 hours. Serve. (Once cooled, bread can be wrapped in double layer of plastic wrap and stored at room temperature for up to 3 days. See freezing instructions below.)

VARIATION

Oatmeal-Honey Sandwich Bread

We prefer our flour blend, but you can substitute 12 ounces of another blend. We strongly recommend weighing the flour; if you opt to measure by volume, you will need 1⅔ cups plus ½ cup King Arthur Gluten-Free Multi-Purpose Flour or 2¼ cups plus 2 tablespoons Bob's Red Mill GF All-Purpose Baking Flour. Note that bread made with King Arthur will be slightly spongy, and bread made with Bob's Red Mill will be denser and slightly wet and will have a distinct bean flavor.

Reduce water to 1¾ cups. Reduce ATK Gluten-Free Flour Blend to 12 ounces (2⅔ cups) and increase oat flour to 6 ounces (2 cups). Substitute 3 tablespoons honey for sugar. Sprinkle top of loaf with 2 tablespoons old-fashioned rolled oats after spraying with water in step 3. Increase baking time to 2 hours.

TEST KITCHEN TIP **Working with Gluten-Free Sandwich Bread Dough**

Most experienced bakers know that bread dough is properly kneaded when it transitions from sticky to smooth. This change doesn't occur when making gluten-free bread dough. The mixing process is important for hydrating the flour and combining the ingredients, but when the dough is properly mixed it will still be quite sticky and it will look like thick cookie dough. As a result, the dough goes right from the mixing bowl to the loaf pan in this recipe. Don't attempt hand kneading on the counter.

Using silicone spatula, scrape dough into greased 8½ by 4½-inch loaf pan. Using wet hands, press dough gently into corners of pan; smooth top of dough and spray with water.

TEST KITCHEN TIP
Cooling and Storing Gluten-Free Bread

Like its traditional counterparts, gluten-free bread needs to cool completely before being sliced, or the interior of the loaf will be gummy. Gluten-free breads have a shorter shelf life than bread made with wheat flour. As baked bread cools, its starches begin to crystallize, trapping water inside the hardened crystal structures. This process of "retrogradation" (more commonly known as staling) explains why bread becomes firm and appears to dry out as it sits on the counter. Gluten-free flour blends have a higher starch content than wheat flour has, so this effect is amplified in gluten-free breads.

We have found that most gluten-free breads will keep for a few days if wrapped tightly in a double layer of plastic wrap. After the first day, the bread is best toasted. As with traditional breads, refrigerating any gluten-free bread will speed up the staling process, so keep them on the counter.

TEST KITCHEN TIP
Freezing Gluten-Free Bread

We have found that freezing fully cooled loaves is a good option for most gluten-free breads. For sandwich breads, we like to slice the bread before freezing so that we can pull individual slices from the freezer as needed. This applies to Classic Sandwich Bread, Oatmeal-Honey Sandwich Bread, Multigrain Sandwich Bread, and Cinnamon-Raisin Bread. For Hearty Country Flax Bread and Olive-Rosemary Bread, freeze leftover bread in a single piece, defrost it at room temperature, and then reheat the bread in a 400-degree oven for about 10 minutes to recrisp the crust. (You can also slice these two breads before freezing and then take out pieces one at a time for toasting.) Don't keep any gluten-free bread in the freezer for longer than one month.

Classic Sandwich Bread

A good gluten-free sandwich bread is hard to come by. Among supermarket options, our tasters felt that most were inedible. (See pages 32–33 for more detail.) Whether store-bought or homemade, most gluten-free loaves are short and dense, but with some clever engineering we were able to create a tall loaf that could actually be used for sandwiches.

1. ADD PSYLLIUM: The gluten proteins in wheat flour build structure in traditional sandwich breads. After testing various options, we concluded that powdered psyllium husk was the best substitute. It acts like a binding agent and strengthens the proteins in gluten-free flours so they can hold gas and steam during baking without weighing the bread down or producing a gummy texture. (See page 21 for more detail about psyllium.)

2. ADD MILK POWDER AND OAT FLOUR: Most sandwich breads are made with milk, but we found that most gluten-free loaves, including this one, rose better with water. To make up for the lost flavor, we turned to milk powder. It added a rich dairy flavor and ensured a brown crust. Bread flour is a common choice for sandwich bread because its high protein content contributes to a better rise and lighter crumb. To increase the protein content in our recipe we tested a variety of whole-grain gluten-free flours before landing on oat flour, which got the job done without imparting an out-of-place flavor.

3. ADD EXTRA WATER AND BAKE IT LONGER: While the hydration level of a typical sandwich bread is around 68 percent (meaning that there are 68 grams of water for every 100 grams of flour), our gluten-free loaves turned out small and dense when we used this hydration level. Adding more water (enough to boost the hydration level to 89 percent) produced more steam and helped create a loaf with good rise. Because the dough is so wet, we found it necessary to extend the baking time and drive off some of the excess moisture once the loaf had risen and set and the steam had done its job.

4. USE A FOIL COLLAR: Because there is less protein in gluten-free bread dough than in traditional bread dough, gluten-free bread has a hard time rising straight up in the oven. In many tests, loaves rose well but then spilled over the sides of the pan, causing a real mess. Many recipes solve this problem by making smaller loaves. Instead, we engineered a taller pan by attaching a foil collar, just as you might do when making a soufflé in a ceramic soufflé dish. The collar, which should extend at least 1 inch above the rim of the pan, ensures that the loaf will rise up rather than out.

Multigrain Sandwich Bread

G-F TESTING LAB

FLOUR SUBSTITUTION	King Arthur Gluten-Free Multi-Purpose Flour 11½ ounces = **1¾ cups plus ⅓ cup**	Bob's Red Mill GF All-Purpose Baking Flour 11½ ounces = **2⅓ cups**
	Note that bread made with King Arthur will have a slightly denser crumb, and bread made with Bob's Red Mill will be a bit drier and will have a distinct bean flavor.	
HOT CEREAL MIX	Bob's Red Mill Gluten-Free Mighty Tasty Hot Cereal contains four grains: brown rice, corn, sweet white sorghum, and buckwheat. Note that other brands of hot cereal mixes may not work the same in this recipe because they all absorb water differently.	
PSYLLIUM HUSK	Do not omit the powdered psyllium husk; it is crucial to the structure of the bread. For more information, see page 21.	

WHY THIS RECIPE WORKS

We were looking for a hearty mulitgrain bread tender enough for sandwiches. The obvious first step was to replace the oat flour in our Classic Sandwich Bread with several grains. We tested a variety of whole-grain flours, alone and in combinations. The more flours we added, the more we liked this bread, but shopping for small amounts of multiple flours was a hassle. To simplify this recipe, we turned to hot cereal mixes, which contain multiple whole grains in one package. The shopping was now easy, but the whole grains were making the loaf quite dense. Extra yeast and baking powder solved this problem. We also had to change the amount of water, as the cereal mix did not absorb the water as easily as the oat flour did in our classic recipe. Now the only thing missing from our bread was the welcome crunch of seeds. Sunflower seeds were able to distinguish themselves in the loaf and added a nutty richness. Two final tweaks gave this bread even more character: using honey instead of granulated sugar, and swapping out the butter for vegetable oil to keep the loaf from overbrowning. (We also reduced the oven temperature from 350 degrees to 325 degrees for the same reason.) Do not substitute soy milk powder for the milk powder in this recipe, as it will negatively impact the flavor and structure of the bread. If you don't eat dairy, you're better off omitting the milk powder, although the structure of the bread will suffer a bit. Note that this recipe calls for an 8½ by 4½-inch loaf pan; if using a 9 by 5-inch loaf pan, the dough will not rise as high and the bread will not be quite as tall.

Multigrain Sandwich Bread

MAKES 1 LOAF

1½ cups warm water (110 degrees)
2 large eggs
2 tablespoons vegetable oil
2 tablespoons honey
11½ ounces (2⅓ cups plus ¼ cup) ATK All-Purpose Gluten-Free Flour Blend (page 7)
4 ounces (¾ cup) Bob's Red Mill Gluten-Free Mighty Tasty Hot Cereal
1½ ounces (½ cup) nonfat dry milk powder
3 tablespoons powdered psyllium husk
1 tablespoon instant or rapid-rise yeast
1 tablespoon baking powder (see page 24)
1½ teaspoons salt
2 tablespoons unsalted sunflower seeds

1. Spray 8½ by 4½-inch loaf pan with vegetable oil spray. Whisk water, eggs, oil, and honey together in bowl. Using stand mixer fitted with paddle, mix flour blend, hot cereal mix, milk powder, psyllium, yeast, baking powder, and salt on low speed until combined. Slowly add water mixture and let dough come together, about 1 minute, scraping down bowl as needed. Increase speed to medium and beat until sticky and uniform, about 6 minutes. Reduce speed to low, add sunflower seeds, and mix until incorporated. (Dough will resemble cookie dough.)

2. Using silicone spatula, scrape dough into prepared loaf pan and press it gently into corners with your wet hands; smooth top of dough and spray with water. Run your finger around entire edge of loaf, pressing down slightly, so that sides are about ½ inch shorter than center. Tightly wrap double layer of aluminum foil around pan so that top edge of foil rests at least 1 inch above rim of pan; secure foil collar with staples. Cover loosely with plastic wrap and let rise at room temperature until dough has risen by 50 percent (½ inch above rim of pan), about 1 hour.

3. Adjust oven rack to middle position and heat oven to 325 degrees. Remove plastic and spray loaf with water. Bake until top is golden, crust is firm, and loaf sounds hollow when tapped, about 1½ hours, rotating pan halfway through baking.

4. Transfer to wire rack and let bread cool in pan for 10 minutes. Remove loaf from pan and let cool completely on rack, about 2 hours. Serve. (Once cooled, bread can be wrapped in double layer of plastic wrap and stored at room temperature for up to 3 days. See freezing instructions on page 268.)

Whole-Grain Sandwich Bread

G-F TESTING LAB

FLOUR SUBSTITUTION	Do not substitute other whole-grain blends for the ATK Whole-Grain Gluten-Free Flour Blend; they will not work in this recipe.
PSYLLIUM HUSK	Psyllium is crucial to the structure of the bread; see page 21 for more information.
BAKING POWDER	Not all brands of baking powder are gluten-free; see page 24 for more information.

WHY THIS RECIPE WORKS

While we were developing our whole-grain gluten-free flour blend, the idea to use it in a sandwich bread recipe was never far from our minds. Teff flour provides the backbone of the blend and lends a wheaty, earthy flavor that mimics the flavor of whole wheat, while flaxseeds add a nutty richness. Our testing had shown that, in comparison with our all-purpose blend, this high-protein flour blend absorbs more liquid, and as expected, our initial loaves turned out dry and dense. We tested the addition of increasing amounts of water until we settled on the right amount. While it may seem finicky, we found that 2 cups plus 2 tablespoons of water worked perfectly. Any more made the bread slightly mushy, while less made the interior crumb taste dry. The earthy flavor of our whole-grain blend certainly made for a hearty-tasting loaf, but we noticed it tasted slightly lean. A side-by-side test of additional butter versus an extra egg yolk showed that the yolk was the winner, providing a rich, but not wet, texture. While we were happy with the flavor, we still felt that the loaf was too dense. Our other gluten-free sandwich breads all include a small amount of baking powder to help the dough rise nicely after being pressed in the loaf pan. We had initially omitted it here, thinking that the higher protein content of the whole-grain blend would translate into a more elastic dough that could rebound nicely after being pressed into the pan. We were wrong. Adding baking powder to the dough quickly fixed this problem and helped the loaf rise well, producing an open and tender crumb. We also learned that variations in kitchen temperature affected how well the loaf rose. To minimize these inconsistencies and make the recipe more foolproof, we employed two old-time baking tricks. First, we created a warm proofing box using the oven. A proofing box simply is a controlled environment with optimal conditions for letting bread rise. Second, we jump-started the yeast in warm water laced with 1 teaspoon of sugar before adding it to the dough. These two tricks also sped up the rising time substantially, from roughly 1 hour to just 30 minutes. Finally, to prevent the loaf from falling slightly as it cooled, we turned the oven off after the baking time and let the loaf cool down slowly in the oven. This gave the starches more time to set up. Note that this recipe calls for an 8½ by 4½-inch loaf pan; if using a 9 by 5-inch loaf pan, the dough will not rise as high and the bread will not be quite as tall. For information on how to shape the dough in the loaf pan, see page 277.

Whole-Grain Sandwich Bread

MAKES 1 LOAF

17	ounces (2 cups plus 2 tablespoons) warm water (110 degrees)
2¼	teaspoons instant or rapid-rise yeast
3	tablespoons plus 1 teaspoon sugar
2	large eggs plus 1 large yolk
2	tablespoons unsalted butter, melted and cooled
19½	ounces (4⅓ cups) ATK Whole-Grain Gluten-Free Flour Blend (page 9)
3	tablespoons powdered psyllium husk
2	teaspoons baking powder
1½	teaspoons salt

1. Adjust oven rack to middle position and heat oven to 200 degrees. As soon as oven reaches 200 degrees, turn it off. (This will be warm proofing box for dough. Do not begin step 2 until oven has been turned off.) Spray 8½ by 4½-inch loaf pan with vegetable oil spray.

2. Combine warm water, yeast, and 1 teaspoon sugar in bowl and let sit until bubbly, about 5 minutes. Whisk in eggs and yolk, and melted butter. Using stand mixer fitted with paddle, mix flour blend, psyllium, baking powder, salt, and remaining 3 tablespoons sugar on low speed until combined, about 1 minute. Slowly add yeast mixture and mix until combined, scraping down bowl as needed, about 1 minute. Increase speed to medium and beat until dough is sticky and uniform, about 6 minutes. (Dough will resemble cookie dough.)

3. Using silicone spatula, scrape dough into prepared pan. Using your wet hands, press dough gently into corners and smooth top. Run your finger around entire edge of loaf, pressing down slightly, so that sides are about ½ inch shorter than center. Cover loosely with plastic wrap, place in warmed oven, and let rise for 10 minutes; do not let plastic touch oven rack.

4. Remove pan from oven and let sit on counter until loaf has risen ½ inch above rim of pan, about 20 minutes. Meanwhile, heat oven to 350 degrees.

5. Remove plastic and spray loaf with water. Bake until top is browned, crust is firm, and loaf sounds hollow when tapped, about 1½ hours, rotating pan halfway through baking. Turn off oven and leave bread in oven for 15 minutes longer.

6. Remove bread from oven and let cool in pan for 10 minutes. Unmold bread onto wire rack and let cool completely, about 3 hours. Serve. (Cooled bread can be wrapped in double layer of plastic wrap and stored at room temperature for up to 3 days or frozen for up to 1 month. See freezing instructions on page 268.)

VARIATION

Dairy-Free Whole-Grain Sandwich Bread
Substitute vegetable oil for melted butter.

TEST KITCHEN TIP **Ensuring a Good Rise**

Unlike traditional bread dough, which gets punched down during rising, gluten-free breads cannot be deflated once they've risen. You have only one chance to get a gluten-free bread to rise, and we've found that the best rise happens right after the dough has been mixed. Gluten-free doughs start out loose and wet but become dramatically more dense as they sit, even if for a short time. Therefore, you want the yeast to work as quickly as possible after the dough has been mixed, while it's still loose and malleable. We've also found that the temperature of the kitchen can affect how quickly and successfully these breads rise. A cold kitchen will cause the bread to rise more slowly and thus have trouble reaching its ideal height. Note that the ultimate height of a loaf isn't just for looks; it also has a substantial effect on the bread's interior texture. A shorter loaf will be much denser and harder. Given all of this, we incorporated two key tricks into all of our bread recipes to ensure a maximum, superquick rise. First, we create a warm proofing box using a warmed (but turned-off) oven. A proofing box is simply a controlled environment with optimal conditions for letting the bread rise. Second, we use instant or rapid-rise yeast (which activates more quickly than dry active yeast) and jump-start it by dissolving it in sweetened, warm water before mixing the dough.

1. Adjust oven rack to middle position and heat oven to 200 degrees. As soon as oven reaches 200 degrees, turn it off. Do not begin to mix dough until oven has been turned off. The oven will be 100 to 150 degrees when proofing the dough.

2. Combine 110-degree water, yeast, and 1 teaspoon sugar (or honey) in bowl. (Note that 1 packet of yeast equals 2¼ teaspoons.)

3. Let yeast mixture sit at room temperature until it begins to bubble and froth, about 5 minutes. Add this mixture to dough as directed in specific recipes.

Honey-Millet Sandwich Bread

✓ WHY THIS RECIPE WORKS

A seed grown in semiarid climates, millet is naturally gluten-free and highly nutritious, and it has a slightly sweet, cornlike flavor. The seed is high in fiber and protein, making it a good addition to gluten-free breads when ground into flour. We loved the idea of featuring this underutilized seed (both whole and ground) in a sandwich bread recipe. We started with a combination of our all-purpose flour blend (the flavor of the whole-grain blend would overpower the millet) and millet flour for the base of this bread. While the millet flour has a great flavor, too much of the flour made our loaf overly tacky and starchy; 6 ounces of millet flour was the right amount to lend a subtle flavor without compromising the texture. A combination of yeast and baking powder was necessary to achieve an open crumb and a higher rise, while psyllium husk and eggs guaranteed a domed loaf that didn't sink after baking. We had been using a small amount of butter but found that replacing it with vegetable oil gave our loaf a cleaner flavor, and to finish we stirred in ½ cup of rinsed millet. The seeds lent an appealing pop and enhanced the subtle flavor of the millet flour. We love this mild bread for making sandwiches, but it is also great served simply with honey butter alongside chili, soup, or stew. Note that this recipe calls for an 8½ by 4½-inch loaf pan; if using a 9 by 5-inch loaf pan, the dough will not rise as high and the bread will not be quite as tall.

Honey-Millet Sandwich Bread

MAKES 1 LOAF

- 14 ounces (1¾ cups) warm water (110 degrees)
- 2¼ teaspoons instant or rapid-rise yeast
- ¼ cup plus 1 teaspoon honey
- 3 large eggs
- 2 tablespoons vegetable oil
- 12 ounces (2⅔ cups) ATK All-Purpose Gluten-Free Flour Blend (page 7)
- 6 ounces (1⅓ cups plus ¼ cup) millet flour
- 3 tablespoons powdered psyllium husk
- 2 teaspoons baking powder
- 1½ teaspoons salt
- ½ cup millet, rinsed

1. Adjust oven rack to middle position and heat oven to 200 degrees. As soon as oven reaches 200 degrees, turn it off. (This will be warm proofing box for dough. Do not begin step 2 until oven has been turned off.) Spray 8½ by 4½-inch loaf pan with vegetable oil spray.

2. Combine warm water, yeast, and 1 teaspoon honey in bowl and let sit until bubbly, about 5 minutes. Whisk in eggs, vegetable oil, and remaining ¼ cup honey. Using stand mixer fitted with paddle, mix flour blend, millet flour, psyllium, baking powder, and salt on low speed until combined, about 1 minute. Slowly add yeast mixture and mix until combined, scraping down bowl as needed, about 1 minute. Increase speed to medium and beat until dough is sticky and uniform, about 6 minutes. Reduce speed to low, add millet, and mix until incorporated, about 1 minute. (Dough will resemble cookie dough.)

3. Using silicone spatula, scrape dough into prepared pan. Using your wet hands, press dough gently into corners and smooth top. Run your finger around entire edge of loaf, pressing down slightly, so that sides are about ½ inch shorter than center. Tightly wrap double layer of aluminum foil around pan so that top edge of foil rests at least 1 inch above rim of pan; secure foil collar with staples. Cover loosely with plastic wrap, place in warmed oven, and let rise for 10 minutes; do not let plastic touch oven rack.

4. Remove pan from oven and let sit on counter until loaf has risen ½ inch above rim of pan, about 20 minutes. Meanwhile, heat oven to 350 degrees.

5. Remove plastic and spray loaf with water. Bake until top is golden, crust is firm, and loaf sounds hollow when tapped, 1 to 1¼ hours, rotating pan halfway through baking.

G-F TESTING LAB

FLOUR SUBSTITUTION	King Arthur Gluten-Free Multi-Purpose Flour 12 ounces = **1⅔ cups plus ½ cup**	Betty Crocker All-Purpose Gluten Free Rice Blend 12 ounces = **2¼ cups plus 2 tablespoons**
	Bread made with King Arthur will rise less and will be more dense; bread made with Betty Crocker will have a slightly spongy and rubbery texture.	
PSYLLIUM HUSK	Psyllium is crucial to the structure of the bread; see page 21 for more information.	
BAKING POWDER	Not all brands of baking powder are gluten-free; see page 24 for more information.	

6. Remove bread from oven and let cool in pan for 10 minutes. Unmold bread onto wire rack and let cool completely, about 3 hours. Serve. (Cooled bread can be wrapped in double layer of plastic wrap and stored at room temperature for up to 3 days or frozen for up to 1 month. See freezing instructions on page 2.)

Honey Butter

MAKES ¼ CUP

We think this butter tastes terrific with the Honey-Millet Sandwich Bread. Store any leftovers in the refrigerator for up to 1 week.

- 4 tablespoons unsalted butter, softened
- 1 tablespoon honey
- ¼ teaspoon salt

Mix all ingredients in bowl until combined.

TEST KITCHEN TIP
Making a Nicely Domed Loaf

After baking hundreds of loaves of gluten-free bread, we uncovered a small trick to help them achieve an iconic, domed top. It is not crucial for the success of the bread, but it will make the loaf look better. If you skip this step, the loaf will taste fine, but the top might be flat or have a slightly uneven rise.

After putting dough into loaf pan, run your finger around edge of loaf, pressing down slightly, so that sides are about ½ inch shorter than center.

TEST KITCHEN TIP **Making a Foil Collar**

Loaf breads that use the ATK All-Purpose Gluten-Free Flour Blend require a foil collar. Because this blend (as opposed to our whole-grain blend) has less protein than wheat flour, the bread has a hard time rising straight up in the oven. In many tests, loaves spilled over the sides of the pan as they baked, causing a real mess. Rather than resign ourselves to short, squat loaves (as many recipes do), we came up with a clever way to make the loaf pan taller.

Tightly wrap double layer of aluminum foil around pan so that top edge of foil rests at least 1 inch above rim of pan; secure foil collar with staples.

Flourless Nut and Seed Loaf

G-F TESTING LAB

OATS	Do not use quick oats; they have a dusty texture that doesn't work in this recipe. Make sure to buy old-fashioned rolled oats that have been processed in a gluten-free facility. For more information, see page 27.
FLAXSEEDS	Both brown and golden flaxseeds will work well here.
PSYLLIUM HUSK	Psyllium is crucial to the structure of the bread; see page 21 for more information.
COCONUT OIL	Vegetable oil or olive oil can be substituted for the coconut oil.

WHY THIS RECIPE WORKS

We wanted to develop a naturally gluten-free bread and set our sights on a flourless nut and seed loaf that would be high in protein and all-around nutritious with a hearty flavor. A slice of this bread, especially toasted and slathered with butter and good jam, would be all you need for breakfast. To start, we toasted the nuts and seeds to enhance their flavor. We then needed to find a way to bind all the nuts and seeds together. Since oats are a morning staple, we thought that creating a binding porridge with them would do the trick. We also used flaxseeds and powdered psyllium husk, which, when hydrated, create a gel with strong binding properties. For flavor, we liked the combination of sunflower seeds, sliced almonds, and pepitas, while maple syrup added a subtle sweetness. Coconut oil complemented the nutty flavor of the loaf. To ensure the bread stayed together, we allowed everything to fully hydrate for a few hours in the loaf pan before baking. But baking this bread in a loaf pan did not allow for enough evaporation, and the inside of the loaf remained wet. To fix this, we baked the loaf for 20 minutes to allow the outside to set before turning it out onto a wire rack set in a rimmed baking sheet and returning it to the oven for 35 to 45 minutes. After letting the loaf cool for a few hours before cutting, we had a rich, nutty loaf perfect for snacking or toasting. Note that this recipe calls for an 8½ by 4½-inch loaf pan; if using a 9 by 5-inch loaf pan, the loaf will not be quite as tall.

Flourless Nut and Seed Loaf

MAKES 1 LOAF

- 1 cup sunflower seeds
- 1 cup sliced almonds
- ½ cup pepitas
- 1¾ cups old-fashioned rolled oats
- ¼ cup whole flaxseeds
- 3 tablespoons powdered psyllium husk
- 12 ounces (1½ cups) water
- 3 tablespoons coconut oil, melted and cooled
- 2 tablespoons maple syrup
- ¾ teaspoon salt

1. Adjust oven rack to middle position and heat oven to 350 degrees. Combine sunflower seeds, almonds, and pepitas on rimmed baking sheet and bake, stirring occasionally, until lightly browned, 10 to 12 minutes.

2. Line bottom of 8½ by 4½-inch loaf pan with parchment paper and spray with vegetable oil spray. Transfer toasted nut-seed mixture to bowl, let cool slightly, then stir in oats, flaxseeds, and psyllium. In separate bowl, whisk water, coconut oil, maple syrup, and salt until well combined. Using silicone spatula, stir water mixture into nut-seed mixture until completely incorporated.

3. Scrape mixture into prepared pan. Using your wet hands, press dough into corners and smooth top. Cover loosely with plastic wrap and let sit at room temperature until mixture is fully hydrated and cohesive, about 2 hours.

4. Adjust oven rack to middle position and heat oven to 350 degrees. Remove plastic and bake loaf for 20 minutes.

5. Invert loaf onto wire rack set inside rimmed baking sheet. Remove loaf pan and discard parchment. Bake loaf (still inverted) until deep golden brown and loaf sounds hollow when tapped, 35 to 45 minutes.

6. Let loaf cool completely on rack, about 2 hours. Serve. (Loaf can be stored at room temperature, uncovered, for up to 3 days; do not wrap. It can also be wrapped in double layer of plastic and frozen for up to 1 month; see freezing instructions on page 268.)

Hearty Country Flax Bread

G-F TESTING LAB

FLOUR SUBSTITUTION	King Arthur Gluten-Free Multi-Purpose Flour 14 ounces = **2⅓ cups plus ¼ cup**	Bob's Red Mill GF All-Purpose Baking Flour 14 ounces = **2½ cups plus ⅓ cup**
	Note that bread made with King Arthur will be slightly gummy, and bread made with Bob's Red Mill will be denser and a bit drier and will have an extremely earthy flavor.	
PSYLLIUM HUSK	Do not omit the powdered psyllium husk; it is crucial to the structure of the bread. For more information, see page 21.	

✓ WHY THIS RECIPE WORKS

A good rustic bread has a chewy but soft interior crumb and a hearty crust. Classic recipes contain as few as four ingredients—flour, water, yeast, and salt. Protein content is especially important when making any rustic bread because these loaves are baked free-form, rather than in a loaf pan. All that protein gives the dough enough structure to rise up (rather than just out). We knew our gluten-free flour blend would need help. As with sandwich breads, we found that psyllium worked better than either xanthan or guar gum at strengthening the protein network, but it was far from sufficient. We needed to supplement our flour blend with higher-protein flour and tested flours made from teff, quinoa, millet, and flax. We had good results with most of these flours, but our tasters preferred the earthy but still mellow flavor of ground flaxseeds. With the addition of flax, we found that the dough did not absorb water as easily so we cut back on the liquid. As with our sandwich breads, we found that a little sugar helped the yeast do its job and that the milk powder improved flavor and browning. While our loaf was tasting better, it was still spreading way too much in the oven and seemed to lack structure. Adding eggs (something standard in sandwich bread but quite unusual in rustic breads) boosted the protein content and helped with structure. Adding baking soda (another unusual addition) helped create a more delicate crumb. (The flaxseeds are slightly acidic, so baking soda worked better than baking powder in this recipe.) The ingredient list was in good shape, but the loaf was still spreading too much during proofing and baking. Up to this point, we had been letting the loaf rise on a piece of parchment and then transferring the loaf (still on the parchment) to a preheated baking stone, just as we would when making conventional rustic bread. We solved our spread problems by transferring the shaped dough to a small skillet for rising and baking. The sides of the pan prevented excess spread and ensured that the loaf emerged from the oven with good height and a light crumb. Placing the skillet on a preheated baking stone in the oven produced a really crisp bottom crust. We had one last problem to tackle—the dough was sometimes splitting during baking. We found that cutting the top of the loaf with a sharp bread knife allowed the crust to expand and prevented the bread from splitting in the oven. Also spraying the loaf with water right before it went into the oven delayed the formation of a crust during the longer baking time, allowing the bread to fully expand without tearing or splitting. Using more yeast than usual (a full tablespoon) helped with the rise, as did starting the loaf in a hot oven (set to 400 degrees) and then turning down the heat so the loaf could cook through. Do not substitute soy milk powder for the milk powder in this recipe, as it will negatively impact the flavor and structure of the bread. If you don't eat dairy, you're better off omitting the milk powder, although the structure of the bread will suffer a bit.

Hearty Country Flax Bread
MAKES 1 LOAF

1¾ cups warm water (110 degrees)
2 large eggs
14 ounces (3 cups plus 2 tablespoons) ATK All-Purpose Gluten-Free Flour Blend (page 7)
3 ounces (¾ cup) ground flaxseeds
1½ ounces (½ cup) nonfat dry milk powder
3 tablespoons powdered psyllium husk
2 tablespoons sugar
1 tablespoon instant or rapid-rise yeast
1½ teaspoons salt
¾ teaspoon baking soda

1. Whisk water and eggs together in bowl. Using stand mixer fitted with paddle, mix flour blend, ground flaxseeds, milk powder, psyllium, sugar, yeast, salt, and baking soda on low speed until combined. Slowly add water mixture and let dough come together, about 1 minute, scraping down bowl as needed. Increase speed to medium and beat until sticky and uniform, about 6 minutes. (Dough will resemble cookie dough.)

2. Spray 18 by 12-inch sheet of parchment paper with vegetable oil spray. Using silicone spatula, transfer dough to prepared parchment and shape into 6½-inch ball with wet hands. Place dough (still on parchment) inside ovensafe 8-inch skillet. Using sharp serrated knife or single-edge razor blade, make two ½-inch-deep, 4-inch-long slashes in X shape across top of dough. Spray dough with water. Cover loosely with plastic wrap and let rise at room temperature until dough has risen by 50 percent, about 2 hours.

3. One hour before baking, adjust oven rack to lowest position, place baking stone on rack, and heat oven to 400 degrees. Remove plastic and spray loaf with water. Reduce oven temperature to 350 degrees and place skillet on baking stone. Bake until top of bread is well browned, crust is firm, and loaf sounds hollow when tapped, about 1½ hours, rotating skillet halfway through baking.

4. Carefully remove loaf from skillet, transfer to wire rack (discard parchment), and let bread cool completely, about 2 hours. Serve. (Once cooled, bread can be wrapped in double layer of plastic wrap and stored at room temperature for up to 3 days. See freezing instructions on page 268.)

SMART SHOPPING **Flaxseeds**

Flaxseeds are similar in size to sesame seeds and have a sweet, wheaty flavor. They are naturally gluten-free and are sold both whole and ground in most supermarkets. Flaxseeds are one of the highest sources known for the omega-3 fatty acid called alpha-linolenic acid (ALA), which is found only in certain plant foods and oils and must be supplied by our diet for good health. Whole seeds have a longer shelf life, but we preferred ground flaxseeds in our bread because we wanted to use them as a flour rather than as a stir-in. As an added bonus, grinding flaxseeds improves the release of nutrients. If you can't find ground flaxseeds, you can grind whole seeds in a spice grinder or food processor. Like other nuts and seeds, store flaxseeds in the freezer.

TEST KITCHEN TIP **Shaping Hearty Country Flax Bread**

Letting our rustic loaf rise and bake in an ovensafe 8-inch skillet helped prevent spread, ensuring our bread had a better, taller rise. A small cast-iron skillet or conventional skillet with a metal handle is ideal for this recipe. If you prefer, use a single-edge razor blade rather than a serrated knife in step 3. Once the dough has been slashed and sprayed with water, cover it loosely with plastic wrap and let it rise as directed.

1. Using silicone spatula, transfer dough to greased parchment and shape into 6½-inch ball with wet hands.

2. Place dough (still on parchment) inside ovensafe 8-inch skillet.

3. Using serrated knife, make two ½-inch-deep, 4-inch-long slashes in X shape across top of dough. Spray dough with water, cover with plastic, and let rise.

Cinnamon-Raisin Bread

WHY THIS RECIPE WORKS

Cinnamon-raisin bread is always appealing—at least in theory. It can be dry, with a scant amount of filling, or overly sweet and gooey, more like cinnamon buns than bread. We wanted to develop a fluffy, sweet loaf with a soft crumb, plenty of raisins, and a generous cinnamon swirl. That said, we didn't want something so sticky that slices couldn't go into the toaster without setting off the smoke alarm. Using our sandwich bread as the base for this recipe, we started by adding an extra tablespoon of sugar, which made the bread plenty sweet. We discovered that the raisins were best added to the finished dough (so they didn't get blown apart during the kneading process). We then switched our focus to the cinnamon filling. Most traditional recipes mix together brown or granulated sugar, cinnamon, and salt and simply spread this mixture over the dough and roll it up tight. But every time we tried this method, our loaves were marred by gaping holes. After way too many failures, we realized that the layer of cinnamon sugar was too thin and ran out during baking. Switching to confectioners' sugar and increasing the amount of cinnamon produced a filling that stayed in place. When powdery confectioners' sugar absorbed water from the dough, it formed a sticky paste. This paste was then thickened by the cornstarch in the sugar and by the cinnamon. Unfortunately the confectioners' sugar did not completely melt. We needed more moisture than could be supplied by the dough. Lightly spraying the filling with water once it was in place guaranteed that the powdery sugar became a paste. Our loaf was close to perfect, but to guarantee that our filling would be in every bite, we divided the dough in half, spread the filling over each piece, then stacked the two pieces in a loaf pan. We finally had the bread we wanted—slightly sweet and evenly streaked with cinnamon sugar, with no holes. Do not substitute soy milk powder for the milk powder in this recipe, as it will negatively impact the flavor and structure of the bread. Note that this recipe calls for an 8½ by 4½-inch loaf pan; if using a 9 by 5-inch loaf pan, the dough will not rise as high and the bread will not be quite as tall.

Cinnamon-Raisin Bread

MAKES 1 LOAF

FILLING

- 2 ounces (½ cup) confectioners' sugar
- 4 teaspoons ground cinnamon
- ½ teaspoon salt

DOUGH

- 2 cups warm water (110 degrees)
- 2 large eggs
- 2 tablespoons unsalted butter, melted and cooled
- 14 ounces (3 cups plus 2 tablespoons) ATK All-Purpose Gluten-Free Flour Blend (page 7)
- 4 ounces (1⅓ cups) gluten-free oat flour
- 1½ ounces (½ cup) nonfat dry milk powder
- 3 tablespoons powdered psyllium husk
- 3 tablespoons granulated sugar
- 2¼ teaspoons instant or rapid-rise yeast
- 2 teaspoons baking powder (see page 24)
- 1½ teaspoons salt
- 1 cup (5 ounces) golden raisins

1. FOR THE FILLING: Combine all ingredients in bowl.

2. FOR THE DOUGH: Spray 8½ by 4½-inch loaf pan with vegetable oil spray. Whisk water, eggs, and melted butter together in bowl. Using stand mixer fitted with paddle, mix flour blend, oat flour, milk powder, psyllium, granulated sugar, yeast, baking powder, and salt on low speed until just combined. Slowly add water mixture and let dough come together, about 1 minute, scraping down bowl as needed. Increase speed to medium and beat until sticky and uniform, about 6 minutes. (Dough will be very sticky.) Reduce speed to low, add raisins, and mix until incorporated, 30 to 60 seconds.

3. Spray large sheet of parchment paper with vegetable oil spray. With your wet hands, transfer half of dough to prepared parchment. Clean and wet your hands again. Pat dough into rough 11 by 8-inch rectangle. Sprinkle half of filling mixture evenly over dough, leaving ½-inch border on all sides; spray filling lightly

G-F TESTING LAB

FLOUR SUBSTITUTION	King Arthur Gluten-Free Multi-Purpose Flour 14 ounces = **2⅓ cups plus ¼ cup**	Bob's Red Mill All-Purpose GF Baking Flour 14 ounces = **2½ cups plus ⅓ cup**
	Note that bread made with King Arthur will be slightly spongy, and bread made with Bob's Red Mill will be denser and slightly wet and will have a distinct bean flavor.	
OAT FLOUR	If you do not have oat flour, you can process 4 ounces old-fashioned rolled oats in a food processor or spice grinder until finely ground, about 1 minute. Do not use quick oats. You can substitute sorghum or millet flour for the oat flour.	
PSYLLIUM HUSK	Do not omit the powdered psyllium husk; it is crucial to the structure of the bread. For more information, see page 16.	

with water. With short side facing you, use parchment to roll dough into tight cylinder. Pinch seam closed and place seam side up in prepared pan. Repeat with second piece of dough and remaining filling; place in pan, seam side down, on top of first piece of dough. Smooth top of dough and spray with water. Tightly wrap double layer of aluminum foil around pan so that top edge of foil rests at least 1 inch above rim of pan; secure foil collar with staples. Cover loosely with plastic wrap and let rise at room temperature until dough has risen by 50 percent (½ inch above rim of pan), about 1 hour.

4. Adjust oven rack to middle position and heat oven to 350 degrees. Remove plastic and spray loaf with water. Bake until top is golden, crust is firm, and loaf sounds hollow when tapped, about 1½ hours, rotating pan halfway through baking.

5. Transfer to wire rack and let bread cool in pan for 10 minutes. Remove loaf from pan and let cool completely on rack, about 2 hours. Serve. (Once cooled, bread can be wrapped in double layer of plastic wrap and stored at room temperature for up to 3 days. See freezing instructions on page 268.)

TEST KITCHEN TIP **Shaping Cinnamon-Raisin Bread**

Dividing the dough in half and spreading the filling over each piece ensures even distribution of the cinnamon sugar filling in the baked loaf. Make sure to spray the filling (once in place) with water. (A plant mister is perfect for this task.) The water turns the filling into a paste that stays in place as the loaf rises and bakes.

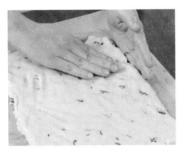

1. With wet hands, transfer half of dough to greased parchment. Clean and wet hands. Pat dough into rough 11 by 8-inch rectangle.

2. Sprinkle half of filling mixture evenly over dough, leaving ½-inch border on all sides.

3. Spray filling lightly with water. Filling should be speckled with water over entire surface.

4. With short side facing you, use parchment to help roll dough into tight cylinder by rolling it gently away from you.

5. Turn loaf seam side up, pinch closed, and place seam side up in prepared pan.

6. Repeat with second piece of dough and remaining filling. Place this piece of dough seam side down on top of first piece. Smooth top and spray with water.

Brioche

G-F TESTING LAB

FLOUR SUBSTITUTION	King Arthur Gluten-Free Multi-Purpose Flour 14½ ounces = **2½ cups plus 2 tablespoons**	Betty Crocker All-Purpose Gluten Free Rice Blend 14½ ounces = **2¾ cups plus 2 tablespoons**
	Brioche made with Betty Crocker will have a slightly gummy and chewy texture.	
OAT FLOUR	Not all brands of oat flour are gluten-free; read the label. Alternatively, 4 ounces (¾ cup plus 2 tablespoons) of sorghum flour can be substituted for the oat flour; we had good luck using Bob's Red Mill "Sweet" White Sorghum Flour.	
PSYLLIUM HUSK	Psyllium is crucial to the structure of the brioche; see page 21 for more information.	
BAKING POWDER	Not all brands of baking powder are gluten-free; see page 24 for more information.	

WHY THIS RECIPE WORKS

We set out to create a tender and plush gluten-free brioche with the same butter-rich flavor and high rise but without the normally labor-intensive process. We looked at our traditional brioche recipe as a jumping-off point and found that it relies on higher-protein flours to help with rise, as the proteins form strong networks to support the weight of the eggs and butter. We needed to achieve a similar height in our gluten-free version, so we added 1⅓ cups of oat flour to boost the protein of our all-purpose gluten-free flour blend, along with 3 tablespoons of psyllium husk to form a strong network and trap the gas and steam formed during baking. For a rich flavor, the average brioche contains up to 50 percent butter (most butter-enriched doughs contain between 10 and 20 percent butter). The high ratio of fat lubricates the wheat proteins in flour and softens the bonds and prevents the dough from becoming tough. Since we did not have to worry about forming strong gluten bonds, we settled on 8 tablespoons of butter (half the amount used in traditional brioche), which added rich flavor without the dough becoming greasy. For our mixing method, instead of adding softened butter slowly to the dough one piece at a time, we found that simply melting the butter and adding it directly to the eggs worked just fine. We used a combination of one egg and three yolks, which added more protein and structure along with the signature eggy flavor. Since the brioche had a lot of water and fat, we needed to bake it a little longer to help dry it out and make sure it did not fall when removed from the oven. Baking the loaf for 70 minutes, then brushing it with an egg wash, allowed us to get the hallmark shiny crust without it becoming too dark. After the loaf was completely baked, we turned the oven off to allow it to dry out a little longer. Now we had a tall and beautiful brioche that was tender and rich-tasting—perfect for a sandwich or for simply slathering with butter and jam. Note that this recipe calls for an 8½ by 4½-inch loaf pan; if using a 9 by 5-inch loaf pan, the dough will not rise as high and the brioche will not be quite as tall. For information on how to shape the dough in the loaf pan and make a foil collar, see page 277.

Brioche

MAKES 1 LOAF

DOUGH

- 16 ounces (2 cups) 1 or 2 percent low-fat milk, heated to 110 degrees
- 2¼ teaspoons instant or rapid-rise yeast
- 3 tablespoons plus 1 teaspoon sugar
- 8 tablespoons unsalted butter, melted and cooled
- 1 large egg plus 3 large yolks
- 14½ ounces (3¼ cups) ATK All-Purpose Gluten-Free Flour Blend (page 7)
- 4 ounces (1⅓ cups) oat flour
- 3 tablespoons powdered psyllium husk
- 2 teaspoons baking powder
- 1½ teaspoons salt

EGG WASH

- 1 large egg
- 1 teaspoon water

1. FOR THE DOUGH: Adjust oven rack to lowest position and heat oven to 200 degrees. As soon as oven reaches 200 degrees, turn it off. (This will be warm proofing box for dough. Do not begin step 2 until oven has been turned off.) Spray 8½ by 4½-inch loaf pan with vegetable oil spray.

2. Combine warm milk, yeast, and 1 teaspoon sugar in bowl and let sit until bubbly, about 5 minutes. Whisk in melted butter and egg and yolks. Using stand mixer fitted with paddle, mix flour blend, oat flour, psyllium, baking powder, salt, and remaining 3 tablespoons sugar on low speed until combined, about 1 minute. Slowly add yeast mixture and mix until combined, scraping down bowl as needed, about 1 minute. Increase speed to medium and beat until dough is sticky and uniform, about 6 minutes. (Dough will resemble cookie dough.)

3. Using silicone spatula, scrape dough into prepared pan. Using your wet hands, press dough gently into corners and smooth top. Run your finger around entire edge of loaf, pressing down slightly, so that sides are about ½ inch shorter than center.

Tightly wrap double layer of aluminum foil around pan so that top edge of foil rests at least 1 inch above rim of pan; secure foil collar with staples. Cover loosely with plastic wrap, place in warmed oven, and let rise for 10 minutes; do not let plastic touch oven rack.

4. Remove pan from oven and let sit on counter until loaf has risen ½ inch above rim of pan, about 20 minutes. Meanwhile, heat oven to 350 degrees.

5. Remove plastic, spray loaf with water, and bake for 1 hour 10 minutes.

6. FOR THE EGG WASH: Beat egg and water together in bowl, then brush gently over top of hot, partially baked bread. Continue to bake until top is deep golden brown, crust is firm, and loaf sounds hollow when tapped, about 20 minutes. Turn off oven and leave bread in oven for 15 minutes longer.

7. Remove bread from oven and let cool in pan for 10 minutes. Unmold bread onto wire rack and let cool completely, about 3 hours. Serve. (Cooled bread can be wrapped in double layer of plastic wrap and stored at room temperature for up to 3 days or frozen for up to 1 month. See freezing instructions on page 268.)

VARIATION
Dairy-Free Brioche
We prefer the flavor and texture of this brioche made with soy milk, but almond milk will also work; do not use rice milk.

Substitute 1 cup unsweetened soy milk and 1 cup water for milk, and Earth Balance Vegan Buttery Sticks for butter.

TEST KITCHEN TIP **Keys to Making Gluten-Free Brioche**

1. Let milk, yeast, and sugar sit until bubbly, about 5 minutes. Whisk melted butter and egg and yolks into bubbly yeast mixture.

2. After loaf has baked for 70 minutes, gently brush egg-water mixture over top and continue to bake for 20 minutes longer.

3. After brioche has finished baking, turn off oven and leave brioche in oven for 15 minutes longer to dry out.

Whole-Grain Sprouted Bread

✓ WHY THIS RECIPE WORKS

For the health-conscious, sprouted grain breads are very appealing, but good luck finding a gluten-free loaf in your local market. Given the success of our Whole-Grain Sandwich Bread (page 272), we were confident we could create a wholesome, hearty, and healthy gluten-free whole-grain sprouted grain bread. There are two common methods for incorporating sprouted grains (and often legumes) into homemade breads: either through sprouted grain flour or by sprouting grains, processing them in a food processor to a mush, and adding the mush to the bread dough. Since we couldn't find sprouted grain flour at our local grocery store, our decision was easy—we would be sprouting grains and processing them ourselves. Thinking that this recipe would need to employ the same tricks we used for our other gluten-free loaves, we put together a working recipe and made sure to include psyllium husk for binding and rise, baking powder and yeast for an open crumb and good rise, and a good amount of water to hydrate the starches and create steam for even more lift during baking. One noticeably absent ingredient was egg; all that sprouted grain mush contributed its own binding power and structure, so eggs weren't necessary. The only question that remained was which grains and/or legumes to sprout. We tested sprouting lentils, corn, oat berries, quinoa, chickpeas, millet, brown rice, and sorghum and landed on three ingredients commonly found in a gluten-free pantry: quinoa, lentils, and millet. Their flavors complemented each other, and the texture they gave the loaf wasn't too tacky or dense. We settled on ¼ cup each of lentils and quinoa and ¾ cup millet; using more of either quinoa or lentils overpowered the delicate flavor of millet, while using any more millet resulted in a loaf that was too starchy. The sprouted grains gave our bread a great flavor, but it also made the bread fairly dense. To open up the crumb a little we tested water amounts until we found the sweet spot (1⅔ cups), but we also found that 1 tablespoon of cider vinegar gave our loaf a better, more even rise. Adding ¼ cup of roasted pepitas and sesame seeds to the dough added a nice crunch and flavor, and sprinkling some over the top before baking made our loaf even more beautiful. This bread can take up to 4 days to make, although most of the time is hands-off. Note that this recipe calls for an 8½ by 4½-inch loaf pan; if using a 9 by 5-inch loaf pan, the dough will not rise as high and the loaf will not be quite as tall. For information on how to shape the dough in the loaf pan, see page 277.

Whole-Grain Sprouted Bread

MAKES 1 LOAF

- ¾ cup millet
- ¼ cup quinoa
- ¼ cup brown lentils, picked over
- 2 cups water for soaking grains, plus 13⅓ ounces (1⅔ cups) warm water (110 degrees) for dough
- ¼ cup roasted, unsalted pepitas
- 2 tablespoons sesame seeds
- 2¼ teaspoons instant or rapid-rise yeast
- 3 tablespoons plus 1 teaspoon honey
- 1 tablespoon cider vinegar
- 14 ounces (3 cups plus 2 tablespoons) ATK Whole-Grain Gluten-Free Flour Blend (page 9)
- 1½ tablespoons powdered psyllium husk
- 1½ teaspoons salt
- 1 teaspoon baking powder

1. Combine millet, quinoa, lentils, and 2 cups water in bowl, cover with plastic wrap, and let soak at room temperature until quinoa starts to sprout, 12 to 24 hours. Drain in fine-mesh strainer, return to bowl, and cover with plastic. Let grains sit at room temperature, rinsing and draining them daily, until each type of grain begins to sprout, 1 to 3 days. (Each individual grain does not need to sprout.)

2. Adjust oven rack to middle position and heat oven to 200 degrees. As soon as oven reaches 200 degrees, turn it off. (This will be warm proofing

G-F TESTING LAB

FLOUR SUBSTITUTION	Do not substitute other whole-grain blends for the ATK Whole-Grain Gluten-Free Flour Blend; they will not work in this recipe.
PSYLLIUM HUSK	Psyllium is crucial to the structure of the bread; see page 21 for more information.
BAKING POWDER	Not all brands of baking powder are gluten-free; see page 24 for more information.

box for dough. Do not begin step 3 until oven has been turned off.) Spray 8½ by 4½-inch loaf pan with vegetable oil spray. Process sprouted grains in food processor to thick, sticky paste, stopping to scrape down bowl often, 2 to 3 minutes. Combine pepitas and sesame seeds in bowl.

3. Combine 13⅓ ounces warm water, yeast, and 1 teaspoon honey in another bowl and let sit until bubbly, about 5 minutes. Whisk in remaining 3 tablespoons honey and vinegar. Using stand mixer fitted with paddle, mix flour blend, psyllium, salt, and baking powder on low speed until combined, about 1 minute. Slowly add yeast mixture and sprouted grain paste and mix until combined, about 1 minute, scraping down bowl as needed. Increase speed to medium and beat until sticky and uniform, about 6 minutes. (Dough will resemble cookie dough.) Reduce speed to low, add ¼ cup seed mixture, and mix until incorporated, 30 to 60 seconds.

4. Using silicone spatula, scrape dough into prepared pan. Using your wet hands, press dough gently into corners and smooth top. Run your finger around entire edge of loaf, pressing down slightly, so that sides are about ½ inch shorter than center. Using serrated knife, cut three ½-inch-deep slashes diagonally across top of dough. Cover loosely with plastic wrap, place in warmed oven, and let rise for 10 minutes; do not let plastic touch oven rack.

5. Remove pan from oven and let sit on counter until loaf has risen ½ inch above rim of pan, about 20 minutes. Meanwhile, heat oven to 350 degrees.

6. Remove plastic, spray loaf with water, and sprinkle with remaining seed mixture. Bake until top is browned, crust is firm, and loaf sounds hollow when tapped, about 2 hours, rotating pan halfway through baking.

7. Remove bread from oven and let cool in pan for 10 minutes. Unmold bread onto wire rack and let cool completely, about 3 hours. Serve. (Cooled bread can be wrapped in double layer of plastic wrap and stored at room temperature for up to 2 days or frozen for up to 1 month. See freezing instructions on page 268.)

TEST KITCHEN TIP **Sprouting Grains for Bread**

1. Combine millet, quinoa, lentils, and 2 cups water in bowl, cover with plastic wrap, and let soak at room temperature until quinoa starts to sprout, 12 to 24 hours.

2. Drain soaked grains in strainer, return to bowl, and cover with plastic. Let grains sit at room temperature, rinsing and draining daily, until each type of grain begins to sprout, 1 to 3 days. (Every individual grain does not need to sprout.)

3. Process sprouted grains in food processor to thick, sticky paste, stopping to scrape down bowl often, 2 to 3 minutes.

Olive-Rosemary Bread

G-F TESTING LAB

FLOUR SUBSTITUTION	King Arthur Gluten-Free Multi-Purpose Flour 12 ounces = **1⅔ cups plus ½ cup**	Bob's Red Mill GF All-Purpose Baking Flour 12 ounces = **2¼ cups plus 2 tablespoons**
	Note that bread made with Bob's Red Mill will have a strong earthy, beany flavor that clashes somewhat with the rosemary in this recipe.	
OAT FLOUR	If you do not have oat flour, you can process 4 ounces old-fashioned rolled oats in a food processor or spice grinder until finely ground, about 1 minute. Do not use quick oats. You can substitute sorghum or millet flour for the oat flour.	
PSYLLIUM HUSK	Do not omit the powdered psyllium husk; it is crucial to the structure of the bread. For more information, see page 21.	

WHY THIS RECIPE WORKS

We used our Hearty Country Flax Bread (page 280) as a starting point for this recipe. While we liked the earthy flavor of ground flax in the country bread, it clashed with the olives and rosemary. We had better results when we replaced the ground flax with milder-tasting oat flour. While the flavors were right, the crumb was very dense and the crust was overly thick. Adding another egg and a few tablespoons of olive oil made the crumb softer, while brushing the loaf with an additional tablespoon of oil just before baking helped to soften the crust. Finally, two teaspoons of lemon juice softened the crumb even further, providing a great contrast to the hearty (but no longer tough) crust. The hydration level in this dough is pretty high, and we found that it needed a longer, slower baking process than the basic country bread. We had the best results baking the loaf in a relatively cool 325-degree oven for 2 hours (yes, this is correct). As with the country bread, this loaf will spread out rather than rise up unless it is proofed and baked in an ovenproof skillet. However, due to the long baking time, we found that placing the skillet on a heated baking stone caused the crust to become too dark and hard. When the dough has risen, simply brush it with oil and place the skillet with the risen dough right into the oven. Do not substitute soy milk powder for the milk powder in this recipe, as it will negatively impact the flavor and structure of the bread. If you don't eat dairy, you're better off omitting the milk powder, although the structure of the bread will suffer a bit. For tips on shaping this bread, see the steps on page 282.

Olive-Rosemary Bread

MAKE 1 LOAF

- 1½ cups warm water (110 degrees)
- 3 large eggs
- 3 tablespoons extra-virgin olive oil
- 2 teaspoons lemon juice
- 12 ounces (2⅔ cups) ATK All-Purpose Gluten-Free Flour Blend (page 7)
- 4 ounces (1⅓ cups) gluten-free oat flour
- 1½ ounces (½ cup) nonfat dry milk powder
- 3 tablespoons powdered psyllium husk
- 2 tablespoons sugar
- 1 tablespoon instant or rapid-rise yeast
- 1 teaspoon salt
- ¾ teaspoon baking soda
- 1 cup pitted kalamata olives, rinsed and chopped
- 2 tablespoons chopped fresh rosemary

1. Whisk water, eggs, 2 tablespoons oil, and lemon juice together in bowl. Using stand mixer fitted with paddle, mix flour blend, oat flour, milk powder, psyllium, sugar, yeast, salt, and baking soda on low speed until combined. Slowly add water mixture and let dough come together, about 1 minute, scraping down bowl as needed. Increase speed to medium and beat until sticky and uniform, about 6 minutes. (Dough will resemble cookie dough.) Stir in olives and rosemary with silicone spatula.

2. Spray 18 by 12-inch sheet of parchment paper with vegetable oil spray. Using silicone spatula, transfer dough to prepared parchment and shape into 6½-inch ball with your wet hands. Place dough (still on parchment) inside ovensafe 8-inch skillet. Using sharp serrated knife or single-edge razor blade, make two ½-inch-deep, 4-inch-long slashes in X shape across top of dough. Spray dough with water. Cover loosely with plastic wrap and let rise at room temperature until dough has risen by 50 percent, about 1½ hours.

3. Adjust oven rack to lowest position and heat oven to 325 degrees. Remove plastic and brush dough with remaining 1 tablespoon olive oil. Bake until top of bread is dark golden brown, crust is firm, and loaf sounds hollow when tapped, about 2 hours, rotating skillet halfway through baking.

4. Carefully remove loaf from skillet, transfer to wire rack (discard parchment), and let bread cool completely, about 2 hours. Serve. (Once cooled, bread can be wrapped in double layer of plastic wrap and stored at room temperature for up to 3 days. See freezing instructions on page 268.)

Baguettes

G-F TESTING LAB

FLOUR SUBSTITUTION	Do not substitute other all-purpose blends for the ATK All-Purpose Gluten-Free Flour Blend; they will not work well in this recipe.
OAT FLOUR	Not all brands of oat flour are gluten-free; read the label. Alternatively, 2 ounces (7 tablespoons) of sorghum flour can be substituted for the oat flour.
PSYLLIUM HUSK	Psyllium is crucial to the structure of the bread; see page 21 for more information.
WATER	Using the correct amount of water is crucial for this recipe; we strongly recommend weighing the water instead of using a liquid measuring cup.
BAGUETTE PAN	This recipe requires a two-loaf perforated baguette pan with 1-inch-deep trenches.

WHY THIS RECIPE WORKS

Making traditional baguettes is daunting for all but the most practiced home bakers, so we wondered whether we could develop a relatively simple gluten-free recipe. We cobbled together a working recipe using our all-purpose gluten-free flour blend, some oat flour for flavor and structure, and ground psyllium husk as a binder. Baguettes traditionally begin with a starter—a small mixture of flour, yeast, and liquid allowed to bubble and ferment—before making the dough in order to give the bread a deeper, richer flavor. We tried two different starters in our recipe, one using our all-purpose blend and another using oat flour. Oddly, the starter made with the all-purpose blend never fermented but rather turned into a rainbow of fuzzy mold. The oat flour starter, however, worked well and added an earthy, sweet fermented flavor to the bread. When testing how long the starter needed to sit, we were happy to find that 30 minutes was long enough to give the bread plenty of flavor. Traditionally, French baguettes also include a substantial amount of water in the dough in order to achieve their hallmark chewy texture and open crumb. To mimic this in our gluten-free version, we tested various amounts of water and found that 8 ounces of water to 10 ounces of flour gave us the chewy, airy crumb we were after. We also learned that measuring the water accurately makes a big difference. If you're off by just a tablespoon or two, the shape and texture of the final loaf will vary dramatically; for accuracy, we recommend weighing the water rather than using a liquid measuring cup. A traditional baguette recipe would never include eggs, but we found that adding a couple of eggs to this gluten-free dough made a big difference. The eggs boosted the protein in the dough to make it stronger and gave the bread a fuller, rounder flavor. We were getting closer to a good baguette, but the crumb was still a bit too dense. Wondering if an alkaline or an acidic ingredient could help open up the crumb, we tried adding them to the dough both separately and together. Adding an alkaline ingredient (baking soda) gave the bread a gummy texture and turned the loaf a strange pink color. Adding an acid (vinegar), however, opened up the crumb nicely, making the airholes larger and more authentic. Testing a few different types of acid—including yogurt, buttermilk, water kefir, milk kefir, lemon juice, rice vinegar, and apple cider vinegar—we found that a mere tablespoon of cider vinegar opened up the crumb just enough without giving the bread a sour flavor. Traditional baguettes bake for only 20 minutes or so, but our gluten-free baguettes required nearly an hour in the oven in order to dry out. To prevent the crust from becoming overly thick and dense during this long baking time, we covered the loaves with a piece of foil (with holes poked into it to help release some of the steam) during the first half of the baking time. Using a very hot oven in addition to the foil gave the baguettes a nice tall oven spring. After we removed the foil, we reduced the oven temperature so that the loaves could dry out and brown evenly. Throughout all of our testing, we tried a variety of shaping methods and found that a perforated baguette pan is crucial because the dough is so wet and slack.

Baguettes

MAKES 2 LOAVES

STARTER

- 2 ounces (⅔ cup) oat flour
- 4 ounces (½ cup) warm water (110 degrees)
- 1½ teaspoons sugar
- ½ teaspoon instant or rapid-rise yeast

DOUGH

- 8 ounces (1¾ cups) ATK All-Purpose Gluten-Free Flour Blend (page 7)
- 7 teaspoons powdered psyllium husk
- 1½ teaspoons sugar
- 1 teaspoon instant or rapid-rise yeast
- ¾ teaspoon salt
- 4 ounces (½ cup) warm water (110 degrees)
- 2 large eggs
- 1 tablespoon cider vinegar

1. FOR THE STARTER: Combine oat flour, warm water, sugar, and yeast in bowl and let sit until bubbly and fragrant, about 30 minutes. Adjust oven rack to middle position and heat oven to 200 degrees. When oven reaches 200 degrees, turn it off. (This will be warm proofing box for dough. Do not begin step 2 until oven has been turned off.)

2. FOR THE DOUGH: Using stand mixer fitted with paddle, mix flour blend, psyllium, sugar, yeast, and salt together on low speed until combined, about 1 minute. Slowly add warm water, eggs, vinegar, and starter and mix until combined, scraping down bowl as needed, about 1 minute. Increase speed to medium and beat until dough is sticky and uniform, about 6 minutes. (Dough will resemble cookie dough.)

3. Scrape down bowl, then scrape half of dough onto clean counter; dough will be very sticky. Using hands, roll into rough 6-inch-long rope. Clean and dry hands, then continue to roll dough into 13-inch-long rope, working from center out to ends and pinching holes together as needed; do not taper ends. Gently transfer loaf to baguette pan. Repeat with remaining dough to form second loaf.

4. Place baguette pan on rimmed baking sheet. Cover loosely with plastic wrap, place in warmed oven, and let rise for 10 minutes; do not let plastic touch oven rack. Remove sheet from oven and let sit on counter until loaves have risen by 50 percent, about 20 minutes. Meanwhile, heat oven to 450 degrees.

5. Remove plastic and cut three 4-inch-long, ½-inch-deep diagonal slashes down length of each loaf using serrated knife. Tent baking sheet loosely with aluminum foil and crimp edges to seal; do not let foil touch top of loaves. Using sharp knife, poke 6 holes in foil. Bake baguettes until lightly browned, about 25 minutes.

6. Carefully remove foil (watch for steam), rotate sheet, and reduce oven temperature to 350 degrees; if necessary, hold oven door open for a few seconds to help it cool down. Continue to bake until baguettes are golden brown, 25 to 35 minutes. Transfer baguettes to wire rack and let cool completely, about 1 hour. Serve. (Cooled bread can be wrapped in double layer of plastic and stored at room temperature for up to 1 day or frozen for up to 1 month. See freezing instructions on page 268.)

TEST KITCHEN TIP **Making Baguettes**

1. Scrape down bowl, then scrape half of dough onto clean counter; dough will be very sticky. Using hands, roll into rough 6-inch-long rope.

2. Washing and drying your hands before continuing to roll dough into 13-inch-long rope is crucial. Dough will become less sticky as you continue to roll it.

3. After dough has risen in perforated baguette pan, cut three 4-inch-long, ½-inch-deep diagonal slashes down length of each loaf using serrated knife.

Baguettes

We wanted baguettes with a crisp, crackly top, a moist, open crumb, and a subtly sweet, earthy tang. To achieve this flavor and texture, we had to employ a few unconventional tricks and ingredients. This is what we learned.

1. USE A STARTER: To produce a flavorful loaf without a lot of hassle, we began with a quick starter of oat flour, sugar, yeast, and warm water. While many starters rely on natural yeast to grow, we discovered that the time required (many days) was not necessary, and with only ½ teaspoon of yeast and a little sugar we achieved the same results with just a 30-minute rest on the counter. We used oat flour because it imparted a subtle sweet, earthy flavor to complement the yeasty fermented tang.

2. ADD CIDER VINEGAR: To help open up the interior texture of the baguette and make the crumb more airy, we added some cider vinegar to the dough. The vinegar strengthened the structure of the rice protein in the flour blend so that it was better able to hold the bubbles in place during baking. But that's not all the vinegar did. It also contains some acetic acid, which sped up the yeast's production of alcohol and carbon dioxide to produce more, and bigger, bubbles. We found that 1 tablespoon of cider vinegar opened up the crumb nicely without overpowering the flavor of the bread.

3. MAKE A WET, STICKY DOUGH: Making the dough extra wet ensures that the bread will have a chewy texture with sizable airholes evenly throughout the loaf. In fact, the dough is so loose that it looks more like cookie dough than bread dough. As the dough is divided and rolled out, however, it becomes much less sticky and easier to work with. Don't be tempted to add extra flour to the mixer to make the dough less sticky; this will only make the bread taste dense and tough. Given the sticky texture of this dough, we don't recommend trying to mix it by hand or substituting a handheld mixer for the stand mixer.

4. REMOVE THE FOIL AND DROP THE OVEN TEMPERATURE FOR THE SECOND HALF OF BAKING: To help with oven spring and prevent the crust from becoming overly thick, we covered the loaves with foil to trap some of the steam during the first half of the baking time. Poking holes in the foil prevents too much steam from building up, which would make the bread wet. We then removed the foil so that the loaves could dry out and brown as they finished baking. Reducing the oven temperature from 450 to 350 degrees at this point prevented the crust from becoming too dark.

Dinner Rolls

FLOUR SUBSTITUTION	King Arthur Gluten-Free Multi-Purpose Flour 15 ounces = **2¾ cups**	Bob's Red Mill GF All-Purpose Baking Flour 15 ounces = **3 cups**
	Note that rolls made with King Arthur will be slightly pasty, and rolls made with Bob's Red Mill will have a strong bean flavor and a darker color. The dough made with Bob's Red Mill will be a bit looser and harder to shape, but the rolls will rise just fine and bake up nicely.	
PSYLLIUM HUSK	Do not omit the powdered psyllium husk; it is crucial to the structure of the rolls. For more information, see page 21.	

WHY THIS RECIPE WORKS

Store-bought gluten-free dinner rolls are tough and bland, and many homemade recipes aren't much better. We wanted rich, tender, pull-apart dinner rolls, so we started with our favorite test kitchen recipe and substituted our gluten-free flour blend plus some psyllium to boost structure. This approach produced rolls with great buttery flavor, but tasters complained that the rolls were greasy. Cutting back on the amount of butter and adding a small amount of nonfat milk powder lent a rich flavor without any added greasiness. The bigger problem was the texture of the crumb—it was dense and a bit tough. The dough needed more liquid. We tested both milk and water, and tasters agreed that the water worked best given all the butter, milk powder, and eggs in the dough. This helped, but our rolls needed something more. Up to this point we had been relying solely on yeast, and we wondered if adding a chemical leavener would create a more open crumb and further tenderize our rolls. We tested various combinations and found that 2 teaspoons of baking powder plus the standard packet of yeast produced rolls with the desired airy crumb. We had one more trick up our sleeve. In other kitchen tests, we discovered the tenderizing effect of lemon juice in our pie dough, so we made one last batch of rolls with some lemon juice in the mix. These rolls were perfect—pillowy soft with a light crumb and rich buttery flavor. The rolls are best eaten the day they are made.

Dinner Rolls

MAKES 8 ROLLS

- 1⅓ cups warm water (110 degrees), plus 1 teaspoon water
- 2 teaspoons lemon juice
- 2 large eggs, plus 1 large yolk
- 15 ounces (3⅓ cups) ATK All-Purpose Gluten-Free Flour Blend (page 7)
- 1½ ounces (½ cup) nonfat dry milk powder
- 2 tablespoons powdered psyllium husk
- 2 tablespoons sugar
- 2¼ teaspoons instant or rapid-rise yeast
- 2 teaspoons baking powder (see page 24)
  Salt
- 6 tablespoons unsalted butter, cut into 6 pieces and softened

1. Spray 9-inch round cake pan with vegetable oil spray. Whisk 1⅓ cups warm water, lemon juice, and 1 egg plus yolk together in bowl. Using stand mixer fitted with paddle, mix flour blend, milk powder, psyllium, sugar, yeast, baking powder, and 1½ teaspoons salt on low speed until combined. Slowly add water mixture and let dough come together, about 1 minute, scraping down bowl as needed. Add butter, increase speed to medium, and beat until sticky and uniform, about 6 minutes.

2. Working with generous ⅓ cup dough at a time, shape into rough rounds using your wet hands; arrange rolls in prepared pan (one in center and seven spaced evenly around edges). Cover loosely with plastic wrap and let rise at room temperature until doubled in size (rolls should press against each other), about 1 hour. (Risen rolls can be refrigerated for up to 4 hours.)

3. Adjust oven rack to middle position and heat oven to 375 degrees. Lightly beat remaining 1 egg, 1 teaspoon water, and pinch salt in bowl until combined. Remove plastic and brush rolls with egg wash. Bake until tops are golden brown, 35 to 40 minutes, rotating pan halfway through baking.

4. Let rolls cool in pan on wire rack for 10 minutes, then invert onto rack; reinvert rolls and let cool for 10 to 15 minutes. Break rolls apart and serve warm.

TEST KITCHEN TIP **Shaping Dinner Rolls**

Baking rolls in cake pan helps them to rise up rather than out. Divide dough into 8 pieces, shape into rounds, and arrange in greased pan with 1 piece of dough in center.

Whole-Grain Dinner Rolls

G-F TESTING LAB

FLOUR SUBSTITUTION	Do not substitute other whole-grain blends for the ATK Whole-Grain Gluten-Free Flour Blend; they will not work in this recipe.
PSYLLIUM HUSK	Psyllium is crucial to the structure of the rolls; see page 21 for more information.

WHY THIS RECIPE WORKS

Knowing that the wheaty flavor of our whole-grain gluten-free flour blend would taste great in a rich, buttery dinner roll, we took our basic dinner roll recipe and swapped in our whole-grain blend. Finding these rolls a bit too greasy, we reduced the butter to 4 tablespoons and added a few egg yolks to make up for the missing richness. Many of our other yeasted breads require a little baking powder for a tall rise, but we found it wasn't necessary here. The whole-grain blend has a higher protein content than that of the all-purpose blend, which makes the dough stronger. Not only does this strong dough translate into a chewier texture, it's also better at trapping the yeast's gas during rising to produce nice, tall rolls. We did, however, like the addition of baking soda. The soda is alkaline, which dissolves a small amount of the rice proteins in the dough and therefore makes the crumb more delicate. Up until now, we had been baking the rolls in a cake pan to create pull-apart rolls, but that wasn't working because the unsupported center roll always collapsed during baking. To solve this, we switched to a muffin tin so that each roll could have pan support during the rise and the bake. To finish, we sprinkled the rolls with chopped sunflower seeds and kosher salt before baking. If using table salt, reduce all salt amounts by half.

Whole-Grain Dinner Rolls

MAKES 12 ROLLS

12	ounces (1½ cups) 1 or 2 percent low-fat milk, heated to 110 degrees
2¼	teaspoons instant or rapid-rise yeast
5	teaspoons sugar
1	large egg plus 2 large yolks
10	ounces (2¼ cups) ATK Whole-Grain Gluten-Free Flour Blend (page 9)
5	teaspoons powdered psyllium husk
	Kosher salt
½	teaspoon baking soda
4	tablespoons unsalted butter, cut into 4 pieces and softened
1	tablespoon raw sunflower seeds, chopped

1. Adjust oven rack to middle position and heat oven to 200 degrees. As soon as oven reaches 200 degrees, turn it off. (This will be warm proofing box for dough. Do not begin step 2 until oven has been turned off.) Spray 12-cup muffin tin with vegetable oil spray.

2. Combine warm milk, yeast, and 1 teaspoon sugar in bowl and let sit until bubbly, about 5 minutes. Whisk in egg and yolks. Using stand mixer fitted with paddle, mix flour blend, psyllium, 2 teaspoons salt, baking soda, and remaining 4 teaspoons sugar on low speed until combined, about 1 minute. Slowly add yeast mixture and mix until combined, scraping down bowl as needed, about 1 minute. Add butter, increase speed to medium, and beat until sticky and uniform, about 6 minutes. (Dough will be very soft and loose.)

3. Working with scant ¼ cup dough at a time, shape into rough rounds using your wet hands and place in prepared muffin tin. Cover loosely with plastic wrap, place in warmed oven, and let rise for 10 minutes; do not let plastic touch oven rack.

4. Remove rolls from oven and let sit on counter until dough has doubled in size, about 20 minutes. Meanwhile, heat oven to 350 degrees.

5. Remove plastic, spray rolls with water, then sprinkle with sunflower seeds and ½ teaspoon salt. Bake until deep golden brown, 30 to 35 minutes, rotating muffin tin halfway through baking.

6. Remove rolls from oven and let cool in tin for 10 minutes. Remove rolls from tin and serve warm. (Rolls can be stored in zipper-lock bag for up to 2 days; they cannot be frozen. To refresh, warm rolls in 350-degree oven for 10 minutes.)

VARIATION

Dairy-Free Whole-Grain Dinner Rolls
We prefer the flavor and texture of these rolls made with soy milk, but almond milk will also work; do not use rice milk.

Substitute ¾ cup unsweetened soy milk and ¾ cup water for milk, and Earth Balance Vegan Buttery Sticks for butter. Omit salt in dough.

Hamburger Rolls

G-F TESTING LAB

FLOUR SUBSTITUTION	King Arthur Gluten-Free Multi-Purpose Flour 12 ounces = **1⅔ cups plus ½ cup**	Betty Crocker All-Purpose Gluten Free Rice Blend 12 ounces = **2¼ cups plus 2 tablespoons**
	Rolls made with Betty Crocker will have a slightly spongy and chewy texture.	
OAT FLOUR	Not all brands of oat flour are gluten-free; read the label. Alternatively, 6 ounces (1⅓ cups) of sorghum flour can be substituted for the oat flour; we had good luck using Bob's Red Mill "Sweet" White Sorghum Flour.	
PSYLLIUM HUSK	Psyllium is crucial to the structure of the rolls; see page 21 for more information.	
BAKING POWDER	Not all brands of baking powder are gluten-free; see page 24 for more information.	

✓ WHY THIS RECIPE WORKS

If you've ever had a store-bought gluten-free hamburger roll, you know how disappointing they can be. Usually dry, crumbly, and stale-tasting, or flat, dense, and tough, these skimpy buns don't have enough structure to stand up to a meaty burger. To start, we employed a handful of tricks we've found to be important to successful gluten-free yeast breads: We added oat flour for a little protein boost, two eggs for structure and richness, psyllium husk powder to create an open crumb and contribute to a sturdy structure, and a combination of yeast and baking powder to encourage the rolls to rise during proofing and baking. These additions made the rolls taste right, but their dry, dense texture still needed work, and they looked more like a dinner roll than a hamburger bun. To fix the dry, dense texture of the rolls, we tested adding more water incrementally beyond the 2 cups in our working recipe. In the end, just ¼ cup additional water made all the difference in opening up the crumb and making the rolls more tender. But the extra water made the dough so slack that the rolls couldn't hold their shape during rising and baking. Even with all the protein boosts and binders we had added to the dough, they just spread out over the pan into pancakes. Rather than tinker with the liquid amount again and wreck the ideal crumb we had created, we decided to think outside of the bun. To help contain the slack dough, we constructed foil collars for each roll so that they could maintain a tall, round shape while proofing and during the first half of baking. Greasing the collars ensured that they released from the partially baked rolls easily. A final spritz of water and a sprinkling of sesame seeds before baking were the final touches for our tender but hearty hamburger rolls.

Hamburger Rolls
MAKES 8 ROLLS

18	ounces (2¼ cups) warm water (110 degrees)
2¼	teaspoons instant or rapid-rise yeast
2	tablespoons plus 1 teaspoon sugar
2	large eggs
2	tablespoons unsalted butter, melted and cooled
12	ounces (2⅔ cups) ATK All-Purpose Gluten-Free Flour Blend (page 7)
6	ounces (2 cups) oat flour
3	tablespoons powdered psyllium husk
2	teaspoons baking powder
1½	teaspoons salt
1	teaspoon sesame seeds

1. Adjust oven rack to middle position and heat oven to 200 degrees. As soon as oven reaches 200 degrees, turn it off. (This will be warm proofing box for dough. Do not begin step 2 until oven has been turned off.) Line rimmed baking sheet with parchment paper and spray with vegetable oil spray. Using double layer of aluminum foil, create eight 13½ by 2-inch strips, then shape each into 4-inch circle and secure with staples. Spray inside of collars with vegetable oil spray and place on prepared sheet.

2. Combine warm water, yeast, and 1 teaspoon sugar in bowl and let sit until bubbly, about 5 minutes. Whisk in eggs and melted butter. Using stand mixer fitted with paddle, mix flour blend, oat flour, psyllium, baking powder, salt, and remaining 2 tablespoons sugar on low speed until combined, about 1 minute. Slowly add yeast mixture and mix until combined, scraping down bowl as needed, about 1 minute. Increase speed to medium and beat until sticky and uniform, about 6 minutes. (Dough will resemble cookie dough.)

3. Working with ½ cup dough at a time, shape each into rough round using your wet hands, and place in foil collar. Cover loosely with plastic wrap, place in warmed oven, and let rise for 10 minutes; do not let plastic touch oven rack.

4. Remove rolls from oven and let sit on counter until dough has doubled in size, about 20 minutes. Meanwhile, heat oven to 400 degrees.

5. Reduce oven temperature to 350 degrees. Remove plastic and adjust foil collars as needed to be flush with pan. Spray rolls with water and sprinkle with sesame seeds. Bake until golden brown and firm, 35 to 40 minutes, rotating sheet and removing foil collars halfway through baking.

6. Transfer rolls to wire rack and let cool completely before serving, about 1 hour. (Split rolls can be wrapped in double layer of plastic wrap and stored at room temperature for up to 2 days, or frozen for up to 1 month. If frozen, microwave at 50 percent power for 1 minute then toast until golden.)

VARIATION
Dairy-Free Hamburger Rolls
Substitute vegetable oil for melted butter.

TEST KITCHEN TIP **Working with Foil Collars**

1. Using double layer of aluminum foil, create eight 13½ by 2-inch strips.

2. Shape each strip into 4-inch circle and secure with staples.

3. Spray inside of collars with vegetable oil spray and place on greased, parchment-lined baking sheet.

4. Working with ½ cup dough at a time, shape into rough rounds using wet hands, and place in foil collars.

5. After rolls have risen, remove plastic wrap and adjust collars as needed to be flush with baking sheet.

6. Remove foil collars halfway through baking time to ensure even browning around edges of rolls.

Hamburger Rolls

Most store-bought gluten-free hamburger rolls are a sad accompaniment to a burger. To create a roll that stood up to even a big pub-style burger, we had to get a little creative in the kitchen.

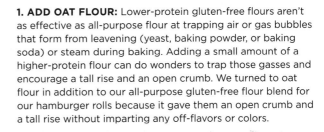

1. ADD OAT FLOUR: Lower-protein gluten-free flours aren't as effective as all-purpose flour at trapping air or gas bubbles that form from leavening (yeast, baking powder, or baking soda) or steam during baking. Adding a small amount of a higher-protein flour can do wonders to trap those gasses and encourage a tall rise and an open crumb. We turned to oat flour in addition to our all-purpose gluten-free flour blend for our hamburger rolls because it gave them an open crumb and a tall rise without imparting any off-flavors or colors.

2. FAST-TRACK THE YEAST: In order to get tall, fluffy rolls, it's important to get the bread rising quickly once the dough is mixed. This is because the dough starts off loose and wet but becomes more dense and dry as it sits (for even a short time), and the yeast has an easier time doing its job while the dough is loose and malleable. To start, we gave the instant yeast a boost by blooming it in warm water laced with sugar before making the dough. Once the dough was made and the rolls were shaped, we kept the yeast working at a fast pace by start-ing the rise in a warm (but turned-off) oven.

3. GET CRAFTY WITH COLLARS: Even with the addition of oat flour, our rolls were spreading too much during proof-ing and baking. We wanted our hamburger rolls to taste and look like the real thing, so using loaf pans or muffin tins were out. We used foil collars with success in some of our sandwich breads to encourage the loaves to rise beyond the loaf pan rim, so we decided to craft free-form collars for the rolls. Not only did the collars encourage the rolls to rise beautifully, they ensured the rolls turned out uniformly.

4. START HOT, THEN TURN DOWN THE HEAT: To get nice browning and a good rise, we found two oven temperatures to be ideal. When the rolls were baked at a moderate heat for an extended amount of time, the bottoms were getting thick and tough, but at a high temperature the rolls were browning too quickly and the crust was getting too hard. Preheating the oven to 400 degrees but dropping the temperature to 350 degrees when putting in the rolls allowed us to achieve good oven spring without overcooking our rolls.

Rustic Bread

G-F TESTING LAB

FLOUR SUBSTITUTION	King Arthur Gluten-Free Multi-Purpose Flour 12 ounces = **1⅔ cups plus ½ cup**	Betty Crocker All-Purpose Gluten Free Rice Blend 12 ounces= **2¼ cups plus 2 tablespoons**
	Bread made with Betty Crocker will have a softer texture and milder flavor.	
OAT FLOUR	Not all brands of oat flour are gluten-free; read the label. Alternatively, 4 ounces (¾ cup plus 2 tablespoons) of sorghum flour can be substituted for the oat flour. We had good luck using Bob's Red Mill "Sweet" White Sorghum Flour.	
PSYLLIUM HUSK	Psyllium is crucial to the structure of the bread; see page 21 for more information.	
WATER	Using the correct amount of water is crucial for this recipe; we strongly recommend weighing the water instead of using a liquid measuring cup.	

WHY THIS RECIPE WORKS

We wanted to develop a recipe for rustic bread with good wheaty flavor, a chewy interior, and a thick, hearty crust. Classic recipes for this type of bread contain as few as four ingredients—water, yeast, salt, and flour—but they rely heavily on the protein in the flour to create an open crumb and give the loaf a nice shape that holds its own without having to bake it in a pan. Knowing that our all-purpose blend would need a protein boost in order to support this kind of loaf, we combined it with a substantial portion of oat flour along with a couple of eggs. To help open the interior crumb of the bread so that it would have large, rustic airholes, rather than the small, tight holes you'd expect in a sandwich bread, we increased the amount of water substantially and made the dough quite wet. To help the wet bread hold on to these larger airholes during rising and baking, we added two key ingredients: psyllium husk and vinegar. The psyllium made the dough stronger and more elastic, and the vinegar also made the dough stronger while speeding up the yeast activity. Focusing next on the flavor, we found our working recipe still tasted too bland. To help give it deeper flavor, we borrowed a technique from our baguette recipe and added a starter. A starter is a small mixture of flour, yeast, and liquid allowed to bubble, ferment, and develop flavor before making the actual bread dough. Using the same 30-minute oat flour starter that we used for the baguettes gave this bread the hearty, wheaty flavor we were after. Up until this point, we had been shaping the dough into one big loaf, but the finished breads were often inconsistent in terms of height and oven spring. Trying a variety of different bread shapes, we found that making two small loaves worked much better. We had one last problem to tackle—baking the bread. With so much water in the dough to provide steam, we had to bake the bread longer to dry out the inside, but this caused the bottom crust to burn. Insulating the baking sheet by placing it inside another baking sheet enabled us to bake the bread for 90 minutes and dry it out but not burn the crust.

Rustic Bread with Sesame Seeds

MAKES 2 LOAVES

STARTER

- 4 ounces (1⅓ cups) oat flour
- 8 ounces (1 cup) warm water (110 degrees)
- 1 tablespoon sugar
- 1 teaspoon instant or rapid-rise yeast

DOUGH

- 12 ounces (2⅔ cups) ATK All-Purpose Gluten-Free Flour Blend (page 7)
- 5 tablespoons powdered psyllium husk
- 1 tablespoon instant or rapid-rise yeast
- 1 tablespoon sugar
- 1½ teaspoons salt
- 9 ounces (1 cup plus 2 tablespoons) warm water (110 degrees)
- 2 large eggs
- 1 tablespoon cider vinegar
- 1 tablespoon sesame seeds

1. FOR THE STARTER: Combine oat flour, warm water, sugar, and yeast in bowl and let sit until bubbly and fragrant, about 30 minutes. Adjust oven rack to middle position and heat oven to 200 degrees. When oven reaches 200 degrees, turn it off. (This will be warm proofing box for dough. Do not begin step 2 until oven has been turned off). Line rimmed baking sheet with parchment paper and place inside second baking sheet.

2. FOR THE DOUGH: Using stand mixer fitted with paddle, mix flour blend, psyllium, yeast, sugar, and salt on low speed until combined, about 1 minute. Slowly add warm water, eggs, vinegar, and starter and mix until combined, scraping down bowl as needed, about 1 minute. Increase speed to medium and beat until dough is sticky and uniform, about 6 minutes. (Dough will be thick and sticky.)

3. Divide dough into 2 equal pieces. Working with 1 piece of dough at a time, roll into rough 6-inch-long rope on clean counter. Dough will be sticky, so clean and dry hands, then gently continue to roll dough into 8-inch-long rope, working from center out to ends and pinching holes together as needed; do not taper ends. Gently transfer loaves to prepared sheet, spaced 4 inches apart.

4. Cover loosely with plastic wrap, place in warmed oven, and let rise for 10 minutes; do not let plastic touch oven rack. Remove from oven and let sit on counter until loaves have risen by 50 percent, about 20 minutes. Meanwhile, heat oven to 350 degrees.

5. Remove plastic and cut three 2-inch-long, ½-inch-deep diagonal slashes down length of each loaf using serrated knife. Spray loaves with water and sprinkle with sesame seeds. Bake until tops are deep golden brown, crusts are firm, and loaves sound hollow when tapped, about 90 minutes, rotating pan halfway through baking.

6. Transfer sheet with loaves to wire rack and let bread cool for 10 minutes. Remove loaves from sheet and let cool completely on rack, about 3 hours. Serve. (Cooled bread can be wrapped in double layer of plastic and stored at room temperature for up to 3 days or frozen for up to 1 month. See freezing instructions on page 268.)

TEST KITCHEN TIP **5 Key Ingredients for Great Gluten-Free Bread**

We've baked well over a thousand loaves of gluten-free bread in search of perfection. Here are the five key ingredients without which good gluten-free bread is just not possible.

GROUND PSYLLIUM HUSK All of our breads call for ground psyllium husk for two reasons. First, it reinforces the protein structure in the dough, much like a glue, so that the dough is stronger and better able to hold on to air bubbles. Second, it helps bind water into the dough, making the crumb more moist. Note that psyllium darkens as it ages, which can discolor the bread.

INSTANT YEAST All of our breads call for instant yeast (aka rapid-rise). Instant yeast is different from active dry yeast because it has been processed more gently, which in turn makes it work faster. Rather than add the instant yeast to the dough in its dried, granular form, we first dissolve it in warm, sweetened water to help speed it up even more. This ensures that the bread has a swift rise with lots of airholes evenly dispersed throughout the loaf.

VINEGAR Our Baguettes and Rustic Bread recipes have a little vinegar added to the dough to help them develop large, airy pockets and a hearty chew. The vinegar has an acidic pH and works on a molecular level to make the rice proteins in the flour blend stronger so that they can hold on to large gas bubbles better. We like cider vinegar because the flavor isn't noticeable in the final bread.

BAKING POWDER Most of our recipes call for baking powder, which is a leavener made of baking soda, an acid (such as cream of tartar), and buffering agents that prevent any reaction from happening until liquid or heat is added. Once activated, it produces gas bubbles that, in addition to the yeast, help bread rise. It is a stronger leavener than baking soda alone because it activates itself twice: once when combined with liquid and a second time when heated. That's why baking powder is often called "double-acting."

BAKING SODA Two of our whole-grain breads call for baking soda, which is a leavener with an alkaline pH. As a leavener, it reacts with any acidity in the dough (including acid created by the fermenting yeast) to create gas that, in addition to the yeast, helps bread rise. Even more important, however, the alkaline pH of the baking soda dissolves some of the proteins in the dough, which makes the bread more tender and soft. This is especially useful in our whole-grain breads (which have a very high protein content) to help soften their tougher texture. We don't add it to any of our breads that use the all-purpose blend, because it makes them mushy and turns them an unappealing purple-pink color.

Whole-Grain Walnut-Cherry Boule

✓ WHY THIS RECIPE WORKS

This walnut-cherry boule is a rustic loaf with a thick, burnished crust and a soft but chewy interior crumb flavored with walnuts and dried cherries. While classic boule recipes rely on the gluten bonds for structure, thereby allowing the dough to rise up instead of out, we had to come up with our own tricks. Starting with our whole-grain gluten-free flour blend was a step in the right direction because its high protein content helped give the dough enough structure to rise. And as with our other yeast breads, we added powdered psyllium husk to strengthen the protein network in the whole-grain flour blend. Using more yeast than usual (4 teaspoons) helped with the rise, as did starting the loaf in a hot oven (400 degrees) and then turning down the heat so it could cook through. We further reinforced the rise by increasing the amount of liquid in the batter, which created a lot of steam in the oven, but we wanted the loaf to rise even higher. Switching from whole to low-fat milk made for a higher rise and a moist crumb, as the bread was no longer weighed down with fat. To help make the interior crumb more delicate, we added baking soda. The soda is alkaline, which dissolved a small amount of the rice proteins in the dough and resulted in a more tender crumb. Proofing and baking the loaf in a small skillet prevented the bread from spreading and allowed us to easily transfer the loaf to the baking stone. Finally, a little bit of sugar helped the yeast do its job and added a subtle sweetness that complemented the earthy flavor of our whole-grain flour blend. You will need an 8-inch ovensafe skillet for this recipe.

Whole-Grain Walnut-Cherry Boule

MAKES 1 LOAF

- 16 ounces (2 cups) 1 or 2 percent low-fat milk, heated to 110 degrees
- 4 teaspoons instant or rapid-rise yeast
- 2 tablespoons plus 1 teaspoon sugar
- 2 large eggs
- 15 ounces (3⅓ cups) ATK Whole-Grain Gluten-Free Flour Blend (page 9)
- 2½ tablespoons powdered psyllium husk
- 1½ teaspoons salt
- ¾ teaspoon baking soda
- 1 cup walnuts, toasted and chopped
- ½ cup dried cherries, chopped

1. Adjust oven rack to middle position and heat oven to 200 degrees. As soon as oven reaches 200 degrees, turn it off. (This will be warm proofing box for dough. Do not begin step 2 until oven has been turned off.)

2. Combine warm milk, yeast, and 1 teaspoon sugar in bowl and let sit until bubbly, about 5 minutes. Whisk in eggs. Using stand mixer fitted with paddle, mix flour blend, psyllium, salt, baking soda, and remaining 2 tablespoons sugar on low speed until combined, about 1 minute. Slowly add yeast mixture and mix until combined, scraping down bowl as needed, about 1 minute. Increase speed to medium and beat until sticky and uniform, about 6 minutes. (Dough will resemble cookie dough.) Reduce speed to low, add walnuts and cherries, and mix until incorporated, 30 to 60 seconds.

3. Spray 18 by 12-inch sheet of parchment paper with vegetable oil spray. Using silicone spatula, transfer dough to prepared parchment. Using wet hands, shape into 6½-inch ball. Transfer dough with parchment to 8-inch ovensafe skillet. Using serrated knife, cut ½-inch-deep X across top of dough. Cover loosely with plastic wrap, place skillet in warmed oven, and let rise for 10 minutes; do not let plastic touch oven rack.

4. Remove skillet from oven and let sit on counter until loaf has risen by 50 percent, about 20 minutes. Meanwhile, place baking stone on rack and heat oven to 400 degrees.

5. Remove plastic and spray loaf with water. Reduce oven temperature to 350 degrees and place skillet on baking stone. Bake until top of bread is well browned, crust is firm, and loaf sounds hollow when tapped, 55 minutes to 1¼ hours, rotating skillet halfway through baking.

G-F TESTING LAB

FLOUR SUBSTITUTION	Do not substitute other whole-grain blends for the ATK Whole-Grain Gluten-Free Flour Blend; they will not work in this recipe.
PSYLLIUM HUSK	Psyllium is crucial to the structure of the bread; see page 21 for more information.

6. Being careful of hot skillet handle, remove skillet from oven. Transfer bread to wire rack, discarding parchment, and let cool completely, about 3 hours. Serve. (Cooled bread can be wrapped in double layer of plastic wrap and stored at room temperature for up to 3 days or frozen for up to 1 month. See freezing instructions on page 268.)

See freezing instructions on page 268.

VARIATION

Dairy-Free Whole-Grain Walnut-Cherry Boule

We prefer the flavor and texture of this boule made with soy milk, but almond milk will also work; do not use rice milk.

Substitute 1 cup unsweetened soy milk and 1 cup water for milk.

TEST KITCHEN TIP **Making Whole-Grain Walnut-Cherry Boule**

1. Using silicone spatula, transfer dough to greased parchment paper and shape with wet hands into 6½-inch ball.

2. Place dough (still on parchment) inside 8-inch ovensafe skillet.

3. Using serrated knife, cut ½-inch-deep X across top of dough. Cover dough with plastic and let rise in turned-off oven.

4. Let dough rise on counter 20 minutes. Meanwhile, heat baking stone in 400-degree oven. After loaf has fully risen, remove plastic and spray loaf with water.

5. Reduce oven temperature to 350 degrees and place skillet with loaf on baking stone.

6. Bake until top of bread is well browned, crust is firm, and loaf sounds hollow when tapped, 55 to 75 minutes, rotating skillet halfway through baking.

English Muffins

G-F TESTING LAB

FLOUR SUBSTITUTION	King Arthur Gluten-Free Multi-Purpose Flour 14 ounces = **2⅓ cups plus ¼ cup**	Bob's Red Mill GF All-Purpose Baking Flour 14 ounces = **2½ cups plus ⅓ cup**
	Note that English muffins made with King Arthur will be slightly starchy, and English muffins made with Bob's Red Mill will be darker and will have a distinct bean flavor.	
OAT FLOUR	If you do not have oat flour, you can process 4 ounces old-fashioned rolled oats in a food processor or spice grinder until finely ground, about 1 minute. Do not use quick oats. You can substitute sorghum or millet flour for the oat flour.	
PSYLLIUM HUSK	Do not omit the powdered psyllium husk; it is crucial to the structure of the muffins. For more information, see page 21.	

WHY THIS RECIPE WORKS

Our Classic Sandwich Bread (page 266) proved to be a good starting point for this recipe—the dough has the necessary flavor and richness—and the classic technique worked well. We portioned the dough into rough balls and let them rise on two rimmed baking sheets until nearly doubled in size. The dough was rather sticky, and we had trouble dusting them with cornmeal (which helps create the distinctive crunch on the exterior of any good English muffin). We found it easier to sprinkle the rimmed baking sheet with cornmeal and then sprinkle more cornmeal over the top of the risen dough rounds. In order to create their distinctive shape and crumb, it's necessary to flatten the dough rounds both before and during griddling. While some classic recipes cook the muffins entirely on the stovetop, we thought the crusts became much too hard. One minute of griddling per side was sufficient. We then transferred the muffins to a baking sheet and finished by baking them in the oven to ensure they were cooked through but not overly browned. Do not substitute soy milk powder for the milk powder in this recipe, as it will negatively impact the flavor and structure of the English muffins.

English Muffins

MAKES 10 MUFFINS

3¾	ounces (¾ cup) cornmeal
2	cups warm water (110 degrees)
2	large eggs
2	tablespoons unsalted butter, melted and cooled
14	ounces (3 cups plus 2 tablespoons) ATK All-Purpose Gluten-Free Flour Blend (page 7)
4	ounces (1⅓ cups) gluten-free oat flour
1½	ounces (½ cup) nonfat dry milk powder
3	tablespoons powdered psyllium husk
2	tablespoons sugar
2¼	teaspoons instant or rapid-rise yeast
2	teaspoons baking powder (see page 24)
1½	teaspoons salt
3	teaspoons vegetable oil

1. Sprinkle ½ cup cornmeal evenly over 2 rimmed baking sheets. Whisk water, eggs, and melted butter together in bowl. Using stand mixer fitted with paddle, mix flour blend, oat flour, milk powder, psyllium, sugar, yeast, baking powder, and salt on low speed until combined. Slowly add water mixture and let dough come together, about 1 minute, scraping down bowl as needed. Increase speed to medium and beat until sticky and uniform, about 6 minutes. (Dough will resemble cookie dough.)

2. Working with ⅓ cup dough at a time, shape into rough balls using your wet hands, and space at least 1½ inches apart on prepared sheets (five per sheet). Cover loosely with lightly greased plastic wrap and let rise at room temperature until doubled in size, about 1 hour.

3. Adjust oven rack to lower-middle position and heat oven to 350 degrees. Remove plastic and, using greased metal spatula, press dough balls into ¾-inch-thick rounds (about 3½ inches in diameter). Dust tops of muffins with remaining ¼ cup cornmeal.

4. Heat 1 teaspoon oil in 12-inch skillet over medium heat until shimmering, about 2 minutes. Wipe out skillet with paper towel, leaving thin film of oil on bottom and sides of pan. Carefully lay 4 muffins in pan and cook until bottoms are just set, about 1 minute, occasionally pressing down on muffins with spatula to prevent doming.

5. Flip muffins and continue to cook until set on second side, about 1 minute longer. Transfer muffins to clean baking sheet lined with parchment. Repeat with remaining 2 teaspoons oil and remaining muffins in 2 more batches, wiping skillet clean before each batch and transferring muffins to same baking sheet.

6. Bake until golden brown and firm, 30 to 35 minutes, rotating sheet halfway through baking. Transfer muffins to wire rack and let cool for at least 20 minutes before splitting with fork and toasting. Serve. (Once cooled, unsplit English muffins can be stored in zipper-lock bag for up to 2 days. See page 349 for freezing instructions.)

Bagels

G-F TESTING LAB

FLOUR SUBSTITUTION	Do not substitute other all-purpose blends for the ATK All-Purpose Gluten-Free Flour Blend; they will not work in this recipe.
OAT FLOUR	Not all brands of oat flour are gluten-free; read the label. Alternatively, 2 ounces (7 tablespoons) of sorghum flour can be substituted for the oat flour.
WATER	Using the correct amount of water is crucial for this recipe; we strongly recommend weighing the water instead of using a liquid measuring cup.
PSYLLIUM HUSK	Psyllium is crucial to the structure of the bagels; see page 21 for more information.
XANTHAN GUM	Xanthan is crucial to the structure of the bagels; see page 21 for more information.

WHY THIS RECIPE WORKS

All too often, the best part of a gluten-free bagel is the cream cheese smeared on top. We knew developing a really good gluten-free bagel with a crisp crust and substantial chew was setting the bar high since even traditional bagels rely on lots of tricks. To start, we compiled a variety of recipes and substituted our all-purpose gluten-free flour blend. The first round of bagels were like small, dense hockey pucks. Despite their problems, bagels that were boiled before baking had a nice crisp crust. The slightly alkaline water (due to the baking soda) cooked the exterior starches on the bagels, giving them a glossy sheen, while the baking soda also helped the bagels brown. We got rid of the multiple proofing steps because with multiple rising steps we were deflating the dough, so we shaped the bagels right out of the mixer and proofed them for just 30 minutes. We then drastically increased the amount of water in the dough from the traditional 55 percent hydration (in glutenous bagels) to 85 percent in hopes that it would open the crumb. The bagels rose high, but when they hit the boiling water they started to fall apart. Psyllium husk powder and xanthan gum made the dough easier to work with, and keeping the boiling time to 10 seconds also helped. Next, we swapped some of our flour blend for high-protein oat flour, which produced a uniform interior crumb. We missed the nutty flavor that malt syrup usually adds to bagels and found that molasses was the perfect substitute. We learned that baking the bagels at 425 degrees for the first half of the baking time ensured a nice rise, then turning down the oven to 350 degrees dried out the interiors without the exteriors getting too dark.

Bagels

MAKES 6 BAGELS

13.3 ounces (1⅔ cups) warm water (110 degrees) for dough, plus 4 quarts for boiling bagels
1 tablespoon instant or rapid-rise yeast
1 tablespoon sugar
3 tablespoons unsalted butter, melted and cooled
1 teaspoon molasses
13½ ounces (3 cups) ATK All-Purpose Gluten-Free Flour Blend (page 7)
2 ounces (⅔ cup) oat flour
1½ tablespoons powdered psyllium husk
2 teaspoons baking powder
1½ teaspoons salt
½ teaspoon xanthan gum
1 tablespoon baking soda

1. Adjust oven rack to middle position and heat oven to 200 degrees. As soon as oven reaches 200 degrees, turn it off. (This will be warm proofing box for dough. Do not begin step 2 until oven has been turned off.) Line rimmed baking sheet with parchment paper and spray with vegetable oil spray.

2. Combine 13.3 ounces warm water, yeast, and sugar in bowl and let sit until bubbly, about 5 minutes. Whisk in melted butter and molasses. Using stand mixer fitted with paddle, mix flour blend, oat flour, psyllium, baking powder, salt, and xanthan gum on low speed until combined, about 1 minute Slowly add yeast mixture and mix until combined, about 1 minute, scraping down bowl as needed. Increase speed to medium and beat until dough is sticky and uniform, about 6 minutes. (Dough will be quite stiff.)

3. Divide dough into 6 equal pieces (5¼ ounces each). Working with 1 piece of dough at a time, roll into 9-inch-long rope (do not taper ends). Bring ends of rope together to form circle, overlapping ends by 1 inch. Gently pinch ends of dough together to seal. Pick up bagel, and using 2 fingers, gently roll seam against counter to reshape; transfer to prepared sheet.

4. Cover loosely with plastic wrap, place sheet in warmed oven, and let rise for 10 minutes; do not let plastic touch oven rack. Remove sheet from oven and let sit on counter until dough is puffy and has risen by 50 percent, about 20 minutes. Meanwhile, heat oven to 425 degrees. Bring 4 quarts water and baking soda to boil in Dutch oven.

5. Working with 1 bagel at a time, place in boiling water and cook for 10 seconds, flipping it over halfway through cooking. Using wire skimmer, return bagels to sheet, right side up, with flat bottoms against pan.

6. Set sheet with bagels inside second rimmed baking sheet. Bake for 15 minutes. Reduce oven temperature to 350 degrees, rotate sheet, and continue to bake until bagels are evenly golden brown, about 20 minutes.

7. Remove bagels from oven and let cool on sheet for 5 minutes. Transfer bagels to wire rack and cool for at least 20 minutes before serving. (Cooled bagels can be stored in zipper-lock bag at room temperature for up to 3 days. They can also be sliced, wrapped in double layer of plastic wrap, and frozen for up to 1 month.)

VARIATIONS

Dairy-Free Bagels

Substitute Earth Balance Vegan Buttery Sticks for butter and reduce salt to 1 teaspoon.

Everything Bagels

Combine 2 tablespoons poppy seeds, 2 tablespoons sesame seeds, 1 tablespoon onion flakes, 2 teaspoons garlic flakes, 2 teaspoons caraway seeds, and ½ teaspoon coarse or pretzel salt in bowl. After bagels have been boiled, sprinkle seed mixture evenly over bagels.

TEST KITCHEN TIP **Making Bagels**

1. Divide dough into 6 equal pieces. Working with 1 piece of dough at a time, roll into 9-inch-long rope (do not taper ends).

2. Bring ends of rope together to form circle, overlapping ends by 1 inch. Gently pinch ends of dough together to seal.

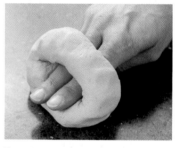

3. Pick up bagel, and using 2 fingers, gently roll seam against counter to reshape; transfer to prepared sheet.

4. Place 1 bagel at a time in boiling water and cook for 10 seconds, flipping bagels halfway through cooking. Using wire skimmer, return bagels to sheet, right side up, with flat bottoms against pan.

5. To provide extra insulation and prevent bagels from getting too dark on bottom during baking, put sheet with bagels inside second rimmed baking sheet.

6. Bake at 425 degrees for 15 minutes. Reduce oven to 350 degrees, rotate sheet, and bake until bagels are evenly golden brown, about 20 minutes.

Light and Fluffy Biscuits

✔ WHY THIS RECIPE WORKS

While gluten development is less important in tender biscuits than in chewy bread, our gluten-free flour blend still fell short. As we did with other breads, we strengthened the protein network with psyllium and added an egg to boost the overall protein content. The biggest challenge was the fat. A biscuit must be buttery, but gluten-free flours just don't absorb fat all that well, and many early attempts were very greasy. A combination of butter and oil was key. (For more information on oil versus butter in baking, see page 533.) Gluten-free flours don't absorb liquid very well either, and we found that biscuits made with buttermilk spread way too much. Switching to thicker yogurt solved the problem. (We prefer whole-milk yogurt, but low-fat yogurt will work, producing slightly drier biscuits.) Tasters missed the tang of the buttermilk, but supplementing the yogurt with a little lemon juice fixed that problem. As with other chemically leavened quick breads and cookies, we found that biscuits were much improved by letting the dough rest for 30 minutes before baking. Not only did the resting time help to thicken the wet dough a bit (making it easier to shape), more importantly it allowed the starches in the flour blend to fully hydrate. If you skip this step the biscuits will have a slightly gritty, starchy texture. Placing the biscuits fairly close together on the baking sheet trapped a little extra steam, which made them just a bit lighter and more tender. Biscuits are best eaten the day they are baked, but they can be frozen (see page 348 for instructions).

Light and Fluffy Biscuits
MAKES 6 BISCUITS

- 9 ounces (2 cups) ATK All-Purpose Gluten-Free Flour Blend (page 7)
- 4 teaspoons baking powder (see page 24)
- 1½ teaspoons powdered psyllium husk
- 1 teaspoon sugar
- ½ teaspoon salt
- ¼ teaspoon baking soda
- 3 tablespoons unsalted butter, chilled and cut into ¼-inch pieces
- ¾ cup plain whole-milk yogurt
- 1 large egg, lightly beaten
- 2 tablespoons vegetable oil
- 2 teaspoons lemon juice

1. Whisk flour blend, baking powder, psyllium, sugar, salt, and baking soda in large bowl until combined. Add butter to flour blend mixture, breaking up chunks with your fingertips until only small, pea-size pieces remain. In separate bowl, whisk yogurt, egg, oil, and lemon juice until combined. Using silicone spatula, stir yogurt mixture into flour mixture until thoroughly combined and no flour pockets remain, about 1 minute. Cover bowl with plastic wrap and let batter rest at room temperature for 30 minutes.

2. Adjust oven rack to middle position and heat oven to 450 degrees. Line rimmed baking sheet with parchment paper and place inside second baking sheet. Using greased ⅓-cup dry measure, scoop heaping amount of batter and drop onto prepared sheet. (Biscuit should measure about 2½ inches in diameter and 1½ inches high.) Repeat with remaining batter, spacing biscuits about ½ inch apart in center of prepared sheet.

3. Bake until golden and crisp, about 15 minutes, rotating sheet halfway through baking. Transfer sheet to wire rack and let cool for 5 to 10 minutes before serving.

VARIATION
Sweet Biscuits
Pair these biscuits with macerated fruit and whipped cream to make shortcakes.

Increase sugar in dough to 2 tablespoons. Sprinkle additional 2 tablespoons sugar evenly over biscuits just before baking.

G-F TESTING LAB

FLOUR SUBSTITUTION	King Arthur Gluten-Free Multi-Purpose Flour 9 ounces = **1½ cups plus 2 tablespoons**	Bob's Red Mill All-Purpose GF Baking Flour 9 ounces = **1½ cups plus ⅓ cup**
	Note that biscuits made with King Arthur will be slightly sandy and a bit starchy and will spread more, and biscuits made with Bob's Red Mill will be coarser and will spread more and have a distinct bean flavor.	
PSYLLIUM HUSK	Do not omit the powdered psyllium husk; it is crucial to the structure of the biscuits. For more information, see page 21.	
RESTING TIME	Do not shortchange the 30-minute rest for the dough; if you do, the biscuits will be gritty and spread too much.	

Biscuits

We wanted a drop biscuit that would offer an easy and quick alternative to a traditional rolled biscuit, but with the same tender texture and buttery flavor. The classic recipe is nothing more than flour, baking powder, baking soda, sugar, and salt mixed with butter and buttermilk. In order to produce an equally tender biscuit with a light, fluffy crumb, we had to rework the ingredient list quite extensively.

1. ADD PSYLLIUM AND EGG FOR STRUCTURE: While traditional biscuits rely on gluten for structure, we had to find another solution. Adding powdered psyllium husk (as we had done in bread recipes) helped strengthen the proteins in gluten-free flours so they could do a better job of trapping gas and steam during baking. However, using too much psyllium imparted an earthy flavor that was out of place in biscuits. An egg provided additional structure along with moisture and elasticity.

2. USE TWO FATS: Butter plays an important role in making biscuits tender and tasty. A batch of fluffy drop biscuits typically relies on at least a stick of butter. We found that our biscuit dough could absorb only 3 tablespoons of butter (the rest just leached out and made the biscuits greasy). With so little fat in the dough, the biscuits were very tough and dry. Two tablespoons of vegetable oil added back some richness, as did replacing the usual buttermilk with thicker, richer whole-milk yogurt.

3. THICKER DAIRY, PLEASE: Biscuits are traditionally made with buttermilk. Because gluten-free flours don't absorb liquid well, we found the dough was very liquid-y and spread too much in the oven. Using less milk didn't work—the starches in the flour never hydrated, and they imparted a gritty texture to the baked biscuits. Switching to thicker yogurt (spiked with a little lemon juice for extra tang) produced a dough with the right consistency, and letting the dough rest for 30 minutes (as we had done with muffins and other chemically leavened bread) allowed the starches to hydrate before baking.

4. DOUBLE UP ON SHEET PANS: A biscuit is typically baked at a high temperature for a short time to achieve a golden crust and nice rise. We struggled to get a nice color on the tops of the biscuits without burning the bottoms. Lowering the oven temperature seemed like a natural solution, but we needed to bake them so long that the inside dried out. We had better luck staying with the high temperature but using a second baking sheet as insulation to keep the bottoms from burning.

Cheddar Cheese Bread

G-F TESTING LAB

FLOUR SUBSTITUTION	King Arthur Gluten-Free Multi-Purpose Flour 12½ ounces = **2¼ cups**	Bob's Red Mill GF All-Purpose Baking Flour 12½ ounces = **2½ cups**

Note that bread made with King Arthur will be somewhat pasty, and bread made with Bob's Red Mill will be wetter and will have a distinct bean flavor.

Studded with pockets of cheese and featuring a crunchy cheese crust, cheddar cheese bread is a comforting loaf that is just as good fresh from the oven as it is transformed into the ultimate grilled cheese. These loaves are typically dense, so we knew we were going to rely heavily on leaveners. Baking powder alone wasn't enough to give this springy dough the right lift, but the addition of a small amount of baking soda did the trick. Tangy sour cream along with cayenne and ground black pepper complemented the sharp cheddar perfectly. Grating the Parmesan on the large holes of a box grater and sprinkling it over the top of the loaf and in the bottom of the pan added a nice texture; do not grate it fine or use pregrated Parmesan. A mild, soft Asiago cheese, crumbled into ¼- to ½-inch pieces, is a nice substitute for the cheddar. The texture of the bread improves as it cools, so resist the urge to slice the loaf while it is piping hot.

Cheddar Cheese Bread

MAKES 1 LOAF

- **3** ounces Parmesan cheese, grated on large holes of box grater (1 cup)
- **12½** ounces (2¾ cups) ATK All-Purpose Gluten-Free Flour Blend (page 7)
- **1** tablespoon baking powder (see page 24)
- **¼** teaspoon baking soda
- **½** teaspoon salt
- **⅛** teaspoon pepper
- **⅛** teaspoon cayenne pepper
- **4** ounces extra-sharp cheddar cheese, cut into ½-inch cubes (1 cup)
- **1¼** cups sour cream
- **3** tablespoons unsalted butter, melted and cooled
- **2** large eggs, lightly beaten

1. Adjust oven rack to middle position and heat oven to 350 degrees. Spray 8½ by 4½-inch loaf pan with vegetable spray, then sprinkle ½ cup Parmesan evenly in bottom of pan.

2. Whisk flour blend, baking powder, baking soda, salt, pepper, and cayenne together in large bowl. Stir in cheddar, breaking up any clumps, until coated with flour mixture. In separate bowl, whisk sour cream, melted butter, and eggs until smooth. Using silicone spatula, stir sour cream mixture into flour mixture until thoroughly combined (batter will be heavy and thick).

3. Scrape batter into prepared pan, smooth top, and sprinkle remaining ½ cup Parmesan evenly over loaf. Bake until deep golden brown and toothpick inserted in center comes out clean, 40 to 45 minutes, rotating pan halfway through baking.

4. Transfer to wire rack and let bread cool in pan for 10 minutes. Remove loaf from pan and let cool on rack for at least 1 hour before serving. (Once cooled, bread can be wrapped in double layer of plastic wrap and stored at room temperature for up to 1 day. To serve, warm in 300-degree oven for 10 minutes.

TEST KITCHEN TIP

Use Two Cheeses for Cheese Bread

The secret to our cheese bread is using two different cheeses prepared two different ways. While most cheese bread recipes call for shredded cheese, we prefer the cheddar cheese cut into small cubes, which create cheesy pockets throughout the bread. Grating Parmesan on the large holes of a box grater and sprinkling it in the pan and on top of the loaf ensure a crunchy crust with good flavor.

Spray 8½ by 4½-inch loaf pan with vegetable spray, then sprinkle ½ cup coarsely grated Parmesan evenly in bottom of pan.

Skillet Cornbread

G-F TESTING LAB

CORNMEAL The test kitchen's favorite cornmeal for baking is finely ground Whole-Grain Arrowhead Mills Cornmeal. This brand has been processed in a gluten-free facility, but not all brands are. Make sure to read the label. See page 26 for more details on cornmeal.

WHY THIS RECIPE WORKS

Unlike its sweet, cakey Northern counterpart, Southern cornbread is thin, crusty, and decidedly savory. It is traditionally made with cornmeal and no flour or sugar, so it is naturally gluten-free from the start. We used yellow cornmeal for potent corn flavor (which we toasted first to bring out its flavor) and, veering from tradition, added a small amount of sugar to enhance the natural sweetness of the corn. Creating a cornmeal mush by moistening the toasted cornmeal with a combination of sour cream and milk (favored over the traditional buttermilk for extra richness) produced a fine, moist crumb. Baking the cornbread in a greased preheated cast-iron skillet gave it a seriously crunchy, golden crust. Using a combination of oil and butter for greasing the skillet (as well as in the batter) struck the perfect balance of flavor and performance—the butter added flavor while the oil raised the smoke point so the butter wouldn't burn. We prefer to use a cast-iron skillet here because it makes the best crust; however, any 10-inch ovensafe skillet will work for this recipe. Cornbread is best served warm.

Skillet Cornbread

SERVES 8 TO 10

11¼	ounces (2¼ cups) cornmeal
1½	cups sour cream
½	cup milk
¼	cup vegetable oil
4	tablespoons unsalted butter
2	tablespoons sugar
1	teaspoon baking powder (see page 24)
1	teaspoon baking soda
¾	teaspoon salt
2	large eggs

1. Adjust oven racks to lower-middle and middle positions and heat oven to 450 degrees. Place 10-inch cast-iron skillet on middle rack and heat for 10 minutes. Meanwhile, spread cornmeal over rimmed baking sheet and toast in oven on lower-middle rack until fragrant and lightly golden, about 5 minutes.

2. Carefully transfer toasted cornmeal to large bowl and whisk in sour cream and milk; set aside. When skillet is hot, add oil and continue to heat until just smoking, about 5 minutes.

3. Using potholders (skillet handle will be hot), remove skillet from oven, carefully add butter, and gently swirl to incorporate. Pour hot oil-butter mixture into cornmeal mixture and whisk to incorporate. Whisk in sugar, baking powder, baking soda, and salt, followed by eggs.

4. Quickly scrape batter into hot skillet and smooth top. Bake on middle rack until top begins to crack and sides are golden brown, 12 to 15 minutes, rotating skillet halfway through baking. Let bread cool in skillet on wire rack for 5 minutes. Remove bread from pan and let cool on rack for at least 10 minutes before serving.

TEST KITCHEN TIP

Ensuring a Well-Browned Bottom Crust

Pouring the batter into a hot, greased cast-iron skillet ensures a crisp crust. Remember the handle will be very hot, so use a potholder.

Working quickly, scrape batter into hot skillet, smooth top with silicone spatula, and return skillet to oven.

Maple-Sorghum Skillet Bread

G-F TESTING LAB

SORGHUM FLOUR	Sorghum flour and sweet white sorghum flour will both work in this bread. The grind, color, and flavor of the sorghum flour will vary slightly from brand to brand; however, all five of the brands we tried produced decent skillet breads. We had good luck using Bob's Red Mill "Sweet" White Sorghum Flour.
CORNMEAL	The test kitchen's favorite cornmeal is Whole-Grain Arrowhead Mills Cornmeal. This brand has been processed in a gluten-free facility, but not all brands are. Make sure to read the label. See page 26 for more information.
BAKING POWDER	Not all brands of baking powder are gluten-free; see page 24 for more information.
XANTHAN GUM	The xanthan gum can be omitted, but the bread will be more crumbly.

WHY THIS RECIPE WORKS

We wanted to create a quick and easy gluten-free skillet bread with a tender, dense crumb and a rough-textured, thick crust—a bread that would be great served alongside chili or barbecue. To start, we zeroed in on sorghum flour, which is increasingly popular in gluten-free baking because of its high protein content and its nutty flavor. We began by modeling our bread after a traditional skillet cornbread but using only sorghum flour and a combination of sour cream, milk, eggs, and maple syrup. This produced a fine, moist crumb more similar to a cake than to a quick bread. Since sorghum flour produces such a light and fluffy texture, we added ¾ cup of yellow cornmeal for its familiar coarse texture. The maple syrup had the added benefits of further enhancing the nutty flavor of the sorghum and contributing to a nicely browned, crisp crust. Baking the bread in a greased preheated cast-iron skillet gave it a seriously crunchy, golden crust. Using a combination of oil and butter for greasing the skillet (as well as for mixing into the batter) proved perfect on two fronts: The butter added flavor while the oil raised the smoke point so the butter wouldn't burn. We prefer to use a cast-iron skillet here because it makes the best crust; however, any 10-inch oven-safe skillet will work for this recipe. This bread is best served warm.

Maple-Sorghum Skillet Bread

MAKES 1 LOAF

- ¼ cup vegetable oil
- 6 ounces (1⅓ cups) sorghum flour
- 3¾ ounces (¾ cup) cornmeal
- 1¼ cups sour cream
- ½ cup whole milk
- ½ cup maple syrup
- 4 tablespoons unsalted butter
- 1 teaspoon baking powder
- ½ teaspoon baking soda
- ¾ teaspoon salt
- ¼ teaspoon xanthan gum
- 2 large eggs

1. Adjust oven rack to middle position and heat oven to 450 degrees. When oven has reached 450 degrees, place 10-inch cast-iron skillet on rack and let heat for 10 minutes. Add oil and continue to heat skillet until just smoking, about 5 minutes.

2. Meanwhile, whisk sorghum flour, cornmeal, sour cream, milk, and maple syrup together in bowl. (Batter will be thick.)

3. Being careful of hot skillet handle, remove skillet from oven. Add butter and gently swirl to incorporate. Pour hot oil-butter mixture into sorghum mixture and whisk to incorporate. Whisk in baking powder, baking soda, salt, and xanthan gum, followed by eggs.

4. Quickly scrape batter into hot skillet and smooth top. Bake until top begins to crack, edges are golden brown, and toothpick inserted in center comes out clean, 20 to 24 minutes, rotating skillet halfway through baking.

5. Being careful of hot skillet handle, remove skillet from oven. Let bread cool in skillet for 5 minutes, then transfer to wire rack and let cool for 20 minutes before serving. (Cooled bread can be wrapped in double layer of plastic wrap and stored at room temperature for up to 2 days; it cannot be frozen.)

VARIATION

Dairy-Free Maple-Sorghum Skillet Bread
We prefer the flavor and texture of this bread made with soy milk, but almond milk will also work; do not use rice milk.

Use dairy-free sour cream. Substitute unsweetened soy milk for milk, and Earth Balance Vegan Buttery Sticks for butter. Omit salt.

Pizza

FLOUR SUBSTITUTION	King Arthur Gluten-Free Multi-Purpose Flour 16 ounces = **2⅔ cups plus ¼ cup**	Bob's Red Mill GF All-Purpose Baking Flour 16 ounces = **2⅔ cups plus ½ cup**
	Note that pizza crust made with King Arthur will be slightly denser and not as chewy, and pizza crust made with Bob's Red Mill will be thicker and more airy and will have a distinct bean flavor.	
ALMOND FLOUR	If you do not have almond flour, you can process 2½ ounces blanched almonds in a food processor until finely ground, about 30 seconds.	
PSYLLIUM HUSK	Do not omit the powdered psyllium husk; it is crucial to the structure of the crust. For more information, see page 21.	

WHY THIS RECIPE WORKS

The best pizza crusts are a study in contrasts: tender and airy on the inside, and crisp and pleasantly chewy on the exterior. The gluten-free pizza crusts we sampled were instead a study in compromise. Even when they were palatable (and many were not), most fell into one of two camps: dense and doughy or thin and cracker-crunchy. We set out to make a gluten-free pizza crust that could stand alongside the best wheat-based crusts. To improve tenderness and produce an open crumb, we increased the amount of water in the dough until it resembled a thick batter; this allowed the dough to expand more fully during fermentation. (To open the crumb even further, we also added a second leavener in the form of baking powder.) But all the extra water required cooking off to avoid gumminess, necessitating the addition of a parbaking step. (When we topped and then baked the raw dough, the cheese and toppings burned before the crust cooked through.) To prevent the exterior of the crust from drying out before the interior was fully cooked during parbaking, we chose a low-and-slow approach: start with a cold oven followed by a long, gentle bake. In order to achieve a crisp exterior, we first tried adding more oil to the dough. This helped, but not enough, and pouring in even more oil just made the crust greasy. A more effective approach was to add richness and fat in the form of almond flour, which provided the crispness and delicate crunch we sought without adding obvious flavor or greasiness.

Pizza Crusts
MAKES 2 PARBAKED CRUSTS

- 16   ounces (3⅓ cups plus ¼ cup) ATK All-Purpose Gluten-Free Flour Blend (page 7)
- 2½   ounces (½ cup plus ⅓ cup) almond flour
- 4½   teaspoons powdered psyllium husk
- 2½   teaspoons baking powder (see page 24)
- 2   teaspoons salt
- 1   teaspoon instant or rapid-rise yeast
- 2½   cups warm water (100 degrees)
- ¼   cup vegetable oil
-   Vegetable oil spray

1. Using stand mixer fitted with paddle, mix flour blend, almond flour, psyllium, baking powder, salt, and yeast on low speed until combined. Slowly add water and oil in steady stream until incorporated. Increase speed to medium and beat until sticky and uniform, about 6 minutes. (Dough will resemble thick batter.)

2. Remove bowl from mixer, cover with plastic wrap, and let stand until inside of dough is bubbly (use large spoon to peer inside dough), about 90 minutes.

3. Adjust oven racks to lower and middle positions. Line 2 baking sheets with parchment paper and spray liberally with vegetable oil spray. Transfer half of dough to center of 1 prepared sheet. Using oil-sprayed spatula, spread dough into 8-inch circle. Spray top of dough with vegetable oil spray, cover with large sheet of plastic, and, using your hands, press dough out to 11½-inch round, about ¼ inch thick, leaving outer ¼ inch slightly thicker than center; remove plastic. Repeat with remaining dough and remaining prepared sheet.

4. Place sheets in oven and set oven temperature to 325 degrees. Bake dough until firm to touch, golden brown on underside, and just beginning to brown on top, 45 to 50 minutes, switching and rotating sheets halfway through baking. Transfer crusts to wire rack and let cool. (Baked and cooled crusts can sit at room temperature for up to 4 hours. Completely cooled crusts can be wrapped first with plastic and then with aluminum foil and frozen for up to 2 weeks. Frozen crusts can be topped and baked as directed in pizza recipes. Note that crusts do not need to thaw before topping and baking.)

Classic Cheese Pizza

MAKES 2 PIZZAS, SERVES 4 TO 6

✔ **WHY THIS RECIPE WORKS**

Once our Pizza Crusts were parbaked and ready to go, we now needed to top and bake them. To keep things simple, we used our no-cook Easy Pizza Sauce. We supplemented the creamy, stretchy mozzarella with sharp, salty Parmesan for flavor. Using a baking stone helped to crisp the crust as it baked. If you do not have a baking stone, use a rimless or inverted baking sheet, heating it in the oven for 30 minutes.

- 1 recipe Pizza Crusts (page 327)
- 1 cup Easy Pizza Sauce (page 333)
- 1 ounce Parmesan cheese, finely grated (½ cup)
- 8 ounces whole-milk mozzarella cheese, shredded (2 cups)

1. One hour before baking pizza, adjust oven rack to upper-middle position, set baking stone on rack, and heat oven to 500 degrees.

2. Transfer 1 parbaked crust to pizza peel. Using back of spoon or ladle, spread ½ cup pizza sauce in thin layer over surface of dough, leaving ¼-inch border around edge. Sprinkle ¼ cup Parmesan evenly over sauce, followed by 1 cup mozzarella. Slide pizza carefully onto stone and bake until crust is well browned and cheese is bubbly and beginning to brown, 10 to 12 minutes. Transfer pizza to wire rack and let cool for 5 minutes before slicing and serving. Repeat with remaining crust, remaining ½ cup pizza sauce, and remaining mozzarella.

VARIATION

Cheese Pizza with Prosciutto and Arugula

Toss 2 cups baby arugula with 2 teaspoons extra-virgin olive oil in bowl and season with salt and pepper to taste. Top each baked pizza with 2 ounces thinly sliced prosciutto cut into 1-inch strips, then top each with 1 cup dressed arugula. Let cool for 5 minutes before slicing and serving.

White Pizza with Ricotta, Sausage, and Bell Pepper

MAKES 2 PIZZAS, SERVES 4 TO 6

✔ **WHY THIS RECIPE WORKS**

For an altogether different take, we left out the red sauce and instead started with a combination of mozzarella and Pecorino as the base of our pizza. We then combined ricotta cheese with fresh herbs, seasonings, and a good dose of garlic and dolloped that over the top of our base. Italian sausage and red bell pepper—softened in the same skillet used to cook the sausage—added heft and color. If you do not have a baking stone, use a rimless or inverted baking sheet, heating it in the oven for 30 minutes.

- 4 ounces (½ cup) whole-milk ricotta cheese
- 2 tablespoons extra-virgin olive oil
- 2 tablespoons heavy cream
- 1 large egg yolk
- 2 garlic cloves, minced
- 1 teaspoon minced fresh oregano
- ½ teaspoon minced fresh thyme
- ⅛ teaspoon salt
- ⅛ teaspoon pepper
  Pinch cayenne pepper
- 1 pound hot or sweet Italian sausage, casings removed
- 1 red bell pepper, stemmed, seeded, and cut into thin strips
- 1 recipe Pizza Crusts (page 327)
- 1 ounce Pecorino Romano cheese, finely grated (½ cup)
- 8 ounces whole-milk mozzarella cheese, shredded (2 cups)

1. One hour before baking pizza, adjust oven rack to upper-middle position, set baking stone on rack, and heat oven to 500 degrees.

2. Whisk ricotta, oil, cream, egg yolk, garlic, oregano, thyme, salt, pepper, and cayenne together in bowl; refrigerate until ready to use. Cook sausage in 12-inch nonstick skillet over medium-high heat, breaking into small pieces with wooden spoon, until browned, about 5 minutes. Using slotted spoon, transfer sausage to paper towel–lined plate. Pour off all but 1 tablespoon fat from skillet, add bell pepper, and cook over medium heat until softened, about 5 minutes; set aside and cool to room temperature.

3. Transfer 1 parbaked crust to pizza peel. Sprinkle with ¼ cup Pecorino, followed by 1 cup mozzarella, leaving ¼-inch border around edge. Using 1 teaspoon measure, dollop half of ricotta cheese mixture evenly over pizza. Sprinkle with half of sausage and half of pepper. Slide pizza carefully onto stone and bake until crust is well browned and cheese is bubbly and beginning to brown, 10 to 12 minutes. Transfer pizza to wire rack and let cool for 5 minutes before slicing and serving. Repeat with remaining crust, remaining Pecorino and mozzarella, remaining ricotta mixture, and remaining sausage and pepper.

TEST KITCHEN TIP **Bake Before Topping**

Extra water in our dough helps it to rise and bake up tender, but all that water poses a problem during baking. The key is to parbake the crust before adding the toppings.

Bake dough until firm to touch, golden brown on underside, and just beginning to brown on top, 45 to 50 minutes. Cool crust before topping and baking again.

TEST KITCHEN TIP **Shaping Pizza Dough**

Our gluten-free pizza dough is much wetter than traditional pizza dough, so it does not double in size as it rises. To determine if the dough is ready for shaping, you must check that air bubbles have formed (meaning the yeast is doing its job). You will need the help of a greased silicone spatula to shape this wet, sticky dough.

1. After dough has proofed for 90 minutes, check to determine if it is ready for shaping. Use large spoon to peer inside dough. If inside of dough is bubbly, it's ready.

2. Transfer half of dough to center of baking sheet lined with greased parchment. Using oil-sprayed spatula, spread dough into 8-inch circle, as though spreading frosting on cake.

3. Spray dough with vegetable oil spray, cover with plastic wrap, and press out to 11½-inch round, about ¼ inch thick, leaving outer ¼ inch slightly thicker than center.

Reinventing Pizza Dough

THE PROBLEM Given that pizza dough does not have to rise as much as yeast breads, we figured this recipe would be fairly easy to transform. We'd replace the wheat flour with our flour blend and add some psyllium to help create a structural network in a dough capable of expanding around the gases produced during fermentation. We'd include the usual yeast, salt, oil, and water, and the dough would rise and bake up just fine, right? Unfortunately, our early tests were quite gummy, especially at the interface between the sauce and crust, and they weren't what you would call light and airy.

MORE LIFT, PLEASE We noticed that while the dough rose well during proofing, it didn't necessarily stay as open by the time it was baked. Rolling or pressing out the dough to make a crust expelled much of the gas, and it never seemed to recover from the handling, even when the dough was left to proof a second time, post-shaping. The first thing we tried was adding more yeast, assuming it would help increase the amount of gas production in the dough and create an open crumb. Yet no matter how much we added, the dough refused to budge. In fact, the only noticeable difference it made was that, in high enough amounts, it gave the dough an unpleasantly yeasty, "overproofed" flavor.

If we couldn't get the crust to hold on to gas the whole time, maybe we could give it a little boost when it mattered most: during baking. To this end, we added a few teaspoons of baking powder to the dough. Sure enough, the leavener, activated by the heat of the oven, gave the dough a bit more of the lift it had been missing.

MORE WATER = GREATER ELASTICITY Traditional pizza dough can be rather stiff right after mixing and yet end up open and easily extensible once fully proofed, which leaves the finished product light and airy once baked. But in the case of our gluten-free pizza dough, things didn't work quite the same way. Even with psyllium in the mix and adding extra leavener, the proteins in the gluten-free flour didn't stretch enough. Maybe increasing the water (so that the dough started out looser) would help?

Even before we baked off the next batches, we could tell that we were onto something: The more water the dough contained, the more it rose during proofing. And as the amount of water increased, the finished crust became more tender and open. In fact, the dough seemed to benefit from the addition of far more water than we'd expected. The best results came when we added nearly double what you might use in a conventional recipe, making the "dough" more like a thick batter.

SHAPING A STICKY DOUGH Of course, more water presented a number of new problems. For one thing, it made shaping the crust rather challenging. Fixing this problem was easy: We went from shaping the dough by hand to spreading it on a baking sheet with a silicone spatula, much like spreading frosting on a cake, and then using a piece of plastic wrap to shape it into a pizza crust.

BAKING OFF EXCESS WATER All that water helped to make the dough more fluid and open during proofing, but it was an unwelcome guest in the oven. In order to remove the excess water, we began parbaking the crusts without sauce or cheese. We started by placing them in a hot oven until they'd dried out and begun to brown on the exterior, but that didn't really do the trick. This produced crusts that might look good on the exterior while remaining gummy inside. So we began lowering the oven temperature and increasing the baking time until the water had been driven off. In the end, we found it best to start the crusts in a cold oven and let them cook through slowly—this prevented the exterior of the crusts from overcooking before the interior was fully baked.

MORE FAT, FROM AN UNUSUAL SOURCE There remained one glaring flaw: the underside of the crust was more tough than crisp, even when parbaked as gently as possible. No problem, we thought, we would just add more oil to the dough. While this did help to crisp things up, it also left the pizza downright greasy. Even though more fat was the answer, the gluten-free flours couldn't absorb more oil. In the end, we achieved the desired crispness by adding almond flour, which boosted the overall fat content in the dough but didn't have the same greasy side effects as more oil. And, best of all, tasters couldn't detect any nut flavor in the finished pizza.

Classic Cheese Pan Pizza

WHY THIS RECIPE WORKS

Unlike its thin-crust cousin, pan pizza has a soft, chewy, thicker crust that can stand up to any topping. We wanted to make this pizza with a rich and flavorful crust and began by using our focaccia recipe (page 334) and splitting it between two pans. A generous amount of oil in the dough as well as 4 tablespoons in each pan gave the crust its richness while also crisping the bottom. We decreased the amount of yeast slightly, as the crust did not need as much lift as focaccia. For a final burst of rise before the crust set, also known as oven spring, we preheated the oven to 475 degrees and then lowered it to 350 degrees when we put the pizza in so the crust could bake through without burning. As we had learned during our focaccia recipe testing, using a baking stone in the oven created a more reliable temperature after decreasing the heat. Although we usually add the sauce and toppings before baking pizza, we found that they weighed down our gluten-free crust and made it soggy, so we baked the crust first and let it cool before topping it. For a simple, no-bake sauce, we simply pureed canned whole tomatoes, garlic, olive oil, red wine vinegar, and spices in the food processor; creamy mozzarella and sharp Parmesan were the perfect toppings. We broiled the topped pizza for a few minutes to melt the cheese and heat the crust through. If you use light-colored cake pans, the crust will not brown as well.

Classic Cheese Pan Pizza

MAKES TWO 9-INCH PIZZAS

- ½ cup plus 3 tablespoons extra-virgin olive oil
- 10.6 ounces (1⅓ cups) warm water (110 degrees)
- 1 tablespoon sugar
- 2¼ teaspoons instant or rapid-rise yeast
- 1 large egg
- 10 ounces (2¼ cups) ATK All-Purpose Gluten-Free Flour Blend (page 7)
- 2 ounces (⅔ cup) oat flour
- 1 tablespoon powdered psyllium husk
- ¾ teaspoon salt
- ½ teaspoon xanthan gum
- 1 cup pizza sauce
- 6 ounces whole-milk mozzarella cheese, shredded (1½ cups)
- 1 ounce Parmesan cheese, grated (½ cup)
- 3 tablespoons chopped fresh basil

1. Adjust oven racks to upper-middle and lower-middle positions and heat oven to 200 degrees. As soon as oven reaches 200 degrees, turn it off. (This will be warm proofing box for dough. Do not begin step 2 until oven has been turned off.) Brush 2 dark 9-inch round cake pans with ¼ cup oil each.

2. Combine warm water, sugar, and yeast in bowl and let sit until bubbly, about 5 minutes. Whisk in remaining 3 tablespoons oil and egg. Using stand mixer fitted with paddle, mix flour blend, oat flour, psyllium, salt, and xanthan gum on low speed until combined, about 1 minute. Slowly add yeast mixture and mix until combined, scraping down bowl as needed, about 1 minute. Increase speed to medium and beat until sticky and uniform, about 6 minutes. (Dough will resemble cookie dough.)

3. Using silicone spatula, divide dough evenly between prepared pans. Using your wet hands, press dough gently into corners and smooth top. Cover loosely with plastic wrap, place on upper rack in warmed oven, and let rise for 10 minutes; do not let plastic touch oven rack.

4. Remove pans from oven and let sit on counter until crusts have risen by 50 percent, about 20 minutes. Meanwhile, place baking stone on lower rack and heat oven to 475 degrees.

5. Reduce oven temperature to 350 degrees. Remove plastic from crusts, place on upper rack (not on stone), and bake until dark golden brown on top and crusts release from pans easily, 45 to 50 minutes, rotating pans halfway through baking.

6. Set wire rack inside rimmed baking sheet. Carefully slide hot crusts out of pans onto prepared rack; let cool for at least 20 minutes or up to 2 hours. (Cooled crusts can be wrapped in double layer of

G-F TESTING LAB

FLOUR SUBSTITUTION	King Arthur Gluten-Free Multi-Purpose Flour 10 ounces = **1½ cups plus ⅓ cup**	Betty Crocker All-Purpose Gluten Free Rice Blend 10 ounces = **2 cups**
	Pizza made with Betty Crocker will have a slightly spongy and chewy texture.	
OAT FLOUR	Not all brands of oat flour are gluten-free; read the label. Alternatively, 2 ounces (7 tablespoons) of sorghum flour can be substituted for the oat flour; we had good luck using Bob's Red Mill "Sweet" White Sorghum Flour.	
PSYLLIUM HUSK	Psyllium is crucial to the structure of the dough; see page 21 for more information.	
XANTHAN GUM	Xanthan is crucial to the structure of the dough; see page 21 for more information.	

plastic wrap and stored at room temperature for up to 1 day or frozen for up to 1 month. If frozen, unwrap and let thaw completely at room temperature before using.)

7. Heat broiler. Spoon ½ cup pizza sauce over top of each crust, leaving ¼-inch border around edge, then sprinkle with mozzarella and Parmesan. Broil pizzas (still on wire rack–lined sheet) on upper rack until cheese is melted, 2 to 3 minutes. Remove pizzas from oven and slide onto cutting board. Sprinkle with basil, slice into quarters, and serve immediately.

VARIATIONS

Pepperoni Pan Pizza
Arrange 2 ounces sliced pepperoni between double layers of coffee filters on plate and microwave until fat begins to render, about 30 seconds. Sprinkle pepperoni on top of cheese before broiling pizzas.

Pan Pizza with Sausage and Peppers
Microwave 4 ounces Italian sausage, casings removed and sausage broken into ½-inch pieces, with ½ green or red bell pepper, cut into ½-inch pieces, and 1 tablespoon water in covered bowl until sausage is no longer pink and bell pepper is crisp-tender, about 4 minutes; drain mixture and transfer to paper towel–lined plate. Sprinkle sausage and pepper mixture over cheese before broiling pizzas.

Easy Pizza Sauce
MAKES 2 CUPS

While it is convenient to use jarred pizza sauce, we think it is almost as easy, and a lot tastier, to whip up your own. Our favorite brand of whole peeled tomatoes is Muir Glen Organic Whole Peeled Tomatoes.

- 1 **(28-ounce) can whole peeled tomatoes, drained with juice reserved**
- 1 **tablespoon extra-virgin olive oil**
- 1 **teaspoon red wine vinegar**
- 2 **garlic cloves, minced**
- 1 **teaspoon dried oregano**
- ½ **teaspoon salt**
- ¼ **teaspoon pepper**

Process drained tomatoes with oil, vinegar, garlic, oregano, salt, and pepper in food processor until smooth, about 30 seconds. Transfer mixture to liquid measuring cup and add reserved tomato juice until sauce measures 2 cups. (Sauce can be refrigerated for up to 1 week or frozen for up to 1 month.)

TEST KITCHEN TIP **Making Pan Pizza**

1. Bake crusts in 350-degree oven, on upper-middle rack (not on stone) until dark golden brown on top and crusts release from pans easily.

2. Using spatula, carefully slide hot crusts out of pans onto wire rack–lined baking sheet. Let crusts cool for at least 20 minutes or up to 2 hours.

3. Spoon ½ cup pizza sauce over top of each cooled crust, leaving ¼-inch border. Sprinkle evenly with cheeses. Broil pizzas until cheese melts, 2 to 3 minutes.

Rosemary Focaccia

G-F TESTING LAB

FLOUR SUBSTITUTION	King Arthur Gluten-Free Multi-Purpose Flour 10 ounces = **1½ cups plus ⅓ cup**	Betty Crocker All-Purpose Gluten Free Rice Blend 10 ounces = **2 cups**
	Focaccia made with Betty Crocker will be very chewy and slightly wet on inside, and the crust will be less crisp.	
OAT FLOUR	Not all brands of oat flour are gluten-free; read the label. Alternatively, 2 ounces (7 tablespoons) of sorghum flour can be substituted for the oat flour; we had good luck using Bob's Red Mill "Sweet" White Sorghum Flour.	
PSYLLIUM HUSK	Psyllium is crucial to the structure of the bread; see page 21 for more information.	
XANTHAN GUM	Xanthan is crucial to the structure of the bread; see page 21 for more information.	

WHY THIS RECIPE WORKS

Focaccia is typically a simple dough containing just flour, yeast, water, salt, and a hefty dose of olive oil for flavor. We decided to tackle hydration first, testing increasing amounts of water and ultimately finding that 1⅓ cups gave us a nice rise without oversaturating the dough. To trap the air bubbles and achieve a good height, we added both psyllium (which helped create an open crumb) and xanthan gum (which gave the bread chew and kept it moist). To achieve the best rise, we had to play with the oven method. Baking the bread at a low temperature for longer led to a flatter bread with a thick, hard crust, while baking the loaf at a high temperature burned the outside before the inside could dry out. We found that preheating the oven to 475 degrees created enough oven spring for a nice rise, while lowering the oven to 350 degrees when adding the bread kept it from burning. During testing, our loaves were turning out with inconsistent heights, which we attributed to the fact that we were using different ovens. The speed that oven temperatures drop varies by oven; to ensure a more reliable oven temperature after decreasing the heat, we heated a baking stone on the rack below the bread. Oiling the top of the finished loaf gave the bread a nice shine and prevented the loaf from deflating under the oil's weight during baking. If you don't have a baking stone, you can use a rimmed baking sheet, but your bread will not rise as high and will be slightly wet. We prefer the coarse texture of kosher salt here; if using table salt, reduce all salt amounts by half.

Rosemary Focaccia

MAKES 1 LOAF

- 5 tablespoons extra-virgin olive oil
- 10.6 ounces (1⅓ cups) warm water (110 degrees)
- 1 tablespoon sugar
- 1 tablespoon instant or rapid-rise yeast
- 1 large egg
- 10 ounces (2¼ cups) ATK All-Purpose Gluten-Free Flour Blend (page 7)
- 2 ounces (⅔ cup) oat flour
- 1 tablespoon powdered psyllium husk
  Kosher salt
- ½ teaspoon xanthan gum
- 1 teaspoon minced fresh rosemary

1. Adjust oven rack to upper-middle and lower-middle positions and heat oven to 200 degrees. As soon as oven reaches 200 degrees, turn it off. (This will be warm proofing box for dough. Do not begin step 2 until oven has been turned off.) Brush 8-inch square baking pan with 1 tablespoon oil.

2. Combine warm water, sugar, and yeast in bowl and let sit until bubbly, about 5 minutes. Whisk in 3 tablespoons oil and egg. Using stand mixer fitted with paddle, mix flour blend, oat flour, psyllium, 1½ teaspoons salt, and xanthan gum on low speed until combined, about 1 minute. Slowly add yeast mixture and mix until combined, scraping down bowl as needed, about 1 minute. Increase speed to medium and beat until sticky and uniform, about 6 minutes. (Dough will resemble cookie dough.)

3. Using silicone spatula, scrape dough into prepared pan. Using your wet hands, press dough gently into corners and smooth top. Cover loosely with plastic wrap, place on upper rack in warmed oven, and let rise for 10 minutes; do not let plastic touch oven rack.

4. Remove pan from oven and let sit on counter until loaf has risen by 50 percent, about 20 minutes. Meanwhile, place baking stone on lower rack and heat oven to 475 degrees.

5. Remove plastic and sprinkle loaf with rosemary and ¼ teaspoon salt. Reduce oven temperature to 350 degrees, place loaf on upper rack (not on stone), and bake until golden brown, 60 to 70 minutes; do not open oven door during baking.

6. Remove bread from oven, brush with remaining 1 tablespoon oil, and let cool in pan for 10 minutes. Unmold bread onto wire rack and let cool completely, about 1 hour. Serve. (Cooled bread can be wrapped in double layer of plastic wrap and stored at room temperature for up to 2 days or frozen for up to 1 month. See freezing instructions on page 268.)

Socca (Chickpea Flatbreads)

G-F TESTING LAB

CHICKPEA FLOUR   As the name suggests, chickpea flour (also sold as garbanzo bean flour) is made from ground whole dried chickpeas. It is sold in most well-stocked supermarkets. See page 22 for more detail.

WHY THIS RECIPE WORKS

Socca is a savory flatbread popular in southern France, where it is served as both an appetizer and a snack. The loose, pancakelike batter comes together in less than a minute—simply whisk together chickpea flour, water, olive oil, salt, and pepper—and it's naturally gluten-free. The biggest variables are the ratios of flour to water and the amount of oil. After several rounds of testing, we concluded that 1½ cups of both chickpea flour and water is best. Olive oil adds flavor, and more is better—up to a point. Any more than 3 tablespoons of oil will make the socca greasy. (More oil is used for cooking the socca.) Traditionally, the batter is poured into a cast-iron skillet and baked in a large, often wood-burning oven. This method produces socca with a blistered top and a smoky flavor, but it doesn't really translate to the home oven. Instead of a crisp top, socca baked this way was dry and limp. After several more failed attempts, we ditched the oven and cast-iron skillet for the stovetop and a nonstick skillet. Up to this point, we had been filling the cast-iron skillet to create one large pancake. The ambient heat ensured the socca was cooked through. On the stovetop, however, the direct heat cooked only the bottom, leaving the top sticky and raw. And flipping the socca wasn't as easy as we'd hoped. We solved this problem by switching to a smaller skillet and using less batter to make several smaller flatbreads. As an added bonus, the smaller flatbreads now had a higher ratio of crunchy crust to tender interior. We loved the simplicity of this dish, and coming up with a few additions to our base proved easy enough. The combination of coriander and lemon highlighted the bright notes of the chickpea flour, while caramelized onions and rosemary gave the socca a more rounded, warm flavor. Serve warm socca drizzled with good olive oil and sprinkled with coarse salt and freshly ground black pepper.

Socca (Chickpea Flatbreads)

MAKES 5 FLATBREADS, SERVES 4 TO 6

- 6¾ ounces (1½ cups) chickpea (garbanzo bean) flour
- ½ teaspoon salt
- ½ teaspoon pepper
- 1½ cups water
- 6 tablespoons plus 1 teaspoon extra-virgin olive oil

1. Adjust oven rack to middle position and heat oven to 200 degrees. Set wire rack in rimmed baking sheet and place in oven. Whisk chickpea flour, salt, and pepper together in bowl. Slowly whisk in water and 3 tablespoons oil until combined and smooth.

2. Heat 2 teaspoons oil in 8-inch nonstick skillet over medium-high heat until shimmering. Add ½ cup batter to skillet, tilting pan to coat bottom evenly. Reduce heat to medium and cook until crisp at edges and golden brown on bottom, 3 to 5 minutes. Flip socca and continue to cook until second side is browned, 2 to 3 minutes. Transfer to wire rack in preheated oven. Repeat with remaining batter and oil. Cut each socca into wedges and serve.

VARIATIONS

Coriander-Lemon Socca
Add 1 teaspoon ground coriander and ½ teaspoon grated lemon zest to chickpea flour in step 1.

Caramelized Onion and Rosemary Socca
Heat 1 tablespoon olive oil in 8-inch nonstick skillet over medium-high heat until shimmering. Add ½ onion, sliced thin, reduce heat to medium, and cook, stirring often, until onion is softened and browned, about 10 minutes. Add 1½ teaspoons chopped fresh rosemary and cook until fragrant, about 30 seconds. Transfer to bowl and let cool slightly, then stir into chickpea flour batter. Wipe skillet clean and use in step 2.

Whole-Grain Crackers

G-F TESTING LAB

FLOUR SUBSTITUTION	Do not substitute other whole-grain blends for the ATK Whole-Grain Gluten-Free Flour Blend; they will not work in this recipe.
BAKING POWDER	Not all brands of baking powder are gluten-free; see page 24 for more information.
XANTHAN GUM	The xanthan gum can be omitted, but the crackers will be less crisp.

WHY THIS RECIPE WORKS

We went into the kitchen to develop a recipe so that we could make our own gluten-free crackers. For our first batch, we combined our whole-grain flour blend, water, a little sugar, and salt, rolled the mixture into a thin sheet, cut it up into squares, and crossed our fingers. This batch was bland, crumbly, and not at all crisp. Fixing the flavor was fairly simple: We added a good dose of extra-virgin olive oil and sesame seeds, and switched to kosher salt (which we also sprinkled over the top before baking). To fix the texture we added an egg white, which crisped up the crackers significantly, as well as xanthan gum, which helped make the dough easier to work with. To keep things simple, instead of tediously cutting each cracker we found that scoring the dough worked just as well. After baking the crackers, we simply broke apart the sheets along the scored lines.

Whole-Grain Crackers

MAKES 8 DOZEN

- 10 ounces (2¼ cups) ATK Whole-Grain Gluten-Free Flour Blend (page 9)
- ¼ cup sesame seeds
- 1 tablespoon sugar
- 1 teaspoon baking powder
- ¼ teaspoon baking soda
  Kosher salt
- ½ teaspoon xanthan gum
- 5 ounces (½ cup plus 2 tablespoons) water
- 6 tablespoons extra-virgin olive oil
- 1 large egg white

1. Adjust oven racks to upper-middle and lower-middle positions and heat oven to 350 degrees. Whisk flour blend, sesame seeds, sugar, baking powder, baking soda, 1 teaspoon salt, and xanthan together in bowl. In separate bowl, whisk water, oil, and egg white until well combined. Using silicone spatula, stir water mixture into flour mixture until dough comes together. (Dough will be malleable and easy to shape.)

2. Divide dough into 2 equal pieces, shape each piece into 4-inch square, and cover with plastic wrap. Working with 1 piece of dough at a time, roll dough between 2 large sheets of parchment paper into 12 by 9-inch rectangle (about ⅛ inch thick). Remove top sheet of parchment. Using sharp knife, score dough into 1½-inch squares. Slide each parchment with dough onto rimmed baking sheet and sprinkle each with 1 teaspoon salt.

3. Bake crackers until firm, 30 to 35 minutes, switching and rotating sheets halfway through baking. Let crackers cool completely on sheets, about 20 minutes. Break crackers apart along scored lines. Serve. (Crackers can be stored in zipper-lock bag at room temperature for up to 1 week.)

VARIATIONS

Whole-Grain Poppy Seed–Thyme Crackers
Substitute poppy seeds for sesame seeds and add 4 teaspoons minced fresh thyme to flour mixture.

Whole-Grain Sesame-Rosemary Crackers
Add 1 teaspoon minced fresh rosemary to flour mixture.

TEST KITCHEN TIP
Making Whole-Grain Crackers

1. Roll dough into 12 by 9-inch rectangle between parchment, remove top sheet, and use knife to score dough into 1½-inch squares.

2. Break apart baked and cooled crackers along scored lines.

Cheddar Cheese Coins

G-F TESTING LAB

FLOUR SUBSTITUTION	King Arthur Gluten-Free Multi-Purpose Flour 7½ ounces = **1¼ cups plus 2 tablespoons**	Betty Crocker All-Purpose Gluten Free Rice Blend 7½ ounces = **1½ cups**

Crackers made with Betty Crocker will have a slightly bitter aftertaste, and the dough will be more difficult to roll into a log in step 2.

✓ WHY THIS RECIPE WORKS

For crisp, cheesy gluten-free crackers, we started with our all-purpose gluten-free flour blend as the base. But in our first tests, the crackers were not crisp enough; we found that adding just 1 tablespoon of cornstarch made a big difference. As for cheese, extra-sharp cheddar turned out to be the right choice: It had a sharp, crowd-pleasing flavor, whereas mild or even sharp cheddar cheese didn't deliver. Paprika and cayenne rounded out the flavors in our cracker, while butter and just 3 tablespoons water were enough to bind the dough. Our first batch of crackers tasted great but left our fingers greasy. The culprit turned out to be the gluten-free flour blend. It doesn't absorb fat as readily as wheat flour does, so we looked at our ingredient list for ways to cut back on the fat. Cheese and butter were the only two sources, and we certainly didn't want to lose any cheese flavor. Instead we cut the butter from 8 to 6 tablespoons, still enough to create a flaky texture without leaving our fingers feeling slick.

Cheddar Cheese Coins
MAKES ABOUT 5 DOZEN

- **8** ounces extra-sharp cheddar cheese, shredded (2 cups)
- **7½** ounces (1⅔ cups) ATK All-Purpose Gluten-Free Flour Blend (page 7)
- **1** tablespoon cornstarch
- **½** teaspoon salt
- **¼** teaspoon paprika
- **⅛** teaspoon cayenne pepper
- **6** tablespoons unsalted butter, cut into 6 pieces and chilled
- **3** tablespoons water

1. Process cheddar, flour blend, cornstarch, salt, paprika, and cayenne in food processor until combined, about 30 seconds. Scatter butter over top and process until mixture resembles wet sand, about 20 seconds. Add water and process until dough ball forms, about 20 seconds. (Dough will be malleable and easy to shape.)

2. Transfer dough to counter and divide into 2 equal pieces. Roll each half into 10-inch log, wrap in plastic wrap, and refrigerate until firm, at least 1 hour or up to 2 days.

3. Adjust oven racks to upper-middle and lower-middle positions and heat oven to 350 degrees. Line 2 rimmed baking sheets with parchment paper. Unwrap logs and slice into ¼-inch-thick coins, giving dough quarter turn after each slice to keep log round. Place coins on prepared sheets, spaced ½ inch apart.

4. Bake until light golden around edges, 22 to 28 minutes, switching and rotating sheets halfway through baking. Let coins cool completely on sheets before serving, about 20 minutes. (Coins can be stored in airtight container at room temperature for up to 2 days.)

VARIATIONS
Pimento Cheese Coins
Increase paprika to 1 tablespoon and cayenne to ½ teaspoon. Add 1 teaspoon garlic powder to food processor with spices.

Mustard, Gruyère, and Caraway Cheese Coins
Substitute Gruyère for cheddar. Add 1 teaspoon caraway seeds to food processor with spices. Substitute 4 tablespoons whole-grain mustard for water.

Everything Cheese Coins
Substitute Gruyère for cheddar. Add 2 tablespoons poppy seeds, 2 teaspoons sesame seeds, 1 teaspoon garlic powder, and 1 teaspoon onion flakes to food processor with spices.

TEST KITCHEN TIP **Cutting Cheese Coins**

Unwrap logs and slice into ¼-inch-thick coins, giving dough quarter turn after each slice to keep log round.

Corn Tortillas

G-F TESTING LAB

MASA HARINA   Maseca is the most widely available brand of masa harina. It is processed in a gluten-free facility. See page 22 for more detail on masa harina.

✅ WHY THIS RECIPE WORKS

Once you've tried homemade corn tortillas, you'll never want to buy the grocery store kind again. Fresh corn tortillas have a lightly sweet flavor and a soft, springy texture. Surprisingly, making tortillas is far easier than most people realize. Most of the recipes we researched were similar—masa harina and water are kneaded together to form a dough, then pressed into thin tortillas (either by hand or with a tortilla press) and toasted in a dry skillet. We then tested the few variables we found in our research, including whether to add salt (yes), and how long to rest the dough before pressing the tortillas (5 minutes so the masa is fully hydrated). Although you can press the dough into tortillas by hand or with a heavy skillet, we found it difficult to get the tortillas uniformly thin without lots of practice. We prefer to use a tortilla press. The dough was still a little finicky to work with, and we found that the addition of vegetable oil (a nontraditional ingredient) made the dough easier to handle. The oil also gave the cooked tortillas a softer texture that our tasters liked. When the tortilla puffs in the skillet after flipping, you know you've done it right: that's a sign that distinct layers are forming, and the finished product will be soft and tender. To reheat tortillas quickly we found it best to use the microwave. Simply stack the tortillas on a plate, sprinkle them with a little water, cover them with a paper towel, and microwave until warm and soft, 1 to 2 minutes. Tortillas can also be reheated one at a time in a skillet.

Corn Tortillas

MAKES ABOUT 22 SMALL TORTILLAS

- 10 ounces (2 cups) masa harina
- 2 teaspoons vegetable oil
- ¼ teaspoon salt
- 1¼ cups warm water, plus more as needed

1. Cut sides of sandwich-size zipper-lock bag but leave bottom seam intact so that bag folds open completely. Line tortilla press with 1 side of open bag. Line large plate with 2 damp dish towels.

2. Mix masa, 1 teaspoon oil, and salt together in medium bowl. Using silicone spatula, stir in water to form soft dough. Using your hands, knead dough in bowl, adding more warm water, 1 tablespoon at a time, as needed, until dough is soft and tacky but not sticky, and has texture of Play-Doh. Cover and set dough aside for 5 minutes.

3. Meanwhile, heat remaining 1 teaspoon oil in 8-inch nonstick skillet over medium-high heat until shimmering. Using paper towel, wipe out skillet, leaving thin film of oil on bottom. Pinch off 1-ounce piece of dough (about 2 tablespoons) and roll into smooth 1¼-inch ball. Cover remaining dough with damp paper towel. Place ball in center of press on open bag, and fold other side of bag over dough. Press ball gently into ¹⁄₁₆-inch-thick tortilla (about 5 inches in diameter). Working quickly, gently peel plastic away from tortilla and carefully place tortilla in hot skillet.

4. Cook tortilla, without moving it, until tortilla moves freely when pan is shaken, about 30 seconds. Flip tortilla over and cook until edges curl and bottom is spotty brown, about 1 minute. Flip tortilla back over and continue to cook until first side is spotty brown and puffs up in center, 30 to 60 seconds. Lay toasted tortilla between damp dish towels; repeat shaping and cooking with remaining dough. (Tortillas can be transferred to zipper-lock bag and refrigerated for up to 5 days.)

TEST KITCHEN TIP **Shaping Tortillas**

Pressing the dough inside a zipper-lock bag that has been cut open at the sides prevents the dough from sticking to the press and makes shaping these tortillas a breeze.

Place 1¼-inch ball of dough in center of tortilla press lined with open plastic bag. Fold other side of bag over dough. Press ball gently into ¹⁄₁₆-inch-thick tortilla.

Arepas (Corn Cakes)

MASAREPA   This precooked corn flour is also known as harina precocida and masa al instante. It is prepared from starchier large kernel white corn (as opposed to the small kernel yellow corn familiar to most Americans). The germ is removed from the kernels during processing, and the kernels are dried and ground to a fine flour. Do not confuse masarepa with masa harina, which is used to make fresh Corn Tortillas (page 342) and Pupusas (page 344). Check labels carefully; not all brands are processed in a gluten-free facility.

Arepas are a type of corn cake popular in Venezuela and Colombia, though iterations exist in other Latin countries. The Venezuelan variety is served as sandwiches that are split open and stuffed with anything from meat and cheese to corn, beans, or even fish. The arepa itself is made using masarepa (naturally gluten-free corn flour) along with water and salt. The dough is shaped into rounds, browned in a skillet with some oil, and finished in the oven. The cooking technique was straightforward enough and we were confident we could come up with a few delicious fillings, so we focused our attention on the ingredient list for the corn cakes. We started by testing the ratio of water to masarepa. Equal parts masarepa to warm water produced a dry, crumbly arepa, while adding significantly more water than masarepa produced a dough that was too loose to shape and fell apart during cooking. In the end, we found that using just a half cup more water than masarepa produced a dough that was easy to shape. Although moist and tender, the arepas were a little dense. A small amount of baking powder (an ingredient typically not used in arepas) lightened their texture just enough. Make either filling while the arepas are baking.

Arepas (Corn Cakes)

MAKES 8 CORN CAKES

- 10 ounces (2 cups) masarepa blanca
- 1 teaspoon salt
- 1 teaspoon baking powder (see page 24)
- 2½ cups warm water
- ¼ cup vegetable oil
- 1 recipe filling (recipes follow)

1. Adjust oven rack to middle position and heat oven to 400 degrees. Whisk masarepa, salt, and baking powder together in bowl. Gradually add water and stir until combined. Using generous ⅓ cup dough, form eight 3-inch rounds, each about ½ inch thick.

2. Heat 2 tablespoons oil in 12-inch nonstick skillet over medium-high heat until shimmering.

Add 4 arepas and cook until golden on both sides, about 4 minutes per side. Transfer to wire rack set in rimmed baking sheet and repeat with remaining 2 tablespoons oil and remaining 4 arepas. (Fried arepas can be refrigerated in zipper-lock bag for up to 3 days or frozen for up to 1 month.)

3. Bake until arepas sound hollow when tapped on bottom, about 10 minutes. (If frozen, do not thaw before baking; increase baking time to 20 minutes.) Split hot arepas open using paring knife or 2 forks, and stuff each with generous 3 tablespoons of filling. Serve immediately.

Chicken and Avocado Filling

MAKES ENOUGH FOR 8 CORN CAKES

- 1 cup shredded rotisserie chicken
- 1 avocado, halved, pitted, and cut into ½-inch pieces
- 2 tablespoons minced fresh cilantro
- 2 scallions, sliced thin
- 1 tablespoon lime juice
- ¼ teaspoon chili powder
  Salt and pepper

Mix all ingredients together in bowl and season with salt and pepper to taste.

Black Bean and Cheese Filling

MAKES ENOUGH FOR 8 CORN CAKES

- 1 (15-ounce) can black beans, rinsed
- 4 ounces Monterey Jack cheese, shredded (1 cup)
- 2 tablespoons minced fresh cilantro
- 2 scallions, sliced thin
- 1 tablespoon lime juice
- ¼ teaspoon chili powder
  Salt and pepper

Using potato masher or fork, mash beans in bowl until most are broken. Stir in Monterey Jack, cilantro, scallions, lime juice, and chili powder and season with salt and pepper to taste.

Pupusas (Stuffed Corn Tortillas)

MASA HARINA   Maseca is the most widely available brand of masa harina. It is processed in a gluten-free facility. See page 22 for more detail on masa harina.

WHY THIS RECIPE WORKS

Pupusas are the ultimate Salvadoran comfort food: a thick, handmade corn tortilla is stuffed with cheese and griddled until golden brown. The stuffed corn tortilla is traditionally topped with curtido, a tart cabbage slaw. While traditionally eaten as a side dish, we think pupusas make a great lunch or light dinner. The dough is similar to the one we use for thin corn tortillas, with a bit more water so it's more malleable and easy to stuff. For the filling, we stuck to the classic combination of cheese, spices, and cilantro. Monterey Jack cheese was the right choice here—just a few minutes in a hot skillet was all it took to melt, and its mild flavor didn't overpower the flavor of the corn flour. Make the curtido before you begin making the pupusas; as the slaw sits, the vinegar, salt, and sugar soften the cabbage and the flavor of the slaw improves.

Pupusas (Stuffed Corn Tortillas)
MAKES 10, SERVES 4 TO 6

TANGY CABBAGE SLAW
- 4 cups shredded green cabbage
- 1 carrot, peeled and shredded
- ¼ cup cider vinegar
- 2 tablespoons water
- 2 tablespoons minced fresh cilantro
- 1 jalapeño chile, stemmed, seeded, and sliced thin
- ⅛ teaspoon minced fresh oregano
- ½ teaspoon sugar
- Salt and pepper

PUPUSAS
- 6 ounces Monterey Jack cheese, shredded (1½ cups)
- 2 tablespoons minced fresh cilantro
- 2 scallions, sliced thin
- 1 tablespoon lime juice
- ¼ teaspoon chili powder
- Salt and pepper
- 10 ounces (2 cups) masa harina
- 2 cups warm water
- 1 teaspoon vegetable oil

1. FOR THE SLAW: Combine cabbage, carrot, vinegar, water, cilantro, jalapeño, oregano, sugar, and ½ teaspoon salt, and pepper to taste in bowl. Cover and refrigerate until cabbage wilts slightly, about 1 hour.

2. FOR THE PUPUSAS: Cut sides of small zipper-lock bag but leave bottom seam intact. Combine Monterey Jack, cilantro, scallions, lime juice, chili powder, and salt and pepper to taste in bowl.

3. Using silicone spatula, stir masa, water, and ¼ teaspoon salt together in medium bowl to form soft dough. Using your hands, knead dough in bowl until soft and slightly tacky, but not sticky, about 1 minute.

4. Heat oil in 12-inch nonstick skillet over medium-high heat until shimmering. Using paper towel, wipe out skillet, leaving thin film of oil. Pinch off 2½-ounce piece of dough (heaping ¼ cup) and roll into ball. Cover remaining dough with damp paper towel. Using your slightly wet hands, flatten into 4-inch-wide round and place 2 tablespoons of cheese mixture in center. Bring up sides of dough around filling and pinch top to seal. Press on pinched seal to flatten into 2½-inch round (about 1 inch thick). Place on 1 side of open zipper-lock bag and fold other side of bag over dough. Using large plate, press dough gently into ¼-inch-thick pupusa. Peel plastic away and place dough in hot skillet. Repeat shaping and filling, cooking 2 pupusas at a time. Cook pupusas until spotty brown on both sides, about 3 minutes per side. Transfer to platter and serve with slaw.

TEST KITCHEN TIP **Filling Pupusas**

Wet hands slightly. Flatten dough ball into 4-inch patty and place 2 tablespoons of cheese mixture in center. Bring up sides of dough around filling and pinch top to seal.

Brazilian Cheese Bread Rolls

G-F TESTING LAB

TAPIOCA STARCH   Tapioca starch is often labeled tapioca flour. See page 24 for details on this
ingredient.

WHY THIS RECIPE WORKS

Brazilian cheese bread rolls (pão de queijo) are small rolls with a crunchy crust and a chewy center. They are typically made with tapioca starch, cheese, milk, oil, and eggs, so they are naturally gluten-free. There are many different approaches to the mixing method. Some recipes heat the batter on the stovetop and transfer it to a stand mixer before adding the eggs (much as you might make the dough for profiteroles or gougères). But we found that this method could be tricky. The heat made the tapioca starch quite gluey, and the dough became hard to handle. We preferred a simpler (and still traditional) approach that calls for making a looser dough (more like pancake batter) in a blender. Rather than shaping the dough by hand, we poured the resulting fluid batter into a greased mini muffin tin that we slid right into the oven. The high liquid content (from both milk and eggs) in the batter created a lot of steam in the oven that helped the rolls to rise. (There's no yeast or chemical leavener in this recipe.) We tested different types of cheese, and it was clear that these small rolls are best made with something potent, so they would pack a punch. We liked the combination of nutty Parmesan and tangy extra-sharp cheddar. These rolls are a fast snack or an accompaniment to dinner, ready in about 30 minutes (including time to heat the oven). They are best eaten warm, but leftovers can be frozen and reheated (see the instructions in sidebar at right).

Brazilian Cheese Bread Rolls
MAKES 24 SMALL ROLLS

- 8   ounces (2 cups) tapioca starch
- 4   ounces extra-sharp cheddar cheese, shredded (1 cup)
- 2   ounces Parmesan cheese, grated (1 cup)
- ⅔   cup whole milk
- ⅓   cup extra-virgin olive oil
- 2   large eggs
- 1   teaspoon salt

1. Adjust oven rack to middle position and heat oven to 375 degrees. Spray 24-cup mini muffin tin with vegetable oil spray. Process all ingredients together in blender until smooth, about 1 minute, scraping down sides of blender jar as needed.

2. Pour batter (about 2 tablespoons per muffin cup) into prepared muffin tin. (Each muffin cup will be nearly full.) Bake rolls until lightly golden and puffed, 17 to 20 minutes, rotating muffin tin halfway through baking. Let rolls cool in muffin tin on wire rack for 3 minutes, then remove rolls from pan. Serve warm.

TEST KITCHEN TIP
Making Cheese Bread Rolls

The "dough" for these Brazilian rolls is very loose and is easily prepared in a blender. Once combined, the batter is poured into a greased mini muffin tin and baked.

1. Process all ingredients in blender until smooth, about 1 minute, scraping down sides of blender jar as needed.

2. Pour batter (about 2 tablespoons per muffin cup) into prepared muffin tin.

TEST KITCHEN TIP
Freezing Biscuits, English Muffins, and Cheese Bread Rolls

Let biscuits, English muffins, and cheese bread rolls cool completely, then wrap individually in a double layer of plastic wrap and then a layer of aluminum foil before freezing. Biscuits can be reheated in a 425-degree oven for 10 minutes. A single English muffin, wrapped in a paper towel, can be microwaved for 20 seconds, then split and toasted. Cheese bread rolls can be reheated in a 375-degree oven for 10 minutes.

COOKIES AND BARS

Chocolate Chip Cookies

G-F TESTING LAB

FLOUR SUBSTITUTION	King Arthur Gluten-Free Multi-Purpose Flour 8 ounces = ¾ **cup plus** ⅔ **cup**	Bob's Red Mill GF All-Purpose Baking Flour 8 ounces = **1½ cups plus 2 tablespoons**
	Cookies made with King Arthur will spread more and be more delicate; cookies made with Bob's Red Mill will spread more and have a distinct bean flavor.	
XANTHAN GUM	Do not omit the xanthan gum; it is crucial to the structure of the cookies. For more information, see page 21.	
RESTING TIME	Do not shortchange the 30-minute rest for the dough; if you do, the cookies will spread too much.	

✓ WHY THIS RECIPE WORKS

We started our testing by swapping in our flour blend for the all-purpose flour in a standard Toll House cookie recipe. It was no surprise that these cookies had problems: They were flat, sandy, and greasy. We'd discovered during our baked goods testing that gluten-free flour blends simply can't absorb as much fat as all-purpose flour can, so cutting back on the butter helped to minimize greasiness. Less butter, along with some xanthan gum, also helped alleviate the spread issue, so the cookies didn't bake up so flat. As for the sandiness, we knew from our gluten-free muffin testing (see Chapter 1) that fixing this problem required a two-step approach. The starches in our blend needed more liquid as well as more time to hydrate and soften, so we added a couple tablespoons of milk and let the dough rest for 30 minutes. This resting time also had a secondary benefit: It gave the sugar time to dissolve, which led to faster caramelization in the oven. And that meant a cookie not just with deeper flavor, but also with a chewier center and crisper edges. Finally, we wanted our cookies to be less cakey and more chewy. We realized that creaming the butter, as the original Toll House recipe directs, was aerating the butter too much. Melting the butter instead, and changing the ratio of brown sugar to granulated sugar, gave our cookies the right chewy texture. The extra brown sugar also gave our cookies a more complex, toffee-like flavor. Bite for bite, this was a chocolate chip cookie that could rival the best versions of the classic. Not all brands of chocolate chips are processed in a gluten-free facility, so read labels carefully.

Chocolate Chip Cookies
MAKES ABOUT 24 COOKIES

- 8 ounces (1¾ cups) ATK All-Purpose Gluten-Free Flour Blend (page 7)
- 1 teaspoon baking soda
- ¾ teaspoon xanthan gum
- ½ teaspoon salt
- 8 tablespoons unsalted butter, melted
- 5¼ ounces (¾ cup packed) light brown sugar
- 2⅓ ounces (⅓ cup) granulated sugar
- 1 large egg
- 2 tablespoons milk
- 1 tablespoon vanilla extract
- 7½ ounces (1¼ cups) semisweet chocolate chips

1. Whisk flour blend, baking soda, xanthan gum, and salt together in medium bowl; set aside. Whisk melted butter, brown sugar, and granulated sugar in large bowl until well combined and smooth. Whisk in egg, milk, and vanilla and continue to whisk until smooth. Stir in flour mixture with silicone spatula and mix until soft, homogeneous dough forms. Fold in chocolate chips. Cover bowl with plastic wrap and let dough rest for 30 minutes. (Dough will be sticky and soft.)

2. Adjust oven rack to middle position and heat oven to 350 degrees. Line 2 baking sheets with parchment paper. Using 2 soupspoons and working with about 1½ tablespoons of dough at a time, portion dough and space 2 inches apart on prepared sheets. Bake cookies, 1 sheet at a time, until golden brown and edges have begun to set but centers are still soft, 11 to 13 minutes, rotating sheet halfway through baking.

3. Let cookies cool on sheet for 5 minutes, then transfer to wire rack. Serve warm or at room temperature. (Cookies are best eaten on day they are baked, but they can be cooled and placed immediately in airtight container and stored at room temperature for up to 1 day.)

TEST KITCHEN TIP
Cooling and Storing Gluten-Free Cookies

Like their traditional counterparts, gluten-free cookies need to briefly cool on the baking sheet when they come out of the oven. This gives them time to set up, reducing the chance they'll break when you slide a spatula underneath. Once they've slightly cooled, move them to a wire rack to finish cooling according to the recipe.

But keep in mind that you don't want to let them sit out for an extended time. Like other gluten-free baked goods, these cookies have a shorter shelf life than cookies made with all-purpose flour. Gluten-free flour blends have a higher starch content, and that starch is very good at absorbing moisture. It continues to absorb the moisture in the cookies over time, making them taste drier and crumble more easily. Consequently, they are best eaten the day they are made.

However, if you do want to store leftover baked cookies, we have found that they will keep acceptably well in an airtight container for a day or two at room temperature. But don't refrigerate any of these cookies because that will make them only drier. And if you do store them, we recommend using a container instead of a zipper-lock bag, and stacking them in as few layers as possible, using parchment in between each layer, since the cookies become more delicate over time and fare better with sturdier protection.

TEST KITCHEN TIP
Freezing Cookie Dough

Given the fact gluten-free cookies don't store all that well—and that a fresh cookie, gluten-free or traditional, is better than an old one—we have found that freezing the cookie dough is a good option in some recipes. For the drop-style cookies, you can freeze portioned and shaped cookie dough as directed in the recipe, then bake off cookies straight from the freezer as you want them. This process applies to Chocolate Chip, Chocolate, Peanut Butter, and Chewy Sugar Cookies. Note that the dough for our Oatmeal-Raisin Cookies doesn't freeze well (the cookies become tough).

For the Holiday Cookies, after making the dough and shaping it into disks, you can wrap each disk in plastic and refrigerate for up to two days or freeze for up to two weeks. Just make sure to defrost frozen dough completely in the refrigerator overnight before rolling it out. The Shortbread dough does not freeze well.

Bars likewise are best eaten the day they are made. Between the starches in the flour blend and the additional moisture, the lemon and raspberry bars just don't keep more than a day; for this brief period you can store raspberry bars at room temperature, and lemon bars in the refrigerator. The brownies will hold well at room temperature for a couple of days.

To bake frozen cookie dough, arrange the dough balls (do not thaw) on parchment-lined baking sheet and bake as directed, increasing baking time by 2 to 5 minutes.

1. After portioning and shaping dough according to recipe, arrange unbaked cookies on baking sheet. Place sheet in freezer.

2. Freeze dough until completely firm, 2 to 3 hours, then transfer to zipper-lock freezer bag and freeze for up to 2 weeks.

Chocolate Chip Cookies

In the pantheon of cookies, chocolate chip cookies are just about everyone's favorite. But gluten-free versions are all too often overly cakey or gritty—a far cry from the classic. Here's how we made gluten-free chocolate chip cookies with a rich, buttery flavor, a crisp exterior, and a tender but not too cakey interior.

1. ADD XANTHAN GUM: Because starches are liquid when hot and don't set up until cool, and because the bonds between the proteins in gluten-free flour blends are weak and few in number, gluten-free cookies don't have the ability to hold their shape like traditional cookies, which have the power of gluten to provide structure, even when hot. To prevent the cookies from spreading all over the baking sheet, we needed to add something to reinforce the weak structure of our gluten-free flour. Just a small amount of xanthan gum did the trick.

2. GET THE SUGAR RATIO RIGHT: We wanted a cookie that was chewy in the center and slightly crisp on the outside. The Toll House cookie recipe calls for equal amounts of granulated sugar and brown sugar. Granulated sugar contributes to a caramelized, crisp texture and provides structure, while brown sugar adds moisture and rich caramel notes. We went up on brown sugar and down on granulated sugar to achieve a perfectly chewy center with crisp edges. Using more brown sugar than white also enhanced the butterscotch flavor notes in this classic cookie.

3. USE LESS BUTTER (AND MELT IT): A traditional chocolate chip cookie recipe has about 12 tablespoons of butter, but our gluten-free version couldn't handle this much fat. That's because our flour blend has more starch and less protein than all-purpose flour has, and it's the proteins that are compatible with fat. We found that 8 tablespoons of butter were the most our cookies could handle; any additional butter couldn't be absorbed and so made the cookies greasy. Creaming aerated the butter, which made the cookies too cakey; melting the butter got us closer to the texture we were after.

4. HYDRATE THE DOUGH: Because we had to decrease the amount of butter in our cookies, the dough had very little liquid to hydrate the flour (remember, butter is about 18 percent water) and we were left with gritty cookies. To solve this problem, we added a small amount of liquid to our dough in the form of milk, and then we let the dough rest to give the starches enough time to absorb the liquid. Two tablespoons of milk and a 30-minute rest hydrated the dough just enough to eliminate grittiness. Resting the dough also helped stiffen it, which improved structure and prevented spread.

Chocolate Cookies

G-F TESTING LAB

FLOUR SUBSTITUTION	King Arthur Gluten-Free Multi-Purpose Flour 4 ounces = **¾ cup**	Bob's Red Mill GF All-Purpose Baking Flour 4 ounces = **½ cup plus ⅓ cup**
	Cookies made with King Arthur will be more cakey and slightly gritty; cookies made with Bob's Red Mill will have a slight bean flavor.	
XANTHAN GUM	Do not omit the xanthan gum; it is crucial to the structure of the cookies. For more information, see page 21.	
CHOCOLATE	Not all brands of chocolate are processed in a gluten-free facility; read the label.	
RESTING TIME	Do not shortchange the 30-minute rest for the dough; if you do, the cookies will spread too much.	

WHY THIS RECIPE WORKS

There are two big issues with most gluten-free cookies (and, really, with gluten-free baking in general): off-flavors and dry, tough textures. But given the huge amount of flavor and moisture melted chocolate can provide, you'd think that making a great gluten-free chocolate cookie would be easy. Not so fast. Even the most promising recipes we tried failed us, with subpar chocolate flavor and a pervasive dry texture. So we started by amping up the chocolate flavor, adding not just melted chocolate but also chips, cocoa powder, and a little espresso powder (which is great for creating more complex chocolate flavor in baked goods). To address the texture, we began by tinkering with the sugar. Cookies made with all granulated sugar were too crisp, but those made with all brown sugar resulted in cookies that were so moist they were flimsy. A compromise was in order. To ensure sufficient structure, our cookies required ¼ cup of granulated sugar (along with xanthan gum). And ¾ cup of brown sugar brought the sweetness to the right level (and made the flavor more complex), while boosting the chewy texture. Still, they weren't chewy enough, so we turned to the butter. We'd just learned from developing our Fudgy Brownies recipe (page 404) that using both unsaturated fat (oil) and saturated fat (butter)—and a higher proportion of unsaturated to saturated—delivered chewier brownies. So wouldn't the same logic apply to our cookies? We switched out 5 tablespoons of butter for vegetable oil, and just as we'd suspected, we got the chewy cookies we were after. And finally, resting the dough for 30 minutes ensured the starches in our flour blend were fully hydrated, preventing any chance of a gritty texture. Dutch-processed or natural unsweetened cocoa powder will work in this recipe.

Chocolate Cookies
MAKES ABOUT 24 COOKIES

- 12 **ounces semisweet chocolate, chopped**
- 4 **ounces (¾ cup plus 2 tablespoons) ATK All-Purpose Gluten-Free Flour Blend (page 7)**
- ¾ **ounce (¼ cup) unsweetened cocoa powder**
- ½ **teaspoon baking soda**
- ½ **teaspoon salt**
- ¼ **teaspoon xanthan gum**
- 5¼ **ounces (¾ cup packed) light brown sugar**
- 1¾ **ounces (¼ cup) granulated sugar**
- 2 **large eggs**
- 5 **tablespoons vegetable oil**
- 2 **tablespoons unsalted butter, melted and cooled**
- 1 **teaspoon vanilla extract**
- ½ **teaspoon instant espresso powder**
- 9 **ounces (1½ cups) bittersweet chocolate chips**

1. Microwave semisweet chocolate in bowl at 50 percent power, stirring occasionally, until melted, 2 to 4 minutes; let cool slightly. In separate bowl, whisk together flour blend, cocoa, baking soda, salt, and xanthan gum; set aside.

2. Whisk brown sugar, granulated sugar, eggs, oil, melted butter, vanilla, and espresso powder in large bowl until well combined and smooth, then whisk in cooled chocolate. Stir in flour mixture with silicone spatula until soft, homogeneous dough forms. Fold in chocolate chips. Cover bowl with plastic wrap and let dough rest for 30 minutes. (Dough will be sticky and soft.)

3. Adjust oven rack to middle position and heat oven to 350 degrees. Line 2 baking sheets with parchment paper. Working with 2 generous tablespoons of dough at a time, roll into balls and space 2 inches apart on prepared sheets. Bake cookies, 1 sheet at a time, until puffed and cracked and edges have begun to set but centers are still soft (cookies will look raw between cracks and seem underdone), 12 to 14 minutes, rotating sheet halfway through baking.

4. Let cookies cool on sheet for 5 minutes, then transfer to wire rack. Serve warm or at room temperature. (Cookies are best eaten on day they are baked, but they can be cooled and placed immediately in airtight container and stored at room temperature for up to 2 days.)

Whole-Grain Chocolate Chip Cookies

G-F TESTING LAB

FLOUR SUBSTITUTION	Do not substitute other whole-grain blends for the ATK Whole-Grain Gluten-Free Flour Blend; they will not work in this recipe.
XANTHAN GUM	Xanthan is crucial to the structure of the cookies; see page 21 for more information.
CHOCOLATE	Not all brands of chocolate are processed in a gluten-free facility; read the label.
RESTING TIME	Do not shortchange the dough's 30-minute rest; if you do, the cookies will spread more and taste gritty.

WHY THIS RECIPE WORKS

We wanted a whole-grain cookie or two in our lineup, and although a whole-grain chocolate chip cookie might not seem like a logical choice, we actually found that chocolate and our teff-heavy blend were a winning combination. The teff lent a rich, caramel flavor and in fact created a great base for the chocolate chip cookies, but the cookies did not spread and were overly gritty, and butter leached out. So we added 2 tablespoons of milk and rested the batter for 30 minutes to hydrate the dough just enough to eliminate grittiness. Resting the dough also improved the structure, and with more baking soda we were able to get the cookies to spread. For a chewy center and a slightly crisp outside we used a combination of sugars. Granulated sugar contributed a caramelized, crisp texture and provided structure, while brown sugar added moisture and enhanced the caramel notes. We went up on brown sugar and down on granulated to achieve a perfectly chewy center with crisp edges. Our traditional recipe has 12 tablespoons of butter, but we knew our gluten-free version couldn't handle that much fat. We found that 8 tablespoons of butter provided richness without making the cookies greasy. A little bit of extra salt and vanilla added the perfect balance of salty caramel flavor.

Whole-Grain Chocolate Chip Cookies

MAKES 24 COOKIES

8	ounces (1¾ cups) ATK Whole-Grain Gluten-Free Flour Blend (page 9)
1¼	teaspoons baking soda
¾	teaspoon xanthan gum
¾	teaspoon salt
8	tablespoons unsalted butter, melted and cooled
4⅔	ounces (⅔ cup packed) light brown sugar
2⅓	ounces (⅓ cup) granulated sugar
1	large egg
2	tablespoons milk
1	tablespoon vanilla extract
7½	ounces (1¼ cups) semisweet chocolate chips

1. Whisk flour blend, baking soda, xanthan gum, and salt together in bowl. In large bowl, whisk melted butter, brown sugar, and granulated sugar together until no lumps remain. Whisk in egg, milk, and vanilla until very smooth. Stir in flour mixture with silicone spatula until dough is completely homogeneous. Fold in chocolate chips. Cover bowl with plastic wrap and let dough rest for 30 minutes. (Dough will be sticky and soft.)

2. Adjust oven rack to middle position and heat oven to 350 degrees. Line 2 baking sheets with parchment paper. Using 2 soupspoons and working with 1½ tablespoons of dough at a time, portion out dough and space 2 inches apart on prepared sheets.

3. Bake cookies, 1 sheet at a time, until golden brown and edges have begun to set but centers are still soft, 12 to 14 minutes, rotating sheet halfway through baking.

4. Let cookies cool on sheet for 5 minutes, then transfer to wire rack. Serve warm or at room temperature. (Cookies can be stored in airtight container at room temperature for up to 1 day.)

VARIATION

Dairy-Free Whole-Grain Chocolate Chip Cookies

We prefer the flavor and texture of these cookies made with soy milk, but almond milk will also work; do not use rice milk.

Reduce salt to ⅛ teaspoon. Substitute Earth Balance Vegan Buttery Sticks for butter, and unsweetened soy milk for milk. Use dairy-free semisweet chocolate chips (or finely chopped chocolate bar).

White Chocolate–Macadamia Nut Cookies

G-F TESTING LAB

FLOUR SUBSTITUTION	King Arthur Gluten-Free Multi-Purpose Flour 8 ounces = **¾ cup plus ⅔ cup**	Betty Crocker All-Purpose Gluten Free Rice Blend 8 ounces = **1½ cups plus 2 tablespoons**
	Cookies made with King Arthur will spread more and will be more delicate; cookies made with Betty Crocker will be drier and the dough will be harder to handle.	
XANTHAN GUM	Xanthan is crucial to the structure of the cookies; see page 21 for more information.	
CHOCOLATE	Not all brands of chocolate are processed in a gluten-free facility; read the label.	
RESTING TIME	Do not shortchange the dough's 30-minute rest; if you do, the cookies will spread more and taste gritty.	

WHY THIS RECIPE WORKS

White chocolate–macadamia nut cookies are an exotic rendition of the classic chocolate chip cookie, but without a good base recipe you may as well eat the stir-ins on their own. Gluten-free cookies tend to be unsatisfying because they're often gritty and greasy, and they spread all over the baking sheet. All these problems are related to the characteristics of gluten-free flours—namely, how they absorb liquids and fats, and their low protein content. First we addressed the greasy nature of our cookies. We know that gluten-free flours simply can't absorb as much butter or oil as wheat flour can, so we scaled down the amount of butter in our recipe. Removing some of the butter made the cookies less greasy, but it also made them taste grittier. We weren't surprised by this result because the reduction of butter made the dough drier. To add some moisture back into the dough, we added 2 tablespoons of milk. We also gave the dough a 30-minute rest before scooping and baking to give the flours time to absorb the liquid and soften.

White Chocolate–Macadamia Nut Cookies

MAKES 24 COOKIES

8	ounces (1¾ cups) ATK All-Purpose Gluten-Free Flour Blend (page 7)
1	teaspoon baking soda
¾	teaspoon xanthan gum
½	teaspoon salt
8	tablespoons unsalted butter, melted and cooled
5¼	ounces (¾ cup packed) light brown sugar
2⅓	ounces (⅓ cup) granulated sugar
1	large egg
2	tablespoons milk
1	tablespoon vanilla extract
¾	cup white chocolate chips
½	cup macadamia nuts, chopped

1. Whisk flour blend, baking soda, xanthan gum, and salt together in bowl. In large bowl, whisk melted butter, brown sugar, and granulated sugar until no lumps remain. Whisk in egg, milk, and vanilla until very smooth. Stir in flour mixture with silicone spatula until dough is completely homogeneous. Fold in white chocolate chips and macadamia nuts. Cover bowl with plastic wrap and let dough rest for 30 minutes. (Dough will be sticky and soft.)

2. Adjust oven rack to middle position and heat oven to 350 degrees. Line 2 baking sheets with parchment paper. Using 2 soupspoons and working with 1½ tablespoons of dough at a time, portion out dough and space 2 inches apart on prepared sheets.

3. Bake cookies, 1 sheet at a time, until golden brown and edges have begun to set but centers are still soft, 12 to 14 minutes, rotating sheet halfway through baking.

4. Let cookies cool on sheet for 5 minutes, then transfer to wire rack. Serve warm or at room temperature. (Cookies can be stored in airtight container at room temperature for up to 1 day.)

VARIATION
Dairy-Free White Chocolate–Macadamia Nut Cookies

We prefer the flavor and texture of these cookies made with soy milk, but almond milk will also work; do not use rice milk.

Substitute vegetable oil for butter, and unsweetened soy milk for milk. Use dairy-free white chocolate chips (or finely chopped chocolate bar).

Chewy Sugar Cookies

G-F TESTING LAB

FLOUR SUBSTITUTION	King Arthur Gluten-Free Multi-Purpose Flour 8 ounces = ¾ cup plus ⅔ cup	Bob's Red Mill GF All-Purpose Baking Flour 8 ounces = 1½ cups plus 2 tablespoons
	Cookies made with King Arthur will spread more and be more delicate; cookies made with Bob's Red Mill will spread more and have a distinct bean flavor.	
ALMOND FLOUR	If you don't have almond flour, you can process 4 ounces blanched almonds in a food processor until finely ground, about 45 seconds.	
XANTHAN GUM	Do not omit the xanthan gum; it is crucial to the structure of the cookies. For more information, see page 21.	
RESTING TIME	Resting the dough for 30 minutes keeps the cookies from spreading too much.	

✓ WHY THIS RECIPE WORKS

Sugar cookies usually rely on just a handful of ingredients—granulated sugar, flour, butter, leavener, and eggs. So when we plugged our flour blend into a recipe, we weren't surprised to find the gluten-free flour's starchy flavor and mouthfeel to be far too noticeable. Plus, these cookies were greasy and stale-tasting, and they spread too much. Fixing the greasiness was easy; we cut back on the butter. But this change made our cookies too lean. We often add dairy products to baked goods for richness and tenderness, so we tried adding heavy cream, but it was too thin and made our dough liquid-y. Likewise when we tried sour cream, we ended up with a soupy dough. Cream cheese, however, enriched the dough without making it loose and was a clear step in the right direction. Letting the dough rest helped avoid grittiness, but to mitigate the starchy flavor we eventually realized we needed to find something to replace a portion of the starchy flour blend. Scanning the long list of gluten-free flours, we realized most were off the table since they either were equally (if not more) starchy or had unwelcome off-flavors. But then we landed on nut flours. Almond flour had a neutral flavor and color that went unnoticed in our cookies. Replacing a portion of our blend with it not only broke up the starchiness, but also gave our cookies a much-needed heft and chew because of the additional protein it contributed. For the leaveners, we found that our cookies needed both baking powder and baking soda. Baking powder provided the right amount of lift, while baking soda helped them spread just enough. Baking soda also gave our cookies the right crackly top, creating bubbles in the dough that rose to the top of each cookie during baking and left fissures behind. And finally, before baking we rolled each portion of dough in sugar for added texture, visual appeal, and a little extra sweetness, then flattened them with the bottom of a measuring cup to ensure even baking. The final dough will be softer than most cookie doughs. For the best results, handle the dough as briefly and as gently as possible when shaping the cookies.

Chewy Sugar Cookies
MAKES ABOUT 24 COOKIES

- **8 ounces (1¾ cups) ATK All-Purpose Gluten-Free Flour Blend (page 7)**
- **4 ounces (1⅓ cups) almond flour**
- **1 teaspoon baking powder (see page 24)**
- **½ teaspoon baking soda**
- **½ teaspoon salt**
- **½ teaspoon xanthan gum**
- **8¾ ounces (1¼ cups) sugar, plus ⅓ cup for rolling**
- **3 ounces cream cheese, softened and cut into 8 pieces**
- **8 tablespoons unsalted butter, melted and still warm**
- **1 large egg**
- **1 tablespoon vanilla extract**

1. Whisk flour blend, almond flour, baking powder, baking soda, salt, and xanthan gum together in medium bowl; set aside. Place 1¼ cups sugar and cream cheese in large bowl. Place remaining ⅓ cup sugar in shallow dish and set aside. Pour warm butter over sugar and cream cheese and whisk to combine (some small lumps of cream cheese will remain but will smooth out later). Whisk in egg and vanilla and continue to whisk until smooth. Stir in flour mixture with silicone spatula and mix until soft, homogeneous dough forms. Cover bowl with plastic wrap and refrigerate until chilled, about 30 minutes. (Dough will be sticky and soft.)

2. Adjust oven rack to middle position and heat oven to 350 degrees. Line 2 baking sheets with parchment paper. Using 2 soupspoons and working with 2 tablespoons of dough at a time, portion 6 balls of dough and place in sugar to coat. Roll each ball in sugar, then space 2 inches apart on prepared sheets. Repeat with remaining dough in batches. Press dough to ½-inch thickness using bottom of measuring cup. Sprinkle tops of cookies evenly with sugar remaining in shallow dish for rolling, using 2 teaspoons for each sheet. (Discard remaining sugar.)

3. Bake cookies, 1 sheet at a time, until edges are set and just beginning to brown, 12 to 14 minutes, rotating sheet halfway through baking. Let cookies cool on sheet for 5 minutes, then transfer to wire rack. Serve warm or at room temperature.

(Cookies are best eaten on day they are baked, but they can be cooled and placed immediately in airtight container and stored at room temperature for up to 1 day.)

TEST KITCHEN TIP **Shaping Sugar Cookies**

Sugar-cookie dough is particularly sticky because of all the sugar it contains. Dropping balls of dough directly into the sugar, then rolling each ball in the sugar shapes them into rounds and gives them their sugary coating in a single, easy step.

1. Using 2 soupspoons and working with 2 tablespoons of dough at a time, portion 6 cookies into shallow dish with sugar.

2. Roll each ball in sugar, then space 2 inches apart on prepared sheets.

TEST KITCHEN TIP **Portioning Drop Cookies**

In our drop-cookie recipes, we often call for portioning dough using soupspoons because we know everyone owns them. But for portioning sticky gluten-free cookie dough, a spring-loaded scoop can be very handy. It not only ensures consistent size and proper yield, but also makes the process faster and easier. We think it's well worth the small investment. The number stamped on the handle of these scoops corresponds to the number of level scoops needed to make 32 ounces. (Remember: 1 ounce equals 2 tablespoons.) Use a #40 scoop in our recipes that call for 1½-tablespoon portions of dough, and a #30 scoop for recipes that use 2-tablespoon (or 2-generous-tablespoon) portions.

SMART SHOPPING
Baking Powder and Baking Soda

Leaveners are critical to gluten-free baking in general (see page 24 for more detail), but with cookies, traditional and gluten-free, they take on very distinct roles. You'll find both baking powder and baking soda used in many of our cookie recipes because together they help create cookies that not only rise but also spread to the right degree. Baking powder is responsible for lift, since it is engineered to produce most of its gas after the cookies go in the oven. But too much lift means humped cookies that bake unevenly. That's where baking soda comes in. It interferes with proteins in the dough and disrupts the structure, causing the cookies to spread. Baking soda also has an aesthetic effect: It delivers cookies with a crackly top.

TEST KITCHEN TIP
Pressing and Baking Cookies

To ensure even baking, we use the bottom of a flat-bottomed dry measuring cup to press each portion of dough for our Chewy Sugar, Oatmeal-Raisin, and Peanut Butter Cookies flat on baking sheets before moving the sheets to the oven. And since the doughs for our Oatmeal-Raisin and Peanut Butter Cookies are particularly moist (and don't have the barrier of a sugar coating like we use in our Chewy Sugar Cookies), in those recipes we also grease the bottom of the measuring cup to prevent sticking.

Using bottom of measuring cup, press each portion of dough to thickness indicated in specific recipe.

Oatmeal-Raisin Cookies

WHY THIS RECIPE WORKS

You'd think creating a gluten-free oatmeal-raisin cookie would be easy. But our favorite test kitchen recipe, which calls for 3 cups of rolled oats, also requires a good amount of flour. When we swapped in our flour blend, we ended up with rock-hard pucks. Between the oats and all the starches in the flour blend, the moisture was getting soaked up entirely. We tried the simplest solution first—adding water to the dough—but this resulted in cookies that were thin and tough. Thinking of ways to add moisture and create a more tender cookie without the spread, we combined a portion of the oats (toasted first to enhance their flavor) with a small amount of water. Within 10 minutes, the oats had soaked up the liquid and softened. We stirred them into the dough, let the dough rest for 30 minutes to hydrate the starches in our flour blend and thus avoid grittiness, then baked off a batch. These cookies set up well and were more tender. But now we had a new problem: Our cookies were too cakey. We took a cue from our Chewy Sugar Cookies (page 363) and substituted almond flour for a few ounces of our flour blend. This gave our cookies richness, heft, and chew without any noticeable almond flavor. (See page 362 for instructions on making your own almond flour.) After portioning the dough onto the baking sheet, flatten the dough balls to ensure that the oats spread out evenly. Do not use quick oats in this recipe.

Oatmeal-Raisin Cookies
MAKES ABOUT 24 COOKIES

- 9 ounces (3 cups) gluten-free old-fashioned rolled oats
- ½ cup warm tap water
- 4 ounces (1⅓ cups) almond flour
- 3 ounces (⅔ cup) ATK All-Purpose Gluten-Free Flour Blend (page 7)
- ½ teaspoon salt
- ½ teaspoon baking powder (see page 24)
- ¼ teaspoon xanthan gum
- ⅛ teaspoon ground nutmeg
- 7 ounces (1 cup packed) brown sugar
- 3½ ounces (½ cup) granulated sugar
- 8 tablespoons unsalted butter, melted and cooled
- 1 large egg, plus 1 large yolk
- 2 tablespoons vegetable oil
- 1 teaspoon vanilla extract
- 1 cup raisins

1. Adjust oven rack to middle position and heat oven to 375 degrees. Spread oats evenly on rimmed baking sheet and bake until fragrant and lightly browned, about 10 minutes, stirring halfway through baking; cool on wire rack. Transfer half of cooled oats to bowl and stir in water. Cover bowl with plastic wrap and let sit until water is absorbed, about 10 minutes.

2. Whisk almond flour, flour blend, salt, baking powder, xanthan gum, and nutmeg together in medium bowl; set aside. Whisk brown sugar, granulated sugar, melted butter, egg and yolk, oil, and vanilla in large bowl until well combined and smooth. Stir in flour mixture, oat-water mixture, and remaining toasted oats using silicone spatula until soft, homogeneous dough forms. Fold in raisins. Cover bowl with plastic and let dough rest for 30 minutes.

3. Adjust oven rack to middle position and heat oven to 325 degrees. Line 2 baking sheets with parchment paper. Working with 2 generous tablespoons of dough at a time, use your damp hands to roll dough into balls and space 2 inches apart on prepared sheets. Press dough to ½-inch thickness using bottom of greased measuring cup. Bake cookies, 1 sheet at a time, until edges are set and beginning to brown but centers are still soft and puffy, 22 to 25 minutes, rotating sheet halfway through baking.

4. Let cookies cool on sheet for 5 minutes, then transfer to wire rack. Serve warm or at room temperature. (Cookies are best eaten on day they are baked, but they can be cooled and placed immediately in airtight container and stored at room temperature for up to 2 days.)

G-F TESTING LAB

FLOUR SUBSTITUTION	King Arthur Gluten-Free Multi-Purpose Flour 3 ounces = ⅓ **cup plus ¼ cup**	Bob's Red Mill GF All-Purpose Baking Flour 3 ounces = ½ **cup plus 2 tablespoons**
	Cookies made with King Arthur will be harder and drier, while cookies made with Bob's Red Mill will be stickier and will have a slight bean flavor.	
XANTHAN GUM	Do not omit the xanthan gum; it is crucial to the structure of the cookies. For more information, see page 21.	
RESTING TIME	Do not shortchange the 30-minute rest for the dough; if you do, the cookies will spread too much.	

Oatmeal-Raisin Cookies

Great oatmeal-raisin cookies should be soft and chewy and have a lot of oat flavor, whether they're made with wheat flour or gluten-free flour. Unfortunately, substituting our flour blend, which is lower in protein and higher in starch compared with all-purpose flour, coupled with the addition of plenty of moisture-absorbing rolled oats, created a dry, tough cookie. To achieve the right balance of tender crumb and slight chew, here's what we did.

1. USE BUTTER AND OIL: A traditional oatmeal-raisin cookie uses butter, not oil. Butter provides good nutty flavor that complements oats, and it provides moisture. Butter (unlike oil) is not a pure fat: It contains about 18 percent water. During baking, that water turns to steam, which gives the cookie a little extra rise and also creates a more tender crumb. However, in our gluten-free version, we found that using only butter for the fat gave us a cookie that had a more cakelike than cookielike texture. Swapping in some oil for butter (we settled on a 4:1 ratio of butter to oil) helped make our cookies less cakey.

2. ADD ALMOND FLOUR: The oil helped to make our cookies less cakey, but they needed to be chewier still, plus, they baked up flat. We looked to our flour blend as the next ingredient to tweak. Just as with all-purpose flour, the proteins in the blend form an elastic structure around the starches. But the low protein content in the blend translates to less structure in the cookie. To boost the protein—and thus give our cookies more substance and chew—we swapped in 4 ounces of high-protein almond flour for a portion of our blend. With about three times as much protein, this substitution made a huge improvement.

3. SKIP THE SODA, ADD THE POWDER: Many cookie recipes contain baking powder and baking soda. Baking soda interferes with proteins in the flour (in both gluten-free and all-purpose flour) that create structure, causing the cookies to spread. We found baking soda didn't do our cookies any favors; the dough spread out into a thin layer around a clump of oats. For even spread and distribution of oats, we were better off omitting the soda and simply pressing each portion of dough into a ½-inch-thick cookie before baking. Baking powder was a keeper, giving our cookies the proper rise and a tender crumb.

4. SOAK THE OATS: The real key to making our cookies soft and tender lay in the amount of moisture in our dough and how it was incorporated. Starchy gluten-free flour blends soak up lots of moisture, as do oats, and the liquid from the eggs, butter, and sugar wasn't enough for this cookie dough. For a dough that was moist but not overly loose, we found the key was adding water to some of the oats and letting them sit for 10 minutes. Once the liquid was absorbed, we stirred the oats into the dough. This gave us just the right soft, tender cookie.

Oatmeal Cookies with Chocolate Chunks

G-F TESTING LAB

FLOUR SUBSTITUTION	King Arthur Gluten-Free Multi-Purpose Flour 3 ounces = ⅓ cup plus ¼ cup	Betty Crocker All-Purpose Gluten Free Rice Blend 3 ounces = ½ cup plus 2 tablespoons
	Cookies made with King Arthur and Betty Crocker will be drier.	
OATS	Not all brands of oats are gluten-free; read the label. Do not substitute quick oats.	
BAKING POWDER	Not all brands of baking powder are gluten-free; see page 24 for more information.	
XANTHAN GUM	Xanthan is crucial to the structure of the cookies; see page 21 for more information.	
CHOCOLATE	Not all brands of chocolate are processed in a gluten-free facility; read the label.	
RESTING TIME	Do not shortchange the dough's 30-minute rest or else the cookies will taste gritty.	

WHY THIS RECIPE WORKS

Creating a recipe for chewy, moist, gluten-free oat cookies turned out to be more challenging than we had anticipated. Packing so much oat flavor in our cookies meant using a full 3 cups of oats, and while our cookies had great oat flavor, they were tough and dry as a result. The oats were soaking up all the available liquid, so instead of stirring them into the cookie dough raw, we decided to beat them at their own game: We soaked half of the oats (toasted first to bring out their full flavor) in warm water before adding them to the dough. This succeeded in creating soft cookies, but now they were too cakey. The cakeyness was thanks to our flour blend, as all the starches in it were giving the cookies a tender, delicate crumb. Substituting 4 ounces of almond flour for a portion of the flour blend contributed additional protein and fat, turning our cookies into the chewy, moist version we were after. Chopping the dried cherries and bittersweet chocolate ensured bright flavor in every bite.

Oatmeal Cookies with Chocolate Chunks and Dried Cherries

MAKES 24 COOKIES

9	ounces (3 cups) old-fashioned rolled oats
½	cup warm tap water
4	ounces (1⅓ cups) almond flour
3	ounces (⅔ cup) ATK All-Purpose Gluten-Free Flour Blend (page 7)
½	teaspoon salt
½	teaspoon baking powder
¼	teaspoon xanthan gum
⅛	teaspoon ground nutmeg
8	tablespoons unsalted butter, melted and cooled
7	ounces (1 cup packed) brown sugar
3½	ounces (½ cup) granulated sugar
1	large egg plus 1 large yolk
2	tablespoons vegetable oil
1	teaspoon vanilla extract
3	ounces bittersweet chocolate, chopped coarse
½	cup dried cherries, chopped

1. Adjust oven rack to middle position and heat oven to 375 degrees. Spread oats onto rimmed baking sheet and bake, stirring occasionally, until fragrant and lightly browned, about 10 minutes; let cool completely.

2. Combine warm water and half of cooled oats in bowl, cover with plastic wrap, and let sit until water is absorbed, about 10 minutes. In separate bowl, whisk almond flour, flour blend, salt, baking powder, xanthan gum, and nutmeg together.

3. In large bowl, whisk melted butter, brown sugar, granulated sugar, egg and yolk, oil, and vanilla until no lumps remain and mixture is very smooth. Stir in oat-water mixture, flour mixture, and remaining toasted oats using silicone spatula until dough is completely homogeneous. Fold in chocolate and dried cherries. Cover bowl with plastic and let dough rest for 30 minutes. (Dough will be sticky and soft.)

4. Adjust oven rack to middle position and heat oven to 325 degrees. Line 2 baking sheets with parchment paper. Working with 2 generous tablespoons of dough at a time, use your damp hands to roll dough into balls and space 2 inches apart on prepared sheets. Press dough to ½-inch thickness using bottom of greased measuring cup.

5. Bake cookies, 1 sheet at a time, until edges are set and beginning to brown but centers are still soft and puffy, 22 to 25 minutes, rotating sheet halfway through baking.

6. Let cookies cool on sheet for 10 minutes, then transfer to wire rack. Serve warm or at room temperature. (Cookies can be stored in airtight container at room temperature for up to 2 days.)

VARIATION
Dairy-Free Oatmeal Cookies with Chocolate Chunks and Dried Cherries
Substitute vegetable oil for butter and use dairy-free bittersweet chocolate.

Chocolate Crinkle Cookies

G-F TESTING LAB

FLOUR SUBSTITUTION	King Arthur Gluten-Free Multi-Purpose Flour 5 ounces = ⅔ **cup plus ¼ cup**	Betty Crocker All-Purpose Gluten Free Rice Blend 5 ounces = **1 cup**
	Cookies made with King Arthur will taste a bit starchy; cookies made with Betty Crocker will be slightly pasty.	
CHOCOLATE	Not all brands of chocolate are processed in a gluten-free facility; read the label.	
BAKING POWDER	Not all brands of baking powder are gluten-free; see page 24 for more information.	
XANTHAN GUM	The xanthan can be omitted, but the cookies will be crumbly and spread more.	
RESTING TIME	Do not shortchange the dough's 30-minute rest; if you do, the dough will be hard to handle.	

✓ WHY THIS RECIPE WORKS

For a gluten-free take on chocolate crinkle cookies that lived up to their name, we used a combination of unsweetened chocolate and cocoa powder (plus a little espresso powder) for a deep, rich chocolate flavor. Using brown sugar instead of granulated lent a more complex, tempered sweetness with a bitter molasses edge that complemented the chocolate. A combination of baking powder and baking soda was key to achieving the hallmark crinkly look. As the cookies baked, the baking soda created bubbles of carbon dioxide that caused the dough to spread and crack, while the baking powder provided lift without deflating. Although these cookies looked great, they were just a little too delicate and crumbly. Adding xanthan gum would prevent the cookies from crumbling apart, but we also intuited that it would create a cakier, less fudgy texture. As a test, we baked a batch with the addition of xanthan gum alone and another with xanthan gum and 2 tablespoons of water. The cookies with just xanthan gum were indeed too cakey. The cookies with the xanthan gum and water, on the other hand, held together and maintained their fudgy texture. To ensure that these cookies were easy to shape and looked perfect every time (the dough was quite sticky), we rolled the cookies in granulated sugar first, followed by confectioners' sugar.

Chocolate Crinkle Cookies
MAKES 22 COOKIES

- 4 ounces unsweetened chocolate, chopped
- 4 tablespoons unsalted butter, cut into 4 pieces
- 5 ounces (1 cup plus 2 tablespoons) ATK All-Purpose Gluten-Free Flour Blend (page 7)
- 1½ ounces (½ cup) Dutch-processed cocoa powder
- ½ teaspoon salt
- ½ teaspoon baking powder
- ¼ teaspoon baking soda
- ¼ teaspoon xanthan gum
- 10½ ounces (1½ cups packed) brown sugar
- 3 large eggs
- 2 tablespoons water
- 4 teaspoons instant espresso powder (optional)
- 1 teaspoon vanilla extract
- 3½ ounces (½ cup) granulated sugar
- 2 ounces (½ cup) confectioners' sugar

1. Microwave chocolate and butter in bowl at 50 percent power, stirring occasionally, until melted, 2 to 4 minutes; let cool slightly. In separate bowl, whisk flour blend, cocoa, salt, baking powder, baking soda, and xanthan gum together.

2. In large bowl, whisk brown sugar, eggs, water, espresso powder (if using), and vanilla together until no lumps remain and mixture is very smooth. Whisk in cooled chocolate mixture until well combined. Stir in flour mixture with silicone spatula until dough is completely homogeneous. Cover bowl with plastic wrap and let dough rest for 30 minutes. (Dough will be very soft and sticky.)

3. Adjust oven rack to middle position and heat oven to 325 degrees. Line 2 baking sheets with parchment paper. Place granulated sugar and confectioners' sugar in separate shallow dishes. Using 2 soupspoons and working with 2 tablespoons of dough at a time, portion 6 pieces of dough and place in granulated sugar. Coat each piece of dough with sugar, then roll into rough balls. Transfer balls to confectioners' sugar, roll to coat evenly, and space 2 inches apart on prepared sheets. Repeat with remaining dough in batches.

4. Bake cookies, 1 sheet at a time, until puffed and cracked and edges have begun to set but centers are still soft (cookies will look raw between cracks and seem underdone), about 12 minutes, rotating sheet halfway through baking.

5. Let cookies cool completely on sheet before serving. (Cookies can be stored in airtight container at room temperature for up to 3 days.)

VARIATION
Dairy-Free Chocolate Crinkle Cookies
Substitute vegetable oil for butter.

Whole-Grain Brown Sugar Cookies

G-F TESTING LAB

FLOUR SUBSTITUTION	Do not substitute other whole-grain blends for the ATK Whole-Grain Gluten-Free Flour Blend; they will not work in this recipe.
BAKING POWDER	Not all brands of baking powder are gluten-free; see page 24 for more information.
XANTHAN GUM	The xanthan can be omitted, but the cookies will spread more and will be less chewy.
RESTING TIME	Do not shortchange the dough's 30-minute rest; if you do, the cookies will spread more and taste gritty.

WHY THIS RECIPE WORKS

Brown sugar cookies are the grown-up version of classic white sugar cookies, featuring slightly crisp edges, chewy centers, and deep, toffeelike sweetness. To make a sophisticated gluten-free brown sugar cookie, we looked to our whole-grain gluten-free flour blend to start. Our first batch of cookies tasted great, but they were far from chewy; instead tasters described them as gritty, dry, and hard. We knew from previous testing that our whole-grain blend needed more liquid to hydrate fully, so we started by adding a small amount of milk to the dough and incorporating a resting time to prevent grittiness. These changes helped to eliminate grittiness and dryness, but the cookies still weren't chewy enough. So we tried increasing the amount of melted butter, adding it incrementally until we settled on 14 tablespoons. Another key to ensuring good chew in these cookies turned out to be erring on the side of underbaking; the cookies had the best chew when we pulled them out of the oven when the edges were just barely set. To finish, we used a combination of granulated sugar and dark brown sugar to coat the dough balls before baking. Brown sugar alone clumped too much, but cutting it with granulated sugar encouraged it to dry out, making it easier to coat the dough balls evenly. Just be sure to combine the sugars early, and break up any sugar clumps before trying to coat the dough balls.

Whole-Grain Brown Sugar Cookies

MAKES 24 COOKIES

ROLLING SUGAR

¼ cup packed dark brown sugar
¼ cup granulated sugar

COOKIES

10½ ounces (2⅓ cups) ATK Whole-Grain Gluten-Free Flour Blend (page 9)
½ teaspoon salt
½ teaspoon baking soda
¼ teaspoon baking powder
¼ teaspoon xanthan gum

10½ ounces (1½ cups packed) dark brown sugar
14 tablespoons unsalted butter, melted and cooled
1 large egg plus 1 large yolk
1 tablespoon milk
1 tablespoon vanilla extract

1. FOR THE ROLLING SUGAR: Combine sugars in shallow dish and crumble with your fingers until no large clumps remain; set aside to dry out.

2. FOR THE COOKIES: Whisk flour blend, salt, baking soda, baking powder, and xanthan gum together in medium bowl. In large bowl, whisk sugar and melted butter until sugar dissolves and no lumps remain. Whisk in egg and yolk, milk, and vanilla until mixture is very smooth and glossy. Stir in flour mixture with silicone spatula until dough is completely homogeneous. Cover bowl with plastic wrap and let dough rest for 30 minutes. (Dough will be sticky and soft.)

3. Adjust oven rack to middle position and heat oven to 350 degrees. Line 3 baking sheets with parchment paper. Working with 2 tablespoons of dough at a time, roll dough into balls and drop into rolling sugar. Coat each dough ball with sugar and space 2½ inches apart on prepared sheets.

4. Bake cookies, 1 sheet at a time, until edges have begun to set but centers are still soft (cookies will look raw between cracks and seem underdone), 12 to 14 minutes, rotating sheet halfway through baking.

5. Let cookies cool on sheet for 5 minutes, then transfer to wire rack. Serve warm or at room temperature. (Cookies can be stored in airtight container at room temperature for up to 1 day.)

VARIATION
Dairy-Free Whole-Grain Brown Sugar Cookies
We prefer the flavor and texture of these cookies made with soy milk, but almond milk will also work; do not use rice milk.

Substitute vegetable oil for butter, and unsweetened soy milk for milk.

Whole-Grain Gingersnaps

FLOUR SUBSTITUTION	Do not substitute other whole-grain blends for the ATK Whole-Grain Gluten-Free Flour Blend; they will not work in this recipe.
BAKING POWDER	Not all brands of baking powder are gluten-free; see page 24 for more information.
XANTHAN GUM	The xanthan can be omitted, but the cookies will be crumbly and spread more.
RESTING TIME	Do not shortchange the dough's 30-minute rest; if you do, the cookies will spread more and taste gritty.

WHY THIS RECIPE WORKS

Most gingersnap recipes don't live up to their name. Once you get past their brittle edges, the cookies turn soft and chewy. We wanted freshly baked gluten-free gingersnaps with a crackly top, a crisp texture, and bold ginger flavor and lingering heat. Our whole-grain gluten-free flour blend seemed to be the right choice here, as its earthy flavor paired well with the spices most often associated with gingersnaps, like cinnamon and cloves, not to mention ginger. For ginger flavor we used a good amount of freshly grated ginger, but found it wasn't enough. We discovered a combination of grated fresh and ground ginger was best, while just ⅛ teaspoon of ground black pepper gave the cookies a little heat. For a crisp, not chewy, gingersnap we knew we would have to limit the amount of moisture in our cookie. To do this, we first looked to the 6 tablespoons of butter in our recipe. Butter is roughly 16 to 18 percent water, and this moisture can make the difference between a cookie that bends and a cookie that snaps. We decided to brown the butter, deepening its rich flavor while simultaneously eliminating its moisture. Next, we looked to sugar. Sugar is hygroscopic, meaning it attracts moisture, and different sugars are more hygroscopic than others. Molasses is often used in gingersnap recipes for its complex, slightly bitter flavor, but it turns out that this type of sugar is the most hygroscopic of all. Making the switch from molasses to dark brown sugar made a huge difference in creating a truly snappy cookie, without a considerable flavor compromise. Finally, to achieve the classic craggy top, we found we needed both baking powder and baking soda.

Whole-Grain Gingersnaps

MAKES 30 COOKIES

- 6 **tablespoons unsalted butter**
- 5¼ **ounces (¾ cup packed) dark brown sugar**
- 1 **tablespoon grated fresh ginger**
- 1 **tablespoon ground ginger**
- ½ **teaspoon ground cinnamon**
- ⅛ **teaspoon ground cloves**
- ⅛ **teaspoon pepper**
- 6 **ounces (1⅓ cups) ATK Whole-Grain Gluten-Free Flour Blend (page 9)**
- 1 **teaspoon baking powder**
- ¼ **teaspoon baking soda**
- ¼ **teaspoon xanthan gum**
- ¼ **teaspoon salt**
- 1 **large egg**
- 3½ **ounces (½ cup) granulated sugar**

1. Melt butter in 10-inch skillet over medium heat. Reduce heat to medium-low and cook, swirling pan constantly, until foaming subsides and butter is just beginning to brown, 2 to 4 minutes. Transfer to large bowl and whisk in brown sugar, fresh ginger, ground ginger, cinnamon, cloves, and pepper until smooth. Let cool slightly, about 2 minutes.

2. Whisk flour blend, baking powder, baking soda, xanthan gum, and salt together in bowl. Whisk egg into butter-spice mixture until well combined. Stir in flour mixture with silicone spatula and mix until dough is completely homogeneous. Cover bowl with plastic wrap and let dough rest for 30 minutes. (Dough will be sticky and soft.)

3. Adjust oven rack to middle position and heat oven to 300 degrees. Line 2 baking sheets with parchment paper. Place granulated sugar in shallow dish. Working with 2 teaspoons of dough at a time, roll dough into balls and drop into sugar. Coat each dough ball with sugar and space 1½ inches apart on prepared sheets.

4. Bake cookies, 1 sheet at a time, until cookies are set, 20 to 25 minutes, rotating sheet halfway through baking.

5. Let cookies cool on sheet for 5 minutes, then transfer to wire rack. Cool completely before serving. (Cookies can be stored in airtight container at room temperature for up to 1 week.)

VARIATION
Dairy-Free Whole-Grain Gingersnaps
Substitute vegetable oil for butter; don't heat oil but instead mix it with brown sugar and spices.

Peanut Butter Cookies

G-F TESTING LAB

FLOUR SUBSTITUTION	King Arthur Gluten-Free Multi-Purpose Flour 8 ounces = ¾ **cup plus** ⅔ **cup**	Bob's Red Mill GF All-Purpose Baking Flour 8 ounces = **1½ cups plus 2 tablespoons**
	Note that cookies made with King Arthur will be denser and spread less, while cookies made with Bob's Red Mill will have a slight bean flavor.	
XANTHAN GUM	Do not omit the xanthan gum; it is crucial to the structure of the cookies. For more information, see page 21.	
RESTING TIME	Do not shortchange the 30-minute rest for the dough; if you do, the cookies will spread too much.	

✓ WHY THIS RECIPE WORKS

Gluten-free or not, most peanut butter cookies are either dry and sandy or overly cakey, and they all come up short on peanut butter flavor. We wanted a chewy, really peanut-buttery cookie that was also gluten-free. We started with the starring ingredient. We were surprised that we preferred commercial peanut butter (like Skippy) over natural-style peanut butters. The cookies made with the commercial varieties had a nice rise, a crisp edge, and a soft center; cookies made with all-natural options were sadly dry and crumbly. And smooth peanut butter won out over chunky since the latter gave the cookies an unappealing coarse texture. We found that we could pack a full cup of peanut butter into our cookies, but only as long as we kept the butter in check to avoid greasiness. To avoid cakey cookies, we used just enough flour to provide the necessary structure and volume. Even with less flour, we found we still needed to rest the dough for 30 minutes to ensure the starches in the flour blend were fully hydrated. Getting the sweeteners just right was key since we didn't want the sugars to overwhelm the peanut butter flavor, plus, they were major players in the final texture. Granulated sugar was necessary for crisp edges and structure (along with xanthan gum), while brown sugar contributed chew and a nice molasses flavor that complemented the peanut butter. The cookies will look underdone after 12 to 14 minutes, but they will set up as they cool. The baking time is very important, and 2 minutes can be the difference between a soft, chewy cookie and a crisp cookie.

Peanut Butter Cookies
MAKES ABOUT 24 COOKIES

- 8 ounces (1¾ cups) ATK All-Purpose Gluten-Free Flour Blend (page 7)
- 1 teaspoon baking soda
- ½ teaspoon salt
- ¼ teaspoon xanthan gum
- 7 ounces (1 cup packed) light brown sugar
- 5¼ ounces (¾ cup) granulated sugar
- 1 cup creamy peanut butter
- 8 tablespoons unsalted butter, melted and still warm
- 2 large eggs
- 1 teaspoon vanilla extract
- ⅓ cup dry-roasted peanuts, chopped fine

1. Whisk flour blend, baking soda, salt, and xanthan gum together in medium bowl; set aside. Combine brown sugar, granulated sugar, and peanut butter in large bowl. Pour warm butter over sugar mixture and whisk to combine. Whisk in eggs and vanilla and continue to whisk until smooth. Stir in flour mixture with silicone spatula and mix until soft, homogeneous dough forms. Cover bowl with plastic wrap and let rest for 30 minutes. (Dough will be slightly shiny and soft.)

2. Adjust oven rack to middle position and heat oven to 325 degrees. Line 2 baking sheets with parchment paper. Working with 2 generous tablespoons of dough at a time, roll into balls and space 2 inches apart on prepared sheets. Press dough to ¾-inch thickness using bottom of greased measuring cup. Sprinkle tops evenly with peanuts.

3. Bake cookies, 1 sheet at a time, until puffed and edges have begun to set but centers are still soft (cookies will look underdone), 12 to 14 minutes, rotating sheet halfway through baking. Let cookies cool on sheet for 5 minutes, then transfer to wire rack. Serve warm or at room temperature. (Cookies are best eaten on day they are baked, but they can be cooled and placed immediately in airtight container and stored at room temperature for up to 1 day.)

Peanut Butter Sandwich Cookies

G-F TESTING LAB

FLOUR SUBSTITUTION	King Arthur Gluten-Free Multi-Purpose Flour 4 ounces = ¾ **cup**	Betty Crocker All-Purpose Gluten Free Rice Blend 4 ounces = ½ **cup plus** ⅓ **cup**
	Cookies made with Betty Crocker will taste similar, but the dough will be soft, wet, and more difficult to handle.	
XANTHAN GUM	Xanthan is crucial to the structure of the cookies; see page 21 for more information.	
RESTING TIME	Do not shortchange the dough's 30-minute rest; if you do, the cookies will spread more and taste gritty.	

WHY THIS RECIPE WORKS

These easy-to-make sandwich cookies feature crunchy cookies and a smooth filling, both packed with big peanut butter flavor. Since our traditional recipe uses very little flour, developing a gluten-free version was simple. We started by just swapping in our all-purpose gluten-free flour blend for the flour. The cookies turned out pretty close to the original, but tasted a bit gritty and spread out too thin as they baked. Resting the batter helped the cookies taste less gritty, and adding xanthan gum reined in the spreading. Satisfied with the cookies' texture, we focused on flavor. To boost the peanut flavor, we added chopped peanuts to the dough. As for the filling, we found that it was hard to spread over the cookies without breaking them. Softening the peanut butter and butter briefly in the microwave before assembling the sandwich cookies solved this problem easily. To make the filling a bit more sweet and help it stay in place once the cookies were assembled, we added some confectioners' sugar. Using salted peanut butter is important; do not use unsalted peanut butter for this recipe.

Peanut Butter Sandwich Cookies

MAKES 24 SANDWICH COOKIES

COOKIES

- 1¼ cups dry-roasted, unsalted peanuts
- 4 ounces (¾ cup plus 2 tablespoons) ATK All-Purpose Gluten-Free Flour Blend (page 7)
- 1 teaspoon baking soda
- ½ teaspoon salt
- ¼ teaspoon xanthan gum
- 3 tablespoons unsalted butter, melted
- ½ cup creamy peanut butter
- 3½ ounces (½ cup) granulated sugar
- 3½ ounces (½ cup packed) light brown sugar
- 3 tablespoons whole milk
- 1 large egg

FILLING

- ¾ cup creamy peanut butter
- 3 tablespoons unsalted butter
- 3 ounces (¾ cup) confectioners' sugar

1. FOR THE COOKIES: Pulse peanuts in food processor until finely chopped, about 8 pulses. Whisk flour blend, baking soda, salt, and xanthan gum together in bowl. In separate bowl, whisk butter, peanut butter, granulated sugar, brown sugar, milk, and egg together. Stir flour mixture into peanut butter mixture with silicone spatula until combined. Stir in peanuts until evenly distributed. Cover bowl with plastic wrap and let dough rest for 30 minutes.

2. Adjust oven racks to upper-middle and lower-middle positions and heat oven to 350 degrees. Line 2 baking sheets with parchment paper. Working with half of dough, keeping other half covered, portion out 2 generous teaspoons of dough, roll into balls, and space 3 inches apart on prepared sheets; dough will be very sticky. Using your damp hands, press dough balls into 2-inch cookies. Repeat with remaining dough.

3. Bake cookies until deep golden brown and firm to touch, 12 to 15 minutes, switching and rotating sheets halfway through baking. Let cookies cool on sheets for 5 minutes, then transfer to wire rack and let cool completely before assembling.

4. FOR THE FILLING: Microwave peanut butter and butter until melted and warm, about 40 seconds. Stir in confectioners' sugar until combined.

5. While filling is warm, place 24 cookies upside down on counter. Place 1 tablespoon filling in center of each cookie. Top each with one of remaining cookies, right side up, and press gently until filling spreads to edges. Let filling set for 1 hour before serving. (Assembled cookies can be stored in airtight container for up to 3 days.)

VARIATION

Dairy-Free Peanut Butter Sandwich Cookies
We prefer the flavor and texture of these cookies made with soy milk, but almond milk will also work; do not use rice milk.

Substitute vegetable oil for butter, and unsweetened soy milk for milk.

Linzer Cookies

G-F TESTING LAB

FLOUR SUBSTITUTION	King Arthur Gluten-Free Multi-Purpose Flour We do not recommend using King Arthur in this recipe.	Betty Crocker All-Purpose Gluten Free Rice Blend 10 ounces = **2 cups**
	Cookies made with King Arthur will be too delicate and break easily during assembly; cookies made with Betty Crocker will be slightly dry.	
XANTHAN GUM	Xanthan is crucial to the structure of the cookies; see page 21 for more information.	
CHILLING TIME	Do not shortchange the dough's chilling times; if you do, the dough will be difficult to work with and the cookies won't hold their shape.	

WHY THIS RECIPE WORKS

These old-world jam cookies rely on ground almonds for their trademark nutty flavor. For our gluten-free linzer cookies we took advantage of the ground almonds for flavor as well as for structural reasons. We were using our all-purpose gluten-free flour blend, but because of the blend's high amount of starch we wound up with a dough that was too soft and sticky. Substituting some almond flour worked to our advantage, adding both flavor and structure since it is high in protein (and the gluten-free flours in our blend are not). In addition to providing some much-needed structure, the almond flour also helped make the dough easier to work with. To achieve a crisp, short texture for our cookies, we opted to cream the butter (melted butter creates a chewy texture in cookies) and swap superfine sugar for granulated (to create a more fine-textured cookie). To prevent the cookies from spreading in the oven, we chilled the dough before rolling and cutting the cookies (which also made the dough easier to work with), and added ¼ teaspoon of xanthan gum. For the raspberry filling, simply spreading jam in between the cookies wasn't enough; when we took a bite, the jam leaked out. Instead, we added a little gelatin to thicken the filling. If you do not have superfine sugar (which is sold in the baking aisle at most supermarkets), process granulated sugar in a food processor for 30 seconds.

Linzer Cookies

MAKES 24 SANDWICH COOKIES

½ teaspoon unflavored gelatin
2 teaspoons grated lemon zest plus
    2 teaspoons juice
½ cup raspberry jam
10 ounces (2¼ cups) ATK All-Purpose
    Gluten-Free Flour Blend (page 7)
8 ounces (2⅔ cups) almond flour
½ teaspoon salt
¼ teaspoon xanthan gum
12 tablespoons unsalted butter, cut into
    12 pieces and softened
7 ounces (1 cup) superfine sugar
1 large egg plus 1 large yolk
2 teaspoons vanilla extract
    Confectioners' sugar

1. Sprinkle gelatin over lemon juice in bowl and let sit until gelatin softens, about 5 minutes. Microwave jam in separate bowl until hot, whisking occasionally, about 30 seconds. Add softened gelatin mixture to hot jam and whisk to dissolve. Cover and refrigerate until needed.

2. Whisk flour blend, almond flour, salt, and xanthan gum together in medium bowl. Using stand mixer fitted with paddle, beat butter, superfine sugar, and lemon zest on medium-high speed until pale and fluffy, about 3 minutes. Add egg and yolk and vanilla, and beat until well combined, about 2 minutes. Reduce speed to low, add flour mixture, and beat until completely incorporated and dough is homogeneous, 2 to 4 minutes, scraping down bowl as needed.

3. Divide dough into 4 equal pieces. Press each piece into 4-inch disk, wrap in plastic wrap, and refrigerate until firm, at least 1 hour or up to 2 days. (Dough can also be frozen for up to 2 weeks; let thaw completely in refrigerator, about 12 hours, before rolling.)

4. Working with 1 piece of dough at a time, roll into 10-inch circle (⅛ inch thick) between 2 large sheets of parchment paper. Slide dough, still between parchment, onto baking sheet and refrigerate until firm, about 30 minutes.

5. Adjust oven rack to middle position and heat oven to 325 degrees. Line 2 baking sheets with parchment paper. Working in batches (keeping remaining dough chilled), use 2½-inch cookie cutter to cut out rounds, and space ¼ inch apart on prepared sheets. Using 1-inch cookie cutter, cut out centers from half of cookies. Scraps should be combined and rerolled once.

6. Bake cookies, 1 sheet at a time, until firm to touch and edges are just beginning to brown, 12 to 15 minutes, rotating sheet halfway through baking. Let cookies cool on sheet for 5 minutes, then transfer to wire rack and let cool completely before assembling. (Unassembled cookies can be stored in airtight container at room temperature for up to 5 days.)

7. Spread 1 teaspoon jam mixture on cookies without cutouts, and top with cut-out cookies to form sandwiches. Dust cookies with confectioners' sugar before serving.

VARIATION

Dairy-Free Linzer Cookies
Substitute Earth Balance Vegan Buttery Sticks for butter.

TEST KITCHEN TIP **Making Linzer Cookies**

1. Soften gelatin in lemon juice. Whisk softened gelatin into hot jam to dissolve. Cover and refrigerate until needed.

2. Divide dough into 4 equal pieces. Press each piece into 4-inch disk, wrap in plastic wrap, and refrigerate until firm, at least 1 hour or up to 2 days.

3. Working with 1 piece of dough at a time, roll into 10-inch circle (⅛ inch thick) between 2 large sheets of parchment paper. Slide dough, still between parchment, onto baking sheet and refrigerate until firm, about 30 minutes.

4. Working in batches (keeping remaining dough chilled), use 2½-inch cookie cutter to cut out rounds, and space ¼ inch apart on prepared sheets.

5. Using 1-inch cookie cutter, cut out centers from half of cookies. These will be tops of cookies.

6. Spread 1 teaspoon jam mixture over cookie bottoms, top with cookie tops, and press lightly. Dust cookies with confectioners' sugar before serving.

Almond Biscotti

✓ WHY THIS RECIPE WORKS

Despite their elegant appearance, these twice-baked cookies are easy to make. Italians like their biscotti dry and hard, while American versions tend to be buttery and more tender. We wanted something in between: a crisp but not tooth-shattering cookie. We began our testing by substituting our all-purpose gluten-free flour blend in a variety of traditional recipes from our archives, and found that just 4 tablespoons of butter gave us rich flavor and a cookie-like texture, while two eggs helped with structure and binding. To avoid crumbly cookies, we added ¾ teaspoon xanthan gum. Adding 2 tablespoons of water and letting the dough rest for 30 minutes before baking eliminated any grittiness. Baking biscotti twice (first as a log, then again as individual cookies) is the traditional method, and it worked well for our gluten-free version. For the second baking, we found that placing the cookies on a wire rack helped them bake through more evenly because the rack allowed air to circulate around the cookies. To punch up the almond flavor, we used both almond and vanilla extracts. A combination of hazelnuts and almonds also works well.

Almond Biscotti

MAKES 24 COOKIES

- 10 ounces (2¼ cups) ATK All-Purpose Gluten-Free Flour Blend (page 7)
- 1 teaspoon baking powder
- ¾ teaspoon xanthan gum
- ½ teaspoon salt
- 7 ounces (1 cup) sugar
- 4 tablespoons unsalted butter, cut into 4 pieces and softened
- 2 large eggs
- 2 tablespoons water
- ½ teaspoon vanilla extract
- ½ teaspoon almond extract
- ¾ cup whole almonds, toasted and chopped coarse

1. Whisk flour blend, baking powder, xanthan gum, and salt together in medium bowl. Using stand mixer fitted with paddle, beat sugar and butter on medium-high speed until pale and fluffy, about 3 minutes. Add eggs, water, vanilla, and almond extract and beat until well combined, about 2 minutes. Reduce speed to low, add flour mixture, and beat until completely incorporated and dough is homogeneous, 2 to 4 minutes, scraping down bowl as needed. (Dough will be sticky and loose.) Add almonds and beat until combined, about 30 seconds. Cover bowl with plastic wrap and let dough rest for 30 minutes.

2. Adjust oven rack to middle position and heat oven to 350 degrees. Line baking sheet with parchment paper. Using silicone spatula, transfer dough to prepared sheet. Using your damp hands, shape dough into 12 by 3½-inch-long rectangle. Bake until golden and just beginning to crack on edges, about 35 minutes, rotating pan halfway through baking.

3. Remove biscotti loaf from oven and let cool for 10 minutes. Reduce oven temperature to 325 degrees. Transfer cooled loaf to cutting board and slice on bias into ½-inch-thick slices using serrated knife. Arrange slices, cut side down, on wire rack set in rimmed baking sheet, spaced ¼ inch apart.

4. Bake biscotti until crisp and lightly golden brown on both sides, about 35 minutes, flipping cookies halfway through baking. Let cool completely before serving. (Cookies can be stored in airtight container at room temperature for up to 3 weeks.)

VARIATIONS

Dairy-Free Almond Biscotti
Omit salt. Substitute Earth Balance Vegan Buttery Sticks for butter.

Anise Biscotti
Substitute 1 teaspoon anise-flavored liqueur (such as ouzo or anisette) for almond extract. Add 1½ teaspoons anise seeds to dough with almonds in step 1.

G-F TESTING LAB

FLOUR SUBSTITUTION	King Arthur Gluten-Free Multi-Purpose Flour 10 ounces = **1½ cups plus ⅓ cup**	Betty Crocker All-Purpose Gluten Free Rice Blend 10 ounces = **2 cups**
	Biscotti made with King Arthur will be fragile and will spread more; biscotti made with Betty Crocker be more crumbly and the dough will be difficult to handle.	
BAKING POWDER	Not all brands of baking powder are gluten-free; see page 24 for more information.	
XANTHAN GUM	Xanthan is crucial to the structure of the biscotti; see page 21 for more information.	
RESTING TIME	Do not shortchange the dough's 30-minute rest; if you do, the cookies won't hold their shape.	

Pistachio Spice Biscotti

Substitute pistachios for almonds. Add 1 teaspoon ground cardamom, ½ teaspoon ground cloves, ½ teaspoon pepper, ¼ teaspoon ground cinnamon, and ¼ teaspoon ground ginger to flour mixture in step 1.

Chocolate-Dipped Biscotti

Microwave 12 ounces bittersweet chocolate in bowl at 50 percent power, stirring occasionally, until melted, 2 to 4 minutes. Dip bottom third of cooled biscotti in chocolate, letting excess chocolate drip back into bowl; transfer to greased wire rack set over parchment paper to catch drips. Let cookies cool until chocolate is set, about 1 hour.

TEST KITCHEN TIP **Making Biscotti**

1. Using silicone spatula, transfer dough to parchment-lined baking sheet.

2. Using damp hands (dough will be very sticky), shape dough into 12 by 3½-inch-long rectangle.

3. Bake until golden and just beginning to crack on edges, about 35 minutes, rotating pan halfway through baking.

4. Reduce oven temperature. After loaf has cooled slightly, transfer to cutting board and slice on bias into ½-inch-thick slices using serrated knife.

5. Arrange slices, cut side down, on wire rack set in rimmed baking sheet, spaced ¼ inch apart.

6. Bake biscotti until crisp and lightly golden brown on both sides, about 35 minutes, flipping cookies halfway through baking. Let cool completely before serving.

Pignoli

ALMONDS   This recipe calls for slivered almonds, which are blanched during processing to remove the brown skin from the nuts. You can use sliced almonds if they have been blanched to remove the somewhat bitter skin.

✓ WHY THIS RECIPE WORKS

With an appealingly light texture from egg whites (no yolks), and a nutty flavor profile that takes them beyond one-note macaroons and meringues, these classic Southern Italian cookies require only a few ingredients, are simple to make, and are also naturally gluten-free. For the base, most recipes we found rely on almond paste, and many call for both honey and granulated sugar for sweeteners. For a deeper, richer almond flavor and more controlled sweetness, we passed over the almond paste in favor of processing slivered almonds with our sweetener and egg whites. We found that granulated sugar alone was best here; honey was too intense and added flavors that tasters felt distracted from the otherwise clean, simple profile of the pignoli. Using slightly more almonds than sugar by volume also helped to keep the sweetness in check. Processing the almonds to a fine consistency was key to making cookies that held together, as any straggling bits of almond disrupted the texture. Some recipes we found added lemon or orange zest, but once again we found that these additions were more a distraction than an asset. Our base was a little sticky, but it was still easy enough to roll into balls, then coat in pine nuts for the classic finish to this Italian after-dinner cookie. There was no need to toast the pine nuts ahead of time since they toasted as the cookies baked. We let the baked cookies cool completely to room temperature to ensure they set up properly. These simple yet elegant cookies are perfect matched with dessert wine or coffee.

Pignoli
MAKES ABOUT 18 COOKIES

- 1⅔ **cups slivered almonds**
- 9⅓ **ounces (1⅓ cups) sugar**
- 2 **large egg whites**
- 1 **cup pine nuts**

1. Adjust oven racks to upper-middle and lower-middle positions and heat oven to 375 degrees. Line 2 baking sheets with parchment paper.

2. Process almonds and sugar in food processor until finely ground, about 30 seconds. Scrape down sides of bowl and add egg whites. Continue to process until smooth (dough will be wet), about 30 seconds; transfer mixture to bowl. Place pine nuts in shallow dish.

3. Working with 1 scant tablespoon dough at a time, roll into balls, roll in pine nuts to coat, and space 2 inches apart on prepared sheets.

4. Bake cookies until light golden brown, 13 to 15 minutes, switching and rotating sheets halfway through baking. Let cookies cool on sheets for 5 minutes, then transfer to wire rack. Let cookies cool to room temperature before serving. (Cookies can be stored in airtight container at room temperature for up to 4 days.)

SMART SHOPPING **Pine Nuts**

Also called piñons (Spanish) or pignoli (Italian), these diminutive nutlike seeds are actually harvested from pine cones. There are two main types of pine nuts: the delicately flavored, torpedo-shaped Mediterranean pine nuts and the more assertive corn kernel–shaped Chinese pine nuts. The less-expensive Chinese variety is more widely available, but both can be used interchangeably. Pine nuts have a mild taste and a slightly waxy texture. They need to be stored with care to prevent rancidity, and are best transferred to an airtight container as soon as their original packaging is opened. They will keep in the refrigerator for up to three months or in the freezer for up to nine months.

Holiday Cookies

G-F TESTING LAB

FLOUR SUBSTITUTION	King Arthur Gluten-Free Multi-Purpose Flour 12½ ounces = **2¼ cups**	Bob's Red Mill GF All-Purpose Baking Flour 12½ ounces = **2½ cups**
	Note that cookies made with King Arthur will be very sandy, while cookies made with Bob's Red Mill will have a strong bean flavor. We don't recommend using store-bought flours in this recipe.	
XANTHAN GUM	Do not omit the xanthan gum; it is crucial to the structure of the cookies. For more information, see page 21.	
CHILLING TIME	Do not shortchange either of the chilling times for the dough; if you do, the cookies will spread too much.	

✔ WHY THIS RECIPE WORKS

To be suitable for decorating, holiday cookies must be thin and crisp. When we used our flour blend in our favorite recipe, we had a whole host of problems. The dough was incredibly sticky, and even when we managed to stamp out a few cookies, they turned out with an unappealing sandy, airy texture. They also lost their shape in the heat of the oven—not surprising given the gluten-free flour blend's high amount of starch, which doesn't set up until cool. Swapping out the granulated sugar in favor of superfine gave our cookies a more even crumb and a crisp texture. And unlike our drop cookies, where we used melted butter for a chewy texture, we opted to cream the butter here for a crisp texture. To make the dough easy to work with, we chilled it twice: before rolling it out, and again before stamping out the cookies. Chilling the dough wasn't enough to ensure cookies that held their shape through baking, so we added a small amount of xanthan gum for structure. If you do not have superfine sugar (which is sold in the baking aisle at most supermarkets), process granulated sugar in the food processor for 30 seconds.

Holiday Cookies

MAKES ABOUT 24 (3-INCH) COOKIES

COOKIES

12½	ounces (2¾ cups) ATK All-Purpose Gluten-Free Flour Blend (page 7)
½	teaspoon salt
¼	teaspoon xanthan gum
16	tablespoons unsalted butter, cut into 16 pieces and softened
7	ounces (1 cup) superfine sugar
1	large egg, plus 1 large yolk
2	teaspoons vanilla extract

GLAZE

1	tablespoon cream cheese, room temperature
2–3	tablespoons milk
6	ounces (1½ cups) confectioners' sugar

1. FOR THE COOKIES: Whisk flour blend, salt, and xanthan gum together in bowl; set aside. Using stand mixer fitted with paddle, beat butter and sugar at medium-high speed until pale and fluffy, about 3 minutes. Add egg, yolk, and vanilla and beat until well combined. Reduce speed to low, add flour mixture, and mix until flour is incorporated and dough comes together, 2 to 4 minutes. Divide dough into 4 equal pieces. Press each piece into 4-inch disk, wrap each disk in plastic wrap, and refrigerate until dough is firm, about 1 hour. (Dough can be refrigerated up to 2 days or frozen for up to 2 weeks; defrost frozen dough in refrigerator before using.)

2. Working with 1 piece of dough at a time, roll ⅛ inch thick between 2 large sheets of parchment paper. Peel parchment from 1 side of dough and place back on dough. Flip dough and parchment over and repeat with second sheet of parchment. Slide dough, still between parchment, onto baking sheet and refrigerate until set, about 30 minutes.

3. Adjust oven rack to middle position and heat oven to 325 degrees. Line 2 baking sheets with parchment paper. Working with 1 sheet of dough at a time, peel parchment from 1 side of dough and cut into desired shapes using cookie cutters; space cookies 1½ inches apart on prepared sheets. Bake cookies, 1 sheet at a time, until firm to touch and edges are just beginning to brown, 12 to 14 minutes, rotating sheet halfway through baking. (Dough scraps can be patted together, chilled, and rerolled once.) Let cookies cool on sheet for 5 minutes, then transfer to wire rack. Let cookies cool to room temperature before glazing.

4. FOR THE GLAZE: Whisk cream cheese and 2 tablespoons milk together in medium bowl until no lumps remain. Add sugar and whisk until smooth, adding remaining 1 tablespoon milk as needed until glaze is thin enough to spread easily. Using back of spoon, drizzle or spread scant teaspoon of glaze onto each cooled cookie. Allow glazed cookies to dry at least 30 minutes. (Cookies are best eaten on day they are baked, but they can be stored in airtight container for up to 2 days.)

Shortbread

G-F TESTING LAB

FLOUR SUBSTITUTION	King Arthur Gluten-Free Multi-Purpose Flour 9 ounces = **1½ cups plus 2 tablespoons**	Bob's Red Mill GF All-Purpose Baking Flour 9 ounces = **1½ cups plus ⅓ cup**
	Note that shortbread made with King Arthur will be denser and slightly sandy, while shortbread made with Bob's Red Mill will be darker in color, drier, and more crumbly, and will have a distinct bean flavor.	
XANTHAN GUM	Do not omit the xanthan gum; it is crucial to the structure of the shortbread. For more information, see page 21.	

WHY THIS RECIPE WORKS

With its short ingredient list—just flour, sugar, salt, and butter—a good shortbread should showcase a rich, buttery flavor, and it should have a dense, slightly sandy texture and a tawny, light brown color. For a traditional shortbread recipe using all-purpose flour, one of the biggest issues is trying to avoid gluten development, which makes the cookies tough. Obviously this wasn't going to be an issue with a gluten-free recipe, but without any gluten we had an entirely different problem: shortbread that was crumbly and had a coarse texture. Adding some xanthan gum provided structure so it wouldn't crumble, and to ensure the shortbread held its shape during cooking, we pressed the dough inside a springform pan collar and baked it in the collar with the clasp open at the start. Swapping in confectioners' sugar for the granulated gave the cookies the right sandy, rather than gritty, texture (resting the dough to hydrate the flour, as we'd done with several of our other cookies, wasn't an option since the shortbread dough contains so little moisture). We wanted to pack in as much butter as we could, and we found that 14 tablespoons was the most fat our flour blend could handle. As for the baking method, to ensure our cookies cooked through without browning too much, we got the best results by preheating the oven at a high temperature, then turning it down to 250 degrees when we put the cookies in. We baked them briefly, just until they were golden, and then cut them (at this stage, they could be cut without shattering). Then we returned the cookies to a turned-off oven, propping the door open to ensure they would simply dry out. Still, they baked slightly unevenly. Stamping a small circle of dough from the center with a biscuit cutter guaranteed even baking.

Shortbread

MAKES 16 WEDGES

- 9 ounces (2 cups) ATK All-Purpose Gluten-Free Flour Blend (page 7)
- 2⅔ ounces (⅔ cup) confectioners' sugar
- 1 teaspoon xanthan gum
- ½ teaspoon salt
- 14 tablespoons unsalted butter, chilled and cut into ¼-inch-thick slices

1. Adjust oven rack to middle position and heat oven to 450 degrees. Using stand mixer fitted with paddle, mix flour blend, sugar, xanthan gum, and salt on low speed until combined, about 5 seconds. Add butter and continue to mix until dough forms and pulls away from sides of bowl, 3 to 5 minutes.

2. Place collar of 9- or 9½-inch springform pan on parchment paper–lined baking sheet (do not use springform pan bottom). Press dough into collar in even ½-inch-thick layer, then smooth top of dough with your damp hands or back of spoon. Place 2-inch biscuit cutter in center of dough and cut out center. Discard extracted dough and replace cutter in center of dough. Open springform collar, but leave it in place.

3. Decrease oven temperature to 250 degrees and bake shortbread until top begins to turn pale golden and edges are golden, 15 to 20 minutes. Remove baking sheet from oven and turn off oven. Remove springform pan collar. Use chef's knife to score surface of shortbread into 16 even wedges, cutting only halfway through shortbread. Using wooden skewer, poke 8 to 10 holes in each wedge. Return shortbread to oven and prop door open with handle of wooden spoon, leaving 1-inch gap at top. Allow shortbread to dry in turned-off oven until pale golden in center (shortbread should be firm but giving to touch), about 1 hour.

4. Transfer sheet to wire rack and let shortbread cool to room temperature, about 1 hour. Cut shortbread at scored marks to separate and serve. (Shortbread is best eaten on day it is baked, but it can be cooled and placed immediately in airtight container and stored at room temperature for up to 2 days.)

TEST KITCHEN TIP **Forming and Baking Shortbread**

Because of the significant amount of butter called for in the recipe, and the starches in our flour blend—both of which become molten in the oven—we bake the shortbread dough inside a springform pan collar to keep it from spreading. Once it has set up, we remove the collar, score the cookies, and continue baking in a turned-off oven to dry them out. To ensure even baking, we also cut a round out of the center of the dough using a biscuit cutter.

1. Press dough into closed upside-down springform pan collar on parchment-lined baking sheet to ½-inch thickness; smooth with your damp hands or back of spoon.

2. Cut hole in center of dough with 2-inch biscuit cutter; replace cutter in hole and discard extracted dough.

3. Open collar. Reduce oven temperature to 250 degrees, transfer sheet to oven, and bake shortbread until top begins to turn pale golden and edges are golden, 15 to 20 minutes.

4. Remove springform pan collar. Score partially baked shortbread into 16 wedges, then poke 8 to 10 holes in each wedge.

5. Return shortbread to turned-off oven to dry; prop door open with wooden spoon or stick.

6. Transfer sheet to wire rack and let shortbread cool to room temperature. Cut shortbread at scored marks.

TEST KITCHEN TIP **Xanthan Gum in Gluten-Free Cookies**

We learned after developing a number of gluten-free muffins and quick breads that our low-protein flour blend needed reinforcement to deliver baked goods with the proper structure. When we started developing our cookie recipes, we found this to be even more important. In the case of our shortbread, the flour blend delivered a crumbly cookie that couldn't hold together, but a teaspoon of xanthan gum provided the necessary reinforcement and elasticity to produce the right texture. Xanthan gum proved even more critical in our drop cookies and Holiday Cookies. Unlike our shortbread, which we bake in a springform pan collar, and our bars, which have baking pans to keep them in check, drop cookies and Holiday Cookies are loose on the baking sheet. Xanthan gum was a must to ensure these cookies didn't spread all over the sheet. See page 21 for more information about xanthan and possible substitutions.

Florentine Lace Cookies

✔️ WHY THIS RECIPE WORKS

With their toasty caramel-almond flavor, flecks of candied citrus, and chocolate drizzle finish, wafer-thin Florentine lace cookies are true showstoppers. And it's not surprising that most recipes are best left to the pros, with much of the process less like simple cookie baking and more like complicated candy making. But given their elegance (in both flavor and looks) and the fact they rely on such a small amount of flour, we agreed that figuring out how to make an approachable gluten-free Florentine was a must. Most recipes start by cooking butter, cream, and either corn syrup or honey in a saucepan until the mixture reaches 238 degrees to make the caramel base. We found we didn't need to futz around with a thermometer if we removed the saucepan from the heat when the mixture was consistently thick, bubbly, and a creamy tan color. At this point, we found that in batch after batch the target temp had been hit, and the resulting cookies were spot-on. Once the base was ready, the rest of the ingredients—typically flour, candied citrus, chopped almonds, vanilla, and a pinch of salt—are stirred in. We simplified things by swapping in orange marmalade for the candied citrus, and because chopped almonds interfered with the fine, lacy texture of the cookies, we ground them in the food processor before adding them to the batter. Flattening each portion before baking ensured evenly shaped, round cookies. For the finishing touch, we melted chocolate in the microwave, then quickly piped a drizzle onto each cookie with the help of a zipper-lock bag with the corner snipped off.

Florentine Lace Cookies

MAKES ABOUT 24 COOKIES

- 2 **cups slivered almonds**
- ¾ **cup heavy cream**
- 4 **tablespoons unsalted butter, cut into 4 pieces**
- 3½ **ounces (½ cup) sugar**
- ¼ **cup orange marmalade**
- 3 **tablespoons ATK All-Purpose Gluten-Free Flour Blend (page 7)**
- 1 **teaspoon vanilla extract**
- ¼ **teaspoon grated orange zest**
- ¼ **teaspoon salt**
- 4 **ounces bittersweet chocolate, chopped fine**

1. Adjust oven racks to upper-middle and lower-middle positions and heat oven to 350 degrees. Line 2 baking sheets with parchment paper. Process almonds in food processor until they resemble coarse sand, about 30 seconds.

2. Bring cream, butter, and sugar to boil in medium saucepan over medium-high heat. Cook, stirring frequently, until mixture begins to thicken, 5 to 6 minutes. Continue to cook, stirring constantly, until mixture begins to brown at edges and is thick enough to leave trail that doesn't immediately fill in when spatula is scraped along pan bottom, 1 to 2 minutes longer (some darker speckles may appear in mixture). Remove pan from heat and stir in ground almonds, marmalade, flour blend, vanilla, zest, and salt until combined.

3. Drop six portions of dough, 1 level tablespoon each onto each onto prepared sheet spaced at least 3½ inches apart. When dough is cool enough to handle, use your damp fingers to press each portion into 2½-inch circle.

4. Bake until deep brown from edge to edge, 15 to 17 minutes, switching and rotating sheets halfway through baking. Transfer baked cookies, still on parchment, to wire rack to cool. Let sheets cool for 10 minutes, line with fresh parchment, then repeat portioning and baking remaining dough.

5. Microwave 3 ounces chocolate in bowl at 50 percent power, stirring frequently, until about two-thirds of chocolate has melted, 1 to 2 minutes. Remove from microwave and add remaining 1 ounce chocolate and stir until melted, returning to microwave for no more than 5 seconds at a time to complete melting if necessary. Transfer chocolate to small zipper-lock bag and snip off corner to make hole no larger than 1/16 inch.

G-F TESTING LAB

FLOUR SUBSTITUTION	King Arthur Gluten-Free Multi-Purpose Flour **3 tablespoons**	Bob's Red Mill GF All-Purpose Baking Flour **3 tablespoons**
	Note that cookies made with King Arthur and Bob's Red Mill will need less time to bake; reduce the baking time by a few minutes. Cookies made with Bob's Red Mill will also be darker in color. Because so little flour blend is used in this recipe, there's no need to weigh it.	
CHOCOLATE	Not all brands of chocolate are processed in a gluten-free facility; make sure to read the label.	

6. Transfer cooled cookies from parchment directly to wire racks. Pipe zigzag of chocolate over surface of each cookie, distributing chocolate evenly among all cookies. Refrigerate until chocolate is set, about 30 minutes. (Cookies can be stored in airtight container at cool room temperature for up to 4 days.)

TEST KITCHEN TIP **Making Florentines**

Most Florentine recipes are incredibly fussy. Our recipe simplifies things, and does so first by avoiding the need for a thermometer when making the caramel base. And for the chocolate drizzle, we found microwaving the chocolate at 50 percent power until it was mostly melted and then adding a little room-temperature chocolate delivered the same results as the involved process of tempering. And finally, we ditched the pastry bag in favor of an everyday zipper-lock bag with the corner snipped off to pipe on the chocolate.

1. Bring cream, butter, and sugar to boil and cook, stirring, until mixture begins to brown at edges and leaves trail that doesn't immediately fill in when spatula is scraped along pan bottom.

2. Off heat, stir in ground almonds, marmalade, flour blend, vanilla, orange zest, and salt until combined.

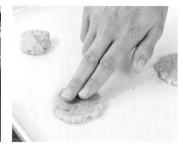

3. Drop 6 level tablespoons of dough onto 2 parchment-lined baking sheets, leaving at least 3½ inches in between. When dough is cool enough to handle, use damp fingers to press each portion into 2½-inch circle.

4. Bake cookies until uniformly brown; transfer on parchment paper to wire racks. Let sheets cool for 10 minutes, then repeat with remaining dough.

5. Microwave most of chocolate at 50 percent power, stirring frequently, until two-thirds melted. Stir in remaining chocolate until melted, microwaving as needed.

6. Pour chocolate into zipper-lock bag, snip off corner, and pipe onto cookies. Refrigerate for 30 minutes to set chocolate.

Lemon Madeleines

G-F TESTING LAB

FLOUR SUBSTITUTION	King Arthur Gluten-Free Multi-Purpose Flour 2½ ounces = **7 tablespoons**	Betty Crocker All-Purpose Gluten Free Rice Blend 2½ ounces = **½ cup**
	Madeleines made with King Arthur will have a coarse crumb; madeleines made with Betty Crocker will be slightly dry and dome dramatically in the center.	
BAKING POWDER	Not all brands of baking powder are gluten-free; see page 24 for more information.	
RESTING TIME	Do not shortchange the batter's 30-minute rest; if you do, the madeleines will taste gritty.	

WHY THIS RECIPE WORKS

Madeleines can be found at nearly every corner coffee shop these days, but those dense, flavorless, prepackaged cookies are a far cry from the buttery, rich tea cakes that originated in France. For gluten-free madeleines that were light and tender, we started by taking our favorite test kitchen recipe and swapping in our all-purpose gluten-free flour blend. Although they tasted delicious, they were also tough and dense. To fix this, we started by adding baking powder, which created rise by producing air bubbles during baking. These air bubbles interrupted the structure of the baked madeleines, giving them a more tender, cakelike crumb. Even with the addition of baking powder, however, our madeleines were still a little tough. Eggs stood out to us as a possible source of this toughness, and after exhaustive testing we found that one whole egg and two yolks got us the closest to our ideal texture, though it still wasn't the light, tender treat we were after. In addition to leaveners, fat and sugar can have a tenderizing effect on baked goods. We didn't notice any change when we adjusted the amount of melted butter we were using, but noticed a significant change when we increased the amount of sugar. Eventually we settled on a full 6 tablespoons of sugar (more sugar than flour blend by weight) for a tender, cakey texture.

Lemon Madeleines
MAKES 12 MADELEINES

- 2½ ounces (⅓ cup plus ¼ cup) ATK All-Purpose Gluten-Free Flour Blend (page 7)
- ¼ teaspoon baking powder
- ⅛ teaspoon salt
- 1 large egg plus 2 large yolks
- 2⅔ ounces (6 tablespoons) granulated sugar
- 4 tablespoons unsalted butter, melted and cooled
- 1 tablespoon grated lemon zest
- 1½ teaspoons vanilla extract
- Confectioners' sugar

1. Whisk flour blend, baking powder, and salt together in medium bowl. Whisk egg and yolks, granulated sugar, melted butter, lemon zest, and vanilla in large bowl until well combined and very smooth. Stir in flour mixture with silicone spatula and mix until flour is completely incorporated and dough is homogeneous, about 1 minute. Cover bowl with plastic wrap and let batter rest for 30 minutes.

2. Adjust oven rack to middle position and heat oven to 375 degrees. Spray madeleine pan thoroughly with vegetable oil spray. Working with generous 2 teaspoons batter at a time, portion batter into molds. Bake madeleines until edges just begin to brown and spring back when pressed lightly, 8 to 10 minutes, rotating pan halfway through baking.

3. Let madeleines cool in pan for 5 minutes. Run thin knife around edges of molds to loosen, then transfer madeleines, ridged side up, to clean dish towel. Let madeleines cool completely.

4. Dust madeleines with confectioners' sugar before serving. (Madeleines can be stored in airtight container at room temperature for up to 2 days.)

VARIATIONS
Dairy-Free Lemon Madeleines
Substitute vegetable oil for butter.

Almond Madeleines
Omit lemon zest. Substitute ½ teaspoon almond extract for vanilla extract.

Orange-Cardamom Madeleines
Omit vanilla. Substitute orange zest for lemon zest, and add ½ teaspoon ground cardamom to sugar mixture in step 1.

Rugelach

FLOUR SUBSTITUTION	King Arthur Gluten-Free Multi-Purpose Flour 5½ ounces= **1 cup**	Betty Crocker All-Purpose Gluten Free Rice Blend 5½ ounces= **1 cup plus 2 tablespoons**
	Rugelach made with King Arthur will be difficult to work with; rugelach made with Betty Crocker will be drier.	
XANTHAN GUM	Xanthan is crucial to the structure of the rugelach; see page 21 for more information.	

✓ WHY THIS RECIPE WORKS

Rugelach are a traditional Jewish treat, part pastry and part cookie, that can be filled with a variety of nuts, jams, and dried fruit. Its dough is similar to that of a standard butter cookie but usually includes some cream cheese for structure, richness, and chew. Our first attempt at making these cookies was a disaster, as the filling melted all over the tray and the cookies lost their shape completely. Reducing the amount of butter from 8 to 6 tablespoons and adding a little xanthan gum helped the cookies hold their shape better. Chilling the dough for 30 minutes before rolling firmed it up and made it easier to work with while also giving the flour blend time to hydrate so that the cookies tasted less gritty. But our rugelach were still a little too tough. To make them more delicate, we added baking soda, which not only tenderized the cookies but also helped them brown better during baking. Finally, we turned our attention to the filling, made of apricot jam, golden raisins, and walnuts, which consistently leaked out during baking. To solve this issue, we used less filling, changed the shape of the cookies from crescents to rolled-and-cut slices, and insulated the bottom of the cookies by baking them on top of two stacked baking sheets. Be sure to sprinkle the cookies with the cinnamon sugar before you transfer them to the baking sheet, or the sugar will burn onto the pan.

Rugelach

MAKES ABOUT 30 COOKIES

DOUGH

- 5½ ounces (1¼ cups) ATK All-Purpose Gluten-Free Flour Blend (page 7)
- 1 tablespoon sugar
- ¾ teaspoon xanthan gum
- ½ teaspoon salt
- ¼ teaspoon baking soda
- 4 ounces cream cheese, cut into ½-inch pieces and chilled
- 6 tablespoons unsalted butter, cut into ½-inch pieces and chilled
- 1 teaspoon vanilla extract

FILLING AND EGG WASH

- 3 tablespoons sugar
- 1½ teaspoons ground cinnamon
- 1 large egg, lightly beaten
- 1 teaspoon water
- 6 tablespoons apricot jam
- ⅓ cup walnuts, toasted and chopped fine
- 3 tablespoons golden raisins, chopped fine

1. FOR THE DOUGH: Process flour blend, sugar, xanthan gum, salt, and baking soda in food processor until combined, about 3 seconds. Add cream cheese, butter, and vanilla and process until dough comes together, about 20 seconds.

2. Divide dough into 3 equal pieces and shape each into 7 by 2-inch rectangle. Wrap each tightly in plastic wrap and refrigerate for at least 30 minutes or up to 2 days. (If dough is too firm after chilling, let soften at room temperature for 15 minutes before rolling.)

3. Working with 1 piece of dough at a time, roll dough between 2 sheets of parchment paper into 12 by 5-inch rectangle (⅛ inch thick). Slide dough, still between parchment, onto baking sheet and refrigerate until sheet of dough is stiff, about 10 minutes.

4. FOR THE FILLING AND EGG WASH: Mix sugar and cinnamon together in bowl. In separate bowl, mix egg with water.

5. Adjust oven rack to middle position and heat oven to 375 degrees. Line rimmed baking sheet with parchment paper, spray with vegetable oil spray, and place inside second baking sheet.

6. Slide 1 sheet of dough, still between parchment, onto counter. Loosen parchment on top, then flip dough over and remove second piece of parchment. Spread 2 tablespoons jam over dough, leaving 1-inch border around edge. Sprinkle with 2 tablespoons walnuts, 1 tablespoon raisins, and 1½ teaspoons cinnamon sugar.

7. With long side facing you, use loosened parchment to roll dough tightly into log. Roll log seam-side down, trim ends, and slice into 1-inch cookies. Brush cookies with egg wash, sprinkle with 1½ teaspoons cinnamon sugar, and transfer to prepared sheet, spaced about 1 inch apart. Repeat with remaining dough and filling; all cookies should fit on 1 sheet. (Unbaked cookies can be frozen for up to 1 month; place on prepared baking sheet and let thaw completely at room temperature, about 1½ hours, before baking.)

8. Bake cookies until golden and slightly puffy, about 20 minutes, rotating sheet halfway through baking. Let cookies cool on sheet for 5 minutes, then transfer to wire rack and let cool completely before serving. (Cookies can be stored in airtight container at room temperature for up to 1 day.)

VARIATIONS

Dairy-Free Rugelach
Omit salt, use dairy-free cream cheese, and substitute Earth Balance Vegan Buttery Sticks for butter.

Blackberry-Almond Rugelach
Omit raisins. Substitute blackberry jam for apricot jam, and toasted, chopped almonds for walnuts.

TEST KITCHEN TIP **Forming Rugelach**

1. Working with 1 piece of dough at a time, roll dough between 2 sheets of parchment paper into 12 by 5-inch rectangle (⅛ inch thick). Refrigerate dough for 10 minutes before filling and rolling cookies.

2. Loosen parchment on top, then flip dough over and remove second piece of parchment.

3. Spread 2 tablespoons jam over dough, leaving 1-inch border around edge. Sprinkle with 2 tablespoons walnuts, 1 tablespoon raisins, and 1½ teaspoons cinnamon sugar.

4. With long side facing you, use loosened parchment to roll dough tightly into log.

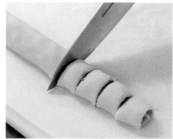

5. With log seam-side down, trim ends and slice into 1-inch cookies.

6. Brush cookies with egg wash, sprinkle evenly with 1½ teaspoons cinnamon sugar, and transfer to prepared sheet.

Rugelach

Making a gluten-free version of rugelach posed many challenges: collapsing, melting cookies; leaking, burning filling; and charred bottoms. Here's how we made gluten-free rugelach with a tangy, flaky dough rolled with the perfect amount of sweet, jammy filling.

1. USE LESS BUTTER AND ADD XANTHAN GUM: Cutting back on the butter helped to minimize greasiness and prevent the rugelach from melting all over the baking sheet. Because starches are liquid when hot and don't set up until cool, and because the protein structures made from our all-purpose gluten-free flour blend are weaker, these cookies don't hold their shape the way that traditional cookies do. To further prevent the cookies from spreading too much, we added a small amount of xanthan gum.

2. CHILL THE DOUGH TWICE: We relied on cream cheese and butter in order to make a tender dough with just the right richness, tang, and chew. But this composition made for a soft, delicate dough. Refrigerating the dough for 30 minutes before rolling it out gave the starches time to fully hydrate and allowed the dough to firm up, which made it easier to roll out. We found that with so much butter and cream cheese, this dough softened again during the rolling process. Chilling it for another 10 minutes after rolling allowed us to fill and cut our cookies easily.

3. USE LESS FILLING: These cookies, stuffed with apricot jam, golden raisins, and toasted walnuts, were consistently leaking during baking. The sugary filling would then burn and glue our cookies to the baking sheet. Because our gluten-free cookies lacked the structure of regular rugelach, they weren't able to support and contain the usual amount of filling. Reducing the amount of filling and finely chopping the golden raisins and walnuts to ensure even distribution solved the problem.

4. USE TWO SHEET PANS: Rugelach typically has a high sugar content in the form of jam, raisins, and cinnamon sugar. Combined with the fact that our flour blend is higher in starch than all-purpose flour (and therefore higher in sugar), this meant that our gluten-free rugelach were constantly burning on the bottom, becoming bitter and overcaramelized. We set the baking sheet in a second baking sheet to insulate the pan and prevent the bottoms of the cookies from burning.

Lime-Glazed Coconut-Cardamom Cookies

G-F TESTING LAB

FLOUR SUBSTITUTION	King Arthur Gluten-Free Multi-Purpose Flour 12 ounces = **1⅔ cups plus ½ cup**	Betty Crocker All-Purpose Gluten Free Rice Blend 12 ounces = **2¼ cups plus 2 tablespoons**
	Cookies made with King Arthur will be very sandy; cookies made with Betty Crocker will be dry and crumbly, and the dough will be wet and difficult to handle.	
XANTHAN GUM	Xanthan is crucial to the structure of the cookies; see page 21 for more information.	
RESTING TIME	Do not shortchange the dough's 30-minute rest; if you do, the cookies will spread more and taste gritty.	

These rich, buttery cookies are flavored with cardamom and lime and topped with a zesty cream cheese glaze and toasted coconut. Using the test kitchen's simple butter cookie recipe as our starting point, we swapped in our gluten-free all-purpose flour blend and added a small amount of xanthan gum for structure. Using one whole egg and one yolk added both richness and tenderness without the binding properties of the extra egg white, which made the cookies tough. A hefty 12 tablespoons of butter provided rich flavor and gave the cookies their signature short texture. To get rid of the sandy texture that plagues most gluten-free baked goods, we added a small amount of milk (just ¼ cup) and let the batter rest for 30 minutes to hydrate. For more flavor, we whipped the lime zest and carda-mom with the sugar and butter to bloom them and cut any harshness. A simple glaze of cream cheese, lime juice, and confectioners' sugar added the per-fect amount of tartness to these cookies, while a toasted coconut topping added crunch.

Lime-Glazed Coconut-Cardamom Cookies

MAKES 40 COOKIES

COOKIES

- 12 ounces (2⅔ cups) ATK All-Purpose Gluten-Free Flour Blend (page 7)
- ½ teaspoon salt
- ½ teaspoon xanthan gum
- 7 ounces (1 cup) granulated sugar
- 12 tablespoons unsalted butter, cut into 12 pieces and softened
- 1 teaspoon ground cardamom
- ½ teaspoon grated lime zest
- ¼ cup milk
- 1 large egg plus 1 large yolk
- 2 teaspoons vanilla extract

TOPPING

- 1½ cups sweetened shredded coconut, chopped fine and toasted
- 3 tablespoons lime juice (2 limes)

- 1 tablespoon cream cheese, softened
- 6 ounces (1½ cups) confectioners' sugar

1. FOR THE COOKIES: Whisk flour blend, salt, and xanthan gum together in medium bowl. Using stand mixer fitted with paddle, beat sugar, butter, cardamom, and lime zest on medium-high speed until pale and fluffy, about 3 minutes. Add milk, egg and yolk, and vanilla and beat until well combined, about 2 minutes. Reduce speed to low, add flour mixture, and beat until completely incorporated and dough is homogeneous, 2 to 4 minutes, scraping down bowl as needed. Cover bowl with plastic wrap and let dough rest for 30 minutes.

2. Adjust oven rack to middle position and heat oven to 325 degrees. Line 2 baking sheets with parchment paper. Working with 1 heaping table-spoon of dough at a time, roll into balls using damp hands, and space 1 inch apart on prepared sheets.

3. Bake cookies, 1 sheet at a time, until firm to touch and lightly golden around edges, 12 to 16 min-utes, rotating sheet halfway through baking. Let cookies cool on sheet for 5 minutes, then transfer to wire rack and cool completely before glazing.

4. FOR THE TOPPING: Place coconut in shallow dish. Whisk 2 tablespoons lime juice and cream cheese together in bowl until smooth, then whisk in sugar until smooth. Add remaining 1 tablespoon lime juice as needed until glaze is easy to spread. Dip tops of cooled cookies into glaze, allowing excess to drip back into bowl, then coat with coco-nut. Let glaze dry completely before serving, about 30 minutes. (Cookies can be stored in airtight con-tainer at room temperature for up to 2 days.)

VARIATION
Dairy-Free Lime-Glazed Coconut-Cardamom Cookies
We prefer the flavor and texture of these cookies made with soy milk, but almond milk will also work; do not use rice milk.

Substitute ½ cup vegetable oil for butter, and unsweetened soy milk for milk. Use dairy-free cream cheese.

Fudgy Brownies

G-F TESTING LAB

FLOUR SUBSTITUTION	King Arthur Gluten-Free Multi-Purpose Flour 4 ounces = ¾ **cup**	Bob's Red Mill GF All-Purpose Baking Flour 4 ounces = ½ **cup plus** ⅓ **cup**
	Note that brownies made with King Arthur will have less structure and be slightly gritty, while brownies made with Bob's Red Mill will have a slight bean flavor.	
XANTHAN GUM	The xanthan gum can be omitted, but the brownies will be more crumbly, will not rise as well, and will sink somewhat in the middle.	
RESTING TIME	Do not shortchange the 30-minute rest for the batter; if you do, the brownies will be gritty.	

☑ WHY THIS RECIPE WORKS

Fudgy brownies contain less flour than cakey ones, so it made sense to start with our favorite recipe for fudgy brownies and use our flour blend instead. With cocoa powder, unsweetened chocolate, and bittersweet chocolate, this recipe delivers intense chocolate flavor. But when made with our flour blend, the brownies were a bit dry and dense (even for a fudgy brownie), and there was a subtle graininess. Cutting back on the amount of flour helped give the brownies the right moist, fudgy texture, and resting the batter for 30 minutes before baking gave the starches in our flour blend time to hydrate and soften. But reducing the amount of flour also had an unwanted side effect: The chocolate flavor fell out of balance. Now our brownies had a bitter edge. Both unsweetened chocolate and cocoa powder were candidates for elimination since they are on the more bitter end of the chocolate spectrum. Brownies made without cocoa lacked structure—so it had to stay. Dropping the unsweetened chocolate was a big step in the right direction, and switching the bittersweet out for semisweet chocolate eliminated the bitter flavor altogether. Not all brands of chocolate are processed in a gluten-free facility, so read labels carefully.

Fudgy Brownies
MAKES 16 BROWNIES

- 4 ounces (¾ cup plus 2 tablespoons) ATK All-Purpose Gluten-Free Flour Blend (page 7)
- ½ teaspoon salt
- ½ teaspoon xanthan gum
- 7 ounces semisweet chocolate, chopped coarse
- 8 tablespoons unsalted butter, cut into 8 pieces
- 3 tablespoons unsweetened cocoa powder
- 8¾ ounces (1¼ cups) sugar
- 3 large eggs
- 2 teaspoons vanilla extract

1. Make foil sling for 8-inch square baking pan by folding 2 long sheets of aluminum foil so each is 8 inches wide. Lay sheets of foil in pan perpendicular to each other, with extra foil hanging over edges of pan. Push foil into corners and up sides of pan, smoothing foil flush to pan; spray with vegetable oil spray.

2. Whisk flour blend, salt, and xanthan gum together in bowl; set aside. Microwave chocolate, butter, and cocoa in bowl at 50 percent power, stirring often, until melted and smooth, 1 to 3 minutes. Let mixture cool slightly.

3. Whisk sugar, eggs, and vanilla together in large bowl. Whisk in cooled chocolate mixture. Stir in flour mixture using silicone spatula and mix until well combined. Scrape batter into prepared pan and smooth top with spatula. Cover pan with plastic wrap and let batter rest for 30 minutes.

4. Adjust oven rack to middle position and heat oven to 350 degrees. Remove plastic and bake until toothpick inserted in center comes out with few moist crumbs attached, 45 to 55 minutes, rotating pan halfway through baking.

5. Let brownies cool completely in pan on wire rack, about 2 hours. Using foil overhang, lift brownies out of pan. Cut into squares and serve. (Brownies are best eaten on day they are baked, but they can be cooled and placed immediately in airtight container and stored at room temperature for up to 2 days.)

TEST KITCHEN TIP **Making a Foil Sling**

A foil sling makes removing bars tidy and easy. Make sure to grease foil sling to prevent sticking.

Lay 2 sheets of foil in pan perpendicular to each other, with extra foil hanging over edges of pan. Push foil into corners and up sides of pan, smoothing foil flush to pan.

Lunchbox Brownies

G-F TESTING LAB

FLOUR SUBSTITUTION	King Arthur Gluten-Free Multi-Purpose Flour 7½ ounces = **1¼ cups plus 2 tablespoons**	Betty Crocker All-Purpose Gluten Free Rice Blend 7½ ounces = **1½ cups**
	Brownies made with King Arthur will be slightly starchy and dry; brownies made with Betty Crocker will slightly dry and spongy.	
BAKING POWDER	Not all brands of baking powder are gluten-free; see page 24 for more information.	
XANTHAN GUM	Xanthan is crucial to the structure of the brownies; see page 21 for more information.	
RESTING TIME	Do not shortchange the batter's 30-minute rest; if you do, the brownies will taste gritty.	

Chewy, chocolaty brownies should be simple and satisfying, but too often the gluten-free versions are dense and remarkably low on chocolate flavor. For simple old-fashioned brownies without a lot of fuss, we used plenty of Dutch-processed cocoa powder for the chocolate flavor and ditched the bar chocolate. We didn't miss the flavor of the bar chocolate and loved the ease of not having to prep it. To bring out the best flavor from the cocoa, we found it important to bloom it with melted butter and oil in the microwave. The real key to our success with this simple brownie, however, was discovering the perfect ratio of oil to butter. We worked to get the right balance of saturated fat (butter) and unsaturated fat (oil) for maximum chew and found that equal parts worked best. We then added an egg yolk in addition to two whole eggs, whose emulsifiers prevented fat from separating and leaking out during baking. A little milk gave the brownies the right amount of moisture, while adding a rest allowed the milk to hydrate the gluten-free flours, eliminating grittiness. A modest amount of all-purpose gluten-free flour blend, plus baking powder and xanthan gum, gave the brownies a structure that was partway between fudgy and chewy. Nailing the baking time was essential—too little time in the oven and the brownies were gummy and underbaked; too much time and they were dry. Thirty minutes in the oven provided the right balance. A tablespoon of vanilla rounded out the flavor of this quick and easy brownie. See page 405 for details on how to make a foil sling.

Lunchbox Brownies

MAKES 16 BARS

7½ ounces (1⅔ cups) ATK All-Purpose Gluten-Free Flour Blend (page 7)
½ teaspoon baking powder
½ teaspoon xanthan gum
½ teaspoon salt
2 ounces (⅔ cup) Dutch-processed cocoa powder

4 tablespoons unsalted butter, cut into 4 pieces
¼ cup vegetable oil
10½ ounces (1½ cups) sugar
2 large eggs plus 1 large yolk
3 tablespoons milk
1 tablespoon vanilla extract

1. Make foil sling for 8-inch square baking pan by folding 2 long sheets of aluminum foil so each is 8 inches wide. Lay sheets of foil in pan perpendicular to each other, with extra foil hanging over edges. Push foil into corners and up sides of pan, smoothing foil flush to pan; spray with vegetable oil spray.

2. Whisk flour blend, baking powder, xanthan gum, and salt together in bowl. In large bowl, microwave cocoa, butter, and oil at 50 percent power until butter has melted and cocoa has dissolved, about 1 minute; let cool slightly. Whisk in sugar, eggs and yolk, milk, and vanilla until very smooth. Stir in flour mixture with silicone spatula until flour is completely incorporated and dough is homogeneous, about 1 minute. Cover bowl with plastic wrap and let dough rest for 30 minutes.

3. Adjust oven rack to middle position and heat oven to 325 degrees. Scrape batter into prepared pan and smooth top with spatula. Bake until toothpick inserted in center comes out with few moist crumbs attached, 30 to 35 minutes, rotating pan halfway through baking.

4. Let brownies cool completely in pan, about 2 hours. Using foil sling, remove brownies from pan. Cut into squares and serve. (Brownies can be stored in airtight container at room temperature for up to 2 days.)

VARIATION
Dairy-Free Lunchbox Brownies
We prefer the flavor and texture of these brownies made with almond milk, but soy milk will also work; do not use rice milk.

Omit salt. Substitute Earth Balance Vegan Buttery Sticks for butter, and unsweetened almond milk for milk. Increase baking time to 35 to 40 minutes.

Blondies

G-F TESTING LAB

FLOUR SUBSTITUTION	King Arthur Gluten-Free Multi-Purpose Flour 8 ounces = **¾ cup plus ⅔ cup**	Betty Crocker All-Purpose Gluten Free Rice Blend 8 ounces = **1½ cups plus 2 tablespoons**
	Blondies made with King Arthur will taste a bit starchy and have very crisp edges; blondies made with Betty Crocker will be a bit dry and crumbly.	
CHOCOLATE	Not all brands of chocolate are processed in a gluten-free facility; read the label.	
BAKING POWDER	Not all brands of baking powder are gluten-free; see page 24 for more information.	
XANTHAN GUM	Xanthan is crucial to the structure of the blondies; see page 21 for more information.	

WHY THIS RECIPE WORKS

Chewy but crisp around the edges, blondies are simply butterscotch-flavored brownies that rely on brown sugar and butter to give them their signature flavor. We began our testing by swapping in our all-purpose gluten-free flour blend in our traditional blondie recipe. It was no surprise that these blondies had problems: They were flat, sandy, and greasy. To start, we scaled way back on the butter, from 12 tablespoons to 7 tablespoons, to eliminate the greasiness. The reduced amount of butter also lightened the batter so that the blondies now had a nice rise. Next we tested mixing methods and found that the key to getting that hallmark blondie "chew" was to use melted butter, rather than creaming the butter with sugar. To fix the sandiness, we added a couple tablespoons of milk, which helped to hydrate and soften the flours. For sweetening, we used a combination of light brown sugar (for its toffee-like flavor) and granulated sugar (for structure). To further enhance the flavor we used a substantial amount of vanilla extract (4 teaspoons), and a little salt to sharpen the sweetness. To add texture and flavor to the bars, we included both semisweet and white chocolate chips. The blondies required a longer than usual baking time to dry them out or else they tasted mushy. See page 405 for details on how to make a foil sling.

Blondies

MAKES 16 BARS

- 8 ounces (1¾ cups) ATK All-Purpose Gluten-Free Flour Blend (page 7)
- ¾ teaspoon salt
- ½ teaspoon baking powder
- ½ teaspoon xanthan gum
- 7 tablespoons unsalted butter, melted and cooled
- 7 ounces (1 cup packed) light brown sugar
- 3½ ounces (½ cup) granulated sugar
- 2 large eggs
- 2 tablespoons milk
- 4 teaspoons vanilla extract
- ½ cup white chocolate chips
- ½ cup semisweet chocolate chips

1. Adjust oven rack to middle position and heat oven to 325 degrees. Make foil sling for 8-inch square baking pan by folding 2 long sheets of aluminum foil so each is 8 inches wide. Lay sheets of foil in pan perpendicular to each other, with extra foil hanging over edges. Push foil into corners and up sides of pan, smoothing foil flush to pan; spray with vegetable oil spray.

2. Whisk flour blend, salt, baking powder, and xanthan gum together in bowl. In large bowl, whisk melted butter, brown sugar, and granulated sugar until no lumps remain. Whisk in eggs, milk, and vanilla until very smooth. Stir in flour mixture with silicone spatula until flour is completely incorporated and batter is homogeneous, about 1 minute. Fold in white chocolate and semisweet chocolate chips. Scrape batter into prepared pan and smooth top with spatula.

3. Bake until deep golden brown and toothpick inserted in center comes out clean, 50 minutes to 1 hour, rotating pan halfway through baking.

4. Let blondies cool completely in pan, about 2 hours. Using foil sling, remove blondies from pan. Cut into squares and serve. (Blondies can be stored in airtight container at room temperature for up to 2 days.)

Lemon Bars

G-F TESTING LAB

FLOUR SUBSTITUTION	King Arthur Gluten-Free Multi-Purpose Flour 6 ounces = ¾ **cup plus** ⅓ **cup**	Bob's Red Mill GF All-Purpose Baking Flour 6 ounces = ⅔ **cup plus** ½ **cup**
	Bars made with King Arthur will be somewhat pasty; bars made with Bob's Red Mill will have a distinct bean flavor and be a bit more crumbly.	
XANTHAN GUM	Do not omit the xanthan gum; it is crucial to the structure of the bars. For more information, see page 21.	

WHY THIS RECIPE WORKS

For our gluten-free version of this classic, we started with the topping. Lemon juice plus zest ensured plenty of bright flavor, while butter and heavy cream added richness. This topping also needed some form of thickener so that it could set up and slice neatly. Some recipes rely on flour, but we found that eggs delivered better results. Seven yolks plus two whole eggs gave our topping a smooth, custard-like texture that set up just enough, and the lemon flavor was pure and clean. Next, we moved on to the base. We knew we wanted something similar to shortbread: a crisp, buttery crust that could support the topping yet slice neatly and easily. We'd just developed a simple shortbread crust using butter, sugar, our flour blend, and xanthan gum for our Raspberry Streusel Bars (page 416), and it worked perfectly here as well. To ensure that the base wouldn't become soggy, we prebaked it just as we had with our Raspberry Streusel Bars, then topped it with the custard and returned the pan to the oven. Letting the bars cool for the full 2 hours was key to ensuring the custard topping set up. See page 405 for details on how to make a foil sling.

Lemon Bars

MAKES 16 BARS

CRUST

- 6 ounces (1⅓ cups) ATK All-Purpose Gluten-Free Flour Blend (page 13)
- 2⅓ ounces (⅓ cup) granulated sugar
- ¼ teaspoon salt
- ¼ teaspoon xanthan gum
- 8 tablespoons unsalted butter, cut into ½-inch pieces and softened

LEMON FILLING

- 2 large eggs, plus 7 large yolks
- 7 ounces (1 cup) plus 2 tablespoons granulated sugar
- ¼ cup grated lemon zest plus ⅔ cup juice (4 lemons)
  Pinch salt

- 4 tablespoons unsalted butter, cut into 4 pieces
- 3 tablespoons heavy cream
  Confectioners' sugar

1. Adjust oven rack to middle position and heat oven to 350 degrees. Make foil sling for 8-inch square baking pan by folding 2 long sheets of aluminum foil so each is 8 inches wide. Lay sheets of foil in pan perpendicular to each other, with extra foil hanging over edges of pan. Push foil into corners and up sides of pan, smoothing foil flush to pan; spray with vegetable oil spray.

2. FOR THE CRUST: Using stand mixer fitted with paddle, mix flour blend, granulated sugar, salt, and xanthan gum on low speed until combined, about 5 seconds. Add butter, 1 piece at a time, and continue to mix until dough forms and pulls away from sides of bowl, 2 to 3 minutes. Distribute mixture evenly into prepared pan and press firmly into even layer using bottom of measuring cup. Bake crust until fragrant and beginning to brown, 25 to 30 minutes, rotating pan halfway through baking. Transfer to wire rack and let cool before adding filling, about 30 minutes (do not turn off oven).

3. FOR THE FILLING: Whisk eggs and yolks together in medium saucepan. Whisk in granulated sugar until combined, then whisk in lemon zest and juice, and salt. Add butter and cook over medium heat, stirring constantly, until mixture thickens slightly and registers 170 degrees, about 5 minutes. Strain mixture immediately into bowl and stir in cream.

4. Pour filling over cooled crust. Bake until filling is shiny and opaque and center jiggles slightly when shaken, 15 to 20 minutes, rotating pan halfway through baking.

5. Let bars cool completely in pan on wire rack, about 2 hours. Using foil overhang, lift bars out of pan, cut into squares, and dust with confectioners' sugar before serving. (Bars are best eaten on day they are baked, but they can be cooled and refrigerated for up to 2 days.)

Key Lime Bars

G-F TESTING LAB

FLOUR SUBSTITUTION	King Arthur Gluten-Free Multi-Purpose Flour 6 ounces = ¾ **cup plus** ⅓ **cup**	Betty Crocker All-Purpose Gluten Free Rice Blend 6 ounces = ⅔ **cup plus** ½ **cup**
	Lime bars made with King Arthur will taste somewhat pasty; lime bars made with Betty Crocker will have a softer, more delicate crust.	
XANTHAN GUM	Xanthan is crucial to the structure of the crust; see page 21 for more information.	

✓ WHY THIS RECIPE WORKS

We wanted to bring all the essence of Key lime pie to a Key lime bar, creating a bar that balanced a tart and creamy topping and a buttery rich base. For the base, we wanted something similar to shortbread: a crisp, buttery crust that could support the topping yet slice neatly and easily. We started with a classic shortbread recipe by mixing pieces of softened butter into our all-purpose gluten-free flour blend, along with sugar and salt, using a stand mixer to ensure a fine crumb. The flavor was exactly what we wanted, but without gluten this base couldn't support the topping. Adding just ¼ teaspoon of xanthan gum gave the crust the structure it needed to hold up and slice neatly without crumbling. As for the filling, it also had to be sturdy and sliceable. By adding cream cheese and an egg yolk to the usual sweetened condensed milk and lime juice and zest, we created a rich and firm filling. Letting the bars cool for a full 2 hours and then refrigerating them for an additional 2 hours were key to ensuring the custard topping set up. You can use either Key limes or regular limes here; Key limes have a delicate flavor, while regular limes have a stronger, more tart flavor. In order to yield ½ cup of juice, you'll need about 20 Key limes or four regular limes; do not substitute bottled lime juice. Be sure to zest the limes before juicing them. See page 405 for details on how to make a foil sling.

Key Lime Bars
MAKES 16 BARS

CRUST

6	ounces (1⅓ cups) ATK All-Purpose Gluten-Free Flour Blend (page 7)
2⅓	ounces (⅓ cup) sugar
¼	teaspoon salt
¼	teaspoon xanthan gum
8	tablespoons unsalted butter, cut into ½-inch pieces and softened
1–2	tablespoons water

FILLING

2	ounces cream cheese, softened
1	tablespoon grated lime zest plus ½ cup juice (4 limes)
	Pinch salt
1	(14-ounce) can sweetened condensed milk
1	large egg yolk
¾	cup sweetened shredded coconut, toasted (optional)

1. Adjust oven rack to middle position and heat oven to 350 degrees. Make foil sling for 8-inch square baking pan by folding 2 long sheets of aluminum foil so each is 8 inches wide. Lay sheets of foil in pan perpendicular to each other, with extra foil hanging over edges. Push foil into corners and up sides of pan, smoothing foil flush to pan; spray with vegetable oil spray.

2. FOR THE CRUST: Using stand mixer fitted with paddle, mix flour blend, sugar, salt, and xanthan gum on low speed until combined. Add butter, 1 piece at a time, and continue to mix until dough forms and pulls away from sides of bowl, 2 to 3 minutes. (Add 1 to 2 tablespoons of water as needed if dough appears dry.)

3. Transfer mixture to prepared pan and press firmly into even layer using bottom of measuring cup. Bake crust until fragrant and beginning to brown, 25 to 30 minutes, rotating pan halfway through baking. Let crust cool for about 30 minutes.

4. FOR THE FILLING: Stir cream cheese, lime zest, and salt together in bowl until well combined and no lumps remain. Whisk in condensed milk until well combined. Whisk in lime juice and egg yolk until very smooth. Pour filling evenly over cooled crust. Bake until bars are set and edges begin to pull away slightly from sides of pan, 15 to 20 minutes, rotating pan halfway through baking.

5. Let bars cool completely in pan, about 2 hours. Cover with foil and refrigerate bars until thoroughly chilled, about 2 hours. Using foil sling, remove bars from pan. Sprinkle with toasted coconut, if using. Cut into squares and serve. (Bars can be refrigerated for up to 2 days; crust will soften.)

Whole-Grain Pecan Bars

G-F TESTING LAB

FLOUR SUBSTITUTION   Do not substitute other whole-grain blends for the ATK Whole-Grain Gluten-Free Flour Blend; they will not work in this recipe.

✔ WHY THIS RECIPE WORKS

To create a gluten-free version of this classic with a buttery crust, gooey filling, and nutty topping, we began our testing by swapping in our whole-grain gluten-free flour blend in the test kitchen's pecan bar recipe. To no surprise, we ran into a couple of problems during our first round of testing. The bars were much too tough as well as sandy and greasy. We started by scaling back the amount of butter in the crust to eliminate the greasiness, because gluten-free flours don't absorb fat well. Still, we were left with a tough, crumbly crust that didn't stand up to the gooey filling. In the next round of testing we found that omitting the baking powder from the crust of our original pecan bar recipe gave us the more tender, cookie-like crust that we had been looking for. Baking powder is normally used in baked goods to provide rise; however, we were trying to get away from a cakelike texture in this particular crust. To fix the sandiness of the crust, we added 2 tablespoons of water to hydrate our flour blend. We also baked the crust before adding the filling so that it could set up and wouldn't turn soggy. Since the ratio of filling to crust is less in bars than in pie, our filling needed to be intensely flavored. To enhance the flavor and cut through the sweetness of these bars, we added a small amount of vanilla and ½ teaspoon of salt. See page 405 for details on how to make a foil sling.

Whole-Grain Pecan Bars

MAKES 16 BARS

CRUST

- 5 ounces (1 cup plus 2 tablespoons) ATK Whole-Grain Gluten-Free Flour Blend (page 9)
- 2⅓ ounces (⅓ cup packed) light brown sugar
- ¼ cup pecans, toasted and chopped coarse
- ½ teaspoon salt
- 4 tablespoons unsalted butter, cut into ¼-inch pieces and chilled
- 2 tablespoons water

FILLING

- 3½ ounces (½ cup packed) light brown sugar
- ⅓ cup light corn syrup
- 4 tablespoons unsalted butter, melted and cooled
- 2 teaspoons vanilla extract
- ½ teaspoon salt
- 1 large egg, lightly beaten
- 1¾ cups pecans, toasted and chopped coarse

1. Adjust oven rack to middle position and heat oven to 350 degrees. Make foil sling for 8-inch square baking pan by folding 2 long sheets of aluminum foil so each is 8 inches wide. Lay sheets of foil in pan perpendicular to each other, with extra foil hanging over edges. Push foil into corners and up sides of pan, smoothing foil flush to pan; spray with vegetable oil spray.

2. FOR THE CRUST: Pulse flour blend, sugar, pecans, and salt in food processor until mixture resembles coarse cornmeal, about 5 pulses. Sprinkle butter and water over top and pulse until mixture again resembles coarse cornmeal, about 8 pulses.

3. Transfer mixture to prepared pan and press firmly into even layer using bottom of measuring cup. Bake until beginning to brown, 20 to 24 minutes, rotating pan halfway through baking.

4. FOR THE FILLING: As soon as crust finishes baking, whisk sugar, corn syrup, melted butter, vanilla, and salt together in bowl until well combined. Whisk in egg until very smooth. Pour mixture over hot crust and sprinkle evenly with pecans. Bake until edges begin to bubble, 25 to 30 minutes.

5. Let bars cool completely in pan, about 2 hours. Using foil sling, remove bars from pan. Cut into squares and serve. (Bars can be stored in airtight container at room temperature for up to 2 days.)

VARIATION

Dairy-Free Whole-Grain Pecan Bars
Omit salt. Substitute Earth Balance Vegan Buttery Sticks for butter.

Raspberry Streusel Bars

G-F TESTING LAB

FLOUR SUBSTITUTION	King Arthur Gluten-Free Multi-Purpose Flour 6 ounces = ¾ **cup plus** ⅓ **cup**	Bob's Red Mill GF All-Purpose Baking Flour 6 ounces = ⅔ **cup plus** ½ **cup**
	Bars made with King Arthur will be somewhat pasty; bars made with Bob's Red Mill will have a bean flavor, be a bit more crumbly, and brown more quickly. If using Bob's Red Mill, you will need to reduce the baking time by a few minutes.	
OATS	Do not use quick oats; they have a dusty texture that doesn't work in this recipe. Make sure to buy old-fashioned rolled oats (see page 27).	
XANTHAN GUM	Do not omit the xanthan gum; it is crucial to the structure of the bars. For more information, see page 21.	

WHY THIS RECIPE WORKS

A raspberry streusel bar should have a sturdy, buttery shortbread-like base, a filling with bright raspberry flavor, and a rich streusel topping that lends texture and stays in place. For the base, we started with butter, our flour blend, and sugar (plus salt for a little flavor). By mixing pieces of softened butter into the dry ingredients using a stand mixer, we ensured the right fine crumb. The flavor was exactly what we wanted, but without gluten this base couldn't support the topping. Adding just ¼ teaspoon of xanthan gum gave the crust the structure it needed to hold up and slice neatly without crumbling. We also baked the crust before adding the fruit and streusel so that it could set up and wouldn't turn soggy from the moisture in the raspberry filling. For the streusel topping, we simply took a portion of our shortbread base mixture and added light brown sugar, pecans, and oats. The last component on our list was the fruit filling. Preserves seemed like a convenient option, but they lost a fair bit of flavor during the cooking process. Fresh berries alone, however, were too tart and loose. For a filling with just the right jammy consistency as well as bright flavor, a combination of preserves and fresh berries, plus a bit of lemon juice, did the trick. After baking the base, all we had to do was spread on the filling, crumble our streusel over the top, and return the pan to the oven for a short stint. See page 405 for details on how to make a foil sling.

Raspberry Streusel Bars

MAKES 16 BARS

6 ounces (1⅓ cups) ATK All-Purpose Gluten-Free Flour Blend (page 7)
2⅓ ounces (⅓ cup) granulated sugar
¼ teaspoon salt
¼ teaspoon xanthan gum
8 tablespoons unsalted butter, cut into ½-inch pieces and softened
2 tablespoons packed light brown sugar
⅓ cup pecans, chopped fine
¼ cup gluten-free old-fashioned rolled oats
6 ounces (½ cup) raspberry preserves
2½ ounces (½ cup) fresh raspberries
1½ teaspoons lemon juice

1. Adjust oven rack to middle position and heat oven to 375 degrees. Make foil sling for 8-inch square baking pan by folding 2 long sheets of aluminum foil so each is 8 inches wide. Lay sheets of foil in pan perpendicular to each other, with extra foil hanging over edges of pan. Push foil into corners and up sides of pan, smoothing foil flush to pan; spray with vegetable oil spray.

2. Using stand mixer fitted with paddle, mix flour blend, granulated sugar, salt, and xanthan gum on low speed until combined, about 5 seconds. Add butter, 1 piece at a time, and continue to mix until dough forms and pulls away from sides of bowl, 2 to 3 minutes.

3. Measure ½ cup dough into medium bowl and set aside. Distribute remaining dough evenly into prepared pan and press firmly into even layer using bottom of measuring cup. Bake until edges begin to brown, 14 to 18 minutes, rotating pan halfway through baking.

4. While crust is baking, add brown sugar, pecans, and oats to reserved dough; use your hands to mix until well incorporated. Pinch mixture with fingers to create hazelnut-size clumps; set streusel aside.

5. Combine preserves, raspberries, and lemon juice in small bowl and mash with fork until combined but some berry pieces remain.

6. Spread filling evenly over hot crust; sprinkle streusel topping evenly over filling (do not press streusel into filling). Return pan to oven and bake until topping is golden brown and filling is bubbling, 22 to 25 minutes. Let bars cool completely in pan on wire rack, 1 to 2 hours. Using foil overhang, lift bars out of pan, cut into squares, and serve. (Bars are best eaten on day they are baked, but they can be cooled and placed immediately in airtight container and stored at room temperature for up to 1 day; crust and streusel will soften.)

Ginger-Fig Streusel Bars

G-F TESTING LAB

FLOUR SUBSTITUTION	King Arthur Gluten-Free Multi-Purpose Flour 6 ounces = ¾ **cup plus ⅓ cup**	Betty Crocker All-Purpose Gluten Free Rice Blend 6 ounces = ⅔ **cup plus ½ cup**
	Fig bars made with King Arthur will taste slightly pasty; fig bars made with Betty Crocker will have a softer, more delicate crust.	
XANTHAN GUM	Xanthan is crucial to the structure of the crust; see page 21 for more information.	
OATS	Not all brands of old-fashioned rolled oats are gluten-free; read the label. Do not substitute quick oats; they will not work in this recipe.	

WHY THIS RECIPE WORKS

For a novel approach to a classic fig bar, we introduced the bright, slightly spicy flavor of ginger and a crisp streusel topping. A streusel bar should have a sturdy, buttery, shortbread-like base and a rich crumble topping that lends texture and stays in place. For the base, we started with butter, our all-purpose gluten-free flour blend, and sugar (plus salt for a little flavor). By mixing pieces of softened butter into the dry ingredients using a stand mixer, a method called reverse creaming, we developed the ideal delicate, short crumb. The buttery flavor was exactly what we wanted, but without gluten this base couldn't support the weight of a filling and topping. Adding just ¼ teaspoon of xanthan gum gave the crust the structure it needed to hold up and slice neatly without crumbling. We also baked the crust before adding the fruit and streusel so that it could set up and wouldn't turn soggy from the moisture in the fig filling. For the streusel topping, we simply took a portion of our shortbread base mixture and added light brown sugar, walnuts, and oats. The last component on our list was the fruit filling. Fig preserves or spread with the addition of lemon juice, lemon zest, and zippy crystallized ginger provided just the right jammy consistency as well as bright flavors we were seeking. After baking the base, all we had to do was spread on the filling, crumble our streusel over the top, and return the pan to the oven for a short stint. See page 405 for details on how to make a foil sling.

Ginger-Fig Streusel Bars

MAKES 16 BARS

- 6 **ounces (1⅓ cups) ATK All-Purpose Gluten-Free Flour Blend (page 7)**
- 2⅓ **ounces (⅓ cup) granulated sugar**
- ½ **teaspoon ground ginger**
- ¼ **teaspoon salt**
- ¼ **teaspoon xanthan gum**
- 8 **tablespoons unsalted butter, cut into ½-inch pieces and softened**
- 2 **tablespoons packed light brown sugar**
- ⅓ **cup walnuts, toasted and chopped fine**
- ¼ **cup old-fashioned rolled oats**
- 9 **ounces (¾ cup) fig preserves**
- 1 **tablespoon minced crystallized ginger**
- ½ **teaspoon grated lemon zest plus 2 teaspoons juice**

1. Adjust oven rack to middle position and heat oven to 375 degrees. Make foil sling for 8-inch square baking pan by folding 2 long sheets of aluminum foil so each is 8 inches wide. Lay sheets of foil in pan perpendicular to each other, with extra foil hanging over edges. Push foil into corners and up sides of pan, smoothing foil flush to pan; spray with vegetable oil spray.

2. Using stand mixer fitted with paddle, mix flour blend, granulated sugar, ground ginger, salt, and xanthan gum on low speed until combined, about 5 seconds. Add butter, 1 piece at a time, and beat until well combined, 2 to 3 minutes.

3. Measure ½ cup dough into medium bowl; set aside for topping. Press remaining mixture evenly into prepared pan using bottom of measuring cup. Bake crust until edges begin to brown, 14 to 18 minutes, rotating pan halfway through baking.

4. Meanwhile, mix brown sugar, walnuts, and oats into reserved dough until well incorporated. In separate bowl, combine preserves, crystallized ginger, and lemon zest and juice.

5. Spread fig preserve mixture evenly over hot crust, then sprinkle with hazelnut-size clumps of oat topping. Bake until topping is golden brown and filling is bubbling, 22 to 25 minutes.

6. Let bars cool completely in pan, 1 to 2 hours. Using foil sling, remove bars from pan. Cut into squares and serve. (Bars can be refrigerated for up to 2 days; crust and streusel will soften.)

Granola Bars

G-F TESTING LAB

OATS Do not use quick oats; they have a dusty texture that doesn't work in this recipe. Make sure to buy old-fashioned rolled oats (see page 27) that have been processed in a gluten-free facility.

WHY THIS RECIPE WORKS

Almost always too sugary and as dry as cardboard, most store-bought granola bars aren't worth the few bucks they cost, so we set out to make our own version of this naturally gluten-free treat. For plenty of flavor and texture, we started by adding sunflower seeds, pepitas, pecans, and coconut flakes to the usual oat base. For our sweetener (as well as some binding power), a combination of brown sugar and maple syrup provided a more complex flavor than granulated sugar alone, and they weren't as cloying as honey. To temper the sweetness further and also help create a crisp texture, we found that stirring in a surprising ingredient—extra-virgin olive oil—was the secret. The flavor and texture in our granola bars were great at this point, but they weren't holding together well enough. We didn't want to add any more sugar or syrup, so we had to consider more creative options. We eventually discovered that we could process some of the oats into a flour, then combine it with the oil and sugars to create a sticky paste that held our bars together. A little flake sea salt elevated the flavors of our bars to the next level. We discovered the granola mixture shattered if we waited until it was cool before cutting the bars. So we cut the bars, still in the pan, shortly after they came out of the oven. They fused back together a bit and required a second cut once cool, but this time they cut cleanly and neatly. You can add ¼ teaspoon table salt if you don't have flake sea salt. See page 405 for details on how to make a foil sling.

Granola Bars
MAKES 16 BARS

- ⅓ **cup maple syrup**
- 1¾ **ounces (¼ cup packed) light brown sugar**
- ¾ **teaspoon flake sea salt**
- ⅓ **cup extra-virgin olive oil**
- 6 **ounces (2 cups) gluten-free old-fashioned rolled oats**
- ½ **cup pecans, chopped fine**
- ½ **cup raw pepitas**
- ½ **cup raw sunflower seeds**
- ½ **cup unsweetened flaked coconut**

1. Adjust oven rack to middle position and heat oven to 300 degrees. Make foil sling for 13 by 9-inch baking pan by folding 2 long sheets of aluminum foil; first sheet should be 13 inches wide and second sheet should be 9 inches wide. Lay sheets of foil in pan perpendicular to each other, with extra foil hanging over edges of pan. Push foil into corners and up sides of pan, smoothing foil flush to pan; spray with vegetable oil spray.

2. Whisk maple syrup, sugar, and salt together in large bowl. Whisk in oil.

3. Process ½ cup oats in food processor until finely ground, 30 to 40 seconds. Transfer to bowl with maple syrup mixture and stir in remaining 1½ cups oats, pecans, pepitas, sunflower seeds, and coconut until all dry ingredients are thoroughly coated.

4. Transfer oat mixture to prepared pan and spread into thin, even layer. Generously spray large metal spatula with oil spray, then firmly compress oat mixture with spatula until very compact. Bake granola bars until deeply golden, about 45 minutes, rotating pan halfway through baking.

5. Let bars cool in pan on wire rack for 15 minutes, then cut, still in pan, into 16 bars. Let cool to room temperature, about 1 hour. Using foil overhang, lift bars out of pan and transfer to cutting board. Using sharp knife, carefully recut bars following original cuts. (Granola bars can be stored at room temperature in airtight container for up to 1 week.)

TEST KITCHEN TIP
Making Crunchy Granola Bars

To make thin, crisp bars, firmly pack the granola mixture in the pan before baking it.

Grease wide metal spatula with vegetable oil spray. Transfer granola bar mixture to prepared pan and press into compact, even layer using spatula.

Whole-Grain Graham Crackers

G-F TESTING LAB

FLOUR SUBSTITUTION	Do not substitute other whole-grain blends for the ATK Whole-Grain Gluten-Free Flour Blend; they will not work in this recipe.
BAKING POWDER	Not all brands of baking powder are gluten-free; see page 24 for more information.
XANTHAN GUM	Xanthan is crucial to the structure of the crackers; see page 21 for more information.
RESTING TIME	Do not shortchange the dough's 30-minute rest; if you do, the dough will be too soft to roll out and cut.

WHY THIS RECIPE WORKS

We wanted to create gluten-free graham crackers with the characteristic crunch, sweet layers, and nutty flavor of the original, but without using graham flour, which is not gluten-free. Using our whole-grain gluten-free flour blend seemed like a natural starting point because its molasses-like flavor and coarse texture are very similar to graham flour. To soften the whole-grain flour blend and prevent the cookies from tasting sandy, we added ¼ cup of milk and let the batter rest on the counter for 30 minutes to hydrate the flours. We also added a little xanthan gum to prevent the cookies from spreading during baking. For a nice rise without making the cookies puffy, a combination of baking powder and baking soda was key. Following the traditional method for making graham crackers, we incorporated 8 tablespoons of chilled butter into the dough, which helped us achieve the signature flaky, tender layers inside the cookie. To add additional depth of flavor, we stirred in a little cinnamon and a combination of sugar, molasses, and a full tablespoon of vanilla. Increasing the amount of sugar slightly, from ½ cup to ⅔ cup, gave us the crisp crunch that is the hallmark of a good graham cracker. Poking the dough with holes before baking helped keep the cookies flat, and scoring the dough made it easy to snap the cookies apart after they baked and cooled. Finally, we found it necessary to bake the cookies on a double sheet pan to prevent them from overbrowning.

Whole-Grain Graham Crackers
MAKES 32 COOKIES

- 12 ounces (2⅔ cups) ATK Whole-Grain Gluten-Free Flour Blend (page 9)
- 4⅔ ounces (⅔ cup) sugar
- 1 teaspoon baking powder
- ½ teaspoon baking soda
- ½ teaspoon salt
- ½ teaspoon xanthan gum
- ¼ teaspoon ground cinnamon
- 8 tablespoons unsalted butter, cut into ½-inch pieces and chilled
- ¼ cup milk
- 2 tablespoons molasses
- 1 tablespoon vanilla extract

1. Process flour blend, sugar, baking powder, baking soda, salt, xanthan gum, and cinnamon in food processor until combined, about 5 seconds. Add butter and process until mixture resembles coarse cornmeal, about 15 seconds. Add milk, molasses, and vanilla, and process until dough comes together, about 20 seconds.

2. Transfer dough to bowl, cover with plastic wrap, and let rest for at least 30 minutes. (Dough can be wrapped in plastic wrap and refrigerated for up to 2 days or frozen for up to 2 weeks. Let refrigerated dough soften at room temperature before rolling. Let frozen dough thaw for 12 hours in refrigerator, then soften at room temperature.)

3. Adjust oven rack to middle position and heat oven to 375 degrees. Set rimmed baking sheet in second baking sheet. Divide dough into 2 equal pieces. Roll 1 piece of dough into rough 17 by 10-inch rectangle (⅛ inch thick) between 2 large sheets of parchment paper. (Keep other dough piece refrigerated.)

4. Discard top sheet parchment. Using knife, trim dough into 14 by 8-inch rectangle. Score dough lightly into sixteen 3½ by 2-inch rectangles. Using tines of fork, prick each rectangle several times.

5. Slide parchment with dough onto prepared sheet. Bake until lightly browned on edges, 12 to 16 minutes, rotating sheet halfway through baking. Let cool on sheet for 5 minutes, then transfer to wire rack and let cool completely. Let baking sheets cool before repeating with remaining dough.

6. Break cookies apart along scored lines and serve. (Cookies can be stored in airtight container at room temperature for up to 3 days.)

VARIATION
Dairy-Free Whole-Grain Graham Crackers
Do not use rice milk.

Omit salt. Substitute Earth Balance Vegan Buttery Sticks for butter, and unsweetened almond or soy milk for milk.

FRUIT DESSERTS, PIES, AND TARTS

Pie Dough

FLOUR SUBSTITUTION	King Arthur Gluten-Free Multi-Purpose Flour 13 ounces (for double crust) = **2¼ cups plus 2 tablespoons** 6½ ounces (for single crust) = **⅔ cup plus ½ cup**	Betty Crocker All-Purpose Gluten Free Rice Blend 13 ounces (for double crust) = **2½ cups plus 2 tablespoons** 6½ ounces (for single crust) = **1⅓ cups**
	Pie dough made with King Arthur will be less sturdy.	
XANTHAN GUM	Xanthan gum is crucial to the structure of the pie dough; see page 21 for more information.	

WHY THIS RECIPE WORKS

Perfect pie dough has just the right balance of tenderness and structure. The former comes from fat, the latter from the long protein chains, called gluten, that form when flour mixes with water. Too little gluten and the dough won't stick together; too much and the crust turns tough. So presumably we would face mostly a structural issue with a gluten-free dough, since gluten-free flours are naturally low in protein. As our first step, we swapped in our gluten-free flour blend for the wheat flour in all the pie dough recipes the test kitchen has developed over the years. We produced workable doughs in every case, but an all-butter dough (which includes sour cream for tenderness) had the necessary richness to stand up to the starchiness of the gluten-free flour blend and was clearly the best starting point. Although we weren't surprised to find that the dough was still too soft and lacked structure, we were taken aback by how tough it was; on its own, the sour cream was not sufficient to tenderize a gluten-free dough. We solved the structural problem easily with the addition of a modest amount of xanthan gum, but flakiness and tenderness were still elusive. In an effort to further tenderize our dough, we tested ingredients that are known to tenderize: baking soda, lemon juice, and vinegar. Vinegar was the clear winner, producing a pie crust that was not only tender, but also light and flaky. This pie dough can be prepared in advance and refrigerated for two days; however, it is not sturdy enough to withstand freezing.

Double-Crust Pie Dough

MAKES ENOUGH FOR ONE 9-INCH DOUBLE-CRUST PIE

- 6   tablespoons ice water
- 3   tablespoons sour cream
- 1   tablespoon rice vinegar
- 13 ounces (2¾ cups plus 2 tablespoons) ATK All-Purpose Gluten-Free Flour Blend (page 7)
- 1   tablespoon sugar
- 1   teaspoon salt
- ½   teaspoon xanthan gum
- 16 tablespoons unsalted butter, cut into ¼-inch pieces and frozen for 10 to 15 minutes

1. Combine ice water, sour cream, and vinegar in bowl. Process flour blend, sugar, salt, and xanthan gum in food processor until combined, about 5 seconds. Scatter butter over top and pulse until crumbs look uniform and distinct pieces of butter are no longer visible, 20 to 30 pulses.

2. Pour half of sour cream mixture over flour mixture and pulse to incorporate, about 3 pulses. Add remaining sour cream mixture and pulse until dough comes together in large pieces around blade, about 20 pulses.

3. Divide dough into 2 equal pieces. Turn each piece of dough onto sheet of plastic wrap and flatten each into 5-inch disk. Wrap each piece tightly in plastic and refrigerate for at least 1 hour or up to 2 days. Before rolling out dough, let it sit on counter to soften slightly, about 30 minutes, before rolling. (Dough cannot be frozen.)

Single-Crust Pie Dough

MAKES ENOUGH FOR ONE 9-INCH SINGLE-CRUST PIE

- 3   tablespoons ice water
- 1½   tablespoons sour cream
- 1½   teaspoons rice vinegar
- 6½   ounces (¾ cup plus ⅔ cup) ATK All-Purpose Gluten-Free Flour Blend (page 7)
- 1½   teaspoons sugar
- ½   teaspoon salt
- ¼   teaspoon xanthan gum
- 8   tablespoons unsalted butter, cut into ¼-inch pieces and frozen for 10 to 15 minutes

1. Combine ice water, sour cream, and vinegar in bowl. Process flour blend, sugar, salt, and xanthan gum in food processor until combined, about 5 seconds. Scatter butter over top and pulse until crumbs look uniform and distinct pieces of butter are no longer visible, 20 to 30 pulses.

2. Pour sour cream mixture over flour mixture and pulse until dough comes together in large pieces around blade, about 20 pulses.

3. Turn dough onto sheet of plastic wrap and flatten into 5-inch disk. Wrap tightly in plastic and refrigerate for at least 1 hour or up to 2 days. Before rolling out dough, let it sit on counter to soften slightly, about 30 minutes, before rolling. (Dough cannot be frozen.)

TEST KITCHEN TIP **Making a Single-Crust Pie**

1. Roll dough into 12-inch circle between 2 large sheets of plastic wrap.

2. Remove top plastic and gently invert dough over 9-inch pie plate.

3. Working around circumference, ease dough into plate by gently lifting plastic wrap with 1 hand while pressing dough into plate bottom with other hand.

4. Remove plastic wrap. Trim excess dough with kitchen shears, leaving ½-inch overhang beyond lip of pie plate.

5. Tuck overhang underneath itself to form tidy, even edge that sits on lip of pie plate.

6. Using index finger of 1 hand and thumb and index finger of other hand, create fluted ridges perpendicular to edge of pie plate.

Pie Dough

Our low-protein gluten-free flour blend was an asset in some aspects of developing our pie dough recipe since less protein means less chance for turning out a tough dough that is hard to roll out. That said, we still needed to strike a balance between adding structure to our dough so it wouldn't crumble and creating the flaky layers that are the hallmark of great pie crust. Here is what we learned.

1. ADD XANTHAN GUM FOR STRUCTURE: In traditional pie dough, you do not want a lot of gluten development because it makes the dough tough, but you do need a little bit for structure. In contrast to all-purpose flour, gluten-free flour blends have less protein, and those proteins also form weaker bonds, resulting in pie dough that has a hard time holding together. The dough needed reinforcement to provide structure and elasticity. To prevent the pie crust from crumbling we added a small amount of xanthan gum, which acts similarly to gluten, and it helped bind the proteins, creating a sturdy network.

2. ADD SOUR CREAM FOR WORKABILITY: The test kitchen's all-butter pie dough includes sour cream for the tenderizing and workability that shortening traditionally adds. In our testing we explored alternatives to the sour cream to see if they would make a difference in any way. We tried adding cream cheese and yogurt. Cream cheese turned our crust tough and rubbery, while yogurt added a tang that tasters didn't like. Sour cream added richness that complemented the butter flavor while keeping the dough workable.

3. ADD VINEGAR FOR FLAKINESS AND TENDERNESS: In our quest for a flaky, tender gluten-free crust, we tested ingredients that are known to tenderize dough, namely baking soda, lemon juice, and vinegar. Baking soda produced a crust that was too crumbly and overly browned. Lemon juice and vinegar produced crusts that were indeed tender, but the crust made with vinegar was also light and flaky. Adding vinegar lowered the pH of the dough, which weakened the bonds just enough to produce a pie crust that was tender, with flaky layers.

4. ROLL BETWEEN SHEETS OF PLASTIC WRAP: Our gluten-free dough was a lot softer than regular pie dough, but we knew that using extra flour blend to roll it out would work against us; this additional flour would have no opportunity to hydrate, which meant, as we learned from our testing of muffins and other baked goods, that we'd end up with a gritty texture. Instead, we simply rolled out the dough between two sheets of plastic wrap to prevent sticking and allow for easy transfer to the pie plate.

Pumpkin Pie

G-F TESTING LAB

FLOUR SUBSTITUTION	See page 426 for information about using various brands of gluten-free flour in the pie dough.

Pumpkin pie filling is naturally gluten-free, so we weren't worried about changing it, but when we used our favorite recipe to bake one in a gluten-free pie crust, we found that the loose, liquid-y filling turned our once-flaky crust gummy and raw-tasting. We needed to start with a thicker filling that would not readily soak into the crust. Cooking the pumpkin mixture briefly on the stovetop drove off some of the moisture that had ruined the crust. As an added bonus, this stint on the stovetop also helped to bloom the spices and intensify their warmth, resulting in the most flavorful pumpkin pie filling we had ever tasted. Next, we made sure that both shell and filling were hot when we assembled the pie, so the custard could begin to firm up almost immediately rather than soaking into the pastry. Finally, we baked the pie quickly, in the lower half of the oven, exposing the bottom of the crust to more intense heat and thus keeping it crisp and flaky. We avoided curdling by taking the pie out of the oven as soon as the center thickened to the point where it no longer sloshed but instead wiggled like gelatin when the pie plate was gently shaken. Timing is important here, as the filling must be prepared while the crust bakes. Be sure to use pumpkin puree, not pumpkin pie filling. The pie may be served slightly warm, chilled, or at room temperature. This pie is best the day it is made.

Pumpkin Pie

SERVES 8

- 1 recipe Single-Crust Pie Dough (page 427)
- 1 (15-ounce) can pumpkin puree
- 7 ounces (1 cup packed) dark brown sugar
- 2 teaspoons ground ginger
- 2 teaspoons ground cinnamon
- 1 teaspoon ground nutmeg
- ½ teaspoon salt
- ¼ teaspoon ground cloves
- ⅔ cup heavy cream
- ⅔ cup whole milk
- 4 large eggs

1. Adjust oven racks to middle and lower positions and heat oven to 375 degrees. Roll dough into 12-inch circle between 2 large sheets of plastic wrap. Remove top plastic, gently invert dough over 9-inch pie plate, and ease dough into plate. Remove remaining plastic and trim dough ½ inch beyond lip of pie plate. Tuck overhanging dough under itself to be flush with edge of pie plate. Crimp dough evenly around edge using your fingers. Cover loosely with plastic and freeze until chilled, about 15 minutes.

2. Remove plastic wrap from chilled crust and bake crust on upper rack until light brown in color, 20 to 25 minutes, rotating pie plate halfway through baking. Transfer pie plate to wire rack. (Crust must still be warm when filling is added.) Increase oven temperature to 425 degrees.

3. While crust bakes, process pumpkin puree, sugar, ginger, cinnamon, nutmeg, salt, and cloves together in food processor until combined, about 1 minute. Transfer pumpkin mixture to medium saucepan (do not clean processor bowl) and bring to simmer over medium-high heat. Cook pumpkin mixture, stirring constantly, until thick and shiny, about 5 minutes. Whisk in cream and milk, return to simmer briefly, then remove from heat.

4. Process eggs in food processor until uniform, about 5 seconds. With machine running, slowly add about half of hot pumpkin mixture through feed tube. Stop machine, add remaining pumpkin, and continue processing mixture until uniform, about 30 seconds longer.

5. Immediately pour warm filling into warm pie crust. (If you have any extra filling, ladle it into pie after 5 minutes of baking, by which time filling will have settled.) Bake on lower rack until filling is puffed and lightly cracked around edges and center wiggles slightly when jiggled, about 25 minutes, rotating pie plate halfway through baking. Let pie cool on wire rack until filling has set, about 2 hours; serve slightly warm or at room temperature.

Pecan Pie

FLOUR SUBSTITUTION	See page 426 for information about using various brands of gluten-free flour in the prebaked pie shell.

WHY THIS RECIPE WORKS

Our favorite pecan pie filling starts on the stovetop over gentle heat to prevent curdling. Then we pour it into a warm partially baked pie crust and bake it in a low 275-degree oven. Jump-starting the cooking of the filling on the stovetop ensures even cooking, and assembling the pie while both the filling and crust are still hot helps the custard to begin firming up immediately, preventing it from soaking into the pastry. But when we tried this with our gluten-free crust, the crust's starches still absorbed moisture from the filling before having the chance to crisp. We found that this crust would need to be fully baked into a flaky shell before the filling could be added, so we baked the empty pie crust to the desired golden-brown color at 375 degrees. We then reduced the oven temperature to 275 degrees, poured the warm pecan filling into the warm crust, and returned the pie to the oven. The sweet, custardy filling still needed close to an hour to set, but we found that the crust didn't overbake at such a low temperature during this time. This pie is best served the day it is made.

Pecan Pie

SERVES 8

- 1 recipe Single-Crust Pie Dough (page 427)
- 6 tablespoons unsalted butter, cut into 6 pieces
- 7 ounces (1 cup packed) dark brown sugar
- ½ teaspoon salt
- 3 large eggs
- ¾ cup light corn syrup
- 1 tablespoon vanilla extract
- 8 ounces (2 cups) pecans, toasted and chopped fine

1. Roll dough into 12-inch circle between 2 large sheets of plastic wrap. Remove top plastic, gently invert dough over 9-inch pie plate, and ease dough into plate. Remove remaining plastic and trim dough ½ inch beyond lip of pie plate. Tuck overhanging dough under itself to be flush with edge of pie plate. Crimp dough evenly around edge using your fingers. Cover loosely with plastic and freeze until chilled, about 15 minutes.

2. Adjust oven rack to lower-middle position and heat oven to 375 degrees. Bake crust until crisp and golden, 25 to 35 minutes, rotating pie plate halfway through baking. Remove crust from oven and let cool slightly. Reduce oven temperature to 275 degrees.

3. Melt butter in heatproof bowl set in skillet of water maintained at just below simmer. Remove bowl from skillet and stir in sugar and salt until butter is absorbed. Whisk in eggs, then corn syrup and vanilla, until smooth. Return bowl to hot water and stir until mixture is shiny and hot to touch and registers 130 degrees. Off heat, stir in pecans.

4. Pour pecan mixture into slightly cooled pie crust and bake until filling looks set but yields like Jell-O when gently pressed with back of spoon, 50 minutes to 1 hour, rotating pie plate halfway through baking.

5. Let pie cool on wire rack until filling has set, about 2 hours. Serve slightly warm or at room temperature.

TEST KITCHEN TIP **Making Pecan Pie Filling**

Cook the butter, sugar, and egg mixture in a heatproof bowl set in a skillet of barely simmering water until the mixture is shiny and hot to the touch before adding the pecans.

Deep-Dish Apple Pie

G-F TESTING LAB

| **FLOUR SUBSTITUTION** | See page 426 for information about using various brands of gluten-free flour in the pie dough. |

WHY THIS RECIPE WORKS

The simplest recipes call for piling sliced apples, tossed with sugar and spices, between two layers of pie dough and baking. This method spelled disaster for our gluten-free pie crust, which absorbed juices shed by the apples. Precooking the apples prevented a flood of juices from ruining the crust. To guarantee a crisp bottom crust, we baked the pie in a metal pie plate on a preheated baking sheet. We like a mix of tart and sweet apples, such as Granny Smiths and Golden Delicious, but you can also use Empires or Cortlands (tart) and Fuji, Jonagolds, or Braeburns (sweet). It's not safe to place a glass (Pyrex) pie plate on a preheated baking sheet. If you must use a glass pie plate, do not preheat the baking sheet; your crust will not be as crisp. This pie is best served the day it is made.

Deep-Dish Apple Pie

SERVES 8

- 2½ pounds Granny Smith apples, peeled, cored, and sliced ¼ inch thick
- 2½ pounds Golden Delicious apples, peeled, cored, and sliced ¼ inch thick
- 3½ ounces (½ cup) plus 1 teaspoon granulated sugar
- 1¾ ounces (¼ cup packed) light brown sugar
- ½ teaspoon grated lemon zest plus 1 tablespoon juice
- ¼ teaspoon salt
- ⅛ teaspoon ground cinnamon
- 1 recipe Double-Crust Pie Dough (page 427)
- 1 large egg white, lightly beaten

1. Toss apples, ½ cup granulated sugar, brown sugar, lemon zest, salt, and cinnamon together in Dutch oven. Cover and cook over medium heat, stirring often, until apples are tender when poked with fork but still hold their shape, 15 to 20 minutes. (Apples and juices should gently simmer during cooking.) Transfer apples and juices to rimmed baking sheet and let cool to room temperature, about 30 minutes. Drain apples thoroughly in colander.

2. Adjust oven rack to lowest position, place foil-lined rimmed baking sheet on rack, and heat oven to 425 degrees. Roll 1 disk of dough into 12-inch circle between 2 large sheets of plastic wrap. Remove top plastic, gently invert dough over 9-inch metal pie plate, and ease dough into plate; remove remaining plastic. Roll other disk of dough into 12-inch circle between 2 large sheets of plastic; remove top plastic.

3. Spread apples into dough-lined pie plate, mounding slightly in middle, and drizzle with lemon juice. Gently invert top crust over filling and remove plastic. Trim dough ½ inch beyond lip of pie plate, pinch dough edges together, and tuck under itself to be flush with edge of pie plate. Crimp dough evenly around edge using your fingers. Cut four 2-inch slits in top crust. Brush pie with egg white and sprinkle with remaining teaspoon sugar.

4. Place pie on preheated baking sheet and bake until crust is dark golden brown, 45 to 55 minutes, rotating sheet halfway through baking. Let pie cool on wire rack to room temperature, about 2 hours; serve slightly warm or at room temperature.

TEST KITCHEN TIP
Topping a Double-Crust Pie

1. Invert top crust over filling and remove plastic; trim excess dough with shears, leaving ½-inch overhang to line up with bottom dough.

2. Pinch top and bottom layers of dough together and fold dough under itself so that edge of fold is flush with outer rim of pie plate.

Dutch Apple Pie

G-F TESTING LAB

FLOUR SUBSTITUTION	King Arthur Gluten-Free Multi-Purpose Flour 4½ ounces = ½ **cup plus ⅓ cup**	Betty Crocker All-Purpose Gluten Free Rice Blend 4½ ounces = ¾ **cup plus 2 tablespoons**
	See page 426 for information about using various brands of gluten-free flour in the prebaked pie shell. Topping made with King Arthur will melt together; topping made with Betty Crocker taste slightly pasty.	
RESTING TIME	Do not shortchange the topping's 30-minute rest; if you do, the topping will be gritty.	

WHY THIS RECIPE WORKS

A Dutch apple pie is known for its rich, cream-thickened filling and sweet streusel topping. For the filling, we followed the procedure for our classic Deep-Dish Apple Pie (page 434). We combined the apples and cream mixture, chilled them (so they wouldn't melt the streusel topping), loaded them into our gluten-free prebaked pie crust, and topped the filling with a basic streusel dough we'd developed for our New York–Style Crumb Cake (page 90). The steam released from the apples turned the topping dense and soggy so we cranked up the oven temperature to 425 degrees, which helped the topping set up before it could absorb excess moisture.

Dutch Apple Pie

SERVES 8

PIE

1	recipe Double-Crust Pie Dough (page 427)
2	tablespoons unsalted butter
2½	pounds Granny Smith apples, peeled, quartered, cored, and sliced crosswise into ¼-inch-thick pieces
2	pounds McIntosh apples, peeled, quartered, cored, and sliced crosswise into ¼-inch-thick pieces
1¾	ounces (¼ cup) granulated sugar
½	teaspoon ground cinnamon
⅛	teaspoon salt
¾	cup golden raisins
½	cup heavy cream

TOPPING

4	tablespoons unsalted butter, melted and still warm
1¾	ounces (¼ cup) granulated sugar
1¾	ounces (¼ cup packed) light brown sugar
1	large egg yolk
2	teaspoons water
½	teaspoon ground cinnamon
	Pinch salt
4½	ounces (1 cup) ATK All-Purpose Gluten-Free Flour Blend (page 7)

1. FOR THE PIE: Roll dough into 12-inch circle between 2 large sheets of plastic wrap. Remove top plastic, gently invert dough over 9-inch pie plate, and ease dough into plate. Remove remaining plastic and trim dough ½ inch beyond lip of pie plate. Tuck overhanging dough under itself to be flush with edge of pie plate. Crimp dough evenly around edge using your fingers. Cover loosely with plastic and freeze until chilled, about 15 minutes.

2. Adjust oven rack to lower-middle position and heat oven to 375 degrees. Bake crust until crisp and golden, 25 to 35 minutes, rotating pie plate halfway through baking. Remove crust from oven and let cool slightly. (Crust can be held at room temperature for up to 1 day before filling.)

3. Melt butter in Dutch oven over medium heat. Stir in apples, sugar, cinnamon, and salt, cover, and cook, stirring occasionally, until apples are softened, 5 to 7 minutes. Add raisins and cook, covered, until some apples have begun to break down, 5 to 7 minutes; transfer to large bowl.

4. Set large colander over now-empty Dutch oven. Transfer cooked apples to colander, let drain for 2 to 3 minutes; return apples to bowl. Stir cream into pot and boil over high heat, stirring occasionally, until thickened and wooden spoon leaves trail in mixture, about 5 minutes. Pour cream mixture over apples and gently combine. Spread apples onto rimmed baking sheet and refrigerate until cold, about 30 minutes.

5. FOR THE TOPPING: While apples cool, whisk melted butter, granulated sugar, brown sugar, egg yolk, water, cinnamon, and salt in bowl to combine. Stir in flour blend with silicone spatula until cohesive dough forms. Cover and let topping rest at room temperature for at least 30 minutes.

6. Adjust oven rack to middle position and heat oven to 425 degrees. Transfer apple mixture to slightly cooled pie shell and press into even layer. Pinch topping into ¼- to ½-inch pieces and sprinkle over top. Place pie on aluminum foil–lined rimmed baking sheet and bake until topping is golden and crisp, 25 to 30 minutes, rotating sheet halfway through baking.

7. Let pie cool on wire rack to room temperature, 2 to 3 hours. Serve.

Blueberry Pie

FLOUR SUBSTITUTION	See page 426 for information about using various brands of gluten-free flour in the pie dough.
TAPIOCA STARCH	Tapioca starch is often labeled tapioca flour. See page 25 for more details on this ingredient. If you do not have tapioca starch, you can substitute instant tapioca or pearl tapioca in the filling; you will need to grind the tapioca to a powder in a spice grinder or mini food processor. If using pearl tapioca, reduce the amount to 5 teaspoons.

✓ WHY THIS RECIPE WORKS

We wanted a pie that had a firm, juicy filling full of fresh blueberry flavor with still plump berries, and we also wanted a crisp, flaky crust. To thicken the pie, we tried cornstarch as well as our gluten-free flour blend but preferred tapioca starch, which was subtle enough to allow the berry flavor to shine through. Too much of it, though, created a congealed mess. Cooking some of the blueberries down to a saucy consistency helped us reduce the amount of tapioca required, as did adding a peeled Granny Smith apple that we shredded on the large holes of a box grater. Rich in pectin, the apple helped thicken the berries naturally. Since gluten-free pie crusts can easily turn soggy, we found that preheating a sheet pan in the oven and baking the pie on the lower rack helped keep the crust crisp. It's not safe to place a glass (Pyrex) pie plate on a preheated baking sheet. If you must use a glass pie plate, do not preheat the baking sheet; note, however, that your crust will not be as crisp. This pie is best served the day it is made.

Blueberry Pie

SERVES 8

30	ounces (6 cups) blueberries
1	Granny Smith apple, peeled, cored, and shredded
5¼	ounces (¾ cup) sugar
2	tablespoons tapioca starch
2	teaspoons grated lemon zest plus 2 teaspoons juice
	Pinch salt
1	recipe Double-Crust Pie Dough (page 427)
1	large egg white, lightly beaten

1. Cook 3 cups blueberries in medium saucepan over medium heat, mashing occasionally with potato masher to help release juices, until half of berries have broken down and mixture is thickened and measures 1½ cups, about 8 minutes. Let cool slightly.

2. Place shredded apple in clean dish towel and wring dry. Combine apple, cooked berry mixture, remaining 3 cups uncooked berries, sugar, tapioca starch, lemon zest and juice, and salt in large bowl.

3. Adjust oven rack to lowest position, place foil-lined rimmed baking sheet on rack, and heat oven to 425 degrees. Roll 1 disk of dough into 12-inch circle between 2 large sheets of plastic wrap. Remove top plastic, gently invert dough over 9-inch metal pie plate, and ease dough into plate; remove remaining plastic. Roll other disk of dough into 12-inch circle between 2 large sheets of plastic. Remove top plastic. Using 1¼-inch round cookie cutter, cut hole in center of dough, then cut out 6 more holes, about 1½ inches from hole in center, evenly spaced around center hole.

4. Spread blueberry mixture evenly into dough-lined pie plate. Gently invert top crust over filling and remove remaining plastic. Trim dough ½ inch beyond lip of pie plate, pinch dough edges together, and tuck under itself to be flush with edge of pie plate. Crimp dough evenly around edge using your fingers. Brush pie with egg white.

5. Place pie on preheated baking sheet and bake until crust is light golden brown, about 25 minutes. Reduce oven temperature to 350 degrees, rotate baking sheet, and continue to bake until juices are bubbling and crust is deep golden brown, 30 to 40 minutes longer. Let pie cool on wire rack to room temperature, about 4 hours. Serve.

TEST KITCHEN TIP **A Pretty Top Crust**

An easy way to make a pretty double-crust blueberry pie is to precut holes in the crust before placing it on the pie. These holes also help with evaporation during baking.

Using 1¼-inch round cookie cutter, cut round from center of dough. Cut another 6 rounds from dough, 1½ inches from edge of center hole and equally spaced around center hole.

Fresh Strawberry Pie

FLOUR SUBSTITUTION	See page 426 for information about using various brands of gluten-free flour in the pie dough.

WHY THIS RECIPE WORKS

To make the glazy filling that would hold our ripe berries in place, we first simmered pureed strawberries with sugar and cornstarch. We tossed this thickened puree with whole, fresh berries and piled them into a baked pie crust, but after a short time the filling became a gloppy mess atop a soggy crust. Increasing the amount of cornstarch dulled the fresh strawberry flavor. Gelatin produced a bouncy filling, while arrowroot and tapioca produced overly thin fillings. Next, we tried tossing the berries with jarred strawberry jam. This offered a reasonably thick texture, but the sweetness was cloying. The solution: make our own "jam" from fresh berries, sugar, and pectin so that we could control the sweetness. This version was better, but pectin alone was still too firm. We remembered the looser texture of our original cornstarch test and decided to combine the two. This method produced just the right supple, lightly clingy glaze that coated the strawberries without sogging out the crust. To account for any imperfect strawberries, the ingredient list calls for more berries than you will need. Make sure the strawberries are at room temperature and dried well so the glaze will adhere properly. For the fruit pectin, we recommend both Sure-Jell for Less or No Sugar Needed Recipes and Ball RealFruit Low or No-Sugar Needed Pectin. The pie is at its best after 2 or 3 hours of chilling; the glaze becomes softer and wetter as it continues to chill, and the crust will become soggy if the pie is refrigerated for more than 5 hours. Serve with whipped cream.

Fresh Strawberry Pie
SERVES 8

- 1   recipe Single-Crust Pie Dough (page 427)
- 3   pounds strawberries, hulled (9 cups)
- 5¼ ounces (¾ cup) sugar
- 2   tablespoons cornstarch
- 1½ teaspoons low-sugar or no-sugar-needed fruit pectin
-     Pinch salt
- 1   tablespoon lemon juice

1. Roll dough into 12-inch circle between 2 large sheets of plastic wrap. Remove top plastic, gently invert dough over 9-inch pie plate, and ease dough into plate. Remove remaining plastic and trim dough ½ inch beyond lip of pie plate. Tuck overhanging dough under itself to be flush with edge of pie plate. Crimp dough evenly around edge using your fingers. Cover loosely with plastic and freeze until chilled, about 15 minutes.

2. Adjust oven rack to lower-middle position and heat oven to 375 degrees. Bake crust until crisp and golden, 25 to 35 minutes, rotating pie plate halfway through baking. Remove crust from oven and let cool completely. (Crust can be held at room temperature for up to 1 day before filling.)

3. Select 6 ounces misshapen, underripe, or otherwise unattractive berries, halving those that are large; you should have about 1½ cups. Process strawberries in food processor to smooth puree, 20 to 30 seconds, scraping down bowl as needed (you should have about ¾ cup puree).

4. Whisk sugar, cornstarch, pectin, and salt together in medium saucepan. Stir in berry puree, making sure to scrape corners of pan. Cook over medium-high heat, stirring constantly with heatproof silicone spatula, and bring to full boil. Boil, scraping bottom and sides of pan to prevent scorching, for 2 minutes to ensure that cornstarch is fully cooked (mixture will appear frothy when it first reaches boil, then will darken and thicken with further cooking). Transfer glaze to large bowl and stir in lemon juice. Let cool until slightly warm.

5. Meanwhile, pick over remaining strawberries and measure out 2 pounds of most attractive ones; halve or quarter any berries larger than 1½ inches. Add strawberries to bowl with glaze and fold in gently with silicone spatula until evenly coated. Scoop strawberry mixture into cooled pie crust, piling into mound. If any cut strawberry sides face up on top, turn them face down. If necessary, rearrange berries so that holes are filled and mound looks attractive. Refrigerate pie until chilled, about 2 hours. Serve.

Strawberry-Rhubarb Pie

G-F TESTING LAB

FLOUR SUBSTITUTION	See page 426 for information about using various brands of gluten-free flour in the pie dough.

WHY THIS RECIPE WORKS

Since the filling for this summery pie is naturally gluten-free, we started by following our traditional recipe but using our flaky double-crust gluten-free pie dough. But the top crust essentially melted into the filling and the vents collapsed, trapping so much steam and moisture that the top crust slid off to the side while the bottom crust sogged out. The starches in our gluten-free flour blend were the likely culprit because they absorb excess moisture so readily. Next we tried making a lattice top but it busted around the perimeter and collapsed into the juicy filling. Reducing the filling on the stovetop wasn't the answer either: The filling became sticky and jammy, and our crust was still soggy. So we considered an entirely new approach. We rolled out our top and bottom crusts and cut out numerous star cookies from the top crust. We parbaked the bottom crust, and fully baked the star cookies. Then we filled the parbaked crust and baked the pie topless. After taking the pie out of the oven, we shingled the baked stars over the top of the pie for a playful finishing touch. Don't let the second piece of pie dough sit on the counter for too long, or it will be too soft to work with. This pie is best served the day it is made.

Strawberry-Rhubarb Pie
SERVES 8

- 1¼ pounds rhubarb, sliced into ½-inch pieces (6 cups)
- 7 ounces (1 cup) plus 1 tablespoon sugar
- 1 pound strawberries, hulled and halved if smaller than 1 inch or quartered if larger than 1 inch (3 cups)
- 1 recipe Double-Crust Pie Dough (page 427)
- 1 large egg white, lightly beaten
- 3 tablespoons low-sugar or no-sugar-needed fruit pectin
- 2 teaspoons cornstarch
  Pinch salt

1. Toss rhubarb with ¾ cup sugar in bowl and microwave until sugar is mostly dissolved, 2½ minutes, stirring mixture halfway through. Stir in 1 cup strawberries and let sit at room temperature, stirring occasionally, for 1 hour.

2. Adjust oven racks to upper-middle and lower-middle positions and heat oven to 375 degrees. Roll 1 disk of dough into 12-inch circle between 2 large sheets of plastic wrap. Remove top plastic, gently invert dough over 9-inch pie plate, and ease dough into plate. Remove remaining plastic and trim dough ½ inch beyond lip of pie plate. Tuck overhanging dough under itself to be flush with edge of pie plate. Crimp dough evenly around edge using your fingers. Cover loosely with plastic and freeze until chilled, about 15 minutes.

3. Line baking sheet with parchment paper. Roll second disk of dough into 12-inch circle between 2 large sheets of plastic wrap. Remove top plastic. Using 3-inch star cookie cutter, cut 14 stars from dough and transfer to prepared baking sheet, spaced ½ inch apart. Brush cookies with egg white and sprinkle with 1 tablespoon sugar.

4. Bake star cookies on upper rack and chilled crust on lower rack until both are crisp and golden, 15 to 20 minutes for stars and 25 to 30 minutes for crust, rotating both halfway through baking. Remove both from oven and let cool slightly. Increase oven temperature to 425 degrees. (Cookies can be held at room temperature for up to 6 hours before turning stale.)

5. Drain rhubarb mixture through fine-mesh strainer into large saucepan, then return mixture to bowl. Add remaining 2 cups strawberries to saucepan and bring to simmer over medium-high heat. Reduce heat to medium-low and simmer until mixture measures 1½ cups, 15 to 25 minutes.

6. Combine remaining ¼ cup sugar, pectin, cornstarch, and salt in bowl, then stir into saucepan. Stir in rhubarb mixture and bring to boil over medium-high heat. Cook, stirring constantly, until filling is thickened and slightly darkened, about 2 minutes. Immediately pour filling into partially baked pie crust.

7. Place pie on aluminum foil–lined baking sheet and bake on lower rack until crust is deep golden brown and filling is bubbling, about 15 minutes, rotating sheet halfway through baking. Transfer pie to wire rack. Shingle star cookies attractively over filling and press gently to adhere. Let pie cool at room temperature until juices have thickened, 2 to 3 hours. Serve.

TEST KITCHEN TIP **Making Strawberry-Rhubarb Pie**

1. Microwave rhubarb and sugar until sugar dissolves, 2½ minutes. Stir in 1 cup of strawberries and let fruit sit for 1 hour to draw out liquid.

2. Using 3-inch star cookie cutter, cut 14 stars from dough. Transfer cookies to parchment-lined baking sheet, then brush with egg white and sprinkle with sugar.

3. Bake star cookies on upper rack and chilled crust on lower rack until both are golden, 15 to 20 minutes for stars and 25 to 30 minutes for crust.

4. After simmering drained rhubarb liquid and remaining strawberries together to thicken and reduce, add pectin–cornstarch mixture and drained rhubarb mixture and cook until thickened.

5. Pour filling immediately into pie crust and bake on foil-lined baking sheet until crust is deep golden brown and filling is bubbling, about 15 minutes.

6. Shingle star cookies attractively over filling and press gently to adhere. Let pie cool at room temperature until juices have thickened, 2 to 3 hours, before serving.

Chocolate Angel Pie

✓ WHY THIS RECIPE WORKS

Having devoted so much time and energy to developing gluten-free versions of our favorite pies and tarts, we were delighted to discover that a delicious classic, chocolate angel pie, is naturally gluten-free, meringue crust and all. The ideal chocolate angel pie should have a light, crisp meringue crust, a filling so chocolaty and satiny it could put a truffle to shame, and plenty of whipped cream to top it off. For an ultracrisp and sliceable meringue, we whipped egg whites with sugar, cornstarch, and vanilla, along with cream of tartar for stability. We baked the meringue at 275 degrees for 1½ hours and then dropped the temperature to 200 degrees for an additional hour in order to cook off excess moisture while preventing the sugars from burning into a dark, tacky meringue. To prevent the crust from sticking to the pan, we relied on a dose of cornstarch to coat the greased pie plate. Next, we needed to boost the chocolate flavor. By making a cooked custard with egg yolks to stabilize our creamy filling, we were able to load nearly a pound of chocolate into the filling. A delicate balance of 9 ounces milk chocolate and 5 ounces bittersweet chocolate lent depth and complexity. To finish, we slathered on lightly sweetened whipped cream and sprinkled a dusting of cocoa powder over the top. With the airy, crisp meringue serving as the perfect gluten-free crust, this heavenly pie is like chocolate sitting on a cloud. Serve the assembled pie within 3 hours of chilling.

Chocolate Angel Pie

SERVES 8 TO 10

FILLING

- 9 ounces milk chocolate, chopped fine
- 5 ounces bittersweet chocolate, chopped fine
- 3 large egg yolks (reserve egg whites for meringue)
- 1½ tablespoons granulated sugar
- ½ teaspoon salt
- ½ cup half-and-half
- 1¼ cups heavy cream, chilled

MERINGUE CRUST

- 1 tablespoon cornstarch, plus extra for pie plate
- 3½ ounces (½ cup) granulated sugar
- 3 large egg whites
- Pinch cream of tartar
- ½ teaspoon vanilla extract

TOPPING

- 1⅓ cups heavy cream, chilled
- 2 tablespoons confectioners' sugar
- Unsweetened cocoa powder

1. FOR THE FILLING: Microwave milk chocolate and bittersweet chocolate in large bowl at 50 percent power, stirring occasionally, until melted, 2 to 4 minutes. Meanwhile, whisk egg yolks, sugar, and salt together in medium bowl. Bring half-and-half to simmer in small saucepan over medium heat. Whisking constantly, slowly add hot half-and-half to egg yolk mixture in 2 additions until incorporated.

2. Return half-and-half mixture to now-empty saucepan and cook over low heat, whisking constantly, until thickened slightly, 30 seconds to 1 minute. Stir half-and-half mixture into melted chocolate until combined. Let cool slightly, about 8 minutes.

3. Using stand mixer fitted with whisk, whip cream on medium-low speed until foamy, about 1 minute. Increase speed to high and whip until soft peaks form, 1 to 3 minutes. Gently whisk one-third of whipped cream into cooled chocolate mixture. Fold in remaining whipped cream until no white streaks remain. Cover and refrigerate at least 3 hours or up to 24 hours.

4. FOR THE MERINGUE CRUST: Adjust oven rack to lower-middle position and heat oven to 275 degrees. Grease 9-inch pie plate and dust well with extra cornstarch, using pastry brush to distribute evenly. Combine sugar and 1 tablespoon cornstarch in bowl. Using stand mixer fitted with whisk, whip egg whites and cream of tartar on medium-low speed until foamy, about 1 minute. Increase speed to medium-high and whip whites to soft, billowy mounds, 1 to 3 minutes. Gradually

G-F TESTING LAB

CHOCOLATE AND COCOA	Not all brands of chocolate and cocoa are processed in a gluten-free facility; read the label.

add sugar mixture and whip until glossy, stiff peaks form, 3 to 5 minutes. Add vanilla to meringue and whip until incorporated.

5. Spread meringue into prepared pie plate, following contours of plate to cover bottom, sides, and edges. Bake for 1½ hours.

6. Rotate pie plate, reduce oven temperature to 200 degrees, and continue to bake until completely dried out, about 1 hour. (Shell will rise above rim of pie plate; some cracking is OK.) Let crust cool completely, about 30 minutes.

7. FOR THE TOPPING: Spread cooled chocolate filling into pie crust. Using stand mixer fitted with whisk, whip cream and sugar on medium-low speed until foamy, about 1 minute. Increase speed to high and whip until stiff peaks form, 1 to 3 minutes. Spread whipped cream evenly over chocolate. Refrigerate until filling is set, about 1 hour. Dust with cocoa before serving.

TEST KITCHEN TIP **Making Chocolate Angel Pie**

1. Cook half-and-half, egg yolks, sugar, and salt together to make custard, then stir custard into bowl of melted chocolate. Let filling cool slightly, about 8 minutes.

2. Whisk some of whipped cream into filling to lighten, then fold in remaining whipped cream until no streaks remain. Cover and refrigerate filling for 3 hours.

3. Using stand mixer fitted with whisk, make meringue by whipping egg whites, cream of tartar, sugar, cornstarch, and vanilla together until glossy, stiff peaks form.

4. Spread meringue into pie plate that has been greased and coated with cornstarch, following contours of plate to cover bottom, sides, and edges.

5. Bake meringue crust for 2½ hours, reducing oven temperature from 275 to 200 degrees after 1½ hours. Let crust cool completely before filling.

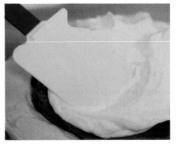

6. Spread cooled chocolate filling into pie crust, then top with whipped cream and refrigerate for 1 hour before serving.

Coconut Cream Pie

G-F TESTING LAB

FLOUR SUBSTITUTION	See page 426 for information about using various brands of gluten-free flour in the prebaked pie shell.

✔ WHY THIS RECIPE WORKS

A great coconut cream pie should be rich and creamy and full of deep, tropical coconut flavor. We tried using 2 cups of coconut milk as the base of our lush custard, simmering it until thickened on the stovetop. While it boasted a concentrated coconut flavor, it turned out fat-laden and unappealing. We substituted light coconut milk, but it was seriously lacking in flavor. Instead, a combination of coconut milk and whole milk gave us just the right silky custard. We still wanted a bit more coconut flavor, however. The solution was simple: adding unsweetened shredded coconut. We simmered it along with the milks to soften it so its texture wouldn't interrupt the smooth filling. Do not use low-fat coconut milk here because it doesn't have enough flavor. Also, don't confuse coconut milk with cream of coconut. The filling should be warm—neither piping hot nor room temperature—when poured into the pie crust.

Coconut Cream Pie

SERVES 8

PIE

1	recipe Single-Crust Pie Dough (page 427)
1	(13.5-ounce) can coconut milk
1	cup whole milk
4⅔	ounces (⅔ cup) sugar
1½	ounces (½ cup) unsweetened shredded coconut
¼	teaspoon salt
5	large egg yolks
¼	cup cornstarch
2	tablespoons unsalted butter, cut into 2 pieces
1½	teaspoons vanilla extract

TOPPING

1½	cups heavy cream, chilled
1½	tablespoons sugar
1½	teaspoons dark rum (optional)
½	teaspoon vanilla extract
1	tablespoon unsweetened shredded coconut, toasted

1. FOR THE PIE: Roll dough into 12-inch circle between 2 large sheets of plastic wrap. Remove top plastic, gently invert dough over 9-inch pie plate, and ease dough into plate. Remove remaining plastic and trim dough ½ inch beyond lip of pie plate. Tuck overhanging dough under itself to be flush with edge of pie plate. Crimp dough evenly around edge using your fingers. Cover loosely with plastic and freeze until chilled, about 15 minutes.

2. Adjust oven rack to lower-middle position and heat oven to 375 degrees. Bake crust until crisp and golden, 25 to 35 minutes, rotating pie plate halfway through baking. Remove crust from oven and let cool completely. (Crust can be held at room temperature for up to 1 day before filling.)

3. Bring coconut milk, whole milk, ⅓ cup sugar, shredded coconut, and salt to simmer in medium saucepan over medium-high heat, stirring occasionally.

4. As coconut milk mixture begins to simmer, whisk egg yolks, cornstarch, and remaining ⅓ cup sugar together in medium bowl until smooth. Slowly whisk 1 cup simmering coconut milk mixture into yolk mixture to temper, then slowly whisk tempered yolk mixture into saucepan. Reduce heat to medium and cook, whisking vigorously, until mixture is thickened and few bubbles burst on surface, about 30 seconds. Off heat, whisk in butter and vanilla. Let mixture cool, stirring often, until just warm, about 5 minutes.

5. Pour coconut filling into completely cooled pie shell. Lay sheet of plastic wrap directly on surface of filling to prevent skin from forming. Refrigerate pie until filling is chilled and set, at least 4 hours or up to 24 hours.

6. FOR THE TOPPING: Before serving, use stand mixer fitted with whisk to whip cream, sugar, rum, if using, and vanilla on medium-low speed until foamy, about 1 minute. Increase speed to high and whip until soft peaks form, 1 to 3 minutes. Spread whipped cream attractively over top of pie, sprinkle with shredded toasted coconut, and serve.

Lemon Meringue Pie

G-F TESTING LAB

FLOUR SUBSTITUTION	See page 426 for information about using various brands of gluten-free flour in the prebaked pie shell.

✓ WHY THIS RECIPE WORKS

A lemon meringue pie worthy of its name features a tart filling that is firm and a tall meringue. We wanted a meringue that didn't puddle on the bottom or "weep" on the top. We discovered that if the filling is piping hot when the meringue is applied, the underside of the meringue will not undercook; if the oven temperature is relatively low, the top of the meringue won't overcook. To further stabilize the meringue, we beat in a small amount of cornstarch. Make the pie crust, let it cool, and then work on the filling. As soon as the filling is made, cover it with plastic wrap to keep it hot and then start working on the meringue topping. You want to add hot filling to the cooled crust and then apply the meringue topping and quickly get the pie into the oven.

Lemon Meringue Pie

SERVES 8

PIE

1	recipe Single-Crust Pie Dough (page 427)
1½	cups water
7	ounces (1 cup) sugar
¼	cup cornstarch
⅛	teaspoon salt
6	large egg yolks
1	tablespoon grated lemon zest plus ½ cup juice (3 lemons)
2	tablespoons unsalted butter, cut into 2 pieces

MERINGUE

⅓	cup water
1	tablespoon cornstarch
4	large egg whites
½	teaspoon vanilla extract
¼	teaspoon cream of tartar
½	cup (3½ ounces) sugar

1. FOR THE PIE: Roll dough into 12-inch circle between 2 large sheets of plastic wrap. Remove top plastic, gently invert dough over 9-inch pie plate, and ease dough into plate. Remove remaining plastic and trim dough 1/2 inch beyond lip of pie plate. Tuck overhanging dough under itself to be flush with edge of pie plate. Crimp dough evenly around edge using your fingers. Cover loosely with plastic and freeze until chilled, about 15 minutes.

2. Adjust oven rack to lower-middle position and heat oven to 375 degrees. Bake crust until crisp and golden, 25 to 35 minutes, rotating pie plate halfway through baking. Remove crust from oven and let cool completely. (Crust can be held at room temperature for up to 1 day.)

3. Adjust oven rack to middle position and reduce oven temperature to 325 degrees. Bring water, sugar, cornstarch, and salt to simmer in large saucepan, whisking constantly. When mixture starts to turn translucent, whisk in egg yolks, 2 at a time. Whisk in lemon zest and juice and butter. Return mixture to brief simmer, then remove from heat. Lay sheet of plastic wrap directly on surface of filling to keep warm and prevent skin from forming.

4. FOR THE MERINGUE: Bring water and cornstarch to simmer in small saucepan and cook, whisking occasionally, until thickened and translucent, 1 to 2 minutes. Remove from heat and let cool slightly. Using stand mixer fitted with whisk, whip egg whites, vanilla, and cream of tartar on medium-low speed until foamy, about 1 minute. Increase speed to medium-high and beat in sugar, 1 tablespoon at a time, until incorporated and mixture forms soft, billowy mounds. Add cornstarch mixture, 1 tablespoon at a time, and continue to beat to glossy, stiff peaks, 2 to 3 minutes.

5. Meanwhile, remove plastic from filling and return to very low heat during last minute or so of beating meringue (to ensure filling is hot).

6. Pour lemon filling into slightly cooled pie crust. Using silicone spatula, immediately distribute meringue evenly around edge and then center of pie, attaching meringue to crust to prevent shrinking. Using back of spoon, create attractive swirls and peaks in meringue. Bake until meringue is light golden brown, about 20 minutes, rotating pie halfway through baking. Let pie cool on wire rack until filling has set, about 2 hours. Serve.

Whole-Grain Free-Form Pear Tart

FLOUR SUBSTITUTION	Do not substitute other whole-grain blends for the ATK Whole-Grain Gluten-Free Flour Blend; they will not work in this recipe.
XANTHAN GUM	Xanthan is crucial to the structure of the tart dough; see page 21 for more information.
PEARS	The pears should be ripe but firm, which means the flesh at the base of the stem should give slightly when gently pressed with a finger. The test kitchen prefers to use Bartlett pears in this recipe, but Bosc pears can also work. Be sure to let the pears drain for 20 minutes, or else the tart will be wet and may leak.

WHY THIS RECIPE WORKS

The problem with free-form tarts is making a dough sturdy enough to hold the fruit without leaking. We thought we would have a fighting chance using our whole-grain gluten-free flour blend because it is so high in protein. Our first step was to test our blend in tart recipes developed by the test kitchen. But most of the tarts suffered from filling that leached out of the crust and scorched in the oven. Structural issues aside, our favorite crust contained a bit of sour cream for tenderness. By increasing the amount of sour cream from ¼ cup to ¾ cup, we made a dough that was more tender and much closer in flavor to real tart dough. Adding a bit of xanthan gum made the dough even easier to handle and helped prevent cracking during shaping and folding. Our traditional recipes for free-form tarts call for chilling the dough after rolling, before filling and baking. But as we folded our chilled gluten-free dough, we could see cracking and tearing. By topping and shaping the more tender gluten-free crust without chilling, we were able to protect the integrity of our tart. As for the fruit, we microwaved our pears with half of the sugar to pull excess moisture out of the fruit so it wouldn't sog out the dough. This tart dough can be prepared in advance and refrigerated for two days or frozen for up to one month.

Whole-Grain Free-Form Pear Tart

MAKES ONE 9-INCH TART, SERVES 6

TART DOUGH

- ¾ cup sour cream
- 1 tablespoon ice water
- 1 teaspoon rice vinegar
- ½ teaspoon vanilla extract
- 7½ ounces (1⅔ cups) ATK Whole-Grain Gluten-Free Flour Blend (page 9)
- 2 tablespoons granulated sugar
- ¾ teaspoon xanthan gum
- ¾ teaspoon salt
- 8 tablespoons unsalted butter, cut into ½-inch pieces and frozen for 10 to 15 minutes

FILLING

- 3 pounds ripe but firm Bartlett or Bosc pears, peeled, halved lengthwise, cored, and each half cut lengthwise into 4 slices
- 3½ ounces (½ cup) granulated sugar
- ¼ cup dried cranberries, chopped coarse
- 1½ tablespoons lemon juice
- ¼ teaspoon ground cinnamon
  Pinch salt
- 1 egg white, lightly beaten
- 1 tablespoon turbinado sugar

1. FOR THE TART DOUGH: Whisk sour cream, ice water, vinegar, and vanilla together in bowl. Process flour blend, sugar, xanthan gum, and salt together in food processor until combined, about 5 seconds. Scatter butter over top and pulse until mixture resembles coarse cornmeal, about 10 pulses.

2. Pour half of sour cream mixture over flour mixture and pulse until incorporated, about 3 pulses. Pour remaining sour cream mixture over flour mixture and pulse until dough comes together, about 6 pulses.

3. Turn dough onto sheet of plastic wrap and flatten into 6-inch disk. Wrap dough tightly and refrigerate for at least 1 hour or up to 2 days. (Dough can also be frozen for up to 1 month; let thaw completely on counter before rolling out.)

4. FOR THE FILLING: Combine pears and ¼ cup granulated sugar in bowl, cover, and microwave, stirring occasionally, until pears are translucent and slightly pliable, 7 to 10 minutes. Transfer to colander and let pears drain for about 20 minutes.

5. Adjust oven rack to upper-middle position and heat oven to 350 degrees. Roll dough into 15-inch circle between 2 large sheets greased parchment paper. Slide onto baking sheet and remove top parchment. If necessary, trim parchment paper to fit sheet.

6. Gently combine cooled pears, remaining ¼ cup sugar, cranberries, lemon juice, cinnamon, and salt in bowl. Mound pear mixture in center of dough, leaving 3-inch border around edge. Using parchment to help, fold outer 3 inches dough over filling, pleating dough every 2 to 3 inches as needed. Brush tart crust with egg white and sprinkle with turbinado sugar.

7. Bake tart until dark brown and crust feels firm, 1 hour to 1 hour 10 minutes, rotating sheet halfway through baking. Let tart cool slightly on baking sheet, about 5 minutes. Slide onto wire rack using parchment, then use spatula to loosen tart from parchment and remove parchment. Let tart cool until juices have thickened, about 25 minutes. Serve warm or at room temperature.

TEST KITCHEN TIP **Making a Whole-Grain Free-Form Tart**

1. Make tart dough in food processor, then refrigerate for at least 1 hour before rolling out.

2. Microwave pears and ¼ cup granulated sugar until pears are translucent and slightly pliable, 7 to 10 minutes. Transfer to colander and let drain.

3. Roll dough into 15-inch circle between 2 large sheets of greased parchment paper. Slide onto baking sheet and remove top parchment.

4. Gently combine cooled pears, remaining ¼ cup granulated sugar, cranberries, lemon juice, cinnamon, and salt in bowl. Mound pear mixture in center of dough, leaving 3-inch border around edge.

5. Using parchment to help, fold outer 3 inches dough over filling, pleating dough every 2 to 3 inches as needed.

6. Brush tart crust with egg white and sprinkle with turbinado sugar.

Tart Shell

WHY THIS RECIPE WORKS

While pie crust is tender and flaky, classic tart crust should be fine-textured, buttery-rich, crisp, and crumbly—it is often described as being similar to shortbread. We began experimenting with our classic recipe (which combines flour, confectioners' sugar, an egg yolk, heavy cream, and a stick of butter), substituting our gluten-free flour blend for the all-purpose flour, but found the crust too sweet and fragile. Adding xanthan gum helped reinforce the structure, but our tart shell was still too crumbly and too sweet (since rice flours, unlike all-purpose flour, have a distinct sweetness). Our next step was to go down on sugar and test adding another egg, egg yolks, and more cream. But still the crust was sandy and overly sweet. Our traditional tart crust uses confectioners' sugar to make the crust more shortbreadlike, but since our working recipe was leaning too far in the shortbread direction, so much so that the crust was almost powdery, we decided to try granulated sugar. Unfortunately, the granulated sugar produced a hard, candied shell. In the end we found that reducing the amount of sugar and using a mix of confectioners' sugar and brown sugar did the trick. We also learned that we didn't need the cream at all—just a very small amount of water was all that was required to bind the dough together. Refer to pages 456–457 when making this recipe.

Tart Shell
MAKES ONE 9-INCH TART SHELL

- 1 **large egg yolk**
- ½ **teaspoon vanilla extract**
- 7 **ounces (1⅓ cups plus ¼ cup) ATK All-Purpose Gluten-Free Flour Blend (page 7)**
- 2⅓ **ounces (⅓ cup packed) light brown sugar**
- 1 **ounce (¼ cup) confectioners' sugar**
- 1 **teaspoon xanthan gum**
- ¼ **teaspoon salt**
- 8 **tablespoons unsalted butter, cut into ¼-inch pieces and chilled**
- 2 **teaspoons ice water**

1. Whisk egg yolk and vanilla together in bowl. Process flour blend, brown sugar, confectioners' sugar, xanthan gum, and salt together in food processor until combined, about 5 seconds. Scatter butter over top and pulse until mixture resembles coarse cornmeal, about 10 pulses.

2. With processor running, add egg yolk mixture and continue to process until dough just starts to come together around processor blade, about 15 seconds. Add 1 teaspoon ice water and pulse until dough comes together. If dough does not come together, add remaining 1 teaspoon ice water and pulse until dough comes together.

3. Turn dough onto sheet of plastic wrap and flatten into 6-inch disk. Wrap dough tightly in plastic and refrigerate for at least 1 hour or up to 2 days. (Dough can also be frozen for up to 2 months; let thaw completely on counter before rolling out.)

4. Let dough sit on counter to soften slightly, about 10 minutes. Spray 9-inch tart pan with removable bottom with vegetable oil spray. Roll dough into 12-inch circle between 2 large sheets plastic wrap. Slide it onto baking sheet and remove top plastic. Place tart pan upside down in center of dough. Holding tart pan and baking sheet firmly, flip over sheet pan, dough, and tart pan and set back on counter. Remove sheet pan and remaining plastic.

5. Run rolling pin over edges of tart pan to cut dough. Gently press dough into bottom of tart pan. Roll dough scraps into ½-inch rope. Line pan edge with rope and gently press into fluted sides. Line pan with plastic and, using measuring cup, gently smooth dough to even thickness. Trim away excess dough above rim of tart pan with paring knife. Cover loosely with plastic wrap and freeze until chilled and firm, about 15 minutes, before baking.

VARIATION
Dairy-Free Tart Shell
Omit salt and substitute Earth Balance Vegan Buttery Sticks for butter.

G-F TESTING LAB

FLOUR SUBSTITUTION	King Arthur Gluten-Free Multi-Purpose Flour 7 ounces = 1¼ **cups**	Betty Crocker All-Purpose Gluten Free Rice Blend We do not recommend using Betty Crocker in this recipe
	The tart shell made with King Arthur will be more crumbly and grainy; the tart shell made with Betty Crocker was too delicate and it crumbled apart during baking.	
XANTHAN GUM	Xanthan gum is crucial to the structure of the tart dough; see page 21 for more information.	

TEST KITCHEN TIP **Making a Tart Shell**

Because our gluten-free tart dough is softer than traditional dough, you need to roll it out between sheets of plastic wrap. We also discovered a supereasy method for getting this dough into the pan: We pressed the tart pan into the dough to cut it, and then inverted the baking sheet along with the tart pan so that the dough fell right into the pan. Make sure to chill the dough before starting this process. If at any point the dough becomes too soft to work with, slip the dough onto a baking sheet and refrigerate it until workable. Note that this dough needs to be lined with greased foil and weighted with pie weights before baking, or else it will puff up in the oven and the sides will shrink down.

1. Roll dough into 12-inch circle between 2 sheets of plastic wrap. Slide onto baking sheet, then carefully remove top sheet of plastic.

2. Place tart pan, bottom side up, in center of dough and press gently so that sharp edge of tart pan cuts dough.

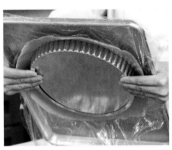

3. Holding tart pan in place, pick up baking sheet and carefully flip it over so that tart pan is right side up on counter. Remove baking sheet and peel off remaining plastic.

4. Run rolling pin over edges of tart pan to cut dough completely. Gently ease and press dough into bottom of pan, reserving scraps.

5. Roll dough scraps into ½-inch rope, line edge of tart pan with rope, and gently press into fluted sides.

6. Line tart pan with plastic wrap and, using measuring cup, gently press and smooth dough to even thickness (sides should be ¼ inch thick). Trim any excess dough with paring knife.

Apple Tart

G-F TESTING LAB

FLOUR SUBSTITUTION	See page 456 for information about using various brands of gluten-free flour in the tart shell.

✓ WHY THIS RECIPE WORKS

This stunning tart features a luxurious apple puree topped with a showstopping spiral fan of apple slices. We added butter and apricot preserves to our apple filling for a rich concentrated puree that reinforced the bright flavor of the fresh apples. Sautéing the apple slices briefly made them pliable for decorating. After baking, we brushed the tart with a quick glaze made by straining the apricot preserves we were already using in the filling. We briefly ran the tart under the broiler to get a burnished finish. You may have extra apple slices after arranging the apples in step 4. If you don't have a potato masher, you can puree the apples in a food processor. To ensure that the outer ring of the pan releases easily from the tart, avoid getting puree and glaze on the crust. The tart is best served the day it is made.

French Apple Tart

SERVES 8

- 1 recipe Tart Shell (page 455)
- ½ cup apricot preserves
- 10 Golden Delicious apples (8 ounces each), peeled and cored
- 3 tablespoons unsalted butter
- 1 tablespoon water
- ¼ teaspoon salt

1. Adjust oven rack to middle position and heat oven to 375 degrees. Set chilled tart pan on rimmed baking sheet. Press greased heavy-duty aluminum foil into tart shell, covering edges to prevent burning, and fill with 1 cup of pie weights. Bake until tart shell is just set, about 25 minutes, rotating sheet halfway through baking. Carefully remove weights and foil and continue to bake tart shell until lightly golden, about 10 minutes. Let tart shell cool completely in pan.

2. Microwave apricot preserves until fluid, about 30 seconds. Strain preserves through fine-mesh strainer into small bowl, reserving solids. Measure out and reserve 3 tablespoons strained preserves for brushing tart.

3. Cut 5 apples lengthwise into quarters, and cut each quarter lengthwise into 4 slices. Melt 1 tablespoon butter in 12-inch skillet over medium heat. Add apple slices and water and toss to combine. Cover and cook, stirring occasionally, until apples begin to turn translucent and are slightly pliable, 3 to 5 minutes. Spread apples out onto large plate and let cool. Do not clean skillet.

4. Cut remaining 5 apples into ½-inch-thick wedges. Melt remaining 2 tablespoons butter in now-empty skillet over medium heat. Add apple wedges, reserved apricot solids and strained apricot preserves, and salt. Cover and cook, stirring occasionally, until apples are very soft, about 10 minutes. Mash apples to puree with potato masher. Continue to cook, stirring occasionally, until puree is reduced to 2 cups, about 5 minutes.

5. Adjust 1 oven rack to lowest position and second rack 5 to 6 inches from broiler element, and heat oven to 375 degrees. Spread apple puree into cooled tart shell and smooth surface. Select 5 thinnest apple slices and set aside for center. Starting at outer edge of tart, arrange remaining slices, tightly overlapping, in concentric circles. Bend reserved slices to fit in center. Bake tart on baking sheet on lower rack for 30 minutes, rotating sheet halfway through baking.

6. Remove tart from oven and heat broiler. While broiler heats, warm reserved preserves in microwave until fluid, about 20 seconds, and brush evenly over apples, avoiding crust. Broil tart, checking every 30 seconds and turning as necessary, until apples are attractively caramelized, 1 to 3 minutes.

7. Transfer baking sheet with tart to wire rack and let cool to room temperature, about 1½ hours. Remove outer metal ring of tart pan, slide thin metal spatula between tart and pan bottom, and carefully slide tart onto serving platter. Cut into wedges and serve.

VARIATION

Dairy-Free French Apple Tart
Use Dairy-Free Tart Shell (page 457) and substitute Earth Balance Vegan Buttery Sticks for butter.

Rustic Walnut Tart

G-F TESTING LAB

FLOUR SUBSTITUTION	See page 456 for information about using various brands of gluten-free flour in the tart shell.

WHY THIS RECIPE WORKS

This rustic yet beautiful tart features our gluten-free tart shell and a simple nut filling made with corn syrup and brown sugar as its base. A hefty amount of vanilla and a hit of bourbon pair nicely with the walnuts. Parbaking the shell ensures that it will be crisp. We also found that it was necessary to line the dough with greased parchment and fill the pan with pie weights, as the shell otherwise puffed up during baking because of the sugar and egg in the dough. The crust also shrank away from the sides of the pan if it was not baked with pie weights. Once filled, the tart should be baked until the filling is just firm enough to slice neatly. Pecans can be substituted for the walnuts if desired. There's no need to toast the nuts before chopping them; the tart bakes long enough to bring out their full flavor. Serve with whipped cream.

Rustic Walnut Tart

SERVES 8 TO 10

1	recipe Tart Shell (page 455)
3½	ounces (½ cup packed) light brown sugar
⅓	cup light corn syrup
4	tablespoons unsalted butter, melted and cooled
1	tablespoon bourbon or dark rum
2	teaspoons vanilla extract
½	teaspoon salt
1	large egg
1¾	cups walnuts, chopped coarse

1. Adjust oven rack to middle position and heat oven to 375 degrees. Set chilled tart pan on rimmed baking sheet. Press greased heavy-duty aluminum foil into tart shell, covering edges to prevent burning, and fill with 1 cup of pie weights. Bake until tart shell is just set, about 15 minutes, rotating sheet halfway through baking. Carefully remove weights and foil and continue to bake tart shell until lightly golden, about 5 minutes. Transfer baking sheet with tart shell to wire rack and let cool while making filling. (Tart shell can be either slightly warm or completely cool when you add filling.)

2. Whisk sugar, corn syrup, melted butter, bourbon, vanilla, and salt together in large bowl until sugar dissolves. Whisk in egg until combined. Pour filling into tart shell and sprinkle evenly with walnuts. Bake tart on baking sheet until filling is set and walnuts begin to brown, 30 to 40 minutes, rotating sheet halfway through baking.

3. Transfer baking sheet with tart to wire rack and let cool to room temperature, about 2 hours. (Tart can be refrigerated for up to 1 day; bring to room temperature before serving.)

4. To serve, remove outer ring of tart pan, slide thin metal spatula between tart and tart pan bottom, and carefully slide tart onto serving platter or cutting board. Slice tart into wedges and serve.

TEST KITCHEN TIP **Prebaking Tart Dough**

Pie weights prevent the dough from melting out of shape or puffing up on the bottom as the tart shell bakes.

Set dough-lined tart pan on large baking sheet. Line with greased parchment paper or double layer of foil and fill shell with pie weights. (Pennies will work in a pinch.)

Nutella Tart

G-F TESTING LAB

| **FLOUR SUBSTITUTION** | See page 456 for information about using various brands of gluten-free flour in the tart shell. |

WHY THIS RECIPE WORKS

For an incredibly easy, incredibly irresistible dessert, we started with a flavor-packed base: Nutella. For a dense and velvety filling, we stirred Nutella into a simple ganache made of chocolate and cream. Nutella and cream alone made a filling that was too soft and didn't set up, but the addition of bittersweet chocolate helped the tart firm up, deepened the chocolate flavor, and tempered the sweetness level. Adding a little butter to the mixture proved important because it ensured that the tart was easy to slice once it was chilled. To cook the filling, we turned to the microwave. Using low power and stirring the mixture often were key; when the power was too high, the filling became grainy. A bottom layer of chopped toasted hazelnuts sprinkled over our fully baked gluten-free tart shell contributed more nutty flavor and a nice crunch. Garnishing this easy tart with whole toasted hazelnuts amped up the elegance factor. If the ganache mixture looks curdled when whisking, add boiling water, 1 tablespoon at a time, and whisk until smooth. Make sure to serve with a dollop of whipped cream to cut the richness of the tart.

Nutella Tart
SERVES 8 TO 10

1	cup hazelnuts
1	recipe Tart Shell (page 455)
1½	cups heavy cream
1¼	cups Nutella
2	ounces bittersweet chocolate, chopped fine
4	tablespoons unsalted butter, cut into 4 pieces

1. Adjust oven rack to middle position and heat oven to 375 degrees. Toast hazelnuts on rimmed baking sheet until skins begin to blister and crack, 15 to 20 minutes. Wrap warm nuts in dish towel and rub gently to remove skins. Reserve 24 whole nuts for garnish, then chop remaining nuts coarsely.

2. Adjust oven rack to middle position and heat oven to 375 degrees. Set chilled tart pan on rimmed baking sheet. Press greased heavy-duty aluminum foil into tart shell, covering edges to prevent burning, and fill with 1 cup of pie weights. Bake until tart shell is just set, about 25 minutes, rotating sheet halfway through baking. Carefully remove weights and foil and continue to bake tart shell until lightly golden, about 10 minutes. Let tart shell cool in pan. (Tart shell can be either slightly warm or completely cool when you add filling.)

3. Combine cream, Nutella, chocolate, and butter in bowl. Cover and microwave at 30 percent power, stirring often, until mixture is smooth and glossy, about 1 minute (do not overheat). Sprinkle chopped hazelnuts into prebaked tart shell. Pour warm Nutella mixture over nuts and smooth top. Refrigerate until filling is just set, about 15 minutes. Arrange reserved whole hazelnuts around edge of tart and continue to refrigerate until filling is firm, at least 1½ hours or up to 1 day.

4. To serve, remove outer ring of tart pan, slide thin metal spatula between tart and tart pan bottom, and carefully slide tart onto serving platter or cutting board. Slice tart into wedges and serve.

TEST KITCHEN TIP **Topping a Nutella Tart**

To ensure that the decorative hazelnuts do not sink to the bottom of the tart, you must first chill the filled tart.

Refrigerate until filling is just set, about 15 minutes. Arrange reserved whole hazelnuts around edge of tart and continue to refrigerate until filling is firm, about 1½ hours.

Lemon Tart

FLOUR SUBSTITUTION	See page 456 for information about using various brands of gluten-free flour in the tart shell.

✔ WHY THIS RECIPE WORKS

The filling for lemon tart, normally a simple stovetop lemon curd, is easy to make and naturally gluten-free, so with our gluten-free tart dough in hand, we thought this recipe would be an easy addition to our gluten-free dessert repertoire. Despite its simplicity, however, there is much that can go wrong with lemon tart: it can slip over the edge of sweet and become cloying; its tartness can grab at your throat; and it can be gluey or eggy or, even worse, metallic-tasting. For a balanced lemon curd with just enough sugar to offset the acidity of the lemons, we used 3 parts sugar to 2 parts lemon juice, plus a whopping ¼ cup of lemon zest for a bright, lemony flavor. To achieve a curd that was creamy and dense with a vibrant yellow color, we used a combination of whole eggs and egg yolks. A few pats of butter, whisked in as we cooked the curd over gentle heat, contributed more richness. For a smooth, light texture, we strained the curd, then stirred in heavy cream before pouring the filling into the prebaked tart shell and baking it until set. Once the lemon curd ingredients have been combined, cook the curd immediately; otherwise, it will have a grainy finished texture. The shell should still be warm when the filling is added. Dust with confectioners' sugar before serving, if desired. This tart is best served on the day it is made.

Lemon Tart

SERVES 8 TO 10

    1   recipe Tart Shell (page 455)
    2   large eggs plus 7 large yolks
    7   ounces (1 cup) sugar
    ¼   cup grated lemon zest plus ⅔ cup juice
        (4 lemons)
        Pinch salt
    4   tablespoons unsalted butter, cut into
        4 pieces
    3   tablespoons heavy cream

1. Adjust oven rack to middle position and heat oven to 375 degrees. Set chilled tart pan on rimmed baking sheet. Press greased heavy-duty aluminum foil into tart shell, covering edges to prevent burning, and fill with 1 cup of pie weights. Bake until tart shell is just set, about 25 minutes, rotating sheet halfway through baking. Carefully remove weights and foil and continue to bake tart shell until lightly golden, about 10 minutes. Transfer sheet to wire rack. (Tart shell must still be warm when filling is added.)

2. Whisk eggs and yolks together in medium saucepan. Whisk in sugar until combined, then whisk in lemon zest and juice and salt. Add butter and cook over medium-low heat, stirring constantly, until mixture thickens slightly and registers 170 degrees. Immediately pour mixture through fine-mesh strainer into bowl and stir in cream.

3. Pour warm lemon filling into warm tart shell. Bake tart on baking sheet until filling is shiny and opaque and center jiggles slightly when shaken, 10 to 15 minutes, rotating sheet halfway through baking. Transfer baking sheet with tart to wire rack and let cool to room temperature, about 2 hours.

4. To serve, remove outer ring of tart pan, slide thin metal spatula between tart and tart pan bottom, and carefully slide tart onto serving platter or cutting board. Slice tart into wedges and serve.

Baked Raspberry Tart

G-F TESTING LAB

FLOUR SUBSTITUTION You can substitute 2½ tablespoons of King Arthur Gluten-Free Multi-Purpose Flour or Betty Crocker All-Purpose Gluten Free Rice Blend; neither will affect the flavor or texture of the filling. See page 456 for information about using various brands of gluten-free flour in the tart shell.

✓ WHY THIS RECIPE WORKS

This rustic raspberry tart mixes fresh berries right into a buttery custard filling before baking. The heat of the oven gently brings together the crisp tart shell, custard, and tangy raspberries into a rich-tasting but simple and beautiful tart. We started by baking our gluten-free tart shell until it was lightly golden brown. We then arranged the raspberries in the base of the cooled shell before pouring our custard mixture on top. Our first attempt at the custard filling was a simple mixture of butter, egg, and sugar. We turned to cornstarch for its gluten-free thickening power. The resulting tart was starchy, coarse, and bland. After replacing the cornstarch with our all-purpose gluten-free flour blend, the custard had a smooth, silky texture. Browning the butter gave it a nice nutty flavor. We rounded out the profile of the filling with heavy cream for richness, a bit of lemon zest and juice for brightness, as well as a moderate amount of vanilla extract and framboise to reinforce the berry flavor. Do not substitute frozen raspberries here. This tart is best served the day it is made.

Baked Raspberry Tart

SERVES 8

1	recipe Tart Shell (page 455)
6	tablespoons unsalted butter, cut into 6 pieces
1	large egg, plus 1 large white
3½	ounces (½ cup) sugar
¼	teaspoon salt
1	teaspoon vanilla extract
1	teaspoon framboise or kirsch (optional)
¼	teaspoon grated lemon zest plus 1½ teaspoons juice
2½	tablespoons ATK All-Purpose Gluten-Free Flour Blend (page 7)
2	tablespoons heavy cream
10	ounces (2 cups) raspberries

1. Adjust oven rack to middle position and heat oven to 375 degrees. Set chilled tart pan on rimmed baking sheet. Press greased heavy-duty aluminum foil into tart shell, covering edges to prevent burning, and fill with 1 cup of pie weights. Bake until tart shell is just set, about 25 minutes, rotating sheet halfway through baking. Carefully remove weights and foil and continue to bake tart shell until lightly golden, about 10 minutes. Let tart shell cool completely in pan.

2. Melt butter in small saucepan over medium heat, stirring occasionally, until butter smells nutty and milk solids are golden brown, about 7 minutes; transfer to bowl and let cool to room temperature.

3. Whisk egg and white together in large bowl until combined. Whisk in sugar and salt until light in color, about 1 minute. Whisk in browned butter, vanilla, framboise (if using), and lemon zest and juice. Whisk in flour blend, followed by cream, until well combined.

4. Arrange raspberries in single layer in bottom of cooled tart shell. Pour filling mixture evenly over raspberries. Bake tart on baking sheet until filling is set (center should not jiggle when shaken) and surface is puffed and deep golden brown, about 35 minutes, rotating sheet halfway through baking.

5. Transfer baking sheet with tart to wire rack and let cool to room temperature, about 1½ hours. Remove outer metal ring of tart pan, slide thin metal spatula between tart and pan bottom, and carefully slide tart onto serving platter. Cut into wedges and serve.

TEST KITCHEN TIP **Making a Raspberry Tart**

Arrange raspberries in single layer in bottom of cooled tart shell. Pour filling mixture evenly over raspberries.

Fresh Fruit Tart

G-F TESTING LAB

| **FLOUR SUBSTITUTION** | See page 456 for information about using various brands of gluten-free flour in the tart shell. |

WHY THIS RECIPE WORKS

Fresh fruit tarts usually offer little substance beyond their dazzling beauty, with rubbery or puddinglike fillings, soggy crusts, and underripe, flavorless fruit. We started by baking the crust until it was golden brown. We then filled the tart with pastry cream, made with half-and-half that was enriched with butter and thickened with just enough cornstarch to keep its shape without becoming gummy. For the fruit, we chose a combination of sliced kiwis, raspberries, and blueberries. The finishing touch: a drizzle of jelly glaze for a glistening presentation. Do not fill the prebaked tart shell until just before serving. Once filled, the tart should be topped with fruit, glazed, and served within 30 minutes.

Fresh Fruit Tart
SERVES 8 TO 10

2	cups half-and-half
3½	ounces (½ cup) sugar
	Pinch salt
½	vanilla bean, halved lengthwise, seeds removed and reserved
5	large egg yolks
3	tablespoons cornstarch
4	tablespoons unsalted butter, cut into ½-inch pieces and chilled
1	recipe Tart Shell (page 455)
2	large kiwis, peeled, halved lengthwise, and sliced ⅜ inch thick
10	ounces (2 cups) raspberries
5	ounces (1 cup) blueberries
½	cup red currant or apple jelly

1. Bring half-and-half, 6 tablespoons sugar, salt, and vanilla bean and seeds to simmer in medium saucepan over medium-high heat, stirring occasionally. As half-and-half mixture begins to simmer, whisk egg yolks, cornstarch, and remaining 2 tablespoons sugar together in medium bowl until smooth. Slowly whisk 1 cup of simmering half-and-half mixture into yolk mixture to temper, then slowly whisk tempered yolk mixture back into pan. Reduce heat to medium and cook, whisking vigorously, until mixture is thickened and few bubbles burst on surface, about 30 seconds.

2. Off heat, remove vanilla bean and whisk in butter. Transfer mixture to clean bowl, lay sheet of plastic wrap directly on surface, and refrigerate until chilled and firm, about 3 hours. (Pastry cream can be refrigerated for up to 2 days.)

3. Meanwhile, adjust oven rack to middle position and heat oven to 375 degrees. Set chilled tart pan on rimmed baking sheet. Press greased heavy-duty aluminum foil into tart shell, covering edges to prevent burning, and fill with 1 cup of pie weights. Bake until tart shell is just set, about 25 minutes, rotating sheet halfway through baking. Carefully remove weights and foil and continue to bake tart shell until lightly golden, about 10 minutes. Let tart shell cool completely in pan.

4. Spread chilled pastry cream evenly over bottom of cooled tart shell. Shingle kiwi slices around edge of tart, then arrange three rows of raspberries inside kiwi. Finally, arrange mound of blueberries in center, and scatter remaining over raspberries.

5. Melt jelly in small saucepan over medium-high heat, stirring occasionally to smooth out any lumps. Using pastry brush, dab melted jelly over fruit. To serve, remove outer ring of tart pan, slide thin metal spatula between tart and tart pan bottom, and carefully slide tart onto serving platter or cutting board. Slice tart into wedges and serve.

VARIATION
Mixed Berry Tart

Omit kiwi and add 2 cups extra berries (including blackberries and/or hulled and quartered strawberries). Combine berries in large zipper-lock bag and toss gently to mix. Carefully spread berries in even layer over filled tart. Glaze and serve as directed.

Strawberry Shortcakes

G-F TESTING LAB

FLOUR SUBSTITUTION	King Arthur Gluten-Free Multi-Purpose Flour 9 ounces = **1½ cups plus 2 tablespoons**	Betty Crocker All-Purpose Gluten Free Rice Blend 9 ounces = **1½ cups plus ⅓ cup**
	Shortcakes made with King Arthur will be slightly sandy and will spread more; shortcakes made with Betty Crocker will be drier and slightly rubbery.	
BAKING POWDER	Not all brands of baking powder are gluten-free; see page 24 for more information.	
PSYLLIUM HUSK	Psyllium is crucial to the structure of the shortcakes; see page 21 for more information.	
RESTING TIME	Do not shortchange the shortcake dough's 30-minute rest or else the shortcakes will taste gritty and mushy.	

✓ WHY THIS RECIPE WORKS

Our idea of the perfect strawberry shortcake is one with a juicy, chunky strawberry filling sandwiched between two halves of a sweet, tender biscuit and served with a dollop of whipped cream. Since the filling isn't cooked, getting the right texture for the strawberries was key. So we quartered the berries and mashed some of them for a filling that had bites of sweet strawberries and plenty of juice. With our filling settled, we moved on to developing a gluten-free biscuit that met our standards. We wanted a drop biscuit that would be easy to make yet offer the same tender texture and buttery flavor as a traditional rolled and cut biscuit. In order to achieve this, we had to tweak the traditional ingredients (flour, baking powder, baking soda, sugar, salt, butter, and buttermilk) quite a bit. We added psyllium husk powder and an egg for the structure and elasticity normally provided by gluten development. We tried making the biscuits with buttermilk but found the dough very liquid-y, and it spread too much in the oven. This is because our flour blend does not absorb liquid to the same degree that all-purpose flour does. We switched to whole-milk yogurt, which, as a thicker liquid, produced a dough with the right consistency. It also helped us achieve a richness and tenderness previously lacking in our biscuits. Since we weren't using buttermilk, we added a squirt of lemon juice to add a little extra tanginess. Our gluten-free flour blend also does not absorb fat well, but we wanted to keep the biscuits buttery. To this end, we used a combination of butter (for flavor) and oil. This kept the fat from leaching out of the biscuit. As with other chemically leavened gluten-free quick breads, we found that a 30-minute rest greatly improved the texture of these biscuits. It not only helped us work with the dough but left enough time for the starches to fully hydrate, giving us biscuits that were tender and sweet instead of gritty and starchy. Once the biscuits were fully cooled, we split them and filled them with our macerated berries and a dollop of slightly sweetened whipped cream.

Strawberry Shortcakes

SERVES 6

STRAWBERRIES

- 2 pounds strawberries, hulled and quartered (6 cups)
- 6 tablespoons granulated sugar

SHORTCAKES

- 9 ounces (2 cups) ATK All-Purpose Gluten-Free Flour Blend (page 7)
- 2 tablespoons granulated sugar
- 4 teaspoons baking powder
- ¼ teaspoon baking soda
- 1½ teaspoons powdered psyllium husk
- ½ teaspoon salt
- 3 tablespoons unsalted butter, cut into ¼-inch pieces and chilled
- ¾ cup plain whole-milk yogurt
- 1 large egg, lightly beaten
- 2 tablespoons vegetable oil
- 2 teaspoons lemon juice
- 1 tablespoon turbinado sugar

WHIPPED CREAM

- 1 cup heavy cream, chilled
- 1 tablespoon granulated sugar
- 1 teaspoon vanilla extract

1. FOR THE STRAWBERRIES: Using potato masher, crush one-third of strawberries with sugar in bowl. Stir in remaining strawberries, cover, and let sit at room temperature while making biscuits, or up to 2 hours.

2. FOR THE SHORTCAKES: Whisk flour blend, granulated sugar, baking powder, baking soda, psyllium, and salt together in large bowl. Using fingers, rub butter into flour mixture until only small pea-size pieces remain. In separate bowl, whisk yogurt, egg, oil, and lemon juice together. Using silicone spatula, stir yogurt mixture into flour mixture until well combined and no flour pockets remain, about 1 minute. Cover with plastic wrap and let rest at room temperature for 30 minutes.

3. Adjust oven rack to middle position and heat oven to 450 degrees. Line rimmed baking sheet with parchment paper and place inside second baking sheet. Using greased 1/3-cup dry measure, scoop out and drop six 2½-inch-wide mounds of dough onto prepared sheet, spaced about 1½ inches apart. Sprinkle with turbinado sugar.

4. Bake biscuits until golden and crisp, about 15 minutes, rotating sheet halfway through baking. Let biscuits cool completely on wire rack, about 30 minutes.

5. FOR THE WHIPPED CREAM: Using stand mixer fitted with whisk, whip cream, sugar, and vanilla on medium-low speed until foamy, about 1 minute. Increase speed to high and whip until stiff peaks form, 1 to 3 minutes.

6. Split each biscuit open through middle. Using slotted spoon, portion strawberries over biscuit bottom. Dollop with whipped cream, cap with biscuit top, and serve immediately.

VARIATION

Peach Shortcakes

Substitute 2 pounds peaches, peeled, pitted, and cut into ¼-inch wedges, for strawberries, and skip step 1. Gently toss three-quarters of peaches with ¼ cup granulated sugar in large bowl and let stand 30 minutes. Toss remaining peaches with 2 tablespoons granulated sugar and 2 tablespoons peach schnapps in separate bowl and microwave, stirring occasionally, until peaches are bubbling, about 1 to 1½ minutes. Using potato masher, crush microwaved peaches and let stand 30 minutes. Add sliced peaches to mashed peaches and combine before assembling shortcakes.

TEST KITCHEN TIP **Making Strawberry Shortcakes**

1. Crush one-third of berries with sugar in bowl with potato masher. Stir in remaining berries, cover, and let sit at room temperature for up to 2 hours.

2. After shortcakes have cooled, split each one open through middle.

3. Using slotted spoon, portion berries over biscuit bottom. Dollop with whipped cream, cap with biscuit top, and serve immediately.

Shortcakes

We wanted a sweet drop biscuit that would offer an easy and quick alternative to a traditional rolled biscuit, but with the same tender texture and buttery flavor. The classic recipe is nothing more than flour, baking powder, baking soda, sugar, and salt mixed with butter and buttermilk. In order to produce an equally tender biscuit with a light, fluffy crumb, we had to rework the ingredient list quite extensively.

1. ADD PSYLLIUM AND EGG FOR STRUCTURE: While traditional biscuits rely on gluten for structure, we had to find another solution. Adding powdered psyllium husk (as we had done in bread recipes) helped strengthen the proteins in gluten-free flours so they could do a better job of trapping gas and steam during baking. However, using too much psyllium imparted an earthy flavor that was out of place in biscuits. An egg provided additional structure along with moisture and elasticity.

2. USE TWO FATS: Butter plays an important role in making biscuits tender and tasty. A batch of fluffy drop biscuits typically relies on at least a stick of butter. We found that our biscuit dough could absorb only 3 tablespoons of butter (the rest just leached out and made the biscuits greasy). With so little fat in the dough, the biscuits were very tough and dry. Two tablespoons of vegetable oil added back some richness, as did replacing the usual buttermilk with thicker, richer whole-milk yogurt.

3. THICKER DAIRY PLEASE: Biscuits are traditionally made with buttermilk. Because gluten-free flours don't absorb liquid well, we found the dough was very liquid-y and spread too much in the oven. Using less milk didn't work—the starches in the flour never hydrated, and they imparted a gritty texture to the baked biscuits. Switching to thicker yogurt (spiked with a little lemon juice for extra tang) produced a dough with the right consistency, and letting the dough rest for 30 minutes (as we had done with muffins and other chemically leavened bread) allowed the starches to hydrate before baking.

4. DOUBLE UP ON SHEET PANS: A biscuit is typically baked at a high temperature for a short time to achieve a golden crust and a nice rise. We struggled to get a nice color on the tops of the biscuits without burning the bottoms. Lowering the oven temperature seemed like a natural solution, but we needed to bake them so long that the insides dried out. We had better luck staying with the high temperature but using a second baking sheet as insulation to keep the bottoms from burning.

Individual Blueberry-Almond Buckles

G-F TESTING LAB

FLOUR SUBSTITUTION	King Arthur Gluten-Free Multi-Purpose Flour 3½ ounces = ½ **cup plus 2 tablespoons**	Bob's Red Mill GF All-Purpose Baking Flour 3½ ounces = **⅔ cup**

Note that buckles made with Bob's Red Mill will have a distinct bean flavor.

✔ WHY THIS RECIPE WORKS

These individual fruit-packed cakes are an easy make-ahead dessert that is especially handy when entertaining. We made the simple batter for these buckles in the food processor, folding in the berries at the end, which kept prep work and dishes to a minimum. This recipe requires very little flour because we grind up nuts to give the batter both flavor and structure; as a result, our gluten-free flour blend worked easily here. It helps too that these buckles are laden with fresh fruit and are meant to be moist and dense and not firm and cakey. Plus, the ramekins help these buckles cook evenly, and we didn't have to worry about soggy centers or even about unmolding. For a nice finishing touch, we topped the buckles with a portion of the nuts before baking. Coating the ramekins with vegetable oil spray prevented the buckles from sticking. Do not substitute frozen berries here. Serve warm with vanilla ice cream or whipped cream.

Individual Blueberry-Almond Buckles

SERVES 8

- 5¼ ounces (¾ cup) sugar
- ½ cup sliced almonds, toasted and chopped coarse
- 4 tablespoons unsalted butter, softened
- ¼ teaspoon salt
- ⅓ cup heavy cream
- 2 large eggs
- ½ teaspoon almond extract
- 3½ ounces (¾ cup) ATK All-Purpose Gluten-Free Flour Blend (page 7)
- ½ teaspoon baking powder (see page 24)
- 15 ounces (3 cups) fresh blueberries

1. Adjust oven rack to middle position and heat oven to 375 degrees. Spray eight 6-ounce ramekins with vegetable oil spray and place on rimmed baking sheet.

2. Process sugar, ¼ cup almonds, butter, and salt together in food processor until finely ground, 10 to 15 seconds. With processor running, add cream, eggs, and almond extract and continue to process until smooth, about 5 seconds. Add flour blend and baking powder and pulse until incorporated, about 5 pulses.

3. Transfer batter to large bowl and gently fold in blueberries. Spoon batter into prepared ramekins and sprinkle evenly with remaining ¼ cup almonds. (Buckles can sit at room temperature, covered with plastic wrap, for up to 2 hours.)

4. Bake buckles until golden and beginning to pull away from sides of ramekins, 25 to 30 minutes, rotating sheet halfway through baking. Let buckles cool on wire rack for 10 minutes before serving.

VARIATIONS

Individual Raspberry-Pistachio Buckles
Don't use frozen raspberries here.

Substitute shelled pistachios for almonds, 1 teaspoon vanilla extract for almond extract, and fresh raspberries for blueberries.

Individual Blackberry-Walnut Buckles
Substitute walnuts for almonds, 1 teaspoon vanilla extract for almond extract, and fresh blackberries for blueberries.

Apple Crisp

FLOUR SUBSTITUTION	King Arthur Gluten-Free Multi-Purpose Flour 1½ ounces = **¼ cup**	Bob's Red Mill GF All-Purpose Baking Flour 1½ ounces = **5 tablespoons**
	Note that topping made with King Arthur will be slightly softer, and topping made with Bob's Red Mill will have a slight bean flavor.	
OATS	Do not use quick oats; they have a dusty texture that doesn't work in this recipe. Make sure to buy old-fashioned rolled oats (see page 27) that have been processed in a gluten-free facility.	

WHY THIS RECIPE WORKS

Thinking this recipe would be easy to make gluten-free since only the topping contains flour, we started by making our classic recipe, which calls for parbaking the topping and the fruit separately and then combining them for a short stint in the oven. When we swapped out all-purpose flour for our gluten-free blend, the topping spread over the baking sheet. The low protein content in our flour blend meant it wasn't able to hold the topping together to form the desired crumbly bits. Recognizing that using less flour would work to our advantage, we experimented with larger amounts of oats and nuts, toasting them and then finely grinding nearly half of them to a flour-like consistency. In the end, we needed just ⅓ cup of flour blend. Given the stability of our new topping, we found that we did not need to parbake it. However, it was critical to parbake the apples because the time they required to cook through was far longer than the time needed to crisp the topping. For just the right, saucy consistency, we grated one apple, which broke down during cooking. We liked the way Golden Delicious apples worked in this recipe, as some broke down and created a saucy filling. You can use pecans or walnuts instead of sliced almonds in the topping. The baked crisp can be kept at room temperature for up to 4 hours; warm crisp in oven before serving.

Apple Crisp
SERVES 6

TOPPING
- ¾ cup gluten-free old-fashioned rolled oats
- ¾ cup sliced almonds
- 1½ ounces (⅓ cup) ATK All-Purpose Gluten-Free Flour Blend (page 7)
- 1¾ ounces (¼ cup packed) brown sugar
- 2 tablespoons granulated sugar
- 2 teaspoons vanilla extract
- 1 teaspoon water
- ⅛ teaspoon salt
- 6 tablespoons unsalted butter, cut into 6 pieces and softened

FILLING
- 4 teaspoons lemon juice
- ¾ teaspoon cornstarch
- 3 pounds Golden Delicious apples (about 6 medium), peeled and cored (5 cut into ½-inch cubes, 1 grated)
- 2⅓ ounces (⅓ cup) granulated sugar
- Pinch salt
- Pinch ground cinnamon
- Pinch ground nutmeg

1. FOR THE TOPPING: Adjust oven rack to middle position and heat oven to 400 degrees. Place oats and nuts in two piles on parchment paper–lined baking sheet, and bake until lightly toasted, 3 to 5 minutes. Remove from oven and cool completely.

2. Pulse ½ cup oats, flour blend, brown sugar, granulated sugar, vanilla, water, and salt in food processor until combined, about 5 pulses. Sprinkle butter and half of almonds over top and process until mixture clumps together into large, crumbly balls, about 30 seconds, stopping halfway through to scrape down bowl. Sprinkle remaining almonds and remaining ¼ cup oats over mixture and combine with 2 quick pulses. Transfer mixture to bowl.

3. FOR THE FILLING: Whisk lemon juice and cornstarch in large bowl until cornstarch is dissolved. Stir in apples, sugar, salt, cinnamon, and nutmeg. Transfer mixture to 8-inch square baking dish, cover tightly with aluminum foil, and bake for 20 minutes.

4. Remove baking dish from oven, uncover, and stir filling well. Pinch topping into grape-size pieces (with some smaller loose bits) and sprinkle over filling. Bake until topping is well browned and fruit is tender and bubbling around edges, 20 to 25 minutes, rotating dish halfway through baking. Let crisp cool on wire rack until warm, about 15 minutes. Serve.

VARIATION
Apple-Cranberry Crisp
Substitute pecans for almonds and add ½ cup dried cranberries to filling along with apples in step 3.

Whole-Grain Cherry Crisp

G-F TESTING LAB

FLOUR SUBSTITUTION	Do not substitute other whole-grain blends for the ATK Whole-Grain Gluten-Free Flour Blend; they will not work in this recipe.
CHERRIES	Make sure to use cherries packed in syrup. Cherries packed in water do not work in this recipe. The cherries in syrup should weigh 4½ pounds before draining.
OATS	Do not use quick oats; they have a dusty texture that doesn't work in this recipe. Make sure to buy old-fashioned rolled oats that have been processed in a gluten-free facility. See page 27 for more information.

WHY THIS RECIPE WORKS

For a satisfyingly rich gluten-free cherry crisp, we decided to pair our cherry filling with a crumble topping made with our whole-grain flour blend. Since fresh sour cherries are available only for one short month of the year, we decided to proceed with jarred or canned cherries, packed in either water or syrup. When testing each type, we drained off all the liquid and added in our own flavorings. Red wine gave us depth and highlighted the rich cherry flavor. A bit of almond extract helped enhance the almonds in the topping. Thickening the cherries was our major hurdle. We tried varying amounts of cornstarch with a wide range of results; 2 tablespoons seemed to work beautifully sometimes but not always. It was clear that these differences were related to whether the cherries were packed in water or syrup. Cherries in syrup thickened up nicely, while cherries in water always seemed, well, watery. Cherries packed in water were out. Moving on, a mixture of toasted oats and almonds paired well with our flour blend for a hearty topping. For just the right consistency, we pulsed in some of the almonds and oats at the end. We parbaked the filling to soften the cherries before adding our topping and popping the assembled crisp back into the oven to finish baking. The result was a sweet, crunchy, perfect crisp.

Whole-Grain Cherry Crisp
SERVES 6

TOPPING
- ¾ cup old-fashioned rolled oats
- ¾ cup sliced almonds
- 1½ ounces (⅓ cup) ATK Whole-Grain Gluten-Free Flour Blend (page 9)
- 1¾ ounces (¼ cup packed) brown sugar
- 2 tablespoons granulated sugar
- 2 teaspoons vanilla extract
- 1 teaspoon water
- ⅛ teaspoon salt
- 6 tablespoons unsalted butter, cut into 6 pieces and softened

FILLING
- 5¼ ounces (¾ cup) granulated sugar
- 2 tablespoons cornstarch
- 4½ pounds pitted sour cherries in syrup, drained (6½ cups)
- 2 tablespoons red wine
- ¼ teaspoon almond extract

1. FOR THE TOPPING: Adjust oven rack to middle position and heat oven to 400 degrees. Place oats and almonds on separate sides of parchment paper–lined baking sheet. Bake until lightly toasted, 3 to 5 minutes; let cool completely on baking sheet.

2. Pulse ½ cup toasted oats, flour blend, brown sugar, granulated sugar, vanilla, water, and salt in food processor until combined, about 5 pulses. Sprinkle butter and ½ cup toasted almonds over top and process until mixture clumps together into large, crumbly balls, about 30 seconds, stopping halfway through to scrape down bowl. Sprinkle remaining ¼ cup almonds and remaining ¼ cup oats over top and pulse to just combine, about 2 pulses; transfer to bowl.

3. FOR THE FILLING: Whisk granulated sugar and cornstarch together in large bowl. Stir in cherries, wine, and almond extract until combined. Transfer fruit mixture to 8-inch square baking dish and cover with aluminum foil. Place on foil-lined rimmed baking sheet and bake until fruit has released its juices, about 20 minutes.

4. Remove baking dish from oven, uncover, and stir gently. Pinch topping into ½-inch pieces (with some smaller loose bits) and sprinkle over fruit. Bake uncovered until topping is well browned and firm and juices are bubbling around edges, 25 to 35 minutes, rotating dish halfway through baking. Let cool on wire rack until warm, about 15 minutes. Serve.

VARIATION
Dairy-Free Whole-Grain Cherry Crisp
In topping, omit salt and substitute Earth Balance Vegan Buttery Sticks for butter.

Peach Cobbler with Cornmeal Biscuits

G-F TESTING LAB

FLOUR SUBSTITUTION	King Arthur Gluten-Free Multi-Purpose Flour 4½ ounces = ½ **cup plus** ⅓ **cup**	Bob's Red Mill GF All-Purpose Baking Flour 4½ ounces = ¾ **cup plus 2 tablespoons**

Note that biscuits made with King Arthur will be a bit pasty, and biscuits made with Bob's Red Mill will be darker in color and more crumbly, will not rise as well, and will have a slight bean flavor.

CORNMEAL	The test kitchen's favorite cornmeal for baking is finely ground Whole-Grain Arrowhead Mills Cornmeal. This brand has been processed in a gluten-free facility, but not all brands are. Make sure to read the label. See page 26 for more details on cornmeal.

WHY THIS RECIPE WORKS

Our first attempts at trying to marry our gluten-free biscuits with peach cobbler filling proved right away that a sturdier biscuit would be in order. Our gluten-free biscuits softened dramatically when paired with the hot filling. Clearly a biscuit that was not made with all flour blend would be a better bet, and the less time it spent atop a hot filling, the better. For this reason, we decided to take another route for our cobbler topping: cornmeal biscuits. Cornmeal paired with an equal amount of our flour blend would make a sturdier biscuit, and we thought the corn flavor would pair well with the peach filling. We started with an old yet beloved cornmeal biscuit recipe, which had very little sugar and baking powder. Increasing both and adding a little baking soda gave us the lift and sturdiness needed for this recipe, while the extra sugar tilted the biscuit to the sweet rather than the savory side—perfect for our cobbler. The baking powder gave us the lift that we needed to form traditional-looking biscuits. We parbaked these biscuits as well as the filling, so they needed to spend only about 5 minutes together in the oven for the perfect cobbler.

Peach Cobbler with Cornmeal Biscuits

SERVES 8

5	ounces (1 cup) cornmeal
4½	ounces (1 cup) ATK Gluten-Free Flour Blend (page 7)
2⅓	ounces (⅓ cup) plus 3 tablespoons sugar, plus extra as needed
2	teaspoons baking powder (see page 24)
¼	teaspoon baking soda
	Salt
8	tablespoons unsalted butter, cut into ¼-inch pieces and chilled
¾	cup buttermilk, chilled
4	pounds ripe but firm peaches, peeled, halved, pitted, and cut into ½-inch wedges
¼	teaspoon ground ginger
⅛	teaspoon ground cinnamon
5	teaspoons lemon juice
1½	teaspoons cornstarch

1. Adjust oven rack to middle position and heat oven to 375 degrees. Line baking sheet with parchment paper. Pulse cornmeal, flour blend, 2 tablespoons sugar, baking powder, baking soda, and ½ teaspoon salt together in food processor until combined, about 5 pulses. Scatter butter pieces over top and pulse until mixture resembles coarse cornmeal with few slightly larger butter lumps, about 10 pulses.

2. Transfer cornmeal mixture to medium bowl, add buttermilk, and stir with fork until dough gathers into moist clumps. Using greased ¼-cup dry measure, scoop out and drop 8 mounds of dough onto prepared baking sheet, spaced about 1 inch apart. Sprinkle 1 tablespoon sugar over top and bake until biscuits are puffed and lightly browned, 25 to 30 minutes. Let biscuits cool slightly on wire rack. (Cooled biscuits can be held at room temperature in sealed zipper-lock bag for up to 2 hours.)

3. Meanwhile, combine peaches, remaining ⅓ cup sugar, ginger, cinnamon, and pinch salt together in Dutch oven. Cover and cook over medium-low heat until peaches have softened and release their juices, 10 to 15 minutes.

4. Whisk lemon juice and cornstarch together in bowl, then stir into peaches and continue to cook, uncovered, until liquid has thickened, 2 to 5 minutes. Season with extra sugar to taste. Transfer to deep-dish pie plate or into 8 individual gratin dishes. (Fruit can be covered with plastic wrap and held at room temperature for up to 1½ hours.)

5. To serve, arrange biscuits on top of peach mixture and bake until heated through, 3 to 5 minutes. Serve immediately.

Blueberry Cobbler with Cornmeal Biscuits

G-F TESTING LAB

FLOUR SUBSTITUTION	King Arthur Gluten-Free Multi-Purpose Flour 4½ ounces = **½ cup plus ⅓ cup**	Betty Crocker All-Purpose Gluten Free Rice Blend 4½ ounces = **¾ cup plus 2 tablespoons**
	Biscuits made with King Arthur will be a bit pasty; biscuits made with Betty Crocker will be drier and a bit pasty.	
CORNMEAL	The test kitchen's favorite cornmeal is Whole-Grain Arrowhead Mills Cornmeal. This brand has been processed in a gluten-free facility, but not all brands are. Make sure to read the label. See page 26 for more information.	
BAKING POWDER	Not all brands of baking powder are gluten-free; see page 24 for more information.	
XANTHAN GUM	Xanthan is crucial to the structure of the biscuits; see page 21 for more information.	

WHY THIS RECIPE WORKS

Because blueberry and corn are such a classic and winning combination, for our gluten-free cobbler we settled on rustic cornmeal drop biscuits instead of traditional biscuits. Equal cup amounts of cornmeal and our all-purpose flour blend proved to be the best starting point, as this combination created a sturdy biscuit that would hold up to our fruit filling. For leaveners, we used both baking soda and baking powder to give us the lift and sturdiness we needed for the biscuits to hold their shape, as well as to keep them from being too dense. As with our traditional cobblers, we found that baking the filling and biscuits separately, then combining them just before serving, gave us a perfectly cooked filling and tender biscuits. Be ready to serve the cobbler as soon as it comes out of the oven; the bottom of the biscuits will become quite soggy if allowed to sit on top of the warm fruit for too long.

Blueberry Cobbler with Cornmeal Biscuits
SERVES 8

BISCUITS

5	ounces (1 cup) cornmeal
4½	ounces (1 cup) ATK All-Purpose Gluten-Free Flour Blend (page 7)
3	tablespoons sugar
2	teaspoons baking powder
¼	teaspoon baking soda
½	teaspoon salt
¼	teaspoon xanthan gum
8	tablespoons unsalted butter, cut into ¼-inch pieces and chilled
¾	cup buttermilk, chilled

FILLING

2⅓	ounces (⅓ cup) sugar
4	teaspoons cornstarch
¼	teaspoon salt
30	ounces (6 cups) blueberries
1½	teaspoons grated lemon zest plus 1 tablespoon juice

1. FOR THE BISCUITS: Adjust oven rack to upper-middle and lower-middle positions and heat oven to 375 degrees. Line baking sheet with parchment paper. Pulse cornmeal, flour blend, 2 tablespoons sugar, baking powder, baking soda, salt, and xanthan gum in food processor until combined, about 5 pulses. Scatter butter pieces over top and pulse until mixture resembles coarse cornmeal with few slightly larger butter lumps, about 10 pulses.

2. Transfer cornmeal mixture to medium bowl, add buttermilk, and stir with fork until dough gathers into moist clumps. Using greased ¼-cup dry measure, scoop out and drop eight 2¼-inch-wide mounds of dough onto prepared sheet, spaced about 1 inch apart. (Do not make biscuits wider or they won't all fit in pie plate when baked.)

3. Sprinkle remaining 1 tablespoon sugar over biscuits and bake on upper rack until biscuits are puffed and lightly browned, 25 to 30 minutes, rotating sheet halfway through baking. Let biscuits cool on wire rack. (Cooled biscuits can be held at room temperature in zipper-lock bag for up to 2 hours.)

4. FOR THE FILLING: Stir sugar, cornstarch, and salt together in large bowl. Gently stir in blueberries and lemon zest and juice until evenly combined. Transfer to 9-inch deep-dish pie plate, cover with aluminum foil, and place on rimmed baking sheet. Bake on lower rack until blueberries are beginning to burst and juices are bubbling around edge, 40 to 50 minutes, stirring halfway through baking.

5. Uncover blueberries and stir gently. Arrange biscuits on top of fruit and continue to bake until biscuits have warmed through, about 5 minutes. Serve immediately.

VARIATION

Dairy-Free Blueberry Cobbler with Cornmeal Biscuits

Do not use soy milk or rice milk in this recipe.

In biscuits, omit salt, substitute Earth Balance Vegan Buttery Sticks for butter, and ¾ cup almond milk mixed with 2 teaspoons lemon juice for buttermilk.

Individual Fresh Berry Gratins with Zabaglione

G-F TESTING LAB

BERRIES   We prefer to make this recipe with a variety of berries but you can use just one type of fruit if you prefer. Do not use frozen berries.

✅ WHY THIS RECIPE WORKS

Berry gratins can be a very humble affair in which fresh fruit is simply dressed up with sweetened bread crumbs and baked, or they can be a bit more sophisticated, as when they are topped with the foamy Italian custard called zabaglione. Since zabaglione, made with egg yolks, sugar, and wine, is naturally gluten-free, we decided to choose this approach. But making the zabaglione takes a little finesse. It requires constant watching so that the mixture doesn't overcook. It also needs to be whisked until it's the ideal thick, creamy texture. We were after a foolproof method for this topping for a gratin that could serve as an elegant finale to a summer meal. We chose to make individual gratins and settled on a mix of berries, which we tossed with sugar and salt to draw out their juices. To prevent a custard with scrambled eggs, we kept the heat low; for the right texture, we whisked until the custard was somewhat thick. As for flavor, traditional Marsala wine gave us an overly sweet zabaglione; crisp, dry Sauvignon Blanc provided a clean flavor that worked better with the berries. Whipped cream worked well as a thickening agent. We spooned our zabaglione over the berries and sprinkled a mixture of brown and granulated sugars on top before broiling for a crackly, caramelized crust.

Individual Fresh Berry Gratins with Zabaglione

SERVES 4

BERRY MIXTURE

- 15 ounces (3 cups) mixed blackberries, blueberries, raspberries, and strawberries (strawberries hulled and halved lengthwise if small, quartered if large)
- 2 teaspoons granulated sugar
  Pinch salt

ZABAGLIONE TOPPING

- 3 large egg yolks
- 3 tablespoons granulated sugar
- 3 tablespoons dry white wine such as Sauvignon Blanc
- 2 teaspoons packed light brown sugar
- 3 tablespoons heavy cream, chilled

1. FOR THE BERRY MIXTURE: Line rimmed baking sheet with aluminum foil. Toss berries, granulated sugar, and salt together in bowl. Divide berry mixture evenly among 4 shallow 6-ounce gratin dishes set on prepared sheet; set aside.

2. FOR THE ZABAGLIONE: Whisk egg yolks, 2 tablespoons plus 1 teaspoon granulated sugar, and wine together in medium bowl until sugar is dissolved, about 1 minute. Set bowl over saucepan of barely simmering water and cook, whisking constantly, until mixture is frothy. Continue to cook, whisking constantly, until mixture is slightly thickened, creamy, and glossy, 5 to 10 minutes (mixture will form loose mounds when dripped from whisk). Remove bowl from saucepan and whisk constantly for 30 seconds to cool slightly. Transfer bowl to refrigerator and chill until egg mixture is completely cool, about 10 minutes.

3. Meanwhile, adjust oven rack 6 inches from broiler element and heat broiler. Combine remaining 2 teaspoons granulated sugar and light brown sugar in bowl.

4. Whisk heavy cream in large bowl until it holds soft peaks, 30 to 90 seconds. Using silicone spatula, gently fold whipped cream into cooled egg mixture. Spoon zabaglione over berries and sprinkle sugar mixture evenly over zabaglione; let stand at room temperature for 10 minutes, until sugar dissolves.

5. Broil until sugar is bubbly and caramelized, 1 to 4 minutes. Serve immediately.

VARIATION

Individual Fresh Berry Gratins with Lemon Zabaglione

Replace 1 tablespoon wine with equal amount lemon juice, and add 1 teaspoon grated lemon zest to egg yolk mixture in step 2.

Individual Pavlovas with Tropical Fruit

G-F TESTING LAB

CREAM OF TARTAR	This white powder sold in the spice aisle ensures that the whipped eggs are both stable and glossy. See page 25 for details on this ingredient.

✔ WHY THIS RECIPE WORKS

These naturally gluten-free meringue shells filled with whipped cream and topped with fresh fruit make a light ending to a meal. The key to this recipe is successfully making the meringues. Individual meringues are easier to shape than one large meringue and easier to serve because there's no slicing required. We portioned out the mixture into small mounds on a baking sheet and used the back of a spoon to create a concave center for holding the whipped cream and fruit. Baking the meringues at 200 degrees for 1½ hours yielded perfectly dry, crisp white shells, but they required gradual cooling off in a turned-off oven to ensure crispness. Adding a tablespoon of sugar to the fruit was necessary to extract some of their juices and create a flavorful syrup that soaked into the meringue and whipped cream. The fruit is the garnish here, so it's worth taking time to cut it into tidy pieces. Avoid making pavlovas on humid days or the meringue shells will turn out sticky.

Individual Pavlovas with Tropical Fruit
SERVES 6

MERINGUES AND FRUIT
- 4 large egg whites, room temperature
- ¾ teaspoon vanilla extract
- ¼ teaspoon cream of tartar
- 7 ounces (1 cup) plus 1 tablespoon sugar
- 1 mango, peeled, pitted, and cut into ¼-inch pieces
- 2 kiwis, peeled, halved lengthwise, and sliced thin
- 1½ cups ½-inch pineapple pieces

WHIPPED CREAM
- 1 cup heavy cream, chilled
- 1 tablespoon sugar
- 1 teaspoon vanilla extract

1. FOR THE MERINGUES: Adjust oven rack to middle position and heat oven to 200 degrees. Line baking sheet with parchment paper.

2. Using stand mixer fitted with whisk, whip egg whites, vanilla, and cream of tartar on medium-low speed until foamy, about 1 minute. Increase speed to medium-high and whip whites to soft, billowy mounds, about 1 minute. Gradually add 1 cup sugar and whip until glossy, stiff peaks form, 1 to 2 minutes.

3. Using ½-cup measure, scoop six ½-cup mounds of meringue onto prepared sheet, spacing them about 1 inch apart. Gently make small, bowl-shaped indentation in each meringue using back of spoon. Bake until meringues are smooth, dry, and firm, about 1½ hours. Turn oven off and leave meringues in oven until completely dry and hard, about 2 hours. (Meringue shells can be stored in airtight container at room temperature for up to 2 weeks.)

4. Gently toss fruit with remaining 1 tablespoon sugar in bowl. Let sit at room temperature until sugar has dissolved and fruit is juicy, about 30 minutes.

5. FOR THE WHIPPED CREAM: Using clean, dry mixer bowl and whisk attachment, whip cream, sugar, and vanilla on medium-low speed until foamy, about 1 minute. Increase speed to high and whip until soft peaks form, 1 to 3 minutes. (Whipped cream can be refrigerated for up to 8 hours; rewhisk before serving.)

6. To assemble, place meringue shells on individual plates and spoon about ⅓ cup whipped cream into each. Top with about ½ cup fruit (some fruit and juice will fall onto plate). Serve immediately.

VARIATIONS

Individual Pavlovas with Mixed Berries
Substitute 1½ cups each raspberries and blueberries and 1 cup blackberries for mango, kiwi, and pineapple.

Individual Pavlovas with Strawberries, Blueberries, and Peaches
Substitute 1 cup strawberries, sliced thin, 1 cup blueberries, and 2 peaches, peeled, halved, pitted, and sliced ¼ inch thick, for mango, kiwi, and pineapple.

CAKES

Yellow Layer Cake

G-F TESTING LAB

FLOUR SUBSTITUTION	King Arthur Gluten-Free Multi-Purpose Flour 11 ounces = **2 cups**	Bob's Red Mill GF All-Purpose Baking Flour 11 ounces = **1⅔ cups plus ½ cup**
	Note that cake made with King Arthur will not rise as well and will have a somewhat grainy, pasty texture, and cake made with Bob's Red Mill will be darker in color and will have a coarser crumb and a distinct bean flavor.	
CHOCOLATE	Not all brands of chocolate are processed in a gluten-free facility; make sure to read the label.	
XANTHAN GUM	Do not omit the xanthan gum; it is crucial to the structure of the cake. For more information, see page 21.	

A good yellow layer cake should melt in the mouth and taste of butter and vanilla. But many of the gluten-free layer cake recipes we tried tasted overly sweet, and most came out dense and gummy. If those problems weren't daunting enough, all of the initial recipes we tried were terribly greasy. The standard amount of butter in a traditional yellow layer cake (two sticks) was way too much. As we have learned time and time again, the starches in gluten-free flour just don't absorb fat (especially butter) all that well. We dramatically reduced the amount of butter in our working recipe, but predictably that left the cake too lean and dry. Replacing the milk or buttermilk used in classic recipes with sour cream was a step in the right direction, but we needed more richness. In the end, we borrowed a trick that works for chocolate cakes—melted chocolate—to help solve this problem. Rather than using unsweetened or bittersweet chocolate (neither acceptable in a yellow cake), we turned to white chocolate, and it worked like a charm, boosting richness without making the cake greasy. With one big problem solved, we now focused on lightening up the crumb. Adding extra baking powder and a bit of baking soda helped give our cake better rise and a tender texture. To create a really fluffy texture, we needed to whip the egg whites with some sugar to create a stable meringue-like mixture that could provide greater lift in the oven. Whipping the egg yolks with a bit more sugar ensured that sufficient air was in the batter. Note the relatively low oven temperature, which we found allowed the layers to cook through without excessive browning. These lofty layers were tender yet sturdy enough to stand up to a thick coating of frosting. Use the Creamy Chocolate Frosting or any of the easy frostings on page 498. See detailed frosting instructions on page 502. Once the cake is frosted, serve it within a few hours.

Yellow Layer Cake

SERVES 10 TO 12

6	ounces white chocolate, chopped
8	tablespoons unsalted butter, cut into 8 pieces
11	ounces (1¾ cups plus ⅔ cup) ATK All-Purpose Gluten-Free Flour Blend (page 7)
1	tablespoon baking powder (see page 24)
1¼	teaspoons xanthan gum
1	teaspoon salt
¼	teaspoon baking soda
4	large eggs, separated
	Pinch cream of tartar
7	ounces (1 cup) sugar
1½	tablespoons vanilla extract
⅔	cup sour cream
4	cups frosting

1. Adjust oven rack to middle position and heat oven to 325 degrees. Grease two 9-inch round cake pans, line bottoms with parchment paper, and grease parchment.

2. Microwave chocolate and butter together in bowl at 50 percent power, stirring occasionally, until melted, about 2 minutes. Whisk mixture until smooth, then set aside to cool slightly. In separate bowl, whisk flour blend, baking powder, xanthan gum, salt, and baking soda until combined.

3. Using stand mixer fitted with whisk, whip egg whites and cream of tartar on medium-low speed until foamy, about 1 minute. Increase speed to medium-high and whip whites to soft, billowy mounds, about 1 minute. Gradually add ½ cup sugar and whip until glossy, stiff peaks form, 2 to 3 minutes; transfer to bowl.

4. Return now-empty bowl to mixer, add egg yolks and vanilla, and whip on medium speed until well blended, about 30 seconds. Gradually add remaining ½ cup sugar, increase mixer speed to high, and whip until very thick and pale yellow, about 2 minutes. Reduce mixer speed to medium, add chocolate mixture and sour cream, and whip until combined, about 30 seconds. Reduce speed to low, slowly add flour blend mixture, and mix until thoroughly combined, about 1 minute.

5. Using silicone spatula, stir one-third of whipped egg whites into batter to lighten. Gently fold in remaining whites until no white streaks remain. Divide batter evenly between prepared pans and smooth tops. Bake until cakes begin to pull away from sides of pans and spring back when pressed lightly, 30 to 32 minutes, rotating pans halfway through baking.

6. Let cakes cool in pans on wire rack for 10 minutes. Run knife around edge of cakes to loosen. Remove cakes from pans, discard parchment, and let cool completely on rack, about 1½ hours. (Cake layers can be wrapped tightly in plastic wrap and stored at room temperature for up to 1 day.)

7. Place 1 cake layer on platter and spread 1½ cups frosting evenly over top using small icing spatula or butter knife. Top with second cake layer, press lightly to adhere, then spread remaining 2½ cups frosting evenly over top and sides. Serve.

VARIATION
Yellow Sheet Cake
Four cups of frosting is enough to generously frost the top and sides of the cake.

Grease 13 by 9-inch baking pan, line bottom with parchment paper, and grease parchment. Scrape all of batter into prepared pan; baking time will not change. Let cake cool completely in pan on wire rack, about 2 hours. Run knife around edge of cake to loosen. Remove cake from pan, discard parchment, transfer to platter, and frost.

TEST KITCHEN TIP **Preparing a Cake Pan**

Gluten-free cakes tend to stick to the pan more than traditional cakes, and often require an extra step of lining the sides of the cake pan with parchment paper in addition to the bottom.

1. Grease pan with oil spray, butter, or shortening. The grease helps parchment paper stay in place, especially on sides of pan.

2. Trim piece of parchment to fit nicely inside cake pan, then lay flat into pan bottom.

3. Cut strips of parchment to match height of cake pan, then lay flat against pan sides.

Yellow Layer Cake

Although the aim of most traditional cakes is minimal gluten development, eliminating gluten altogether presents myriad problems of its own. To achieve the tall, fluffy layers of a classic yellow layer cake without gluten, we had to take a different approach to both ingredients and mixing method.

1. INCORPORATE MELTED WHITE CHOCOLATE: It was essential to reduce the fat in our gluten-free cake in order to combat greasiness, but simply using less butter left the layers tasting a bit too lean and dry. To replace some of the fat and moisture without leaving a greasy texture, we melted white chocolate with the butter in the microwave and then whisked the mixture until smooth and incorporated it into the batter. This emulsified combination added flavor and richness to the cake without turning it greasy.

2. ADD XANTHAN GUM FOR STRUCTURE: Because there was no gluten development to support the cake as it baked, we needed help creating structure. Xanthan gum proved essential to giving the cake the support and structure it needed to rise and set in the oven. However, there was a limit to the power of xanthan. Yes, it helped to build structure, but the cake was still dense and heavy. We turned to the eggs to solve this problem.

3. WHIP EGG WHITES AND SUGAR: We needed to find another way to add extra lift and support for these wide, flat cake layers. Focusing on the mixing method, we found that separating out the egg whites and whipping them into stiff peaks easily solved this problem. Adding cream of tartar and sugar to the whites as they whipped helped create a stable meringue-like mixture that did not deflate when folded into the cake batter. Whipping the egg yolks with additional sugar also helped to ensure that as much air as possible was trapped in the batter, giving it a light, fluffy texture.

4. USE SOUR CREAM: Buttermilk is often used in traditional yellow cakes for moisture and flavor, but in this cake it made the batter too loose and resulted in layers that were dense and gummy. Instead, we used sour cream, which gave us a thicker batter that baked up taller and fluffier. And the sour cream helped make the crumb especially tender. The tang of the sour cream also helped balance the sweetness of the white chocolate.

Birthday Cupcakes

G-F TESTING LAB

FLOUR SUBSTITUTION	King Arthur Gluten-Free Multi-Purpose Flour 6½ ounces = ⅔ **cup plus ½ cup**	Betty Crocker All-Purpose Gluten Free Rice Blend 6½ ounces = **1⅓ cups**
	Note that cupcakes made with King Arthur will not rise as well and will taste slightly pasty; cupcakes made with Betty Crocker will be slightly drier and pasty.	
CHOCOLATE	Not all brands of chocolate are processed in a gluten-free facility; make sure to read the label.	
XANTHAN GUM	Do not omit the xanthan gum; it is crucial to the structure of the cupcakes. For more information, see page 21.	

WHY THIS RECIPE WORKS

In our quest for tender cupcakes with a slightly domed top and a light, open crumb, we began with our Yellow Layer Cake (page 490). We immediately found that we didn't need to whip the egg whites. In fact, whipping the eggs was creating a huge dome, which made frosting the cupcakes a challenge. In addition, the cupcakes were so fluffy that they fell apart in our hands. Using the easiest mixing method (combining everything in a bowl) was a step in the right direction—the cupcakes were more compact and less crumbly. Unfortunately, they were still doming too much. We needed the baking soda for browning and tenderness but found we could reduce the amount of baking powder substantially. While these adjustments had solved the structural problems in these little cakes, the change in mixing method meant that the butter wasn't getting emulsified into the batter. In the end, we swapped the butter for oil, as we had done in many other gluten-free cakes (see page 533 for more details). Thankfully, the white chocolate and sour cream kept the cupcakes plenty rich, so tasters didn't miss the butter flavor, especially when the cakes were piled high with frosting. Use the scaled-down frosting variations for cupcakes on page 498 or page 499. Once the cupcakes are frosted, serve them within a few hours.

Birthday Cupcakes
MAKES 12 CUPCAKES

4	ounces white chocolate, chopped
6	tablespoons vegetable oil
6½	ounces (¾ cup plus ⅔ cup) ATK All-Purpose Gluten-Free Flour Blend (page 7)
1	teaspoon baking powder (see page 24)
⅛	teaspoon baking soda
½	teaspoon xanthan gum
½	teaspoon salt
2	large eggs
2	teaspoons vanilla extract
3½	ounces (½ cup) sugar
⅓	cup sour cream
2	cups frosting

1. Adjust oven rack to middle position and heat oven to 325 degrees. Line 12-cup muffin tin with paper or foil liners.

2. Microwave white chocolate and oil together in bowl at 50 percent power, stirring occasionally, until melted, about 2 minutes. Whisk mixture until smooth, then set aside to cool slightly. In separate bowl, whisk flour blend, baking powder, baking soda, xanthan gum, and salt together.

3. In large bowl, whisk eggs and vanilla together. Whisk in sugar until well combined. Whisk in cooled chocolate mixture and sour cream until combined. Whisk in flour blend mixture until batter is thoroughly combined and smooth.

4. Using ice cream scoop or large spoon, portion batter evenly into prepared muffin tin. Bake until cupcakes are set on top and spring back when pressed lightly, 20 to 22 minutes, rotating muffin tin halfway through baking. Let cupcakes cool in muffin tin on wire rack for 10 minutes. Remove cupcakes from tin and let cool completely, about 1 hour. (Unfrosted cupcakes can be stored in airtight container at room temperature for up to 1 day.)

5. Spread or pipe frosting over top of cupcakes and serve.

VARIATIONS
Rainbow Sprinkle Cupcakes
In step 2, after combining ingredients to make batter, gently whisk ¼ cup rainbow sprinkles into batter until thoroughly incorporated. Proceed with recipe as directed. To frost, use Easy Vanilla Frosting for Cupcakes recipe on page 498 and stir 2 tablespoons rainbow sprinkles into frosting before spreading or piping onto cupcakes.

Dairy-Free Birthday Cupcakes
We had good luck using Milkless Polar Dream White chocolate bar.

Use dairy-free white chocolate and dairy-free sour cream. Substitute Dairy-Free Cream Cheese Frosting (page 499) for frosting.

Dark Chocolate Cupcakes

G-F TESTING LAB

FLOUR SUBSTITUTION	King Arthur Gluten-Free Multi-Purpose Flour 3½ ounces = **½ cup plus 2 tablespoons**	Bob's Red Mill GF All-Purpose Baking Flour 3½ ounces = **⅔ cup**
	Note that cupcakes made with Bob's Red Mill will have a slightly coarser crumb and an earthy flavor.	
CHOCOLATE AND COCOA	Not all brands of chocolate and cocoa are processed in a gluten-free facility; make sure to read the label.	
XANTHAN GUM	Do not omit the xanthan gum; it is crucial to the structure of the cupcakes. For more information, see page 21.	

WHY THIS RECIPE WORKS

The ultimate chocolate cupcakes are moist and tender with rich chocolate flavor. Taking a cue from the success of our moist and tender Chocolate Layer Cake (page 500), we scaled the recipe to fit in a standard 12-cup muffin tin and simply adjusted the baking time. The combination of rich chocolate flavor and light, fluffy crumb once again fooled tasters into thinking these cupcakes couldn't possibly be gluten-free. Use the scaled-down frosting variations for cupcakes on page 498 or page 499. Once the cupcakes are frosted, serve them within a few hours.

Dark Chocolate Cupcakes
MAKES 12 CUPCAKES

- ½ cup vegetable oil
- 3 ounces bittersweet chocolate, chopped
- 1 ounce (⅓ cup) unsweetened cocoa powder
- 3½ ounces (¾ cup) ATK All-Purpose Gluten-Free Flour Blend (page 7)
- ¾ teaspoon baking powder (see page 24)
- ½ teaspoon baking soda
- ½ teaspoon xanthan gum
- ½ teaspoon salt
- 2 large eggs
- 1 teaspoon vanilla extract
- 5¼ ounces (¾ cup) sugar
- ½ cup whole milk
- 2 cups frosting

1. Adjust oven rack to lower-middle position and heat oven to 350 degrees. Line 12-cup muffin tin with paper or foil liners.

2. Microwave oil, chocolate, and cocoa together in bowl at 50 percent power, stirring occasionally, until melted, about 2 minutes. Whisk mixture until smooth, then set aside to cool slightly. In separate bowl, whisk flour blend, baking powder, baking soda, xanthan gum, and salt together.

3. In large bowl, whisk eggs and vanilla together. Whisk in sugar until well combined. Whisk in cooled chocolate mixture and milk until combined. Whisk in flour blend mixture until batter is thoroughly combined and smooth.

4. Using ice cream scoop or large spoon, portion batter evenly into prepared muffin tin. Bake until toothpick inserted into center of cupcakes comes out clean, 16 to 18 minutes, rotating muffin tin halfway through baking. Let cupcakes cool in muffin tin on wire rack for 10 minutes. Remove cupcakes from tin and let cool completely, about 1 hour. (Unfrosted cupcakes can be stored in airtight container at room temperature for up to 1 day.)

5. Spread or pipe (see page 499) frosting over top of cupcakes and serve.

SMART SHOPPING **Cocoa Powder**

This potent source of chocolate flavor is nothing more than unsweetened chocolate with much of the fat removed. Cocoa powder comes in natural and Dutched versions. Dutch-processed cocoa has been treated with an alkaline substance to make it less acidic (Dutching also darkens the cocoa's color). In some cases, the type of cocoa can make a noticeable difference, but for the recipes in this book we had good results with both regular (natural) brands as well as Dutched cocoas. Our favorite brand of natural cocoa is Hershey's Natural Unsweetened Cocoa; our favorite Dutch-processed cocoa is Droste Cocoa.

Frostings

Creamy Chocolate Frosting

MAKES 4 CUPS

This not-too-sweet frosting relies on egg whites and sugar heated over a double boiler until thickened and foamy. Knobs of softened butter are then added, and the mixture is beaten until silky and light. Cool the chocolate to between 85 and 100 degrees before adding it as the final step in this recipe.

4⅔   ounces (⅔ cup) sugar
4   large egg whites
    Pinch salt
24   tablespoons (3 sticks) unsalted butter, cut into 24 pieces and softened
12   ounces bittersweet chocolate, melted and cooled
1   teaspoon vanilla extract

1. Combine sugar, egg whites, and salt in bowl of stand mixer; place bowl over pan of simmering water. Whisking gently but constantly, heat mixture until slightly thickened and foamy and it registers 150 degrees, 2 to 3 minutes.

2. Place bowl in stand mixer fitted with whisk. Beat mixture on medium speed until it has consistency of shaving cream and has cooled slightly, about 5 minutes. Add butter, 1 piece at a time, until smooth and creamy. (Frosting may look curdled after half of butter has been added; it will smooth out with additional butter.)

3. Once all butter is added, add cooled melted chocolate and vanilla and mix until combined. Increase speed to medium-high and beat until light and fluffy, about 30 seconds, scraping beater and sides of bowl with silicone spatula as necessary. If frosting seems too soft after adding chocolate, chill it briefly in refrigerator, then rewhip until creamy.

VARIATION
Creamy Chocolate Frosting for Cupcakes
This variation will yield enough for 12 cupcakes.

Cut all ingredient amounts by half; follow procedure as directed.

Easy Vanilla Frosting

MAKES 4 CUPS

Even if you omit the added salt, salted butter will ruin this recipe. The heavy cream is a simple refinement that gives this fast frosting a silky quality—don't omit it.

24   tablespoons (3 sticks) unsalted butter, cut into 24 pieces and softened
3   tablespoons heavy cream
2½   teaspoons vanilla extract
¼   teaspoon salt
12   ounces (3 cups) confectioners' sugar

1. Using stand mixer fitted with whisk, whip butter, cream, vanilla, and salt together on medium-high speed until smooth, 1 to 2 minutes. Reduce mixer speed to medium-low, slowly add sugar, and whip until incorporated and smooth, 1 to 2 minutes.

2. Increase speed to medium-high and whip frosting until light and fluffy, 3 to 5 minutes.

VARIATIONS
Easy Vanilla Frosting for Cupcakes
This variation will yield enough for 12 cupcakes.

Cut all ingredient amounts by half; follow procedure as directed.

Coffee Frosting
Add 2 tablespoons instant espresso or instant coffee to butter mixture before beating. (For cupcakes, add just 1 tablespoon instant espresso or instant coffee.)

Almond Frosting
Add 2 teaspoons almond extract to butter mixture before beating. (For cupcakes, add just 1 teaspoon almond extract.)

Coconut Frosting
Add 1 tablespoon coconut extract to butter mixture before beating. (For cupcakes, add just 1½ teaspoons coconut extract.)

Cream Cheese Frosting

MAKES ABOUT 4 CUPS

Low-fat cream cheese will make the frosting soupy. If the frosting becomes soft, refrigerate it until firm.

- 16 ounces cream cheese, softened
- 10 tablespoons unsalted butter, cut into 10 pieces and softened
- 2 tablespoons sour cream
- 1½ teaspoons vanilla extract
- ¼ teaspoon salt
- 8 ounces (2 cups) confectioners' sugar

1. Using stand mixer fitted with whisk, whip cream cheese, butter, sour cream, vanilla, and salt on medium-high speed until smooth, 1 to 2 minutes. Reduce mixer speed to medium-low, slowly add sugar, and whip until smooth, 1 to 2 minutes.

2. Increase speed to medium-high and whip frosting until light and fluffy, 3 to 5 minutes.

VARIATION

Cream Cheese Frosting for Cupcakes

This variation will yield enough for 12 cupcakes.

Cut all ingredient amounts by half; follow procedure as directed.

TEST KITCHEN TIP

Piping Frosting onto Cupcakes

Frosting cupcakes with a small icing spatula or butter knife is certainly easy, but for an extra-special presentation consider using a pastry bag fitted with a large star tip.

Swirl frosting into tall pile on top of cupcake, starting at outer edge of cupcake and working toward center.

Chocolate Layer Cake

G-F TESTING LAB

FLOUR SUBSTITUTION	King Arthur Gluten-Free Multi-Purpose Flour 7 ounces = **1¼ cups**	Bob's Red Mill GF All-Purpose Baking Flour 7 ounces = **1¼ cups plus 2 tablespoons**
	Note that cake made with Bob's Red Mill will have a slightly coarser crumb and an earthy flavor.	
CHOCOLATE AND COCOA	Not all brands of chocolate and cocoa are processed in a gluten-free facility; make sure to read the label.	
XANTHAN GUM	Do not omit the xanthan gum; it is crucial to the structure of the cake. For more information, see page 21.	

WHY THIS RECIPE WORKS

Everyone loves a rich-tasting chocolate cake, but too often the gluten-free translation is less than appealing. We wanted fluffy, tender, moist layers that baked up tall and sturdy. A combination of cocoa powder and melted bittersweet chocolate provided the best flavor, but we were afraid the melted chocolate was weighing down our cakes. When we made cake with all cocoa powder, the results were dry and dense, with a very flat chocolate flavor. Instead, we kept the chocolate and cocoa combination and traded the traditional butter for oil, which had proven successful in other gluten-free cakes. This not only gave our cake better texture, but also produced a richer, cleaner chocolate flavor. Another combination of ingredients was necessary for leavening our rich layers: baking powder, baking soda, and xanthan gum. The soda helped to keep the cake tender, while the powder gave it lift, and the xanthan gum provided necessary structure. Chocolate cake recipes often call for sour cream to add moisture and richness, but this cake batter was already thick and plenty rich. Switching to whole milk gave us better results. Once frosted, our rich chocolate layer cake was an impressive sight. Use the Creamy Chocolate Frosting or any of the easy frostings on page 498. See detailed frosting instructions on page 502. Once the cake is frosted, serve it within a few hours.

Chocolate Layer Cake

SERVES 10 TO 12

- 1 cup vegetable oil
- 6 ounces bittersweet chocolate, chopped
- 2 ounces (⅔ cup) unsweetened cocoa powder
- 7 ounces (1⅓ cups plus ¼ cup) ATK All-Purpose Gluten-Free Flour Blend (page 7)
- 1½ teaspoons baking powder (see page 24)
- 1 teaspoon baking soda
- 1 teaspoon xanthan gum
- 1 teaspoon salt
- 4 large eggs
- 2 teaspoons vanilla extract
- 10½ ounces (1½ cups) sugar
- 1 cup whole milk
- 4 cups frosting

1. Adjust oven rack to lower-middle position and heat oven to 350 degrees. Grease two 9-inch round cake pans, line bottoms with parchment paper, and grease parchment.

2. Microwave oil, chocolate, and cocoa together in bowl at 50 percent power, stirring occasionally, until melted, about 2 minutes. Whisk mixture until smooth, then set aside to cool slightly. In separate bowl, whisk flour blend, baking powder, baking soda, xanthan gum, and salt together.

3. In large bowl, whisk eggs and vanilla together. Whisk in sugar until well combined. Whisk in cooled chocolate mixture and milk until combined. Whisk in flour blend mixture until batter is thoroughly combined and smooth.

4. Divide batter evenly between prepared pans and smooth tops. Bake until toothpick inserted into center of cake comes out clean, 30 to 32 minutes, rotating pans halfway through baking.

5. Let cakes cool in pans on wire rack for 10 minutes. Run knife around edge of cakes to loosen. Remove cakes from pans, discard parchment, and let cool completely on rack, about 1½ hours. (Cake layers can be wrapped tightly in plastic wrap and stored at room temperature for up to 1 day.)

6. Place 1 cake layer on platter and spread 1½ cups frosting evenly over top using small icing spatula or butter knife. Top with second cake layer, press lightly to adhere, then spread remaining 2½ cups frosting evenly over top and sides. Serve.

VARIATION

Chocolate Sheet Cake

Four cups of frosting is enough to generously frost the top and sides of the cake.

Grease 13 by 9-inch baking pan, line bottom with parchment paper, and grease parchment. Scrape all of batter into prepared pan; baking time will not change. Let cake cool completely in pan on wire rack, about 2 hours. Run knife around edge of cake to loosen. Remove cake from pan, discard parchment, transfer to platter, and frost.

TEST KITCHEN TIP **Frosting a Layer Cake**

The steps below outline the test kitchen's basic method for frosting a layer cake. A rotating cake stand makes this process a bit easier, but any flat platter can be used. The four strips of parchment paper help keep the platter neat and clean. If you notice that the cake layers are covered with loose crumbs, use a pastry brush to gently brush the crumbs away before you start. (If left in place, the crumbs will become embedded in the frosting and mar the appearance of the cake.) We like to use an offset spatula when frosting any cake. The wide, flexible blade lets you spread the icing with minimal pressure. For a particularly smooth finish, dip the spatula in hot water when performing step 6. And for a more homestyle appearance, don't smooth out the frosting as shown in step 6; instead, use a soupspoon to create billowy swirls in the frosting. Simply press the back of the spoon into the frosting, then gently twirl the spoon as you lift it away.

1. Cover edges of cake platter with strips of parchment paper to help keep it clean. Slide pieces of parchment out from under cake once frosting job is done.

2. Dollop small amount of frosting in center of platter to help anchor bottom cake layer to platter and prevent it from sliding around.

3. Place cake layer on platter, dollop 1½ cups frosting in center, and spread it into even layer right to edge of cake.

4. Lay second cake layer on top and brush away any large crumbs. Dollop more frosting on top and spread lightly to edge of cake.

5. Gather several tablespoons frosting on tip of icing spatula, and gently smear onto side of cake. Use gentle motions, don't press too hard on cake, and clean spatula as needed.

6. Gently run edge of spatula around sides to smooth out bumps and tidy area where top and sides of cake merge.

Chocolate Cream Cupcakes

✔ WHY THIS RECIPE WORKS

Hostess CupCakes were a childhood favorite for most of us here in the test kitchen, so we wanted to develop a gluten-free version that would live up to our fond memories of the original. First, we focused on creating a tender, moist cupcake with deep chocolate flavor. A combination of cocoa powder and melted bittersweet chocolate provided the best chocolaty flavor, but we were faced with an overly delicate and greasy texture. Suspecting that butter was the culprit, we swapped it out for oil, which coats the gluten-free flour particles more consistently; this is because the water in butter weakens the bonds between the fat and the protein of the flour, creating pools of grease. To make a stronger cake that could support the cream filling, we added an extra egg. Content with the rich chocolate flavor and tender yet sturdy crumb of our cupcake, we turned our attention to developing a sweet, creamy filling that wouldn't dribble out. Combining marshmallow crème and the right amount of gelatin gave us the base for a perfect creamy filling. We tried to inject the filling into the center of the baked cupcakes with a pastry bag, but the cakes cracked open and spilled filling out the sides. Instead, we used a paring knife to cut inverted cones from the tops of the cupcakes, added the filling, and plugged the holes with the top rounds. For a shiny, fudgy glaze to finish the cupcakes, we melted semisweet chocolate chips with butter. To finish the look of these cakes, we couldn't resist piping some curlicues across the top of each cupcake using some extra filling.

Chocolate Cream Cupcakes

MAKES 12 CUPCAKES

CUPCAKES

- ½ cup vegetable oil
- 3 ounces bittersweet chocolate, chopped
- 1 ounce (⅓ cup) Dutch-processed cocoa powder
- 3½ ounces (¾ cup) ATK All-Purpose Gluten-Free Flour Blend (page 7)
- ¾ teaspoon baking powder
- ½ teaspoon baking soda
- ½ teaspoon xanthan gum
- ½ teaspoon salt
- 3 large eggs
- 1 teaspoon vanilla extract
- 5¼ ounces (¾ cup) sugar
- ⅓ cup whole milk

FILLING AND GLAZE

- 1 teaspoon unflavored gelatin
- 3 tablespoons water
- 4 tablespoons unsalted butter, softened, plus 3 tablespoons unsalted butter
- 1 teaspoon vanilla extract
  Pinch salt
- 1¼ cups marshmallow crème
- ½ cup semisweet chocolate chips

1. FOR THE CUPCAKES: Adjust oven rack to lower-middle position and heat oven to 350 degrees. Line 12-cup muffin tin with paper liners.

2. Microwave oil, chocolate, and cocoa together in bowl at 50 percent power, stirring often, until chocolate is melted, about 2 minutes; whisk smooth and let cool slightly. In separate bowl, whisk flour blend, baking powder, baking soda, xanthan gum, and salt together.

3. In large bowl, whisk eggs and vanilla together. Whisk in sugar until well combined. Whisk in cooled chocolate mixture and milk until combined. Whisk in flour blend mixture until batter is thoroughly combined and smooth.

4. Portion batter evenly into prepared muffin tin. Bake until toothpick inserted into center of cupcakes comes out clean, 16 to 18 minutes, rotating muffin tin halfway through baking. Let cupcakes cool in muffin tin for 10 minutes, then transfer to wire rack and let cool completely, about 1 hour. (Unfilled and unglazed cupcakes can be stored in airtight container at room temperature for up to 1 day.)

5. FOR THE FILLING AND GLAZE: Sprinkle gelatin over water in large bowl and let sit until gelatin is softened, about 5 minutes. Microwave until mixture

G-F TESTING LAB

FLOUR SUBSTITUTION	King Arthur Gluten-Free Multi-Purpose Flour 3½ ounces = **½ cup plus 2 tablespoons**	Betty Crocker All-Purpose Gluten Free Rice Blend 3½ ounces = **⅔ cup**
	Cupcakes made with King Arthur will be slightly drier and crumbly; cupcakes made with Betty Crocker will be slightly drier and spongy.	
CHOCOLATE	Not all brands of chocolate are processed in a gluten-free facility; read the label.	
BAKING POWDER	Not all brands of baking powder are gluten-free; see page 24 for more information.	
XANTHAN GUM	Xanthan is crucial to the structure of the cupcakes; see page 21 for more information.	
MARSHMALLOW CRÈME	Not all brands of marshmallow crème are processed in a gluten-free facility; read the label.	

is bubbling around edges and gelatin dissolves, about 30 seconds. Whisk in softened butter, vanilla, and salt until combined. Let mixture cool until just warm to touch, about 5 minutes, then whisk in marshmallow crème until smooth; refrigerate until set, about 30 minutes.

6. Transfer ⅓ cup filling into pastry bag fitted with small plain tip for garnishing finished cupcakes (or zipper-lock bag; trim corner of bag before piping). Reserve remaining mixture for filling cupcakes. Microwave chocolate and 3 tablespoons butter in bowl at 50 percent power, stirring often, until melted, about 30 seconds. Let glaze cool to room temperature, about 10 minutes.

7. Cut cone-shaped piece from center of each cupcake and fill with 1 tablespoon filling. Cut off tip of cone, then replace on cupcakes and press lightly to adhere. Frost each cupcake with 2 teaspoons cooled glaze and let sit for 10 minutes. Pipe curlicues across top of cupcakes with filling in pastry bag, and serve.

TEST KITCHEN TIP **Making Chocolate Cream Cupcakes**

1. Using paring knife, cut cone-shaped piece from center of each cupcake.

2. Cut off all but top ¼ inch of cone, leaving circular disk of cake.

3. Fill each cupcake with 1 tablespoon filling.

4. Replace disk of cake and press lightly to adhere.

5. Frost each cupcake with 2 teaspoons cooled glaze and let sit for 10 minutes.

6. Pipe curlicues across top of cupcakes with filling in pastry bag, and serve.

Red Velvet Cupcakes

G-F TESTING LAB

FLOUR SUBSTITUTION	King Arthur Gluten-Free Multi-Purpose Flour 6 ounces = ¾ **cup plus** ⅓ **cup**	Bob's Red Mill GF All-Purpose Baking Flour 6 ounces = ⅔ **cup plus** ½ **cup**
	Note that cupcakes made with King Arthur will be slightly pasty, and cupcakes made with Bob's Red Mill will have an earthy flavor.	
COCOA	Not all brands of cocoa are processed in a gluten-free facility; make sure to read the label.	
XANTHAN GUM	Do not omit the xanthan gum; it is crucial to the structure of the cupcakes. For more information, see page 21.	

WHY THIS RECIPE WORKS

Red velvet cupcakes derive their color from food dye mixed with cocoa powder, and their tender texture from the reaction that occurs when buttermilk and vinegar are combined with baking soda. As with our Birthday Cupcakes (page 494), we achieved a moister, more tender crumb with oil instead of butter, especially when we used rich sour cream as the dairy element. The vinegar in the classic recipe didn't work the same way in the gluten-free version, especially with sour cream in the mix instead of buttermilk. We eventually discovered we could make these cupcakes without it. The combination of baking powder and baking soda used in traditional recipes was key, as was adding a little xanthan gum to keep these little cakes from crumbling when you eat them. For a cupcake with more chocolate flavor, we bumped up the cocoa powder from the usual tablespoon or two to a full ¼ cup. Once the cupcakes are frosted, serve them within a few hours.

Red Velvet Cupcakes
MAKES 12 CUPCAKES

- 6 ounces (1⅓ cups) ATK All-Purpose Gluten-Free Flour Blend (page 7)
- ¾ ounce (¼ cup) unsweetened cocoa powder
- 1 teaspoon baking powder (see page 24)
- ½ teaspoon salt
- ¼ teaspoon xanthan gum
- ⅛ teaspoon baking soda
- 8¾ ounces (1¼ cups) sugar
- ⅔ cup sour cream
- 6 tablespoons vegetable oil
- 2 large eggs
- 1 tablespoon red food coloring
- 1½ teaspoons vanilla extract
- 1 recipe Cream Cheese Frosting for Cupcakes (page 499)

1. Adjust oven rack to middle position and heat oven to 350 degrees. Line 12-cup muffin tin with paper or foil liners. Whisk flour blend, cocoa, baking powder, salt, xanthan gum, and baking soda together in bowl.

2. In large bowl, whisk sugar, sour cream, oil, eggs, food coloring, and vanilla together until combined. Whisk in flour blend mixture until batter is thoroughly combined and smooth.

3. Using ice cream scoop or large spoon, portion batter evenly into prepared muffin tin. Bake until toothpick inserted into center of cupcakes comes out clean, 18 to 20 minutes, rotating muffin tin halfway through baking. Let cupcakes cool in muffin tin on wire rack for 10 minutes. Remove cupcakes from tin and let cool completely, about 1 hour. (Unfrosted cupcakes can be stored in airtight container at room temperature for up to 1 day.)

4. Spread or pipe (see page 499) frosting over top of cupcakes and serve.

Carrot Sheet Cake

FLOUR SUBSTITUTION	King Arthur Gluten-Free Multi-Purpose Flour 12½ ounces = **2¼ cups**	Bob's Red Mill GF All-Purpose Baking Flour 12½ ounces = **2½ cups**

Note that cake made with King Arthur will taste a bit starchy, and cake made with Bob's Red Mill will have a mild bean flavor.

WHY THIS RECIPE WORKS

Carrot cake is typically a bowl cake made with oil rather than butter, and our early testing confirmed that this direction would work. As usual, we needed to go down on oil to account for our flour blend's inability to absorb fat. After many rounds of testing, we landed on ¾ cup of vegetable oil—half as much as we use in the test kitchen's favorite carrot cake recipe with wheat flour. With so little fat, the cake was a bit dry. We solved this problem by using more brown sugar (and less granulated sugar). We not only liked the molasses flavor provided by the brown sugar but also the extra moisture it added. We found that the simplest mixing method was the food processor. We used the processor fitted with the shredding disk to prepare the carrots, then swapped out the blade to combine the eggs, sugars, and oil. The whirring blade of the food processor ensured that the oil and eggs were well emulsified, which helped keep the oil from making the cake heavy or dense. (If you don't own a food processor, shred the carrots on a box grater and use an electric mixer to combine the eggs, sugars, and oil.) Once frosted, serve the cake within a few hours.

Carrot Sheet Cake
SERVES 15

12½ ounces (2¾ cups) ATK All-Purpose Gluten-Free Flour Blend (page 7)

1¼ teaspoons baking powder (see page 24)

1 teaspoon baking soda

1¼ teaspoons ground cinnamon

½ teaspoon ground nutmeg

½ teaspoon salt

⅛ teaspoon ground cloves

1 pound carrots, peeled

7 ounces (1 cup) granulated sugar

7 ounces (1 cup packed) light brown sugar

4 large eggs

¾ cup vegetable oil

1 cup pecans or walnuts, toasted and chopped (optional)

1 recipe Cream Cheese Frosting (page 499)

1. Adjust oven rack to middle position and heat oven to 350 degrees. Grease 13 by 9-inch baking pan, line bottom with parchment paper, and grease parchment. Whisk flour blend, baking powder, baking soda, cinnamon, nutmeg, salt, and cloves together in large bowl.

2. In food processor fitted with large shredding disk, shred carrots; transfer carrots to bowl (you should have about 3 cups). Wipe out food processor bowl and fit with metal blade. Process granulated sugar, brown sugar, and eggs until frothy and thoroughly combined, about 20 seconds. With processor running, add oil in steady stream. Process until egg mixture is light in color and well emulsified, about 20 seconds.

3. Transfer egg mixture to large bowl. Using silicone spatula, stir in shredded carrots, flour blend mixture, and nuts, if using, until thoroughly incorporated. Pour batter into prepared pan. Bake until toothpick inserted into center of cake comes out clean, 35 to 40 minutes, rotating pan halfway through baking.

4. Let cake cool completely in pan on wire rack, about 2 hours. Run knife around edge of cake to loosen. Remove cake from pan, discard parchment, and transfer to platter. (Cake can be wrapped tightly in plastic wrap and stored at room temperature for up to 1 day.)

5. Spread frosting evenly over top, and sides if desired, using small icing spatula. Serve.

VARIATION
Carrot Layer Cake
See page 502 for instructions on frosting a layer cake.

Grease two 9-inch round cake pans, line bottoms with parchment paper, and grease parchment. Divide batter evenly between pans and reduce baking time to 25 to 30 minutes. Let cakes cool in pans on wire rack for 10 minutes. Run knife around edges of cakes to loosen. Remove cakes from pans, discard parchment, and let cool completely on rack, about 1½ hours, before frosting.

Whole-Grain Carrot Cupcakes

G-F TESTING LAB

FLOUR SUBSTITUTION	Do not substitute other whole-grain blends for the ATK Whole-Grain Gluten-Free Flour Blend; they will not work in this recipe.
BAKING POWDER	Not all brands of baking powder are gluten-free; see page 24 for more information.
XANTHAN GUM	The xanthan can be omitted, but the cupcakes will be more crumbly.
RESTING TIME	Do not shortchange the batter's 30-minute rest; if you do, the cupcakes will taste wet and mushy.

WHY THIS RECIPE WORKS

We set out to transform an old-time favorite, classic carrot cake, into a gluten-free cupcake. We were after a tender, open crumb and slightly domed tops—which can be quite challenging in gluten-free baked goods. We started with our whole-grain gluten-free flour blend because we thought that its earthy flavor would pair well with the natural sweetness of carrots. We began our testing using the test kitchen's favorite carrot cake recipe, swapping in our whole-grain blend and portioning the batter out into cupcake liners. Unfortunately, this first batch was not successful and produced cupcakes that were overly sweet, dense, and gummy with flat, crystallized tops. Thinking that the sugars were partly to blame here, we focused on them first. The original recipe had equal amounts of granulated and brown sugar, and after testing various amounts and ratios of them both we found that going down on the brown sugar got us heading in the right direction. Looking next to the carrots, we found that they released their moisture during baking, which caused the cupcakes to taste wet and mushy. To encourage the carrots to release this moisture before baking, we stirred them into the batter and then let the batter rest for 30 minutes. Giving the batter a good stir after this rest helped to reincorporate this moisture evenly. In addition to the natural moisture from the carrots, we added a few tablespoons of milk to loosen up the batter, which made the cupcakes taller and more tender. We prefer these cupcakes with cream cheese frosting but Easy Vanilla Frosting for Cupcakes (page 498) will also work here.

Whole-Grain Carrot Cupcakes
MAKES 12 CUPCAKES

- 7½ ounces (1⅔ cups) ATK Whole-Grain Gluten-Free Flour Blend (page 9)
- 1 teaspoon baking powder
- ½ teaspoon baking soda
- ¼ teaspoon ground nutmeg
- ¼ teaspoon salt
- ⅛ teaspoon xanthan gum
- ⅛ teaspoon ground cinnamon
  Pinch ground cloves
- 3½ ounces (½ cup) granulated sugar
- 1¾ ounces (¼ cup packed) light brown sugar
- 2 large eggs
- 3 tablespoons 1 or 2 percent low-fat milk
- ⅓ cup vegetable oil
- 8 ounces carrots, peeled and shredded (1½ cups)
- 1 recipe Cream Cheese Frosting for Cupcakes (page 499)

1. Whisk flour blend, baking powder, baking soda, nutmeg, salt, xanthan gum, cinnamon, and cloves together in bowl.

2. In separate bowl, whisk granulated sugar, brown sugar, eggs, milk, and oil together until thoroughly combined. Using silicone spatula, stir in shredded carrots and flour blend mixture until thoroughly incorporated. Cover bowl with plastic wrap and let batter rest at room temperature for 30 minutes.

3. Adjust oven rack to middle position and heat oven to 350 degrees. Line 12-cup muffin tin with paper liners. Stir batter to recombine, and portion evenly into prepared muffin tin. Bake until toothpick inserted into center of cupcakes comes out clean, 18 to 22 minutes, rotating muffin tin halfway through baking.

4. Let cupcakes cool in muffin tin for 10 minutes, then transfer to wire rack and let cool completely, about 1 hour. (Unfrosted cupcakes can be stored in airtight container at room temperature for up to 1 day.) Spread or pipe frosting onto cupcakes before serving.

VARIATION
Dairy-Free Whole-Grain Carrot Cupcakes
We prefer the flavor and texture of these cupcakes made with soy milk, but almond milk will also work; do not use rice milk.

Substitute unsweetened soy milk for milk. Substitute scaled-down recipe of Dairy-Free Cream Cheese Frosting (page 499) for frosting.

Lemon Layer Cake

G-F TESTING LAB

FLOUR SUBSTITUTION	King Arthur Gluten-Free Multi-Purpose Flour 9 ounces = **1½ cups plus 2 tablespoons**	Betty Crocker All-Purpose Gluten Free Rice Blend 9 ounces = **1½ cups plus ⅓ cup**
	Cake made with Betty Crocker will be slightly spongy and rubbery.	
BAKING POWDER	Not all brands of baking powder are gluten-free; see page 24 for more information.	
XANTHAN GUM	Xanthan gum is crucial to the structure of the cake; see page 21 for more information.	

WHY THIS RECIPE WORKS

For an exceptional gluten-free dessert, nothing fits the bill like a sophisticated lemon layer cake. We wanted to produce a delicate dessert, with creamy lemon curd dividing layers of tender cake, all draped in swirls of meringue-like frosting. For our base, we started with the test kitchen's recipe for an airy egg white–based butter cake, swapping in our all-purpose gluten-free flour blend. Using a reverse creaming method (softened butter is added piece by piece to the dry ingredients, typically done to prevent gluten development) gave this cake a fine crumb and a tender texture. But it turned out too tender; the cake started to collapse under the weight of the lemon curd. The edges were tough and chewy, and the bottom of the cake had a sticky, greasy layer of separated butter and eggs. First, we modified the mixing method because we weren't worried about overdeveloping gluten. We melted the butter and incorporated it with the other wet ingredients; this helped the starches of the gluten-free flour best absorb the fat so that it wouldn't leach out. Next, the addition of xanthan gum helped to build a stronger cake without compromising the airy, light texture, while baking soda helped produce a fluffier yet strong crumb. Looking to eliminate the tough edges of the cake layers, we noted that the bottom of the cake didn't have this chewy quality because of the parchment paper lining the bottom of the pan. Lining the sides of the pan with parchment as well helped resolve this issue. For instructions on how to line the sides of a cake pan with parchment, see page 492.

Lemon Layer Cake
SERVES 10 TO 12

FILLING
- ¾ cup lemon juice (4 lemons)
- ¾ teaspoon unflavored gelatin
- 7¾ ounces (1 cup plus 2 tablespoons) sugar
  Pinch salt
- 3 large eggs plus 4 large yolks
- 6 tablespoons unsalted butter, cut into ½-inch cubes and frozen

CAKE
- 1 cup whole milk
- 8 tablespoons unsalted butter, melted
- 5 large egg whites
- 2 teaspoons vanilla extract
- 9 ounces (2 cups) ATK All-Purpose Gluten-Free Flour Blend (page 7)
- 8¾ ounces (1¼ cups) sugar
- 1 tablespoon baking powder
- ½ teaspoon baking soda
- 1 teaspoon salt
- ¾ teaspoon xanthan gum

ICING
- 2 large egg whites
- 7 ounces (1 cup) sugar
- ¼ cup water
- 1 tablespoon lemon juice
- 1 tablespoon corn syrup

1. FOR THE FILLING: Measure 1 tablespoon lemon juice into bowl, sprinkle gelatin over top, and let sit until gelatin softens, about 5 minutes. Heat remaining lemon juice, sugar, and salt in medium saucepan over medium-high heat, stirring occasionally, until sugar dissolves and mixture is hot but not boiling, about 1 minute.

2. Whisk eggs and yolks together in medium bowl until combined, then slowly whisk in hot lemon-sugar mixture. Return mixture to saucepan and cook over medium-low heat, stirring constantly, until mixture is thickened and registers 170 degrees, and spatula scraped along bottom of pan leaves trail, 4 to 6 minutes.

3. Off heat, stir in gelatin mixture until dissolved. Stir in frozen butter until incorporated. Strain mixture through fine-mesh strainer into bowl (you should have 2 cups). Press plastic wrap directly onto surface of mixture and refrigerate until firm and spreadable, at least 4 hours. (Filling can be refrigerated for up to 1 day; fold with silicone spatula to loosen before using.)

4. FOR THE CAKE: Adjust oven rack to middle position and heat oven to 350 degrees. Grease two

9-inch round cake pans. Line bottoms with parchment paper, and line sides with strips of parchment, then grease parchment.

5. Whisk milk, melted butter, egg whites, and vanilla together in bowl. Using stand mixer fitted with paddle, mix flour blend, sugar, baking powder, baking soda, salt, and xanthan gum on low speed until combined, about 1 minute. Add all but ½ cup milk mixture, increase speed to medium, and beat until pale and fluffy, scraping down bowl as needed, about 1½ minutes. Reduce speed to medium-low, add remaining ½ cup milk mixture, and beat until incorporated, about 1 minute. Give batter final stir by hand. Divide batter evenly between prepared pans, and smooth tops.

6. Bake until cakes are light golden and spring back when pressed lightly, 30 to 35 minutes, rotating pans halfway through baking. Let cakes cool in pans for 10 minutes. Remove cakes from pans, discard parchment, transfer to wire rack, and let cool completely, about 1½ hours. (Unfrosted cakes can be wrapped tightly with plastic wrap and stored at room temperature for up to 1 day.)

7. Using long serrated knife, cut each layer in half evenly into 2 thin layers. Line edges of cake platter with 4 strips of parchment to keep platter clean. Place 1 bottom cake layer on platter and spread ⅔ cup filling evenly over top, leaving ½-inch border at edge. Repeat with 2 more cake layers and remaining 1⅓ cups filling. Top with remaining cake layer, cut side down, and press gently to adhere. Smooth out any filling that has leaked out sides.

8. FOR THE ICING: Combine all ingredients in clean mixer bowl. Set bowl over saucepan filled with 1 inch of barely simmering water (do not let bottom of bowl touch water). Cook, whisking constantly, until mixture registers 160 degrees, 5 to 10 minutes.

9. Remove bowl from heat. Using stand mixer fitted with whisk, whip warm egg white mixture on medium speed until soft peaks form, about 5 minutes. Increase speed to medium-high and continue to whip until mixture has cooled to room temperature and stiff, glossy peaks form, 5 to 7 minutes. Frost cake with icing using back of spoon to create billowy swirls. Remove parchment strips and serve.

VARIATION

Dairy-Free Lemon Layer Cake

We prefer the flavor and texture of this cake made with almond milk, but soy milk will also work; do not use rice milk.

Omit salt. Substitute Earth Balance Vegan Buttery Sticks for butter, and unsweetened almond milk for milk.

TEST KITCHEN TIP **Cutting and Stacking a Layer Cake**

1. Measure height of cake and use paring knife to mark midpoint at several places around sides of cake.

2. Using marks as guide, score entire circumference of cake with long serrated knife.

3. Following scored line, run knife around cake several times, slowly cutting inward, to slice layers apart.

Lemon Layer Cake

The trick to a good lemon layer cake is making layers that are strong enough to support the heavy curd while maintaining a light and airy crumb.

1. LINE THE SIDES AND BOTTOMS OF THE CAKE PANS: Throughout much of our testing, we noticed a tough, candy-like texture around the sides of the cake. We figured that it would disappear as we tinkered with the recipe, but it didn't. Finding this crust unappealing, even underneath all of the billowy frosting, we realized that the bottom of the cake didn't possess this chewy quality thanks to the parchment paper lining the pan bottom. Adding a lining of parchment paper around the edge of the cake pan to protect the sides of the cake solved this problem.

2. ADD XANTHAN GUM AND BAKING SODA: In order for the thin layers of cake to support the heavy curd, they need to be very strong. Adding a substantial amount of xanthan gum gave the cake necessary structure and support. To help prevent this sturdy cake from tasting overly dense, we added some baking soda in addition to the baking powder to help with lift and to help tenderize the crumb.

3. MELT THE BUTTER: Rather than start the mixing method by creaming the butter with the sugar or the dry ingredients, we found it better to melt the butter and add it to the liquid ingredients. We then simply beat the liquid and dry ingredients together, which encouraged the flour to absorb the butter so that the cake didn't taste greasy.

4. BEAT THE CAKE BATTER VIGOROUSLY: To help build as much structure and incorporate as much air as possible into the cake batter (which translates to a sturdy but airy cake) we whipped the wet ingredients into the dry ingredients for a total of 2½ minutes. This extra whipping also ensured that the cake batter was well mixed and emulsified. We added most of the liquid at the outset, leaving just a small amount to be added at the end, in order to prevent the batter from splattering out of the bowl during mixing.

Whole-Grain Brown Sugar Layer Cake

G-F TESTING LAB

FLOUR SUBSTITUTION	Do not substitute other whole-grain blends for the ATK Whole-Grain Gluten-Free Flour Blend; they will not work in this recipe.
BAKING POWDER	Not all brands of baking powder are gluten-free; see page 24 for more information.
XANTHAN GUM	Xanthan gum is crucial to the structure of the cake; see page 21 for more information.

WHY THIS RECIPE WORKS

Sweet and buttery, brown sugar cake makes delicious use of our whole-grain gluten-free flour blend. To offset the heaviness of our whole-grain blend, we used a few tricks. Replacing some of the brown sugar with granulated lightened the texture without sacrificing the caramel flavor. Low-fat milk lightened the batter; we bolstered it with a little sour cream, which helped the structure of the cake without leaching fat. For leavening, we included a whole tablespoon of baking powder plus a little baking soda. Finally, using an electric mixer helped the brown sugar fully dissolve in the batter and incorporated lots of air, helping to keep our cake light. Extra baking time ensured the cake wasn't gummy. Be sure to use soft, fresh brown sugar so that it incorporates well. We prefer the flavor of cream cheese frosting on this cake, but Easy Vanilla Frosting (page 498) also works well.

Whole-Grain Brown Sugar Layer Cake
SERVES 10 TO 12

12½	ounces (2¾ cups) ATK Whole-Grain Gluten-Free Flour Blend (page 9)
1	tablespoon baking powder
¼	teaspoon baking soda
1½	teaspoons salt
½	teaspoon ground cinnamon
½	teaspoon xanthan gum
¾	cup 1 or 2 percent low-fat milk
½	cup sour cream
2	tablespoons vanilla extract
10½	ounces (1½ cups packed) dark brown sugar
1¾	ounces (¼ cup) granulated sugar
10	tablespoons unsalted butter, melted
4	large eggs
1	recipe Cream Cheese Frosting (page 499)

1. Adjust oven rack to middle position and heat oven to 325 degrees. Grease two 9-inch round cake pans, line bottoms with parchment paper, and line sides with strips of parchment. Grease parchment.

2. Combine flour blend, baking powder, baking soda, salt, cinnamon, and xanthan gum in bowl. In separate bowl, whisk milk, sour cream, and vanilla together until combined. Using stand mixer fitted with whisk, whip brown sugar, granulated sugar, and melted butter at medium speed until smooth, about 1 minute. Add eggs, 1 at a time, and whip until combined, scraping down bowl as needed.

3. Reduce speed to low and add flour blend mixture in 3 additions, alternating with milk mixture in 2 additions. Scrape down bowl thoroughly. Increase speed to medium-high and whip batter until light and fluffy and no clumps of brown sugar remain, about 4 minutes. Give batter final stir by hand.

4. Scrape batter into prepared pans and smooth tops. Bake until toothpick inserted in centers comes out clean, about 30 minutes, then bake for 15 minutes longer, rotating pans halfway through baking.

5. Let cakes cool in pans for 10 minutes. Remove cakes from pans, discard parchment, transfer to wire rack, and let cool completely, about 2 hours. (Unfrosted cakes can be wrapped tightly with plastic wrap and stored at room temperature for up to 1 day.)

6. Line edges of cake platter with 4 strips of parchment to keep platter clean, and place dab of frosting in center to anchor cake. Place 1 cake layer on platter and spread 1½ cups frosting evenly over top. Top with second cake layer, press lightly to adhere, then spread 1 cup frosting evenly over top. Spread remaining 1½ cups frosting evenly over sides of cake. To smooth frosting, run edge of offset spatula around cake sides and over top. Carefully remove parchment strips and serve.

VARIATION

Dairy-Free Whole-Grain Brown Sugar Layer Cake

We prefer the flavor and texture of this cake made with soy milk, but almond milk will also work; do not use rice milk.

Use dairy-free sour cream. Substitute unsweetened soy milk for milk, vegetable oil for butter, and Dairy-Free Cream Cheese Frosting (page 499) for frosting.

Gingerbread Cake

G-F TESTING LAB

FLOUR SUBSTITUTION	King Arthur Gluten-Free Multi-Purpose Flour 13 ounces = **2¼ cups plus 2 tablespoons**	Bob's Red Mill GF All-Purpose Baking Flour 13 ounces = **2½ cups plus 2 tablespoons**

Note that cake made with King Arthur will not rise as well and will be a bit denser, and cake made with Bob's Red Mill will be wetter, will not dome properly, and will have a slight bean flavor.

WHY THIS RECIPE WORKS

Old-fashioned gingerbread cake is rather austere (there's no frosting) but satisfying nonetheless because of the complex ginger and spice flavors. Employing both ground ginger and grated fresh ginger as well as cinnamon and black pepper ensured the cake had sufficient punch. Most recipes rely on molasses as well as brown and granulated sugars, and we saw no reason to depart from tradition. Melted butter imparted a greasy texture, so we switched to vegetable oil supplemented with a significant helping of sour cream (1¼ cups), as we had done in other cake recipes. (See page 533 for more on why gluten-free flours have a hard time absorbing melted butter.) During testing, the center of the cake occasionally collapsed. Up to this point, we had been scraping the batter into a large rectangular baking pan. Would switching to a tube pan (which heats from the outside as well as the center hole) help? As we hoped, the cake rose better (and there was no longer a center that could sink), but the texture was still heavy and dense. Adding more eggs (four in total) upped the protein content and ensured a better rise, as did using a lot of baking powder (4 teaspoons) as well as ¾ teaspoon of baking soda. The switch to the tube pan made us reconsider our original unwillingness to frost this cake. Yes, a dusting of confectioners' sugar would be a sufficient finish, but mixing that sugar with maple syrup (plus a little water and a pinch of salt) was just as easy and so much better. The glaze dribbled down the sides of this statuesque cake, adding both drama and yet another layer of flavor.

Gingerbread Cake

SERVES 12

CAKE

- 1¼ cups sour cream
- 4 large eggs
- ⅔ cup molasses
- 3½ ounces (½ cup packed) light brown sugar
- 3½ ounces (½ cup) granulated sugar
- ⅓ cup vegetable oil
- 1 tablespoon grated fresh ginger
- 13 ounces (2¾ cups plus 2 tablespoons) ATK All-Purpose Gluten-Free Flour Blend (page 7)
- 4 teaspoons baking powder (see page 24)
- 1 tablespoon ground ginger
- ¾ teaspoon baking soda
- ½ teaspoon salt
- ¼ teaspoon ground cinnamon
- ⅛ teaspoon pepper

GLAZE

- 4 ounces (1 cup) confectioners' sugar
- 5 teaspoons water
- 1 tablespoon maple syrup
  Pinch salt

1. FOR THE CAKE: Adjust oven rack to middle position and heat oven to 350 degrees. Grease 16-cup tube pan.

2. Whisk sour cream, eggs, molasses, brown sugar, granulated sugar, oil, and fresh ginger together in bowl until combined. In large bowl, whisk flour blend, baking powder, ground ginger, baking soda, salt, cinnamon, and pepper together. Whisk sour cream mixture into flour blend mixture until batter is thoroughly combined and smooth.

3. Pour batter into prepared pan and smooth top. Bake until top of cake is just firm to touch and skewer inserted into center comes out clean, 45 to 50 minutes, rotating pan halfway through baking. Let cake cool in pan on wire rack, about 1½ hours. Run thin knife around edge of cake to loosen, then remove cake from pan and return it to wire rack.

4. FOR THE GLAZE: Whisk all ingredients together until smooth. Pour glaze evenly over top of cooled cake. Let glaze set for 20 minutes before serving. (Cake can be wrapped in plastic wrap and stored at room temperature for up to 2 days.)

Applesauce Snack Cake

G-F TESTING LAB

FLOUR SUBSTITUTION	King Arthur Gluten-Free Multi-Purpose Flour 7½ ounces = **1¼ cups plus 2 tablespoons**	Bob's Red Mill GF All-Purpose Baking Flour 7½ ounces = **1½ cups**
	Note that cake made with King Arthur will not rise as well and will be denser and slightly pasty, and cake made with Bob's Red Mill will have a coarser crumb, will be slightly drier, and will have a distinct bean flavor.	
XANTHAN GUM	The xanthan gum can be omitted, but the cake will be more crumbly and will not rise quite as well.	

WHY THIS RECIPE WORKS

One of the test kitchen's favorite cakes is a decidedly humble affair—an applesauce snack cake that is permeated with the sweet flavor of apples and infused with warm spice notes. Three-quarters of a cup of applesauce guaranteed robust apple flavor as well as the moistness needed, and small amounts of cinnamon, nutmeg, and cloves offered subtle spice flavor. Tasters preferred a modest of amount of sugar, and a mix of granulated and brown sugar lent more complexity to this simple cake. The biggest problem we faced was greasiness. We tried using oil rather than butter, but we really missed the buttery flavor in this unfrosted cake. Trimming the amount of butter from a whole stick to just half a stick solved the problem and preserved enough of the butter flavor to satisfy our tasters. Adding two extra eggs replaced some of the lost richness (without contributing any greasiness) and introduced more protein to the mix, which meant a sturdier crumb and a better rise. Supplementing the baking soda in the classic recipe with baking powder ensured there was enough leavener (especially in the oven) to create a stable cake with a tender, open crumb. Sprinkling a little cinnamon sugar over the baked cake while it was still warm produced a crunchy, sweet crust.

Applesauce Snack Cake
SERVES 8

- 7½ ounces (1⅔ cups) ATK All-Purpose Gluten-Free Flour Blend (page 7)
- 2 teaspoons baking powder (see page 24)
- 1 teaspoon baking soda
- ¼ teaspoon xanthan gum
- 3 large eggs
- 3½ ounces (½ cup) plus 1 tablespoon granulated sugar
- 1¾ ounces (¼ cup packed) light brown sugar
- ½ teaspoon salt
- ½ teaspoon plus pinch ground cinnamon
- ¼ teaspoon ground nutmeg
- ⅛ teaspoon ground cloves
- 4 tablespoons unsalted butter, melted and cooled
- ¾ cup unsweetened applesauce, room temperature
- 1 teaspoon vanilla extract

1. Adjust oven rack to middle position and heat oven to 325 degrees. Grease 8-inch square cake pan, line bottom with parchment paper, and grease parchment. Whisk flour blend, baking powder, baking soda, and xanthan gum together in bowl to combine.

2. In large bowl, whisk eggs, ½ cup granulated sugar, brown sugar, salt, ½ teaspoon cinnamon, nutmeg, and cloves together until well combined and light-colored, about 20 seconds. Whisk in melted butter until combined. Whisk in applesauce and vanilla to combine. Whisk in flour blend mixture until batter is thoroughly combined and smooth.

3. Pour batter into prepared pan. Bake until toothpick inserted into center of cake comes out clean, 30 to 35 minutes, rotating pan halfway through baking.

4. Mix remaining 1 tablespoon sugar with remaining pinch cinnamon, and sprinkle evenly over warm cake. Let cake cool completely in pan on wire rack, about 2 hours. Run thin knife around edge of cake to loosen. Remove cake from pan, discarding parchment, and transfer to platter. Serve. (Cake can be wrapped tightly in plastic wrap and stored at room temperature for up to 1 day.)

VARIATION

Ginger-Cardamom Applesauce Snack Cake
Substitute ½ teaspoon ground ginger and ¼ teaspoon ground cardamom for cinnamon, nutmeg, and cloves. Substitute 1 tablespoon finely chopped crystallized ginger for cinnamon in step 4.

Rustic Plum Torte

G-F TESTING LAB

FLOUR SUBSTITUTION	King Arthur Gluten-Free Multi-Purpose Flour 4½ ounces = ½ **cup plus** ⅓ **cup**	Bob's Red Mill GF All-Purpose Baking Flour 4½ ounces = ¾ **cup plus 2 tablespoons**
	Note that torte made with Bob's Red Mill will have a slight bean flavor.	
XANTHAN GUM	The xanthan gum can be omitted, but the torte will be more crumbly.	

Many European cuisines have recipes for dense, single-layer cakes topped with seasonal fruit, and we particularly like the version made in Austria and Germany with summer plums. After an initial round of testing, we settled on a batter in which ground almonds replaced some of the flour. The high protein content of the almonds compensated for the low protein content in our gluten-free flour blend. The ground nuts also made the batter quite thick and thus better able to support the fruit. We also found that a little xanthan gum was necessary to build structure. As for the plums, we poached them in a few tablespoons of jelly and brandy to brighten their flavor. (Don't add this liquid to the cake pan; however, it can be reserved and served with the finished cake, ideally over a scoop of vanilla ice cream.) The cake can be served with ice cream or whipped cream. This cake is best served the day it is made.

Rustic Plum Torte

SERVES 8

- 3 tablespoons brandy
- 2 tablespoons red currant jelly or seedless raspberry jam
- 1 pound red or black plums, halved, pitted, and cut into 8 wedges
- 5¼ ounces (¾ cup) granulated sugar
- ⅓ cup slivered almonds
- 4½ ounces (1 cup) ATK All-Purpose Gluten-Free Flour Blend (page 7)
- ½ teaspoon baking powder (see page 24)
- ¼ teaspoon salt
- ¼ teaspoon xanthan gum
- 6 tablespoons unsalted butter, cut into 6 pieces and softened
- 1 large egg plus 1 large yolk
- 1 teaspoon vanilla extract
- ½ teaspoon almond extract
  Confectioners' sugar

1. Cook brandy and jelly together in 10-inch nonstick skillet over medium heat until thick and syrupy, 2 to 3 minutes. Remove skillet from heat and place plums cut side down in syrup. Return skillet to medium heat and cook, shaking pan to prevent plums from sticking, until plums release their juices and liquid reduces to thick syrup, about 5 minutes. Let plums cool in skillet, about 20 minutes.

2. Adjust oven rack to middle position and heat oven to 350 degrees. Grease 9-inch springform pan, line bottom with parchment, and grease parchment.

3. Process granulated sugar and almonds together in food processor until nuts are finely ground, about 1 minute. Add flour blend, baking powder, salt, and xanthan gum and pulse to combine, about 5 pulses. Add butter and pulse until mixture resembles coarse sand, about 10 pulses. Add egg, yolk, vanilla, and almond extract and process until smooth, about 5 seconds, scraping down bowl if needed (batter will be very thick and heavy).

4. Scrape batter into prepared pan and smooth top. Stir plums to coat with syrup, then arrange wedges in two rings over top of cake. Bake until cake is golden brown, 40 to 50 minutes, rotating pan halfway through baking.

5. Run knife around edge of cake to loosen. Let cake cool in pan on wire rack for at least 30 minutes. Remove cake from pan, discard parchment, and transfer to serving platter. Dust with confectioners' sugar and serve warm or at room temperature.

Whole-Grain Apple Upside-Down Cake

G-F TESTING LAB

FLOUR SUBSTITUTION	Do not substitute other whole-grain blends for the ATK Whole-Grain Gluten-Free Flour Blend; they will not work in this recipe.
BAKING POWDER	Not all brands of baking powder are gluten-free; see page 24 for more information.
XANTHAN GUM	Xanthan is crucial to the structure of the cake; see page 21 for more information.

WHY THIS RECIPE WORKS

Our gluten-free upside-down cake pairs sweet apples with a rich whole-grain cake. We knew we'd need a cake sturdy enough to stand up to the thick fruit topping. To start, we precooked the apples to thicken their juices and to make a thick caramel glaze. Then we turned to the cake. Although gluten-free flours are generally highly absorbent, they do have trouble absorbing fat, so we made some changes to avoid a greasy, dense cake. We reduced the amount of butter in the traditional recipe and added xanthan gum. This helped, but the cake was still dense and heavy so we tried swapping out some of the sour cream for low-fat milk. This lightened up the cake, opened up the crumb, and helped the cake to rise while keeping it sturdy yet tender. Be sure to let the cake cool fully in the pan.

Whole-Grain Apple Upside-Down Cake

SERVES 8

TOPPING

 4 tablespoons unsalted butter,
   cut into 4 pieces
3½ ounces (½ cup packed) light brown sugar
1½ pounds Granny Smith apples, peeled, cored,
   and cut into ½-inch-thick wedges
 ⅛ teaspoon salt

CAKE

 5 tablespoons 1 or 2 percent low-fat milk
 ¼ cup sour cream
 1 large egg plus 1 large yolk
 ½ teaspoon vanilla extract
 6 ounces (1⅓ cups) ATK Whole-Grain
   Gluten-Free Flour Blend (page 9)
5¼ ounces (¾ cup) granulated sugar
 ½ teaspoon ground cinnamon
 ½ teaspoon baking powder
 ¼ teaspoon baking soda
 ¼ teaspoon xanthan gum
 ¼ teaspoon salt
 6 tablespoons unsalted butter, cut into
   6 pieces and softened

1. Adjust oven rack to middle position and heat oven to 350 degrees. Grease 9-inch round cake pan.

2. FOR THE TOPPING: Melt butter in 12-inch skillet over medium-high heat. Stir in sugar and cook, swirling pan occasionally, until sugar is dark brown, about 2 minutes. Stir in apples and salt and cook, stirring often, until apples have softened slightly and juices are thickened and syrupy, 5 to 7 minutes. Scrape apple mixture into prepared pan and lightly press into even layer.

3. FOR THE CAKE: Whisk milk, sour cream, egg and yolk, and vanilla together in bowl. Using stand mixer fitted with paddle, mix flour blend, sugar, cinnamon, baking powder, baking soda, xanthan gum, and salt on low speed until combined, about 1 minute. Add butter, 1 piece at a time, and mix until mixture resembles moist crumbs, about 2 minutes.

4. Add half of milk mixture, increase speed to medium, and beat until light and fluffy, about 1 minute. Reduce speed to medium-low, add remaining milk mixture, and beat until incorporated, about 30 seconds. Give batter final stir by hand.

5. Spoon batter over apples and gently spread into even layer. Bake until toothpick inserted into center comes out clean, 35 to 40 minutes, rotating pan halfway through baking, then continue to bake 10 minutes longer.

6. Let cake cool in pan, about 2 hours. Run thin knife around edge of cake to loosen. Place serving platter over top of cake pan, invert cake, and let sit until cake releases from pan, about 1 minute. Gently remove cake pan and serve.

VARIATION

Dairy-Free Whole-Grain Apple Upside-Down Cake

We prefer the flavor and texture of this cake made with almond milk. Do not substitute soy or rice milk in this recipe.

In topping and cake, substitute Earth Balance Vegan Buttery Sticks for butter and omit salt. In cake, substitute unsweetened almond milk for milk and use dairy-free sour cream.

Rosemary Polenta Cake with Clementines

G-F TESTING LAB

FLOUR SUBSTITUTION	King Arthur Gluten-Free Multi-Purpose Flour 5½ ounces = **1 cup**	Betty Crocker All-Purpose Gluten Free Rice Blend 5½ ounces = **1 cup plus 2 tablespoons**
	Cake made with King Arthur will be dense and will taste starchy; cake made with Betty Crocker will be slightly dry and crumbly.	
INSTANT POLENTA	Not all brands of instant polenta are processed in a gluten-free facility; read the label.	
BAKING POWDER	Not all brands of baking powder are gluten-free; see page 24 for more information.	
XANTHAN GUM	Xanthan is crucial to the structure of the cake; see page 21 for more information.	

WHY THIS RECIPE WORKS

Topping this rustic polenta cake with a crown of honey whipped cream and clementines transforms it to special occasion status. Because the cake is usually made with more polenta than flour, we thought it would be easy to make it gluten-free. We were wrong. Simply swapping in our all-purpose gluten-free flour blend produced a cake that was overly heavy and crumbly—more like cornbread, less like cake. Our flour blend did not stand up well to the weight of the polenta. Adding more flour blend and reducing the amount of polenta helped to lighten up the texture a bit, but the cake was still pretty dry and dense. So we increased the amount of liquid (rosemary-steeped milk, for flavor) used to make the polenta. This worked well, and the looser batter translated into a moister cake. We also moved to a creaming method where the butter and sugar are first beaten together until fluffy, which helped transform the heavy batter into a lovely cake.

Rosemary Polenta Cake with Clementines

SERVES 8

CAKE

- 1¼ cups whole milk
- 2 sprigs fresh rosemary
- 7 ounces (1¼ cups) instant polenta
- 2 large eggs
- ¼ cup honey
- 2 teaspoons vanilla extract
- 5½ ounces (1¼ cups) ATK All-Purpose Gluten-Free Flour Blend (page 7)
- 1 teaspoon baking powder
- ½ teaspoon salt
- ¼ teaspoon xanthan gum
- 8 tablespoons unsalted butter, softened
- 5¼ ounces (¾ cup) sugar

WHIPPED CREAM AND CLEMENTINES

- ½ cup heavy cream
- 1 tablespoon honey
- 4 clementines, peeled and sliced ⅛ inch thick

1. FOR THE CAKE: Adjust oven rack to middle position and heat oven to 350 degrees. Grease 9-inch round cake pan, then line bottom with parchment paper.

2. Bring milk and rosemary sprigs to simmer in medium saucepan, then steep off heat for 10 minutes; discard rosemary. Toast polenta on rimmed baking sheet in oven until fragrant, about 10 minutes. Whisk polenta into milk until combined.

3. Whisk eggs, honey, and vanilla together in bowl. In separate bowl, whisk flour blend, baking powder, salt, and xanthan gum together. Using stand mixer fitted with paddle, beat butter and sugar on medium-high speed until pale and fluffy, about 3 minutes. Reduce speed to low and add egg mixture, scraping down bowl as needed. Add flour blend mixture and beat until combined, about 1 minute. Break up any large clumps of polenta, then beat into batter until combined, about 30 seconds. Increase speed to medium and beat until smooth, about 2 minutes.

4. Scrape batter into prepared pan. Bake until toothpick inserted into center comes out clean, 30 to 35 minutes, rotating pan halfway through baking.

5. Let cake cool in pan for 10 minutes. Remove cake from pan, discard parchment, transfer to wire rack, and let cool completely, about 2 hours. (Unfrosted cake can be wrapped tightly with plastic wrap and stored at room temperature for up to 2 days.)

6. FOR THE WHIPPED CREAM AND CLEMENTINES: Using stand mixer fitted with whisk, whip cream and honey on medium-low speed until foamy, about 1 minute. Increase speed to high and whip until soft peaks form, 1 to 3 minutes. Spread over top of cake, leaving ¼-inch border at edge. Shingle clementines over top. Use serrated knife to cut slices for serving.

VARIATION

Dairy-Free Rosemary Polenta Cake

We prefer the flavor and texture of this cake made with soy milk, but almond milk will also work; do not use rice milk.

Substitute unsweetened soy milk for milk, Earth Balance Vegan Buttery Sticks for butter, and dairy-free whipped topping for whipped cream with honey. Omit salt.

Almond Cake

G-F TESTING LAB

FLOUR SUBSTITUTION	King Arthur Gluten-Free Multi-Purpose Flour 4½ ounces = **½ cup plus ⅓ cup**	Bob's Red Mill GF All-Purpose Baking Flour 4½ ounces = **¾ cup plus 2 tablespoons**

Note that cake made with Bob's Red Mill will be crumbly and have a distinct bean flavor.

WHY THIS RECIPE WORKS

Almond cake is typically a simple, unfrosted single-layer cake with rich nut flavor. It is both elegant and casual. Despite the bold almond flavor and beautiful appearance, most traditional almond cakes are heavy and dense and come across more as a sweet confection than as a cake. Most recipes are made with almond paste and flour, plus sugar and eggs. By switching out the traditional almond paste for ground almonds, we reduced the sweetness quotient and boosted the nut flavor. This swap also made the cake lighter and less candylike. Traditional recipes don't contain much flour, so using our gluten-free flour blend worked fairly well, although we found it necessary to use an extra egg to boost the protein content and thus improve the structure of the cake. If blanched sliced almonds cannot be found, use 1 cup of slivered almonds in the cake and ⅓ cup of unblanched sliced almonds for the topping. This cake is very sticky, so be sure to grease and flour the cake pan well. Serve with Orange Crème Fraiche or simply dust with confectioners' sugar. Refer to page 530 when making this recipe.

Almond Cake

SERVES 8 TO 10

- 1½ cups plus ⅓ cup blanched sliced almonds, toasted
- 4½ ounces (1 cup) ATK All-Purpose Gluten-Free Flour Blend (page 7)
- ¾ teaspoon salt
- ¼ teaspoon baking powder (see page 24)
- ⅛ teaspoon baking soda
- 4 large eggs
- 7 ounces (1 cup) plus 2 tablespoons sugar
- 1 tablespoon plus ½ teaspoon grated lemon zest (2 lemons)
- 1 teaspoon almond extract
- 4 tablespoons unsalted butter, melted
- 4 tablespoons vegetable oil

1. Adjust oven rack to middle position and heat oven to 300 degrees. Grease and flour 9-inch round cake pan and line bottom with parchment paper. Pulse 1½ cups almonds, flour blend, salt, baking powder, and baking soda in food processor until almonds are finely ground, 10 to 15 pulses; transfer to bowl.

2. Place eggs, 1 cup sugar, 1 tablespoon zest, and almond extract in now-empty food processor and process for 2 minutes. With processor running, add melted butter, followed by oil, in steady stream, until incorporated. Add almond-flour mixture and pulse until fully combined, 4 to 5 pulses.

3. Scrape batter into prepared pan, smooth top, and sprinkle with remaining ⅓ cup almonds. Using fingers, combine remaining 2 tablespoons sugar and remaining ½ teaspoon lemon zest in bowl until fragrant, then sprinkle over top.

4. Bake until center of cake is set and toothpick inserted into center comes out clean, 55 minutes to 1 hour 5 minutes, rotating pan after 40 minutes. Let cake cool in pan on wire rack for 15 minutes. Run knife around edge of cake to loosen. Remove cake from pan, discard parchment, and let cool completely on rack, about 1½ hours. Serve. (Cake can be wrapped tightly in plastic wrap and stored at room temperature for up to 2 days.)

Orange Crème Fraiche

MAKES ABOUT 2 CUPS

- 2 oranges
- 8 ounces (1 cup) crème fraiche
- 2 tablespoons sugar
- ⅛ teaspoon salt

Grate 1 teaspoon zest from oranges; set aside. Cut away remaining peel and pith from oranges. Over bowl, use paring knife to slice between membranes to release segments. Cut segments into ¼-inch pieces, place in fine-mesh strainer, and let drain. Whisk orange zest, crème fraiche, sugar, and salt together in medium bowl. Fold in strained orange pieces, cover, and refrigerate until chilled, about 1 hour, before serving.

Rebuilding an Italian Classic

THE PROBLEM This Italian favorite, typically made with almond paste or ground almonds plus sugar, a little flour, butter, and eggs, is a sweet, dense, almost pound cake–like cake. We set our sights on developing a gluten-free version, thinking it would be an easy task given how little flour it typically requires. Using the test kitchen's most recent almond cake recipe as a starting point, we simply replaced the all-purpose wheat flour with an equal amount of our gluten-free flour blend. The result? A very dense, flat, and greasy cake. Developing a gluten-free version of this cake was not going to be a simple fix. Here's what we learned.

TOAST AND GRIND ALMONDS A key factor in this recipe is infusing the cake with deep almond flavor. Marzipan, ground almonds, almond extract, and almond paste are often used either alone or in combination. Taking a hard look at almond paste, we zeroed in on the fact that it is made of 50 percent almonds and 50 percent sugar. Given that our flour blend is already on the sweet side as a result of its two rice flours, the addition of almond paste made the cake cloyingly sweet. Grinding sliced almonds seemed like a much better route and would help us control the sweetness. Toasting the almonds deepened their flavor and made them easier to grind, plus, the ground almonds helped give the cake a nice texture. We still needed to reduce the amount of sugar to 1 cup (most recipes call for 1¼ to 1½ cups).

THE CREAMING ISSUE Traditional almond cakes cream butter and sugar before incorporating the eggs and dry ingredients. This method relies on the flour to produce gluten and create structure. Obviously we needed a different approach. We first turned to the egg foam method, which requires whipping the eggs and sugar for a full 2 minutes before incorporating melted butter and flour; beating the eggs like this not only incorporated lots of air but unraveled their protein strands so they could hold on to that air. This created the lift and structure that would normally come from gluten. But it

was actually a bit too much lift for this particular cake, which is not supposed to be tall and fluffy. Was there a middle ground?

USE THE FOOD PROCESSOR We wanted to stay true to the dense, rich texture that is the hallmark of this cake. Since we were already grinding the almonds in the food processor, we tried using it to whip and aerate the sugar and eggs, wondering if it would make a difference. Not only could we successfully whip the eggs and sugar in the food processor, but unlike the mixer, its sharp blade damaged some of the protein strands of the eggs, resulting in less overall lift. Now we had the moist interior we were looking for without all the unintended fluffiness.

A MIX OF BUTTER AND OIL Now that we were making the cake batter in the food processor, we needed to switch from softened butter to melted butter. We have found that our flour blend does not absorb fat in the same way that all-purpose flour does. To combat greasiness, we ended up using less butter, but that also made the cake a bit dry. Vegetable oil actually does a better job than butter of creating a moist crumb. (Oil-based carrot cakes are a good example of this phenomenon.) Replacing half the butter with oil helped keep the cake moist while still providing the flavor benefits associated with butter.

Lemon Pound Cake

✓ WHY THIS RECIPE WORKS

Making a superior lemon pound cake (fine-crumbed, rich, moist, and buttery) is not an easy feat. That's because the classic recipe—with just flour, butter, sugar, and eggs—contains no leavener. Using the test kitchen's favorite recipe as our guide, we began our testing by simply subbing in our gluten-free flour blend for all-purpose flour. The resulting cake was overly tender (it crumbled too easily), greasy, and gummy. Adding a bit of xanthan gum improved the structure so the cake didn't crumble. Reducing the amount of butter (the classic recipe contains two sticks) helped with the greasiness, but it also made the cake dry. We tried oil, but tasters rejected this swap—pound cake must taste buttery. We switched gears and looked to replace some of the butter with something else. After several rounds of testing, we ended up swapping out one stick of butter for an equal amount of cream cheese. Unlike butter, which separates into water and fat in the oven, cream cheese—which is much more stable—didn't cause the greasiness problem that plagued our all-butter gluten-free pound cakes. To get the most lemon flavor, we pulsed the zest in the food processor with the sugar. Since we were already using our food processor, we found that we could mix the batter with it as well, as it ensured a perfect emulsification of the eggs, sugar, and melted butter. The crumb was still a tad gummy and heavy, but adding a small amount of baking powder increased lift and produced a consistent crumb with just the right density.

Lemon Pound Cake

SERVES 8

CAKE

- 7   ounces (1⅓ cups plus ¼ cup) ATK All-Purpose Gluten-Free Flour Blend (page 7)
- 1   teaspoon baking powder (see page 24)
- ½   teaspoon salt
- ¼   teaspoon xanthan gum
- 8¾ ounces (1¼ cups) granulated sugar
- 2   tablespoons grated lemon zest plus 1 tablespoon juice (2 lemons)
- 4   large eggs
- 4   ounces cream cheese
- 1½ teaspoons vanilla extract
- 8   tablespoons unsalted butter, melted

GLAZE

- 2   ounces (½ cup) confectioners' sugar, sifted
- 2   teaspoons lemon juice

1. FOR THE CAKE: Adjust oven rack to middle position and heat oven to 350 degrees. Grease and flour 8½ by 4½-inch loaf pan. Whisk flour blend, baking powder, salt, and xanthan gum together in bowl.

2. Pulse sugar and zest together in food processor until combined, about 5 pulses. Add lemon juice, eggs, cream cheese, and vanilla and process until combined, about 15 seconds. With processor running, add melted butter in steady stream until combined, about 20 seconds. Transfer mixture to large bowl. Add flour blend mixture and whisk until batter is thoroughly combined and smooth.

3. Pour batter into prepared pan. Bake 15 minutes. Reduce oven temperature to 325 degrees and continue to bake until cake is golden brown and toothpick inserted into center comes out clean, about 40 minutes, rotating pan halfway through baking. Let cake cool in pan on wire rack for 10 minutes. Run knife around edge of cake to loosen. Remove cake from pan and let cool completely on rack, about 2 hours.

4. FOR THE GLAZE: Whisk sugar and lemon juice together in bowl until smooth. Spread glaze over cake, allowing some to drip down sides. Let glaze set for at least 15 minutes before serving. (Cake can be wrapped in plastic wrap and stored at room temperature for up to 2 days.)

VARIATION

Lemon-Poppy Seed Pound Cake
Add ⅓ cup poppy seeds to batter with flour blend mixture in step 2.

G-F TESTING LAB

FLOUR SUBSTITUTION	King Arthur Gluten-Free Multi-Purpose Flour 7 ounces = 1¼ **cups**	Bob's Red Mill GF All-Purpose Baking Flour 7 ounces = 1¼ **cups plus 2 tablespoons**

Note that pound cake made with King Arthur will not rise as much and will be denser, and pound cake made with Bob's Red Mill will have a coarser crumb and a distinct bean flavor.

XANTHAN GUM	Do not omit the xanthan gum; it is crucial to the structure of the cake. For more information, see page 21.

TEST KITCHEN TIP **Making Lemon Pound Cake**

There are three main challenges in creating a great lemon pound cake—getting enough lemon flavor, incorporating the fat to make an emulsified batter, and adding the flour to what's already a thick batter. Grinding the lemon zest with the sugar in a food processor releases a ton of flavor, and the whirring blade of the food processor also does a great job of incorporating the melted butter into the batter. Unfortunately, the food processor doesn't do a very job good of incorporating the flour evenly to produce a smooth batter. Moving operations to a large bowl and using a whisk enables you to incorporate the flour easily and evenly.

1. Pulse sugar and zest in food processor until combined, about 5 pulses. The sugar breaks down zest so its essential oils are evenly distributed in cake batter.

2. Add lemon juice, eggs, cream cheese, and vanilla and process until combined, about 15 seconds. With machine running, add melted butter through feed tube in steady stream until combined, about 20 seconds.

3. Transfer mixture to large bowl. Add flour blend mixture and whisk until batter is thoroughly combined and smooth.

TEST KITCHEN TIP **Baking with Butter versus Oil**

In the test kitchen, our preference is to use butter rather than oil in most baked goods, including cakes. In most recipes, butter tastes better. (There are exceptions, such as carrot cake, which is typically made with oil to ensure a very moist, very tender crumb.) But as we developed gluten-free cakes, we found that oil generally worked better, and butter was the "exception."

That's because the butter imparted a greasy texture to many cakes and cupcakes. In some recipes, we simply replaced the butter with oil and added sour cream for some dairy richness. In other recipes, we kept the butter but looked to other solutions to mitigate greasiness. For example, in our Lemon Pound Cake we replaced half the butter with cream cheese.

But the question lingered: Why does butter make baked goods feel and taste greasy when oil doesn't, especially since oil is 100 percent fat and butter is just 80 percent fat (the rest is mostly water)? Shouldn't butter, which has less fat, make baked goods less greasy?

The answer, as we learned, has to do with how butter and oil interact with the proteins in the flour. When oil is mixed with flour, it evenly coats the flour particles, producing baked goods with a consistent crumb. (Oil also tends to make baked goods that are a bit more compact and thus a bit moister.) In contrast, butter coats the flour particles unevenly, and small clumps of fat end up pooling together. It turns out that the water in the butter is actually the problem—it weakens the bonds between the fat in the butter and the protein molecules in the flour. (And the problem is exacerbated in gluten-free recipes because the flour has so little protein to begin with.) It's these unattached pools of butter that end up giving gluten-free baked goods their oily mouthfeel and greasy texture.

Lavender Tea Cakes

G-F TESTING LAB

FLOUR SUBSTITUTION	King Arthur Gluten-Free Multi-Purpose Flour 3½ ounces = ½ **cup plus 2 tablespoons**	Betty Crocker All-Purpose Gluten Free Rice Blend 3½ ounces = ⅔ **cup**
	Cakes made with King Arthur will be denser and slightly pasty; cakes made with Betty Crocker will be drier and more chewy.	
BAKING POWDER	Not all brands of baking powder are gluten-free; see page 24 for more information.	
XANTHAN GUM	Xanthan gum is crucial to the structure of the cakes; see page 21 for more information.	

✔ WHY THIS RECIPE WORKS

With their buttery crumb, these lavender-infused glazed tea cakes are a perfect teatime treat. We started with our gluten-free pound cake, simply portioning the batter into a muffin tin—which did not work. First, the leavening needed adjustment. The original recipe contained baking powder only, so we reduced the amount for a more modest rise and added baking soda for a more tender crumb. For a boost of elegant flavor, we pulsed dried lavender blossoms with sugar, then we continued to use the food processor to mix a well-emulsified batter. The cakes were really sticking to the muffin tin, no matter how well we greased it; we had better luck brushing the pan with a mixture of butter and sugar. This both made the pan nonstick and created a crisp exterior on the cakes. We then draped each cake in a simple glaze. For a sophisticated final touch, decorate the cakes with candied violets.

Lavender Tea Cakes with Vanilla Bean Glaze
MAKES 12 TEA CAKES

CAKE RELEASE
- 2 tablespoons granulated sugar
- 2 tablespoons unsalted butter, melted

CAKES
- 3½ ounces (¾ cup) ATK All-Purpose Gluten-Free Flour Blend (page 7)
- ¼ teaspoon baking powder
- ¼ teaspoon baking soda
- ¼ teaspoon salt
- ⅛ teaspoon xanthan gum
- 4⅓ ounces (½ cup plus 2 tablespoons) granulated sugar
- 1 teaspoon dried lavender
- 2 large eggs
- 2 ounces cream cheese
- 1½ teaspoons water
- ¾ teaspoon vanilla extract
- 4 tablespoons unsalted butter, melted

GLAZE
- 1 vanilla bean
- 7 ounces (1¾ cups) confectioners' sugar
- 2–4 tablespoons milk

1. FOR THE CAKE RELEASE: Adjust oven rack to middle position and heat oven to 325 degrees. Whisk sugar and melted butter together in bowl. Brush 12-cup muffin tin with butter-sugar mixture.

2. FOR THE CAKES: Combine flour blend, baking powder, baking soda, salt, and xanthan gum in bowl.

3. Process sugar and lavender together in food processor for 30 seconds. Add eggs, cream cheese, water, and vanilla and process to combine, about 15 seconds. With processor running, add melted butter, about 20 seconds. Scrape down sides of bowl, add flour blend mixture, and process until batter is smooth, about 15 seconds.

4. Portion batter evenly into prepared muffin tin. Bake until cakes are golden brown and toothpick inserted into center of cakes comes out clean, about 15 minutes, rotating pan halfway through baking.

5. Let cakes cool in muffin tin for 10 minutes. Invert muffin tin over wire rack and gently tap pan several times to help cakes release. Let cakes cool completely on rack, flat side up, about 30 minutes. (Unfrosted cakes can be stored in airtight container at room temperature for up to 1 day.)

6. FOR THE GLAZE: Cut vanilla bean in half lengthwise. Using tip of paring knife, scrape out seeds. Whisk vanilla seeds, sugar, and 2 tablespoons milk together in bowl until smooth. Gradually add remaining 2 tablespoons milk as needed until glaze is thick but still pourable. Spoon glaze over flat side of each cooled cake, letting some drip down sides. Let glaze set for 10 minutes before serving.

VARIATION
Dairy-Free Lavender Tea Cakes with Glaze
We prefer the flavor of these cakes made with soy milk, but almond milk will also work; do not use rice milk.

In cake release and cakes, substitute vegetable oil for butter. In cakes, use dairy-free cream cheese. In glaze, substitute unsweetened soy milk for milk.

Lemon Bundt Cake

FLOUR SUBSTITUTION	King Arthur Gluten-Free Multi-Purpose Flour 15 ounces = **2¾ cups**	Betty Crocker All-Purpose Gluten Free Rice Blend 15 ounces = **3 cups**
	Cake made with King Arthur will be drier and more coarse; cake made with Betty Crocker will be slightly rubbery and will have a darker exterior crust.	
BAKING POWDER	Not all brands of baking powder are gluten-free; see page 24 for more information.	
XANTHAN GUM	Xanthan gum is crucial to the structure of the cake; see page 21 for more information.	

WHY THIS RECIPE WORKS

To develop a sturdy yet tender lemon Bundt cake, we had to attack our traditional recipe on all fronts. Since many of our gluten-free cakes were more successful using melted butter and a simple bowl method, we started there. The resulting cake was greasy and heavy, even when we went down on the amount of butter. The traditional creaming method helped this issue and got us closer to a light and even crumb, but the cake was too crumbly. To create better structure, we added a bit of xanthan gum and another egg. Our all-purpose gluten-free flour blend is mostly white rice flour, which is naturally sweeter than all-purpose flour, so we needed to reduce the amount of sugar in the cake. A healthy dose of lemon juice and zest cut the sweetness even more and amplified the lemon flavor. And finally, because we were using so much lemon juice, whole milk, rather than buttermilk, provided the best texture and cleanest flavor. A simple glaze gave the cake an extra burst of lemony flavor.

Lemon Bundt Cake

SERVES 12

CAKE RELEASE

- **2 tablespoons unsalted butter, melted**
- **1 tablespoon ATK All-Purpose Gluten-Free Flour Blend (page 7)**

CAKE

- **15 ounces (3⅓ cups) ATK All-Purpose Gluten-Free Flour Blend (page 7)**
- **1 teaspoon salt**
- **1 teaspoon baking powder**
- **½ teaspoon baking soda**
- **¼ teaspoon xanthan gum**
- **¾ cup whole milk**
- **3 tablespoons lemon zest plus ⅓ cup juice (3 lemons)**
- **2 teaspoons vanilla extract**
- **12 tablespoons unsalted butter, softened**
- **10½ ounces (1½ cups) granulated sugar**
- **4 large eggs**

GLAZE

- **4 ounces (1 cup) confectioners' sugar**
- **4–6 teaspoons lemon juice**

1. FOR THE CAKE RELEASE: Adjust oven rack to lower-middle position and heat oven to 350 degrees. Whisk melted butter and flour blend together in bowl to make paste. Brush paste thoroughly into 12-cup nonstick Bundt pan, without leaving clumps.

2. FOR THE CAKE: Whisk flour blend, salt, baking powder, baking soda, and xanthan gum together in bowl. In separate bowl, whisk milk, lemon zest and juice, and vanilla together.

3. Using stand mixer fitted with paddle, beat softened butter and sugar on medium-high speed until pale and fluffy, about 3 minutes. Add eggs, 1 at a time, and beat until combined. Reduce speed to low and add flour blend mixture in 3 additions, alternating with milk mixture in 2 additions, scraping down bowl as needed. Give batter final stir by hand.

4. Scrape batter into prepared pan, smooth top, and gently tap pan on counter to settle batter. Bake cake until wooden skewer inserted in center comes out with few crumbs attached, 45 to 55 minutes, rotating pan halfway through baking.

5. Let cake cool in pan for 10 minutes. Run thin knife around edges of cake to loosen. Gently turn cake out onto wire rack and let cool completely, about 2 hours. (Cake can be wrapped tightly with plastic wrap and stored at room temperature for up to 2 days.)

6. FOR THE GLAZE: Whisk sugar and 4 teaspoons lemon juice together in bowl until smooth. Gradually add remaining 2 teaspoons lemon juice until glaze is thick but pourable. Drizzle glaze over cake, letting it drip down sides, and let set for 10 minutes. Serve.

VARIATION

Dairy-Free Lemon Bundt Cake

We prefer the flavor and texture of this cake made with soy milk, but almond milk will also work; do not use rice milk.

In cake release, substitute vegetable oil for melted butter. In cake, substitute unsweetened soy milk for milk, and ½ cup vegetable oil for butter.

Chocolate-Hazelnut Torte

G-F TESTING LAB

FLOUR SUBSTITUTION	King Arthur Gluten-Free Multi-Purpose Flour **2 tablespoons**	Betty Crocker All-Purpose Gluten Free Rice Blend **2 tablespoons**
CHOCOLATE	Not all brands of chocolate are processed in a gluten-free facility; read the label.	

This decadent chocolate-hazelnut torte has a crackly, meringue-like top and a dense, moist interior. It is based on a delicate balance of eggs, butter, sugar, chocolate, and ground nuts, with just a small amount of flour to create a structure slightly cakier and lighter than a flourless chocolate cake. We substituted our all-purpose gluten-free flour blend for the all-purpose flour in our standard recipe and were pleasantly surprised to find that our blend provided the structural support the cake needed. The key to this cake's texture is really determined by the quantity and texture of the nuts. We preferred the more refined texture of a cake made with toasted, finely ground nuts; we ground them in a food processor along with some sugar to prevent them from clumping. For lift, this cake relies solely on beaten eggs—it contains no other leaveners. To maximize the lift, we separated the eggs. We beat the egg yolks into the batter to provide body and richness and then whipped the whites separately to stiff peaks and folded them into the batter for lightness. Baking this cake in a springform pan made for easy removal. To toast and skin hazelnuts easily, combine the hazelnuts, 3 cups water, and ¼ cup baking soda in a small saucepan and boil for 4 minutes; drain, rinse, and rub the nuts in a dish towel to remove the skins before toasting for 15 minutes in a 350-degree oven. For neat, professional-looking pieces of cake, clean the knife thoroughly between slices.

Chocolate-Hazelnut Torte

SERVES 8

6	ounces bittersweet chocolate, chopped coarse
1⅓	cups hazelnuts, skinned and toasted
7	ounces (1 cup) granulated sugar
2	tablespoons ATK All-Purpose Gluten-Free Flour Blend (page 7)
¼	teaspoon salt
8	tablespoons unsalted butter, softened
5	large eggs, separated, plus 1 large yolk
⅛	teaspoon cream of tartar
	Confectioners' sugar

1. Adjust oven rack to middle position and heat oven to 350 degrees. Grease 9-inch springform pan, line bottom with parchment paper, and grease parchment. Melt chocolate in microwave at 50 percent power, stirring often, about 2 minutes; let cool.

2. Process hazelnuts, ¼ cup granulated sugar, flour blend, and salt together in food processor until nuts are very finely ground, about 15 seconds.

3. Using stand mixer fitted with paddle, beat butter and remaining ¾ cup granulated sugar together at medium-high speed until light and fluffy, about 3 minutes. Beat in yolks, one at a time, until combined, about 30 seconds. Reduce mixer speed to low and beat in melted chocolate, followed by ground hazelnut mixture, until incorporated, about 1 minute.

4. In clean mixer bowl fitted with whisk, whip egg whites and cream of tartar at medium-low speed until frothy, about 1 minute. Increase speed to medium-high and whip until stiff peaks form, 3 to 4 minutes.

5. Gently fold one-third of whipped egg whites into chocolate batter until only few streaks remain. Repeat twice more with remaining egg whites, and continue to fold batter until no streaks remain.

6. Scrape batter into prepared pan, smooth top, and gently tap pan on counter to settle batter. Bake until toothpick inserted into center comes out clean, about 40 minutes, rotating pan halfway through baking.

7. Immediately run thin knife around edge of cake and let cake cool completely in pan, about 3 hours. (Cooled cake can be wrapped with plastic wrap and stored at room temperature for up to 2 days.) Remove sides of pan, gently slide thin metal spatula between parchment and pan bottom to loosen, then slide torte onto platter and remove parchment. Before serving, dust with confectioners' sugar.

VARIATION

Dairy-Free Chocolate-Hazelnut Torte
We had good luck using Scharffen Berger bittersweet chocolate.

Use dairy-free chocolate. Omit salt and substitute Earth Balance Vegan Buttery Sticks for butter.

Molten Chocolate Cakes

G-F TESTING LAB

FLOUR SUBSTITUTION	King Arthur Gluten-Free Multi-Purpose Flour **2 tablespoons**	Betty Crocker All-Purpose Gluten Free Rice Blend **2 tablespoons**
CHOCOLATE	Not all brands of chocolate are processed in a gluten-free facility; read the label.	

✓ WHY THIS RECIPE WORKS

Molten chocolate cakes are a classic restaurant show-stopper. We set out to develop a practical gluten-free recipe for these elegant cakes that home cooks could easily master. To create a decadent yet light cake, we started by beating whole eggs and sugar together to create a thick foam before adding the melted butter and chocolate. This delivered the rich, moist texture we were looking for without weighing it down. While many molten chocolate cakes contain no flour, we found that a modest 2 tablespoons of our all-purpose gluten-free flour blend provided just enough structure for our cakes to walk the line between a soufflé and a fudgy cake. To create the perfect lava center, we found that many recipes simply underbake the cakes, leaving the center as partially raw batter. Not only was the thought of consuming partially raw eggs unsettling to some, but achieving the ideal gooeyness hinged on the exact cooking time and temperature of these cakes (leaving little room for oven variations or error). Other recipes call for inserting a spoonful of chocolate ganache into the middle of each cake before baking, but this required making a separate ganache. To keep this recipe simple, we just pressed a piece of bittersweet chocolate into the center of each cake before placing them in the oven, where the chocolate melted into the ideal oozing molten center. As a bonus, we found that the batter can be made ahead and poured into ramekins and refrigerated, then baked just before serving. Serve with lightly sweetened whipped cream and fresh berries.

Molten Chocolate Cakes

SERVES 8

CAKE RELEASE

- 1 tablespoon unsalted butter, softened
- 1 tablespoon Dutch-processed cocoa powder

CAKES

- 10 ounces bittersweet chocolate, chopped coarse, plus 4 ounces, broken into 8 equal pieces
- 8 tablespoons unsalted butter
- 5 large eggs plus 1 large yolk
- 3½ ounces (½ cup) granulated sugar
- 1 teaspoon vanilla extract
- ½ teaspoon salt
- 2 tablespoons ATK All-Purpose Gluten-Free Flour Blend (page 7)
  Confectioners' sugar

1. FOR THE CAKE RELEASE: Adjust oven rack to middle position and heat oven to 400 degrees. Mix softened butter and cocoa together to make paste. Brush paste evenly inside eight 6-ounce ramekins.

2. FOR THE CAKES: Microwave 10 ounces chopped chocolate and butter in bowl at 50 percent power, stirring often, until melted, about 2 minutes; whisk smooth and let cool slightly.

3. Using stand mixer fitted with whisk, whip eggs and yolk, granulated sugar, vanilla, and salt together at high speed until volume nearly triples, color is very light, and mixture drops from whisk in smooth, thick ribbon, 5 to 7 minutes. Reduce speed to low, add melted chocolate mixture and flour blend, and mix until incorporated, about 1 minute, stopping to scrape bottom of bowl halfway through mixing.

4. Give batter final stir by hand. Portion batter evenly into prepared ramekins. Gently press broken chocolate piece into center of each ramekin to submerge, breaking up any large pieces as needed. (Ramekins can be covered with plastic wrap and refrigerated for up to 8 hours.)

5. Place ramekins on rimmed baking sheet and bake until cakes have puffed above rims of ramekins, have thin crust on top, and jiggle slightly in center when gently shaken, 11 to 14 minutes (for refrigerated cakes, increase baking time to 15 to 20 minutes). Dust with confectioners' sugar and serve immediately.

VARIATION
Dairy-Free Molten Chocolate Cakes
We had good luck using Scharffen Berger bittersweet chocolate.

In cake release, substitute vegetable oil for butter. In cakes, substitute ⅓ cup vegetable oil for butter and use dairy-free chocolate.

Whole-Grain Sticky Toffee Pudding Cakes

G-F TESTING LAB

FLOUR SUBSTITUTION	Do not substitute other whole-grain blends for the ATK Whole-Grain Gluten-Free Flour Blend; they will not work in this recipe.
BAKING POWDER	Not all brands of baking powder are gluten-free; see page 21 for more information.
RESTING TIME	Do not shortchange the batter's 30-minute rest or else the cakes will taste gritty.

✓ WHY THIS RECIPE WORKS

Sticky toffee pudding is a richly flavored sponge cake full of dates in a sweet toffee sauce. We thought that the earthy, molasses-like flavors of our whole-grain gluten-free flour blend would work well in these cakes. Our existing recipe for sticky toffee pudding cakes achieves its moist crumb by baking the filled ramekins in a water bath, covered with aluminum foil to seal in the steam. The additional moisture made our gluten-free cakes mushy and wet because the flours in our blend absorb more moisture than wheat flour does. Minus the water bath, our cakes turned out tender and delicate but were now gritty. The starches in our blend needed time to soften, so we rested the batter. For fruity date flavor, we used the soaking liquid from the dates in the batter and pulsed half of the dates so that every bite of cake had both bits and chunks of sticky dates.

Whole-Grain Sticky Toffee Pudding Cakes
SERVES 8

PUDDING CAKES
- 8 ounces (1¾ cups) ATK Whole-Grain Gluten-Free Flour Blend (page 9)
- ½ teaspoon baking powder
- ½ teaspoon salt
- ¾ cup warm water
- ½ teaspoon baking soda
- 1⅓ cups pitted whole dates, sliced ¼ inch thick
- 5¼ ounces (¾ cup packed) light brown sugar
- 2 large eggs
- 1½ teaspoons vanilla extract
- 4 tablespoons unsalted butter, melted

TOFFEE SAUCE
- 8 tablespoons unsalted butter
- 7 ounces (1 cup packed) light brown sugar
- ⅔ cup heavy cream
- 1 tablespoon rum

1. FOR THE PUDDING CAKES: Whisk flour blend, baking powder, and salt together in bowl. Whisk warm water and baking soda together in small bowl, add ⅔ cup dates, and soak for 5 minutes. Drain dates and reserve soaking liquid.

2. Pulse remaining ⅔ cup dates and sugar in food processor to combine, about 5 pulses. Add eggs, vanilla, and date soaking liquid and process to combine, about 5 seconds. With processor running, slowly add melted butter until incorporated. Add flour blend mixture and pulse to combine, about 5 pulses. Transfer batter to bowl, stir in softened dates, cover, and let rest for 30 minutes.

3. Adjust oven rack to middle position and heat oven to 350 degrees. Grease eight 6-ounce ramekins and place on wire rack set in rimmed baking sheet. Portion batter evenly among prepared ramekins. (Ramekins can be covered individually with plastic wrap and refrigerated for up to 8 hours.)

4. Place sheet in oven and bake until tops of cakes are set and toothpick inserted into center of each cake comes out clean, 30 to 35 minutes, rotating pan halfway through baking (for refrigerated cakes, increase baking time to 35 to 40 minutes).

5. FOR THE TOFFEE SAUCE: Meanwhile, melt butter in medium saucepan over medium heat. Whisk in sugar and cook, stirring occasionally, until sugar is dissolved and mixture looks puffy, 3 to 4 minutes. Slowly whisk in cream and rum, reduce heat to medium-low, and simmer until frothy, about 3 minutes. Remove from heat and cover to keep warm. (Sauce can be refrigerated in airtight container for up to 2 days; reheat in microwave, about 3 minutes.)

6. Let cakes cool in ramekins for 10 minutes. Run thin knife around edges of ramekins to loosen cakes, then flip out onto individual plates or bowls. Drizzle with warm toffee sauce and serve.

VARIATION

Dairy-Free Whole-Grain Sticky Toffee Pudding Cakes

We had good luck using Silk Soy Creamer.

In cakes and toffee sauce, substitute Earth Balance Vegan Buttery Sticks for butter. In toffee sauce, substitute plain soy creamer for heavy cream.

Flourless Chocolate Cake

G-F TESTING LAB

CHOCOLATE   Not all brands of chocolate are processed in a gluten-free facility; make sure to read the label.

WHY THIS RECIPE WORKS

Flourless chocolate cake should serve as an ultimate expression of pure chocolate flavor, with a rich, dense texture that still retains some delicacy. Unfortunately, many versions are too heavy, while others are gritty. Yes, this cake should be rich, but it shouldn't be leaden, and it must be smooth and creamy. We found it imperative to whip the eggs in order to lighten the batter. Baking the cake in a water bath created a gentle moist-heat environment that ensured a smooth, creamy result. It's also important to remove the cake from the oven while it is still a little underdone. The cake will continue to cook and firm up as it cools. Good-quality chocolate is very important to the flavor and texture of this cake. You can substitute ¼ cup warm water mixed with 1 teaspoon instant espresso or instant coffee for the strong coffee. If substituting an 8-inch springform pan, increase the baking time to 22 to 25 minutes. This cake is very rich, so small slices are best. For neat, professional-looking slices, clean the knife thoroughly after each cut.

Flourless Chocolate Cake

SERVES 12 TO 14

1	pound bittersweet chocolate, chopped
16	tablespoons unsalted butter, cut into 16 pieces
¼	cup strong coffee
8	large eggs, room temperature
	Confectioners' sugar
10	ounces (2 cups) raspberries

1. Adjust oven rack to lower-middle position and heat oven to 325 degrees. Grease 9-inch springform pan, then line bottom with parchment paper. Wrap outside of pan with two 18-inch square pieces heavy-duty aluminum foil. Lay dish towel in bottom of roasting pan and place wrapped cake pan on towel. Bring kettle of water to boil.

2. Microwave chocolate, butter, and coffee in large bowl at 50 percent, stirring often, until melted, 1 to 3 minutes; set aside to cool slightly.

3. Using stand mixer fitted with whisk, whip eggs on medium-low speed until frothy, about 1 minute. Increase speed to high and whip until eggs are very thick and pale yellow, 5 to 10 minutes. Gently fold one-third of whipped eggs into chocolate mixture with silicone spatula until few streaks remain. Repeat twice more with remaining whipped eggs and continue to fold batter until no streaks remain.

4. Scrape batter into prepared pan and smooth top. Set roasting pan on oven rack and pour boiling water into roasting pan until it reaches about halfway up sides of springform pan. Bake cake until edges are just beginning to set, a thin crust has formed over top, and cake registers 140 degrees about 1 inch from edge, 18 to 20 minutes. (Do not overbake.)

5. Let cake cool in roasting pan for 45 minutes, then transfer to wire rack and let cool until barely warm, 2½ to 3 hours, running knife around edge of cake every hour or so. Wrap pan tightly in plastic wrap and refrigerate until set, at least 12 hours and up to 2 days.

6. About 30 minutes before serving, run knife around edge of cake and remove sides of pan. Carefully slide cake, still on parchment, onto serving platter. Before serving, dust with confectioners' sugar and garnish with raspberries.

TEST KITCHEN TIP **Setting Up a Water Bath**

Some cakes are baked in a "water bath," which means that the cake pan is partially immersed in water to ensure gentle heating. A water bath reduces the risk of overcooking cheesecakes and other delicate flourless cakes. Wrap the springform pan with two pieces of foil to prevent leaking.

Line roasting pan with dish towel. Place springform pan in roasting pan, fill, place pan in oven, and carefully add boiling water until it reaches halfway up sides of springform pan.

New York-Style Cheesecake

G-F TESTING LAB

FLOUR SUBSTITUTION	Do not substitute other whole-grain blends for the ATK Whole-Grain Gluten-Free Flour Blend; they will not work in this recipe.
XANTHAN GUM	The xanthan gum can be omitted, but the crust will be much less crisp.

WHY THIS RECIPE WORKS

Classic New York cheesecake owes its distinctive browned top, puffed perimeter, and luxurious texture to a risky baking technique: It typically spends the first 10 minutes in a 500-degree oven, after which the oven is turned down to 200 degrees for the remainder of the baking time. Success with this method is dependent on the oven temperature falling at a very specific rate—too fast and the cheesecake will be soupy; too slow and it will be burned, cracked, and grainy. For success every time, we turned the conventional method on its head: We baked the cheesecake for about 3 hours at the lower temperature and then removed it from the oven while we heated the oven to 500 degrees. Finishing the cake at the higher temperature produced the proper appearance and texture—but without the risk. Having discovered the secret to a perfectly velvety cheesecake, we were ready to build a simple gluten-free graham cracker crust. We ordered every brand of gluten-free graham crackers and cookies we could get our hands on and plugged them into our favorite crust recipe. Theoretically, any and all of these options would be an easy substitution for a classic crust. Instead, each brand performed catastrophically: One melted into a brittle toffee, another became chewy and greasy, while another never bound together at all, resulting in a dusty pile of crumbs in the pan. It was clear that we couldn't create a consistent graham cracker crust relying on the widely inconsistent gluten-free products on the market. Next, we tried using ground Rice Chex cereal as our "cookie" crumb. While we had better luck developing an appropriate texture for our crust, we couldn't get past the iconic cereal flavor. Instead, we decided to make a press-in dough for a buttery cookie crust using our whole-grain gluten-free flour blend. It gave our cheesecake a base with a firm texture and rich, wheaty flavor as well as a sturdy yet short crumb able to withstand prolonged contact with the wet filling without turning soggy. This cheesecake takes at least 12 hours to make (including chilling),

so we recommend making it the day before serving. An accurate oven thermometer and instant-read thermometer are essential. To ensure proper baking, check that the oven thermometer is holding steady at 200 degrees and refrain from frequently taking the temperature of the cheesecake (unless it is within a few degrees of 165, allow 20 minutes between checking). Keep a close eye on the cheesecake in step 6 to prevent overbrowning.

New York–Style Cheesecake
SERVES 12 TO 16

WHOLE-GRAIN CRUST
6 tablespoons unsalted butter, melted
4 ounces (¾ cup plus 2 tablespoons) ATK Whole-Grain Gluten-Free Flour Blend (page 9)
2⅓ ounces (⅓ cup) sugar
⅛ teaspoon salt
⅛ teaspoon xanthan gum

FILLING
2½ pounds cream cheese, softened
10½ ounces (1½ cups) sugar
⅛ teaspoon salt
⅓ cup sour cream
2 teaspoons lemon juice
2 teaspoons vanilla extract
6 large eggs plus 2 large yolks

1. FOR THE WHOLE-GRAIN CRUST: Adjust oven racks to upper-middle and lower-middle positions and heat oven to 325 degrees. Brush bottom of 9-inch springform pan with ½ tablespoon butter.

2. In large bowl, whisk flour blend, sugar, salt, and xanthan gum together until combined. Whisk in 5 tablespoons butter until fully incorporated and mixture resembles wet sand. Using your hands, press crumb mixture evenly into pan bottom. Using bottom of dry measuring cup, firmly pack crust into pan. Bake on lower rack until edges begin to darken and crust is firm on top, 22 to 25 minutes; let cool completely. Reduce oven temperature to 200 degrees.

3. FOR THE FILLING: Using stand mixer fitted with paddle, beat cream cheese, ¾ cup sugar, and salt at medium-low speed until combined, about 1 minute. Beat in remaining ¾ cup sugar until combined, about 1 minute. Scrape beater and bowl well. Add sour cream, lemon juice, and vanilla and beat at low speed until combined, about 1 minute. Add egg yolks and beat at medium-low speed until thoroughly combined, about 1 minute. Scrape beater and bowl. Add whole eggs, 2 at a time, beating until thoroughly combined, about 30 seconds after each addition.

4. Strain filling through fine-mesh strainer into bowl, using silicone spatula to help batter pass through strainer. Brush sides of springform pan with remaining ½ tablespoon melted butter. Pour filling into crust and set aside for 10 minutes to allow air bubbles to rise to top. Gently draw tines of fork across surface of cake to pop air bubbles that have risen to surface.

5. When oven thermometer reads 200 degrees, bake cheesecake on lower rack for 45 minutes. After 45 minutes, remove cake from oven and use toothpick to pierce any bubbles that have risen to surface. Return to oven and continue to bake until center registers 165 degrees, 2¼ to 2¾ hours longer.

6. Remove cake from oven and increase oven temperature to 500 degrees. When oven is 500 degrees, bake cheesecake on upper rack until top is evenly browned, 4 to 12 minutes. Let cool for 5 minutes, then run thin knife between cheesecake and side of pan. Let cheesecake cool until barely warm, 2½ to 3 hours. Wrap tightly in plastic wrap and refrigerate until cold and firmly set, at least 6 hours. (Cake can be refrigerated for up to 2 days.)

7. To unmold cheesecake, remove sides of pan. Slide thin metal spatula between crust and pan bottom to loosen, then slide cheesecake onto serving plate. Let cheesecake stand at room temperature for about 30 minutes. Serve.

TEST KITCHEN TIP **Making New York–Style Cheesecake**

1. Pour filling into crust and set aside for 10 minutes to allow air bubbles to rise to top. Gently draw tines of fork across surface of cake to pop air bubbles that have risen to surface.

2. After 45 minutes, remove cake from oven and use toothpick to pierce any bubbles that have risen to surface. Return to oven and continue to bake until center registers 165 degrees, 2¼ to 2¾ hours longer.

3. Remove cake from oven and increase oven temperature to 500 degrees. When oven is 500 degrees, bake cheesecake on upper rack until top is evenly browned, 4 to 12 minutes.

Weight-to-Volume Equivalents for G-F Flours

Different brands of wheat flour all contain the same ingredients, so they measure out the same. However, different gluten-free flour brands contain different ingredients, which will pack differently. For this reason, weight-to-volume equivalents vary from brand to brand, as you can see from the information below.

You can avoid this problem if you simply weigh your flour (this is how our recipes are written). Ten ounces of gluten-free flour blend is the same, no matter the brand. If you decide to measure flour by volume, the G-F Testing Lab feature gives you relevant conversion information.

Note that these flour blends are not always interchangeable in our recipes. For details, see the G-F Testing Lab notes for each recipe.

OUNCES	ATK Whole-Grain Flour Blend / ATK All-Purpose Flour Blend	Betty Crocker All-Purpose Gluten Free Rice Blend / Bob's Red Mill GF All-Purpose Baking Flour	King Arthur Gluten-Free Multi-Purpose Flour
1	3½ tablespoons	3 tablespoons	3 tablespoons
1.5	⅓ cup	5 tablespoons	¼ cup
2	7 tablespoons	6 tablespoons	6 tablespoons
2.5	⅓ cup plus ¼ cup	½ cup	7 tablespoons
3	⅔ cup	½ cup plus 2 tablespoons	⅓ cup plus ¼ cup
3.5	¾ cup	⅔ cup	½ cup plus 2 tablespoons
4	¾ cup plus 2 tablespoons	½ cup plus ⅓ cup	¾ cup
4.5	**1 cup**	¾ cup plus 2 tablespoons	½ cup plus ⅓ cup
5	1 cup plus 2 tablespoons	**1 cup**	⅔ cup plus ¼ cup
5.5	1¼ cups	1 cup plus 2 tablespoons	**1 cup**
6	1⅓ cups	⅔ cup plus ½ cup	¾ cup plus ⅓ cup
6.5	¾ cup plus ⅔ cup	1⅓ cups	⅔ cup plus ½ cup
7	1⅓ cups plus ¼ cup	1¼ cups plus 2 tablespoons	1¼ cups
7.5	1⅔ cups	1½ cups	1¼ cups plus 2 tablespoons
8	1¾ cups	1½ cups plus 2 tablespoons	¾ cup plus ⅔ cup
8.5	1¾ cups plus 2 tablespoons	1⅔ cups	1⅓ cups plus ¼ cup
9	**2 cups**	1½ cups plus ⅓ cup	1½ cups plus 2 tablespoons
9.5	2 cups plus 2 tablespoons	1¾ cups plus 2 tablespoons	1¾ cups
10	2¼ cups	**2 cups**	1½ cups plus ⅓ cup
10.5	2⅓ cups	2 cups plus 2 tablespoons	1⅔ cups plus ¼ cup
11	1¾ cups plus ⅔ cup	1⅔ cups plus ½ cup	**2 cups**
11.5	2⅓ cups plus ¼ cup	2⅓ cups	1¾ cups plus ⅓ cup
12	2⅔ cups	2¼ cups plus 2 tablespoons	1⅔ cups plus ½ cup
12.5	2¾ cups	2½ cups	2¼ cups
13	2¾ cups plus 2 tablespoons	2½ cups plus 2 tablespoons	2¼ cups plus 2 tablespoons
13.5	**3 cups**	2⅔ cups	1¾ cups plus ⅔ cup
14	3 cups plus 2 tablespoons	2½ cups plus ⅓ cup	2⅓ cups plus ¼ cup
14.5	3¼ cups	2¾ cups plus 2 tablespoons	2½ cups plus 2 tablespoons
15	3⅓ cups	**3 cups**	2¾ cups
15.5	2¾ cups plus ⅔ cup	3 cups plus 2 tablespoons	2½ cups plus ⅓ cup
16	3⅓ cups plus ¼ cup	2⅔ cups plus ½ cup	2⅔ cups plus ¼ cup
16.5	3⅔ cups	3⅓ cups	**3 cups**

Conversions and Equivalents

The recipes in this book were developed using standard U.S. measures following U.S. government guidelines. The charts below offer equivalents for U.S. and metric measures. All conversions are approximate and have been rounded up or down to the nearest whole number.

EXAMPLE:

1 teaspoon = 4.9292 milliliters, rounded up to 5 milliliters

1 ounce = 28.3495 grams, rounded down to 28 grams

VOLUME CONVERSIONS

U.S.	METRIC
1 teaspoon	5 milliliters
2 teaspoons	10 milliliters
1 tablespoon	15 milliliters
2 tablespoons	30 milliliters
¼ cup	59 milliliters
⅓ cup	79 milliliters
½ cup	118 milliliters
¾ cup	177 milliliters
1 cup	237 milliliters
1¼ cups	296 milliliters
1½ cups	355 milliliters
2 cups (1 pint)	473 milliliters
2½ cups	591 milliliters
3 cups	710 milliliters
4 cups (1 quart)	0.946 liter
1.06 quarts	1 liter
4 quarts (1 gallon)	3.8 liters

WEIGHT CONVERSIONS

OUNCES	GRAMS
½	14
¾	21
1	28
1½	43
2	57
2½	71
3	85
3½	99
4	113
4½	128
5	142
6	170
7	198
8	227
9	255
10	283
12	340
16 (1 pound)	454

CONVERSIONS FOR INGREDIENTS COMMONLY USED IN BAKING

Baking is an exacting science. Because measuring by weight is far more accurate than measuring by volume, and thus more likely to achieve reliable results, in our recipes we provide ounce measures in addition to cup measures for many ingredients. Refer to the chart below to convert these measures into grams.

INGREDIENT	OUNCES	GRAMS
1 cup granulated (white) sugar	7	198
1 cup packed brown sugar (light or dark)	7	198
1 cup confectioners' sugar	4	113
1 cup cocoa powder	3	85
4 tablespoons butter* (½ stick, or ¼ cup)	2	57
8 tablespoons butter* (1 stick, or ½ cup)	4	113
16 tablespoons butter* (2 sticks, or 1 cup)	8	227

* In the United States, butter is sold both salted and unsalted. We generally recommend unsalted butter. If you are using salted butter, take this into consideration before adding salt to a recipe.

OVEN TEMPERATURES

FAHRENHEIT	CELSIUS	GAS MARK
225	105	¼
250	120	½
275	135	1
300	150	2
325	165	3
350	180	4
375	190	5
400	200	6
425	220	7
450	230	8
475	245	9

CONVERTING TEMPERATURES FROM AN INSTANT-READ THERMOMETER

We include doneness temperatures in many of the recipes in this book. We recommend an instant-read thermometer for the job. Refer to the above table to convert Fahrenheit degrees to Celsius. Or, for temperatures not represented in the chart, use this simple formula:

Subtract 32 degrees from the Fahrenheit reading, then divide the result by 1.8 to find the Celsius reading.

EXAMPLE:
"Roast chicken until thighs register 175 degrees."
To convert:
$175°F - 32 = 143°$
$143° \div 1.8 = 79.44°C$, rounded down to $79°C$

Nutritional Information for Our Recipes

Analyzing recipes for their nutritional values is a tricky business, and we did our best to be as realistic and accurate as possible throughout this book. We were absolutely strict about measuring when cooking and never resorted to guessing or estimating. And we never made the portion sizes unreasonably small to make the nutritional numbers appear lower. We also didn't play games when analyzing the recipes in the nutritional program to make the numbers look better. To calculate the nutritional values of our recipes per serving, we used The Food Processor SQL by ESHA Research. When using this program, we entered all the ingredients, including optional ones, using weights for important ingredients such as meat, cheese, and most vegetables. We also used all of our preferred brands in these analyses. Yet there are two tricky ingredients to be mindful of when analyzing a recipe that require some special rules of their own: salt and fat.

When the recipe called for seasoning with an unspecified amount of salt and pepper (often raw meat), we added ½ teaspoon salt and ¼ teaspoon pepper to the analysis. We did not, however, include additional salt or pepper in our analysis when the food was "seasoned to taste" at the end of cooking. As for fat, it can be difficult to accurately predict the amount of oil absorbed during frying. We compared our recipes, without any added cooking fat, to similar foods in The Food Processor SQL to estimate how much fat was absorbed during cooking. We found a good rule of thumb to be that most foods absorb 10 percent of their weight in oil on average. (The exception to this rule is our recipe for Polenta Fries, which are shallow fried and not deep fried. For this recipe we used 5 percent of the recipe's weight to account for the oil absorption.) We then added the estimated amount of fat back into our nutritional analysis to calculate our final numbers.

Note: Unless otherwise indicated, information applies to a single serving. If there is a range in the serving size in the recipe, we used the highest number of servings to calculate the nutritional values.

	Cal	Fat	Sat Fat	Chol	Sodium	Carb	Fiber	Protein
GLUTEN-FREE BASICS								
America's Test Kitchen All-Purpose Gluten-Free Flour Blend (1 ounce)	100	0g	0g	0mg	10mg	23g	1g	1g
America's Test Kitchen Whole-Grain Gluten-Free Flour Blend (1 ounce)	110	2.5g	0g	0mg	0mg	19g	4g	4g
A GOOD START								
Buttermilk Pancakes (1 pancake)	120	4g	2g	30mg	260mg	18g	0g	3g
Whole-Grain Pancakes (1 pancake)	140	6g	1.5g	25mg	180mg	17g	3g	4g
Dairy-Free Whole-Grain Pancakes (1 pancake)	130	6g	0.5g	20mg	170mg	16g	3g	4g
Buckwheat Blueberry Pancakes (1 pancake)	140	5g	2.5g	45mg	230mg	19g	1g	3g
Fluffy Oat Pancakes (1 pancake)	120	4.5g	1.5g	30mg	190mg	14g	2g	4g
Dairy-Free Fluffy Oat Pancakes (1 pancake)	120	5g	0.5g	25mg	190mg	13g	2g	4g
Johnnycakes (1 johnnycake)	80	4.5g	1.5g	5mg	150mg	10g	1g	1g
Dairy-Free Johnnycakes (1 johnnycake)	70	3.5g	0.5g	0mg	160mg	10g	1g	1g
Maple Butter (1 tablespoon)	90	9g	6g	25mg	115mg	3g	0g	0g
Lemon Ricotta Pancakes (1 pancake)	120	6g	3.5g	45mg	190mg	12g	0g	5g
Pear-Blackberry Pancake Topping (½ cup)	70	0g	0g	0mg	25mg	18g	4g	1g
Crepes with Lemon and Sugar (1 crepe)	160	6g	3g	60mg	120mg	24g	1g	4g
Crepes with Bananas and Nutella (1 crepe)	200	7g	3.5g	60mg	120mg	29g	1g	4g
Crepes with Honey and Toasted Almonds (1 crepe)	190	8g	3g	60mg	260mg	25g	1g	5g
Buttermilk Waffles (1 waffle)	430	13g	7g	140mg	520mg	64g	1g	10g
Whole-Grain Waffles (1 waffle)	590	25g	6g	160mg	520mg	76g	11g	20g
Dairy-Free Whole-Grain Waffles (1 waffle)	580	27g	2.5g	140mg	530mg	71g	12g	17g

	Cal	Fat	Sat Fat	Chol	Sodium	Carb	Fiber	Protein
Blueberry Muffins	250	9g	5g	70mg	240mg	38g	1g	3g
Whole-Grain Blueberry Muffins	320	16g	8g	80mg	400mg	41g	4g	6g
Dairy-Free Whole-Grain Blueberry Muffins	300	14g	1.5g	45mg	440mg	41g	5g	5g
Cranberry-Orange Pecan Muffins	280	12g	6g	70mg	240mg	38g	2g	4g
Coconut-Cashew Muffins	350	19g	10g	70mg	270mg	41g	2g	5g
Dairy-Free Coconut-Cashew Muffins	360	21g	6g	45mg	280mg	41g	2g	5g
Corn Muffins	310	15g	9g	70mg	290mg	40g	2g	4g
Dairy-Free Corn Muffins	340	18g	3.5g	30mg	380mg	43g	2g	5g
Millet-Cherry Almond Muffins	260	10g	5g	70mg	240mg	41g	2g	4g
Currant Scones	330	16g	10g	70mg	350mg	43g	1g	3g
Dairy-Free Currant Scones	350	17g	7g	30mg	470mg	46g	1g	4g
Banana Bread (⅔" slice)	290	12g	5g	50mg	330mg	45g	2g	4g
Date-Nut Bread (⅔" slice)	300	12g	4.5g	45mg	330mg	43g	2g	5g
Dairy-Free Date-Nut Bread (⅔" slice)	310	14g	1.5g	30mg	320mg	43g	2g	4g
Pumpkin Bread (⅔" slice)	220	11g	2g	35mg	380mg	29g	1g	3g
Whole-Grain Chai Spice Bread (⅔" slice)	300	14g	6g	55mg	460mg	39g	4g	6g
Dairy-Free Whole-Grain Chai Spice Bread (⅔" slice)	310	16g	1.5g	30mg	460mg	38g	4g	6g
Coffee Cake	320	14g	7g	75mg	330mg	43g	1g	3g
Whole-Grain Gingerbread Coffee Cake	300	12g	6g	60mg	500mg	44g	3g	5g
Dairy-Free Whole-Grain Gingerbread Coffee Cake	290	11g	3.5g	35mg	530mg	44g	3g	5g
New York–Style Crumb Cake	500	24g	14g	150mg	230mg	64g	1g	5g
Dairy-Free New York–Style Crumb Cake	500	25g	10g	95mg	390mg	64g	1g	5g
Yeasted Doughnuts	380	17g	4.5g	50mg	190mg	54g	2g	4g
Dairy-Free Yeasted Doughnuts	380	17g	3g	35mg	210mg	54g	2g	4g
Cinnamon Sugar–Glazed Doughnuts	390	17g	4g	50mg	190mg	56g	2g	4g
Vanilla-Glazed Doughnuts	390	17g	4g	50mg	190mg	56g	2g	4g
Chocolate-Glazed Doughnuts	480	21g	7g	55mg	200mg	69g	3g	5g
Popovers	200	8g	3.5g	135mg	270mg	23g	1g	7g
10-Minute Steel-Cut Oatmeal	170	3g	0g	0mg	150mg	29g	5g	7g
Apple-Cinnamon 10-Minute Steel-Cut Oatmeal	340	14g	2g	5mg	310mg	46g	7g	10g
Cranberry-Orange 10-Minute Steel-Cut Oatmeal	360	10g	1.5g	5mg	310mg	59g	7g	11g
Carrot-Spice 10-Minute Steel-Cut Oatmeal	380	14g	2g	5mg	490mg	58g	8g	10g
Millet Porridge with Maple Syrup	260	4g	1g	5mg	105mg	49g	8g	8g
Millet Porridge with Dried Cherries and Pecans	400	14g	2g	5mg	110mg	61g	11g	10g
Millet Porridge with Coconut and Bananas	410	18g	14g	0mg	115mg	58g	11g	8g
Hot Quinoa Breakfast Cereal with Blueberries and Almonds	210	8g	0.5g	0mg	75mg	29g	5g	7g
Hot Quinoa Breakfast Cereal with Raspberries and Sunflower Seeds	200	7g	1.5g	5mg	70mg	28g	5g	8g
Hot Quinoa Breakfast Cereal with Golden Raisins and Pistachios	250	8g	1.5g	5mg	75mg	38g	4g	8g
Three-Grain Breakfast Porridge	370	5g	1.5g	5mg	340mg	73g	7g	10g
Dairy-Free Three-Grain Breakfast Porridge	370	5g	1.5g	5mg	340mg	73g	7g	10g
Three-Grain Breakfast Porridge with Blueberries and Maple	410	5g	1.5g	5mg	340mg	83g	9g	11g
Three-Grain Breakfast Porridge with Tahini and Apricots	590	15g	2.5g	5mg	350mg	104g	11g	15g
Almond Granola with Dried Fruit (½ cup)	340	16g	1.5g	0mg	70mg	43g	6g	8g

	Cal	Fat	Sat Fat	Chol	Sodium	Carb	Fiber	Protein
Quinoa Granola with Sunflower Seeds and Almonds (½ cup)	345	19g	8g	0mg	70mg	36g	5g	8g
Quinoa Granola with Pecans, Espresso, and Chocolate (½ cup)	400	26g	12.5g	0mg	70mg	39g	5g	6.5g
Quinoa Granola with Pepitas, Cayenne, and Golden Raisins (½ cup)	355	20g	8g	0mg	75mg	37.5g	5g	8.5g

GRAINS

	Cal	Fat	Sat Fat	Chol	Sodium	Carb	Fiber	Protein
Coconut Rice with Bok Choy and Lime	230	8g	5g	0mg	800mg	36g	2g	4g
Basmati Rice Pilaf	180	3g	0g	0mg	100mg	35g	1g	3g
Herbed Basmati Rice Pilaf	180	3g	0g	0mg	100mg	35g	1g	3g
Basmati Rice Pilaf with Peas, Scallions, and Lemon	190	3g	0g	0mg	100mg	37g	2g	4g
Basmati Rice Pilaf with Currants and Toasted Almonds	200	2.5g	0g	0mg	100mg	41g	2g	4g
Hearty Baked Brown Rice with Onions and Roasted Red Peppers	240	6g	1.5g	5mg	650mg	41g	2g	7g
Hearty Baked Brown Rice with Black Beans and Cilantro	250	4.5g	0.5g	0mg	630mg	45g	4g	7g
Hearty Baked Brown Rice with Peas, Feta, and Mint	250	6g	2.5g	10mg	600mg	41g	3g	8g
Wild Rice Pilaf with Pecans and Cranberries	360	12g	3.5g	10mg	430mg	57g	3g	7g
Wild Rice Pilaf with Scallions, Cilantro, and Almonds	310	9g	3g	10mg	430mg	48g	2g	8g
Black Rice Salad with Snap Peas and Ginger-Sesame Vinaigrette	310	14g	2g	0mg	450mg	44g	5g	6g
Brown Rice Bowls with Roasted Carrots, Kale, and Fried Eggs	480	25g	4.5g	185mg	590mg	51g	6g	13g
Indonesian-Style Fried Rice	480	17g	2g	125mg	1380mg	67g	4g	14g
Miso Brown Rice Cakes	440	17g	2g	95mg	880mg	60g	3g	11g
Sriracha Mayonnaise (1 tablespoon)	70	7g	1g	5mg	110mg	1g	0g	0g
Almost Hands-Free Risotto with Parmesan and Herbs	390	11g	6g	25mg	940mg	55g	3g	11g
Almost Hands-Free Risotto with Chicken and Herbs	520	16g	7g	95mg	980mg	55g	3g	31g
Creamy Parmesan Polenta	310	15g	8g	35mg	1410mg	31g	3g	16g
Sautéed Cherry Tomato and Fresh Mozzarella Topping	250	20g	8g	30mg	130mg	7g	2g	9g
Broccoli Rabe, Sun-Dried Tomato, and Pine Nut Topping	190	17g	2g	0mg	380mg	8g	1g	4g
Wild Mushroom and Rosemary Topping	150	13g	4.5g	15mg	55mg	7g	1g	2g
Quinoa Pilaf with Herbs and Lemon	200	6g	2.5g	10mg	300mg	29g	3g	6g
Quinoa Pilaf with Chile, Queso Fresco, and Peanuts	300	15g	5g	15mg	370mg	33g	5g	11g
Quinoa Pilaf with Apricots, Pistachios, and Aged Gouda	310	14g	5g	20mg	370mg	37g	5g	11g
Quinoa Pilaf with Olives, Raisins, and Cilantro	230	7g	2.5g	10mg	400mg	35g	4g	6g
Quinoa Pilaf with Shiitakes, Edamame, and Ginger	230	8g	1g	0mg	300mg	31g	4g	8g
Rainbow Quinoa Pilaf with Swiss Chard and Carrots	240	7g	0g	0mg	500mg	36g	4g	6g
Rainbow Quinoa Pilaf with Bell Pepper, Lime, and Cilantro	230	7g	0g	0mg	410mg	35g	3g	6g
Quinoa Salad with Red Bell Pepper and Cilantro	200	6g	1g	0mg	220mg	30g	4g	6g
Quinoa, Black Bean, and Mango Salad with Lime Dressing	450	27g	3.5g	0mg	350mg	45g	8g	9g
Quinoa Patties with Spinach and Sun-Dried Tomatoes (1 patty)	190	11g	2.5g	55mg	380mg	17g	2g	6g
Kasha Pilaf with Caramelized Onions	260	12g	1.5g	0mg	10mg	36g	4g	6g
Creamy Cheesy Millet	210	8g	2.5g	10mg	580mg	27g	6g	10g
Curried Millet Pilaf	260	7g	1g	5mg	310mg	44g	9g	8g
Millet Salad with Corn and Queso Fresco	230	9g	1.5g	0mg	320mg	31g	3g	5g
Millet Salad with Oranges, Olives, and Almonds	260	12g	1.5g	0mg	420mg	33g	5g	5g
Millet Salad with Endive, Blueberries, and Goat Cheese	310	17g	4.5g	10mg	380mg	34g	5g	8g
Millet Cakes with Spinach and Carrots	350	15g	2g	50mg	410mg	46g	8g	10g

	Cal	Fat	Sat Fat	Chol	Sodium	Carb	Fiber	Protein
Dairy-Free Millet Cakes with Spinach and Carrots	360	14g	1.5g	45mg	400mg	47g	8g	10g
Cucumber-Yogurt Sauce (1 tablespoon)	10	1g	0g	0mg	0mg	0g	0g	1g
Buckwheat Tabbouleh	270	15g	2g	0mg	610mg	30g	5g	6g
Buckwheat Bowls with Lemon-Yogurt Sauce	510	26g	4g	5mg	620mg	60g	10g	13g
Dairy-Free Buckwheat Bowls with Lemon-Yogurt Sauce	520	26g	3.5g	0mg	610mg	61g	11g	13g
Oat Berry Pilaf with Walnuts and Gorgonzola	310	17g	3g	10mg	230mg	39g	6g	12g
Oat Berry, Chickpea, and Arugula Salad	220	11g	2.5g	10mg	550mg	28g	5g	9g
Oat Berry and Mushroom Risotto	130	4.5g	0g	0mg	440mg	24g	4g	7g
Polenta Fries	270	16g	1g	0mg	590mg	27g	2g	3g
Herb Mayonnaise (1 tablespoon)	80	9g	1g	5mg	70mg	0g	0g	0g

PASTA

	Cal	Fat	Sat Fat	Chol	Sodium	Carb	Fiber	Protein
Fresh Pasta	230	6g	1.5g	125mg	440mg	39g	2g	7g
Fresh Pasta al Limone	420	25g	7g	140mg	800mg	40g	2g	11g
Fresh Pasta with Tomato–Brown Butter Sauce	330	14g	6g	145mg	880mg	45g	3g	8g
Fresh Pasta Alfredo	500	34g	19g	220mg	780mg	41g	2g	11g
Penne with Spiced Butter, Cauliflower, and Pine Nuts	710	38g	13g	45mg	650mg	82g	9g	15g
Fusilli with Basil Pesto	580	30g	4g	5mg	560mg	67g	4g	12g
Fusilli with Kale–Sunflower Seed Pesto	600	29g	5g	10mg	690mg	68g	4g	16g
Fusilli with Roasted Red Pepper Pesto	530	24g	3.5g	5mg	1170mg	67g	3g	11g
Fusilli with Spring Vegetable Cream Sauce	750	34g	16g	85mg	1050mg	91g	9g	18g
Spaghetti with Puttanesca Sauce	490	12g	1g	5mg	1240mg	84g	8g	14g
Spaghetti and Meatballs	810	32g	10g	130mg	1400mg	91g	9g	38g
Penne with Sausage and Red Pepper Ragu	630	16g	4g	35mg	1260mg	86g	7g	30g
Penne with Weeknight Meat Sauce	730	25g	8g	80mg	1790mg	91g	8g	36g
Soba Noodles with Pork, Shiitakes, and Bok Choy	550	16g	3.5g	85mg	1600mg	68g	7g	37g
Soba Noodles with Roasted Eggplant and Sesame	510	23g	2.5g	0mg	1240mg	70g	9g	11g
Drunken Noodles with Chicken	740	18g	2g	60mg	1730mg	118g	4g	28g
Singapore Noodles with Shrimp	420	9g	1g	105mg	1930mg	63g	5g	21g
Pad Thai with Shrimp	560	25g	3.5g	175mg	1090mg	67g	4g	22g
Spicy Basil Noodles with Crispy Tofu, Snap Peas, and Bell Pepper	820	32g	2.5g	0mg	1190mg	116g	6g	20g

COMFORT FOODS

	Cal	Fat	Sat Fat	Chol	Sodium	Carb	Fiber	Protein
Lasagna with Hearty Tomato-Meat Sauce	680	38g	20g	150mg	1010mg	45g	4g	37g
Spinach and Tomato Lasagna	550	24g	13g	115mg	1180mg	48g	6g	29g
Vegetable Lasagna	500	25g	11g	75mg	1130mg	43g	5g	23g
Chicken Parmesan	620	41g	9g	125mg	1150mg	25g	4g	36g
Eggplant Parmesan	500	31g	8g	110mg	970mg	39g	6g	16g
Easy Stovetop Macaroni and Cheese	850	45g	23g	225mg	970mg	75g	3g	37g
Baked Macaroni and Cheese	1130	67g	40g	185mg	1240mg	86g	3g	45g
All-American Meatloaf	500	32g	11g	170mg	830mg	23g	1g	30g
Cheesy Southwestern Meatloaf	490	25g	11g	220mg	1140mg	23g	2g	41g
Fried Chicken	1000	53g	12g	250mg	1100mg	57g	2g	72g
Batter-Fried Fish	420	27g	3g	75mg	670mg	15g	0g	32g
Tartar Sauce (1 tablespoon)	310	33g	4.5g	15mg	430mg	3g	0g	0g
New England Clam Chowder	430	20g	11g	110mg	1180mg	37g	3g	23g
Quicker New England Clam Chowder	380	19g	10g	85mg	1260mg	38g	3g	14g

	Cal	Fat	Sat Fat	Chol	Sodium	Carb	Fiber	Protein
Breaded Pork Cutlets	430	29g	4.5g	105mg	310mg	16g	0g	28g
Lemon-Thyme Breaded Pork Cutlets	430	29g	4.5g	105mg	310mg	16g	0g	28g
Crispy Pan-Fried Pork Chops	540	27g	4.5g	115mg	520mg	31g	1g	42g
Crispy Chicken Fingers	570	30g	4g	210mg	550mg	28g	1g	43g
Pecan-Crusted Chicken	550	32g	9g	115mg	450mg	27g	4g	38g
Buffalo Chicken Wings	380	27g	10g	185mg	1520mg	3g	0g	28g
Chicken Wings with Sweet and Spicy Thai Sauce	400	22g	6g	165mg	1080mg	20g	0g	28g
Orange-Flavored Chicken	900	53g	10g	160mg	1420mg	65g	1g	40g
Chicken Enchiladas (1 enchilada)	290	18g	8g	65mg	690mg	17g	3g	16g
Chicken and Dumplings	520	20g	6g	160mg	1080mg	46g	4g	36g
Dairy-Free Chicken and Dumplings	520	20g	4.5g	140mg	1140mg	46g	4g	36g
Chicken Pot Pie	550	30g	17g	160mg	500mg	38g	2g	29g
Beef Pot Pie	630	30g	13g	150mg	1110mg	41g	3g	43g
Cheese Quiche	380	27g	16g	185mg	450mg	23g	1g	12g
Quiche Lorraine	450	33g	18g	195mg	550mg	24g	1g	15g
Leek and Goat Cheese Quiche	400	28g	17g	185mg	430mg	25g	1g	11g
Asparagus and Gruyère Quiche	400	27g	16g	190mg	460mg	24g	2g	14g
Spinach and Feta Quiche	380	26g	15g	185mg	550mg	24g	1g	12g
Shepherd's Pie	470	18g	9g	125mg	1010mg	44g	4g	30g
Vegetable Pot Pie with Crumble Topping	680	37g	22g	115mg	1330mg	71g	11g	15g
Strata with Spinach and Gruyère	400	24g	10g	200mg	600mg	26g	2g	18g
Strata with Sausage, Mushrooms, and Monterey Jack Cheese	460	30g	11g	260mg	750mg	26g	1g	20g
Tamale Pie	410	22g	7g	70mg	770mg	32g	5g	25g
Golden Cornbread and Sausage Stuffing	420	23g	12g	140mg	840mg	39g	3g	15g
Wild Rice Dressing	360	21g	12g	90mg	390mg	34g	1g	8g

BREAD, PIZZA, AND CRACKERS

	Cal	Fat	Sat Fat	Chol	Sodium	Carb	Fiber	Protein
Classic Sandwich Bread (½" slice)	160	3g	1g	25mg	360mg	29g	3g	4g
Oatmeal-Honey Sandwich Bread (½" slice)	170	3g	1g	25mg	360mg	29g	3g	5g
Multigrain Sandwich Bread (½" slice)	150	3.5g	0g	25mg	380mg	27g	3g	4g
Whole-Grain Sandwich Bread (½" slice)	180	5g	1g	40mg	290mg	28g	6g	6g
Dairy-Free Whole-Grain Sandwich Bread (½" slice)	180	6g	0g	35mg	290mg	28g	6g	6g
Honey-Millet Sandwich Bread (½" slice)	200	5g	0g	35mg	290mg	33g	7g	6g
Honey Butter (1 tablespoon)	120	11g	7g	30mg	150mg	4g	0g	0g
Flourless Nut and Seed Loaf (½" slice)	180	12g	3.5g	0mg	110mg	14g	4g	5g
Hearty Country Flax Bread (⅔" slice)	200	4.5g	0.5g	30mg	480mg	35g	5g	6g
Cinnamon-Raisin Bread (½" slice)	210	3g	1g	25mg	430mg	41g	3g	4g
Brioche (½" slice)	220	8g	4g	75mg	310mg	31g	3g	5g
Dairy-Free Brioche (½" slice)	280	12g	5g	60mg	360mg	39g	4g	5g
Whole-Grain Sprouted Bread (½" slice)	180	4.5g	0g	0mg	250mg	32g	6g	7g
Olive-Rosemary Bread (⅔" slice)	220	6g	1g	45mg	420mg	35g	4g	6g
Baguettes (1" slice)	50	0.5g	0g	15mg	85mg	10g	1g	1g
Dinner Rolls	340	11g	6g	90mg	730mg	51g	3g	7g
Whole-Grain Dinner Rolls	170	7g	3g	60mg	310mg	21g	4g	6g
Dairy-Free Whole-Grain Dinner Rolls	170	8g	2g	45mg	350mg	20g	4g	5g
Hamburger Rolls	310	6g	2g	55mg	590mg	54g	6g	7g
Dairy-Free Hamburger Rolls	310	7g	0.5g	45mg	590mg	54g	6g	7g

	Cal	Fat	Sat Fat	Chol	Sodium	Carb	Fiber	Protein
Rustic Bread with Sesame Seeds (1" slice)	130	1.5g	0g	25mg	240mg	26g	4g	3g
Whole-Grain Walnut-Cherry Boule (⅔" slice)	260	10g	1g	35mg	400mg	36g	8g	9g
Dairy-Free Whole-Grain Walnut-Cherry Boule (⅔" slice)	250	10g	1g	30mg	390mg	34g	8g	8g
English Muffins	300	6g	2g	45mg	570mg	54g	5g	8g
Bagels	340	7g	3.5g	15mg	1360mg	62g	5g	5g
Dairy-Free Bagels	340	7g	2.5g	0mg	1230mg	62g	5g	5g
Everything Bagels	380	10g	4g	15mg	1540mg	65g	6g	7g
Light and Fluffy Biscuits	280	12g	5g	50mg	580mg	37g	1g	4g
Sweet Biscuits	310	12g	5g	50mg	580mg	45g	1g	4g
Cheddar Cheese Bread (½" slice)	190	10g	6g	50mg	340mg	18g	0g	6g
Skillet Cornbread	280	18g	7g	65mg	370mg	29g	3g	5g
Maple-Sorghum Skillet Bread (2" piece)	180	10g	4g	40mg	190mg	21g	1g	3g
Dairy-Free Maple-Sorghum Skillet Bread (2" piece)	150	7g	1.5g	25mg	220mg	20g	1g	3g
Classic Cheese Pizza	300	14g	4g	15mg	780mg	35g	3g	8g
Cheese Pizza with Prosciutto and Arugula	330	16g	4.5g	25mg	1030mg	35g	3g	11g
White Pizza with Ricotta, Sausage, and Bell Pepper	410	23g	8g	60mg	880mg	34g	3g	16g
Classic Cheese Pan Pizza (1 slice)	430	27g	7g	40mg	440mg	37g	3g	9g
Pepperoni Pan Pizza (1 slice)	470	30g	8g	50mg	570mg	37g	3g	11g
Pan Pizza with Sausage and Peppers (1 slice)	460	28g	7g	45mg	520mg	37g	3g	12g
Rosemary Focaccia (per 2" square)	130	5g	0.5g	10mg	135mg	18g	1g	2g
Socca (Chickpea Flatbreads) (1 flatbread)	300	20g	2.5g	0mg	240mg	23g	6g	8g
Coriander-Lemon Socca (1 flatbread)	300	20g	2.5g	0mg	240mg	23g	7g	8g
Caramelized Onion and Rosemary Socca (1 flatbread)	330	23g	3g	0mg	240mg	24g	7g	8g
Whole-Grain Crackers (6 crackers)	130	8g	0.5g	0mg	125mg	13g	3g	3g
Whole-Grain Poppy Seed–Thyme Crackers (6 crackers)	130	8g	1g	0mg	120mg	13g	3g	3g
Whole-Grain Sesame-Rosemary Crackers (6 crackers)	130	8g	0.5g	0mg	125mg	13g	3g	3g
Cheddar Cheese Coins (6 crackers)	230	14g	9g	40mg	270mg	18g	0g	7g
Pimento Cheese Coins (6 crackers)	230	14g	9g	40mg	270mg	18g	1g	7g
Mustard, Gruyère, and Caraway Cheese Coins (6 crackers)	250	15g	8g	45mg	410mg	18g	1g	8g
Everything Cheese Coins (6 crackers)	250	15g	9g	45mg	290mg	19g	1g	8g
Corn Tortillas (1 tortilla)	50	1g	0g	0mg	25mg	9g	1g	1g
Arepas (Corn Cakes) (1 cake)	190	7g	0.5g	0mg	350mg	28g	0g	3g
Chicken and Avocado Filling (filling for 1 corn cake)	70	4.5g	0.5g	15mg	20mg	3g	2g	6g
Black Bean and Cheese Filling (filling for 1 corn cake)	80	4.5g	2.5g	15mg	210mg	5g	2g	5g
Pupusas (Stuffed Corn Tortillas) (1 tortilla)	180	7g	3g	20mg	320mg	24g	3g	7g
Brazilian Cheese Bread Rolls (1 roll)	100	6g	2g	25mg	180mg	9g	0g	3g

COOKIES AND BARS (Nutritional information based on one cookie or bar)

	Cal	Fat	Sat Fat	Chol	Sodium	Carb	Fiber	Protein
Chocolate Chip Cookies	150	6g	4g	20mg	110mg	23g	1g	1g
Chocolate Cookies	210	12g	6g	20mg	85mg	28g	2g	3g
Whole-Grain Chocolate Chip Cookies	150	7g	4g	20mg	140mg	21g	2g	2g
Dairy-Free Whole-Grain Chocolate Chip Cookies	150	7g	3g	10mg	120mg	21g	2g	2g
White Chocolate–Macadamia Nut Cookies	160	8g	4g	20mg	115mg	20g	0g	1g
Dairy-Free White Chocolate–Macadamia Nut Cookies	160	9g	2g	10mg	115mg	20g	1g	1g
Chewy Sugar Cookies	160	8g	3.5g	20mg	110mg	22g	1g	2g
Oatmeal-Raisin Cookies	200	8g	3g	25mg	70mg	28g	2g	3g

	Cal	Fat	Sat Fat	Chol	Sodium	Carb	Fiber	Protein
Oatmeal Cookies with Chocolate Chunks and Dried Cherries	200	9g	3.5g	25mg	65mg	28g	2g	3g
Dairy-Free Oatmeal Cookies with Chocolate Chunks and Dried Cherries	170	6g	1g	15mg	65mg	28g	2g	3g
Chocolate Crinkle Cookies	160	6g	3.5g	30mg	95mg	28g	1g	2g
Dairy-Free Chocolate Crinkle Cookies	170	6g	2.5g	25mg	95mg	28g	1g	2g
Whole-Grain Brown Sugar Cookies	180	8g	4g	35mg	85mg	25g	2g	2g
Dairy-Free Whole-Grain Brown Sugar Cookies	170	10g	0.5g	15mg	85mg	21g	2g	2g
Whole-Grain Gingersnaps	80	3g	1.5g	10mg	50mg	12g	1g	1g
Dairy-Free Whole-Grain Gingersnaps	80	3.5g	0g	5mg	50mg	12g	1g	1g
Peanut Butter Cookies	200	11g	3.5g	25mg	160mg	25g	1g	4g
Peanut Butter Sandwich Cookies	210	14g	4g	15mg	160mg	20g	1g	5g
Dairy-Free Peanut Butter Sandwich Cookies	220	14g	2.5g	10mg	160mg	20g	1g	5g
Linzer Cookies	200	11g	4g	30mg	60mg	24g	1g	3g
Dairy-Free Linzer Cookies	200	11g	2.5g	15mg	120mg	24g	1g	3g
Almond Biscotti	120	4.5g	1.5g	20mg	55mg	19g	1g	2g
Dairy-Free Almond Biscotti	120	4.5g	1g	15mg	75mg	19g	1g	2g
Anise Biscotti	120	4.5g	1.5g	20mg	55mg	19g	1g	2g
Pistachio Spice Biscotti	120	4g	1.5g	20mg	55mg	19g	1g	2g
Chocolate-Dipped Biscotti	190	10g	4.5g	20mg	55mg	26g	2g	3g
Pignoli	170	10g	1g	0mg	5mg	18g	2g	4g
Holiday Cookies	190	8g	5g	35mg	60mg	27g	0g	1g
Shortbread	160	10g	6g	25mg	80mg	18g	0g	1g
Florentine Lace Cookies	140	11g	4g	15mg	30mg	12g	2g	2g
Lemon Madeleines	100	5g	2.5g	55mg	45mg	11g	0g	1g
Dairy-Free Lemon Madeleines	100	6g	0.5g	45mg	45mg	11g	0g	1g
Almond Madeleines	90	5g	2.5g	55mg	45mg	11g	0g	1g
Orange-Cardamom Madeleines	90	5g	2.5g	55mg	45mg	11g	0g	1g
Rugelach	90	5g	2g	15mg	65mg	9g	0g	1g
Dairy-Free Rugelach	100	7g	2.5g	10mg	45mg	9g	0g	1g
Blackberry-Almond Rugelach	90	5g	2g	15mg	65mg	10g	1g	1g
Lime-Glazed Coconut-Cardamom Cookies	120	5g	3.5g	20mg	45mg	18g	0g	1g
Dairy-Free Lime-Glazed Coconut-Cardamom Cookies	110	4.5g	1.5g	10mg	45mg	18g	0g	1g
Fudgy Brownies	210	10g	6g	50mg	90mg	30g	1g	2g
Lunchbox Brownies	200	8g	3g	45mg	105mg	31g	1g	2g
Dairy-Free Lunchbox Brownies	200	8g	2g	35mg	60mg	31g	1g	2g
Blondies	230	9g	5g	40mg	150mg	37g	1g	2g
Lemon Bars	230	12g	7g	130mg	65mg	28g	0g	3g
Key Lime Bars	220	11g	7g	40mg	105mg	29g	0g	3g
Whole-Grain Pecan Bars	230	15g	4.5g	25mg	160mg	23g	2g	3g
Dairy-Free Whole-Grain Pecan Bars	220	14g	2.5g	10mg	60mg	23g	2g	3g
Raspberry Streusel Bars	160	8g	3.5g	15mg	40mg	23g	1g	1g
Ginger-Fig Streusel Bars	190	7g	3.5g	15mg	60mg	29g	1g	1g
Granola Bars	200	14g	4g	0mg	100mg	17g	3g	4g
Whole-Grain Graham Crackers	90	3.5g	2g	10mg	70mg	12g	1g	1g
Dairy-Free Whole-Grain Graham Crackers	90	3.5g	1g	0mg	65mg	12g	1g	1g

	Cal	Fat	Sat Fat	Chol	Sodium	Carb	Fiber	Protein
FRUIT DESSERTS, PIES, AND TARTS								
Double-Crust Pie Dough	380	23g	15g	60mg	310mg	39g	1g	2g
Single-Crust Pie Dough	190	12g	7g	30mg	160mg	19g	1g	1g
Pumpkin Pie	420	22g	13g	155mg	360mg	50g	3g	6g
Pecan Pie	680	42g	15g	125mg	360mg	73g	3g	6g
Deep-Dish Apple Pie	600	24g	15g	60mg	400mg	95g	7g	4g
Dutch Apple Pie	620	26g	16g	95mg	230mg	96g	7g	4g
Blueberry Pie	530	24g	15g	60mg	340mg	77g	4g	4g
Fresh Strawberry Pie	330	12g	7g	30mg	180mg	54g	4g	2g
Strawberry-Rhubarb Pie	510	24g	15g	60mg	400mg	72g	3g	4g
Chocolate Angel Pie	510	38g	23g	150mg	190mg	41g	2g	6g
Coconut Cream Pie	630	47g	32g	220mg	270mg	47g	2g	6g
Lemon Meringue Pie	430	18g	10g	175mg	230mg	63g	1g	5g
Whole-Grain Free-Form Pear Tart	550	23g	12g	50mg	340mg	87g	12g	7g
Tart Shell	200	10g	6g	40mg	70mg	26g	1g	1g
French Apple Tart	450	16g	10g	65mg	170mg	76g	6g	2g
Rustic Walnut Tart	460	28g	10g	75mg	200mg	47g	2g	5g
Nutella Tart	610	46g	21g	105mg	95mg	48g	3g	5g
Lemon Tart	390	20g	11g	225mg	105mg	48g	1g	5g
Baked Raspberry Tart	420	22g	14g	105mg	180mg	51g	3g	3g
Fresh Fruit Tart	450	22g	13g	165mg	110mg	59g	3g	5g
Mixed Berry Tart	450	22g	13g	165mg	110mg	58g	4g	5g
Strawberry Shortcakes	540	28g	14g	105mg	600mg	69g	4g	6g
Peach Shortcakes	550	28g	14g	105mg	600mg	72g	4g	6g
Individual Blueberry-Almond Buckles	290	14g	6g	75mg	130mg	38g	2g	4g
Individual Raspberry-Pistachio Buckles	290	15g	7g	75mg	130mg	38g	4g	5g
Individual Blackberry-Walnut Buckles	290	16g	7g	75mg	130mg	35g	3g	4g
Apple Crisp	470	18g	8g	30mg	85mg	71g	8g	5g
Apple-Cranberry Crisp	520	22g	8g	30mg	85mg	79g	9g	4g
Whole-Grain Cherry Crisp	390	14g	6g	25mg	45mg	62g	5g	6g
Dairy-Free Whole-Grain Cherry Crisp	390	14g	4g	0mg	100mg	62g	5g	6g
Peach Cobbler with Cornmeal Biscuits	370	13g	7g	30mg	330mg	63g	5g	5g
Blueberry Cobbler with Cornmeal Biscuits	350	12g	7g	30mg	400mg	58g	5g	4g
Dairy-Free Blueberry Cobbler with Cornmeal Biscuits	340	12g	4.5g	0mg	370mg	57g	5g	3g
Individual Fresh Berry Gratins with Zabaglione	190	8g	4g	155mg	50mg	26g	4g	3g
Individual Fresh Berry Gratins with Lemon Zabaglione	190	8g	4g	155mg	50mg	27g	4g	3g
Individual Pavlovas with Tropical Fruit	360	15g	9g	55mg	55mg	54g	2g	4g
Individual Pavlovas with Mixed Berries	340	15g	9g	55mg	55mg	50g	4g	4g
Individual Pavlovas with Strawberries, Blueberries, and Peaches	340	15g	9g	55mg	55mg	50g	2g	4g
CAKES								
Classic Yellow Layer Cake	730	47g	28g	155mg	420mg	75g	3g	7g
Yellow Sheet Cake	730	47g	28g	155mg	420mg	75g	3g	7g
Birthday Cupcakes with Vanilla Frosting	390	24g	11g	70mg	200mg	41g	0g	3g
Rainbow Sprinkle Cupcakes	420	25g	11g	70mg	180mg	45g	0g	3g
Dairy-Free Rainbow Sprinkle Cupcakes	420	25g	11g	65mg	200mg	45g	0g	3g

	Cal	Fat	Sat Fat	Chol	Sodium	Carb	Fiber	Protein
Dark Chocolate Cupcakes with Frosting	400	28g	12g	60mg	210mg	40g	3g	4g
Coffee Frosting	120	9g	6g	25mg	20mg	11g	0g	0g
Almond Frosting	120	9g	6g	25mg	20mg	11g	0g	0g
Coconut Frosting	120	9g	6g	25mg	20mg	11g	0g	0g
Cream Cheese Frosting for Cupcakes	110	9g	5g	25mg	65mg	8g	0g	1g
Chocolate Layer Cake with Frosting	800	57g	24g	125mg	420mg	80g	6g	7g
Chocolate Sheet Cake with Frosting	800	57g	24g	125mg	420mg	80g	6g	7g
Chocolate Cream Cupcakes	360	23g	9g	65mg	210mg	40g	2g	4g
Red Velvet Cupcakes	380	22g	9g	70mg	250mg	44g	1g	3g
Carrot Sheet Cake	600	37g	13g	105mg	390mg	66g	2g	6g
Carrot Layer Cake	600	37g	13g	105mg	390mg	66g	2g	6g
Whole-Grain Carrot Cupcakes	350	21g	8g	65mg	300mg	37g	3g	5g
Dairy-Free Whole-Grain Carrot Cupcakes	350	21g	8g	65mg	300mg	37g	3g	5g
Lemon Layer Cake	480	17g	9g	145mg	450mg	77g	1g	6g
Dairy-Free Lemon Layer Cake	470	16g	6g	110mg	600mg	76g	1g	6g
Whole-Grain Brown Sugar Layer Cake	660	38g	22g	160mg	640mg	70g	4g	10g
Dairy-Free Whole-Grain Brown Sugar Layer Cake	680	41g	17g	130mg	680mg	70g	4g	10g
Gingerbread Cake	390	12g	3.5g	70mg	390mg	66g	1g	4g
Applesauce Snack Cake	270	8g	4g	85mg	450mg	44g	1g	4g
Ginger-Cardamom Applesauce Snack Cake	270	8g	4g	85mg	450mg	46g	1g	4g
Rustic Plum Torte	310	12g	6g	70mg	120mg	43g	2g	3g
Whole-Grain Apple Upside-Down Cake	400	18g	10g	85mg	200mg	57g	5g	5g
Dairy-Free Whole-Grain Apple Upside-Down Cake	400	18g	7g	45mg	270mg	57g	5g	5g
Rosemary Polenta Cake with Clementines	390	15g	9g	80mg	200mg	58g	3g	5g
Dairy-Free Rosemary Polenta Cake with Clementines	340	10g	4g	35mg	290mg	56g	3g	5g
Almond Cake	350	21g	4.5g	85mg	230mg	37g	2g	7g
Orange Crème Fraiche	70	6g	3.5g	20mg	25mg	4g	0g	1g
Lemon Pound Cake	430	19g	11g	140mg	290mg	59g	1g	5g
Lemon–Poppy Seed Pound Cake	460	21g	11g	140mg	290mg	61g	2g	6g
Lavender Tea Cakes with Vanilla Bean Glaze	220	8g	5g	50mg	115mg	36g	0g	2g
Dairy-Free Lavender Tea Cakes with Vanilla Bean Glaze	230	9g	1.5g	30mg	120mg	36g	0g	2g
Lemon Bundt Cake	400	14g	8g	95mg	330mg	64g	1g	4g
Dairy-Free Lemon Bundt Cake	380	12g	1g	60mg	330mg	64g	1g	4g
Chocolate-Hazelnut Torte	370	25g	10g	135mg	95mg	36g	4g	7g
Dairy-Free Chocolate-Hazelnut Torte	380	27g	9g	110mg	190mg	33g	4g	8g
Molten Chocolate Cakes	440	31g	17g	175mg	190mg	46g	5g	7g
Dairy-Free Chocolate Molten Cakes	470	37g	19g	140mg	330mg	37g	6g	10g
Whole-Grain Sticky Toffee Pudding Cakes	580	28g	15g	120mg	290mg	78g	5g	6g
Dairy-Free Whole-Grain Sticky Toffee Pudding Cakes	530	21g	7g	45mg	470mg	79g	5g	6g
Flourless Chocolate Cake	310	25g	14g	140mg	40mg	23g	4g	5g
New York–Style Cheesecake	450	33g	19g	185mg	290mg	30g	1g	9g

Index

D

Dairy-free substitutions, 36
Dark Chocolate Cupcakes, *496, 497*
Date(s)
-Nut Bread, *78, 79*
Whole-Grain Sticky Toffee Pudding Cakes, *542, 543*
Deep-Dish Apple Pie, *434, 435*
Desserts
Apple-Cranberry Crisp, 477
Apple Crisp, *476*, 477
Baked Raspberry Tart, *466, 467*
Blueberry Cobbler with Cornmeal Biscuits, *482, 483*
Blueberry Pie, *438*, 439
Chocolate Angel Pie, 445–47, *446*
Coconut Cream Pie, *448, 449*
Deep-Dish Apple Pie, *434*, 435
Dutch Apple Pie, *436, 437*
French Apple Tart, *458, 459*
Fresh Fruit Tart, *468, 469*
Fresh Strawberry Pie, *440, 441*
Individual Blackberry-Walnut Buckles, 475
Individual Blueberry-Almond Buckles, *474*, 475
Individual Fresh Berry Gratins with Lemon Zabaglione, 485
Individual Fresh Berry Gratins with Zabaglione, *484*, 485
Individual Pavlovas with Mixed Berries, 487
Individual Pavlovas with Strawberries, Blueberries, and Peaches, 487
Individual Pavlovas with Tropical Fruit, *486*, 487
Individual Raspberry-Pistachio Buckles, 475
Lemon Meringue Pie, *450*, 451
Lemon Tart, *464, 465*
Mixed Berry Tart, 469
Nutella Tart, *462, 463*
Peach Cobbler with Cornmeal Biscuits, *480*, 481
Peach Shortcakes, 472
Pecan Pie, *432*, 433
Pumpkin Pie, *430*, 431
Rustic Walnut Tart, *460, 461*
Strawberry-Rhubarb Pie, *442*, 443–44

Desserts (cont.)
Strawberry Shortcakes, *470*, 471–73
Whole-Grain Cherry Crisp, *478*, 479
Whole-Grain Free-Form Pear Tart, *452*, 453–54
see also Bars; Cakes; Cookies
Dinner Rolls, *298*, 299
Dinner Rolls, Whole-Grain, *300*, 301
Dips
Herb Mayonnaise, *160*, 161
Sriracha Mayonnaise, *124*, 125
Tartar Sauce, 221, *222*
Double-Crust Pie Dough, *426*, 427–29
Doughnuts, Yeasted, *92*, 93–95
Chocolate-Glazed, 94
Cinnamon Sugar–Glazed, 94
Vanilla-Glazed, 94
Dressing, Wild Rice, *262*, 263
Drunken Noodles with Chicken, *188*, 189
Dumplings, Chicken and, *240*, 241–42
Dutch Apple Pie, *436, 437*

E

Easy Pizza Sauce, 333
Easy Stovetop Macaroni and Cheese, *210*, 211
Easy Vanilla Frosting, 498
Edamame, Shiitakes, and Ginger, Quinoa Pilaf with, 133
Eggplant
Parmesan, 207–9, *208*
Roasted, and Sesame, Soba Noodles with, *186*, 187
Vegetable Lasagna, *202*, 203
Eggs
for baking recipes, 16
Fried, Roasted Carrots, and Kale, Brown Rice Bowls with, *120, 121*
Indonesian-Style Fried Rice, *122*, 123
Pad Thai with Shrimp, *192, 193*
Enchiladas, Chicken, *238*, 239
Endive, Blueberries, and Goat Cheese, Millet Salad with, 147